THE GREAT BOOK OF
SPORTS CARS

OVER 200 OF THE WORLD'S GREATEST AUTOMOBILES

BY THE AUTO EDITORS OF CONSUMER GUIDE®

PORTLAND HOUSE

DEAN BATCHELOR • CHRIS POOLE • GRAHAM ROBSON

h   g   f   e   d   c   b   a

ISBN 0-517-63377-9

This edition published by Portland House, a
division of dilithium Press, Ltd., distributed
by Crown Publishers, Inc., 225 Park Avenue
South, New York, New York 10003

Library of Congress Catalog Card Number: 87-63423

CREDITS

Principal Authors
Dean Batchelor
Chris Poole
Graham Robson

Photography
The editors gratefully acknowledge the
photographers who helped make this
book possible. They are listed below,
along with the page number(s) of their
photos:

Bob Cavallo—14, 242 **Roger Hill**—14
Tom McClellan—16 **Sam Griffith**—18,
52, 60, 128, 130, 158, 162, 178, 186, 188,
190, 192, 196, 198, 202, 208, 240, 298, 378
Mirco Decet—20, 56, 62, 64, 66, 68, 70,
72, 74, 94, 96, 98, 100, 102, 104, 108, 110,
136, 206, 210, 216, 228, 252, 254, 258, 260,
312, 322, 394, 396, 398, 400, 402, 406, 410,
412 **Douglas Mitchel**—22, 30, 36, 58, 86,
184, 194, 212, 218, 232, 258, 266, 292, 360,
362 **Vince Manocchi**—24, 112, 114, 116,
118, 120, 122, 124, 150, 152, 154, 226, 306,
380, 382, 384 **David Gooley**—30, 42, 44,
76, 84, 92, 134, 156, 220, 230, 236, 238,
256, 316, 318, 320, 374, 410 **Nicky
Wright**—30, 38, 54, 76, 78, 82, 146, 164,
214, 220, 222, 262, 280, 302, 304, 310, 336,
364, 386, 388, 392, 398 **Roland Flessner**—
32, 132, 142, 200, 286, 296, 326, 354, 356
Dean Batchelor—46, 156, 176, 334 **Franco
Rossi**—66, 244, 246, 248 **Andre Van De
Putte**—48, 160, 166, 168, 170 **Bud
Juneau**—86, 88, 292, 314, 324, 344 **Randy
Lorentzen**—92 **Laura Prince**—106 **Joseph
H. Wherry**—138, 208, 290, 312, 328, 392,
400, 404, 412, 416 **Mitch Frumkin**—146
Mike Segal—158 **Jan Borgfelt**—182, 308,
414 **Bill Bailey**—194 **Bert E. Johnson**—
212 **Richard Spiegelman**—234 **Dennis
Doty**—236, 238 **Gary Versteege**—264,
272, 274, 276, 278, 282 **Fred Chamberlain**—268 **Derek Bell**—270 **Bob Ten-
ney**—284 **Milt Kieft**—344 **Mel Winer**—
350 **Alex Gabbard**—364, 366, 368, 370,
372

Owners
Special thanks to the owners of the cars
featured in this book for their enthusiastic
cooperation. Listed by car type, they are:

1953-63 AC Ace & Aceca—**Edsel H.
Pfabe** 1957-64 AC Ace-Bristol & Aceca-
Bristol—**Tony Voiture, Graham Porter**

1962-68 AC Shelby Cobra 260/289 & AC 289—**Don Kraft** 1965-67 AC Shelby Cobra 427—**Ed Coughlin** 1947-52 Alfa Romeo 6C 2500—**Walter Neumayer** 1950-58 Alfa Romeo 1900—**Gary Clark** 1958-68 Alfa Romeo 2000 & 2600—**Chris Savill, Richard Mothersill** 1946-49 Allard K1—**Domino's Rear View Mirror Museum** 1950-52 Allard K2—**Ray & Kitty McLaughlin** 1971-85 Alpine-Renault A310—**Ray & Carole Banicki, Wilfried Taubert** 1968-70 American Motors AMX—**James Lojewski** 1954-61 Arnolt-Bristol—**Tom Mittler** 1950-53 Aston Martin DB2—**Donald Murr** 1953-57 Aston Martin DB2/4—**Harry Woodnorth Automobiles** 1957-59 Aston Martin DB Mark III—**R.S. Williams Ltd.** 1958-63 Aston Martin DB4—**R.S. Williams Ltd.** 1959-63 Aston Martin DB4GT & DB4GT Zagato—**R.S. Williams Ltd.** 1963-65 Aston Martin DB5 & Volante—**R.S. Williams Ltd.** 1953-56 Austin-Healey 100/4—**Mike Hopkins** 1956-59 Austin-Healey 100 Six—**Len Wilby** 1958-61 Austin-Healey Sprite—**James A. Mathews** 1959-67 Austin-Healey 3000—**Mike Hopkins, Fernhurst Motors** 1963-69 Bizzarrini GT Strada 5300—**John Ling** 1956-59 BMW 507—**James L. Roman, Terry Knudsen** 1968-77 BMW 2800CS, 2.5CS & 3.0CS/CSi/CSL—**Stephen Rouke, Tom Jervis** 1965-67 Bristol 409—**Kelly Classics** 1953-55 Chevrolet Corvette—**Dorothy & Gordon Clemmer** 1956-57 Chevrolet Corvette—**Robert & Diane Adams** 1958-60 Chevrolet Corvette—**Thomas & Mae Crockatt** 1961-62 Chevrolet Corvette—**Richard Carpenter** 1963-67 Chevrolet Corvette Sting Ray—**Tom Schay** 1968-77 Chevrolet Corvette Stingray—**Frank Capolupo** 1978-82 Chevrolet Corvette—**Gordon & Dorothy Clemmer, Edward E. Ortiz** 1947-52 Cisitalia 202 Gran Sport—**Ben Rose** 1971-75 Citroën SM—**George Jarmusz** 1952-55 Cunningham C-3 Continental—**Briggs Cunningham** 1961-69 Datsun 1500 Sports/ 1600/2000—**Dr. John J. Deviny** 1971-88 DeTomaso Pantera—**Stauffer Classics, Ltd.** 1954-58 Facel Vega & FVS—**Paul Sable** 1959-61 Facel Vega HK500—**B. J. Davidson** 1962-64 Facel Vega Facel II—**Joanne Fisher** 1947-53 Ferrari 166—**Dr. Henry Smith** 1950-53 Ferrari 195 & 212—**Ken Hutchison, Edsel H. Pfabe** 1950-55 Ferrari 340/342/375 America—**Wayne Golomb** 1953-54 Ferrari 250 Europa—**Dennis Machul** 1954-62 Ferrari 250 GT Long-Wheelbase—**Joe Marchetti** 1956-59 Ferrari 410 Superamerica—**Chris LaPorte** 1960-64 Ferrari 400 Superamerica—**Dr. Ronald Mulacek** 1964-65 Ferrari 250/275 LM—**Lou Sellyei** 1964-67 Ferrari 275 GTB/GTS—**Michael Feldman** 1967-71 Ferrari 365 GT 2+2—**Gunnar Elmgren** 1967-69 Ferrari Dino 206 GT—**John R. Kissinger** 1968-74 Ferrari 365 GTB/4 "Daytona" & 365 GTS/4 "Daytona Spider"—**Ed McCoughlin** 1969-73 Ferrari Dino 246 GT/246 GTS—**Richard Giacobett** 1974-88 Ferrari 365 GT4 2+2/400i/412i—**Continental Motors** 1973-79 Ferrari Dino 308 GT4—**Bob Cortese & John Wagner** 1974-85 Ferrari 365 GT4 BB & 512 BB/BBi—**Chuck Jordan, Hillary Rabb** 1975-88 Ferrari 308/308i GTB/GTS & 328 GTB/GTS—**Continental Motors** 1980-88 Ferrari Mondial 8/3.2 Mondial—**Continental Motors** 1985-88 Ferrari Testarossa—**Continental Motors** 1984-87 Ferrari GTO—**John Weinberger** 1968-85 Fiat 124 Sports/Spider 2000—**Rebecca Monk, Arnold Ness** 1955-57 Ford Thunderbird—**Leonard Nowosel, Alan Wendland** 1946-54 Healey—**Don Griffiths** 1948-54 Jaguar XK120—**Dan & Barb Pankratz** 1954-57 Jaguar XK140—**Anthony Holland** 1957-61 Jaguar XK150/XK150S—**Allen Hendry, R. Woodley** 1961-71 Jaguar E-Type—**Bruce Sears** 1971-75 Jaguar E-Type Series III V-12—**David Snyder** 1975-88 Jaguar XJS—**European Motors of Bellevue** 1972-76 Jensen-Healey & Jensen GT—**Yvette Hampton, Michael W. McBroom** 1954 Kaiser-Darrin—**Jerry Johnson** 1948-54 Kurtis—**David Hill** 1964-68 Lamborghini 350 GT/400 GT—**Jack Kellam** 1966-73 Lamborghini Miura/Miura S/Miura SV—**Jack Kellam** 1966-73 Lamborghini Espada—**Harry Woodnorth Automobiles** 1968-70 Lamborghini Islero—**Tony Voiture** 1962-74 Lotus Elan & Elan +2—**Steven Tillack** 1966-75 Lotus Europa—**Edsel H. Pfabe** 1976-88 Lotus Esprit & Esprit Turbo—**Bell & Colville** 1946-50 Maserati A6/1500—**Domino's Rear View Mirror Museum** 1951-57 Maserati A6G & A6G/2000—**Peter Kaus** 1957-64 Maserati 3500GT/GTI—**John R. Richter** 1962-66 Maserati Sebring—**Bob Rudinsky** 1963-70 Maserati Mistral—**Dave Couling** 1965-73 Maserati Mexico—**Robert Ellingson** 1966-73 Maserati Ghibli—**Frank Mandarano, Larry Brackett** 1969-74 Maserati Indy—**Major John Mood** 1971-80 Maserati Bora—**Dr. Dale Bloomquist** 1972-83 Maserati Merak—**Classic Car Centre** 1974-82 Maserati Khamsin—**Dr. Richard Goldman** 1977-83 Maserati Kyalami—**Frank Baumann** 1954-63 Mercedes-Benz 190SL—**Darl & Mary McAllister** 1954-63 Mercedes-Benz 300SL—**Allan Gordon, Dean Watts** 1963-71 Mercedes-Benz 230SL /250SL/280SL—**Jud Stone** 1945-49 MG TC—**Ben Rose** 1949-53 MG TD—**Robert Connole** 1953-55 MG TF & TF 1500—**Bob & Alice Wirth** 1955-62 MGA & MGA DeLuxe—**Whitehill Motors, Chris Starr** 1961-79 MG Midget—**Ake Andersson** 1962-80 MGB & MGB GT—**Roger Jerram, Fernhurst Mtrs. Co.** 1967-69 MGC & MGC GT—**Scott Davis, Newlands Mtrs.** 1967-77 Monteverdi 375-Series—**Norman T. Jarrett** 1950-68 Morgan Plus 4—**Kenneth Scotland** 1955-88 Morgan 4/4—**Evelyn Willburn** 1963-66 Morgan Plus 4 Plus—**Evelyn & John Willburn** 1951-54 Nash-Healey—**Gordon McGregor, Gerald Newton** 1968-73 Opel GT—**Roger & Carol Erickson** 1960-65 Porsche 356B/356C—**C. A. Stoddard** 1965-69/1976 Porsche 912/912E—**Dan & Barb Pankratz** 1970-76 Porsche 914 & 914/6—**Patrick I. Garvey, Michael F. Hartmann** 1966-70 Saab Sonett II—**A. J. Sutton** 1970-74 Saab Sonett III—**David C. Newkirk** 1967-69 Shelby GT-350/GT-500/GT-500KR—**Raymond C. Hamilton, Jeff Murr** 1965-70 Toyota 2000GT—**W. P. Keeler** 1946-49 Triumph 1800/2000 Roadster—**Duffy & Kelly Nopenz** 1953-55 Triumph TR2—**Mr. Gillamders, Mr. Ressler** 1955-57 Triumph TR3—**Mr. Lodawer** 1958-62 Triumph TR3A & TR3B—**Mr. Schaffer** 1961-67 Triumph TR4/TR4A—**Adrian Thompson** 1962-67 Triumph Spitfire Mark 1 & 2—**Philippa Newnham** 1966-68 Triumph GT6—**Doug & Peggie Roberts** 1967-68 Triumph TR5 Pl/TR250—**David C. & Linda Betz, Fernhurst Mtrs.** 1969-76 Triumph TR6—**Howard Shimon** 1968-73 Triumph GT6 Mark 2/GT6+ & GT6 Mark 3—**Ann Page** 1970-80 Triumph Spitfire Mark IV & 1500—**Bill & Luette Young** 1980-81 Triumph TR8—**Ron & Penny Cooper** 1967-71 TVR Tuscan—**George Rappelyea** 1972-79 TVR 2500/3000M & Taimar—**Richard Pietruska** 1980-88 TVR Tasmin Family—**Paula McCoy** 1961-71 Volvo P1800/1800S/1800E—**Adrian Praag** 1971-73 Volvo 1800ES—**Daisywagen Motors**

CONTENTS

CONTENTS

Even after more than 40 years, few subjects spark more heated debate among enthusiasts than what constitutes a "sports car." Since this is a book about such cars—one we hope you'll find "great" in more than just scope—we thought it appropriate to begin with some thoughts on that.

Time was when the definition was pretty clear-cut. In the good old days of the late Forties and early Fifties, a "sports car" was a roadster—that is, a two-seat open car with a detachable soft top and side curtains instead of roll-up door windows—mainly for driving fun and sometimes for high performance. Practicality was a secondary consideration, if indeed it figured in at all.

Also implicit in the term was the notion that although intended primarily for road use, a sports car could be driven in competition—what we now call motorsports—with a minimum of modification. The ideal always was that you drove to the track or rally course, picked up your winner's trophy, then motored home in the same car.

Not that this "race-and ride" concept was new. Cars like the Mercer Raceabout and Stutz Bearcat embodied it in the late Teens and Twenties, while the Thirties witnessed the birth of hot rods in American backyards, usually cobbled together from Ford Model T and flathead V-8 bits, typically for a very different kind of motorsport—drag racing—but exciting and very personal cars nevertheless.

Still, what most Americans think of as "sports cars" didn't appear until the early postwar years, when returning GIs brought home T-Series MGs, assorted Morgans, and other British models. Never mind that these were mainly prewar designs with technology that was woefully outmoded even for the late Forties. They made an indelible impression on the American consciousness.

And why not? For one thing, they looked sensational: classic long-hood/short-deck proportions, often set off by traditional wire-spoke wheels, always with a snug cockpit with seating for two. Many seemed to be doing 100 mph just standing still, though most couldn't actually approach that.

But they *were* appealingly different, with such novel "foreign" features as tachometer, floorshift, fold-down windshields in some cases—and handling that was simply a revelation to Americans weaned on the big and clumsy Detroit iron of the day. If the ride was rock-hard, amenities minimal, weather protection crude, engines noisy—well, it was all part of the sports-car mystique.

It wasn't long before sports-car owners began waving in friendly camaraderie whenever they'd encounter each other on the road. Many soon began meeting in social events—and on race tracks—all across the land, thanks to a new organization, the Sports Car Club of America. By the early Fifties, all but one of the major Detroit automakers had responded to the growing craze by issuing sporty production models of their own. While most were merely accessorized versions of workaday family fare, a few were genuine sports cars.

Naturally, you'll find the likes of the Crosley Hot Shot and Nash-Healey covered here, along with a host of European models. But in truth, this should really be titled *The Great Book of Sports* and GT *Cars*, for many of the entries are more strictly *gran turismo* than sports. In fact, most "sports cars" built after 1960 or so are better described by that Italian term, for they were designed mainly for touring in the grand manner—

The 356C was the last of a distinguished line that established Porsche as a world class sports-carmaker.

coupes and convertibles furnished with all the comforts, including a small back seat sometimes and, in cases like Ferrari, able to travel at indecently high speeds.

That the GT concept should win out over *pur sang* sports car was almost inevitable. Two-seaters accounted for a mere 0.25-percent of the total U.S. market in the early Fifties, but because of the huge importance of these sales, European makers began designing their sports and GT cars to suit American tastes, adding more creature comforts and all-round practicality as time passed.

Meantime, advancing technology was changing the nature of motorsports. By the mid-Sixties certainly, being truly competitive in the top echelons of racing required very specialized designs bearing little relationship to a manufacturer's road-going models, thus sounding the death knell for the traditional "race-and-ride" sports car. While a few newer production cars still fit that hallowed ideal (the Porsche 911 and its many derivatives come to mind), their numbers are dwindling.

So nowadays, what's often trumpeted as a sports car—be

it Mazda RX-7, Pontiac Fiero, or Ferrari Testarossa—is more properly described as a GT. Of course, "GT" has been abused as much as "sports car" over the years, having been applied to a number of vehicles that are neither grand nor particularly good tourers, but that's another story.

All this is to say that in the absence of hard-and-fast rules, the authors and editors have used their own best judgement in selecting cars for this book. Also, because postwar models command the greatest interest by far among today's enthusiasts, all of the cars profiled here went into production no earlier than 1945.

Inevitably, some readers will question some of our choices, while others may question why certain models were left out. We might, for example, have included a number of American "ponycars" from the Sixties and early Seventies—the various Ford Mustangs, Chevy Camaros, Plymouth Barracudas, *et al.*—but chose not to because they somehow didn't seem to fit the spirit of either "sports car" or "GT." As for the ones we *did* choose . . . well, we think they make their own case.

1988 Lamborghini Countach 5000 Quattrovalvole.

There's little else you need to know as you read through these pages, but a few words on organization and technical matters are in order.

First, contents are arranged *alphabetically* by make and *chronologically* within makes by year of a model's public introduction. We deviate from the latter in cases like the Lotus Esprit by listing initial year of production where this is significantly later than public announcement.

While not intended to be exhaustive, specifications have been thoroughly researched, using contemporary published reports as well as "standard works," both American and European. Technical features not listed under specifications are found in the text.

Specifications terms are self-explanatory, but readers should note that "A-arm" and "wishbone" are used synonymously and that all front suspensions may be considered as being independent unless a description such as "rigid axle" makes this patently impossible. The same applies to rear suspensions. Unless otherwise stated, torque ratings are always in the same unit of measurement as engine horsepower, i.e., net, DIN, SAE gross or SAE net.

As an aid to collectors, we've tried to provide production figures that are as specific as possible. The reader should assume *model year* production for all entries unless otherwise noted.

Last but not least, special thanks to the owners of the cars featured here, not only for their cooperation with photography but for preserving their machines in such beautiful condition. That takes a lot of time, effort, and money, and all us enthusiasts are all the richer for it.

Regardless of how *you* define "sports car," you're sure to find many of your favorites here, and perhaps even add a few to your list. We hope so, because enjoyment is mainly what this book is all about—which is why we call it *The Great Book of Sports Cars*. Happy motoring, and happy motoring memories new and old.

The Auto Editors of CONSUMER GUIDE®   *January, 1988*

1953-1963
AC ACE AND ACECA

Although tiny AC of Thames Ditton (near London) had built up a fine reputation by the early Fifties, it had developed a very staid image. Reason: its products were hopelessly behind the times. For example, its existing 2.0-liter car retained old-fashioned beam-axle front suspension, and the firm's light-alloy six-cylinder engine dated back to 1919. AC owners Charles and Derek Hurlock were desperately looking for inspiration and a new model. Fortunately for us, they found both.

The result was AC's sudden transformation into a successful sports-car builder, though it happened almost by chance. On a "friend of a friend" basis, the hand-built Tojeiro, a British racing sports car, was demonstrated to the Hurlocks, who promptly bought up the production rights and began making a road car of it. In fact, they tried two Tojeiros, one with a race-tuned Lea-Francis engine, the other with a 2.0-liter Bristol unit.

The basis of the Tojeiro design was a simple ladder-style chassis built up of large diameter tubes and with wishbone and transverse-leaf-spring independent suspension front and rear. The race cars were graced with sleek two-seat "barchetta" bodies unashamedly modelled on those of the most recent racing Ferraris. What attracted the Hurlocks to the Tojeiro design was that little investment would be needed to tool up for chassis production, while the body could easily be produced at AC's own coachbuilding facility.

By using an evolution of the ancient 2.0-liter six and a Moss gearbox, the Hurlocks were able to transform the racing Tojeiro into a relatively civilized roadgoing sports car. The project came together with astonishing speed. The deal wasn't hatched until the summer of 1953, yet the prototype, called AC Ace, was displayed at the London Motor Show in October and deliveries began the following year. The only real changes made in that frenzied development period were raising the original headlamp position (to meet international regulations for minimum height) and abandoning rack-and-pinion steering for a cam-gear system.

AC's light-alloy overhead-cam engine, which had a mere 40 horsepower at 3000 rpm when introduced, was persuaded to produce 85 bhp at 4500 rpm for the Ace, enough to give the graceful new car a top speed of 103 mph. In the next few years, this remarkable old soldier would be tuned even more, to 90 bhp in 1955, and finally to 102 bhp in 1958.

With the open two-seater in production (later to become even more famous as the basis of the Shelby Cobra), AC decided to produce a fastback coupe version. This was the Aceca, its name, like Ace, revived from a famous AC of the Thirties. Revealed in late 1954 and in production by mid-1955, the Aceca, naturally enough, looked rather like Ferrari's contemporary 166 and 212 models, a happy coincidence.

Once these two models were established, AC was up to building five cars a week. The chassis soon had such a good reputation that there were persistent demands for more power. With the AC engine near the end of its development life, alternative power had to be found, and AC eventually "bought in" the ex-BMW Bristol engine (see Ace- and Aceca-Bristol).

Nevertheless, and in spite of in-house competition from other derivatives, the AC-engined Ace and Aceca sold steadily until the autumn of 1963, by which time Thames Ditton was preoccupied with building engineless Cobras for Carroll Shelby in California.

Both models improved along the way. Front disc brakes were fitted from 1956-57, at which time an electrically actuated overdrive became optional. Later, the old Moss gearbox was dropped in favor of Triumph TR3A gears inside a case of AC's own design. As a halfway measure between the two body types, a detachable hardtop was also made available for the Ace.

SPECIFICATIONS

Engine: sohc I-6, 121 cid/1991 cc, 85/90/102 bhp @ 4500-5000 rpm, 105/110 lbs-ft @ 2750/2500 rpm

Transmission:	4-speed manual (with optional overdrive from 1956)
Suspension, front:	independent, double wishbones, transverse leaf spring
Suspension, rear:	independent, double wishbones, transverse leaf spring
Brakes:	front/rear drums; front discs/rear drums from 1956
Wheelbase (in.):	90.0
Weight (lbs):	1685 (Ace), 1840 (Aceca)
Top speed (mph):	103 (Ace), 102 (Aceca)
0-60 mph (sec):	11.4 (Ace), 13.4 (Aceca)
Production:	**Ace** 220 **Aceca** 150

*Opposite page: Ace roadster and companion Aceca fastback were tiny AC's first proper cars. Styling, especially nose, drew heavily from Touring's early Ferrari Barchettas. 2.0-liter six (**lower right**) gave respectable go. **Above:** Cockpit is sports-car spartan.*

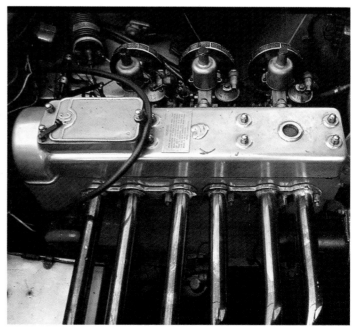

1957-1964
AC ACE-BRISTOL AND
ACECA-BRISTOL

British race-driver Ken Rudd constructed the very first Ace-Bristol, but his hybrid was quickly adopted by the AC factory. First shown in autumn 1956, the Ace-Bristol and the companion Aceca-Bristol were in production by the spring of 1957. Because it was not only more powerful than AC's own engine but capable of a lot more power-tuning, the Bristol unit made these cars, especially the Ace, much more suited for competition.

The roots of the Bristol design go back to the Thirties, when BMW engine design chief Fritz Feider produced a series of six-cylinder engines that culminated in the 1971-cc unit of the fabled 328. After World War II, Bristol of England "acquired" the design by somewhat dubious means (see Bristol 401) and manufactured it in the UK. By the mid-1950s, Bristol was happy to supply this noble engine to other automakers.

Complete with three downdraft Solex carburetors, the Bristol engine was tall but fit comfortably under the Ace/Aceca hood. It had pushrod overhead valve actuation (via complex linkages), part-spherical combustion chambers, and a very long stroke. Despite all this, it was amazingly flexible and high-revving.

For its AC application the engine was normally supplied in 105-horsepower "100C2" guise, but it could also be supplied with 120, 125, or 130 bhp. All versions teamed with Bristol's own 4-speed manual gearbox, but apart from this, very few changes were made—or needed—for the transplant.

Compared with the AC-engine cars, the Bristol-powered Ace and Aceca had a lot more performance but were only a few pounds heavier, so they generally recorded similar fuel consumption figures. It was thus not surprising that though more expensive, they soon began outselling the earlier models, and eventually came to dominate the scene at Thames Ditton.

Naturally, chassis and other improvements were shared with the AC-engine cars. Both Ace- and Aceca-Bristol were offered right from the start with Laycock overdrive (which operated on top, third, and second gears) as an option, and got front-wheel disc brakes as standard during 1957. Although basic styling was not changed, the Ace could be ordered with a curved, instead of flat, windshield beginning in 1958. You could also order a cowl for covering part of the radiator air intake, which reduced drag slightly and increased top speed to more than 120 mph.

In 1961, Bristol dropped a bombshell on the British specialty car market by announcing its new 407 with Chrysler hemi V-8 power—and would soon phase out the old six. This meant that the AC-Bristols were living on borrowed time and that AC needed to find an alternative engine fast. Eventually, AC wedged in the 2553-cc six from the British Ford Zephyr (allied to a Moss gearbox), offered in various stages of tune from 90 to 170 bhp (SAE). It proved very unsuccessful though: only 46 such cars were ever produced.

By 1962, assembly of the Bristol-engine cars was cut back to accommodate the buildup of Shelby Cobra production, though the last of the type wasn't actually built until spring 1964.

SPECIFICATIONS

Engine: Bristol ohv I-6, 120 cid/1971 cc, 105/120/125/130 bhp @ 4750/5750/6200 rpm, 120/122/123/128 lbs-ft @ 3750/4250/5000 rpm

Transmission:	4-speed manual (with optional overdrive from 1956)
Suspension, front:	independent, double wishbones, transverse leaf spring
Suspension, rear:	independent, double wishbones, transverse leaf spring
Brakes:	front/rear drums; front discs/rear drums from 1956
Wheelbase (in.):	90.0
Weight (lbs):	1685 (Ace), 1840 (Aceca)
Top speed (mph):	117 (Ace), 116 (Aceca) (125-bhp models)
0-60 mph (sec):	9.1 (Ace), 10.3 (Aceca)
Production:	**Ace** 466 **Aceca** 169

*Bristol-powered Ace roadster (**opposite**) and Aceca coupe looked little different from their AC-engine cousins.*

1962-1968 AC SHELBY COBRA 260/289 AND AC 289

Though the Cobra's conception, development, and production history are well known, there's still a little controversy over the name and the way the cars were built. But there's no disputing its originator: American Carroll Shelby, the former Ferrari race driver and occasional chicken farmer.

Shelby conceived the idea of shoehorning Ford's forthcoming new small-block V-8 into the light and lively AC Ace in 1961. The first car was completed in February 1962, and deliveries to American customers began later that same year. This and subsequent Cobra models would be built over just a five-year period, but they were among the most charismatic and fearsome roadgoing sports cars ever produced. The British liked to call them AC Cobras, while Americans preferred Shelby-AC Cobra or plain Shelby-Cobra. Today, they're remembered mainly—and vividly—as Cobra.

That first Cobra's basic chassis, suspension, and body design differed little from that of the Ace and Ace-Bristol roadsters that the British firm had been building for some years. As luck would have it, Shelby approached AC about supplying engineless Aces just as Bristol engine supplies began to decline and AC was trying to decide what to do next.

By the time Ace development, such as it was, had been completed, the chassis had been stiffened up a little (much of it shared with late-model Acecas) and a

Salisbury final drive (Jaguar E-Type/Mk X type) complete with limited-slip differential had been installed. Cobra styling was almost exactly the same as that of the latter-day Ace, with the final, smaller grille but flared wheelarches to accommodate wider tires.

All Cobras had four-wheel disc brakes. Inboard rear brakes were contemplated, but production cars had outboard units. The steering box was canted over to clear the Ford engine, but steering and suspension geometry changes were minimal otherwise. Assembly took place in the UK except for engines and gearboxes, which were installed once the cars arrived at Shelby's small assembly operation in Venice, California.

The engine, of course, was the lightweight, compact thinwall V-8 from Ford's new 1962 Fairlane intermediate, initially sized at 260 cubic inches and fitted to the first 75 Cobras built. Mated to it was a 4-speed Borg-Warner all-synchromesh manual transmission. The next 51 cars were equipped with the 289-cid small-block enlargement. Then, as later, the AC chassis really wasn't rigid enough to handle the engine's torque, so not all of the Cobra's wheels stayed on the ground at all times. But this only made an already exciting car even more of a challenge to drive well.

The next Cobras, called "Mark II" by AC designers, were built from the beginning of 1963. They retained the original transverse-leaf-spring Ace chassis and the 289 engine but featured rack-and-pinion steering, a definite improvement. Exactly 528 cars were built before the old Ace chassis was discontinued.

Although the original plan called for the Cobra to be sold only in the U.S., it didn't last long. The first right-hand-drive cars were completed as early as summer 1963, though it wasn't until the end of 1964 that AC officially launched the 289 model on the British market. The cars were also sold in Europe.

The original Ace-chassis Cobra ended in early 1965, when production changed over to the truly ferocious Cobra 427, built on a new chassis dubbed "Mark III." But the small-block Cobra lived on in Europe as a 289 version of the new platform called AC 289. Just 27 were built before all Cobra production ceased in December 1968.

SPECIFICATIONS

Engines: all Ford U.S. ohv V-8, 260 cid/4261 cc, 260 bhp @ 5800 rpm, 269 lbs-ft @ 4800 rpm (SAE gross); 289 cid/4727 cc, 271 bhp @ 6000 rpm, 314 lbs-ft @ 3400 rpm

Transmission:	4-speed manual
Suspension, front:	independent, double wishbones, transverse leaf spring
Suspension, rear:	independent, double wishbones, transverse leaf spring
Brakes:	front/rear discs
Wheelbase (in.):	90.0
Weight (lbs):	2100-2315
Top speed (mph):	138 (289 model)
0-60 mph (sec):	5.5 (289 model)

Production: 260 V-8 75 **289 V-8** 51 **"Mk II"** 528 **"Mk III" AC 289** 27

Opposite page and below: Cobras are often customized in some way. Note this example's non-stock roll bar and chrome wire wheels.

1965-1967
AC SHELBY COBRA 427

The AC/Shelby-Cobra had been designed so quickly that most of its chassis, suspension, and general structure was a virtual carryover from the last of the British six-cylinder Aces. After only three years, therefore, a much more purpose-built Cobra, the Mark III, was introduced.

Although the two Mark III models—289 and 427—looked basically alike, they differed in almost every other respect. The most obvious one was the engine of the new 427 model, named for the cubic-inch displacement of its big-block Ford V-8. In addition, it sported a new chassis, new suspension system, and important changes to the bodyshell. With this brutish engine, the Cobra Mark III was sold only in the U.S. Its European cousin, the AC 289, retained the small-block V-8 of the earlier Mark II Cobra (see previous entry).

Both Mark IIIs continued with the basic ladder-style tubular chassis inherited from the AC Ace, though with larger-diameter tubes spaced further apart. Coil springs replaced the old transverse leaf springs front and rear, still acting on classic, independent double wishbones. Shelby and Ford publicity at the time suggested that this suspension had been computer-generated, but the more prosaic truth is that it was conventionally designed by Bob Negstadt of Shelby-America and Alan Turner of AC. Regardless, the result was more favorable geometry for sharper steering, plus handling that was about as good as this Fifties-vintage chassis could deliver.

With racing in mind—and following the old American axiom that "there's no substitute for cubic inches"—Shelby's team pursued maximum power by stuffing in the largest V-8 they could. Thus, the small-block 289 V-8 gave way to the massive 427-cid Ford "semi-hemi," a close relative of the engine used in Ford's NASCAR racers and modified for the GT40 Mark II and Le Mans-winning Mark IV World Manufacturers Championship cars.

But wait. Although the ultimate Cobra was always known as the "427," it seems that many of them were actually built with the low-stress low-output 428 engine. So what difference does a cubic inch make? Plenty, for these engines had completely different cylinder dimensions (427 bore/stroke = 4.24 × 3.78 in., 428 = 4.14 × 3.98 in.) and cylinder head castings. In short, the 427 was a racing engine, while the 428 was designed for the big Galaxie and Thunderbird passenger cars—considerably heavier than the 427 and by no means as "tuneable."

The Cobra 427 body was similar to that of the Mark III AC 289 and included many common sections. However, wider track dimensions and much fatter tires made it necessary to flare the wheelarches considerably, swelling overall width by seven inches compared to the Mark II shell. This and the burly engine made the 427 a muscular monster that looked as aggressive as it sounded and was only slightly slower than an Atlas rocket.

In fact, the 427's performance was little short of staggering. Even "customer" cars had 390 bhp, while race tuning could provide up to 480 bhp and a pavement-peeling 480 lbs-ft of torque. For its three years of production, the Cobra 427 was undoubtedly the wildest and most exciting machine on American roads. Come to that, it still is.

Alas, sales ran down, so production did too, in 1967. For 1968, the Cobra name (which now belonged to Ford, not Carroll Shelby) began to appear on hopped-up Mustang engines.

In truth, any Cobra, but especially the 427, was too fast for its chassis, and not nearly as refined—or as reliable—as it should have been. Yet because of their rarity and shattering performance, Shelby's high-performance hybrids continued to grow in stature and collectibility as the years passed. Demand quickly outstripped supply, resulting in a slew of Cobra replicas in the Seventies and especially the Eighties. Most employed different and—believe it or not—even cruder chassis designs.

Fortunately, the small but persistent demand for *real* Cobra motoring prompted Brian Angliss and his UK-based Autokraft company to build "Mark IV" Cobras using surviving original tooling purchased from AC, which Autokraft has since acquired. These cars now have Ford's official sanction, which only goes to show that some legends simply will not be consigned to history.

Low stance, bulging stern, and hulking tires give big-block Cobras a menacing appearance. Acceleration is just as intimidating.

SPECIFICATIONS

Engines: all Ford U.S. ohv V-8, 427 cid/6997 cc, 390 bhp @ 5200 rpm, 475 lbs-ft @ 3700 rpm (SAE gross); 428 cid/7014 cc, 355 bhp @ 5400 rpm, 420 lbs-ft @ 3200 rpm (SAE gross)

Transmission:	4-speed manual
Suspension, front:	independent, double wishbones, coil springs
Suspension, rear:	independent, double wishbones, coil springs
Brakes:	front/rear discs
Wheelbase (in.):	90.0
Weight (lbs):	2530
Top speed (mph):	165
0-60 mph (sec):	4.2
Production:	348 (numbered chassis)

1965-1973 AC 428

It was in 1965, as Cobra sales peaked, that the AC company had its next bright idea. The latest coil-spring Cobra chassis provided excellent roadholding and could be tuned for a softer, more "boulevard" ride than in the sports cars. Why not, thought Derek Hurlock, use it as the basis for a modern, luxuriously equipped GT?

Hurlock began scouting the various specialist coachbuilders and finally chose the Italian house of Frua. For its new GT, AC merely lengthened the Cobra wheelbase by six inches — easy to do with such a simple parallel-tube layout — and slotted in Ford's 428-cubic-inch big-block V-8. As a concession to its softer, more refined character, the new model would be offered with Ford's C-6 3-speed automatic transmission as well as manual gearbox. Christened AC 428, the car was considerably bulkier than previous ACs, yet deliberately designed as a two-seater. Perhaps AC's unhappy experience with the 2 + 2 Greyhound coupes of 1959-1963 had something to do with this decision.

In other respects, the new car's chassis was like that of the Mark III Cobra, with four-wheel disc brakes, all-independent suspension via coil-spring/damper units and wishbones, and rack-and-pinion steering, though center-lock wire wheels were chosen instead of cast alloys. Despite hefty curb weight, there was no provision for power steering.

The first 428, a prototype convertible, was revealed at the London Motor Show in 1965, but much more development work was needed before sales actually began over a year later. By then, the convertible had been joined by a glassy fastback coupe with the same lower-body styling. In overall appearance, the 428 was much like the contemporary Maserati Mistral, also a Frua design. Frua at the time was also supplying bodies to Monteverdi, and since AC didn't actually impose any of its own styling ideas, the 428's similarity was, perhaps, no surprise. It is said that some body panels and glass were shared by all three.

The 428 was much larger and heavier than any previous AC. It was certainly a lot more expensive. The main reason was all the shipping involved. Building the 428 required importing Ford drivetrains from Detroit; building and then sending the rolling chassis to Italy, where Frua added the body and completed final assembly; then bringing the finished cars back to the UK for final testing and inspection. As they used to say at Avanti, the car traveled so much during production that it was out of warranty by the time it reached the customer.

For all that, sales were meager. Who, after all, was likely to buy an Italian-bodied American-powered car from a tiny British concern when they could get a genuine Italian thoroughbred with a high-revving twincam engine and a famous badge for the same money? By 1973, when the car was dropped, only 58 coupes and 28 convertibles had been produced. The oil crisis, existing and impending EEC and USA regulations, an unsuccessful battle against labor problems in Italy, and AC's inability to undercut the pricing of firms like Aston Martin all contributed to the 428's demise.

Few of these cars seem to have survived. Yet though rarer than original Cobras, their collector-market prices have long been quite reasonable, which suggests that interest has peaked. A pity, for the 428 is a lot faster than you'd think and has bags of style and exclusivity. One can only wonder how it might have fared with a "designer" label.

SPECIFICATIONS

Engine: Ford U.S. ohv V-8, 428 cid/7014 cc, 345 bhp @ 4600 rpm, 462 lbs-ft @ 2800 rpm (SAE gross)

Transmissions:	4-speed manual or Ford U.S. 3-speed automatic
Suspension, front:	independent, double wishbones, coil springs
Suspension, rear:	independent, double wishbones, coil springs
Brakes:	front/rear discs
Wheelbase (in.):	96.0
Weight (lbs):	3155
Top speed (mph):	140
0-60 mph (sec):	5.9-6.2

Production: coupe 58 **convertible** 28 (some sources list 51 coupes and 29 convertibles)

This 1971-registered 428 coupe shows off the Frua styling that was quite similar to that of the Maserati Mistral and concurrent Monteverdis. It's said some body panels and glass were the same on all three. Low-stressed Ford big-block V-8 (above) delivered 6-second 0-60 mph go.

1947-1952
ALFA ROMEO 6C 2500

By 1947, Alfa Romeo had dug out from the rubble left by the Allied bombing of its factory in Portello, a suburb of Milan, and resumed civilian car production with the Tipo 6C 2500. This dohc six-cylinder design was essentially an evolution of the prewar 6C 2500, which was built as a Turismo (five-passenger sedan), Sport, and Super Sport in 1939-43.

Called *Freccia d'Oro,* meaning Golden Arrow, the new series included a five-passenger berlina (sedan), two-place coupe and cabriolet, and four-seat convertible. These were the last Alfa Romeos built with separate frame and body, and the marque's last coachbuilt cars, with bodies supplied by Touring, Pinin Farina, Stabilimenti Farina, and Boneschi.

These cars were typical of contemporary Alfa engineering practice in having parallel-trailing-arm front suspension, previously seen on Alfa and Auto Union Grand Prix cars and later to be familiar on the Volkswagen Beetle, Porsche 356, and various Aston Martins. Springing was by coils. The independent rear suspension was by swing axles with longitudinal torsion bars. Shock absorbers were tubular-hydraulic all around, and brakes were of the drum type. The rugged frame holding all this together was of channel section, with a sturdy X-member. A four-speed synchromesh transmission was controlled by a shift lever on the steering column. Interestingly, all Freccia d'Oros were built with right-hand drive.

Looking more French than Italian in three-quarter view, this Farina-bodied two-seat cabriolet was one of four body types offered in Alfa's postwar 6C 2500 series. Dashboard design is very late-Forties. Minor trim and other details varied. Some cars have a radio instead of gauges in the dash center.

Under the hood were six inline pistons working in a cast-iron block which had its crankshaft carried in seven main bearings. The cast-aluminum cylinder head supported two camshafts operating one inlet and one exhaust valve per cylinder; combustion chambers were hemispherical. Drive for the camshafts was by chain from the front of the crankshaft to a sprocket just below the camshafts, which in turn rotated the shafts via spur gears. Carburetion varied from a single Solex instrument on the Turismo to three sidedraft Webers on the Sport and Super Sport. Horsepower naturally varied too: 87 bhp at 4600 rpm for the Turismo; the Sport had 95 bhp (at the same revs) from 1939-1946 but only 90 from 1947 to 1952; the Super Sport offered 110 bhp at 4800 rpm, the SS Corsa 125 at 4800. A special version, the Competizione (1946-50) packed 145 bhp at 5500 rpm.

These 6C 2500 Alfa Romeos weren't great cars, as they were rather large and ponderous, but they were milestones in the genesis of postwar car design. American enthusiasts saw them pictured in early issues of magazines like *Road & Track* and *Speed Age*, as well as *The Autocar* and *The Motor* from England. With bodywork by the cream of Italy's carrozzeria, they were beautiful cars, so much cleaner and more refined than the ones we saw on the streets of our own hometowns. And when we found technical specifications or underhood photos, we also discovered that their engines had twin overhead camshafts—quite exotic for the day, at least in America. The only domestic cars powered by this type of engine were Indianapolis racers and, on a smaller scale, the dirt-track midgets of Frank Kurtis. There was also the dohc Duesenberg straight eight of the Thirties, but how many Yanks had actually seen one of those?

The combination of a racing-type twincam engine within all those lovely Latin lines was real dream stuff to a generation of budding U.S. car enthusiasts. Few 6C 2500s found their way to the U.S. But though seen only in magazines for the most part, they helped generate much of America's postwar enthusiasm for Italian cars, reason enough to remember them here.

SPECIFICATIONS

Engines: all dohc I-6, 149 cid/2443 cc, 90 bhp @ 4600 rpm (Sport), 110 bhp @ 4600 rpm (Super Sport), 145 bhp @ 5500 rpm (Competizione); torque NA

Transmission:	4-speed manual (all-synchromesh Competizione; others, synchromesh on III-IV only)
Suspension, front:	independent, parallel trailing arms, coil springs
Suspension, rear:	independent, swing axles, longitudinal torsion bars
Brakes:	front/rear drums
Wheelbase (in.):	106.0 SS, 118.0 others
Weight (lbs):	3410 (Sport), 3080 (SS), 1870 (Competizione)
Top speed (mph):	96 (Sport), 103 (SS), 125 (Competizione)
0-60 mph (sec):	NA

Production: (calendar year) **1947** 486 **1948** 451 **1949** 414 **1950-52** approx. 100

1950-1958
ALFA ROMEO 1900

The 1900 was not only Alfa Romeo's first new postwar design but the first Alfa with unit construction. Berlina (sedan) bodies were produced at the factory, but various coupe and cabriolet styles were offered by Ghia, Boano, Farina, Vignale, Castagna, and Bertone, with the majority produced by Carrozzeria Touring. Though all-new, the 1900 retained some of Alfa's traditional engineering philosophy, particularly in its twincam four-cylinder engine and the 4-speed all-synchromesh transmission of the last 6C 2500.

Initially, the 1900 engine had a bore and stroke of 82.55 × 88 mm giving 1884-cc displacement, hence the model designation. For 1953-58, dimensions grew to 84.5 × 88 mm for a total 1975 cc, a bit oversize but still called a 1900. Unlike the 2500 six, the 1900's dual overhead camshafts were totally chain driven. There were numerous other detail changes, but basic construction was preserved, with cast-iron block and cast-aluminum head.

Drive was taken through a single-disc clutch and the 4-speed transmission to a live rear axle. The 2500's swing axles were abandoned because the 1900 was to be a much higher-volume model, reasonably priced for an Alfa, and the live axle was more appropriate to assembly-line production. Rear axle positioning was by a single lower trailing arm on each side and a triangulated link between floorpan and the top of the differential case, an arrangement that persists at Alfa—albeit with variations—to this day. Front suspension was also new, still independent but with upper and lower transverse A-arms and anti-roll bar. Coil springs and tubular shock absorbers were used all around, and brakes were aluminum drums with cast-iron liners.

In addition to being the marque's first series-produced car, the 1900 broke new ground for Alfa in its left-hand drive. This did not reflect any company foot-dragging. Quite simply, Alfa Romeo had primarily built competition-oriented automobiles prior to 1950, and most two-seat racing cars had the steering wheel on the right. It's still true today. There are two reasons for it. First, most closed-circuit road races are run in a clockwise direction, so positioning the wheel on the right is advantageous because it puts the driver on the inside of most turns. It also places him on the "pit side" of the car for faster entry, exit, and easier conversing with the team manager during pit stops.

The 1900 was not conceived as a competition car, but in May 1950, Piero Taruffi and Felice Bonetto drove stock single-carb berlinas to 5th and 9th overall in the first running of the *Carrera Panamericana* (Mexican Road Race). These 90-horsepower Alfas, which the factory rated at only 93 mph flat out, averaged 77.8 and 76.5 mph, respectively, for the 2178 miles covered in the race from Ciudad Juarez on the U.S. border to El Ocotal on the Guatemala border.

After the berlina arrived as the company's bread-and-butter production model, 1900-series chassis and floorpan assemblies duly went out to the coachbuilders for lighter, more exotic bodywork. These coachbuilt styles seemed to be made mostly of aluminum (sedan bodies were steel) and this, plus somewhat trimmer overall size, made the coupe and cabriolet considerably lighter than the sedans.

A berlina Super appeared in 1953 with a slightly larger engine. Rated horsepower was unchanged, but the added displacement made the powerplant slightly more flexible. The Sprint, offered as a Touring-bodied coupe and Farina cabriolet, arrived in 1951 with 100 bhp at 5500 rpm. This was raised to 115 for the Super Sprint of 1954, when displacement was raised to 1975 cc.

Mention should be made of three very special 1953-54 show cars on the 1900 SS chassis. These were built by Carrozzeria Nuccio Bertone under the designation *Berlina Aerodinamica Technica* (aerodynamic sedan study) or B.A.T. This project spawned numerous ideas committed to many renderings and sketches, but only three cars— B.A.T. 5, B.A.T. 7, and B.A.T. 9—were actually built. All still exist, by the way, in the U.S.

The B.A.T. series was an interesting experiment in automotive aerodynamics, characterized by rounded front ends designed for minimal air disturbance and smooth bodywork swept back to wildly exaggerated tailfins. They were the ultimate show-stoppers in their day and beautifully executed, but of no real value as transportation. Visibility was poor, crash protection nil, creature comforts marginal. Yet they were some of the most exciting designs to come from any coachbuilder, let alone on a fairly ordinary production chassis.

SPECIFICATIONS

Engines: all dohc I-4; **1952-53:** 114.9 cid/1884 cc, 100 bhp @ 5500 rpm, torque NA; **1954-58:** 129.5 cid/1975 cc, 115 bhp @ 5500 rpm, torque NA

Transmissions:	4-speed manual (5-speed manual 1954-58 Super Sprint)
Suspension, front:	independent, parallel unequal-length A-arms, coil springs, anti-roll bar
Suspension, rear:	live axle on single lower trailing arms with upper triangulated link to center of differential, coil springs
Brakes:	front/rear drums
Wheelbase (in.):	98.5
Weight (lbs):	approx. 2200 (Sprint), 2420 (cabriolet)
Top speed (mph):	100 (Sprint cabriolet), 106 (Sprint coupe), 112 (SS)
0-60 mph (sec):	NA
Production:	21,304 incl. 949 **Sprint**, 854 **Super Sprint**

Opposite: A surprising number of Italian coachbuilders exhibited their artistry on the Alfa 1900 chassis—witness this clean-lined coupe by Castagna circa 1954. Above: Twincam engines were an Alfa tradition by the mid-Fifties.

1952-1960
ALFA ROMEO
DISCO VOLANTE

UFOs were unheard of in the early Fifties. Back then, people thought they saw flying saucers. An Italian would have reported such a sighting as a *disco volante*. Closer to earth but just as incredible were the handful of Alfa Romeos that carried this name. They certainly seemed like something from outer space and were even meant to fly—on the race tracks of Europe.

Though Alfa had pinned its early postwar hopes on the 1900 series of 1950, it also planned a line of larger, deluxe touring cars powered by a new 2995-cc six—basically the 1900 four with two extra cylinders, the same 82.5-mm bore and a longer 92-mm stroke (versus 88 mm). This senior line never materialized (though Alfa would get around to a six, the 2600 series, in 1962), but the firm needed an image boost (the 1900 sedan was far from lovely), so it decided to build a batch of 3.0-liter engines for a group of lightweight racers based on the 1900 chassis (modified via Alfin-type brakes with four extra-wide leading shoes). Thanks to their unusually smooth, aerodynamic bodywork, these cars were soon dubbed *disco volante* by factory hands, and the name stuck.

Perhaps hedging its bets, Alfa also built three four-cylinder Discos (officially, Tipo C52), with a 1900 engine bored out to 85 mm and 1997 cc. (The larger-capacity cars were designated 6C 3000CM, for six-cylinder 3000-cc *Cortemaggiore*.) Both versions were slated to contest the 1952 Le Mans 24 Hours, but no Disco raced until the following year's Mille Miglia, when one four and three sixes were entered, the latter with an enlarged 3576-cc engine (bore and stroke: 88 × 98 mm). Despite broken steering towards the end, the legendary Juan Manuel Fangio drove a six-cylinder coupe to second behind a 4.1-liter Ferrari, the only Disco to finish.

Alas, Alfa's image-polisher would score only one other triumph: the 1953 *Supercortemaggiore* at Merano, which Fangio won outright in a 3.0-liter roadster. In between were non-finishes at Le Mans and Spa and withdrawal of the entire team before the Nurburgring 1000 Kilometers.

The story would have ended right there had Alfa not sold off all but the original prototype and Fangio's *Supercortemaggiore* car (still on display in the company's Milan museum). Exact numbers are hard to come by, but nine Discos were apparently built: three C52s and six CMs. It's believed the former comprised two spiders and one coupe, the latter two spiders and four coupes. It's their fate that still fascinates enthusiasts today.

Soon after the Discos were retired, one coupe was purchased by Joakim Bonnier, then Alfa's Swedish distributor, who had it fitted with a new roadster body by Zagato. This car eventually found its way to America, where Rodger Ward (later to win the Indy 500) and Bruce Kessler raced it for owner Shelly Spindel. A fourth car, rebodied by Carrozzeria Boano, was sold in 1955 to Argentine dictator Juan Peron. A fifth Disco, with Ghia coachwork, seems to have disappeared, and it's still equally hard to determine what happened to a sixth car.

The remaining Disco was destined for all the glory, its six-cylinder chassis (the one originally developed for the proposed senior line) becoming the foundation for a series of stunning aerodynamic exercises by Pinin Farina. The first, dubbed "Superflow," was a rounded, low-slung coupe with sharp tailfins, a glassy "bubbletop" with gullwing-type upper doors, and semi-open front wheels (portions of the fender tops were cut away, replaced by clear plastic). This was naturally followed by "Superflow II," a somewhat more conventional version. Its main innovation was plastic fins that appeared to be body color from outside but were transparent when viewed from inside, so as not to hinder driver vision astern. Next came a roadster of the same general style but with large faired-in headrests and no fins. Common to all three (built between 1956 and '59) was the longitudinal, concave bodyside sculpturing that PF would apply to the production Giulia Duetto of 1967 (still around today as the 2000 Spider Veloce).

The final effort was yet another smooth bubbletop coupe, this time with twin transparent roof sections (one above each seat) that slid back on rails for open-air motoring, an early expression of the T-top idea. The tail was similar to that of the previous roadster and, again, predictive of the Duetto's. First seen at the 1960 Geneva Show, this Disco ended up on a used-car lot in Denver only a year later but was rescued.

Like the Bertone B.A.T. Alfas, the Disco Volantes remain interesting commentaries on Fifties thinking about aerodynamics. They wouldn't be the last wild-looking Alfa one-offs, but they were surprisingly practical. Too bad that none saw series production, but let's hope that Alfa can still manage similar dreams in the future. Would you believe an Alfa UFO?

*Alfa retained two of the nine Disco Volantes built. Both can be seen at the company's Milan museum. **Above and opposite top:** The original racing prototype. "Flying saucer" nickname is obvious from the squat, shapely body lines. **Opposite bottom:** Fangio gave the Disco its only race win with this coupe in the 1953 Supercortemaggiore.*

SPECIFICATIONS

Engines: dohc I-4, 122 cid/1997 cc, 158 bhp @ 6500 rpm, torque NA; dohc I-6, 183 cid/2995 cc, 230 bhp @ 6500 rpm, torque NA; 213 cid/3495 cc, 246 bhp @ 6500 rpm, torque NA

Transmissions:	4-speed manual (2.0/3.0-liter), 5-speed manual (3.5-liter)
Suspension, front:	upper and lower unequal-length A-arms, coil springs, anti-roll bar
Suspension, rear:	De Dion live axle, coil springs, anti-roll bar
Brakes:	front/rear drums (Alfin-type, inboard at rear)
Wheelbase (in.):	87.4 (2.0-liter), 88.6 (3.0/3.5-liter)
Weight (lbs):	1620-2115 (dry weight with racing bodywork)
Top speed (mph):	137-159 (with racing bodywork)
0-60 mph (sec):	NA

Production: 2.0-liter **spider** 2 **coupe** 1 3.0/3.5-liter **spider** 2 **coupe** 4

1954-1963 ALFA ROMEO GIULIETTA

The introduction of Alfa Romeo's Giulietta, in 1954, has to rank as one of the most curious in automotive history. Plans had been underway for some time to create a smaller companion for the 1900, with a berlina (sedan) being the first order of business. Unfortunately, Alfa was, as ever, short on development money, so a plan was conceived to sell securities that would carry the going rate, in Italy, for this type of investment. As an added inducement, it was announced that a drawing would be held among the shareholders; those with the winning numbers would receive a new Giulietta. It worked, and the needed capital was raised.

But again unfortunately, Alfa was new to volume production and its problems, and development of the new model fell further and further behind schedule. Mechanical components were being made, but there was still no sign of a finished, saleable car. The lucky numbers were finally announced, company officials hoping this would ease the tension, but it only angered the winners, who wanted their prizes right away. Once the press started calling the scheme a scandal, government-owned Alfa knew it had to do something—fast.

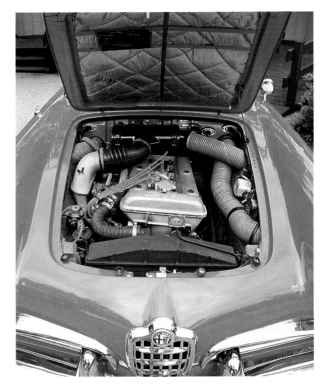

That something turned out to be a contract with Nuccio Bertone Carrozzeria for a small run of 2+2 Giulietta-based Sprint coupes, with the first to be ready for the Turin show in the spring of 1954. That it *was* ready, and displayed, is a triumph over intrigue, egos, poor planning, and ordinary glitches that seem to plague any new design. Alfa initially ordered only a few hundred bodies from Bertone, to satisfy the winners of the drawing, then upped it to 1000, and finally 6000, when it realized that the Giulietta was a hit.

The mainstay, a factory-designed berlina, quickly followed the Sprint into production. By mid-1955, a two-seat spider version had been designed and was being built by Pinin Farina. Sprint had now become synonymous with coupe at Alfa, while Spider (Ferrari and Porsche spelled it Spyder) was an open car, usually a roadster but, in this case, one with roll-up windows. (These terms often confuse historians and enthusiasts, alike, especially as the 1900 Sprint had been both a coupe and cabriolet.) Despite their different architects, all three body styles shared a family resemblance and continued the mechanical design philosophy of the superseded 1900.

At 1290 cc, the Giulietta's twincam four was smaller and less powerful than the 1900, having 80 horsepower at 6300 rpm. Still, the Giulietta Sprint was good for 102.5 mph, and because it was lighter (1936 pounds) and much more maneuverable, it was faster over a given circuit than the 1900. Only a single engine tune was offered at first, but 1956 brought 90-bhp Veloce versions of all three models, with claimed top speeds of up to 111.8 mph. Their extra horsepower was achieved by a change in cam timing, higher compression (from 8.5 to 9.1:1), substituting twin Weber carburetors for the single Solex, and adding steel-tube exhaust headers.

Like the 1900, the Giulietta employed unit construction. Its suspension components were new, but geometry was much the same: unequal-length A-arms in front and a live rear axle on single low-mount trailing arms, with further location provided by a triangulated link attached to the top of the differential; coil springs were used all around. Brakes, large-diameter Alfin drums, were carried over from the 1900.

The Giulietta continued through 1965, but gained 1570 cc Giulia running mates beginning in 1962. After that, only the Giulias were sent to America, though the Giuliettas continued for another three years in Europe.

Though the 1900 had been the first mass-market Alfa, it was the Giulietta that really established the marque in the minds of many enthusiasts, particularly Americans. It was the Giulietta that legendary import-car impresario Max Hoffman chose to sell when he became Alfa Romeo's U.S. distributor.

The Giuliettas were handsome, great fun to drive, and had enough technical interest to satisfy the most critical of enthusiast drivers. They didn't have independent rear suspension like a Porsche, but neither did Ferrari, Aston Martin, or Maserati in those days. Yet that was really all they gave away, and that didn't seem to make much difference except in the most extreme situations. The handling of these cars was so nimble and predictable that it took a real idiot to get one off the road.

Besides the three standard models, the Giulietta series included two special-body offerings: the curvy 1957-62 Sprint Speciale by Bertone and the Sprint Zagato (SZ) of 1959-61, named for that coachbuilder. With engines tuned to 115 bhp at 6500 rpm, both cars were good for about 124 mph.

SPECIFICATIONS

Engine: all dohc I-4, 78.7 cid/1290 cc, 80 bhp @ 6300 rpm, 90 bhp @ 6500 rpm (Veloce), 115 bhp @ 6500 rpm (SS,SZ), 86.8 lbs-ft @ 4500 rpm (Veloce)

Transmissions:	4-speed manual (5-speed SS, SZ)
Suspension, front:	independent, unequal-length A-arms, coil springs
Suspension, rear:	live axle on single lower trailing arms with upper triangulated link to center of differential, coil springs
Brakes:	front/rear aluminum drums with cast-iron liners
Wheelbase (in.):	93.7 (Spider, SS and SZ: 88.6)
Weight (lbs):	1936-1969 (Sprint) 1892-1903 (Spider)
Top speed (mph):	103 (Sprint, Spider), 112 (Spider Veloce), 124 (SS and SZ)
0-60 mph (sec):	11.0 (Spider Veloce)

Production: Sprint 27,142 **Spider** 17,096 **Sprint Speciale and Zagato** 1576

This page, from top: Farina roadster, Bertone Sprint coupe, Zagato SS. All these are "late" (101-Series) Giuliettas from 1959-62.

29

1958-1968 ALFA ROMEO 2000 & 2600

By 1958, the 1900 was the "senior" Alfa Romeo and in need of an update. Its successor arrived that year as the 2000 (internal designation: Series 102), with new bodywork wrapped around what was basically the 1900 engine and running gear. First out were a berlina, designed and built by the factory, and a dashing spider with bodywork by Carrozzeria Touring. A Sprint coupe designed by Bertone completed the range in 1960.

All three, but particularly the spider, bore a family resemblance to contemporary Giuliettas. The Sprint was a harbinger of the 2600 and Giulia Sprint models to come, having a notchback 2+2 body with minimal A- and C-pillars and an almost non-existent B-pillar. The result was a very light, airy greenhouse with lots of glass area. But though these were the best-looking production Alfas yet and extremely comfortable touring cars, their weight and relatively low power made them slower than the Giuliettas and less fun to drive.

The 2000's dohc four-cylinder engine was essentially the same as the second-series 1900 unit, with cast-iron block, aluminum head, and 1975 cc from an 84.5-mm bore and 88-mm stroke. The Berlina engine, with a single downdraft Solex carburetor, produced 105 horsepower at 5300 rpm, while the Sprint and Spider versions put out 115 bhp at 5900 via twin Solex sidedraft instruments.

If a bit on the conservative side, the 2000 Sprint and Spider reflected the best of then-current Italian styling. Mechanically, they were obviously products of racing experience, with their twincam engines, large Alfin brakes, well-developed suspension, and quick, positive steering. But at 2640 pounds for the Sprint and 2596 for the Spider, neither had the sort of power-to-weight ratio for the sparkling performance expected from a firm like Alfa Romeo.

Only a little over 7000 of the 2000-series cars were built through 1962. The Spider accounted for almost half (outpacing even the sedan), though it was built for the full five years versus only three for the Sprint.

In an effort to regain the model spread lost by concentrating so heavily on its Giulietta/Giulia series, Alfa Romeo gave its senior 2000 line a new six-cylinder engine in 1962. Typically Alfa, it had chain-driven double overhead camshafts, cast-iron block, and aluminum head, but was developed more from the smaller Giulietta.

Though physically longer than the 2.0-liter four, the 2.5 six fit into the engine compartment with surprising ease, suggesting that Alfa engineers may well have had this move in mind when they created the 2000 four years earlier. Bore and stroke measured 83 × 79.6 mm, making this Alfa's first oversquare engine. The Tipo 161 and 162 prototype racing cars of 1939 and 1941 had "square" engines (62 mm bore and stroke), but most Alfa power units had been long-stroke designs. With actual displacement of 2584 cc, the new six was rated at 145 horsepower at 5900 rpm.

Bodywork for the 2600 was identical with the 2000 series except for minor trim changes. The factory-built berlina (sedan), Bertone Sprint coupe, and Touring Spider were later joined by a striking Zagato coupe with a jutting, rounded nose.

With its punchier new engine and consequently superior power-to-weight ratio, the 2600 series was more entertaining than the 2000 and more commercially successful, though not by much. The big problem was that a Giulietta cost about half as much, yet was twice as much fun to drive. Still, the large Alfas were excellent cross-country cruisers: quiet, comfortable, relatively roomy, and with traditional Alfa Romeo handling that always made the driver feel secure on any road. Unfortunately, high weight meant they had to struggle to reach cruising speed.

Both 2600 and Giulia arrived with four-wheel disc brakes, something new for Alfa. In addition to being safer, they were a real advantage in competition or sport driving, frequently enabling the Alfas to win through better braking when they couldn't do it by superior speed. Stamped-steel disc wheels were still standard, as on all postwar production Alfas. For unknown reasons, Borrani center-lock knock-off wire wheels, so common on other Italian sports and GT cars, were not offered as standard Alfa equipment. Still, the cars didn't suffer visually, and the disc wheels were certainly cheaper and easier to maintain.

Alfa 2600s weren't sold in the U.S. due to high prices but found favor among Alfisti in Britain, hence this righthand-drive Bertone Sprint coupe (opposite page, top) and Touring roadster. Both looked like grownup Giulias, which was probably deliberate. Disc wheels shown here were standard, but Borrani wires were available. Coupe cabin is lush.

SPECIFICATIONS

Engines: 2000: dohc I-4, 120.5 cid/1975 cc, 115 bhp @ 5700-5900 rpm, torque NA; **Disco Volante/Sportiva:** 121.8 cid/1997.4 cc, 158/138 bhp @ 6500 rpm, torque NA; **2600:** dohc I-6, 157.6 cid/2854 cc, 145 bhp @ 5900 rpm, torque NA

Transmission:	5-speed all-synchromesh manual (4-speed on Disco Volante)
Suspension, front:	independent, unequal-length A-arms, coil springs, anti-roll bar
Suspension, rear:	live axle on single lower trailing arms with upper triangulated link to center of differential, coil springs
Brakes:	front/rear aluminum drums with cast iron liners (2000), front/rear discs (2600)
Wheelbase (in.):	101.6 (Sprint), 98.4 (Spider)
Weight (lbs):	2640 (2000 Sprint), 2695 (2000 Spider), 2013 (Sportiva), 1617 (Disco Volante), 2816 (2600 Sprint), 2864 (2600 Spider)
Top speed (mph):	109 (2000), 137 (Sportiva), 135-140 (Disco Volante), 125 (2600)
0-60 mph (sec):	NA

Production: 2000 Spider 3443 **2000 Sprint** 700 **2600 Spider** 2255 **2600 Sprint** 6999 **SZ** 105

1962-1988
ALFA ROMEO GIULIA

Alfa Romeo's 1600 Giulia engine (actually 1570 cc) was introduced in 1962 in the 101-series Giulietta bodies. At first, this engine was the Giulias' only real distinction aside from minor trim changes. But the extra displacement and resulting extra torque made for a more pleasurable car that was easier to drive. The engine block was now aluminum, with cast-iron cylinder liners, and a 5-speed, all-synchromesh gearbox was standard.

By 1963, a new 105-series Giulia berlina and Sprint were on sale with all-new bodywork, the berlina's still designed and built by the factory, the Sprint by Bertone. Accompanying this more attractive styling was revised suspension. At the front, the previous unequal-length A-arms were replaced by a single lower A-arm and separate upper links that permitted caster adjustment. At the rear, the triangulated link gave way to a T-shape device for lateral location; it also minimized axle windup in hard acceleration and braking.

The new series brought a major style change to the Sprint coupe body, an elegantly simple piece of work by Bertone designer Giorgio Giugiaro, destined for international fame in the Seventies as head of his own studio, Ital Design. Unlike previous Sprints, however, the 105-series body was manufactured and assembled with the rest of the car in the new Alfa Romeo factory at Arese, on the outskirts of Milan, alongside Giulia sedans. Alfa christened it Sprint GT to avoid confusion with the 101-series model.

The 1966 Geneva show saw the debut of a new small Alfa spider. Dubbed "Duetto," this Pininfarina design was inspired by a styling exercise on a 3.5-liter Disco Volante chassis, seen at Geneva in 1959. The rounded front and rear, connected by a wide full-length bodyside groove, generated decidedly mixed feelings among *Alfisti*. Pininfarina also built the production Duetto bodies under contract.

These two models finally took the Giulia completely away from the old 101-series look. Meanwhile, the limited-production Bertone-built Sprint Speciale continued with almost no change in appearance, though it received all the mechanical updates applied to its linemates.

There was also an entirely new Sprint Zagato model. Now called GTZ, it was considerably better-looking than its Giulietta predecessor, with obvious signs of having been designed for high-speed work. Its engine and running gear were standard Giulia, albeit extensively modified for racing, and rear suspension was fully independent. The smooth, slightly bulbous fastback coupe was dominated by a truncated, Kamm-type tail.

Nineteen sixty-five brought further variations of the Sprint GT in the four-place GTC convertible and the GTA, a lightened, hopped-up racing special. A similar GTA 1300 Junior was built starting in 1968 for class racing in Europe.

Giulia displacement swelled to 1779 cc in 1969, but Alfa called the cars "1750," no doubt to evoke memories of the successful, highly acclaimed 1750 sports-racers of prewar days. This engine was offered in all 105-series body styles and further aided the small Alfas' overall flexibility, though horsepower and torque were not greatly increased. The Duetto was now simply called Spider. In 1971 it was given a chopped, Kamm-style tail, which changed its appearance considerably. In fact, there's still a distinct difference of opinion among Alfa fanciers as to whether this change was for the better.

Because of American emission standards and other bureaucratic requirements, no Alfas were marketed in the U.S. for 1972. When the 1973 models appeared, the Giulia engine had been further enlarged, to 1962 cc, for a revised group of 115-series 2000 models. Spica mechanical fuel injection was adopted for the American market in the interest of improved driveability and cleaner exhaust (dual sidedraft Weber carburetors continued in Europe). Alas, Sprint production ended the following year, but the Spider continues at this writing and, probably, for the foreseeable future.

There's been a great deal of speculation about how long Alfa Romeo will hang on to this design. As a car, the Spider is now 22 years old, though it has seen continuing mechanical improvements (such as adoption of Bosch electronic injection for 1982 U.S. models). But in spite of various body changes, it's really six years older visually. Moreover, nothing about it is state of the art. The chassis has been developed about as far as it can go without full independent rear suspension, and many observers think there's no hope at all for the body. Yet largely on the strength of the Spider's timeless open-air appeal, Alfa enjoyed a U.S. sales resurgence during 1986-87 despite the car's archaic qualities.

Now that wealthy Fiat owns the company, Alfa boosters are hoping for a new Spider in the near future. We are too.

SPECIFICATIONS

Engines: all dohc I-4; **1962-68 Giulia 1600 (101/105-Series):** 95.7 cid/1570 cc, 104 bhp @ 6200 rpm (122 bhp @ 6000 rpm Sprint GT), 103 lbs-ft @ 3000 rpm (Sprint GT); **1969-72 "1750" (105-Series):** 108.5 cid/1779 cc, 132 bhp @ 5500 rpm (132 bhp @ 5500 rpm Sprint GTV and Spider), 132 lbs-ft @ 2900 rpm (Spider); **1973-88 2000 (105/115-Series):** 119.7 cid/1962 cc, 116 bhp (SAE net) @ 5000 rpm (129 bhp @ 5800 rpm Spider Veloce), 116-122 lbs-ft @ 2500-4000 rpm (132 lbs-ft @ 3500 rpm Sprint GTV)

Transmission:	5-speed all-synchromesh manual
Suspension, front:	independent, unequal-length A-arms, coil springs, anti-roll bar
Suspension, rear:	live axle on single lower trailing arms with upper triangulated link to center of differential, coil springs
Brakes:	front/rear discs
Wheelbase (in.):	92.5 (Sprint), 88.6 (Spider)
Weight (lbs):	2180-2300
Top speed (mph):	115 (1750 Spider), 110 (2000)
0-60 mph (sec):	10.6-12.2 (Giulia), 9.9 (1750), 9.6-10.0 (2000)
Production:	NA

Opposite top: *Zagato-bodied Giulia GTZ coupes like this one often saw weekend race action.* **Other photos:** *The 2000 Spider Veloce in 1986 U.S. form. Styling remains distinctive, if busier than on earlier Duettos and 1750s.*

1972-1975
ALFA ROMEO
MONTREAL

Canada's Expo '67, held in Montreal and often mistakenly referred to as the Montreal World's Fair, witnessed the birth of a very special Alfa Romeo. The Italian firm had been asked to develop a car to represent the automobile industry, and rose to the occasion in magnificent fashion, albeit with the design help of Carrozzeria Bertone.

Named Montreal in honor of its venue, the show car was based on the 105-series Giulia chassis, but Bertone's fastback coupe body featured a column of large air slots behind each door that suggested a mid-engine configuration. It was reported at the show that while the display car was a one-of-a-kind prototype, it had been designed with possible production in mind.

A production version was eventually shown, though not until 1970. Appearance was little altered, but a major change had occurred in the motive power. Nestled under the hood up front was a new 2593-cc four-cam, aluminum-block V-8 with Spica mechanical fuel injection. Producing 200 DIN (230 SAE) horsepower at 6500 rpm, it was, in fact, nothing less than a detuned version of Alfa's T33 racing engine. At 2830 pounds, the Montreal weighed about 470 pounds more than the Giulia 2000 GTV, its closest stablemate. That gave it a power-to-weight ratio of just 12.1 lbs/bhp (SAE) while the lighter Giulia 2000 came in at about 20 lbs/bhp. Like the show car, the production Montreal used the Giulia suspension, which meant lower A-arms and upper transverse and trailing links at the front, and a live rear axle with lower trailing arms and an upper T-bar from chassis to differential case for lateral location. Wheelbase was the same as that of the Giugiaro-designed 105/115-series Sprint coupe, while overall length was some four inches less.

Despite its conventional front-engine/rear-drive layout, the production Montreal retained the show car's distinctive C-pillar slots for cockpit ventilation. These conferred a unique if somewhat busy look, as did the front, which had three separate openings: a central one shaped like the traditional Alfa Romeo shield, and one on each side that surrounded the quad headlights. The lights themselves were partly hidden behind slatted grilles reaching up into the nose.

Any Alfa Romeo owner, particularly one familiar with the Giulias, would feel right at home in the Montreal, noting how many items were the same in both cars. Unfortunately, minor instruments are difficult to read quickly, clustered under the large speedometer and tach in twin pods. In typical Italian fashion, the steering wheel is raked forward more than most American or British drivers are used to and want. This had led to nasty comments from automotive journalists over the years about Italians being built like apes, with long arms and short legs.

This misconception reflects a lack of knowledge about the Italian driving style. One of this book's authors was fortunate in being able to take a ride around Alfa's test track in a Montreal with one of the company's best drivers at the wheel. He sat, with the seat well back, in a relaxed position, gripping the lower rim of the wheel gently. Shuffling the wheel between right and left hand as we went round the track at a blistering pace, he never once raised either hand above the lower third of the wheel, so there was no need for the wheel to be in a more vertical position.

By contrast, American, British, and German drivers typically hold the wheel with hands at the nine-and-three-o'clock or ten-and-two positions, so a near-vertical wheel is almost mandatory for best control. Judging by our ride with the Alfa tester, Italian enthusiasts do it differently, and the wheel position of their cars suits them perfectly.

Another thing we learned during that drive was the high degree to which Alfa Romeo had developed its live-rear-axle setup. A car with the Montreal's performance potential—130+ mph—would seem to demand independent rear suspension or, at the very least, De Dion linkage, but at no time during our spirited run did we sense the need for anything more than this well-controlled live axle. Of course, that was in early 1971. There's been a lot of engineering progress since then, and all-independent suspension is now more or less the sports-car norm.

As for the Montreal, it's difficult to figure why Alfa even bothered. It received virtually no promotion or advertising and little development (the car was never certified for U.S. sale), so demand was meager and the car short-lived. There wasn't even a direct replacement. Alfa's financial and managerial problems of the day largely account for all this, but it's still sad.

In the end, the Montreal was nothing more than a sideline—a high-buck GT aimed at the likes of Porsche's 911 and the Mercedes SL, quickly discarded as unprofitable. Today it stands as a rare and singular Alfa Romeo, and something to celebrate.

SPECIFICATIONS

Engine:	dohc V-8, 180 cid/2953 cc, 230 bhp @ 6500 rpm, 174 lbs-ft @ 4750 rpm (SAE gross)
Transmission:	ZF 5-speed manual
Suspension, front:	lower A-arms, upper lateral and trailing links, coil springs, anti-roll bar
Suspension, rear:	live axle, single lower trailing arms, upper T-bar to top of differential, coil springs
Brakes:	front/rear disc
Wheelbase (in.):	92.5
Weight (lbs):	2830
Top speed (mph):	132
0-60 mph (sec):	8.0
Production:	3925

This is the Expo '67 Bertone prototype that led to the production Montreal. Aft door quarter windows were eliminated and changes made to nose, tail, beltline height, and rear wheelarches. Only the one show car was built.

1981-1986
ALFA ROMEO GTV-6

When the Giulia Sprint GTV was dropped from production in 1974, Alfa introduced the Alfetta GT fastback coupe to replace it. Virtually everything was new. Only the dohc four-cylinder engine with Spica fuel injection was retained. The Alfetta's independent front suspension was similar to the GTV's, but had longitudinal torsion bars in place of coil springs. Drive was carried to a 5-speed transmission in unit with the differential to form a rear transaxle that was part of a De Dion assembly with coil springs. Brakes were disc all around, with the rears moved inboard to reduce unsprung weight.

The Alfetta GT came to the U.S. in 1975 with the 1962-cc engine, but was offered in Europe with a choice of 1.6-, 1.8-, and 2.0-liter engines. The designation became GTV in 1976, then changed to Sprint Veloce in 1978.

All shared the same fastback coupe body, again by Bertone. While roomier than previous Alfa coupes, it wasn't noted as an aesthetic success. It also wasn't quite large enough to provide practical transportation for four, and wasn't sleek enough to be either a true GT or sports car. And though it looked like it should have had a hatchback, it didn't. However, these models were the best-handling Alfas to date, partly because of excellent suspension geometry and partly because of the near-equal fore/aft weight distribution conferred by the rear transaxle.

In 1981, this car took on a new image and a new powerplant to become the GTV-6. Exterior sheetmetal and appearance remained much as before, but structure,

The 1986 U.S. GTV-6 shows few basic styling differences from the predecessor Alfetta GT, but V-6 provides more spirited performance.

suspension, brakes, transaxle, wheels, and tires were all upgraded to cope with a bigger and more potent engine. It turned out to be a sterling new 60-degree V-6, with a single overhead camshaft on each bank, driven by toothed belt, plus Bosch L-Jetronic fuel injection (specified for both the American and European versions). Inclined valves above hemispherical chambers were retained, but were now actuated by a rather complicated arrangement. The camshafts were directly over the intake valves, but worked the exhaust valves via tappets, transverse pushrods, and rocker arms. Displacement was 2492 cc from a bore of 88 mm and a stroke of 68.3 mm, a far cry from Alfa's long-stroke engines of old. Rated horsepower was 154 (SAE) at 5500 rpm with 152 lbs-ft torque at 3200 rpm, enough to propel the 2840-pound GTV-6 from 0 to 60 mph in 8.4 seconds and on to a top speed of 125 mph.

The interior wasn't overlooked either. A tilt wheel, leather upholstery, higher-grade carpeting, and standard air conditioning all made the driver feel good, even if they didn't contribute to performance. Even more welcome was a new dashboard with all instruments placed directly in front of the driver, eliminating the odd arrangement of previous models in which the speedometer and minor gauges were inconveniently placed in the center of the dash.

The shift mechanism to the rear-mounted transmission was thought to be somewhat soft and rubbery. Complaints were voiced about the twin-disc clutch being grabby, though it never slipped. But these are things that could be changed through development, and were.

The best part of the GTV-6 was its excellent balance and overall handling. Critics and Alfa loyalists alike wondered why this suspension couldn't be put under the Spider. It could, of course, but Alfa management didn't want to go any further with their convertible.

Whether the GTV-6 will be replaced is uncertain in the wake of Alfa Romeo's takeover by Fiat in 1987. If we're lucky, the new owners will replace this spirited but aesthetically awkward coupe with something truly modern—dare we say futuristic?—and that should be well worth waiting for.

SPECIFICATIONS

Engine: sohc V-6, 154.8 cid/2492 cc, 154 bhp @ 5500 rpm, 152 lbs-ft @ 3200 rpm (SAE net)

Transmission:	5-speed manual
Suspension, front:	lower A-arms, upper transverse arms and trailing links, torsion bars, anti-roll bar
Suspension, rear:	De Dion transaxle with angled trailing links, Watt linkage, coil springs, anti-roll bar
Brakes:	front/rear disc (inboard at rear)
Wheelbase (in.):	94.5
Weight (lbs):	2840
Top speed (mph):	125
0-60 mph (sec):	8.4
Production:	NA

1946-1949
ALLARD K1

Sydney Allard was 19 years old in 1929, a member of a London family who owned a garage that sold British Ford cars. Sydney raced a three-wheel Morgan Super Sports at the Brooklands circuit that year, but with very little success. Deciding he needed an extra wheel, he added one to create the first Allard special.

Sydney's first fling with a Ford, a relationship that would last as long as he built cars, came in 1932 when he bought a new four-cylinder Model B and installed a highly modified Model BB truck engine. That car went so well that he began to think of what he might do with one of Ford's V-8s, particularly in a lightweight chassis. Through an incredible coincidence, Allard found just the car he had been looking for at the Tourist Trophy race in Ards, Ireland, in 1934. The area Ford distributor had shown up with two shiny specials fitted with the American flathead engine, and Allard bought one without a second thought.

Allard campaigned the car for two seasons in track races, rallies, and hillclimbs. But success in somebody else's car wasn't enough. Allard wanted to build his own.

The opportunity came in 1936 when he bought a wrecked '35 Ford coupe. After towing it home on a Friday, he started dismantling and rebuilding it on Monday. By Saturday, the first car to carry the name Allard Special was running. It followed a pattern that Sydney would continue to use in future years. The frame was shortened, lightened, and fitted with a 1932 Ford front-axle assembly, which was lighter than the '35 unit. Unlike later Allards though, this chassis was topped with a Bugatti Type 51 body. This oddball hybrid was a winner from the start. During the winter, suspension engineer Leslie Bellamy designed the now-infamous split-front-axle independent suspension that was to become a trademark of all early Allards.

World War II found the Allard garage repairing and maintaining British army trucks; as soon as hostilities were over, Sydney again turned to car building, but with a new seriousness. Like so many others in postwar England, his major problem was a lack of materials, particularly steel and aluminum. This was one of the many reasons why Allard relied so heavily on proprietary parts for his cars. His choice of Ford components rather than some other make's stemmed from a combination of availability, cost, and his own familiarity with them.

Designated K1, Allard's first postwar car was largely a carryover from the limited-production prewar J1 except for a six-inch-longer wheelbase. The engine (a British-built 221-cubic-inch Ford V-8 with 85 horsepower) was virtually stock. Transmission, driveshaft, rear axle, and brakes were also stock Ford, as was the front axle. However, the last was split in the center to create a swing-axle type independent front suspension. A torque tube and beam axle located the rear wheels; front and rear springing was by Ford's antiquated transverse leafs. The frame was made up from stamped-steel channel sections by Thomsons of Wolverton specially for Allard. Side rails and cross-members were designed to fit the existing Ford suspension pieces, because there was no thought at that time of using anything but Ford running gear and chassis components.

Most early Allards—the K, L, and M two- and four-place models—looked much the same. Some have compared them to the BMW 328, with the same sort of squarish "waterfall" grille and separate fenders front and rear. All were right-hand drive, of course. The four-place models had roll-up windows. Bodies, all built by Allard, employed a wood-frame overlaid with steel panels.

As far as we know, the K1 was never offered for sale outside England, although company records show a few going to Brazil, Argentina, Belgium, Australia, and possibly three to the U.S. As expected, the vast majority were sold in England and Scotland. Some K1s carried Canadian Mercury V-8s instead of the British Ford unit.

The K-series was really a stepping-stone model for Allard, who would go on to even greater fame and success with the J2 competition model.

SPECIFICATIONS

Engines: Ford Britain L-Head V-8, 221 cid/3622 cc, 85/95 bhp @ 3600 rpm; Canadian Mercury L-head V-8, 239 cid/3917 cc, 95/100 bhp @ 3600 rpm

Transmission:	3-speed manual (synchromesh on II-III)
Suspension, front:	solid axle split in center, transverse leaf spring
Suspension, rear:	live axle, transverse leaf spring
Brakes:	front/rear drums
Wheelbase (in.):	106.0
Weight (lbs):	2460
Top speed (mph):	NA
0-60 mph (sec):	NA
Production:	151

This K1 doesn't look like the home-built special it is. Unique "waterfall" grille was characteristic of Allard's early-postwar roadgoing models.

1950-1951
ALLARD J2

The postwar resurgence of England's auto industry was hard on many. The car companies seemed to be seeking the most profit per pound of scarce materials rather than trying to develop new models, so buyers didn't have a great choice of cars—or many great ones either.

As bad as this may have been for the public, it was good for Sydney Allard's fledgling business. Allard was also smart enough to realize that this situation wouldn't last forever, and that he'd better get cracking on a new and better car before things changed. Allard went to the U.S. on a research trip, and came home with an important fact he hadn't known before: Americans wouldn't buy his existing K, L, or M models, but they might buy an updated version of his original J. The result was the J2, the car that put Allards in the winner's circle and Sydney's name on the sports-car racing map.

Retaining the J1's 100-inch wheelbase and the split I-beam front axle used in all Allards since World War II, the J2 featured coils instead of the old transverse leaf springs front and rear, plus a De Dion rear axle with quick-change center section and inboard 12-inch Alfin drum brakes. The radius rods that had previously helped locate a live rear axle now served as locating members for the De Dion dead-axle beam. Dry weight could be as low as 2000 pounds, but never went over 2600 even with one of the big new American V-8s such as Cadillac or Chrysler.

Having improved the chassis, Allard turned his attention to the powerplant. His "off-the-shelf" engine, the flathead Ford V-8, was 18 years old in 1950, and thus no longer suitable for a serious competition car despite an enormous amount of available speed equipment—at least for U.S. buyers. (Import restrictions kept it from being sold in England.) By coincidence, an overhead-valve conversion for the flathead Ford/Mercury V-8 was being created in New York City by Zora Arkus-Duntov (in a loft he shared with Luigi Chinetti, soon to be U.S. Ferrari distributor). Duntov's design, a pushrod-and-rocker-arm system much like that of the first Chrysler hemi V-8 engines, worked well in some American hot rods at places like Bonneville and El Mirage Dry Lake, but nobody in England, it seemed, could make this Ardun engine produce reliable power for any length of time. Thus, the J2 arrived with a choice of flathead Ford or Mercury, the Ardun ohv conversion, or the new ohv Cadillac or Chrysler V-8s. It soon became obvious that the last were the ones to have, and the Ardun engine was dropped from production after about 75 J2s were so equipped.

For all its faults, the J2 was a simple, reliable competition machine. As with his previous cars, Allard used as many proprietary parts as possible, most of which were understressed and seldom caused trouble. Those that broke were easily and cheaply replaced, so it was no great problem to maintain a racing schedule with this rugged, very dependable car. The frame remained a channel-section stamped-steel affair, with cross-members for supporting radiator, engine, transmission, front and rear axles, and the rudimentary body with its bolt-on rear fenders and cycle-type front fenders.

Cars were made with either left- or right-hand drive depending on the work order and ultimate destination. With their proprietary Ford axles, early Allards naturally had the same 56-inch track dimensions as contemporary Fords, but rear track was reduced to 52 inches with the J2's De Dion axle. This sometimes made the car look as though it "crab-tracked" when in fact it was going dead straight.

The J2 was a very basic car for touring or racing, little more than a British hot rod. But it was fast (especially with Cadillac or Chrysler power), exciting (for race watchers as well as drivers) and, until overwhelmed by the more sophisticated and far costlier Ferraris, Maseratis, and Mercedes, was usually the car to beat at most any event.

SPECIFICATIONS

Engines: Ford U.S. L-head V-8, 239 cid/3917 cc, 100 bhp @ 3600 rpm, 181 lbs-ft @ 2000 rpm (140-bhp Ardun ohv conversion); Cadillac ohv V-8, 331 cid/5420 cc, 160 bhp @ 3800 rpm, 312 lbs-ft @ 1800 rpm; Chrysler ohv V-8, 331 cid/5420 cc, 180 bhp @ 4000 rpm, 312 lbs-ft @ 2000 rpm

Transmission:	3-speed manual (synchromesh on II-III)
Suspension, front:	solid axle split in center, coil springs
Suspension, rear:	De Dion axle (with Allard quick-change differential), coil springs
Brakes:	front/rear drums
Wheelbase (in.):	100.0
Weight (lbs):	2000-2600
Top speed (mph):	NA
0-60 mph (sec):	NA
Production:	90

J2 was a more modern version of the race-and-ride J1 but still employed as many borrowed components as Sydney Allard could manage. This example recalls the heyday of J2 racing, which is the way most were used. Performance was formidable with Yankee V-8s.

1950-1952
ALLARD K2

Nineteen-fifty brought out an improved version of Sydney Allard's roadgoing K1 sports car. Logically designated K2, it retained a live rear axle with transverse leaf spring and a split front axle, now on twin coil springs instead of the single transverse leaf. Also new was a smoother, two/three-seat aluminum body with cut-down doors and a tail treatment not far removed from that of the Jaguar XK120. From there forward, however, the K2 was its own car, sharing a style with nothing but other Allards. The front fenders were what some designers call the "clamshell" type and carried flush headlights. The front bodysides, with three portholes *a la* Buick, joined to a rounded nose with a squarish, vertical-bar grille. Set well back from this was a small flat hood panel. Typical of Allard practice to date, stamped-steel disc wheels were standard, and short bumperettes protected the easily dented body front and rear.

Inside, the K2 was pretty stark but more "luxurious" than any previous two-seat Allards—more like the four-passenger L, M, and P models—with full instrumentation and a choice of right- or left-hand drive.

Underneath, frame rails and cross-members were stamped specially for Allard by Thomsons of Wolverhampton, not made up from Ford pieces, though engine, transmission, and both axles continued to come from Ford. Also retained was a front axle split in the center to create the now-famous Allard swing-axle ifs, while the rear axle was shortened to provide a narrower rear track.

Buick-style portholes and rather odd proportioning marked the Allard K2. Like the predecessor K1, most carried proprietary British and American flathead Ford V-8s. This example has been treated to a supercharger and protruding dual exhausts.

The K2 was offered with four engines, all based on the Ford/Mercury flathead V-8: a 221-inch version with 85 horsepower, the same with 90 bhp (presumably via high-compression heads and dual intake manifold), a 239-cid block with Ardun ohv heads and a rated 140 bhp, and a bored-out 266.8-cid Mercury unit with Allard aluminum heads and 110 bhp. Unlike the J2, no ohv American V-8s were available here.

Allard made his own speed equipment for the Ford engine because of England's exorbitant import duty on U.S. parts, though he based them on the American items. His cylinder heads, for example, were copied from Eddie Edmunds, his dual intake manifold from Eddie Meyer.

Americans who bought an Allard with a "Mercury" engine soon found that it really had the 1937/early-'38 Ford 21-stud unit, with the water pump in the block and the water outlets in the center of the cylinder heads. Those who tried to put American speed equipment on the British-built V-8 often found things didn't fit right, and a 24-stud Edelbrock head, for example, wouldn't fit at all. The intake manifolds were interchangeable, so that was no problem.

Like so many other Allards, the K2s were little more than British-style hot rods, modeled on the American concept but designed more for touring or road racing than sheer straight-line performance. American hot rodders bought '32 Ford roadsters and went to work; British hot rodders just bought Allards. Undoubtedly, Sydney Allard would have felt right at home in Los Angeles or on El Mirage Dry Lake, and Yankee speed demons would have found him a kindred spirit.

Allard built 119 K2s through 1952, and a substantial number of them were sold in the United States. (Curiously, the first two, sold in February 1950, went to Uruguay.) This isn't surprising given the Ford heritage of most Allards, many of which received extreme engine modifications after reaching these shores. The ready availability of flathead-Ford speed equipment and wide knowledge of how to use it made a lot of Allards a lot faster than Sydney ever dreamed.

SPECIFICATIONS

Engines: Ford Britain L-head V-8, 221 cid/3622 cc, 85/90 bhp (140 bhp Ardun ohv conversion); American Mercury L-head V-8, 239 cid/3917 cc, 95/100 bhp @ 3600 rpm

Transmission:	3-speed manual (synchromesh on II-III)
Suspension, front:	solid axle split in center, coil springs
Suspension, rear:	live axle, transverse leaf spring
Brakes:	front/rear drums
Wheelbase (in.):	106.0
Weight (lbs):	2460
Top speed (mph):	NA
0-60 mph (sec):	NA
Production:	119

1952-1954 ALLARD K3

Having been very successful in building competition-oriented cars, Sydney Allard turned to the design and production of a more serious touring model in 1952. The result was the new K3, generally offered with the buyer's choice of engine, with engine mounts then fitted to suit. Allard kept his unique split-axle independent front suspension and borrowed his J2's wider De Dion rear axle. Otherwise, the K3 frame was totally new. Made with a pair of stacked chrome-moly tubes as side rails, heavily gusseted with steel plates, it was both lighter and stronger than the previous stamped-steel channel-section chassis.

Bodywork, too, was all-new, being a modern "envelope" type with integral rather than separate fenders. Inside was a bench seat that could accommodate three in relative comfort.

Though built on a wheelbase six inches shorter than the K2's, the K3 seemed bigger than it really was. It was too often compared with the contemporary MG, Triumph, Porsche, and Austin-Healey, all of which made the Allard seem huge when, in fact, its main bulk was in width (tracks were 56.5 inches front, 58.5 inches rear) and weight (2580 pounds at the curb).

Road & Track magazine tested a K3 in October 1954 and gave it high marks for acceleration, handling (weight distribution was 50/50), and steering. However, the editors complained that the wheels wouldn't turn far enough in either direction and suggested that parallel parking was a definite problem, let alone running a gymkhana. They also felt that the clutch and transmission were weak points and criticized the aluminum body's susceptibility to damage from flying gravel. The cockpit came in for the most criticism despite its greater room. The doors didn't open wide enough, there was no provision for heating or defrosting, and the windshield wipers were inadequate. Worse, ventilation with the top and windows up was totally inadequate, and with top up and windows down, the car couldn't be driven more than 35 miles per hour without the top flapping to the passengers' distraction. So although Allard had intended this as a sporting, fast, and comfortable tourer that could be sold in all countries, it was apparent that the K3 needed much more development. Not surprisingly, most K3s came to the U.S. Two went to Mexico and Canada, and one each to Germany, Venezuela, Colombia, Guatemala, India, Belgium, and England.

For its day, the K3 was reasonably well finished, if still not as good as cars from the volume manufacturers. Allard had discovered, to his dismay, that what passed for good fit and finish in a competition car was a far cry from what was needed for a saleable road car.

This reflected a big problem. While Sydney Allard had many "better ideas," his company was seriously undercapitalized, lacking both the facilities and manpower to develop his designs fully. This didn't seem to matter with his competition cars, particularly in the early 1950s, when racing didn't have anywhere near the sophistication it does today, but it made producing a competitive road car extremely difficult. When a customer paid well over $5000 for a car (the K3 sold for about $5300 in the U.S.), he expected to get something he could proudly show off to his friends. In that respect, the K3 was an embarrassment in many ways.

Early publicity had indicated that the K3 was available with English Ford V-8, American Mercury V-8, Chrysler hemi V-8, or Jaguar XK dohc six. Yet even that choice of powerplants and Allard's proven race record still weren't enough to make this car the commercial success he thought it would be. The last K3 left the Allard factory on October 8, 1954. Total production was just 61. Still, it would prove to be neither the most nor least successful of Sydney's memorable hybrids.

SPECIFICATIONS

Engines: Ford Britain L-head V-8, 221 cid/3622 cc, 85 bhp; American Mercury L-head V-8, 239 cid/3917 cc, 95/100 bhp @ 3600 rpm; Chrysler ohv V-8, 331 cid/5420 cc, 180 bhp @ 4000 rpm, 312 lbs-ft @ 2000 rpm; Jaguar dohc I-6, 210 cid/3442 cc, 160 bhp @ 5200 rpm

Transmissions:	3-speed manual (4-speed with Jaguar engine)
Suspension, front:	solid axle split in center, radius rods, coil springs
Suspension, rear:	De Dion axle, coil springs
Brakes:	front/rear drums
Wheelbase (in.):	100.0
Weight (lbs):	2580
Top speed (mph):	115 (est. with Chrysler engine)
0-60 mph (sec):	8.6 (est. with Chrysler engine)
Production:	61 (some sources list 62)

K3 was Sydney Allard's first attempt at modern sports-car styling, which bore a passing resemblance to the contemporary Cunningham C2. Many design flaws precluded high sales. Jaguar XK six and Chrysler hemi V-8 were available, delivered great go.

1952-1954 ALLARD J2X

As far as we know, Sydney Allard's first J2X carried chassis number 2138 and was delivered to a buyer in London on September 7, 1951. The second one went to America on November 21. Thus began a production run that would see just 83 cars. The last one left the factory on November 29, 1954, destined for the U.S.

The main visual difference between the J2X and the earlier J2 was their spare tire location: hidden in a compartment low in the back on the J2, an exposed side-mount (just forward of the cockpit) on J2X. The differences were as few underneath, but far more important. Typical Allard suspension—split I-beam front axle, De Dion rear with long radius rods to the chassis—was retained, as were all-round coil springs and inboard rear brakes. In front, the "trailing" radius rods had been moved from behind the axle to a position in front of the axle ("leading" rods), which necessitated a six-inch frame extension at the front. This explains the "X" designation (for extended) as wheelbase remained at 100 inches, as on the J2. It also allowed the engine to be mounted 7.5 inches further forward, which added considerably to cockpit footroom and made the car handle much better at the same time.

As before, engine choices were L-head Mercury V-8, the same with Ardun overhead valves, and ohv Cadillac or Chrysler V-8s. The vast majority of J2Xs were ordered with the last, since the Ford engine, with or without ohv, was no longer a viable contender in the horsepower race.

Most J2Xs also seemed to have center-lock, knock-off wire wheels rather than the stamped-steel discs of the J2, though this is not a hard and fast identification point. The J2X was conceived as a competition car that *might* be used for touring, while the J2 was the other way around (though more of them probably raced than toured).

At speed, a J2 or J2X was a spectacular sight: rear end hunkered down from the torque of a big Cadillac V-8, front end in the air, the caster angle caused by the swing-axle ifs making the front wheels look "knock-kneed" as the car weaved and dodged its way along. They may not have been as exciting to drive fast as they looked from the sidelines, but drivers we've talked to admit that while the De Dion rear axle kept the back end pretty much under control, the same thing couldn't be said for the front. Staying on course in either of these beasts was often a matter of aim and hope.

Regardless, they won races, sometimes looking deceptively casual in the process. Spectators at early races from Watkins Glen and Bridgehampton to Torry Pines and Pebble Beach remember Fred Wacker, Mike Graham, and Bill Pollack as being the primary practitioners of the Allard driving art, the last at the wheel of Tom Carstens' black number-14 J2X complete with chrome-plated luggage rack and whitewall tires!

They were cars to root for, those Allards—British hot rods with big American V-8s, something a great many racegoers could readily identify with. They were not "giant killers" because they were giants themselves, but they were the epitome of low-dollar racing in their day—backyard challengers to the ever-increasing number of costly, multi-cylinder, high-technology Ferraris.

And unfortunately, Sydney Allard could no longer keep pace. By 1954, you either bought a Ferrari, Porsche, Maserati or Aston Martin if you wanted to win races, or you built your own cars with a lot of money and know-how, as Briggs Cunningham did.

The Allards' days have passed, but they will be fondly remembered and missed. Racing was fun then.

SPECIFICATIONS

Engines: American Mercury L-head V-8, 239 cid/3917 cc, 120 bhp @ 3600 rpm; Chrysler ohv V-8, 331 cid/5420 cc, 180-235 bhp @ 4000-4400 rpm, 312-330 lbs-ft @ 2000-2600 rpm; Cadillac ohv V-8, 331 cid/5420 cc, 190-230 bhp @ 4000-4400 rpm, 322-330 lbs-ft @ 2200-2700 rpm

Transmission:	3-speed manual
Suspension, front:	solid axle split in center, radius rods, coil springs
Suspension, rear:	De Dion axle with Allard quick-change differential, coil springs
Brakes:	front/rear drums
Wheelbase (in.):	100.0
Weight (lbs):	2500
Top speed (mph):	125 (est. with Chrysler engine)
0-60 mph (sec):	8.0 (est. with Chrysler engine)
Production:	83

Purposeful is the only way to describe the most famous of Allards, the J2X. Extended wheelbase, sidemount spare, and more forward engine made it a better racer than the J2.

1971-1985
ALPINE-RENAULT A310

The first "private enterprise" Alpine-Renaults, designed and manufactured by Jean Redele's company in Dieppe, France, appeared in the early Fifties. By the Sixties, Alpine was much closer to the Renault factory technically and commercially. Its mainstays in these years were the A108 and A110 series, fast but fragile rear-engine coupes with Renault running gear and fiberglass bodies. But these were cramped little two-seaters more suited to racing or European rallying than normal road work.

A new model was long overdue by 1971, and Alpine-Renault surprised everyone that year with the new A310, a much larger, more spacious, and altogether more practical machine. It was so different from the 1957-vintage A108/A110 that both the old and new models continued in production for a number of years. The former were high-strung two-seaters for youngbloods (rather the "Corvette types" of France), the latter more sophisticated long-distance GTs.

Even so, the A310 followed the established—and famous—Alpine-Renault formula in many ways: rear-mounted engine, steel backbone chassis with all-independent suspension, many standard components from the Renault parts bin, separate fiberglass body. Compared with the A110, it was longer, wider, and far roomier, with genuine 2+2 seating and graceful, modern styling (some compared its front end to that of the Ferrari Daytona).

The original A310 used the most powerful Renault production engine then available, the overhead-valve 1.6-liter four from the R16, matched to a 5-speed all-synchromesh transaxle. Automatic wasn't available, and never would be. This chassis was capable of handling a lot more power. Even so, the four's 127 bhp gave the French coupe a 131-mph top speed.

Unfortunately, the A310 was dogged by quality control problems early on, and many prospective customers shunned its rear-engine layout (the DeLorean encountered similar resistance in the Eighties, though it never seemed to bother Porsche's 911). Then came the first Energy Crisis in 1973-74, which only compounded the sales difficulties. As a result, Alpine-Renault soon found itself in financial hot water. But Renault came to the rescue by buying the firm, and Alpine has seen steady expansion ever since.

Autumn 1976 brought the definitive A310, powered by a new 90-degree V-6. This engine, jointly developed by Peugeot, Renault, and Volvo and used in so many other cars in the late Seventies/early Eighties (including the DeLorean), suited the A310's character very well indeed. It offered an easy 150 bhp, pushing top speed up to about 137 mph and making this the world's quickest rear-engine production car apart from the Porsche 911. Exactly 2334 four-cylinder A310s had been built in five years, but the new V-6 sold even better, helped by further improvements: standard 5-speed gearbox in 1979, upgraded interior appointments from late 1982. Production continued at Dieppe until 1985, when the A310 gave way to the new GTA. Sales were confined largely to Europe (mainly France and Germany), but a few A310s made it to the U.S. via the infamous "gray market" of the late Seventies/early Eighties.

Whether four-cylinder or V-6, the A310 was essentially a car for younger, more tolerant drivers. No matter how hard Renault tried to disguise the rear-engine location, it couldn't banish the layout's characteristic tail-out handling behavior, which could feel quite spooky in some circumstances. Nevertheless, the A310 always sold well by Alpine-Renault standards, and the small purpose-built factory was kept busy to the very end. Clearly, Renault judged the A310 a success, for its successor was very much the same type of car.

*A310 looked chunkier and more aggressive than the earlier A108/A110 and was the first Alpine-Renault with +2 seating. Appearance was unchanged over 14 years, but late V-6 models (**opposite bottom**) had a rear spoiler and various detail revisions.*

SPECIFICATIONS

Engines: Renault ohv I-4, 98 cid/1605 cc, 127 bhp (DIN) @ 6250 rpm, 108 lbs-ft @ 5000 rpm; "PRV" sohc V-6, 162.5 cid/2664 cc, 150 bhp (DIN) @ 6000 rpm, 150 lbs-ft @ 3500 rpm

Transmission:	4/5-speed manual
Suspension, front:	upper and lower A-arms, coil springs, anti-roll bar
Suspension, rear:	upper and lower A-arms, coil springs, anti-roll bar
Brakes:	front discs/rear drums (rear discs on V-6)
Wheelbase (in.):	89.4
Weight (lbs):	2075 (1.6-liter), 2240 (V-6)
Top speed (mph):	131 (1.6-liter), 137 (V-6)
0-60 mph (sec):	8.1 (1.6-liter), 7.5 (V-6)
Production:	**1.6-liter** 2334 **V-6** NA

1985-1988 ALPINE-RENAULT GTA

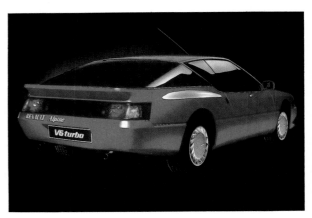

Renault allowed the Alpine-Renault A310 V-6 to run more than eight years before fielding a stunning replacement intended to carry the marque into the 1990s. Although this new GTA is similar in many ways, it has a lot that's completely new. It's certainly the most professional A-R yet. Where the A310 had been created on the cheap by Jean Redele's company, the GTA was designed by Renault itself, using every computer-assisted technique available. Moreover, the A310 was intended strictly for local consumption, while the GTA was planned for export appeal, particularly in the lucrative U.S. market.

First, though, the similarities. The A310 used a steel backbone frame, with the engine slung out behind and driving the rear wheels. Its fiberglass body afforded 2+2 (or, more charitably, close-coupled four-seat) accommodation. The GTA keeps this design faith in a more modern idiom. In addition, it's larger and roomier: three inches longer in wheelbase, four inches wider, two inches taller.

Structurally, the GTA is altogether more integrated than the A310, as it should be, coming from Renault. For example, its backbone frame uses much thinner metal, while the A310's entirely separate body has been axed in favor of fiberglass panels bonded to the chassis, resulting in a steel/fiberglass monocoque. As if to dispel the fiction that fiberglass body cars are necessarily light, the GTA weighs in at 2540 pounds, with the bodyshell accounting for 575 pounds of it, about 20 percent.

Compared with the A310, the GTA's styling was very carefully considered to optimize aerodynamics. Still, headlamps continue with sloping glass covers, and a low front "chin" spoiler and smartly integrated rear spoiler are also retained. But shape makes all the difference, and the GTA boosts a coefficient of drag (Cd) of only 0.28. Interestingly, Renault claims that the more significant CdA air-resistance figure (Cd × frontal area) is 5.1 square feet for the GTA, the lowest of any production car in the world. It is in such details that the GTA is so obviously a product of Renault rather than Alpine-Renault, and it made an immediate impression.

Mechanically, the GTA marked a further evolution of the A310. Power is still provided by the PRV V-6, but there are now two versions. The basic GTA carries a normally aspirated 2849-cc unit with Renault's own unique combination of single and twin-choke carburetors, good for 160 bhp at 5750 rpm. But the big news was availability of the 200-bhp 2458-cc turbocharged engine from the big Renault 25 sedan, which gives the GTA 150 mph flat out. As in the A310, both engines mount longitudinally and drive forward to an all-indirect Renault 5-speed gearbox. Automatic is again conspicuous by its absence, which brings us back to more similarities: all-independent suspension by coil springs and double wishbones, all-disc brakes, rack-and-pinion steering (albeit with standard power assist). To trim the tail-heavy handling (front/rear weight distribution is 39/63 percent), Renault specifies larger tires for the rear than the front, also as before except that both are bigger here: 195/50VR-15 fore, massive 255/45VR-15 rubber aft.

Although the GTA feels like a much better car than the A310, its handling still occasionally betrays that heavy rearward weight bias. Closing the throttle in tight corners can result in a spin, as it does on many Porsche 911s, though it's hardly hurt the sales of those cars. And make no mistake: the GTA is as fast as it looks, especially the Turbo. Yet because of the rear-engine position, it's surprisingly quiet when driven briskly. There's also no doubt that it has more interior space than its obvious rivals. Renault believe they've produced a better car than the 911, though only time will tell.

Sad to say, the GTA won't be sold in North America after all, even though designed for U.S. standards and intended to be the new flagship of Renault's American-market fleet. The reason, of course, is the 1987 Chrysler Corporation buyout of Renault's 46-percent stake in American Motors and, more to point, the close similarities in price and target audience between the GTA and Chrysler's long-delayed Maserati-built TC. Understandably, Chrysler doesn't need two $30,000 sports cars (it'll have trouble enough with one). And, corporate pride being what it is, any automaker will prefer its own product over one from an erstwhile rival, even one picked up as part of an acquisition.

So the GTA has been locked out of the U.S. market (just as Renault itself will be eventually), and it's too bad. It's cars like this that make life more interesting for enthusiasts, and American buffs will be that much poorer for lack of the GTA.

Alpine-Renault GTA was slated for U.S. sale but was cancelled by Chrysler Corporation's buyout of Renault's equity in American Motors. Hot Turbo version (above) reaches near 150 mph.

SPECIFICATIONS

Engines: all "PRV" sohc V-6; 174 cid/2849 cc, 160 bhp (DIN) @ 5750 rpm, 166 lbs-ft @ 3500 rpm; 150 cid/2458 cc, 200 bhp (DIN) @ 5750 rpm, 214 lbs-ft @ 2500 rpm (turbocharged) (All ratings for European models without catalytic converter.)

Transmission:	5-speed manual
Suspension, front:	upper and lower A-arms, coil springs, anti-roll bar
Suspension, rear:	upper and lower A-arms, coil springs, anti-roll bar
Brakes:	front/rear discs
Wheelbase (in.):	92.1
Weight (lbs):	2620
Top speed (mph):	149 (Turbo)
0-60 mph (sec):	6.3
Production:	NA (production continues at this writing)

1968-1970
AMERICAN MOTORS AMX

Richard A. Teague has always been a "two-seater kind of guy," and the production AMX was his car. It originated in late 1965 when the American Motors styling director worked up four non-running show cars at the behest of company chairman Roy D. Chapin, Jr., who wanted to show the public that AMC was a going concern capable of more exciting stuff than the workaday economy sedans for which it was noted.

Included in this quartet, which toured the nation as "Project IV," was a slick fastback coupe that Teague named AMX (logically, for "American Motors Experimental"). Its most novel feature was the "Ramble Seat," an updated version of the old rumble-seat idea, with a rear windscreen and a pair of auxiliary bucket seats that could be flipped up to accommodate two extra passengers *al fresco*. There was also a small, conventional back seat, leading Teague to call the package a "2+2+2." With its taut, eager styling, the AMX met with such overwhelming response that AMC contracted Vignale of Italy to build a running model.

Meantime, Teague was working on the Javelin, AMC's reply to the Ford Mustang, giving it much of the AMX show car's styling flavor. Being at AMC, and Packard before that, Teague was used to doing big things on small budgets, and he hatched a brilliant idea: take 12 vertical inches out of the new 109-inch-wheelbase Javelin to create a two-seater that could be tooled for very little money, thus providing even more of the image-boosting excitement Chapin was seeking.

The result appeared in February 1968, *sans* "Ramble Seat" but still called AMX. Though its Javelin heritage was obvious, Teague gave it a "faster" back, a different grille, longer hood, and racy rear-fender creases. AMC engineers gave it their biggest powerplant ever: a 390-cubic-inch enlargement of the thinwall V-8 previously available as a 290 (1966) and 343 (1967), which were standard and optional, respectively.

With two seats and a wheelbase an inch shorter than Corvette's, the AMX was often seen by the press as a Corvette competitor, though AMC never called it a "sports car." But like the '57 T-Bird, it *could* be a high-performance car. To prove it, AMC hired Land Speed Record ace Craig Breedlove and wife Lee to take a couple of AMXs out for a spin on a Texas track. "Spin" they did, streaking 24 straight hours to 106 new national and international speed records while averaging 140.7 mph. The Breedloves later hit 189 mph in a USAC-sponsored run at Bonneville. Soon, AMXs were cleaning up on the dragstrips (thanks to Lou Downy, Shirley Shahan, and others) and in amateur sports-car competition (though one was nosed out by a Corvette for the 1969 SCCA national championship).

The AMX generated lots of excitement but not many sales, something AMC had halfway expected. The '69s were predictably little changed apart from a $52 higher base price, new and *very* bright "Big Bad" colors, and an optional "Go" package. Volume improved but slightly, so AMC decided to bail out after the 1970 models, which carried revised frontal styling that added two inches to overall length, plus "power blister" hood, high-back seats, and AMC's new 360 V-8 as standard. Alas, production plunged to half the previous year's. Teague tried to keep the car alive, mocking up an AMX version of his restyled humped-fender '71 Javelin, but to no avail.

Still, Teague managed a moral victory in two exciting mid-engine exercises, the non-running AMX/2 of 1969 and the follow-up 1970 AMX/3, of which six were built. The latter, developed with help from Italian sports-car engineer Giotto Bizzarrini and BMW, had all-independent wishbone suspension, big four-wheel disc brakes, a 340-bhp 390 engine, and handsome styling—perhaps Teague's best effort ever and chosen over a competitive (and rather dull) proposal by Giorgetto Giugiaro.

The AMX/3 might have seen limited production, but AMC was on a downhill slide by 1970 and had no money for that or even a continuation of the Javelin-based AMX. Now there's no more AMC, and Teague is retired.

But not to a rocking chair. Among his many and varied current activities is the occasional presentation to AMX enthusiasts—which is only fitting. After all, they're his kind of people.

SPECIFICATIONS

Engines: all ohv V-8; **1968-69:** 290 cid/4752 cc, 225 bhp @ 4700 rpm, 300 lbs-ft @ 3200 rpm; 343 cid/5621 cc, 280 bhp @ 4800 rpm, 365 lbs-ft @ 3000 rpm; 390 cid/6391 cc, 315 bhp @ 4600 rpm, 425 lbs-ft @ 3200 rpm; **1970:** 360 cid/5899 cc, 290 bhp @ 4800 rpm, 395 lbs-ft @ 3200 rpm; 390 cid/6391 cc, 325 bhp @ 5400 rpm, 420 lbs-ft @ 3200 rpm; 390 cid/6391 cc, 340 bhp @ 5100 rpm, 430 lbs-ft @ 3600 rpm

Transmissions:	3/4-speed manual, 3-speed automatic
Suspension, front:	unequal-length A-arms, coil springs
Suspension, rear:	live axle, semi-elliptic leaf springs
Brakes:	front discs/rear drums
Wheelbase (in.):	97.0
Weight (lbs):	3245-3395
Top speed (mph):	120-130
0-60 mph (sec):	6.7-9.0
Production:	**1968** 6725 **1969** 8293 **1970** 4116

*Dorsal racing stripes were part of AMX's "Go" package option for '69. Javelin-based two-seater was a real stormer with optional 390 V-8 (**opposite top**).*

1954-1961 ARNOLT-BRISTOL

Chicago has had its fair share of interesting characters over the years. Take S.H. "Wacky" Arnolt. In the Fifties, Arnolt operated a profitable Windy City foreign-car dealership and was also vice-president of Bertone, the renowned Italian coachbuilding firm. Having already built a little-known Bertone-bodied sports car based on the T-series MG (the Arnolt-MG), Wacky conceived the idea of a similar hybrid using the British Bristol chassis. To that end, he visited the London Motor Show in October 1953 and talked to Bristol executives. Following these discussions, Arnolt visited the Bristol factory, acquired a Bristol 404 rolling chassis, and shipped it to Italy so that Bertone could design a two-seat body to suit. The result was the Arnolt-Bristol, which went on sale in 1954 through another of Wacky's many enterprises.

The Arnolt-Bristol was an interesting amalgam of contemporary Bristol chassis engineering and Bertone styling and body construction. The 96-inch-wheelbase chassis was basically the 404 platform, a sturdy box-section affair with transverse front leaf spring and a carefully located live rear axle. However, the A-B packed more power than the 404, carrying a tuned version of Bristol's Type BS1 sports-racing engine, a six-cylinder unit that harked back to the prewar BMW 328. Output was 130 horsepower (Bristol touring-car engines were usually rated at 105 bhp in this period). Gearbox and brakes came from Bristol's earlier 403 coupe-sedan. To use the modern vernacular, the Arnolt-Bristol was a real "parts bin" job.

Bristol sent rolling chassis to Bertone, which topped them with either open two-seater or closely related fastback coupe bodies. Completed cars were then shipped to Chicago. The fastback would prove very rare (it is thought that only two were built). The open version was offered in two forms. The stark $3994 Bolide, with cut-down windshield and no soft top, was essentially a ready-made "club racer." An extra $750 bought a Deluxe model with more complete trim. The coupe, though still small inside, noisy, and somewhat uncomfortable to drive, had full weather protection and wind-down windows. The styling, all swooping curves with a rather pinched nose and mouth, was typical of Bertone in the Fifties.

Because Arnolt-Bristols were built mostly by hand in limited quantities (only 142 over seven years), specifications varied. Early examples had conventional steel disc wheels, but later cars were supplied with center-lock discs, presumably for faster changes at pit stops.

Though demand was never high, the Arnolt-Bristol was a remarkably long-lived specialty sports car. Light weight and ample power gave it good acceleration, and this coupled with excellent balance and fine manners made it a racing natural. Its first competition win came in the 2.0-liter class at the 1955 Sebring 12 Hours (repeated the following year), and A-Bs were still winning races—or at least their class—well into the Sixties.

By that time, though, routine chassis supplies had ceased (Bristol was about to stop building its distinctive BMW-based six anyway) and even Wacky was gone (he died in 1960). With little impetus to develop a successor model, the marque disappeared, but not before a final A-B was built from leftover parts and delivered in 1964.

Though 12 cars were lost to a warehouse fire, a high proportion of the remaining 130 Arnolt-Bristols survive today. Among them are two interesting "few-of-a-kind" variations: an aluminum-bodied semi-racer, of which five were originally built, and another four roadsters equipped with 283-cubic-inch Corvette V-8s.

Elusive, expensive, and immensely desirable, the Arnolt-Bristol remains a footnote in the pages of automotive history, but a memorable one. Like Chicago, it had a lot of class that was rarely appreciated.

SPECIFICATIONS

Engine: Bristol ohv I-6; 120 cid/1971 cc, 130 bhp (net) @ 5500 rpm, 128 lbs-ft @ 5000 rpm

Transmission:	4-speed manual
Suspension, front:	double wishbones, transverse leaf spring
Suspension, rear:	live axle, A-bracket, radius arms, torsion bars
Brakes:	front/rear drums
Wheelbase (in.):	96.0
Weight (lbs):	2050-2315
Top speed (mph):	107
0-60 mph (sec):	10.1

Production: 142; includes 2 coupes (some sources list 3) and 12 cars destroyed in warehouse fire

Most Arnolt-Bristols were roadsters like this Bolide, designed for weekend competition duty and fitted out accordingly here. Bertone used near-identical lines for a one-off Arnolt-Aston Martin built on a DB2 chassis in the mid-Fifties.

1948-1950
ASTON MARTIN DB1

Tiny Aston Martin was in financial trouble by the time industrialist David Brown bought it in 1947. Of course, the firm already had a checkered history. The very first Aston Martin was built in 1914, though sales didn't begin until 1921, while the Thirties brought hard times, several changes of ownership, and no radically new models.

But by 1947 there was a new design, laid down during and after the war by Claude Hill. Code-named "Atom," it featured a box-section multi-tube chassis with all-coil suspension—independent trailing arms at the front and a live rear axle located by radius rods—plus a 2.0-liter four-cylinder engine with pushrod-actuated overhead valves. Trouble was, the old Aston Martin company (then based at Feltham in Middlesex, near London's still-small Heathrow airport) couldn't afford to tool up for production. But the David Brown takeover made fresh funds available, and the Atom duly arrived on the market in 1948 as the DB1, the designation obviously standing for "David Brown, first model." However, it was only intended as an interim offering. Brown had also acquired Lagonda in 1947 and was busy getting out an all-new Lagonda sedan whose twincam engine would power a forthcoming new Aston.

Though nicely engineered, the DB1 chassis was suited to only very limited production. This undoubtedly made the whole car quite expensive to build. It certainly wasn't a profitable project, but that didn't seem to matter. As Brown later admitted, he'd bought Aston and Lagonda merely to "have a bit of fun."

In truth, the DBI was underpowered and only 15 were ever sold. Its 2.0-liter engine produced a respectable 90 horsepower (SAE), but this was largely negated by the heavy four-seat convertible bodywork fitted to most examples. However, there was one light—and successful—DB1: a sparsely equipped two-seat sports racer that won the Belgian Spa 24-Hour race in 1948 in the capable hands of "Jock" Horsefall and Leslie Johnson. No replicas, however, were ever produced.

The standard convertible shell was styled by ex-Lagonda employee Frank Feeley, who had been responsible for such luscious creations as the Thirties V-12 Lagondas and the new 2.6-liter Lagonda sedan then reaching production. The DB1 bore the characteristic front-end treatment that would be carried forward on the more famous DB2, and had long, sweeping lines.

The DB1 engine was never used in any other Aston or Lagonda. And since no tooling and few spare parts were ever produced, keeping this British rarity on the road won't be easy or cheap. Such is the price of history.

SPECIFICATIONS

Engine: ohv I-4, 120 cid/1970 cc, 90 bhp (SAE gross) @ 4750 rpm, torque NA

Transmission:	4-speed manual
Suspension, front:	trailing arms, coil springs, anti-roll bar
Suspension, rear:	live axle, radius rods, Panhard rod, coil springs
Brakes:	front/rear drums
Wheelbase (in.):	108.0
Weight (lbs):	2240
Top speed (mph):	85-95
0-60 mph (sec):	NA
Production:	15 (some sources list 14)

Also known as Two-Liter Sports, the first David Brown Aston was handsome in its way and not that fast, but it bridged the gap between prewar Astons and later DBs.

1950-1953
ASTON MARTIN DB2

Though the DB1 carried a "David Brown" label, it was the much faster, sleeker, and more successful DB2 that was the first *real* David Brown Aston. Brown, who'd made his fortune in transmissions and farm tractors, decided to have "a bit of fun" in 1947 by acquiring the financially ailing Aston Martin and Lagonda motor companies. Both were located just west of London, both were saddled with antiquated facilities, and neither could afford to put its new designs into production. Brown took control, moved Lagonda business into the Aston Martin factory at Feltham, and began to look to the future.

What he inherited with these acquisitions were a fine new Aston Martin chassis and a splendid 2.6-liter twincam six-cylinder engine from Lagonda. The engine had been designed under the guidance of the legendary W.O. Bentley, Lagonda's technical director since 1935. In an inspired move, Brown had the Aston DB1 chassis modified to accept the Lagonda engine and transmission. The result was an excellent new Aston, the DB2. This car and its descendants would carry Aston Martin successfully through the Fifties.

Three DB2 prototypes were built in 1949, given smooth fastback coupe bodies (shaped by Frank Feeley, who'd styled the DB1), and entered at that year's Le Mans 24-Hour race in France. Two ran the four-cylinder DB1 engine, the other the new

Lagonda six. There was no success that first time out but, two weeks later, the six-cylinder prototype finished third overall at the Spa 24-Hour race in Belgium.

Conceived as a rather spartan open and closed two-seater, the DB2 was more civilized when it went on sale in 1950, with proper bumpers and more complete equipment. Its multi-tube chassis was an evolution of the DB1 design, still with trailing-arm independent front suspension but revised rear axle location. Like all the best British sports cars of the day, it also had center-lock wire wheels. The engine produced 105 horsepower in standard form, but a 125-bhp "Vantage" version was later offered at extra cost. The 4-speed manual gearbox, a David Brown Industries product, was available with either steering-column or floor-mounted shifter.

Though undoubtedly beautiful, the DB2 was initially more a competition car than a full-fledged road machine. Its aluminum body, with panels handcrafted at Feltham, featured a hinged front section—hood, nose and both fenders—that tilted forward for engine access, handy for the track. The coupe's rearward vision was restricted by a small backlight, and there was no exterior access to the luggage space. The only opening rear panel was a top-hinged lid covering the spare tire compartment. Some thought the drophead coupe looked even better than the fixed-top model, but only 49 of the 409 DB2s built were open.

Pundits, owners, and magazine road testers all agreed that, though an expensive proposition, the DB2 had a superb chassis, great performance, and an immense amount of character. Even better, it became progressively more civilized over its four-year production run. Original racing-oriented features like engine bay-louvers were abandoned in favor of more and better-quality trim and improved seating. The simple three-piece grille was displaced by a more stylish one-piece design in 1951.

At Aston Martin, however, there was never much time for a design to settle in. Thus, the DB2 was displaced in 1953 by an even more refined version, the DB2/4.

SPECIFICATIONS

Engine: dohc I-6, 157.4 cid/2580 cc, 105 bhp (SAE) @ 5000 rpm, 125 lbs-ft @ 3000 rpm (Vantage: 125 bhp @ 5000 rpm, 144 lbs-ft @ 2400 rpm)

Transmission:	4-speed manual
Suspension, front:	trailing arms, coil springs, anti-roll bar
Suspension, rear:	live axle, radius rods, Panhard rod, coil springs
Brakes:	front/rear drums
Wheelbase (in.):	99.0
Weight (lbs):	2660
Top speed (mph):	110
0-60 mph (sec):	12.4
Production:	410 (some sources list 411)

The first true Aston DB was offered as a fastback or this handsome drophead. Both were strictly two-seaters.

1953-1957
ASTON MARTIN DB2/4

The DB2/4 bowed in the autumn of 1953 to replace the DB2, and was an altogether better version of it. The designation tells the main story, for this was still the "David Brown" Aston, only now with four seats. Of course, it helped to have a sense of humor about that, because wheelbase was unchanged, and squeezing in those extra seats required a good deal of shuffling, including a smaller fuel tank repositioned above the spare. In fact, there was really no room for a rear passenger's legs with the front seats pushed all the way back.

As before, there were coupe and convertible body styles, but the coupe's appearance was subtly altered. A one-piece windshield replaced the previous divided glass, and the rear roofline was bulged out to provide some semblance of headroom for those unfortunate enough to have to ride in the new back seat. The biggest improvement was a new top-hinged hatchback—the first ever fitted to a sporting car, by the way—for access to a much-enlarged luggage area. As on so many of today's cars, the rear seatback could be folded forward for even more cargo space. Coupe bodies were contracted to H.J. Mulliner and Sons of Birmingham, famous for its Rolls-Royce coachwork and which had recently begun building TR2 shells for Standard-Triumph. Under the hood, the more powerful 125-horsepower Vantage engine was now standard.

The result of all this was an exciting sports tourer that was more practical and versatile than ever. Independent tests showed the DB2/4 capable of 111 mph maximum and 12.6 seconds in the 0-60 mph sprint, making this a fast car by early-Fifties standards. No wonder sales surged.

Demand swelled even more beginning in mid-1954 when a larger 2922-cc engine with 140 bhp became available. A third body style arrived in 1955, a notchback coupe version of the convertible. By that time, Mulliner had moved closer to Standard-Triumph (which would take over the coachmaker in 1958), so David Brown shifted coupe body production to Tickford at Newport Pagnell, which already built the convertible; final assembly continued at Feltham for the time being. With this change came a conventional hood and front fenders fixed to the chassis.

Naturally enough, this second-generation DB2/4 became known as the Mark II, and was built for two years. It was capable of 120 mph, which was almost on a par with the much heavier and less nimble Jaguar XK140, yet retained the same feline roadholding of earlier DB-series Astons. It's interesting to recall that these cars were sold with drum brakes, for disc-brake technology was still in its infancy.

Though DB2/4 production was low by most any standard, this was a successful car for Aston Martin. Exactly 566 "Mark Is" were built, 199 Mark IIs.

At its peak, the DB2/4 was being produced at the rate of six or seven a week even though it was strictly a handbuilt car. Of course, it's very collectible today, but David Brown had an even better Aston in the works, the DB Mark III.

"/4" signified new +2 seating in the revised DB2. Practical rear hatch (above) was also new, and unusual for the mid-Fifties. Cabin (left) was considerably plusher and comfier.

SPECIFICATIONS

Engines: dohc I-6; **1953-54 "Mk I":** 157.4 cid/2580 cc, 125 bhp (SAE) @ 5000 rpm, 144 lbs-ft @ 2400 rpm; **1954-57 Mk II:** 178 cid/2922 cc, 140 bhp (SAE) @ 5000 rpm, 178 lbs-ft @ 3000 rpm

Transmission:	4-speed manual
Suspension, front:	trailing arms, coil springs, anti-roll bar
Suspension, rear:	live axle, radius rods, Panhard rod, coil springs
Brakes:	front/rear drums
Wheelbase (in.):	99.0
Weight (lbs):	2270
Top speed (mph):	120 (Mk II)
0-60 mph (sec):	11.1 (Mk II)
Production:	**1953-54 "Mk I"** 566 **1954-57 MK II** 199

1957-59 ASTON MARTIN DB MARK III

The DB Mark III, third and final derivative of the DB2 Aston Martin, appeared in March 1957 (originally for export only) and was produced for two years. Almost everything about its technical development, equipment, and marketing was logical except the name. After the DB2/4 and DB2/4 Mark II, it rightly should have been called DB2/4 Mk III, but it wasn't. Neither could it be the DB3, for that designation had been used on a sports-racing car in the early 1950s.

So, the short-lived DB Mk III carried a name that made little sense in the progression of Aston Martins built before or after. But that doesn't detract at all from the last, excellent flowering of the basic DB2 design: faster, more secure, and better-looking than ever. Styling was only slightly altered compared with the DB2/4 Mk II. The nose and grille were more delicately sculptured and very graceful, visually quite

similar to that of the aforementioned DB3S sports racer. At the rear were modestly revised fenders incorporating the taillamps of the Rootes-built Humber Hawk. Inside, a new instrument panel designed by Frank Feeley grouped all gauges directly ahead of the driver instead of in the center.

But the most notable improvements showed up in the engine, transmission, and brakes. Standard horsepower was up to 162, and a more efficient twin exhaust and dual SU carbs were optional to boost that to 178 bhp. In 1958, both gave way to a final version of the 3.0-liter "Bentley/Lagonda" engine with triple Weber or SU carbs and higher compression (8.68 vs. 8.16:1) for 180 or 195 bhp. Girling front disc brakes were optional through the first 100 cars, then standard, while electric overdrive for the manual gearbox and a new Borg-Warner automatic transmission also became optional extras.

By this time, Aston Martin had decided to concentrate assembly at the old Tickford factory at Newport Pagnell. All DB4-series cars (see entries) were assembled there, as were the last DB Mk IIIs. Although the DB Mk III was primarily intended as a fast, superbly finished road car, it could be ordered with all manner of competition-oriented goodies: special engine, close-ratio gearbox, engine oil cooler, competition clutch and suspension, and an extra-large (33.6 U.S.-gallon) fuel tank. It was the sort of car that contract team drivers like Stirling Moss were proud to use on the road.

SPECIFICATIONS

Engines: all dohc I-6, 178 cid/2922 cc; **1957-58 "DBA":** 162 bhp (SAE) or 178 bhp (twin carburetors) @ 5500 rpm, 180 lbs-ft @ 4000 rpm; **1958-59 "DBB":** 180 bhp (twin/triple SU carbs) or 195 bhp (triple Weber or SU carbs) (SAE) @ 5500 rpm, torque NA

Transmissions:	4-speed manual with optional overdrive, optional Borg-Warner 3-speed automatic
Suspension, front:	trailing arms, coil springs, anti-roll bar
Suspension, rear:	live axle, radius rods, Panhard rod, coil springs
Brakes:	front discs/rear drums
Wheelbase (in.):	99.0
Weight (lbs):	2800
Top speed (mph):	119 (162-bhp engine)
0-60 mph (sec):	9.3 (162-bhp engine)
Production:	551 (incl. one 214-bhp competition special)

Mark III was the final evolution of the original DB2. Coupe styling foreshadows that of the coming DB4/DB5. Drophead (left) gained more upright top. DB3S (opposite top) was a hairy sports-racer. Only 19 were built.

1958-1963
ASTON MARTIN DB4

The DB2 had been on sale five years before Aston Martin began contemplating a successor. Christened DB4, it was all-new, which helps explain why it took three years to be finalized, delaying its public launch until autumn 1958.

Key personalities behind the new model were general manager John Wyer (who would mastermind the birth of the Ford GT40 in the Sixties), chassis designer Harold Beach, and engine designer Tadek Marek. David Brown himself took a major step forward by agreeing to the development of an entirely new car, for every major component in the DB4 was new, and there was never any thought of compromise by using carryover parts.

Wyer concentrated as much of the new model's manufacturing and assembly as he could in the modernized Newport Pagnell factory. One unanticipated consequence, however, was that longtime stylist Frank Feeley declined to move to Buckinghamshire, forcing Aston Martin Lagonda to seek outside design help.

The DB4 chassis was simpler and more rigid than that of the DB2s. Wheelbase was an inch shorter but tracks were wider, and improved packaging allowed more reasonable four-place seating. The previous multi-tube design was abandoned for Aston's first pressed-steel platform-type frame, which in one form or another would persist at Aston through the Sixties and Seventies.

Conventional coil-spring/double-wishbone independent front suspension was retained along with rack-and-pinion steering. Chassis engineer Beach had wanted to use a De Dion rear end, but this would have to wait a full decade and an ordinary live axle was used instead.

Under the DB4 hood was a big, rugged, and visually beautiful twincam six inspired by, but altogether larger than, the Jaguar XK engine. Displacement was 3.7 liters even in its original form, good for a dead-reliable 240 bhp, though a lot more was possible (and realized in future models). Because this was much too lusty for the existing DB2 transmission, a new David Brown 4-speed unit was produced to suit. A few automatic-transmission cars were also produced towards the end of the model run. Naturally, there were disc brakes all around. A good thing, too, for even early DB4s weighed nearly 3000 pounds and were capable of 141 mph.

DB4 styling and body construction were "imported" from Italy. Carrozzeria Touring of Milan, which had already produced several Aston specials, was hired to design the car and supply bodies for it built according to the firm's patented "super light" principles. This *Superleggera* construction employed aluminum panels over a lattice of small tubes laid out to define the body shape, an ideal process for a small-volume producer like Aston.

Initially, the DB4 had a Mark III-like grille, shaped rather like a squashed loaf of bread seen head-on, flanked by single headlamps on the corners of the front fenders, but this treatment would undergo five minor variations over the subsequent five years. Series 1 cars' rear-hinged hoods changed to front-hinged on Series 2 models (built from January 1960). The Series 3 (from April 1961) had minor cosmetic changes, while the Series 4 (from September that same year) had a new-style grille and the high-power Vantage models received headlamps recessed behind sloping covers. The final Series 5 (from September 1962) had more legroom and trunk space and a higher roofline. A four-seat convertible joined the introductory fastback coupe style in late 1961.

DB4 running changes also encompassed mechanicals. Overdrive was added as an option beginning with Series 2, while the Series 4 offered a tuned 266-bhp option called Vantage. A slew of axle ratios was available right from the first, almost anything the customer demanded.

Though the DB4 was much larger, heavier, and costlier than the DB Mark III it eventually displaced, it was the first truly modern Aston and very popular because of it. A total of 1113 were produced—a new high-water mark for the firm—before the closely related DB5 took over in late 1963.

SPECIFICATIONS

Engines: all dohc I-6, 224 cid/3670 cc, 240 bhp (SAE) @ 5500 rpm, 240 lbs-ft @ 4250 rpm; **Vantage** (from 9/61): 266 bhp @ 5750 rpm, torque NA

Transmissions:	4-speed manual with optional overdrive or optional Borg-Warner 3-speed automatic
Suspension, front:	upper-and-lower A-arms, coil springs, anti-roll bar
Suspension, rear:	live axle, Watt linkage, radius rods, coil springs
Brakes:	front/rear discs
Wheelbase (in.):	98.0
Weight (lbs):	2885
Top speed (mph):	141 (240-bhp engine)
0-60 mph (sec):	8.5 (240-bhp engine)

Production: "Series 1" 149 **"Series 2"** 351 **"Series 3"** 165 (incl. 3 302-bhp GT-engine models) **"Series 4"** 260 (incl. 30 convertibles) **"Series 5"** 185 (incl. 185 convertibles) *(Note: "Series" nomenclature by Aston Martin Owners Club; not used by factory.)*

Above: The DB4 wasn't designed to race, though some obviously did. Opposite: Offered less than two years, the handsome DB4 convertible saw only 215 copies.

1959-1963
ASTON MARTIN DB4GT
AND DB4GT ZAGATO

Aston Martin reached the pinnacle of sports-car racing in 1959. Helped by victory in that year's Le Mans 24 Hours, it won the World Manufacturer's Championship with the very special DBR 1/2. Of course, ordinary folk couldn't buy a DBR 1/2, but they continually asked for faster and more specialized DB4s. AM responded between 1959 and 1963 with two distinctly different cars.

A year after the DB4 arrived, a modified version called DB4GT was announced, a prototype having already won a production-car race at the British Silverstone circuit in early '59. Trimmer than the DB4 in both size and weight, this new high-performance Aston rode a five-inch shorter wheelbase. Its cabin was cut down accordingly with shorter doors and no rear seats. More visual distinction was provided by a more rounded nose/front-fender ensemble, with headlights recessed behind Plexiglas covers. Trim and equipment were simplified where possible, so weight dropped from the DB4's nominal 2885 pounds to 2705. Under the hood was a new version of the all-alloy 3.7-liter six with high-lift camshafts, higher compression (9.0:1), and three dual-choke Weber carburetors. Output was a smashing 302 horsepower at 6000 rpm, enough for a top speed of more than 140 mph.

A handful of super-light DB4GTs was also produced for favored racing teams. In long-distance contests like the British Tourist Trophy race they proved almost as fast and nimble as the famous Ferrari 250GT Berlinettas. Still, the DB4GT was too heavy and, crazy as it sounds, too well equipped to be a competitive racer. Though 75 roadgoing models were built in little more than a year—which, by Aston's standards, made this a successful and profitable project—it was time to try harder.

What emerged was a curvy new Zagato-bodied variation, logically designated DB4GT Zagato and first seen in late 1960. Nothing could be done to reduce chassis size and weight (nor did prevailing homologation requirements permit it), but the Italian coachbuilder produced a very light fastback coupe shell that was quite unmistakable. Its overall appearance was marked by the curious combination of curves and angles associated with this *carrozzeria*, definitely smoother than the standard-issue GT and a little bulbous. Yet despite show-car styling, and publicity claims to the contrary, this was a circuit racer that might, if you insisted, be driven on the road. The fact that only 19 were called for (with a good number of detail differences among them) suggests that most GTZ's were used on the track.

The Zagato body was completely different from the DB4GT's in both style and construction. Normally the car was supplied without bumpers, though you could get them if you insisted. Rolling chassis were sent to Italy for body installation, but painting and final assembly were performed at Newport Pagnell.

As for its engine, the Zagato was treated to a new-design cylinder head with twin spark plugs for each cylinder and still higher compression (9.7:1), which pushed peak power to 314 bhp at 6000 rpm. As the body weighed about 100 pounds less than the normal DB4GT's, and likely suffered less air drag, the Zagato was that much more competitive on the track. Had Aston Martin mounted a serious competition program for this car, it might have had the measure of Ferrari.

But there was no money for that because Aston was still a tiny operation, smaller even than Enzo's company (though Ferrari had grown quite a bit by this time, relatively speaking). And in the high-stakes, high-visibility world of European road racing (or any form of racing, for that matter), better to make no effort than a half-hearted one. Besides, Aston had already proven its point by winning Le Mans and the '59 championship.

Though lighter than the standard DB4, the short-wheelbase two-seat DB4GT was too heavy and well equipped to be a serious track competitor. The even lighter Zagato-bodied GT (right) was more competitive, but Aston never mounted a serious campaign.

SPECIFICATIONS

Engines: all dohc I-6, 224 cid 3670 cc; **DB4GT:** 302 bhp (SAE) @ 6000 rpm, 240 lbs-ft @ 5000 rpm; **Zagato:** 314 bhp @ 6000 rpm, 278 lbs-ft @ 5000 rpm

Transmission:	4-speed manual
Suspension, front:	upper-and-lower A-arms coil springs anti-roll bar
Suspension, rear:	live axle, Watt linkage, radius rods, coil springs
Brakes:	front/rear discs
Wheelbase (in.):	93.0
Weight (lbs):	2705 (DB4GT), approx. 2600 (Zagato)
Top speed (mph):	142 (DB4GT), 153 (Zagato)
0-60 mph (sec):	6.4 (DB4GT), 6.1 (Zagato)
Production:	**DB4GT** 75 **DB4GT Zagato** 19

1963-1965
ASTON MARTIN DB5
AND VOLANTE

After five years, the DB4 had evolved so far from its origins that it deserved a new name. It got one in the autumn of 1963: DB5. But though it retained the basic chassis, body style, and running gear of late-model DB4s, Aston's newest was once again a different car in many respects. Interestingly, it would be built for only two years and 1021 examples yet became one of the most famous of all Astons. Such is the power of Hollywood. A specially equipped DB5 served as James Bond's spy car in the film *Goldfinger*, thus instantly making this model an international star.

The best way to begin describing the DB5 is to start with the DB4 from which it was developed. The solid 98-inch-wheelbase pressed-steel platform chassis and the basic dohc six-cylinder engine were retained, as was the choice of four-seat coupe and slightly less spacious convertible models. However, a 4-mm bore increase swelled engine displacement from 3670 to 3995 cc. In original standard form (with three SU carburetors), the DB5 thus carried a rated 282 horsepower. The coupe, complete with headlamps recessed behind sloping covers, looked almost exactly like the last of the DB4s, while the convertible now adopted this treatment (DB4 Convertibles always had exposed headlamps). A detachable steel hardtop remained optional for it. As before, both models carried Touring Superleggera bodies.

Initial DB5 transmission choices were as for late DB4s: 4-speed David Brown manual gearbox, the same with extra-cost electric overdrive, and optional 3-speed Borg-Warner automatic. But there was also a third option now, an all-synchromesh ZF 5-speed manual (also used in six-cylinder Maseratis of the period) in which fifth gear was effectively an overdrive. It became standard by mid-1964 and the 4-speed and separate overdrive vanished.

Autumn of 1964 brought a more powerful engine as a new Vantage option. Breathing through a trio of twin-choke Weber carburetors, it was rated at no less than 325 bhp, and was to be the most popular Aston "Big Six" for the remaining years of its life.

Another interesting DB5 footnote concerns the dozen "shooting brake" (station wagon) conversions produced by Harold Radford, the London-based coachbuilders. Built in 1965, they now have considerable rarity value. The convertible was somewhat revised that same year, with quarter bumpers front and rear rather than full-width blades, an additional oil-cooler air intake at the front (under the license plate), and its own surname: Volante ("flying" in Italian). Only 37 were built before the production changeover to the successor DB6.

By this time, the Aston Martin DB was not only faster but significantly heavier than ever. The typical DB5 coupe weighed nearly 3300 pounds, 400 more than the DB4 of five years earlier. Even so, it was still good for about 140 mph. But the extra heft showed up in heavier fuel consumption, and most owners found they could do no better than about 15 mpg.

Though definitely a hand-built thoroughbred in the best British tradition, the DB5 was a dinosaur in some respects. For example, air conditioning wasn't available. Neither was power steering, so you needed strong arms to get the best out of the car on twisty roads. Strong legs didn't hurt either. The DB5's combination of Italian styling and oh-so-British appointments had undeniable charm, but its shortcomings seemed more intolerable—and less professional—as the years passed. Correcting them was the mission for Aston's next-generation design, the DB6.

The James Bond film Goldfinger *made the DB5 an instant celebrity. Both coupe (**bottom**) and newly named Volante convertible offered more power, fresh styling, and greater comfort.*

SPECIFICATIONS

Engines: dohc I-6, 243.7 cid/3995 cc, 282 bhp (SAE) @ 5500 rpm, 288 lbs-ft @ 3850 rpm (Vantage option: 325 bhp @ 5750 rpm, torque NA)

Transmissions:	4-speed manual with optional overdrive, optional 5-speed manual (standard from mid-1964), optional Borg-Warner 3-speed automatic
Suspension, front:	upper-and-lower A-arms, coil springs, anti-roll bar
Suspension, rear:	live axle, Watt linkage, radius rods, coil springs
Brakes:	front/rear discs
Wheelbase (in.):	98.0
Weight (lbs):	3235
Top speed (mph):	141
0-60 mph (sec):	8.1
Production:	Coupe 886 Volante (convertible) 123
Shooting Brake	(Radford conversion): 12

1965-1970
ASTON MARTIN DB6
& VOLANTE

Just two years after introduction, the Aston Martin DB5 stepped aside for the larger, plusher DB6. Inevitably, the new model was less sporting than its predecessors, if undeniably more practical and still quite potent.

Bowing in late 1965, the DB6 retained Aston's then-seven-year-old basic chassis design, but with a 3.75-inch longer wheelbase and a relocated rear axle (as usual, by Salisbury). The platform stretch was given over entirely to additional rear seat space. Running gear and suspension were virtual DB5 carryovers, but all drivetrain combinations—282- and 325-horsepower engines with either ZF manual or Borg-Warner automatic transmission—now cost the same, and "Powr-Lok" limited-slip differential (first used by Aston on the DB4GT) and chrome wire wheels were standard. Announced shortly after the car itself was first-time availability of power steering, a welcome option.

From the front, the DB6 looked much like the DB5, but was quite a departure from the cowl back, if still recognizably Aston. The designers aimed to provide more passenger space, especially in the small "+2" rear, and improve aerodynamic stability. Accordingly, the DB6 windshield was higher and more vertical than the DB5's so the roofline could be raised for increased headroom. The familiar coupe remained a fastback style, but rear quarter windows now swept up instead of down, and the tapered tail of old gave way to a modern, abruptly chopped Kamm-style treatment much like that of the Ferrari 250 Berlinetta Lusso or 275 GTB.

Other recognition points included the return of front-door quarter windows, an oil-cooler air scoop low on the nose, and quarter-bumpers at each corner. Inside were the usual dazzling—and rather haphazardly placed—instruments, sweet-smelling leather upholstery, and top-quality British carpeting.

Though overall length was up two inches, the DB6 weighed about the same as the DB5 even though Aston now abandoned Touring's patented *Superleggera* construction. Henceforth, all Astons would have conventional bodies, with aluminum skins and steel floor and inner panels.

The DB6 was apparently slipperier than the DB5, for top speed was up to 148-150 mph in 325-bhp Vantage guise, making it the equal of the more charismatic Ferraris and Maseratis of these years, at least for all-out speed. In fast touring, the British car was still somewhat "trucky" compared with its Latin rivals—more work in spirited driving, though easier to manage than previous Astons.

Per recent practice, a new Volante convertible arrived about a year behind the DB6 coupe. Unlike the "interim" Volante built on the DB5 chassis with a DB6-style rear end, this one had the longer wheelbase and a new power-operated top mechanism. Both body styles then continued with virtually no appearance changes through the end of the series in 1970.

Aston's next generation, the DBS, had been on the scene three years by then, but the DB6 had one last hurrah beginning in the autumn of 1969. That's when an updated Mark II version appeared with flared wheelarches to accommodate fatter DBS-type wheels and tires. At the same time, AE-Brico fuel injection arrived as a new option, but it was a very unreliable system and found few takers. Almost all DB6s so equipped have since been fitted with carburetors.

Incidentally, the Radford works again turned out a handful of DB6 "Shooting Brake" (wagon) conversions. These closely resembled the dozen DB5-based examples, but only half as many were built, just six in all.

With the end of DB6 production in November 1970 came the end of the great line begun with the DB2 in 1950. The torch had already passed to a more modern Aston, a design that's with us yet. For that story, read on.

SPECIFICATIONS

Engine: dohc I-6, 243.7 cid/3995 cc, 282 bhp (SAE) @ 5500 rpm, 288 lbs-ft @ 3850 rpm (Vantage option: 325 bhp @ 5750 rpm, torque NA)

Transmissions:	ZF 5-speed overdrive manual or Borg-Warner 3-speed automatic
Suspension, front:	upper-and-lower A-arms, coil springs, anti-roll bar
Suspension, rear:	live axle, Watt linkage, radius rods, coil springs
Brakes:	front/rear discs
Wheelbase (in.):	101.7
Weight (lbs):	3250
Top speed (mph):	148 (Vantage)
0-60 mph (sec):	6.5 (Vantage)

Production: **Coupe** 1321 **Volante** (convertible) 140 **Shooting Brake** (Radford conversion) 6

DB6 looked much like DB5 except for higher rooflines and new Kamm-style tail treatment. Volante convertible arrived a year behind the familiar 2+2 coupe.

1967-1973
ASTON MARTIN DBS &
AM VANTAGE

David Brown's Aston Martin concern held out for every possible sale before discarding a car design, thus hoping to realize maximum return on investment. This helps explain why the DB2 family lasted seven years, the DB4 generation 12. Thus, when the DBS arrived in September 1967, it was only the third truly new Aston in 18 years. Even then, it wasn't all-new, for much of its chassis and running gear came straight from the existing DB6 in concept if not always detail.

Work on the DBS began in 1966, a year that saw Aston's fortunes at a low ebb. Touring, the firm's Italian design and body contractor, suffered a financial collapse just after it had completed a pair of promising prototype coupes now known as DBSC, while a government credit squeeze in England deflated demand for costly cars like the DB6. Brown, however, could still afford his "bit of fun" and put the rush on yet another new design.

This styling assignment was handed to the ambitious young William Towns, who'd been hired at Newport Pagnell only to design seats. Towns knew that Brown wanted not only a new Aston coupe but a new Lagonda sedan as well, so he conjured up two closely related proposals, one for each model, differing mainly in wheelbase and roof and nose styling. By sheer persistence, he got his coupe approved. (The erstwhile Lagonda only progressed as far as a couple of prototypes.) Towns left plenty of underhood space for a brand-new V-8 then under development, though it wouldn't materialize until 1969.

Because capital reserves were low and the sense of urgency high, the new DBS (the "DB7" designation was ruled out to emphasize just how new) rode the DB6 chassis, albeit with an extra inch of wheelbase and a significant 4.5 inches of front and rear track. Front suspension and the still-optional power steering were as before,

but engineer Harold Beach finally won his battle for a De Dion rear suspension. Running gear—standard and Vantage engines with manual or automatic transmission—were also per DB6. So was the troublesome AE-Brico fuel injection option, which garnered as few orders here.

Though the new fastback coupe body showed familiar Aston shapes in its grille and side window openings, it had a crisp, clean "extruded" look, with curved bodysides and a rather angular superstructure that nevertheless harmonized well. Quad headlamps were set within a full-width eggcrate grille, and center-lock wire wheels were on hand—or rather, on ground—as usual. Overall, there was no trace of Italian influence, yet the DBS was as smart and modern as anything from Turin and offered significantly more passenger space than the DB6 despite being slightly shorter. It remains the basis of the Aston V-8s still in production at this writing, though a convertible was not part of the picture in the late Sixties; that came much later.

Because of its bulk, the DBS was unavoidably heavier than the DB6—by a whopping 510 pounds—so its performance and gas mileage were predictably that much worse. Still, it could do nearly 150 mph flat out, 0-60 mph acceleration remained respectable at 8.5 seconds, and roadholding was excellent, a benefit of the wider track. On the down side, handling was cumbersome without the optional power steering. In fact, all controls—shifter, steering, brakes—demanded somewhat "masculine" effort, a good description of Aston character if plainly sexist. Fuel consumption declined to an appalling 10 miles per U.S. gallon, though few worried about it much because gas was still plentiful and cheap.

The promised V-8 duly appeared in a companion model called DBS-V8 (which later prompted some to dub the six-cylinder version "DBS-6"). However, the DBS continued, albeit with no significant changes, until 1972.

Which just happened to be a watershed year for Aston Martin Lagonda, as David Brown stopped having "fun" and sold his interests to Company Developments, Ltd. At that point, the DBS was renamed Vantage and received the 325-bhp engine as standard equipment. It also got a mild facelift, with larger dual headlights flanking a narrowed grille bearing a simple black mesh insert.

The Vantage died after 14 months, lasting through July 1973 and accounting for a mere 70 of the total DBS-series production run of 857 units. With it died the splendid Aston Martin twincam six, sad to say. All subsequent Astons have used the 1969-vintage V-8.

SPECIFICATIONS

Engine: dohc I-6, 243.7 cid/3995 cc, 282 bhp (SAE) @ 5500 rpm, 288 lbs-ft @ 3850 rpm (Vantage option: 325 bhp @ 5750 rpm)

Transmissions:	ZF 5-speed manual or Borg-Warner 3-speed automatic
Suspension, front:	upper-and-lower A-arms, coil springs, anti-roll bar
Suspension, rear:	De Dion live axle with Watt linkage, radius arms, coil springs
Brakes:	front/rear discs
Wheelbase (in.):	102.8
Weight (lbs):	3760
Top speed (mph):	148 (Vantage)
0-60 mph (sec):	8.6
Production:	**DBS** 787 **AM Vantage** 70

Opposite top and bottom: Early DBS Astons had four headlamps. Below and opposite center: The restyled 1972-73 AM Vantage had a two-lamp front and the 325-bhp twincam six but was much the same otherwise.

1969-1988 ASTON MARTIN DBS V-8/AM V-8, VANTAGE & VOLANTE

The six-cylinder Aston Martin DBS appeared in 1967 but had always been planned around a new V-8. This powerful 5.3-liter unit, with light-alloy block and heads and twin overhead camshafts per cylinder bank, was actually unveiled that same year for racing, but didn't see production until the autumn of 1969. It has powered every Aston and Lagonda built since.

Aston enthusiasts had waited a long time for something like the V-8, and they weren't disappointed. It was—and is—a magnificent powerplant: very muscular and torquey, and quite reliable with proper servicing. It's also quite expensive—built mostly by hand, in fact—which keeps production at Newport Pagnell down to no more than four or five cars a week.

You could distinguish between the six-cylinder and V-8 DBS by the latter's standard cast-alloy wheels—and much greater performance: 0-60 mph was now a mere 6.0-second affair, top speed a blistering 150 mph. The V-8 transformed the DBS from being very fast to stupendously fast—one of the two or three quickest cars in the world. Because rival makers often claimed optimistic (and sometimes unbelievable) power and performance figures in the late Sixties, Aston refused to quote any at all, stating only that the V-8 was "sufficient" and allowing its performance to speak for itself.

Nevertheless, the V-8 initially delivered an estimated 350-375 horsepower with standard Bosch electronic fuel injection which, as experience soon showed, was rather finicky to maintain. As with the six-cylinder model it was offered with 5-speed manual (ZF) or 3-speed automatic transmission, only the latter was now the well-known Chrysler TorqueFlite. Chassis specifications were as for the six-cylinder car except that its optional power steering was standard.

The DBS V-8 has been in production nearly two decades now, surviving several management and ownership changes in the process. Today's version doesn't seem all that different from the original, but it's seen a fair number of changes over the years.

The first came in 1972, when David Brown sold Aston Martin Lagonda to Company Developments, Ltd. The DBS V-8 was renamed Aston Martin V-8 and received the facelifted six-cylinder model's new two-lamp nose with narrowed black-mesh grille, and a hood "power bulge" (replacing the former scoop). From summer 1973, the engine reverted to carburetors, a quartet of twin-choke Webers that actually improved both performance and driveability. These continued into the Eighties, when fuel injection returned, a more modern Bosch system. (Incidentally, there was a six-month period in 1974-75 when no Astons of any kind were built, pending the arrival of new management and fresh capital.) Power was boosted by an advertised "15 percent" in 1977, and though emissions controls have since taken a toll, recent official figures list output at 309 bhp net.

That same year, 1977, brought a souped-up Vantage V-8, a British reply to Italian supercars like the Lamborghini Countach and Ferrari Berlinetta Boxer. It was easily identified by a deep front airdam with engine-cooling slots, big Cibié driving lamps ahead of a blanked-off grille, fat Pirelli P7 tires, and added-on (later faired-in) rear lip spoiler. Suspension was modified to suit to the new tires and the higher performance of a V-8 tweaked to 400 bhp initially; current output is 406 bhp. Given the right conditions the Vantage can exceed 170 mph, thus vying with the legendary V-12 Ferrari Daytona as the world's fastest-ever front-engine production car.

Aston hadn't offered a Volante convertible since the last DB6 model in 1970, but June 1978 brought a new drop-top version of Bill Towns' original DBS design, looking just as good—maybe better—than the fastback coupe, which by that time was an elderly 11 years old. Supplied with most every luxury, the Volante was first offered with just the normal-tune V-8, but has been available with Vantage power since 1986.

Although big and heavy (around 4100 pounds at the curb with all options), the V-8 Astons are beautifully balanced and handle surprisingly well, though they're still high-effort tourers, "man's" cars rather than a "woman's" in the best Aston tradition. If you could forget about price (well over $100,000 by the early Eighties) and attracting unwanted police attention, you could throw one around with the same abandon as an MG Midget—but at considerably higher speeds, of course.

How long they'll hang around is questionable at this writing. Aston recently renewed ties with Zagato in Italy for a limited run of special-body coupes (50) and convertibles (25), and this could possibly spawn a replacement for the Towns' design. But it won't render the hairy-chested V-8 Astons collector's items. They achieved that status long ago, and it's well deserved.

SPECIFICATIONS

Engines: dohc V-8, 325.9 cid/5340 cc; output not available, but estimated at 350-375 bhp (SAE gross) for initial fuel-injected engine to 406 bhp (SAE net) for current Vantage version

Transmissions:	5-speed manual or 3-speed automatic
Suspension, front:	upper and lower A-arms, coil springs, anti-roll bar
Suspension, rear:	De Dion live axle, radius arms, coil springs
Brakes:	front/rear discs
Wheelbase (in.):	102.8
Weight (lbs):	3800-4000
Top speed (mph):	145 (carbureted V-8), 170 (Vantage)
0-60 mph (sec):	6.2 (carbureted V-8), 5.4 (Vantage)

Production: **DBS V-8** (4/70-5/72) 399 **AM V-8 "Series 2"** (4/72-5/73) 286 **"Series 3"** (8/73-9/78) 973 **"Series 4"** (10/78-12/85) 299 **Volante** approx. 350 (through 12/85) **V-8 Vantage** approx. 215 (through 12/85; includes 43 **"Series 3,"** 172 **"Series 4"**)

*Below: Early DBS V-8s looked like the six-cylinder DBS but had more go, of course. **Opposite:** Volante appeared in 1978, has been offered with potent Vantage V-8 since 1986.*

1953-1956 AUSTIN-HEALEY 100/4

Britain's Healeys—the cars, that is—were looking pretty long in the tooth by 1952, so Donald Healey—their famed builder—began casting around for a new design that would allow him to expand his business. To do this, he reasoned, he needed to buy cheaper components and build more cars so that he could sell each at a lower price. But the romance of this little story is that when the eventual Healey 100 was shown in prototype form at the 1952 London Motor Show, BMC managing director Leonard Lord made Healey an offer he couldn't refuse. Thus was born the Austin-Healey, a car that would have been made in the hundreds at Warwick but that ended up being built at Longbridge in the tens of thousands. Sports-car devotees have been grateful ever since.

There were several good reasons why Len Lord was so attracted to this car. The sleek, beautiful two-seat roadster was rugged and straightforward, and designed around lightly modified Austin A90 running gear and suspension. Since the A90 wasn't selling well at the time, Lord's liking for the new Healey was quite understandable.

The Healey 100 had what looked like a steel body atop a separate chassis with box-section side-members, but these were actually welded together on initial assembly. BMC ultimately awarded the body/chassis contract to the Jensen brothers, Dick and Alan, who'd been building their own sports cars at a small plant in West Bromwich. Front suspension was coil-spring independent. At the rear was a beam axle mounted above the side-members, with rather restricted movement; a Panhard rod helped semi-elliptic leaf springs locate the axle itself. Center-lock wire wheels were standard.

Driveline comprised the A90's 2.66-liter 90-horsepower all-iron four matched to a 4-speed gearbox with the top gear simply blanked off. However, it was allied to electrically actuated Laycock overdrive operating on top (third) and second gears, giving a dexterous driver five forward ratios to play with. Body design was Donald's own, albeit refined by Buckinghamshire coachbuilder Tickford, and was unmistakable. A modern "envelope" style, it featured smooth flowing lines, distinctive shell-shape grille, and a one-piece windshield that could be laid back for bugs-in-the-teeth traditionalists.

A-H assembly began at the Austin factory near Birmingham in the spring of 1953, and U.S. exports soon followed. Right away, it was clear that the car had performance and handling to match its good looks. It could easily top the magic "ton," hence the 100 designation. Even better, it stepped into a sparsely populated market sector, priced comfortably below the Jaguar XK120 but well above the Triumph's new TR2.

Two problems quickly surfaced: excess engine heat in the cockpit and limited ground clearance, mostly due to a low-riding exhaust system. Neither would ever really be solved through this basic design's long 15-year production life.

Though the four-cylinder Austin-Healey was built for only 3½ years, there were four distinct variations. The original car, built until the autumn of 1955, was coded (and is now colloquially known as) BN1. The following year, it gained a new 4-speed gearbox (still with overdrive) to become the BN2. Meantime, the Healey company (not BMC) developed and further refined a racing BN1 in 1954-55. Called 100S (S for Sebring), it featured a stripped all-aluminum body *sans* bumpers and had a much-modified 132-bhp engine. Only 50 were built, all intended (and mostly used) in competition. There were also 1159 examples of the 100M, a BN2 conversion with 110 bhp, duo-tone paint, and assorted body and chassis modifications.

The Healey 100 succeeded in establishing a fine reputation very quickly indeed, especially in the U.S., where enthusiasts found it offered everything a contemporary MG didn't. In fact, most of the more than 14,000 BN1s and BN2s built were sold in America, making the name Austin-Healey a permanent part of sports-car love and lore.

Above: Healey 100/4 appearance was virtually unchanged through the model run. Right: A BN1 shows its standard lay-back windshield.

SPECIFICATIONS

Engines: ohv I-4, 162.3 cid/2660 cid, 90 bhp (net) @ 4000 rpm, 144 lbs-ft @ 4000 rpm; **100M:** 110 bhp @ 4500 rpm, torque NA; **100S:** 132 bhp @ 4700 rpm, torque NA

Transmissions:	3-speed (1953-55) or 4-speed (1955-56) manual with Laycock de Normanville electric overdrive
Suspension, front:	wishbones, coil springs, anti-roll bar
Suspension, rear:	live axle, Panhard rod, semi-elliptic leaf springs
Brakes:	front/rear drums (front/rear discs on 100S)
Wheelbase (in.):	90.0
Weight (lbs):	2015-2150
Top speed (mph):	103-110 (100S: 126)
0-60 mph (sec):	10.3 (100S: 7.8)

Production: BN1 (1953-55) 10,688 (incl. 55 100S) **BN2** (1955-56) 3924 (incl. 1159 100M)

1956-1959
AUSTIN-HEALEY 100 SIX

From the first, BMC saw the Austin-Healey as an integral part of the lineup, so when the firm's engine strategy changed, it was clear that the big sports car would too. It was thus no surprise that the 100/4 became the 100 Six in 1956. The old A90 four was considered obsolete. In its place was a new straight six of about the same size. But there was much more to the new model than just two extra cylinders and more low-rpm torque, for the Healey family, at BMC's behest, took the opportunity to freshen up the car end to end.

U.S. market feedback suggested buyers wanted more cabin space than the 100/4 had, so the redesign included a two-inch wheelbase stretch and the repositioning of some components in the tail to make room for the addition of tiny "+2" rear bucket seats. These may have been virtually useless for anything except parcels, but they met the demands of the sales force. Styling was much the same aside from a new oval grille, fixed windscreen, choice of wire-spoke or steel-disc wheels, and a bulged hood with a small functional air intake at the front.

The big difference, of course, was the new six-cylinder engine. This was BMC's corporate C-Series large-car unit, which had some design similarities—but few common components—with the B-Series four used in the MGA sports car. A big, heavy 2.64-liter cast-iron job with overhead valvegear, it was, according to the claimed figures, more powerful than the old big four (102 vs. 90 horsepower). A 4-speed

gearbox was standard, as on the ousted BN2, but on this new car, designated BN4, overdrive was an optional extra.

Alas, the 100 Six was a disappointment in its first year or so of production. Considerably heavier than the 100/4 (2435 pounds vs. 2150), it not only felt but was less lively. It didn't seem to handle as well either, and somehow came off as less of a sports car than its predecessors.

But autumn 1957 brought two important developments. First came a major strategic move as BMC decided to centralize assembly of all its sports cars; this meant that Austin-Healey production moved 50 miles south, from Longbridge to the MG factory at Abingdon. At about the same time (the phase-in point was neither tidy nor exact) there appeared a much-improved engine, with a revised cylinder head and more efficient manifolding that boosted peak power to 117 bhp and afforded a more sporting torque delivery. The difference was perhaps more marked than the figures suggest, for road tests pointed to an 8-mph gain in top speed and acceleration restored to something like BN2 levels.

Then, the two-seater returned as an addition to the line. Designated BN6, it reflected the sort of "second thoughts" backpedalling that would increasingly come to characterize BMC marketing. Moreover, BN4 assembly was suspended for a time, then resumed once existing inventory was cleared (most in the U.S., presumably).

Still, these were exciting years for Austin-Healey, especially once the little "frogeye" Sprite arrived in 1958 to take the marque into high-volume territory for the first time. With two different models in the showrooms, enthusiasts began to refer to the 100 Six (and its successors) as the "Big Healey."

By that point, the disappointing BN4 had been forgotten, and the reputation and sales of the latest six-cylinder Healeys continued to mount. As in 1953, these were sports cars with great character and style that not only performed well but made all the right noises. They would be a tough act to follow, but BMC thought it could do just that. It did. The Austin-Healey 3000 was at hand.

SPECIFICATIONS

Engine: ohv I-6, 161 cid/2639 cc, 102/117 bhp (net) @ 4600/4750 rpm, 142/144 lbs-ft @ 2400/3000 rpm

Transmission:	4-speed manual with optional Laycock de Normanville electric overdrive
Suspension, front:	wishbones, coil springs, anti-roll bar
Suspension, rear:	live axle, Panhard rod, semi-elliptic leaf springs
Brakes:	front/rear drums
Wheelbase (in.):	92.0
Weight (lbs):	2435
Top speed (mph):	102 ("early"), 111 ("late")
0-60 mph (sec):	11.2 ("late"), 12.9 ("early")
Production:	**BN4** 10,289 **BN6** 4150

A two-inch wheelbase stretch made room for a tiny seat in the 100 Six. Two extra cylinders didn't improve performance much.

1958-1961 AUSTIN-HEALEY SPRITE

Few cars have been more adroitly timed—or more *right* for their time—than the original Austin-Healey Sprite, the beloved "Bugeye." It was conceived to fill an obvious market gap that existed by the time the genuinely small sporting MGs, the Midgets of the Thirties and Forties, had evolved into the larger, costlier, more modern and "mature" MGA of the Fifties.

BMC chairman Sir Leonard Lord rarely missed a commercial trick, and invited the Healey family to design a small, back-to-basics sports car that would complement, rather than compete with, the popular MGA. As this collaboration had already led to the Austin-Healey 100, which was selling very well in the U.S., Lord was convinced that the new small Healey would have similar success. As it turned out, he was right.

Donald Healey and sons went to work at Warwick, though their creation was finalized by MG at Abingdon and put into production there beginning in mid-1958. The "olde worlde" Berkshire works thus found itself building three different sports cars: the MGA, the Austin-Healey 100 Six, and the new Sprite. BMC delved into its big box of registered trademarks for the model name, which had graced a Riley sports car of the Thirties. (The Nuffield Organisation had acquired Riley in 1938, then joined Austin in 1952 to form BMC.)

Riding an 80-inch wheelbase, the Sprite was tiny by the standards of its day (and ours, come to that) though larger and heavier than Thirties' Midgets. Alfa Romeo and Fiat had already produced unit-construction sports cars (both on shortened mass-market sedan platforms) but the Sprite was the first unitized British sports car. It was, of course, a spare two-seat roadster but, with a 1460-pound curb weight, wasn't all that light for its size.

To keep the Sprite structure as simple and rigid as possible, the Healeys omitted an external trunklid; you loaded luggage through the cockpit by folding down the seats. Front sheetmetal—hood, fenders, and surrounding panels—was hinged at the firewall to lift up as a unit, thus providing almost unrestricted access to engine and front suspension. Doors were mere shells (scooped out for storage) to which sliding side curtains could be attached. Per British tradition, the soft top was of the "build-it-yourself" variety, though an optional bolt-on hardtop was offered soon after introduction.

What everybody noticed, of course, was the protruding headlamps that gave the Sprite a "bugeye" or "frogeye" look, hence the nicknames that persist to this day. This appearance distinction was quite accidental. Retractable lights had been contemplated (prototypes had them) but were cancelled at the last minute as too costly (so was a fold-down windshield), by which time it was too late to change the styling.

Cost considerations also dictated off-the-shelf running gear and chassis components, a mixture of items from two small BMC family sedans. The Morris Minor 1000 donated its rack-and-pinion steering, while the Sprite's 4-speed gearbox, firmed-up front suspension, and venerable BMC A-series four-cylinder engine came from the Austin A35. The last also contributed its rear suspension, with a live axle located by upper radius arms and cantilevered quarter-elliptic leaf springs.

The result was a cheeky little car with enormous character and *joie de vivre*. With its rudimentary rear end, the Bugeye could be darty and prone to oversteer, but since the steering was so responsive—and top speed only 80 mph—it rarely got away from you. And because it could be flung about with abandon, the Sprite was perfect for slaloms, gymkhanas, and other competition, and demand from weekend warriors soon prompted all sorts of hop-up and handling goodies from aftermarket sources. Much-modified Sprites, with front disc brakes, heated engines, and smoothed-out bodywork competed gamely but with distinction against far larger and more powerful machines at places like Sebring and Daytona.

Inherent mechanical sturdiness and race-and-ride versatility helped sales, but price was the big factor. At about $1500 new, the Sprite was cheap—$1000 or so less than an MGA and Triumph TR3—and a whale of a buy. Alas, it wouldn't last long: just three years and near 49,000 units. Its successor, the Sprite Mark II of 1961 (also cloned for a new MG Midget), was much the same car with extra amenities and more conventional, square-rigged styling.

But Len Lord's bargain-basement roadster had done its job, reestablishing a popular market class while teaching an entire generation what *real* sports-car motoring was all about. While it's likely that fewer than half the original Bugeyes survive today, it's almost possible to build a new one from scratch, so numerous are the reproductions of virtually everything—mechanical parts, body panels, trim, the works. That "cheap wheels" can inspire such long-lived affection may be surprising, but then, the Bugeye was much more than the sum of its humble parts.

Last-minute cancellation of planned hidden headlamps gave early Sprites their distinctive "bugeye" look (top). Cockpit (above) was appropriately spartan. Good proportioning (opposite) belies the car's tiny size.

SPECIFICATIONS

Engine: ohv I-4, 57.9 cid/948 cc, 43 bhp (net) @ 5200 rpm, 52 lbs-ft @ 3300 rpm

Transmission:	4-speed manual
Suspension, front:	wishbones, coil springs
Suspension, rear:	live axle, quarter-elliptic leaf springs
Brakes:	front/rear drums
Wheelbase (in.):	80.0
Weight (lbs):	1460
Top speed (mph):	80
0-60 mph (sec):	20.9
Production:	48,999

1959-1967
AUSTIN-HEALEY 3000

Though we list the Austin-Healey 3000 as a separate family, it was little more than a 100 Six with a bigger engine and better brakes. It was only in the Sixties that more significant changes came along. Thus, the "Big Healey" formula established in 1956 wasn't altered conceptually in its 12 years. From the first 100 Six to the last 3000, these were rugged sports cars with a 92-inch wheelbase and a heavy but reliable engine—not to mention a hairy-chested, rumbly personality and smooth styling. The 3000, introduced in the spring of 1959, spanned nearly nine of those dozen years. In that time came Mark II, Convertible, and Mark III models, plus assorted running changes in engine, chassis, gearbox, and body construction. But almost all these developments were logical and improved the basic car. We can also be thankful that they didn't change its character.

Initially, the 3000's main distinctions were an enlarged engine with 2912 cc and 124 horsepower, plus front-disc brakes (drums continued at the rear). These changes mirrored those made that same year to another Abingdon-built sports car, the MG MGA. As before, there were two roadster styles: two-seater BN7 and BT7 2+2.

Two years later, BMC announced the 3000 Mk II, for which the engine was given three SU carburetors. Rated output rose to 132 bhp but magazine tests showed no

*Above: Two-tone paint, as on this Mark II, was fairly common on 3000s. **Below:** Mark III had windwings, wind-up windows, and new top.*

gain in performance, and since the setup was tricky to keep in tune, BMC dropped it a year later. Also during the Mk II run, a new type of gearbox casing and linkage were adopted with a more direct-acting selector mechanism.

At the end of summer 1962, the Mk II became Mk II Convertible, the body getting its first (and only) re-jig. Without changing overall apperance, BMC gave it a slightly more curved windshield, roll-up door windows, and a proper fold-away soft top. The two-seater was discarded and all 3000s were now 2+2s. The engine, modified yet again, reverted to twin SU carburetors yet suffered no power loss. All in all, the new Convertible was a more modern and practical package.

The Big Healey saw one more major revision in the spring of 1964 with the advent of the 3000 Mk III. Boasting even more power—148 bhp—from the same-size engine, it featured a restyled dashboard with wood paneling, and a between-the-seats center console. A "Phase II" version arrived later in the year with modified rear-axle location (now by radius arms) and chassis alterations allowing more suspension travel.

Built at Abingdon from early 1964 to the winter of 1967-68, the Mk III was undoubtedly the best of the breed—and the fastest: top speed was about 120 mph. Snug and well equipped, it was equally comfortable open and closed.

Of course, not even the most popular cars go on forever, and the Big Healey was beginning to look a bit old-fashioned by the mid-Sixties. Even so, no fewer than 5494 Mk IIIs were produced in 1966, the highest one-year tally since 1960, when the original 3000 was at its sales peak. But by then, BMC faced new U.S. safety and emission regulations and decided that modifying the Big Healey to meet them wasn't worth the money. Thus, except for a single car assembled in 1968, the Big Healey was consigned to history at the end of 1967.

SPECIFICATIONS

Engines: ohv I-6, 177 cid/2912 cc, 124/132/131/148 bhp (net) @ 4600/4750/5250 rpm, 162/167/158/165 lbs-ft @ 2700/3000/3500 rpm

Transmission:	4-speed manual with optional Laycock de Normanville electric overdrive
Suspension, front:	wishbones, coil springs, anti-roll bar
Suspension, rear:	live axle, Panhard rod or (from 1964) radius rods, semi-elliptic leaf springs
Brakes:	front discs/rear drums
Wheelbase (in.):	92.0
Weight (lbs):	2460-2550
Top speed (mph):	114-121
0-60 mph (sec):	9.8-11.4

Production: "Mk I" 13,650 **Mk II** 5450 **Mk II Convertible** 6113 **Mk III** 17,704

1963-1969 BIZZARRINI GT STRADA 5300

In the early Sixties, the name of Giotto Bizzarrini seemed to crop up all over the Italian supercar industry, the engineer being involved with Ferrari, Lamborghini, Iso and his own little carmaking concern in the space of just a few short years. That the car bearing his name should bear a close resemblance to the Bizzarrini-designed Iso Grifo, therefore, should hardly come as a surprise.

Bizzarrini was one of Ferrari's most respected engineers in the late Fifties/early Sixties. When chief engineer Carlo Chiti and several other experienced hands left the Maranello company, Bizzarrini did too, trucking off to Livorno to work freelance. Soon afterward, he was commissioned by Ferruccio Lamborghini's fledgling firm to design a Ferrari-like V-12 and hired to lay out a new chassis for Iso of Milan.

This chassis was the true ancestor of the Bizzarrini GT's. Typical of period Italian practice, it was a fabricated pressed-steel platform to which was attached an all-independent coil-spring suspension with De Dion rear geometry. Power was provided by a 327-cubic-inch Chevrolet Corvette V-8 tuned for 300 or 365 horsepower (SAE). Iso's first Bizzarrini-designed chassis was unveiled with the Rivolta coupe in 1962.

At the same time, Bizzarrini was working on a short-wheelbase version of this chassis that ultimately formed the basis for his GT Strada 5300. The same basic platform with four-barrel 365-bhp Corvette power was also slated for Iso's forthcoming Grifo A3L, a two-seat derivative of the four-place Rivolta. Both cars were unveiled in prototype form at the Turin Motor Show of November 1963, with the future Bizzarrini titled Iso A3C "competition coupe." Though the A3C and A3L had clearly been styled by the same hands—those of Giorgetto Giugiaro at Bertone—they were completely different in detail.

Confused? It gets better. Badged as an Iso, the future Bizzarrini appeared at the 1964 Le Mans 24 Hours, finishing 14th at an average 106.75 mph. This racer carried an aluminum body with headlamps recessed behind sloping plastic covers, and a grille composed of two wide slots. Wheels were cast alloy, and engine cooling vents appeared on the flanks immediately behind the front wheelarches. Meantime, the Grifo went on sale with the same general Bertone lines and similar front-fender exhaust grids, only its body was made of steel, had exposed headlamps and a less radical nose, and sported a more luxuriously trimmed interior. Everyone noticed the obvious relationship between the two cars, but the "competition coupe" was now offered as a limited-edition road car with a new Bizzarrini badge, and no one, least of all Iso, seemed to mind.

Bizzarrini's tiny premises couldn't build more than a few cars at a time, so the "production" GT Strada 5300 (the name means "road" in Italian, the number represents the Corvette engine's cubic-centimeter displacement) was strictly a hand-assembled affair. Rolling chassis came from Iso, while the Bertone-styled body was built by BBM in Modena. Bizzarrini simply put them together.

The result was a low-slung high-performer with vivid acceleration and a 145-mph top speed. Fuel "economy" was only 12 miles per U.S. gallon, a definite drawback in Europe with its less-available, higher-priced gasoline. Then again, this was the sort of car likely to be bought only by rich *poseurs*, so who cared?

It's not clear how many of these cars were actually completed, though the figure of 149 quoted by one source seems rather high. What is clear is that very few survive. In any case, Bizzarrini himself quickly lost interest in this project and turned his attention to the smaller GT Europa 1900, an equally rare but more humble machine powered by a 1.9-liter four-cylinder engine from Opel of Germany.

Low and squat, the Bizzarrini GT began life as an Iso, hence its styling resemblance to the Grifo and use of the same Chevrolet Corvette 327 V-8. Bertone supplied bodies, but Bizzarrini's small assembly facilities limited production to probably no more than 100—making this beautiful survivor a modern rarity. Note "front midships" engine position.

SPECIFICATIONS

Engine: Chevrolet ohv V-8, 327 cid/5354 cc, 365 bhp (SAE) @ 6000 rpm, 376 lbs-ft @ 3500 rpm

Transmission:	4-speed manual
Suspension, front:	wishbones, coil springs, anti-roll bar
Suspension, rear:	De Dion axle, Watt linkage, radius arms, coil springs
Brakes:	front/rear discs
Wheelbase (in.):	96.5
Weight (lbs):	2760
Top speed (mph):	145
0-60 mph (sec):	6.4
Production:	NA

1956-1959
BMW 507

Born in 1916 as an aircraft-engine manufacturer, Bavarian Motor Works had branched out into motorcycles by the late Twenties and was looking to expand into the auto business. It got the chance when the Dixi company in Eisenach proposed that BMW take it over, thus giving the Bavarian firm a license-built version of the British Austin Seven. BMW soon developed cars of its own that moved far beyond that humble little rattletrap, building a reputation for superb engineering in the process. This naturally embraced sporting models, of which the most famous and successful were the six-cylinder Type 328 and 327 of the immediate prewar years.

But then came World War II, and BMW emerged as divided as defeated Germany itself. Some of its prewar facilities were irrevocably lost behind the Iron Curtain in the new state of East Germany, while those that remained in free West Germany had been devastated by Allied bombing. Rebuilding from this rubble was slow and painful, and it wasn't until 1951 that BMW was able to return to car production, though it did so with a new postwar design.

Designated 501, this was a big, bulbous sedan that was altogether too costly for the German market at the time, though BMW was still far too small to field a cheaper, high-volume product, and complex construction more or less dictated a lofty price. The 501 chassis, for example, was a massive box-section affair with tubular cross-members and torsion-bar independent-front/live-axle-rear suspension. Power came from an updated version of the prewar six with its complicated valvetrain. Nevertheless, the "Baroque Angel," as it came to be called, sold well enough to give BMW at least a toehold in the car business, and the firm followed up in 1954 with a new 2.6-liter pushrod V-8 for a derivative model, the 502.

What happened next was something of a surprise for such a struggling outfit: a return to sports cars. At the urging of influential U.S. foreign-car baron Max Hoffman,

BMW recruited German-American industrial designer Count Albrecht Goertz to come up with a pair of sporty models using 502 chassis and running gear. Goertz worked quickly, and the results appeared in September 1955 as the 503 and 507. The former, offered in cabriolet and closed coupe styles, was a smooth if sedate 2+2 tourer rather than an out-and-out sports car. That role was left to the dashing 507.

Conceived as an open two-seater, the 507 shared the big sedans' steering, suspension and track dimensions but rode a wheelbase shortened by no fewer than 16 inches. It also shared the 502 V-8, albeit tuned to 150 net horsepower, teamed with 4-speed gearbox. Early 500-series BMWs employed a remote-mounted transmission, but the 507's gearbox was always in unit. Veteran BMW engineer Fritz Fiedler designed the chassis along 501/502 lines, though the structure was all-new (and shared with the 503).

The 503 was neat and clean, but it positively paled next to the 507. Here was styling as elegant and exciting as anything from Ferrari, Jaguar, or Mercedes-Benz— and completely unmistakable, a glamorous new image-leader for BMW. Compared with the Baroque Angel, it looked like something from the next century. As with the American Corvette and Thunderbird, an optional lift-off steel hardtop was offered to supplement the standard folding roof, and looked great. In typical Teutonic fashion, the 507 was fully equipped and solidly detailed but heavier than its lean looks implied. In fact, it and the 503 weighed little less than the big sedans.

Those who drove the 507 were exhilarated by its straightline performance but disappointed in the rather ponderous handling and the all-drum brakes (improved by substituting front discs on the last few examples). Top speed was 120+ mph— good going for the available power (and testimony, perhaps, to the aerodynamic efficiency of Goertz's styling)—but with more than 2900 pounds at the curb, the 507 was not as nimble as it could have been.

The 507 was never intended to make real money—and at an astronomical $9000 in the U.S., it didn't. As a result, production ended after less than three years and a mere 253 units. But as the most memorable BMW of these years, the 507 was important to the firm's fortunes because it helped revive BMW's prewar reputation for fast, durable, uniquely styled road cars with impeccable engineering credentials.

In fact, it's fair to say that the 507 is the granddaddy of today's "Ultimate Driving Machines," even if it didn't sire them directly. That it's also recognized as a classic in its own right is only fair too, for it was and always will be.

SPECIFICATIONS

Engine: ohv V-8, 193.3 cid/3168 cc, 150 bhp @ 5000 rpm, 173 lbs-ft @ 2000 rpm

Transmission:	4-speed manual
Suspension, front:	wishbones, torsion bars, anti-roll bar
Suspension, rear:	live axle, radius rods, A-bracket, torsion bars
Brakes:	front/rear drums (front discs on late examples)
Wheelbase (in.):	97.6
Weight (lbs):	2935
Top speed (mph):	124
0-60 mph (sec):	8.8
Production:	253

Curvy 507 was a remarkable achievement for a BMW that was struggling to survive in the mid-Fifties. Highish curb weight took the edge off performance despite 150-bhp V-8.

1968-1977
BMW 2800CS, 2.5CS &
3.0CS/CSi/CSL

A key part of BMW's startling sales success in the Seventies and Eighties was its introduction of a new engine family in the Sixties, with hemispherical combustion chambers, opposed valves in crossflow cylinder heads, and overhead-camshaft valvegear. The first of these appeared in late 1961 to power the make-or-break "New Generation" 1500 sedan. Since then, it's been built with both four and six cylinders in displacements from 1.5 to 3.4 liters, and remains an important building block at BMW today.

As this engine grew, the original "New Generation" sedan evolved through 1600, 1800, and 2000 derivatives. A new CS coupe variation arrived in 1965, combining the 2000 sedan's running gear, floorpan, and some inner panels with a handsome new pillarless body designed by BMW's Wilhelm Hofmeister and executed by Karmann of Osnabrück. Unfortunately, this 2000CS had but a 120-horsepower four and was thus somewhat underpowered, while its face was one only Frau Hofmeister could have loved.

But BMW is nothing if not persistent, and in late 1968 it corrected most every 2000CS flaw in a six-cylinder successor, the 2800CS. To accommodate the longer engine, new sheetmetal was grafted onto the existing body ahead of the cowl, adding 2.9 inches in wheelbase but nearly five inches to overall length. Together with a better-integrated "twin-kidney" grille motif and four headlamps, this simple change yielded more balanced proportions that completely transformed the coupe from ugly duckling to beautiful swan. Retained from the 2000CS were BMW's now-characteristic full-length, chrome-trimmed creaseline just below the belt, plus a gently wrapped rear window and horizontal taillamps.

Even better, the 2800CS went as well as it looked. The new six (borrowed from the 2800 sedan, introduced at the same time) delivered a rated 170 horsepower from its 170 cubic inches—the hallowed "1 hp per cu. in." ideal. It not only made for performance of a much higher order than the 2.0-liter four but was smoother, less fussy, very torquey, and an aural delight. It also fulfilled another requisite of a truly great engine by being terrific to look at. All-independent coil-spring suspension with front MacPherson struts and rear semi-trailing arms was continued per established BMW practice, combining a supple ride with good handling and roadholding.

Karmann continued to build CS bodies and handle final assembly in Osnabrück. Interiors were trimmed neatly, if not luxuriously, with top-quality materials in the

German manner. As in the 2000CS, the rear seat was more "+2" than adult-size, though most grown-ups riding there wouldn't complain on short trips and the glassy cabin ensured that no one suffered claustrophobia. Adding to the spacious feel was a roomy front cabin with generously wide individual seats and the now-customary low-profile BMW dash.

This handsome package followed another recent Munich tradition by continuing for a good number of years, albeit with various displacement changes to accommodate market demand and, as time passed, preserve performance in the face of power-sapping safety and emissions regulations. Thus, the 2800CS gave way to the 3.0CS in 1971, followed shortly by the 3.0CSi with Bosch D-Jetronic fuel injection. (BMW model designations in this period reflected displacement in liters rather than cubic centimeters.) Both also had disc brakes at the rear as well as the front (replacing the 2800's drums).

Also appearing in '71 was a lightweight, detrimmed competition special, the 3.0CSL, with aluminum substituted for steel in many body panels. Late 1972 brought fuel injection as well as a small bore increase that boosted capacity to 3003 cc. A year later, displacement was stretched to 3153 cc for a third CSL, which was available with various eye-catching aerodynamic addenda including a rear spoiler between shark-like fins, front-fender strakes, and front airdam. The CSLs were quite successful in road racing on both sides of the Atlantic, carrying BMW's *blau-und-weiss* banner against archrival Porsche, among others, and winning the European Touring Car Championship in several years.

At the other extreme, BMW responded to the first "Energy Crisis" with the downmarket 2.5CS of mid-1974. This had a smaller, less powerful version of the "big-block" six (as initially offered in the 1968 big-sedan generation) and lacked a few frills, but sold for DM 6000 less than the 3.0-liter CS. But though it continued through the end of the Hofmeister coupes in 1975, it saw only 844 copies, making it one of the rarer BMWs of modern times.

All of these cars are fast, but some are outstandingly quick. The 2800CS could reach 128 mph, while the injected 3.0CSi was good for nearly 140 mph and 7.5 seconds in the 0-60 mph test. Surprisingly, the CSL was little faster than this in roadgoing trim, but then the winged and bespoilered jobs looked like they should have been on a racetrack anyway.

Aside from performance, plus styling that has held up amazingly well over the years, the best thing about owning one of these BMWs is that their running gear comes straight from the counterpart sedans, which means that the coupes are no more difficult or expensive to maintain. But even BMW now admits that the Karmann bodies tended to severe rust after a few years, and squeaks, rattles, and air leaks are common, as with most pillarless body styles. This may explain why the replacement 6-Series was built in-house, where BMW could keep a better eye on quality.

With a little care and feeding, though, any of these six-cylinder coupes will return a lot of driving pleasure while testifying to its owner's discerning good taste. You can't say that about every car, especially those from the Seventies.

*Main photos: 2800CS was the four-cylinder 2000CS with a longer front and smooth six-cylinder power. **Opposite top:** By 1971, BMW was racing it in lightweight 3.0CSL form.*

SPECIFICATIONS

Engines: all sohc I-6; **2.5CS** (1974-77): 152 cid/2494 cc, 150 bhp (DIN) @ 6000 rpm; **2800CS** (1968-71): 170 cid/2788 cc, 170 bhp (DIN) @ 6000 rpm; **3.0CS/CSi** (1971-75): 182 cid/2985 cc, 180 bhp (DIN) @ 6000 rpm (CS)/200 bhp (DIN) @ 5500 rpm (CSi); **3.0CSL** (1971-72): 182 cid/2985 cc, 206 bhp (DIN) @ 6600 rpm; **3.0CSL** (1972-73): 183 cid/3003 cc, 206 bhp (DIN) @ 6600 rpm; **3.0CSL** (1973-75): 192 cid/3153 cc, 206 bhp (DIN) @ 6600 rpm; **Torque:** 155 lbs-ft (2.5CS) to 211 lbs-ft (3.0CSL)

Transmissions:	4-speed manual or 3-speed automatic (except CSL)
Suspension, front:	MacPherson struts, lower wishbones, coil springs
Suspension, rear:	semi-trailing arms, coil springs
Brakes:	front/rear discs (rear drums on 2800CS)
Wheelbase (in.):	103.3
Weight (lbs):	2775-3085
Top speed (mph):	128-139
0-60 mph (sec):	7.5-11.0

Production: 2800CS (1968-71) 9399 **3.0CS** (1971-75) 11,063 (some sources list 10,088) **3.0CSi** (1971-75) 8199 **3.0CSL** (1971-75) 1039 (some sources list 1096) **2.5CS** (1974-77) 844

1976-1988
BMW 6-SERIES

It's seen more engine changes than a cross-country freight train, but the BMW 6-Series remains a thing of beauty and a driving joy. It originated in 1973 to succeed the aging Wilhelm Hofmeister-styled coupes that began with the four-cylinder 2000CS. Development work was initiated under chief engineer Bernhard Osswald and completed by his successor, Karlheinz Radermacher. What bowed at the Geneva Salon in March 1976 was essentially a rebodied version of the recently introduced 5-Series sedan, powered by the M-52 "big-block" six of the superseded 2800CS/3.0CS coupes.

Penned by the artistic Paul Bracq, 6-Series styling was—and is—modern and handsome, with BMW's familiar "twin-kidney" grille, broad hood and deck areas, and tall, glassy greenhouse. Unlike its pillarless predecessors, the 6-Series had B-posts, though they were quite thin and, finished in matte-black, hardly noticeable. Karmann continued to supply bodies, but final assembly now took place at BMW's Dingolfing factory, not the coachbuilder's Osnabrück works.

Chassis design followed the well-established formula laid down with the pivotal "New Class" sedans of 1962: all-coil suspension with front MacPherson struts and rear semi-trailing arms, plus recirculating-ball steering. As BMW's new flagship, the 6-Series got disc brakes at the rear as well as the front. It also introduced two innovations: variable-assist power steering, which decreases boost as engine speed increases for better road feel, and the comprehensive Check Control warning-light system that keeps tabs on engine systems, fluid levels, and exterior light bulbs. (Both would spread to other BMW models.) The 2+2 cabin featured a pair of deeply bucketed rear seats separated by an extension of the front center console, which in turn mated with a new angled-middle "Cockpit Design" dash (now another BMW hallmark).

The 6-Series arrived in Europe with the existing 3.0-liter carbureted six as the 630CS. Initial transmission choices comprised 4-speed Getrag manual or 3-speed ZF automatic. The U.S. version appeared for model year 1977 as the 630CSi, the "i" denoting Bosch L-Jetronic fuel injection, necessary to maintain some semblance of performance in the face of stiffening federal emissions standards.

Though critics loved the 6-Series' handling, comfort, and refinement, they judged outright performance disappointing. But BMW was ready with a more powerful, 3.2-liter engine, substituted on both sides of the Atlantic for 1978. Curiously, these cars were badged 633CSi, not the more logical "632CSi."

Since then, the 6-Series has evolved through increasingly potent powerplants with chassis upgrades to match. The first came with the European 635CSi of 1978, identified by special front and rear spoilers, discreet bodyside striping, and wider, lacy-spoke Mahle-BBS alloy wheels, plus a 3.5-liter 218-bhp M-90 engine and close-ratio 5-speed manual gearbox. Alas, a 635 didn't reach North America until 1985 and was much tamer, though it boasted three important chassis changes: "double-pivot" front control arms and "Track Link" rear suspension (borrowed for 1983 6s from the big 7-Series sedans to reduce oversteer tendencies in hard cornering) and Bosch anti-lock braking system (ABS). By this time, all 6s had standard 5-speed manual and optional 4-speed automatic transmissions, the latter with electronic shift control.

More exciting was the limited-production M635CSi, presented at Frankfurt in September 1983. Developed by BMW's Motorsport arm (hence the "M"), it packed a modified version of the twincam, 24-valve M-88 powerplant from the mid-engine M1 (see entry). Performance was vivid to say the least: just 6.4 seconds 0-100 km/h (62 mph) and a blistering 158 mph maximum.

For 1987, BMW finally brought this *autobahn* stormer to North America as the M6, losing little performance in the process. Though luxuriously furnished—twin air conditioners, eight-way power front sports seats, eight-speaker sound system, hand-stitched leather on seats, dash, and door panels—it's *blitz schnell* off the line and cruises easily at 140 mph. Desirable?

In exchange for less performance, less money bought you the equally posh U.S.-market 1987 L6, available only with automatic. Standard manual transmission returned for the renamed '88-model 635CSi, which offered more power via the higher-compression engine from the big second-generation 735i sedan. Closer-fitting bumpers were among several updates throughout.

Alas, nothing lasts forever, and BMW's new 5-Series sedan (scheduled for early-'88 release at this writing) inevitably means that this beautiful *bolide* will be replaced (reportedly by a smooth all-new high-tech design). The good news is that the 6-Series we've come to know and love should continue through 1990 at least. It'll be one tough act to follow.

SPECIFICATIONS

Engines: all sohc I-6; **630CS** (1976-79, Europe only): 182 cid/2985 cc, 185 bhp (DIN) @ 5800 rpm, 188 lbs-ft @ 3500 rpm; **630CSi** (1977): 182 cid/2985 cc, 176 bhp (SAE net) @ 5600 rpm, 185 lbs-ft @ 4500 rpm; **633CSi** (1978-84): 196 cid/3210 cc, 176-181 bhp (SAE net) @ 5500-6000 rpm, 196 lbs-ft @ 4000 rpm; **628CSi** (1980-87, Europe only): 170 cid/2788 cc, 184 bhp (DIN) @ 5800 rpm, 177 lbs-ft @ 4200 rpm; **635CSi/L6** (1978-87): 209 cid/3430 cc, 182 bhp @ 5400 rpm, 214 lbs-ft @ 4000 rpm; **M635CSi/M6** (1983-88): dohc I-6, 211 cid/3453 cc, 256 bhp (SAE net) @ 6500 rpm, 243 lbs-ft @ 4500 rpm; **635CSi** (1988): 209 cid/3430 cc, 208 bhp @ 5700 rpm, 225 bhp @ 4000 rpm, torque NA

Transmissions:	4/5-speed manual or 3/4-speed automatic
Suspension, front:	MacPherson struts, coil springs, lower control arms (double-pivot from 1983), anti-roll bar
Suspension, rear:	semi-trailing arms (with Track Links from 1983), coil springs, anti-roll bar
Brakes:	front/rear discs
Wheelbase (in.):	103.4
Weight (lbs):	3195-3570
Top speed (mph):	125-150
0-60 mph (sec):	6.8-9.0

Production: 630CS/630CSi 32,292 (1978-82 calendar-year sales) **Others** NA (production continues at this writing)

The 6-Series' basic looks have been little altered over more than 10 years but have stood the test of time well. Here, the editors' 1986 test car. After one year as L6, the "base" U.S. model is renamed 635CSi for 1988.

1978-1981 BMW M1

Some cars don't get the chance they deserve. The M1, BMW's first—and so far only—mid-engine production car, was one of them. Though conceived as a "homologation special" for production-class sports-car competition, it was never actually campaigned by the factory, whose motorsport policy veered toward building Formula 1 engines soon after the M1 was finalized. In the end, only 450 examples were built, almost all of them fully equipped road cars. Needless to say, they've already become prized collector's items.

The M1 (which stands for "mid-engine car, first type") originated in 1975 as BMW's counterattack against the Porsche 911s then cleaning up in various sports-racing series. Even so, the only part BMW actually contributed was the engine: a much-modified 4-valves-per-cylinder version of its straight six, designated M-88.

Aside from the gullwing Turbo experimental of 1972, BMW had no experience with "middies," so it hired Lamborghini in Italy to design, develop, and produce M1. Giorgetto Giugiaro's Ital Design (then also involved with the ill-starred DeLorean) was contracted for bodywork styling and construction. Ital was told to retain some "BMW identity," which explains the use of the familiar "twin-kidney" grille motif. Still, the overall result was somewhat heavy-handed compared to Paul Brache's Turbo (especially around the rear quarters), lacking its grace and excitement. Perhaps Giugiaro's staff had had an off day.

The use of Italian specialist know-how should have worked brilliantly, but it didn't. Lamborghini welcomed contracts like this because it was on the financial brink at the time. As if by design, it slipped over the edge shortly after the M1 was locked up, leaving BMW no choice but to regroup. Accordingly, construction was farmed out to two other Italian firms: Marchesi, for the multi-tube chassis, and Trasformazione Italiana Resina, for the fiberglass body. Final assembly was shifted to Baur, the German coachbuilder long associated with BMW.

But by then it was 1979 (the M1 debuted at the Paris Salon in October '78) and BMW was wearying of a project that wasn't likely to generate the publicity—or victories—expected of it. The M1's sole moment in the competition spotlight came with the 1979-80 "Procar" series, a sort of European International Race of Champions staged before major Grands Prix. In it, F1 drivers competed against each other and a few non-GP pilots in identically prepared M1s, a sort of pre-race side show. It was almost as if BMW was ashamed of what it had done.

And more's the pity, because the M1 was a superb modern supercar by any standard. As in Lamborghini's Miura and Countach, the engine sat longitudinally behind a two-seat cockpit to drive the rear wheels via a 5-speed transaxle (by ZF). Suspension was naturally all-independent, with coil springs and twin A-arms at each corner. Brakes were big discs all around, while massive 16-inch-diameter wheels and tires were wider at the rear than at the front, as is common in tail-heavy high-performers. The results of all this were vice-free handling, very high cornering grip, and excellent stopping power—in short, real racetrack ability.

That's hardly surprising when you consider that the M1 was developed in three versions: a 277-horsepower road car, built mainly to satisfy the 400-unit homologation minimum; a Group 4 racer with 470 bhp and suitable body and chassis modifications; and a Group 5 car with about 850 bhp from a reduced-capacity (3.2-liter) turbocharged engine (the others had normally aspirated 3.5-liter powerplants). The Group 4 version was the one run in Procar.

"Production" M1s were pretty plush, their comprehensive equipment running to air conditioning and full carpeting. They were—and are—as nice on the road as any Ferrari Boxer and probably better built. The highly reliable 24-valve M-88 engine is another plus for would-be owners. In fact, this is a pretty young power unit with a lot of development potential as yet unexplored. As proof, a revised rendition powers the limited-production M5 sedan and M635CSi/M6 coupe built by BMW's Motorsport division.

The tragedy of the M1 is that this great car was abandoned before it could prove itself. Will BMW again attempt something so specialized? At this writing, indications are that it will, but the car won't necessarily be mid-engined, and you can bet it won't be built in collaboration with a shaky outfit.

SPECIFICATIONS

Engine: dohc I-6 with 4 valves/cylinder, 210.7 cid/3453 cc, 277 bhp (DIN) @ 6500 rpm, 243 lbs-ft @ 5000 rpm

Transmission:	ZF 5-speed transaxle
Suspension, front:	double A-arms, coil springs
Suspension, rear:	double A-arms, coil springs
Brakes:	front/rear discs
Wheelbase (in.):	100.8
Weight (lbs):	2865-3120
Top speed (mph):	162
0-60 mph (sec):	5.5

Production: 450 (incl. Group 4 and Group 5 competition models)

The first of the now-famous "M-cars" was also the first mid-engine production BMW. In revised form, M1's 24-valve twincam six would power the late-Eighties M5 sedan and M6 coupe.

1949-1953
BRISTOL 401 & 402

Bristol, the famous British aircraft-engine maker, watched its business fall off rapidly after World War II as military contracts ran out, and turned to building high-quality cars. It happened almost by chance. Somehow the firm managed to acquire the services of long-time BMW engineer Dr. Fritz Fiedler, as well as blueprints for and several examples of late-Thirties BMW cars. A key figure in these acquisitions was H.J. Aldington, whose Frazer-Nash concern had been BMW's UK distributor before the war and would build postwar sports cars using Bristol's "purloined" engine and transmission designs.

Bristol's first automobile emerged at the 1947 Geneva Salon as the Type 400. It was pretty dull stuff, too heavy for its available power and stylistically dated. But it was built with precision and the best materials money could buy—and was priced accordingly, of course. But Bristol wasn't planning to outproduce General Motors—or even Rolls-Royce. Just a few cars built patiently for a discerning monied elite would do fine, thank you.

The 400 set a pattern for future Bristols in other ways. Its chassis, for example, has continued without significant change for some 40 years now. A sturdy, advanced box-section structure based on the prewar BMW 326 design, it employed steel floor members for extra torsional rigidity and spanned a 114-inch wheelbase. Front suspension was independent via a Ford-like transverse leaf spring. Longitudinal torsion bars sprung a live rear axle located by radius rods and A-bracket. Steering was rack-and-pinion, *very* rare for the period.

Under the hood was an evolution of the legendary 2.0-liter inline six from BMW's prewar 328 sports car, with the same complicated "cross-pushrod" valvegear, hemispherical combustion chambers, and downdraft intake ports. It was a tall but efficient powerplant, initially rated at 80 horsepower.

Topping all this was a fulsome "almost four-seat" coupe body clearly patterned on that of the prewar 327 Autenreith coupe. The similarities even extended to the grille, a slim, BMW-like "twin-kidney" affair.

After 700 examples through late 1949, the 400 gave way to the logically designated 401. Aside from a nominal 5 extra horsepower, its main distinction was more streamlined styling "such as might be expected from an aircraft builder intent on showing his skill," as a Bristol historian put it. However, the new body design came not from Bristol but Carrozzeria Touring of Italy, and thus had the coachmaker's patented *Superleggera* construction (aluminum body panels attached to a strong, multi-tube framework). Though still a two-door 2 + 2, the 401 looked more aerodynamic than the 400, and undoubtedly was. Its top speed was somewhat higher, now 95 mph, while mildly modified examples could do 100 mph.

It was with this smooth-lined machine that Bristol began to make its mark among GT cars—and in motorsport. The 401 competed in rallies, but was still hampered by comparatively high weight despite its new "superlight" body.

Accompanying the 401 was a derivative convertible designated 402. Pinin Farina had a hand in modifying the coupe's lines, but the result was less than satisfying, especially the longer, more rounded rump. Bristol itself handled this model's body building. Chassis and running gear came straight from the 401. Though a little garish by Bristol standards, the 402 was nicely detailed. Its soft top folded completely away, and removable cant rails were provided for snug wind and weather sealing between the top and the upper edges of the side windows.

The 401/402 saw lower production than the 400, just 650 coupes and a mere 24 convertibles. Not that this bothered Bristol. In fact, the firm had something even better to show as early as 1953. Well, at least it was faster.

SPECIFICATIONS

Engine: ohv I-6, 120.3 cid/1971 cc, 85 bhp (net) @ 4500 rpm, 107 lbs-ft @ 3500 rpm

Transmission:	4-speed manual
Suspension, front:	wishbones, transverse leaf spring
Suspension, rear:	live axle, radius arms, A-bracket, torsion bars
Brakes:	front/rear drums
Wheelbase (in.):	114.0
Weight (lbs):	2670
Top speed (mph):	95
0-60 mph (sec):	17.4
Production:	401 650 402 24

If Boeing had tried its hand at a car in the late Forties, it might have produced something like the British-built Bristol. The 401 was a more stylish version of the original 400 model, with lightweight body and BMW's prewar 2.0-liter six. The 402 was a brief convertible offshoot.

1953-1955
BRISTOL 403

Four years after Bristol put its 401 on sale, the prestigious British aero-enginemaker-turned-automaker was ready with something better. But the firm saw no need for anything radically different given its chosen low-volume/high-price market (that would follow a few years later with the 405), so the new 403 was no more than a thoughtful update.

Launched in May 1953, the 403 looked almost identical to the 401. Appearance changes were limited to silver grille bars (still in BMW-style "twin-kidney" surrounds) and new red model badges (instead of yellow) on trunklid and hoodsides—all very subtle. There was also no companion convertible this time.

Mechanical changes were more substantive, encompassing drivetrain, brakes, suspension, even the heater. Because of the ex-BMW engine's numerous racing successes (mostly in Frazer-Nash cars), Bristol now knew a great deal about its performance potential. Though the firm simply reprofiled the camshaft and fitted larger, sturdier main bearings for the 403, it gained 15 horsepower, now up to 100 bhp total, plus a little more torque, that made for easier low-speed slogging and more eager mid-range response. Continued from late 401s was an improved gearbox with Borg-Warner synchromesh. As before, a flywheel was incorporated in first gear, and the shift lever was long and willowy. Late 403s carried a more satisfying remote-control linkage with a shorter shifter. Chassis changes included the addition of a front anti-roll bar to trim the handling, and the use of larger, heat-dissipating Alfin drums for the brakes.

With its extra power, the 403 was even more the sports tourer than the 401. The factory claimed a 100-mph top speed, though no magazine road-test figures exist to back it up.

There's not much more to say about the 403, except that it was the shortest-lived Bristol to date, lasting just two years. Production totalled exactly 300, all built at the Filton factory near the facilities then being erected for manufacturing Brittania turbo-prop aircraft.

Prewar BMW origins remained in the Bristol 403, looking little different from the 401 but boasting 15 extra horsepower, good for a top speed of around 100 mph.

SPECIFICATIONS

Engine: ohv I-6, 120.3 cid/1971 cc, 100 bhp (net) @ 4500 rpm, 117 lbs-ft @ 3500 rpm

Transmission:	4-speed manual
Suspension, front:	wishbones, transverse leaf spring
Suspension, rear:	live axle, radius arms, A-bracket, torsion bars
Brakes:	front/rear drums
Wheelbase (in.):	114.0
Weight (lbs):	2670
Top speed (mph):	approx. 100
0-60 mph (sec):	approx. 15.0
Production:	300

1953-1958
BRISTOL 404

Bristol had been building cars for six years by 1953, so its reputation was well and truly established. About all its cars lacked was outright performance, and a new model launched that year would take care of that.

Designated 404, Bristol's latest was soon nicknamed the "Businessman's Express," for it was a compact two-seat fastback coupe with a top speed of more than 110 mph. Trouble was, only rich executives could afford it, which helped keep sales very low even for a Bristol. Another problem was Jaguar's XK120/140 coupes (see entries), which were faster yet cost half as much.

The 404 rode a short-wheelbase version of the familiar Bristol chassis (96 inches versus 114). The BMW-inspired six was normally supplied in 105-horsepower tune, slightly higher than in the 403, and there was a new 125-bhp option to make this the most potent Bristol yet. Brakes were also improved, with new Alfin drums and, on early examples, dual hydraulic circuits.

Styling was both smoother and more modern than the 403's, with tiny tailfins that were obviously flash rather than function. In profile, the simple grille resembled the

leading-edge air intakes of Bristol's unsuccessful Brabazon airliner. The Bristol-built body was a clever mixture of steel and light-alloy panels over a wood frame, and introduced a packaging feature that would become a Bristol hallmark: a housing in the left front fender for the spare tire. That was matched on the right by a hatch concealing the battery and most electrical components, mounted on shelves no less.

Few got to drive the 404, but those who did loved its balance, character, and thoroughbred manners. Still, a two-seat Bristol proved just about impossible to sell.

Not to worry, though. A year after the 404 arrived, Bristol introduced its first-ever four-door sedan, the 405, basically the standard-wheelbase 403 chassis with the 105-bhp 404 engine. The four-door also shared frontal styling with the two-seater, but its generously proportioned body was a notchback style with rounded lines that made the 405 look more aerodynamically efficient than the 403 it replaced. It was definitely roomier inside, and airier too, thanks to a modest increase in glass area. Body construction again mixed steel and aluminum panels over a wood framework. Aside from a few more horsepower, the only mechanical difference from the 403 was standard electrically actuated Laycock de Normanville overdrive (effective on top gear only).

Though the 405 was a versatile, high-quality executive sedan, it wasn't as fast as most competitors. No cars were ever released for press appraisal, but a 105-mph top speed seems reasonable—and not all that impressive. Still, Bristol patrons thought this a dandy successor to the 403, and the 405 sold well by the standards of this tiny company. While the 404 lasted through just 40 units built over three years, the 405 saw 294 units in four years. A promised 404 convertible never materialized, but Abbotts of Farnham produced about 46 open 405s with two-door coachwork.

SPECIFICATIONS

Engine: ohv I-6, 120.3 cid/1971 cc, 105/125 bhp (net) @ 4500 rpm, 117 lbs-ft @ 3500 rpm

Transmission:	4-speed manual
Suspension, front:	wishbones, transverse leaf spring
Suspension, rear:	live axle, radius arms, A-bracket, torsion bars
Brakes:	front/rear drums
Wheelbase (in.):	96.0
Weight (lbs):	2265
Top speed (mph):	110 +
0-60 mph (sec):	est. 13.5
Production:	40

Opposite: Lighter, short-wheelbase 404 was the most sporting Bristol yet. **Below:** The 405 was its equally sporty sedan sibling.

1958-1961 BRISTOL 406

After five years of attempting to "divide and conquer" with the split-wheelbase 404/405 arrangement, Bristol returned to a single long-chassis coupe in 1958, albeit with more contemporary styling. In fact, the new 406 was the first Bristol that looked like it had been designed by an automaker instead of an aircraftmaker.

This was a transition model in many ways, which gives it minor historical distinction. On one hand, the 406 set the style pattern for future models well into the Seventies, yet was the last Bristol to use the aging "cross-pushrod" six inherited from BMW, and the only six-cylinder Bristol with more than 2.0-liter displacement.

Steadily rising weight (now at 3010 pounds versus 2670 for the 401) and its negative effect on performance was behind the engine size increase. This was accomplished by stretching both bore and stroke (from 66 × 96 to 69 × 100 mm) for a total 2216 cubic centimeters versus the previous 1971. Even so, rated horsepower was unchanged, though torque improved and peaked 500 rpm lower for a small gain in mid-range performance. As on the 405, drive was to the rear wheels through a 4-speed manual gearbox with electric overdrive.

Predictably, the 406 chassis was much like that of previous Bristols, with the same 114-inch wheelbase and curious wishbone/transverse-leaf independent front suspension. But signs of progress were evident elsewhere. Track widened by two inches front and rear, and there was a new rear axle located laterally by a more modern Watt linkage instead of the previous A-bracket, with single forward-facing torque arms to handle fore/aft loads. Springing remained by longitudinal torsion bars. An important safety item new to Bristol was four-wheel disc brakes, big 11.25-inch-diameter Dunlop units.

Some Bristol partisans were horrified by the new 406 styling, though others muttered that it was overdue. It was far from pretty—especially the gaping "big-

mouth" front—but at least the angular notchback body wasn't stuffy, and Bristol would get around to cleaning up details. The bodies themselves, now supplied by a London builder, employed steel inner panels overlaid with aluminum skins.

The 406 was less slippery than the 405 but made up for it by being considerably roomier despite riding the traditional Bristol wheelbase. For example, it stood 2.5 inches taller for a consequent gain in headroom, especially noticeable in the rear. It was also quite a bit longer—by over a foot, in fact—most of it apparently in the front fenders. Still, this only made it easier to retain one of the 404's more novel features: a spare tire neatly hidden in the left front fender; a similar compartment in the right fender housed battery, brake servo unit, and windshield washer-fluid reservoir.

Perhaps the Bristol had grown too large. The 406 was certainly still too heavy despite its larger engine. But Bristol had an answer to the performance problem—an expensive one—in the form of six lightweight Zagato-bodied specials endowed with tuned 130-bhp engines. With the extra muscle and 540 pounds less weight than the standard 406, they could reach 125 mph (versus only 105), though their four-seat coupe bodywork looked as bizarre as anything this Italian studio ever did. If you run across one of these today, consider it a miracle.

As for the standard issue, the critics were right. Though its handling, steering, and ride were all quite impeccable, the 406 had to be rowed along with the gearlever for maximum performance—which wasn't all that "max."

Still, the addition of disc brakes and the new rear suspension meant the aging Bristol chassis could now handle a lot more power. The only questions were, would Bristol provide it, and if so, when? The answers were yes and 1961.

SPECIFICATIONS

Engine: ohv I-6, 135.2 cid/2216 cc, 105 bhp (net) @ 4700 rpm, 120 lbs-ft @ 3000 rpm

Transmission:	4-speed manual with electric overdrive
Suspension, front:	wishbones, transverse leaf spring
Suspension, rear:	live axle, Watt linkage, radius arms, torsion bars
Brakes:	front/rear discs
Wheelbase (in.):	114.0
Weight (lbs):	3010
Top speed (mph):	approx. 105
0-60 mph (sec):	NA (not quoted)
Production:	292

The updated 406 was the first square-rigged Bristol and the last with six-cylinder power. All-disc brakes were laudable for the day.

1961-1963
BRISTOL 407

Great though it was, BMW's prewar cross-pushrod six couldn't last forever in a postwar world increasingly dominated by high-tech, high-compression V-8s. By the end of the Fifties, it had reached the end of its development road. Bristol Cars—which was still making it, after all—knew this only too well. And with its cars seeming to put on weight each year, a larger, more potent engine was clearly needed.

The firm duly went to the trouble of designing one, a replacement six-cylinder unit designated Type 160, Bristol's first automotive engine. But cars were still a sideline operation for the British aircraft company. And with the car subsidiary's low annual volume, tooling up a new engine would have cost far more than it was worth—or than the firm could afford.

Accordingly, management cancelled the Type 160 and suggested its engineers look around for a suitable proprietary engine. As Bristol also wanted to offer automatic transmission on its next-generation cars, America was the obvious place to start looking.

After lengthy deliberation, Bristol settled on the efficient, thoroughly proven hemi-head V-8 and matching 3-speed TorqueFlite automatic from Chrysler Corporation. Trouble was, Chrysler wasn't building hemis anymore, at least not for cars, and Bristol would have to contend with high tariffs and complex regulations if drivelines were imported direct from the U.S. But the problem was easily solved: Chrysler would send engines from Canada—part of the Commonwealth, you know—built to Bristol specifications.

The result of this alliance appeared in the autumn of 1961 as the 407, first in the long line of Chrysler-powered Bristols that extends to this day. As was almost expected by now, Bristol's latest retained the 114-inch-wheelbase chassis that had originated way back in the Thirties, albeit with all the improvements applied to the outgoing 406. And the 407 had an improvement of its own: a new wishbone/coil-spring front suspension, thus ousting the old transverse-leaf setup at last. Rack-and-pinion steering was abandoned in favor of cam-and-roller, something of a retrograde step but also necessitated by the bulkier, heavier engine.

The Bristol V-8 wasn't pulled from any shelf in Highland Park. For one thing, it was sized at 313 cubic inches, a displacement not previously seen in Chrysler's U.S. lineups. For another, Bristol insisted on hemi heads, not the cheaper and more common polyspherical kind, plus mechanical instead of hydraulic tappets, a different camshaft profile, and a larger-capacity sump. Even the much-vaunted TorqueFlite automatic, then barely six years old, was modified somewhat for this application.

But the effort paid off. Though it tipped the scales at close to 3600 pounds, the 407 was the quickest Bristol yet, the V-8's quoted 250 SAE horsepower seeing it to 122 mph. Standing-start acceleration was similarly improved.

So was Bristol styling. Though the basic 406 shell was retained (and still supplied by the London-based Jones Brothers company), the shorter engine permitted a lower, flatter hood, and there were detail revisions elsewhere. Fortunately, perhaps, there were no Zagato specials.

An irony of the 407 is that it gave Bristol Cars a big image boost just as Bristol Aeroplane Company decided to abandon automobiles, selling the carmaking operation to Anthony Crook and Sir George White. Crook would ultimately take complete control of Bristol Cars, and still runs it in a very personal way at this writing.

With the 407, Bristol no longer meant "just" an expensive, superbly built, fully equipped four-seat touring coupe but a car that was genuinely exciting to drive—a "gentleman's sports car" in every sense. Considering how it started, Bristol had come a mighty long way.

SPECIFICATIONS

Engine: Chrysler Canada ohv V-8, 313 cid/5130 cc, 250 bhp (SAE) @ 4400 rpm, 340 lbs-ft @ 2800 rpm

Transmission:	Chrysler TorqueFlite 3-speed automatic
Suspension, front:	wishbones, coil springs, anti-roll bar
Suspension, rear:	live axle, Watt linkage, radius arms, torsion bars
Brakes:	front/rear discs
Wheelbase (in.):	114.0
Weight (lbs):	3585
Top speed (mph):	122
0-60 mph (sec):	9.9
Production:	300

Specially built Canadian Chrysler hemi V-8 transformed the Bristol 406 into a true high-performer, the 407. Full instrumentation was as expected from this airplane maker.

1963-1965 BRISTOL 408

Squared-up front distinguished Bristol's 408 from the previous 407. Standard adjustable shock absorbers was the only chassis alteration.

With the V-8-powered 407, Bristol Cars began a period of rapid change, not just in technical specifications but styling and model turnover. Bristol had issued just seven models in the 16 years before 1963, but would go through five in the following eight years.

Though basically a warmed-over 407, the 408 that was introduced in 1963 was sufficiently changed to justify a new type number. Most of the alterations involved body design, basically the 407 outline with a more squared-up nose and flatter hood and roof. The most noteworthy mechanical change was adoption of adjustable Armstrong telescopic shock absorbers at the rear, thus enabling the driver to compensate for heavy loads in the trunk and resulting fore/aft attitude changes. Other chassis specs and running gear were as before, though the last few of the 300-odd cars built carried the successor 409 model's drivetrain.

While the giant American automakers would consider frequent running changes in a low-volume model as suicidally incompetent, Bristol Cars, like other contemporary European specialist producers, built its products mostly by hand and had very little tooling to amortize over a longer production run. Thus, even fairly frequent running changes were not only possible but economic.

Besides, Bristols had always sold on the basis of exclusivity, and customers for "bespoke" cars such as this liked to feel that improvements were always being made. Call it snob appeal or one-upmanship, but the fact is that many buyers enjoyed being able to point out the subtleties of the latest model to friends, never mind that further changes might soon render it "yesterday's" model.

It's also true of handbuilt cars that no two are ever completely alike, which enhances the aura of exclusivity as much as limited production. And when you're paying upwards of $12,000 for a car, which is what the 408 cost new—a lot of money in '63—it's nice to feel you're getting something unique. Bristol buyers did and still do, one reason the firm survives today.

SPECIFICATIONS

Engine: Chrysler Canada ohv V-8, 313 cid/5130 cc, 250 bhp (SAE) @ 4400 rpm, 340 lbs-ft @ 2800 rpm

Transmission:	Chrysler TorqueFlite 3-speed automatic
Suspension, front:	wishbones, coil springs, anti-roll bar
Suspension, rear:	live axle, Watt linkage, radius arms, torsion bars
Brakes:	front/rear discs
Wheelbase (in.):	114.0
Weight (lbs):	3585
Top speed (mph):	122
0-60 mph (sec):	9.9
Production:	approx. 300

1965-1967
BRISTOL 409

Continuing its Sixties policy of fairly frequent model changes, Bristol dropped the 408 after only two years in favor of the new 409. This was a more ambitious update than the previous one, though it bore few alterations to styling or equipment.

The same could be said of the chassis: still the proven, 114-inch-wheelbase box-section platform design with wishbone-and-coil-spring independent front suspension and a well-located Salisbury live rear axle on torsion bars. What warranted the new model number was a Canadian Chrysler V-8 enlarged by a mere 5 cubic inches and sporting the same nominal power ratings as the previous 313-cid version. Still, there must have been some "hidden" gains in power and torque since 1961 (or perhaps the latest styling was more aerodynamic) for top speed was now up by 8 mph, to 130 mph, and 0-60 mph acceleration was quicker by 1.1 seconds.

More significant, the revised powerplant was mounted further back in the chassis, which improved fore/aft weight distribution. So did a light-alloy case for the TorqueFlite transmission (replacing cast iron), which contributed to a modest 60-pound reduction in curb weight. Also new was a second-gear hold feature, allowing the driver to delay the automatic upshift into third for faster standing-start pickup.

At the same time, suspension was softened with lower spring rates, though geometry was adjusted to minimize negative effects on handling. There was also a change in the braking department: still four-wheel discs but supplied by Girling rather than Dunlop. Reason? Dunlop was closing out its brake business and Girling was taking it over.

Like earlier Bristols, first-year 409s were available only with manual steering, but optional ZF power assist became available in late 1966 and it appreciably changed the car's character. Of course, refinement had been steadily improving over the years, but this latest Bristol was more civilized and "gentlemanly" than even its most recent forebears—equally at home charging down a fast highway or slipping quietly through the urban jungle. The successor Type 410 and 411 models would take this trend several steps further.

SPECIFICATIONS

Engine: Chrysler Canada ohv V-8, 318 cid/5211 cc, 250 bhp (SAE) @ 4400 rpm, 340 lbs-ft @ 2800 rpm

Transmission:	Chrysler TorqueFlite 3-speed automatic
Suspension, front:	wishbones, coil springs, anti-roll bar
Suspension, rear:	live axle, Watt linkage, radius arms, torsion bars
Brakes:	front/rear discs
Wheelbase (in.):	114.0
Weight (lbs):	3525
Top speed (mph):	130
0-60 mph (sec):	8.8
Production:	approx. 300

Suspension revisions and a slightly larger Chrysler V-8 were the 409's main improvements. Relative narrowness betrays Bristol's Thirties-era ex-BMW chassis design.

107

1967-1969
BRISTOL 410

Bristol Cars adhered to its remarkable (for a low-volume producer) two-year model-change cycle of the late Sixties by transforming the 409 into the 410. Though very closely related to its predecessor, this new Bristol was superior in several ways. Air conditioning became available—but not standard equipment—at last, paint was switched from enamel to acrylic, and controls for the Chrysler TorqueFlite automatic transmission were switched from the American company's infamous pushbuttons to a conventional floor-mount quadrant.

The 410 received no major styling or mechanical changes except for an important update to the Girling all-disc hydraulic brake system: new "fail-safe" twin independent circuits. Top speed remained 130 mph, which seemed quite adequate for the more mature buyers attracted to—and able to afford—this car.

Though not initially publicized, the 410 handled significantly better than the 409, as suspension was modified in every detail, from bushings to shock-absorber rates, to take advantage of the superior capabilities of modern radial tires. Another factor was undoubtedly the switch from 16- to 15-inch-diameter wheels, which lowered the center of gravity for crisper, flatter cornering.

As ever, this Bristol was built strictly to order, but 410 demand was apparently as solid as that of earlier models. The firm again completed some 300 cars in two years before moving on to its next offering, the 411.

SPECIFICATIONS

Engine: Chrysler Canada ohv V-8, 318 cid/5211 cc, 250 bhp (SAE) @ 4400 rpm, 340 lbs-ft @ 2800 rpm

Transmission:	Chrysler TorqueFlite 3-speed automatic
Suspension, front:	wishbones, coil springs, anti-roll bar
Suspension, rear:	live axle, Watt linkage, radius arms, torsion bars
Brakes:	front/rear discs
Wheelbase (in.):	114.0
Weight (lbs):	3525
Top speed (mph):	130
0-60 mph (sec):	8.8
Production:	approx. 300

Bristol's 410 was mainly a plusher 409. Stodgy styling was offset by smooth GT performance and careful craftsmanship.

1969-1976
BRISTOL 411

Again in 1969, a new Bristol appeared just two years after its predecessor debuted. But the days of biennial model changes were over, and the new 411 would remain in production for the next six years, the longest-lived Bristol to date.

Also once more, the Bristol chassis and squarish four-seat coupe body were little changed. That the former was still around at the turn of the Seventies now seems truly remarkable. Remember that Bristol had copied this box-section platform from a late-Thirties BMW design and had first put it on sale, under the original 400 model, in 1947. The intervening 23 years had seen changes to front suspension and rear-axle location, but basic structure, the 114-inch wheelbase, and the cars' general stance had all stayed the same. Even so, Bristol followed through on its suspension tuning for the 410 model by making radial tires standard on the 411.

There was one other change, and it was literally a big one, as the Chrysler 318-cubic-inch hemi-head V-8 was exchanged for the same firm's heavier but considerably more potent 383-cid wedge-head unit. The result was an extra 85 horsepower and a *lot* more torque. While this engine had long been a staple in Chrysler's U.S. lineup, it was also familiar in the UK, having powered various Jensens over the years, including the limited-production Vignale-bodied Interceptor and four-wheel-drive FF grand touring coupes of the late Sixties. Here, as there, it was teamed with Chrysler's latest TorqueFlite automatic transmission.

Even if it did increase weight, the 383 made the 411 appreciably faster than any previous Bristol. Magazine road tests reported a healthy 10-mph gain in top speed—now a thrilling 140 mph—and standing-start acceleration of around 7 seconds flat, enough to rival that of the larger Ferraris and Maseratis of the period and very much in American "muscle car" territory.

In appearance, of course, the 411 was about the farthest thing from a muscle car you could imagine: as conservative as any Bristol, resolutely blocky, and rather staid. At least it was cleaner than recent Bristols and more attractive for it. More modest bodyside chrome strips—one on the rear fender, the other trailing into the door from atop the front wheelarch—replaced the former full-length twin strips, the rear end was simplified (bringing a slightly larger trunk), and there was a bit more rake to windshield and backlight.

The 411 was subtly but sensibly refined in succeeding years. Late 1970 brought a Mark 2 version with automatic self-levelling rear suspension, achieved via load-sensitive compensating struts powered by an engine-driven hydraulic pump. The big V-8 already drove the power steering and still-optional air conditioning, but it was designed for this sort of workload and didn't mind the extra job. Wider wheels all-round accompanied this upgrade.

As if to return to its two-year cycle, Bristol launched the 411 Mk 3 in 1972, marked by a lower-profile nose with very powerful seven-inch-diameter quad headlamps (replacing the familiar dual head/driving lamps foursome) mounted horizontally in an oval cavity either side of a rather awkward square grille. A slim paint stripe replaced the previous front-fender chrome trim, though rocker panel moldings remained. At the rear were no fewer than four exhaust outlets, the result of minor tuning changes.

But the Mk 3 didn't last long, for 1973 brought the revised Mk 4 with the latest 400-cid evolution of the Chrysler 383. This was adopted to meet European emissions standards (less stringent than America's but just as vexing to automakers and also tightening every year) and permit the use of British-grade "two-star" leaded regular gasoline. Rear styling was revised yet again, now quite plain.

After a short run of minimally modified Mk 5 models, the 411 was laid to rest in 1976. Bristol's production pace slowed by about a third, to an average three cars per week, so only 600 411s were built in a little over six years.

SPECIFICATIONS

Engines: all Chrysler ohv V-8; **1969-73:** 383 cid/6277 cc, 335 bhp (SAE gross) @ 4400 rpm, 425 lbs-ft @ 3400 rpm; **1973-76:** 400 cid/6556 cc, 264 bhp (SAE net) @ 4800 rpm, 335 lbs-ft @ 3600 rpm

Transmission:	Chrysler TorqueFlite 3-speed automatic
Suspension, front:	wishbones, coil springs, anti-roll bar
Suspension, rear:	live axle, Watt linkage, radius rods, torsion bars
Brakes:	front/rear discs
Wheelbase (in.):	114.0
Weight (lbs):	3775
Top speed (mph):	138 (383)
0-60 mph (sec):	7.0 (383)
Production:	600

The 411 was the final evolution of Bristol's 406. Lines were cleaner if still conservative, go and gadgets more plentiful than ever.

1953-1955 CHEVROLET CORVETTE

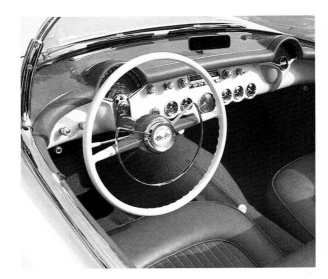

Dream cars were big in Fifties Detroit, but only General Motors built some you could actually buy. Take 1953, when a quartet of sporty convertibles from the travelling Motorama show went on sale. Three of them—Buick Skylark, Cadillac Eldorado, and Oldsmobile Fiesta—were big and flashy, but the fourth was a trim two-seat roadster with a body made of that new wonder material, fiberglass. It was, of course, the Chevrolet Corvette.

Its genesis is well known. In late fall of 1951, Harley Earl, GM's legendary design chief, began sketching ideas for a simple, two-seat sporty car priced to sell at around $1850, about what a Chevy sedan cost at the time. Within a year he'd convinced company brass that his idea merited a full-blown, super-secret development program. Perhaps to confuse the press, it was dubbed "Project Opel," after GM's German subsidiary.

To hold down cost, veteran Chevy engineer Maurice Olley, with an assist from Bob McLean, cut down a standard Chevrolet passenger-car chassis to a 102-inch wheelbase, identical with that of the XK120 (one of Earl's favorites). Next, Olley coaxed 150 horsepower from Chevy's aged "Blue Flame Six" via triple carburetors, higher compression, solid (versus hydraulic) valve lifters, and high-lift camshaft. Chevy didn't have a manual transmission that could handle this power, so 2-speed Powerglide automatic was used instead. Despite all the parts borrowing, the eventual production Corvette had its own X-member frame with box-section side rails, outboard-mounted rear leaf springs (for better cornering stability), Hotchkiss instead of torque-tube drive, and an engine set 13 inches further back than in other Chevys (for better weight distribution and thus handling).

It also looked considerably different, which was the Corvette's main mission: to reverse Chevy's image as a builder of mundane people-movers. By the time of the first 1953 Motorama, in January at New York's Waldorf-Astoria Hotel, Earl had penned a sleek, rounded body with a toothy grille, mesh stone guards over inset headlamps, a trendy wrapped windshield, and thrusting "jet-pod" taillamps. A soft top folded out of sight beneath a solid lift-up panel, while European-style side curtains replaced roll-up door windows.

That Motorama Corvette generated lots of interest, not least because it looked like a production prototype. It was, and Chevy Division general manager Thomas H. Keating duly announced that it *would* be built, albeit in limited numbers, though this may have been planned all along. Regardless, the show car was little altered for production, which began June 30, 1953, on a small auxiliary line at Chevy's Flint, Michigan plant. Fiberglass was retained for its lower cost and greater manufacturing flexibility compared to steel bodywork, though the decision came quite late.

Alas, this dream-car-come-true quickly turned into something of a nightmare for Chevy. Assembly-line problems with the complex body (no fewer than 46 separate pieces) and lack of plant capacity kept 1953 production to just 315 cars. Yet you couldn't really buy one because they were earmarked for VIPs and dealer promotion. Purists, meantime, chided the "plastic" body, tepid six-cylinder performance, and gimmicky styling, while non-enthusiasts disliked the impracticalities of side curtains, a small trunk, and only two seats.

Without changing it much, Chevy made the Corvette more readily available for 1954, transferring production to larger facilities in St. Louis. But though 10 times '53 volume, 1954 output was less than a third the projected total, leaving Chevy with some 1500 unsold cars at year's end. The Corvette might have died right there had it not been for pleas by Earl and Edward N. Cole, who'd arrived from Cadillac in 1952 to become Chevy chief engineer.

And Cole had what would prove to be the Corvette's salvation: the brilliant overhead-valve V-8 he'd developed for Chevy's all-new 1955 passenger cars. It gave the Corvette almost 30 percent more horsepower, yet weighed 30 pounds *less* than the old six. Even better was a new 3-speed manual transmission for 1955, plus some adroit chassis tuning by recently hired Belgian-born engineer Zora Arkus-Duntov. The result was a much faster, more exciting and more roadable Corvette. For all that, and a price cut from $3513 to $2799, only 674 of the '55s were built.

Better things were coming, but the 1953-55 Corvette is still revered as the progenitor of America's first truly successful sports car. That, and as a happy accident for which we can all be grateful.

SPECIFICATIONS

Engines: 1953-55: ohv I-6, 235.5 cid/3859 cc, 150 bhp @ 4200 rpm, 223 lbs-ft @ 2400 rpm; **1955:** ohv V-8, 265 cid/4343 cc, 195 bhp @ 5000 rpm, 260 lbs-ft @ 2800 rpm

Transmissions:	2-speed automatic (1953-55), 3-speed manual (1955)
Suspension front:	unequal-length A-arms, coil springs, anti-roll bar
Suspension rear:	live axle, semi-elliptic leaf springs
Brakes:	front/rear drums
Wheelbase (in.):	102.0
Weight (lbs)	2840-2850
Top speed (mph):	107 mph (six), 119 (V-8)
0-60 mph (sec):	11.0 (six), 8.7 (V-8)
Production:	**1953** 315 **1954** 3640 **1955** 674

All 1953 Corvettes had Polo White exteriors and Sportsman Red interiors. Though tweaked, Chevy's reliable old "Blue Flame Six" (above) could provide only middling performance.

1956-1957 CHEVROLET CORVETTE

Had it not been for the Ford Thunderbird, we might not have a Corvette today. In early 1955, profit-minded General Motors executives were ready to kill off Chevrolet's fiberglass-bodied two-seater, which since its 1953 debut had not made the hoped-for impression on America's admittedly miniscule sports-car market. But Dearborn's posh "personal" car was a challenge GM could not let go unanswered, so Corvette was granted a stay of execution.

Enthusiasts have been grateful ever since, for the reprieve brought a renaissance. With the all-new second-generation design of 1956-57, Chevy could at last rightfully proclaim Corvette as "America's only true sports car"—as indeed it did.

Compared to its slab-sided predecessor, the '56 was stunning. GM design director Harley Earl came up with fresh new styling that was tasteful in an age of garishness yet sexy, low-slung, and distinctly American. Its only questionable elements were phony air scoops atop the front fenders, dummy knock-off hubs on the wheel covers (carried over from 1953-55), and a dash that was more flash than function. Still, the '56 looked more like the serious sports car it was, yet it was also more civilized, with new seats, roll-up door glass (no more clumsy side curtains), and an optional lift-off hardtop (previewed on a 1954 Motorama Corvette) for sedan-like weather protection.

Beneath this finery was a chassis heavily reworked by engineering wizard Zora Arkus-Duntov. Without upsetting the '55's near-equal front/rear weight distribution (52/48 percent), he tightened up both steering response and handling. Though understeer was still a tad excessive and the cast-iron all-drum brakes "faded into oblivion" in hard stops, as one magazine stated, the Vette was now as quick through turns as it was in on straights.

And quick it was. Chevy's superb 265-cubic-inch V-8, designed by Harry Barr and Edward N. Cole, had been an option fitted to all but six of the '55 models. Now it was standard—and up to 210 horsepower in normal tune or 225 bhp with high-lift cam, twin four-barrel carburetors, and dual exhausts. The close-ratio 3-speed manual gearbox, introduced late in the '55 run, was standard now too, replacing Powerglide automatic, which shifted to the options sheet. The most potent '56 could hit 60 mph from rest in a swift 7.5 seconds and top 120 mph.

There was no need to change the handsome styling for '57, but Chevy upped performance by boring out its V-8 from 3.75 to 3.875 inches (stroke remained at 3.00 inches). The result was 283 cid in five engines offering 220 bhp up to an amazing 283 bhp, the latter courtesy of new "Ramjet" fuel injection. A 4-speed Borg-Warner manual transmission arrived in May at $188 extra, and combined with axle ratios as low as 4.11:1 to make the "fuelie" '57 thunderingly fast. Published road tests showed 0-60 in 5.7 seconds, 0-100 mph in 16.8 seconds, the standing quarter-mile in 14.3 seconds at 96 mph, and a maximum 132 mph plus. Alas, mechanical bugs and a $500 price limited injection installations to only 240 units.

Chevy also offered a $725 "heavy-duty racing suspension" package for '57, comprising high-rate springs and shocks, front anti-roll bar, quick steering, and ceramic-metallic brake linings with finned ventilated drums. Add one of the high-power engines and you had a Corvette virtually ready to race right off the showroom floor.

Indeed, these were the years when Corvette began to make its mark in international competition. Dr. Richard Thompson won the Sports Car Club of America C-Production national championship in 1956, then took the '57 crown in B-Production, where the Vette qualified by dint of its larger engine. John Fitch's '56 was the fastest modified car at that year's Daytona Speed Weeks, a Corvette finished 9th in the gruelling 12 Hours of Sebring in '56, and another came home 2nd (behind a Mercedes 300SL) at Pebble Beach that same year. Chevy's 1957 Sebring assault saw production Corvettes finish 1-2 in the GT class and 12th and 15th overall.

It was all symbolic of a dramatic metamorphosis. Said one European writer: "Before Sebring . . . the Corvette was regarded as a plastic toy. After Sebring, even the most biased were forced to admit that [it was] one of the world's finest sports cars. . . ."

That included buyers, who happily took 3467 of the '56s and 6339 of the '57s, a far cry from 1955's 674-unit low. The Corvette's future was assured.

SPECIFICATIONS

Engines: all ohv V-8; **1956:** 265 cid/4343 cc, 210/225 bhp @ 5200 rpm, 270 lbs-ft @ 3600 rpm; **1957:** 283 cid/4638 cc; 220 bhp @ 4800 rpm, 300 lbs-ft @ 3000 rpm; 245 bhp @ 5000 rpm, 300 lbs-ft @ 3800 rpm; 250 bhp @ 5000 rpm, 305 lbs-ft @ 3800 rpm; 270 bhp @ 6000 rpm, 285 lbs-ft @ 4200 rpm; 283 bhp @ 6200 rpm, 290 lbs-ft @ 4400 rpm

Transmissions:	3/4-speed manual or 2-speed automatic
Suspension, front:	unequal-length A-arms, coil springs, anti-roll bar
Suspension, rear:	live axle, semi-elliptic leaf springs
Brakes:	front/rear drums
Wheelbase (in.):	102.0
Weight (lbs):	2880
Top speed (mph):	121-129 (1956), 115-130 (1957)
0-60 mph (sec):	7.3-8.9 (1956), 5.7-8.0 (1957)
Production:	**1956** 3467 **1957** 6339

Second-generation Corvette was one of the first Fifties cars to attain collector status. The main reasons are definitive period styling and terrific small-block V-8.

1958-1960 CHEVROLET CORVETTE

It's easy to dismiss the 1958-60 Corvette as a hokier, heftier version of the memorable second generation—mainly because it was. And indeed, even Corvette enthusiasts overlooked it for years. Lately, however, these cars have come to be appreciated and for very sound reasons. Not the least of these is the fact that this was the Corvette that assured a permanent place in the Chevrolet line for "America's only true sports car."

Nineteen fifty-eight was hardly a vintage year for Detroit styling, but Harley Earl's valedictory Corvette could have fared much worse. Wheelbase was unchanged on the mostly new '58 model but, in the spirit of the times, overall length went up 10 inches, width more than two inches, and curb weight 200 pounds. The basic shape was broadly the same as 1956-57 but busier and shinier, with quad headlamps (all the rage that year), a dummy air scoop ahead of each concave bodyside "cove" (decorated with chrome windsplits no less), simulated louvers on the hood, and equally silly longitudinal chrome strips on the trunklid.

Yet beneath all the glitz were some genuine improvements. Bumpers, for example, were newly mounted on long brackets instead of directly to the body, thus giving better protection, while a redesigned cockpit grouped all instruments directly ahead of the driver for the first time. Also featured were a new passenger grab bar, locking glovebox, and self-seeking "Wonder Bar" radio.

Bigger and plusher it may have been, but the '58 was still a vivid performer—no surprise, since the '57 engine lineup returned with few changes. The top fuel-injected 283 V-8 actually gained 7 horsepower for a total of 290, thus exceeding the hallowed "1 hp per cu in." benchmark reached the previous year. Also carried over was a wide array of performance options, many bargain-priced: Positraction limited-slip differential ($48.45), metallic brake linings ($26.90), 4-speed manual transmission ($188.30), and heavy-duty suspension and brakes ($425.05). Inflation plagued the national economy in '58, yet base price remained reasonable at $3631.

Perhaps surprisingly, critics generally liked the '58. Buyers certainly did. Model year production gained 2829 units over the '57 tally as the Corvette actually turned a profit for the first time.

Volume rose another 500 units for '59, when Chevy smoothed the washboard hood, deleted the chrome backstraps, and added trailing radius rods to counteract rear axle windup in hard acceleration, the year's only noteworthy mechanical change. Despite rumors of a smaller all-new model with independent rear suspension, this basic package continued for 1960 as Corvette production broke the magic 10,000-unit barrier for the first time.

That year brought even higher compression on the top fuelie engine (11.0:1) for an incredible 315 bhp, plus aluminum clutch housings for manual-shift models (saving 18 pounds) and aluminum radiators for cars with the high-power "Duntov cam" engines. A larger 24-gallon fuel tank was a new option, but the extra-cost heavy-duty suspension vanished in favor of a larger front anti-roll bar and a new standard rear bar. An extra inch of wheel travel in rebound further contributed to a smoother ride and more neutral handling. High-silicon aluminum cylinder heads were briefly offered at extra cost for fuel-injected engines, then withdrawn because of warping problems.

Though Corvette was moving away from *pur sang* sports car and toward plush GT, the third generation proved no less a track competitor than the second-generation cars. Highlights include a GT-class win and 12th overall at Sebring '58, national SCCA B-Production championships in 1958-59, fastest in the sports-car division at the 1958 Pikes Peak Hill Climb, and a slew of victories by privateers. Thanks to the Auto Manufacturers Association mid-1957 edict, Chevy was officially "out of racing" now, though not above lending under-the-table support to those campaigning its cars. Among them was sportsman Briggs Cunningham, who gave the Corvette its finest racing hour yet when one of his three team cars (driven by John Fitch and Bob Grossman) finished 8th overall in the 1960 running of the prestigious 24 Hours of Le Mans.

With achievements like that, not to mention great style and flashing performance, the 1958-60 Corvette surely deserves the enthusiast recognition it has belatedly come to enjoy. It may not be "first among equals," but it *is* a Corvette, and for many car lovers, that's all that counts.

SPECIFICATIONS

Engines: all ohv V-8, 283 cid/4638 cc; **1958-60:** 230 bhp @ 4800 rpm, 300 lbs-ft @ 3000 rpm; 245 bhp @ 5000 rpm, 300 lbs-ft @ 3800 rpm; 270 bhp @ 6000 rpm, 285 lbs-ft @ 4200 rpm; **1958-59:** 250 bhp @ 5000 rpm, 305 lbs-ft @ 3800 rpm; 290 bhp @ 6200 rpm, 290 lbs-ft @ 4400 rpm; **1960:** 275 bhp @ 5200 rpm, 290 lbs-ft @ 4200 rpm; 315 bhp @ 6200 rpm, 295 lbs-ft @ 4700 rpm

Transmissions:	3/4-speed manual, 2-speed automatic
Suspension, front:	unequal-length A-arms, coil springs, anti-roll bar
Suspension, rear:	live axle, coil springs
Brakes:	front drums/rear drums
Wheelbase (in.):	102.0
Weight (lbs):	3085
Top speed (mph):	103-128
0-60 mph (sec):	6.6-9.2
Production:	**1958** 9168 **1959** 9670 **1960** 10,261

Third-generation Corvette styling changed little, though fake hood louvers and chrome decklid trim vanished after '58. This 1960 example was one of over 10,000 sold that model year, a benchmark that helped assure Corvette a permanent place in the Chevy line. Note contrast-color "coves" here.

1961-1962 CHEVROLET CORVETTE

If Chevrolet and Zora Arkus-Duntov had had their way, the 1960 Corvette would have been very different. Beginning in 1957, Chevy contemplated a smaller, lighter Vette called the "Q-model." With a rear transaxle (which meant independent rear suspension) and inboard brakes, it was quite radical for the time, especially in Detroit. A full-size mockup soon took shape bearing a remarkable resemblance to the production Sting Ray then six years away.

But the Q-model was abandoned when the 1958 recession put a big dent in car sales that proved slow to recover. Besides, Chevy had other fish to fry: its new 1960 rear-engine Corvair compact, prompted by the upsurge in import sales during said recession. There was nothing to do, then, but soldier on with the third-generation Corvette while designers and engineers set about creating another all-new, albeit less radical, replacement for it.

Fortunately, General Motors had just the designer who could breathe new life into the existing Corvette: William L. Mitchell, who succeeded Harley Earl, his boss and mentor, as head of GM Styling on Earl's retirement in 1958. What emerged was not only the ultimate development of the original 1953 concept but arguably the best Corvettes since 1956-57.

Appearing for 1961, Mitchell's makeover was simple but effective. He simply restyled the area behind the doors along the lines of his late-Fifties Stingray racing car (which was built on the "mule" chassis salvaged from 1957's unsuccessful Corvette SS effort at Sebring). The flowing "ducktail" not only increased luggage space by some 20 percent but mated handsomely with the 1958-60 frontal styling, which Mitchell simplified by substituting mesh for the familiar chrome "teeth" in the grille

cavity and replacing the traditional round nose medallion with a crossed-flags emblem and "Corvette" in big block letters.

Corvette powerteams stood pat for the third straight year as Chevy continued to emphasize refinements for '61: standard-equipment sunvisors, new higher-capacity aluminum-core radiator, side-mount expansion tanks, a wider choice of axle ratios. Base price was up to $3934, but that dough got you a lot of go. Even the mildest 283 V-8 with Powerglide was good for 7.7 seconds 0-60 mph and nearly 110 mph flat out; order the optional 315-bhp "fuelie" and 4-speed manual and you'd hit 60 mph from standstill in well under six seconds and see the far side of 130 mph. In case anyone doubted its prowess, a near-stock '61 finished 11th in that year's Sebring 12 Hours against considerably costlier and more exotic machinery.

With the all-new Sting Ray nearing completion, refinement was again the keynote for '62. However, Chevy gave a sneak preview of things to come by offering the next Corvette's engines in the last of the "traditional" models. There were four in all—one fuelie and three with carburetors—all based on a 283 bored and stroked to 327 cubic inches and offering from 250 to a thumping 360 horsepower. More good news was optional availability of sintered-metallic brake linings, almost mandatory with the new engines' higher performance, and a standard-equipment heater (previously extra at an outrageous $102.25). Styling was cleaner than ever, as Mitchell eliminated the chrome outline around the bodyside "coves" and their optional two-toning, substituted ribbed-aluminum appliqués for the windsplits on the dummy reverse front-fender scoops, blacked in the grille and its flanking cutouts, and added ribbed-aluminum rocker-panel appliqués.

Corvette continued its winning ways on the track and in the showroom for '62. Dr. Dick Thompson, the "flying dentist," won the SCCA's national A-Production championship that year, and Don Yenko captured the B-Production crown. More important to GM managers, Corvette production continued its steady climb, from 1961's record 10,000-plus to over 14,500 units. No question now: the Vette was here to stay.

But not the basic design laid down a decade before. In retrospect, then, the 1961-62 models represent a turning point in the history of America's sports car: the last Corvettes not available with factory air or power brakes at any price, the last with external trunklids and, in the case of the '62s, the first with the 327 V-8 that would be the heart of Corvette power through 1965. In all, a satisfying and successful conclusion to the first chapter of Chevy's great sports-car experiment.

Bill Mitchell gave Harley Earl's '58 Corvette a new lease on life with simple but effective style changes for '61. Sting Ray-inspired "ducktail" **(below)** *was the most obvious. Nose* **(opposite bottom)** *was freshened too.*

SPECIFICATIONS

Engines: all ohv V-8; **1961:** 283 cid/4638 cc; 230 bhp @ 4800 rpm, 300 lbs-ft @ 3000 rpm; 245 bhp @ 5000 rpm, 300 lbs-ft @ 3800 rpm; 270 bhp @ 6000 rpm, 285 lbs-ft @ 4200 rpm; 275 bhp @ 5200 rpm, 290 lbs-ft @ 4200 rpm; 315 bhp @ 6200 rpm, 295 lbs-ft @ 4700 rpm; **1962:** 327 cid/5359 cc; 250 bhp @ 4400 rpm, 350 lbs-ft @ 2800 rpm; 300 bhp @ 5000 rpm, 360 lbs-ft @ 3200 rpm; 340 bhp @ 6000 rpm, 344 lbs-ft @ 4000 rpm; 360 bhp @ 6000 rpm, 352 lbs-ft @ 4000 rpm

Transmissions:	3/4-speed manual, 2-speed automatic
Suspension, front:	unequal-length A-arms, coil springs, anti-roll bar
Suspension, rear:	live axle, semi-elliptic leaf springs
Brakes:	front/rear drums
Wheelbase (in.):	102.0
Weight (lbs):	3020-3085
Top speed (mph):	109-128
0-60 mph (sec):	5.5-7.7
Production:	**1961** 10,939 **1962** 14,531

1963-1967 CHEVROLET CORVETTE STING RAY

Who can forget the Sting Ray? Certainly not the army of enthusiasts who regard it as the most desirable Corvette ever built. It was, of course, very desirable when new: the first real departure in the Corvette's 10-year history, a styling showpiece and an engineering masterpiece.

Introduced for 1963, the Sting Ray took both its name and general shape from Bill Mitchell's late-Fifties Stingray racer and was quite unlike any other car on the road. Apart from four wheels and two seats, the only things it shared with the '62 Corvette were steering, front suspension, four 327 V-8s, and fiberglass bodywork. Most everything else was changed, and definitely for the better.

It began with a slight reduction in overall length and a wheelbase pared four inches. Curb weight was reduced too, thanks to a new ladder-type frame (replacing the heavy old X-member affair) and despite a new steel-reinforced cage that made for a stronger, safer cockpit. Brakes were still drums, though they were self-adjusting now and the fronts were wider.

But the big news was independent rear suspension, a first for a modern U.S. production car. Cleverly engineered by Zora Arkus-Duntov, it comprised a frame-mounted differential with U-jointed half-shafts acting on a single transverse leaf spring; differential-mounted control arms extended laterally and slightly forward to the hub carriers to limit fore/aft movement, and a pair of trailing radius rods was fitted behind. It was elegantly simple, relatively cheap, and highly effective.

As for the styling, it still turns heads, so you can imagine its impact in long-ago '63. The customary roadster gained a dramatic fastback coupe companion, with a vertically split rear window that proved quite controversial. Duntov lobbied against the divider bar, saying it hampered outward vision, while Mitchell huffed that "if you take that off you might as well forget the whole thing." Duntov ultimately won, leaving the split-window coupe a one-year model—and highly prized because of it.

The Sting Ray quickly proved the fastest and most roadable Corvette yet—and the most popular: 1963 sales were nearly twice the record '62 total. Performance had less to do with this than the wider market appeal resulting from more creature comforts than ever: leather upholstery, power steering, power brakes (at last), AM/FM radio, even air conditioning were all optional. Now a Vette could be a posh GT, all-out screamer, or both.

Over the next four years, the Sting Ray evolved through progressively cleaner styling, more power, and greater mechanical sophistication. Appearance was tidied up by either removing what little nonsense there was or making it functional (as with the dummy front-fender vents after 1964). The fuelie small-block delivered up to 395 horsepower for 1964, while '65 brought optional 4-wheel disc brakes (for stopping power to match steadily escalating performance) and Corvette's first big-block V-8, the 425-bhp 396-cid "Mark IV." The next year brought a bored-out 427 that one magazine reported could do 4.8 seconds 0-60 mph and top 140 mph—not bad for a civilized, fully equipped machine selling for around $4500.

Corvette set new sales records in all but one of the Sting Ray years, peaking in 1966 at nearly 28,000. Horsepower seemed to set yearly records too. That peak came with 1967's stupendous L88, an aluminum-head 427 with 12.5:1 compression, wild cam, and big four-barrel carb, rated at no less than 560 bhp. Only 20 cars were so equipped, but they were symbolic of how far the Vette had come.

Of course, many of these high-power Sting Rays went racing, though they often bowed to Carroll Shelby's stark, super-quick Cobras. Still, there were bright spots. Don Yenko was SCCA national B-Production champ in 1963, a Roger Penske car won its class at Nassau '65, and 1966 saw Sting Rays finish 12th overall in the Daytona Continental and 9th at Sebring.

The '63's year-old engines aside, the Sting Ray stands as the only all-new Corvette between the 1953 Motorama original and the 1984 model. Moreover, its chassis would endure with only minor changes for a full two decades, surely a tribute to the genius and foresight of its designers, especially Duntov.

But in the hearts of car lovers everywhere, the Sting Ray itself will always endure. It was—and is—very special, the kind of car that happens only once in a lifetime.

SPECIFICATIONS

Engines: all ohv V-8; **327 cid/5359 cc—1963-65:** 250 bhp @ 4400 rpm, 350 lbs-ft @ 2800 rpm; 300 bhp @ 5000 rpm, 360 lbs-ft @ 3200 rpm; **1963:** 340 bhp @ 6000 rpm, 344 lbs-ft @ 4000 rpm; 360 bhp @ 6000 rpm, 352 lbs-ft @ 4000 rpm; **1964-65:** 365 bhp @ 6200 rpm, 350 lbs-ft @ 4000 rpm; 375 bhp @ 6200 rpm, 350 lbs-ft @ 4400 rpm; **1966-67:** 350 bhp @ 5800 rpm, 360 lbs-ft @ 3000 rpm; **396 cid/6489 cc—1965:** 425 bhp @ 6400 rpm, 415 lbs-ft @ 4000 rpm; **427 cid/6997 cc—1966-67:** 390 bhp @ 5400 rpm, 460 lbs-ft @ 3600 rpm; **1966:** 425 bhp @ 6400 rpm, 460 lbs-ft @ 4000 rpm; **1967:** 435 bhp @ 5800 rpm, 460 lbs-ft @ 4000 rpm

Transmissions:	3/4-speed manual, 2-speed automatic
Suspension, front:	unequal-length A-arms, coil springs, anti-roll bar
Suspension, rear:	half-shafts, lateral arms, trailing radius rods, transverse semi-elliptic leaf spring (anti-roll bar with 396 or 427 engines)
Brakes:	front/rear drums (1963-64); front/rear discs (1965-67)
Wheelbase (in.):	98.0
Weight (lbs):	3050-3270
Top speed (mph):	105-150
0-60 mph (sec):	5.4-8.0

Production: 1963 21,513 **1964** 22,229 **1965** 23,562 **1966** 27,720 **1967** 22,940

Above and opposite: First-ever Corvette coupe arrived with the all-new 1963 Sting Ray generation. Split rear window proved controversial, was deleted after this one year, making this model a prime collectible now. **Left:** A 427-powered '67 roadster with optional factory side exhaust.

1968-1977 CHEVROLET CORVETTE STINGRAY

Chevrolet probably didn't plan it, but the fifth-generation Corvette lasted a long time—so long, in fact, that we're limiting ourselves here to its first 10 years. That's fitting, because the car's fortunes in this decade were decidedly mixed.

The Sting Ray was a tough act to follow, and not everyone liked its 1968 follow-up. Arriving for the first year of federal safety and emissions standards, it combined a new, 7-inch-longer body with essentially carryover engines and chassis. Styling, previewed by the 1965 Mako Shark II show car, was all humpy and muscular, with fulsome front and rear fenders housing 7-inch-wide wheels for better roadholding. Coupe and convertible returned, the former a new notchback style with an innovative "T-top" whose twin panels could be removed to create a semi-convertible. The main mechanical changes involved standardizing the previously optional all-disc brakes and substituting General Motors' fine 3-speed Turbo Hydra-Matic for the archaic 2-speed Powerglide automatic.

The fifth-generation Vette would have bowed for 1967 had Zora Arkus-Duntov not held it up to work out some kinks. Still, the '68s had problems. The most glaring was poor workmanship, which led one motor-noter to label his press car "unfit to road test." Others judged the new design needlessly gimmicky, its dashboard awash in winking lights, a trouble-prone pop-up cowl panel hiding the wipers. A narrower cockpit, a penalty of the wasp-waisted styling, didn't win any friends. Neither did inadequate cooling on big-block cars. For all that, the '68 set another Corvette sales record: more than 28,500 units.

The tally was nearly 38,800 for '69, when the Stingray name returned (as one word) after a year's absence. Duntov did his best to correct flaws, finding a little more cockpit space (smaller steering wheel, slimmer door panels), adding an override so the wiper panel could be left up in freezing weather, reworking other assorted bits. Emissions considerations prompted lower compression ratios and a small-block V-8 stroked to 350 cubic inches, while a fourth 427 option appeared with 430 horsepower. Even wilder were the aluminum-head L88, with 500 bhp and a stiff $1032 price, and the all-aluminum ZL-1 big-block, a virtual Can-Am racing engine. Production? Just 116 and a mere two, respectively.

Total Corvette volume plunged some 50 percent for 1970, thanks to an auto workers strike. The car itself was again little changed, though Chevy cleaned up more details and offered the 370-bhp solid-lifter LT-1 small-block promised for '69. The main news for '71 was a big-block punched out to 454 cid, again in line with emissions standards that were increasingly sapping power from all Detroit engines. Even so, lower compression left the top LS-5 version at 365 bhp, the high-compression LS-6 at 425 bhp.

Inflation, rising gas prices, and soaring insurance rates were sapping performance-car sales by now. Corvette was no exception, its 1972 volume not even equalling '69's. A switch to more realistic SAE net power ratings made engines seem punier—which they were—and the LS-6 was cancelled along with the fiber-optic exterior-light monitors. However, an anti-theft alarm system option was now standardized, a belated nod to the Vette's high "thievability."

The '73s gained a body-color nose of pliable plastic to meet the government's new 5-mph impact-protection rule, plus more insulation and new chassis mounts for quietness. The coupe's drop-down rear window, a feature since '68, went away. So did all engines save a pair of 350s and one big-block. Rear-impact standards dictated a new body-color tail on the '74s, which arrived with the Middle East oil embargo, even higher gas prices, and long lines at the pumps. Yet while other cars suffered sales drops, Corvette kept climbing.

But it kept slipping too. Both the LT-1 and the last big-block options vanished after '74. Worse, the roadster disappeared after '75, a victim of steadily falling demand. Changes were few through 1977, yet sales continued strong. The '76s broke 1969's record at over 46,500, followed by an improbable 49,000-plus of the '77s.

Clearly, Chevy had made a silk purse of the sow's-ear '68 and reaped the rewards. But enthusiasts were still awaiting an all-new Vette. A pair of 1972 rotary-engine show cars strongly hinted it could be a mid-engine design. Perhaps in time for Corvette's 25th birthday in 1978? Ah, that's the *next* part of the story.

SPECIFICATIONS

Engines: all ohv V-8; **327 cid/5359 cc—1968:** 300 bhp @ 5000 rpm, 360 lbs-ft @ 3400 rpm; 350 bhp @ 5800 rpm, 360 lbs-ft @ 3600 rpm; **350 cid/5735 cc—1969-70:** 300 bhp @ 4800 rpm, 380 lbs-ft @ 3400 rpm; 350 bhp @ 5600 rpm, 380 lbs-ft @ 3600 rpm; 370 bhp @ 6000 rpm, 380 lbs-ft @ 4000 rpm; **1971-72:** 270 bhp @ 4800 rpm, 360 lbs-ft @ 3200 rpm; 330 bhp @ 5600 rpm, 360 lbs-ft @ 4000 rpm; **1973-74:** 195 bhp @ 4400 rpm, 275 lbs-ft @ 2800 rpm; 250 bhp @ 5200 rpm, 285 lbs-ft @ 4000 rpm; **1975:** 165 bhp @ 3800 rpm, 270 lbs-ft @ 2400 rpm; 205 bhp @ 4800 rpm, 255 lbs-ft @ 3600 rpm; **1976-77:** 180 bhp @ 4000 rpm, 270 lbs-ft @ 2400 rpm; 210 bhp @ 5200 rpm, 255 lbs-ft @ 3600 rpm; **427 cid/6997 cc—1968-69:** 390 bhp @ 5400 rpm, 460 lbs-ft @ 3600 rpm; 400 bhp @ 5400 rpm, 460 lbs-ft @ 3600 rpm; 435 bhp @ 5800 rpm, 460 lbs-ft @ 4000 rpm; **1969:** 430 bhp @ 5200 rpm, 460 lbs-ft @ 4000 rpm; **454 cid/7440 cc—1970:** 390 bhp @ 4800 rpm, 500 lbs-ft @ 3400 rpm; 465 bhp @ 5200 rpm, torque NA; **1971-72:** 365 bhp @ 4800 rpm, 465 lbs-ft @ 3200 rpm; **1971:** 425 bhp @ 5600 rpm, 475 lbs-ft @ 4000 rpm; **1973-74:** 270 bhp @ 4400 rpm, 390 lbs-ft @ 2800 rpm

Transmissions:	3/4-speed manual, 3-speed automatic
Suspension, front:	unequal-length A-arms, coil springs, anti-roll bar
Suspension, rear:	half-shafts, lateral arms, trailing radius rods, transverse semi-elliptic leaf spring (anti-roll bar optional)
Brakes:	front/rear discs
Wheelbase (in.):	98.0
Weight (lbs):	3280-3530
Top speed (mph):	110-135
0-60 mph (sec):	5.5-7.5

Production: 1968 28,566 **1969** 38,762 **1970** 17,316 **1971** 21,801 **1972** 27,004 **1973** 34,464 **1974** 37,502 **1975** 38,465 **1976** 46,558 **1977** 49,213

Fifth-generation Corvette was judged too bulky and flashy, but T-top roof was predictive. Styling changed only in detail through 1972, but horsepower declined after 1970 owing to a shrinking hot-car market and escalating insurance premiums.

1978-1982 CHEVROLET CORVETTE

A radical new mid-engine Corvette did not appear for 1978, but how close it came for 1980. Its basis would have been the Aerovette, the renamed V-8-powered iteration of Bill Mitchell's 1972 four-rotor Wankel-engine idea car. Mitchell lobbied hard for a production derivative, and General Motors president Thomas Murphy actually approved one for 1980. By the end of 1977, Aerovette-based clay models were complete and tooling ready to be ordered.

But it was not to be. The project lost its key supporter when Mitchell retired in '77. Zora Arkus-Duntov, another booster, had retired at the end of '74, and his successor as Corvette chief engineer, David R. McLellan, preferred a "front mid-engine" layout for reasons of packaging, manufacturing, performance, and cost.

Indeed, cost is what ultimately killed the Aerovette—never mind that mid-engine design had not proven to be the wave of the sports-car future that some had predicted in the late Sixties. GM accordingly regrouped and, by mid-1978, McLellan and his crew were working on a more conventional new Corvette.

Of course, this meant that the fifth-generation would have to hold on awhile—no problem really, what with sales still strong. Still, GM decided to spend some money on rejuvenating the old warrior to mark Corvette's 25th birthday.

The '78 thus received one big change—a new fastback roofline with a huge wraparound rear window—and a host of minor ones (mostly to the cockpit). It was no longer a Stingray, but it was the '78 Indy 500 pace car, and Chevrolet celebrated by building 6200 replicas with special paint, leather interior, and owner-applied regalia decals. To Chevy's chagrin, quick-buck artists were quick to convert standard models into bogus replicas, creating no little confusion. There was also a Silver Anniversary Edition, actually a trim package and not all that different from stock. Engine choices were down to two 350 V-8s: standard 185-horsepower L48 and extra-cost 220-bhp L82.

Corvette mostly marked time for '79. By now it was quite plush for a sports car: power windows, air, tilt steering wheel, power door locks, and AM/FM stereo were all included in a base price that inflation swelled from $9645 to $12,313 in just one year. Yet despite that and poor mileage at a time when gas was again becoming scarcer and costlier, sales leaped to over 50,000 that season.

Relatively high weight had long been a fifth-generation problem, so Corvette went on a diet for 1980, shedding some 250 pounds through greater use of plastics and by substituting aluminum for steel in the differential housing and front frame cross-member. Aerodynamics improved via a new sloped nose with integral spoiler, plus a faired-in rear spoiler.

More weight-saving occurred for '81. The rear transverse leaf spring was now made of fiberglass—just like the body—paring 33 pounds. Door windows and the optional see-through T-tops had thinner glass. A stainless-steel exhaust manifold replaced the former cast-iron affair. There was now just one 350, a new L81 version with magnesium rocker covers, GM's Computer Command Control engine management system, and the same 190 bhp as before. Government fuel-economy mandates dictated a lockup torque converter for the optional automatic transmission. Inflation now pushed base price past $15,000, but that included six-way power driver's seat. Perhaps the year's biggest news, however, was the historic transfer of Corvette production from St. Louis to a new high-tech plant in Bowling Green, Kentucky. With it came promises of improved workmanship, long a Corvette failing.

It also suggested that there really *would* be a new Corvette after all—but not before the fifth-generation put in its 15th and final appearance. At least the '82 offered a sneak preview of the new model's drivetrain. For the first time since 1965, fuel injection returned to a production Vette for a revised 350 dubbed L83. And for the first time since 1955, there was no manual gearbox, just a new 4-speed automatic with torque-converter lockup on all forward gears save first. But the kicker was another limited-production job tellingly named "Collector's Edition," with lift-up rear window (belatedly) and unique trim. It was the costliest Vette yet at a towering $22,538, a far cry from the $4663 it took to buy a '68.

Thus ended the remarkable fifth-generation Corvette. If it hung on too long, as some say, it was because it managed to remain exciting—and thus popular—through some dull yet difficult times. It was, more than anything, a survivor, and you can't say that about every car.

SPECIFICATIONS

Engines: all ohv V-8; **350 cid/5735 cc—1978:** 185 bhp @ 4000 rpm, 280 lbs-ft @ 2400 rpm; 220 bhp @ 5200 rpm, 260 lbs-ft @ 3600 rpm; **1979:** 195 bhp @ 4000 rpm, 285 lbs-ft @ 3200 rpm; 225 bhp @ 5200 rpm, 270 lbs-ft @ 3600 rpm; **1980-81:** 190 bhp @ 4400 rpm, 280 lbs-ft @ 2400 rpm; **1980:** 230 bhp @ 5200 rpm, 275 lbs-ft @ 3600 rpm; **1982:** 200 bhp @ 4200 rpm, 285 lbs-ft @ 2800 rpm; **305 cid/5002 cc—1980:** 180 bhp @ 4200 rpm, 255 lbs-ft @ 2000 rpm

Transmissions:	4-speed manual or 3/4-speed automatic
Suspension, front:	unequal-length A-arms, coil springs, anti-roll bar
Suspension, rear:	half-shafts, lateral arms, trailing radius rods, transverse semi-elliptic leaf spring
Brakes:	front/rear discs
Wheelbase (in.):	98.0
Weight (lbs):	3370-3530
Top speed (mph):	125-130
0-60 mph (sec):	6.5-9.2

Production: **1978** 46,776 **1979** 53,807 **1980** 40,614 **1981** 45,631 **1982** 25,407

Above: This is a genuine 1978 Indy Pace Car replica, but quick-buck artists seeing an instant collectible made bogus ones from stock Corvettes. Right: 1982's Collector Edition was a fifth-generation farewell, with special paint, rear hatch window, aluminum wheels, plush cockpit.

1984-1988 CHEVROLET CORVETTE

Few cars have been more eagerly anticipated than the sixth-generation Corvette. After all, it had been 15 years since the last really new design and, after waiting so long, enthusiasts naturally expected great things from its successor. This Corvette has generally delivered, although like any charismatic figure, it's not been without controversy.

Historians huffed when the sixth-generation arrived in early '83 as a 1984 model (mainly for emissions-certification reasons), thus depriving them of a 30th-anniversary Corvette. Some observers, (former GM styling chief Bill Mitchell among them) criticized appearance as bland, but most liked it. Created under the direction of Jerry Palmer, it was clean, contemporary, recognizably Corvette, and 23.7 percent more aerodynamically efficient—in all, quite a feat. A lift-up hatch window was retained from the '82 Collector Edition, but the T-top gave way to a one-piece Targa roof, and a new front-hinged "clamshell" hood/front-fender assembly offered superb engine access.

That engine was still the '82's L83 V-8, initially teamed only with 4-speed converter-lockup Turbo Hydra-Matic. But the autobox was now an optional alternative to a new "4+3 Overdrive" manual. Created by Vette specialist Doug Nash, it was basically a normal 4-speed with a second planetary gearset actuated by engine electronics, providing gas-saving overdrive ratios in all gears save first.

The rest of the car was equally new. Developed under chief Corvette engineer Dave McLellan, it had a new "uniframe" structure, with a Lotus-like backbone chassis welded to an upper "birdcage" for greatly increased rigidity. The front suspension retained unequal-length A-arm geometry, but with a single transverse plastic leaf spring instead of individual coils. At the rear was a new five-link setup comprising upper and lower longitudinal links, twin lateral strut rods from differential to hub carriers, another transverse plastic spring, and the usual tie rods and half-shafts. Steering switched from recirculating-ball to rack-and-pinion. Big four-wheel disc brakes continued, albeit a new design by the Anglo-American Girlock company. Tires were Goodyear's new ultra-sticky P255/50VR-16 Eagle GTs with unidirectional "gatorback" tread, running on wide cast-alloy wheels.

Weight-saving was a high priority, so the '84 used more lightweight materials (including beautiful aluminum forgings for suspension components) than any previous Corvette. But though 250 pounds lighter than the '82, it was some 300 pounds heavier than expected despite reductions of two inches in wheelbase and 8.8 inches in overall length.

Still, Palmer and McLellan had done their homework. The '84 offered more passenger and cargo space, better outward vision, and all the comfort and luxury any GT could hope for. Alas, it also had complicated digital-and-graphic electronic instruments that were hard to read, especially on a sunny day.

A harsh ride—even harsher with the Z51 handling option—emphasized the new structure's surprising flex. A record base price—initially $23,360—also drew barbs. But that was about it. "A world-class sports car with few rivals in performance," said *Consumer Guide*® magazine.

Chevy tended to details for '85, gaining 25 horsepower by switching from twin-throttle-body to "Tuned Port" injection, softening both standard and optional suspensions, adding oil cooler and gas-pressurized shock absorbers. The '86s were even better. The brakes received Bosch anti-lock control for stopping power to match the stupendous cornering power, while the engine got aluminum cylinder heads, higher compression (9.5:1 versus 9.0), and dual exhausts.

But the big event of 1986 was the mid-season return of the Corvette roadster after a 10-year absence, just in time to pace the Indy 500. Because the sixth-generation had been designed for a topless model, structural stiffening was straightforward, mainly an X-member below the floorpan and reinforcements around the cockpit. For '87, both models were treated to roller valve lifters that added another 10 horses to the evergreen 350 V-8, and a new in-cockpit electronic tire-pressure monitoring system option. The '88s gained another 5 horses via modified heads and camshaft, plus beefier brakes and restyled wheels including newly optional 17-inch rims wearing high-speed P255/50ZR tires.

That's the sixth-generation story so far, but there's more to come. Chevy already sanctions a twin-turbo conversion (by Callaway) and a 400-bhp "wide-body" model should be added by '89. The mind boggles at what could happen before the *next* new Vette.

Sixth-generation Corvette has seen little external change since the initial 1984 coupe (top). Mid-1986 saw the roadster (center) return after 10 years; it paced the Indy 500. The '88 (above and opposite) boasts 245 bhp and a new 17-inch wheel option.

SPECIFICATIONS

Engines: all ohv V-8, 350 cid/5735 cc; **1984:** 205 bhp @ 4200 rpm, 290 lbs-ft @ 2800 rpm; **1985-86:** 230 bhp @ 4000 rpm, 330 lbs-ft @ 3200 rpm; **1987:** 240 bhp @ 4000 rpm, 345 lbs-ft @ 3200 rpm; **1988:** 245 bhp @ 4000 rpm, 345 lbs-ft @ 3200 rpm

Transmissions:	"4+3" overdrive manual or 4-speed automatic
Suspension, front:	unequal-length upper and lower A-arms, transverse semi-elliptic leaf spring, anti-roll bar
Suspension, rear:	half-shafts, upper and lower longitudinal links, twin lateral strut rods, tie rods, transverse semi-elliptic leaf spring, anti-roll bar
Brakes:	front/rear discs
Wheelbase (in.):	96.2
Weight (lbs):	3190-3280
Top speed (mph):	150+
0-60 mph (sec):	5.8

Production: 1984 approx. 20,000 **1985** 39,729 **1986** 35,109 **1987** 25,266

1947-1952 CISITALIA 202 GRAN SPORT

When fashion mogul John Weitz decided to build a "designer" sports car in the early Eighties, he just might have had Cisitalia in mind. Piero Dusio, an ingenious salesman and former soccer star, had formed *Consorzio Industriale Sportiva Italia* to make sporting goods, primarily bicycles, tennis rackets and clothing. By 1946, however, it was also building cars, a reflection of Dusio's passion for automobile racing.

Not surprisingly, Cisitalia's first cars were single-seat 1100-cc racers based on cheap and commonly available Fiat mechanical components. About 50 were built in two years, and so dominated their class that Dusio formed a traveling "circus" with 16 cars performing and some of the best Italian drivers of the day. Two of Italy's best engineers were responsible for the design: Dante Giacosa, later chief engineer at Fiat, and Giovanni Savonuzzi, then of Fiat's experimental-aircraft division. These Cisitalias preceded the more popular Italian-designed Formula Junior race cars by more than a decade.

Encouraged by his success, and apparently ignoring the fact that his efforts hadn't been noticed much outside Italy, Dusio embarked on a more ambitious program: a two-seat sports car. Again he used Fiat components, but this and the chassis were the sole legacies of the *monoposto* competition machines. The chassis was of space-frame construction—light and strong but slow and expensive to build—with independent front suspension and a live rear axle. Front geometry was borrowed from Fiat's minicar, the beloved "Toppolino" (mouse), with a lower A-arm on each side and a single transverse leaf spring, the latter also providing upper wheel location. Semi-elliptic leafs sprung the rear. All-round drum brakes came from Fiat's workaday 1100-series family models, but were more than adequate for the new Cisitalia's light weight and modest performance. The engine, also Fiat 1100, was fortified by means of higher compression, dual downdraft Weber carburetors and dry-sump lubrication.

The first two-seat Cisitalias were lightweight racing coupes and roadsters with aluminum bodies bearing rear fender skirts and large tailfins. Like the single-seaters, they were successful in their class, and in expert hands could sometimes beat faster,

more powerful cars. Famed pilot Tazio Nuvolari was particularly successful in a Cisitalia.

But though attractive, these no-nonsense racers were literally ill-equipped to double as road cars, a business Dusio also wanted to get into. To help him do that, he wisely turned for development help to Giovanni Battista Giuseppe Farina, better known by his family nickname, ''Pinin.'' The result was a beautiful little fastback coupe that has since become a legend.

The reason, of course, is Farina's trend-setting body design, with modern flush-fender sides and a simple front end predictive of his early Ferraris. Named Type 202 Gran Sport, this car was stylistically very advanced for the late Forties and a real work of art. New York City's renowned Museum of Modern Art made that description official in 1951 by selecting the Cisitalia as one of the 10 best automotive designs of all time, and putting one on permanent display. As you might expect, it still looks good today: smooth, well-proportioned, simple, and unaffected. Its only questionable element is the Buick-like portholes at the top rear of some front fenders (one or two per side, depending on year).

Essentially a roadgoing version of the racing two-seater, the GS coupe was soon joined by a companion cabriolet. But prices were prohibitive for the time—$5000 and $7000, respectively—especially for small-displacement cars that weren't all that fast. They were beautiful and fun to drive, but there weren't that many people in Italy or anywhere else able or willing to pay such sums, even for a work of art. Consider that by 1949, for about half what the Cisitalia convertible cost, you could have Jaguar's sleek and sexy XK120 roadster, a genuine 120-mph car with a twincam six. And for $2000 less than the coupe you could get a Porsche 356 which, while not that much faster, at least had all-independent suspension.

While its beauty wasn't only skin deep, the Gran Sport simply didn't have the muscle to attract many sales in the high-flying, horsepower-crazy market of the day, and the high price was hard to justify even for a car that looked *that* good, especially when it used a lot of mass-production parts and almost any old American car could run rings around it.

The postscript to this story is a sad one. Hastened by development costs for a planned Grand Prix racer, Cisitalia ran out of funds in 1949 and Dusio moved operations to Argentina. He built cars there, but of a very different stripe. Meantime, Gran Sport production was slated to resume in Italy under new ownership, and did, but the cars were basically cobbled-up amalgams of special bodies and workaday chassis and drivetrains. Production was sporadic in any case, though it continued as late as 1965.

With all this, serious enthusiasts will look no further than the Italian-made cars, though they'll have to look hard to find one. In all those years, only 170 Gran Sports were completed, including a mere 17 cabriolets.

SPECIFICATIONS

Engine: Fiat ohv I-4, 66.4 cid/1089 cc, 66 bhp @ 5500 rpm, torque NA

Transmission:	4-speed manual
Suspension, front:	lower A-arms, transverse leaf spring
Suspension, rear:	live axle, semi-elliptic leaf springs
Brakes:	front/rear drums
Wheelbase (in.):	NA
Weight (lbs):	1960
Top speed (mph):	approx. 100
0-60 mph (sec):	NA
Production:	**Coupe** 153 **Cabriolet** 17

Literal works of art, the Pinin Farina-styled Cisitalia convertible (left) *and coupe were scarce new and are even rarer now. Trend-setting design conceals Fiat mechanicals.*

1971-1975
CITROËN SM

Citroën, the veteran French automaker, was into "high tech" long before we'd ever heard the term. It pioneered front-wheel drive with its famous *Traction Avant* sedans of 1934. Next came the futuristic DS19 of 1955, with a high-pressure hydraulic system for powering the brakes as well as a unique oleopneumatic suspension system with integral self-levelling. By the Sixties, Citroën had a reputation for cars engineered like no other.

Though Citroën had been toying with the idea of a fast sporty coupe, its four-cylinder engines just weren't up to the job. But in 1968, Citroën took over Maserati, the famed Italian sports-car builder, and suddenly the idea seemed plausible.

Soon after this merger was formalized, Citroën learned how resourceful, speedy, and efficient Maserati's designers could be. Accordingly, it asked the Italians to develop a new high-performance engine of about 2.7 liters (French car taxes took a vertical leap above 2.8-liters displacement) that might power a sportier Citroën *and* a new Maserati.

The result was a 90-degree V-6 with twin overhead camshafts per cylinder bank, actually a close relative of Maserati's existing right-angle quad-cam V-8. With 170 bhp in standard form, it was deemed suitable not only for the new Citroën but a downmarket version of Maserati's mid-engine Bora. The latter, called Merak, was tuned initially for 190 horsepower, later 220 bhp.

Citroën, meantime, set about designing its own new GT, which emerged as the SM (for "Sport Maserati"). Riding a 116.1-inch wheelbase and measuring a grand 192.8 inches long overall, it was a heavy (3200-pound), extravagantly equipped 2 + 2 styled along the lines of the DS sedans, with a low, shapely nose and abbreviated overhangs front and rear. Setting it apart was a sloped roofline ending in a high tail, with a lift-up hatch incorporating a large, curved backlight.

Unusual even for Citroën, the SM had no fewer than six headlights (basically a conventional quad-lamp system plus auxiliary driving lights), with the inboard units linked to the steering so that they'd turn with the front wheels—shades of the Tucker! European models mounted this luminary sextet behind a full-width transparent cover, with a center section for the license plate. Both cover and driving lamps were omitted for the American market as not meeting federal regulations.

The SM's V-6 sat longitudinally behind the front-wheel centerline to drive through a beefy 5-speed gearbox (also used in the Merak as well as the later mid-engine Lotus Esprit and Peugeot's mid-Eighties 205 Turbo 16 Group B rally car). As on the big Citroëns, brakes (here, four-wheel discs) and all-independent suspension continued to be powered hydraulically from engine-driven pumps, but now the steering was too. Lightning quick (a mere 2.0 turns lock-to-lock), it would self-center at rest without any driver assistance—a bit unnerving to the uninitiated.

As always, Citroën's oleopneumatic suspension breathed a literal sigh of relief after engine shutoff, eventually letting the car settle on its bump stops as internal pressure eased. Conversely, the system could be "pumped up" so as to raise the car to maximum wheel travel in rebound, which made for a *very* stiff ride but facilitated tire changes (and fording streams). Inside was a typically Citroën dash, with oval instrument dials, unconventional minor controls, and the ever-present floor-mounted brake "button" that had virtually no movement no matter how hard you pressed (the hydraulics did all the work).

Alas, the SM was knocked for a loop by the 1973-74 energy crisis, which rendered fast tourers like this almost unsaleable for a time and led to big financial trouble for

*Typically Citroën, the sporty SM went its own way in styling and features. Unique oleopneumatic suspension could vary ride height over a towering range (**above**). Maserati designed SM V-6 (**above center**) and used it to power its own mid-engine Merak two-seater.*

the Citroën/Maserati "marriage," prompting Citroën to withdraw from the U.S. market after 1974. SM production limped along for about another year, then ceased following Citroën's acquisition by Peugeot. Later SMs were fitted with fuel injection, raising V-6 output to 178 bhp. There was also a 3.0-liter version (mainly for export) with 180 bhp, offered only with Borg-Warner 3-speed automatic.

Road & Track magazine named the SM "one of the ten best cars in the world" in 1971, perhaps a dubious accolade in light of subsequent events, though it was easily justified at the time. Even in initial carbureted form, the big fastback Cit could reach 130 mph, and its "magic carpet" ride all but obliterated surface irregularities at such speeds.

Like the DS sedans, of course, the SM demanded a totally different driving technique. Its steering, for example, is not only super-quick but super-light, so it's easy to turn too sharply into a corner. It's just as easy to stand the car on its nose by being overly enthusiastic with the pressure-sensitive brake button. But if you could adjust to its idiosyncrasies, the SM was an ideal choice for long, fast journeys across Europe—which was, after all, what it was designed for. High-speed performance is relaxed, aided by unusually good aerodynamics (long a Citroën passion) and that smooth, supple ride.

Though not a commercial success, the SM was an interesting departure for Citroën and somewhat influential. Its styling helped shape the DS-series' CX successor, while its engineering continued in the Merak (which also used the complete SM dash) and Maserati Khamsin even after Citroën and Maserati divorced. Citroën hasn't attempted anything like this since (and may not ever), leaving the weird and wonderful SM a singular sports coupe of endless "high-tech" fascination.

SPECIFICATIONS

Engines: all Maserati dohc V-6; 163 cid/2670 cc, 170 bhp (DIN) @ 5500 rpm, 172 lbs-ft @ 4000 rpm (178 bhp, 164 lbs-ft with fuel injection); 181 cid/2965 cc, 180 bhp (DIN) @ 4750 rpm, 181 lbs-ft @ 4000 rpm

Transmissions:	5-speed manual or 3-speed automatic
Suspension, front:	wishbones, hydropneumatic struts (with self-levelling and ride-height control)
Suspension, rear:	trailing arms, hydropneumatic struts (with self-levelling and ride-height control)
Brakes:	front/rear discs
Wheelbase (in.):	116.1
Weight (lbs):	3200
Top speed (mph):	139 (2.7 injection)
0-60 mph (sec):	9.3 (2.7 injection)
Production:	12,920

1949-1952 CROSLEY HOT SHOT & SUPER SPORTS

Cincinnati radio-and-refrigerator magnate Powel Crosley, Jr., entered the car business in 1939 with dreams of an American *Volkswagen:* a small, cheap economy model that would make every family a two-car family. Prewar Crosleys were cute but crude little boxes with two-cylinder engines, mechanical brakes, very basic equipment, and prices as low as $299. Powel even sold them in his appliance stores as well as through auto dealerships.

Postwar Crosleys tried to be more like "real" cars: 28 inches longer, more impressively styled, somewhat better equipped (but not much), and more powerful, with an overhead-cam four derived from the copper-brazed "CoBra" unit that had been developed for wartime helicopters and was made of sheetmetal. Despite this engine's near-predictable durability problems, Crosley did relatively well in the postwar seller's market, building some 5000 cars for 1946 and over 19,000 for '47. In a burst of optimism, Powel Crosley predicted annual sales would soon reach 80,000. Production did climb for 1948—to 28,374 units—but would go no higher. The very next year, Crosley volume plunged nearly 75 percent in the face of a sated market and new models from larger, more prosperous rivals.

Seeking salvation, Crosley turned to more specialized products in 1949. First came the versatile "FarmORoad" utility, followed by, of all things, a sports car. Aptly named Hot Shot, this bare-bones two-seat roadster spanned a four-inch-longer wheelbase than Crosley's other cars but shared their drivetrain and chassis. What made it interesting was a racy, uniquely styled body featuring cut-away sides, a bulbous nose flanked by freestanding headlamps, and a spare tire jauntily carried on a stubby, trunkless tail.

Though blessed with only 26 horses, the Hot Shot lived up to its name with surprisingly good performance, due largely to its bantamweight build and sparse equipment. It was no race car in stock tune but, all things considered, it was a good goer. The typical example could do 0-60 mph in 20 seconds, the standing quarter-mile in 25 seconds at 66 mph,   and 77 mph top. Being a Crosley, it was dirt cheap: just $849. The scarcely quicker MG-TC sold for twice as much.

By this time, Crosley had abandoned the trouble-prone CoBra engine for a sturdier CIBA (Cast-Iron Block Assembly) version. With five main bearings, full-pressure lubrication, and a safe 10,000-rpm limit, it looked a natural for souping up. Accessory houses soon obliged with a slew of low-cost bolt-ons that halved the stock model's 0-60 mph time and upped top speed to a genuine 100 mph. Braje, for instance, listed a full-race cam for $25, headers for $28, and dual manifolds with Amal motorcycle carburetors for $60. Vertex and H&C sold high-performance ignition systems, and S.CO.T offered a Roots-type supercharger that more than doubled horsepower. Happily, the CIBA engine was well up to such muscle-building.

So was the Hot Shot chassis, which delivered nimble handling and leech-like roadholding despite primitive suspension. Brakes were another story. All 1949-50 Crosleys used aircraft-derived Goodyear-Hawley "spot" discs in front. They resisted fade but lacked proper sealing, and thus often froze when exposed to salt or road grime. A switch to all-round Bendix drums for 1951-52 solved the problem, and were more than a match for even a modified Hot Shot's performance.

Which could be formidable. The Crosley's finest hour came in 1950 when one of that year's new Super Sports, basically a Hot Shot with accessory doors, won the Index of Performance at the inaugural Sebring 12-hour race. A similar car entered by American sportsman Briggs Cunningham might have repeated the feat at the prestigious Le Mans 24 Hours in '51, but retired with electrical problems.

Crosley itself retired at the end of 1952, a victim of plummeting sales in a "bigger is better" market. The Hot Shot was up to $952 by then, while the Super Sports had risen from an initial $925 to $1029. Still, these were astonishingly low prices considering the cars' performance potential and high "fun quotient." They should have sold like hotcakes. And they might have had they been built by one of the Big Three.

But they didn't and they weren't, which probably explains why these remain America's "forgotten" early-postwar sports cars. Too bad. They were appealing little giant-killers fully worthy of the term. Come to that, they still are.

*Name script aside, Super Sports (**opposite bottom**) differed from Hot Shot in having doors. Both were as tiny and spartan as Crosley's passenger cars, but lighter and thus faster. Numerous aftermarket parts made them surprising track performers.*

SPECIFICATIONS

Engine: ohv I-4, 44 cid/721 cc, 26.5 bhp @ 5400 rpm, 32.5 lbs-ft @ 3000 rpm

Transmission:	3-speed manual
Suspension, front:	I-beam axle, semi-elliptic leaf springs
Suspension, rear:	live axle, quarter-elliptic leaf springs
Brakes:	front/rear drums (1949 Hot Shot); front/rear discs (others)
Wheelbase (in.):	85.0
Weight (lbs):	1180-1240
Top speed (mph):	80
0-60 mph (sec):	20.0

Production: 1949 752 (Hot Shot only) **1950** 742 **1951** 646 **1952** 358

1952-1955 CUNNINGHAM C-3 CONTINENTAL

Hollywood could make a movie about Briggs Swift Cunningham, and should. The son of a Cincinnati banker and godson of the Proctor half of Proctor & Gamble, he cut a dashing figure in high society. He knew all the "right" people (many as rich as himself) and had a passion for sports: golfing, flying, yachting especially—and sports cars. After joining the infant Sports Car Club of America in the early postwar years, Briggs drove to second at Watkins Glen in 1948 in his unique "Bumerc," a rebuilt Mercedes SSK with Buick power.

Then Briggs got *serious*. Having met Phil Walters and Bill Frick at the Glen, he acquired their services as driver/engineers by buying their small company, hoping to enter their hybrid "Fordillac" in the 1950 running of the Le Mans 24 Hours, the world's premier endurance race. But the Fordillac didn't qualify, so Briggs fielded two cars powered by Cadillac's new ohv V-8. One was a big special-bodied streamliner (nicknamed *Le Monstre* by appreciative French racegoers), the other a stock 1950 Coupe de Ville. Against all odds, the latter finished 10th overall, the special 11th.

Buoyed by this success, Briggs turned to crafting his own sports-racing cars, setting up a company in West Palm Beach, Florida that same year. "We don't intend to build two types of car, one for racing and the other for touring," he said. "Our policy is to concentrate on one model readily adaptable for both purposes." Before it was all over in 1955, he'd develop several.

The first, logically tagged C-1, was a smooth, low-slung roadster that looked like a cross between the early Ferrari Barchettas and some of the later Ghia-bodied Chrysler specials. Power was supplied by Chrysler's 331-cubic-inch hemi-head V-8, mounted in a strong tubular-steel chassis with independent coil-spring front suspension, De Dion rear end, generous 105-inch wheelbase, and broad 58-inch front and rear tracks. Only one C-1 was completed, equipped for road use, rather lavishly so by European standards.

Next came the evolutionary C-2. Only three were built, all racers designated C-2R. Walters and Fitch drove one at Le Mans '51, but had to settle for 18th overall.

Late that year, Briggs decided to make the C-2 more of a road car and sell it in limited numbers. The resulting C-3 would be offered as a coupe in addition to the usual roadster at respective base prices of $9000 and $8000. Also planned was a $2915 racing package comprising four-carburetor manifold, ported and polished heads, oil cooler, competition brakes, and racing bumperettes and grille screen. But by the time a prototype coupe was finished, someone had figured out that each C-3 would cost $15,000 just to build.

That was no way to run things, so in early 1952, Cunningham contracted with

the Alfredo Vignale coachworks of Turin, Italy to build C-3 bodies to a new design by Giovanni Michelotti. With this, the projected base price was dropped back to $9000.

What emerged was an American *gran turismo* as elegant and exciting as anything from Europe. The C-3's ladder-type tube chassis (with modified Ford front suspension) was almost identical with the C-2's, but the De Dion rear end gave way to a coil-sprung Chrysler live axle located by parallel trailing arms. Brakes were a combination of 11-inch-diameter Mercury drums and Delco actuating mechanisms. Wheelbase remained at 105 inches initially, but was later stretched two inches for more proper 2+2 seating. The V-8 used was basically as supplied by Chrysler Industrial except for Cunningham's own log-type manifolds with four Zenith downdraft carburetors.

Inside and out, the C-3 bore more than a passing resemblance to other Michelotti/Vignale designs of the period, particularly some early Ferraris. The bodywork was distinctively Vignale though, one of the coachbuilder's better efforts in these years. Pleated-leather seats graced the cockpit, while the dash was dominated by a large speedometer and matching combination gauge with clock; a small tachometer was mounted between and slightly above the main dials. Luggage had to be carried inside, because the spare tire and fuel tank occupied most of the normal trunk space.

The first C-3 coupe, named Continental, was finished in time for the Cunningham team to drive to the Glen in September 1952. It then toured U.S. auto shows while a second car was displayed at the Paris Salon that October.

"Production" got underway by early 1953. Unfortunately, while the Palm Beach works could build a chassis a week, Vignale needed almost two months to complete the rest of the car. A planned cabriolet derivative was shown at Geneva in March while assembly continued at this snail's pace. Ultimately, just nine cabrios and 18 coupes would be built, the former carrying a delivered price of exactly $11,422.50. It was as close as Briggs ever got to a production model.

Of course, the *real* reason for all this was to give Cunningham a contender in production-class racing, though the C-3 was really too big and heavy to be much of a threat. Briggs' remaining competition efforts would be made with further variations on his original theme: the C-4R and C-4RK, C-5R, and C-6R.

Nevertheless, the C-3 was svelte and compact next to most contemporary American cars, and it was a styling *tour de force*. Arthur Drexler, then director of New York's Museum of Modern Art, put the coupe on his list of the world's 10 best designs. For a discerning, monied few, the C-3 was a terrific buy, and it sold as quickly as the Cunningham company could build it.

Still, it might have made *real* money with a lower price or more sophisticated running gear. A Cadillac, Lincoln, or Chrysler could carry twice the people for half the money—and in greater comfort over long distances—while some of those able to pay the lofty price doubtless shunned the Cunningham as just a bunch of Yankee parts in a fancy foreign wrapper. The C-3 was probably every bit as good as a contemporary Ferrari—maybe better in some respects—but it wasn't Italian. And while the Chrysler hemi was likely the best engine of its day, it had pushrods, rocker arms, and only one camshaft. Anyone spending $12,000 for a car in the early Fifties wanted something exotic, even if it *wasn't* reliable.

A pity. They missed a *very* good car.

A true transatlantic effort, the lovely Cunningham C-3 Continental combined Italian styling with American V-8 muscle. Arthur Drexler, director of New York's Museum of Modern Art named it one of the world's 10 best designs. Chrysler hemi (above) made performance formidable.

SPECIFICATIONS

Engine: Chrysler ohv V-8, 331 cid/5420 cc; **1952-53:** 220 bhp @ 4000 rpm; **1953-55:** 235 bhp @ 4400 rpm; torque NA

Transmissions:	Cadillac 3-speed manual or Chrysler semi-automatic
Suspension, front:	upper-and-lower A-arms, coil springs (Ford)
Suspension, rear:	Chrysler live axle, parallel trailing arms, coil springs
Brakes:	front/rear Mercury drums
Wheelbase (in.):	105.0/107.0
Weight (lbs):	approx. 3500
Top speed (mph):	120
0-60 mph (sec):	6.9-8.5
Production:	**Coupe** 18 **Cabriolet** 9

1959-1964 DAIMLER SP250

Daimler of England was born more than 90 years ago as an offshoot of the German company that survives today as Daimler-Benz. Yet in all that time it has rarely attempted sporting cars, and then only in tiny numbers. The SP250 was the firm's second such effort in the postwar years (after the mid-Fifties Conquest convertible) and far more successful. But it was also something of a fluke, quite out of character with other Daimlers of the day.

Owned by the BSA group for many years, Daimler in the late Fifties was still mainly a "carriage trade" builder of staid, expensive sedans and limousines. But then BSA inexplicably changed Daimler's new-model strategy and its management, a shakeup that would have far-reaching implications. Jack Sangster became chairman, and Edward Turner, famed designer of BSA motorcycles, was drafted to develop new powerplants. The result was a brace of V-8s and plans for a new two-seater.

As a relative stranger to the field, Daimler looked at existing sports cars, being careful not to copy any one *too* much. Ultimately, the design team settled on a separate chassis topped by a Corvette-style fiberglass body and powered by the smaller, 2.5-liter version of their new V-8. Design and testing proceeded through 1958, followed by a somewhat premature introduction at the New York Auto Show in March 1959 as the "Dart." As Dodge was already using that name and objected, Daimler adopted the prosaic title "Sports 250" (later just SP250, reflecting engine displacement in cubic centimeters divided by 10). Production was underway before the end of the year, making this a high-speed achievement for such a small automaker, if tarnished by mediocre workmanship on early examples.

Chassis and suspension design (including some components) were lifted from Triumph's contemporary TR3A, which also inspired the 4-speed gearbox. (Daimler hadn't built a manual transmission of its own for some 30 years by that time, and it needed a "blueprint" from *somewhere*.) Borg-Warner automatic became optional in 1961.

The V-8 was far more original. Patterned after one of Turner's more recent motorcycle engines, it featured hemispherical combustion chambers and opposed valves with complex overhead actuation. Output was 140 horsepower, which looked right and, by all accounts, was.

The styling wasn't—gimmicky and loaded with period clichés. A wide-grin oval grille bearing a prominent "V" announced a droopy, MGA-style nose with headlamps rather awkwardly thrust out from the front fenders. The windshield was a semi-wrapped affair, and the tail bore trendy fins *a la* the recently announced Sunbeam Alpine. At least the Daimler had wind-up windows at a time when other British sports cars were still making do with clumsy side curtains, and a rigid lift-off hardtop was available to supplement the folding fabric roof.

Sales started in early 1960 and were quite shaky. Blessed with a good power-to-weight ratio, the SP250 was fast (up to 122 mph all out), but it handled with the same skittishness as the TR3A it copied, and body flex was so extreme on early examples that doors sometimes flew open without warning in vigorous cornering. So though sufficiently rapid to be selected by several British police departments for pursuit duty, the SP250 was not likely to approach TR3A or Austin-Healey 3000 sales, a realization that became obvious within the first few months.

Not that it would matter much. In June 1960, BSA sold Daimler to Sir William Lyons and Jaguar, which quickly began reorganizing the combined businesses with the aim of building more Jaguars. Then too, Jaguar was getting ready to bow its sensational new E-Type, which considerably dimmed the Daimler's long-term prospects.

Still, Jaguar tried hard to improve the SP250. In fact, the car was effectively reintroduced in April 1961 with what became known as the "B-Specification," which entailed a much stiffer bodyshell and standard front and rear bumpers. More body improvements followed in 1963 for a "C-Specification" model. But nothing seemed able to counter those initial quality horror stories, and the SP250 was unceremoniously dropped in mid-1964 after fewer than 2700 units. Needless to say, there was no successor.

Daimler SP250 had fiberglass bodywork like Corvette, mixed styling elements of MGA and Sunbeam Alpine. Small V-8 (right) delivered good go, but body flex and a Triumph TR3A-style suspension compromised handling.

SPECIFICATIONS

Engine: ohv V-8, 155.5 cid/2548 cc, 140 bhp (SAE gross) @ 5800 rpm, 155 lbs-ft @ 3600 rpm

Transmissions:	4-speed manual or 3-speed automatic
Suspension, front:	wishbones, coil springs
Suspension, rear:	live axle, semi-elliptic leaf springs
Brakes:	front/rear discs
Wheelbase (in.):	92.0
Weight (lbs):	2220
Top speed (mph):	121
0-60 mph (sec):	10.2
Production:	2648

1961-1969 DATSUN 1500 SPORTS/ 1600/2000

Remember the cars the Japanese *used* to build? Even if you do, it's helpful to recall them now and then, for there's no better way to appreciate how far the Japanese industry has come—or how quickly. Nissan's first sports cars are a case in point.

Nissan Motor Corporation wasn't officially organized until 1934, though its origins go all the way back to 1911. Its earliest car, the 1914 DAT, eventually led to the Datson and, in 1934, the name Datsun. The firm's late-Thirties models were mostly scaled-down British and American designs (including a true "joint-venture" car patterned on the American Graham Crusader), while reworked British Austin A40s, built under license, led a halting recovery in the early postwar years. Amazingly, Nissan didn't get around to a new postwar design of its own until 1958, the Datsun Bluebird sedan.

But bigger and better things weren't long in coming. The very next year brought a new open two-seater, catering to a traditional Japanese fondness for such cars. Designated S211, it replaced the original Datsun Sports that had been built in small numbers for domestic sale since 1952. It was also the first Datsun to bear the poetic Fairlady name that's still in use today, though the car itself was nothing to write sonnets about. Carrying a 60-horsepower 1189-cc four, it was sized like an Austin-Healey Sprite yet wasn't as peppy or agile. Worse, it tried to look like a big Healey. Somehow, production continued through 1963.

Meantime, the 1961 Tokyo Motor Show brought a surprise: an all-new Datsun roadster, the Fairlady 1500. More grown up and civilized than the S211, it offered better performance and more "international" styling in a conventional but well-equipped package that would remain popular through the end of the Sixties. Today, we recognize this generation as significant in paving the sports-car path that ultimately led Nissan to the history-making 240Z.

Designated SP310, the new Fairlady roadster looked rather like the MGB it predated by a full year, with the same neat, squarish, slab-sided body lines and scooped headlamp nacelles. At first it was a *three*-seater, with a single sideways-facing rear bucket, though that feature was dropped by 1963.

Specifications were resolutely orthodox. The separate box-section frame with cruciform center bracing employed coil-and-wishbone front suspension, a live rear axle on semi-elliptic leaf springs, and drum brakes all-round. The drivetrain was just as ordinary, though new: a 71-bhp inline four mated to a 4-speed gearbox.

As was Japanese custom even in those long-ago days, the Fairlady 1500 was fully equipped and priced to sell. Standard amenities like wind-up windows, radio, heater, and snap-on tonneau put it way ahead of most European contemporaries in value for money, and workmanship was at least their equal, if not better. Still, with only 95 mph maximum, the 1500 wasn't a true performance rival for established British and Italian sports cars.

Nissan wasted little time in making it one. Twin SU carburetors (license-built by Hitachi) arrived in 1963, adding 10 horses. Then in September 1964, the 1500 gave way to an uprated 1600 model (CSP311) with 1595 cc and 96 bhp, plus all-synchro gearbox, a more modern diaphragm-spring clutch, and front disc brakes. Smoother, quieter, and faster (top speed was a genuine 100 mph), the 1600 sold like hotcakes, especially in the U.S. May 1965 brought a five-main-bearing crankshaft for a refined edition (SP311). Sold in the U.S. as the Datsun 1600, it had the same engine but was an inch shorter, a half-inch narrower and about two inches higher.

By this time, American emissions regulations were in sight, and Nissan's product line was not only expanding but moving up the size and displacement scale. These factors prompted a final evolution of the British-inspired roadster, the 2000 (SR311). Introduced in 1967, it logically carried a 2.0-liter engine, the new Type U20 overhead-cam four with no less than 135 bhp, mated to a new 5-speed gearbox. Weighing little more than the 1600, it could reach an easy 110 mph. (There was also a limited-production 145-bhp competition version capable of over 125 mph.) At under $3000, it was a whale of a buy and surprisingly able on the track. Like the 1600s, modified 2000s quickly found their way into SCCA racing, and a young Hannu Mikkola even drove one in the Monte Carlo Rally.

All things considered, these simple sporting Datsuns were a big success, one reason you still see them running around today. Like most Japanese cars of the Sixties, they weren't original in design, but they were definitely good value, built to last, and just plain fun. Perhaps things haven't changed so much after all.

The Datsun roadster was sometimes described as a copy of the MGB, but it debuted before the MG. The 2000, with 135-145 bhp, was fast for its day.

SPECIFICATIONS

Engines: all ohv I-4; **1961-65:** 90.8 cid/1488 cc, 71-85 bhp (SAE) @ 5000 rpm, 83-92 lbs-ft @ 3200-4400 rpm; **1965-69:** 97.3 cid/1595 cc, 96 bhp (SAE) @ 6000 rpm, 103 lbs-ft @ 4000 rpm; **1967-69:** ohc I-4, 121 cid/1982 cc, 135-145 bhp @ 6000 rpm, 145 lbs-ft @ 4000 rpm

Transmissions:	4-speed manual (1500/1600), 5-speed manual (2000)
Suspension, front:	wishbones, coil springs, anti-roll bar
Suspension, rear:	live axle, semi-elliptic leaf springs
Brakes:	front/rear drums (1500), front discs/ rear drums (1600/2000)
Wheelbase (in.):	89.9
Weight (lbs):	2030-2110
Top speed (mph):	95-127
0-60 mph (sec):	10.2-15.5
Production:	approx. 40,000

1969-1978
DATSUN 240Z/260Z/280Z

Having dramatically expanded both model offerings and sales in the Sixties, Nissan turned to innovation in the Seventies. Its small front-wheel-drive Cherry (which would come to America as the F-10) showed that the company could field competitive (if ungainly) mass-market cars. But it was the 240Z that showed what this Japanese firm could *really* do, solidly establishing Nissan as what we now call a "world-class" automaker.

The 240Z was carefully conceived, progressing from good idea to production reality over five years. It was called Fairlady Z when launched in Japan in early 1969. The 240 designation was chosen for other markets, corresponding to engine displacement (in liters, multipled by 10), though some say it was the car's project number. Unlike the 1600/2000 roadsters it replaced, the Z was a sleek and sexy fastback coupe, more technically advanced, and designed very much with an eye to export sale, particularly in North America.

Designated Model S30, the original Z-car was shaped at least in part by industrial designer Count Albrecht Goertz, who'd been associated with Raymond Loewy and had styled the two-seat 507 and four-seat 503 for BMW. Strangely, Nissan later tried to shrug off Goertz's involvement until the threat of legal action forced it to "come clean."

In any case, the 240Z was a sensation, not least because of its price. Smooth, civilized, capable, and fully equipped, it was a truly *modern* sports car, worthy of comparison with Jaguar's E-Type yet much cheaper. In fact, at just $3526 when it landed on U.S. shores in 1970, the 240Z was simply astonishing value-for-money, and it was this as much as its obvious abilities that sent auto writers into gales of praise and buyers streaming into Datsun showrooms.

Except for its engine and standard 5-speed overdrive manual transmission (the latter inherited from the 2000 roadster) the 240Z was all-new—altogether beefier, faster, and more long-legged than previous Nissan sports cars. If not exactly original, the styling was adroit, blending elements of the curvaceous E-Type with overtones of Toyota's abortive 2000GT. Journalists picked at details (mostly a profusion of badges and rather tacky wheel covers), but most everything else was just right.

The long nose was dictated partly by the powerplant, a 2.4-liter single-overhead-cam inline six borrowed from a domestic-market Datsun sedan, tuned to produce 151 horsepower in U.S. trim. Chassis specifications were bang up-to-date: all-independent suspension via MacPherson struts, wishbones, and coil springs; rack-and-pinion

*Strictly stock first-generation Zs are hard to find nowadays, the cars invite personalization as much as ever with items like front airdams (**above**) and rear-window louvers (**below**). Wheels on both these examples are also non-stock. Styling still looks good in today's "aero age," is reflected in successor ZX models.*

steering; front-disc/rear-drum brakes. Cockpit design was rather American, especially the Corvette-style dashboard, though that hardly hurt U.S. sales.

Neither did equipment, which set a new standard for this price class. From the first, air conditioning and automatic transmission were optional—items BMC and Triumph hadn't even attempted with the big Healeys and TRs—while full instrumentation, wall-to-wall carpeting, reclining bucket seats, radio, and a proper climate system were all standard.

Of course, none of this would have mattered had performance not matched the styling, but the 240Z delivered. Many compared it with the late, lamented Healey 3000 in overall character, while others merely raved about the 125-mph top speed, nimble handling, secure roadholding, comfortable ride, and refinement unheard of in a sports car of this price.

In fact, a major reason for the 240Z's instant success was that it was more GT than traditional sports car (reinforced by the absence of a soft-top version), a sort of poor man's E-Type. That was no bad thing, of course, and Nissan soon found it couldn't build Zs fast enough. High reliability, a trait never associated with the Jaguar, turned the sales clamor into a stampede.

Demand would remain mostly strong through the end of this design in 1978. Some Americans and Europeans were aware of, but never got a chance to buy, the interesting, Japan-only 2.0-liter and twincam derivatives. What they did get were minor year-to-year improvements, a second body choice, and two displacement increases.

The original 240, which eventually sold in the U.S. at the phenomenal rate of 50,000 units a year, continued into 1973, when the engine was enlarged to 2.6 liters to offset power losses from tightening U.S. emissions limits. Unfortunately, it didn't. Appropriately called 260Z (officially, Type GLS30 in U.S. trim), it had slightly less horsepower and torque. Federal regulations also dictated bigger, heavier bumpers that added unwanted weight, particularly up front, thus further diminishing go and making the optional power steering almost mandatory for easy handling.

The 260 also marked the start of the Z's slow but inexorable transformation from sports car to GT. As if to signal this trend, Nissan introduced a stretched-wheelbase version with a pair of tiny "+2" rear seats. Styling inevitably suffered (as it did on Jaguar's E-Type 2+2), though sales were initially good.

Displacement rose to 2.8 liters for the final variations on this theme, the U.S.-only 280Z and 280Z 2+2, released in 1975. (The 260 continued in both Europe and Japan.) With 150 bhp (SAE net), the larger engine brought performance back to near 240 levels, and Nissan responded to complaints of poor 260 engine driveability by junking carburetors in favor of Bosch electronic fuel injection.

After eight years and more than 540,000 units, the original Z-car came to an end in late 1978. More than any other, this was the car that proved Nissan could build not just transportation but interesting, even exciting cars. Now it was time for a change, though it wouldn't necessarily be for the better.

SPECIFICATIONS

Engines: all sohc I-6; **1969-73:** 146 cid/2393 cc, 151 bhp (SAE) @ 5600 rpm, 146 lbs-ft @ 4400 rpm; **1973-75:** 156.5 cid/2565 cc, 139 bhp (SAE net) @ 5200 rpm, 137 lbs-ft @ 4400 rpm; **1975-78:** 168 cid/2753 cc, 149 bhp (SAE net) @ 5600 rpm, 163 lbs-ft @ 4400 rpm

Transmissions:	5-speed manual or 3-speed automatic
Suspension, front:	MacPherson struts, lower wishbones, coil springs, anti-roll bar
Suspension, rear:	Chapman struts, lower wishbones, coil springs, anti-roll bar
Brakes:	front discs/rear drums
Wheelbase (in.):	90.7 (2-seater) 102.6 (2+2)
Weight (lbs):	2300-2800
Top speed (mph):	115-125
0-60 mph (sec):	8.0-10.0
Production:	540,000+

1978-1983 DATSUN 280ZX

The original Datsun Z-car sold so well that a successor was never in doubt. Christened 280ZX, it didn't last as long—five years instead of seven—but sold relatively better. In 1979-80, Nissan moved over 140,000 in the U.S. alone. The ZX was also much more popular in Europe than the 260Z it replaced there and in Japan. It only goes to show that the public recognizes an attractive package more than the motoring press, which wasn't nearly so enthusiastic about the second-generation design.

Like the 260/280Z, the ZX was offered as a two-seater (designated Type HSL130 in U.S. trim) and 2+2 (Type HGLS130). Japanese introduction took place in the summer of 1978. U.S. sales began the following November for the 1979 model year.

Because styling continuity was deemed important for sales, the ZX looked much like its predecessor—so much so that some wondered whether it wasn't merely the old car with a new skin. It wasn't. The styling, an in-house job this time, was beefier and busier, while the all-steel unit body/chassis structure was not just completely different but more spacious and practical. In U.S. form, the only carry over components were engine and driveline, but the 2.8-liter powerplant was now extended to all markets. The American version arrived with 135 horsepower (SAE net) compared to 140 bhp for European models; the former was boosted to 145 bhp for 1981.

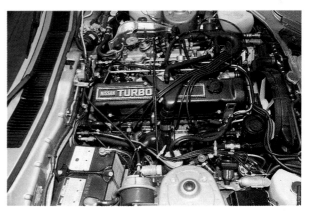

The ZX marked Nissan's first use of wind-tunnel testing during design development. It didn't *look* any slipperier than previous Zs (quite the contrary to some eyes) but it was. It also weighed about the same despite meeting all the latest U.S. "crash" standards, though it was still a bit overweight, all things considered. Nissan tacitly admitted as much by fitting a larger fuel tank and a secondary fuel gauge that measured just the final fourth of it. Dimensionally, wheelbase lengthened by 0.6-inch on the two-seater and shriveled by 3.4 inches on the 2+2. There were similar changes in overall length, while width increased but fractionally.

Production economics dictated more component sharing than on the original Z, so ZX suspension was borrowed from Nissan's upmarket 810 sedans. MacPherson struts, lower lateral arms, and coil springs returned up front with compliance rather than tension struts. The big change was at the rear, where simpler BMW-style semi-trailing arms substituted for Chapman struts and lower A-arms, and the entire

assembly was newly mounted on a separate subframe. All-round coil springs continued. In response to road-test criticisms, rear brakes were switched from drums to discs, and there were now two types of steering: manual rack-and-pinion or power-assisted recirculating-ball (licensed by ZF). As before, it was generally agreed that the latter should have been standard for proper handling, but U.S. customers got it without paying extra only if they bought a 2+2.

Nissan fought hard to maintain Z-car performance in the face of ever-tightening emissions requirements, and mostly succeeded. *Road & Track* magazine, for example, recorded a top speed of 121 mph for the debut-year two-seater and 9.2 seconds in the 0-60 mph run. Alas, the ZX was definitely softer on the road than even the last of the original Zs, if still sporty enough to win wide favor. Said *R&T*: "Today's Z-car is not yesterday's Z-car, and though purists will mourn the passing of the sports car Z, enthusiasts will rejoice for the GT Z."

Indeed, the ZX was downright luxurious for a sporting car, available right from the start with power windows, four-speaker stereo system with "joystick" balance control, electrically remote-adjustable door mirrors, plush velour upholstery, even cruise control. *Consumer Guide®* magazine's auto editors accurately termed it "the Ford LTD of sports cars."

The ZX also became something of a Japanese Corvette. First came a Vette-style T-bar roof option for 1980 two-seaters, extended to the 2+2 for 1981. Within a year, it was accounting for some 50 percent of all U.S. ZX sales. Even closer to America's sports car for performance was the ZX Turbo, introduced in two-seat automatic form at mid-model year '81 and also offered as a 2+2 for 1982-83, along with manual transmission. With 180 bhp in U.S. trim—a 25 percent gain—it could outdrag a Porsche 924 Turbo, leaping from rest to 60 mph in 7.4 seconds (versus 9.2) and bounding on to a 129-mph maximum (127 for the Porsche). If not the ultimate rocketship, the blown ZX was certainly fast enough for 55-mph America.

But by this time, the enthusiastic press had come around to *Consumer Guide®*'s point of view. "Fundamentally," said a 1981 *R&T* comparison test, "the Datsun has less 'soul,' if that matters, than the *pur sang* Alfa [GTV-6] and Porsche and also what felt like about 800 lbs more weight (actually 150) . . . . Meet the world's best boulevard sports car, one that can just about hold its end up with the real racers."

Damning with faint praise? Yes, but there was no denying that the 280ZX was just about unbeatable as a GT. And despite price escalation over the years, it offered the same high value, relatively speaking, as the pioneering 240Z.

In the end, though, the ZX was really too conservative and it aged with disarming speed. By 1984, enthusiasts were hoping not just for another new Z but one with "soul." What they got was another cautious evolution, the Nissan 300ZX (see entry)—so they're still wishin' and a-hopin.'

The editors' test 280ZX Turbo 2+2 from 1983. Rear seat (opposite top) was predictably tight, performance good from inline six (opposite center) despite high weight.

SPECIFICATIONS

Engines: all sohc I-6, 168 cid/2753 cc; **1979-83:** 135/145 bhp (SAE net) @ 5200 rpm, 149/156 lbs-ft @ 4000 rpm; **1981-83 Turbo:** 180 bhp (SAE net) @ 5600 rpm, 203 lbs-ft @ 2800 rpm

Transmissions:	5-speed manual, 3-speed automatic
Suspension, front:	MacPherson struts, lower lateral arms, compliance struts, coil springs, anti-roll bar
Suspension, rear:	semi-trailing arms, coil springs, anti-roll bar
Brakes:	front/rear discs
Wheelbase (in.):	91.3 (2-seater), 99.2 (2+2)
Weight (lbs):	2825-2950
Top speed (mph):	121-129
0-60 mph (sec):	7.4-9.2
Production:	approx. 415,000 worldwide

1967-1971
DeTOMASO MANGUSTA

Alejandro de Tomaso was an Argentinian race-car driver who emigrated to Italy to build competition machines after first settling in the United States, where he married and continued racing for a time (with his wife). In the Seventies he built DeTomaso Automobili into a small power in the motor industry of his adopted country. Today it owns Maserati and Innocenti, and also builds DeTomaso cars as well as Benelli and Moto Guzzi motorcycles.

But in the early Sixties, Alejandro was struggling to make the shift from race-car constructor to road-car manufacturer, producing prototypes that always seemed to have a lot of potential but no future. Accordingly, no one took much notice when he revealed a Ford-powered mid-engine coupe in November 1966. Yet this car, the Mangusta, would become his first series-production model, thus laying the foundation for DeTomaso's future mini auto empire.

The Mangusta ("mongoose" in Italian) wasn't Alejandro's first roadgoing sports car. That was the Vallelunga, which appeared in 1964. A smallish open two-seater, it featured a novel "backbone" chassis with all-independent A-arm suspension and a midships-mounted 1.5-liter British Ford four-cylinder engine. Alejandro hoped to sell copies or at least interest a major automaker in production rights, but could do neither.

Then, a turning point. In 1965, DeTomaso persuaded young Giorgio Giugiaro, formerly of Bertone but then working at the house of Ghia, to design a closed body for the Vallelunga chassis. It attracted attention and Ghia built a few prototypes, only to discover that lack of chassis rigidity around the drivetrain created insoluble vibration problems. This left the Vallelunga stillborn but Alejandro with a valuable contact.

It didn't take long to pay off. Determined to make his chassis work, DeTomaso decided to try a scaled-up version with a small-block V-8 from Ford Dearborn. American racing specialist Pete Brock designed an open competition body for it with an eye to the 1966 Sebring 12 Hours, but the car never made it to Florida. Again thwarted but still undaunted, Alejandro turned to Ghia for a show car based on this "big" chassis.

Meantime, Giotto Bizzarrini (whose name crops up in connection with Ferrari, Iso, and Lamborghini) had just designed a mid-engine chassis of his own, for which Giugiaro had created shapely coachwork of elegant simplicity. This proposed P538

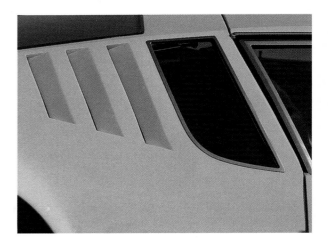

"Bizzarrini" was never built, but Giugiaro's styling was applied to DeTomaso's show car, essentially the Mangusta prototype.

First displayed at the 1966 Turin Show as the Ghia Mangusta, the result was stunning: wide and wickedly sleek, low to the ground, sexy and sophisticated. Happily, nary a line was changed for production. Highlights included a simple grille with two or four headlamps (depending on country of sale), a *very* wide hood, big cast-alloy wheels hulking beneath aggressively flared fenders, and a fastback tail with a distinctive dorsal rib on which twin engine access covers were hinged gullwing-style.

The Mangusta chassis was a classic example of the mid-engine layout then sweeping the competition scene. The powerful 289-cubic-inch Ford engine, tuned as for the new Shelby-Mustang GT-350, sat longitudinally behind a rather cramped two-seat cockpit and ahead of the rear-wheel centerline, driving through a ZF 5-speed transaxle of the type found in such cars as the Ford GT40 endurance racers. The chassis was still DeTomaso's pressed-steel backbone affair, with box-section and tubular superstructures carrying engine/transaxle, suspension, steering, and seat mounts.

Some say that this design was influenced by that of Mickey Thompson's unsuccessful 1964 Indy race car, others that Alejandro had merely mimicked Colin Chapman's Lotus Elan chassis. Regardless, the Mangusta's backbone platform was too flexible for the muscular V-8, and the resulting erratic suspension geometry made handling unpredictable. A rearward weight bias—no less than 68 percent—hardly helped.

Later, at the suggestion of consultant Gian Paolo Dallara, the talented Lamborghini engineer, DeTomaso tried to compensate by fitting much wider rear tires (225-section versus 185 front), but it wasn't enough. Ground clearance was very limited and roll center low, but the chassis flex gave the Mangusta a mind of its own: sometimes it understeered, sometimes it oversteered. Needless to say, high-speed driving could be tricky business, especially on slippery surfaces.

Not that this was any great surprise for what was essentially a detuned race car. Which brings up the Mangusta's other chief failing: lack of practicality. Even for a high-performance GT, it didn't have nearly enough passenger and luggage space, and outward vision was difficult, especially astern. What it *did* have, of course, was speed aplenty—DeTomaso claimed a 155-mph maximum—plus that gorgeous Giugiaro body and, thanks to the low-cost proprietary drivetrain, a reasonable price: $11,500.

Flawed though it was, the Mangusta was a car Alejandro could sell. His wife gave him the means. Her brother, as it happened, was a director in the American firm of Rowan Controls, and she persuaded him to have Rowan buy not only the DeTomaso factory but Ghia as well. Alejandro soon had 300 orders in hand, and the Mangusta went into production during 1967. By 1971, another 100 or so had been sold in Europe. DeTomaso was on his way at last.

*Low and dramatic, the first successful roadgoing DeTomaso was penned by Giorgio Giugiaro, then of the Ghia studios. Doors were conventional, but gullwing-style engine cover (**opposite center**) made the Mangusta unique. Ford thought about a badge-engineered Shelby version of this design to replace the original Cobra, but it came to nothing.*

SPECIFICATIONS

Engine: Ford (U.S.) ohv V-8, 289 cid/4727 cc, 306 bhp (SAE gross) @ 6200 rpm, 392 lbs-ft @ 3500 rpm

Transmission:	ZF 5-speed manual
Suspension, front:	wishbones, coil springs
Suspension, rear:	wishbones, radius arms, coil springs
Brakes:	front/rear discs
Wheelbase (in.):	98.4
Weight (lbs):	2915
Top speed (mph):	155
0-60 mph (sec):	NA
Production:	approx. 400

1971-1988
DeTOMASO PANTERA

Having made a small start as an automaker with the Mangusta, Alejandro deTomaso turned to a more ambitious project: a mid-engine supercar for the American market, built in unheard-of numbers for an Italian specialist producer. Its name: Pantera.

Revealed at the New York Auto Show in March 1970, the Pantera originated as simply the Mangusta's replacement, with new bodywork over the same sort of chassis with Ford V-8 power. But DeTomaso knew that Ford was seeking a successor to its roadgoing GT40 for the European market, and an exotic "image car" for its U.S. Lincoln-Mercury dealers to sell alongside the imported Capri. The Pantera fit both bills, so Alejandro proposed supplying the new model in quantity to Ford for U.S. sale; he'd handle distribution elsewhere. Included was the implication that if the deal worked out well for all concerned, Ford just might be able to buy into Ghia and DeTomaso Automobili, both of which he controlled. Dearborn agreed (and ultimately bought Ghia, in 1974).

Consultant engineer Giampaolo Dallara had given up on the Mangusta chassis, so the Pantera received a newly designed pressed-steel unitized structure (which would cause a lot of pain for restorers in subsequent years). The extra tooling expense was justified by high anticipated U.S. demand, and DeTomaso quickly geared up to build cars by the thousands, not hundreds. Vignale in Turin was tapped as body supplier, with final assembly to be completed at the DeTomaso factory in Modena. Predictably, the styling assignment was again handed to Ghia, this time to American Tom Tjaarda. The result was more practical than the Mangusta yet just as sleek despite no change to overall length.

Chassis design was much as before, but weight distribution was much more favorable, with a "mere" 58-percent rear bias. So, unequal-size tires were retained: 185-section in front, 215-section rear. Dearborn's desire for easy servicing and high reliability dictated more standard Ford components, so power was supplied by the H.O. (high-output) version of the American 5.7-liter/351-cubic-inch "Cleveland" V-8, mated to the usual 5-speed ZF transaxle. Horsepower was initially rated at 310 in U.S. form and 330 for European models. Emasculating emissions controls would bring the former down to 250 bhp by 1973.

Though hardly spacious by absolute standards, the Pantera was at least roomier than the Mangusta. Reflecting Ford input, detail engineering was more thorough and professional, equipment more complete. Even air conditioning was included, unusual

for a low-volume Latin but necessary to satisfy U.S. buyers. Practicality also dictated more conventional body construction, with a single engine lid, hinged at the cockpit end, instead of the Mangusta's flamboyant gullwing panels.

The Pantera made quite a splash when it reached the U.S. for model year 1971. The reason was price. At around $10,000, it offered all the panache of a Ferrari or Maserati for far less, plus a rugged, well-known American engine that could be serviced almost anywhere. It even came with Ford's normal new-car warranty.

A good thing too, because the Pantera was something less than a dream come true. Its Italian style, mid-engine sophistication, and fine handling were undeniable, but so were its cramped cockpit, peculiar driving position, and indifferent workmanship. Worse, complaints about engine overheating and excess cabin heat surfaced early, and performance wasn't all it should have been, at least in U.S. form. European models, unfettered by "detox" gear, could beat 160 mph, but American Panteras weren't nearly as fast. Then too, that simple Yankee iron was hardly a bragging point when everyone knew that *real* Italian exotics had all-aluminum engines with overhead cams.

Despite DeTomaso's clever dealing, the Pantera was designed with a curious disregard for pending U.S. safety and emissions standards. An ugly black-rubber nose guard and bigger back bumpers were in place by 1974, but the '75 standards would have required a major redesign, including a new powerteam. Ford bean-counters deemed it too costly for the car's modest sales rate, rendered even more modest by the 1973-74 gas crisis. As a result, U.S. Pantera imports were halted after 1974, though not before Dearborn stylists mocked up a full-size proposal for a rebodied replacement.

Lincoln-Mercury says it sold 6091 Panteras in four years, but some historians—and cynics—think this exaggerated. In fact, some sources list the 1971-74 total as only 5629 units.

Regardless, the Pantera carried on for Europe (it proved especially popular in Germany), and is still in production at this writing, albeit at much-reduced levels, no more than 100-150 per year. It's seen remarkably little change since '74 apart from a switch to Ford Australia engines (once Dearborn quit offering 351s), higher prices (now near $60,000), and the advent of the bespoiled, "ground effects" GT5 model, a reply to the Lamborghini Countach. Interim offerings comprised a "base" L model and the more aggressive-looking GTS.

Unlike most Seventies-car stories, this one has a happy ending for U.S. enthusiasts as Pantera imports have resumed, though on a more limited basis (about 50 units annually) and through private auspices, not Ford's. The car was recertified in 1981 by two Americans operating under the Panteramerica banner in Santa Monica, California, but distribution has since passed to Stauffer Classics, Ltd. of Blue Mounds, Wisconsin.

Thus, you once again can buy a brand-new Pantera, this time with 300 or 350 U.S.-legal horsepower. If that's not good news, we don't know what is.

SPECIFICATIONS

Engines: all Ford ohv V-8 (U.S. 1971-80, Australia 1980-87), 351 cid/5763 cc, 250-350 bhp (SAE net) @ 5400-6000 rpm, 325-330 lbs-ft @ 3600-3800 rpm

Transmission:	ZF 5-speed manual (in rear transaxle)
Suspension, front:	upper and lower wishbones, coil springs, anti-roll bar
Suspension, rear:	upper and lower wishbones, radius rods, coil springs, anti-roll bar
Brakes:	front/rear discs
Wheelbase (in.):	99.0
Weight (lbs):	3100-3300
Top speed (mph):	140-160
0-60 mph (sec):	5.2-7.5
Production:	est. 9500 through 1987

*DeTomaso's first commercial success has seen remarkably little change over nearly two decades. Clean original lines **(below)** were penned by Tom Tjaarda at Ghia. Later GTS and GT5 models sprouted spoilers and flared fenders **(opposite top)**. Cockpit is cozy.*

1954-1958
FACEL VEGA & FVS

A patriot and motoring enthusiast, Jean Daninos resolved to build a new postwar car that would return his native France to prominence in the GT field. The tricolor certainly had few high-performers by the early Fifties. Deutch-Bonnet and Alpine-Renault were hardly in Ferrari's league, Bugatti and Delage were moribund, and Talbot-Lago was soldiering on, nearly bankrupt, with its old 4.5-liter GS.

Daninos was in an excellent position to correct this situation. Before World War II he'd founded *Forges et Ateliers de Construction d'Eure et de Loire*—FACEL for short—and it had built most everything *including* the kitchen sink: scooters, office furniture, military vehicle bodies, combustion chambers for deHavilland and Rolls-Royce jet engines. By 1954 it employed 2000 workers at four factories, and was also building car bodies for Delahaye, Ford France, Panhard, and Simca. Lending impetus to Daninos's idea was surplus production capacity at his Colombes facility, created when Panhard cancelled a new model.

High postwar taxes severely limited French-market demand for cars with rated horsepower above 15 *cheveaux*, so the new GT would have to survive largely on export sales. What better way to assure that than by using foreign mechanical components? Daninos first tried putting a smooth new coupe body on the 4.3-liter Bentley chassis for the 1951 Paris Auto Show. This Facel-Bentley was well received, and six were ultimately built. But Bentley chassis weren't cheap, and Facel could make its own. Moreover, it was already producing attractive 2 + 2 hardtop bodies for the Ford France Comète/Monte Carlo. Why not a larger version with a few distinctive touches?

The result of all this was the first Facel Vega, introduced in July 1954. The chassis was a simple but rugged tubular affair with channel- and box-section reinforcements around the engine bay and rear axle. It's credited to Lance Macklin, a recent member of the HWM racing team with Stirling Moss and Mike Collins, and son of Sir Noel Macklin of Railton fame. M. Brasseur helped with the body styling but, as *The Autocar* noted, Daninos himself was "the project engineer, designer, and indeed the driving force behind the whole enterprise."

For power, Daninos selected what was technically the world's best V-8: the Chrysler Corporation hemi in its 276-cubic-inch DeSoto version, basically stock but rated at 180 horsepower for this application. It drove the rear wheels through either a French-made Pont-à-Mousson 4-speed manual or Chrysler automatic transmission (2-speed PowerFlite initially, 3-speed TorqueFlite after 1956). Suspension was conventional: independent with coil springs up front and a live axle on semi-elliptic leafs at the rear. Steering was cam-and-roller, the hypoid final drive came from Salisbury, and slotted steel or Robergel wire wheels ventilated 11-inch-diameter aluminum drum brakes all-round.

Intended as a big and brawny *routes nationale* cruiser, not a "turn-on-a-dime" sports car, the Vega was massively engineered and thus heavy (over 3700 pounds), but could easily exceed 100 mph. The cabin was rather undersized but lush, with leather trim and an impressive array of instruments and switches. A predictive feature was the fold-down rear seatbacks for interior access to the trunk, which had a regular external lid.

There was nothing regular about the Vega's workmanship—it was impeccable. Body panel fit was faultless, rust-resistant stainless steel was used for brightwork, and interior materials were of the highest quality. No wonder the price was a lofty $7000—about as much as a contemporary Rolls-Royce Silver Dawn—and that only 46 Vegas were built through 1955.

At least Daninos had the good sense to target California, land of the rich and famous, as his prime export market, choosing Charles Hornburg, the west coast Jaguar distributor, as his main dealer. Later, for the east coast, Daninos signed on import-car baron Max Hoffman, who'd continue to sell Facels through 1963.

Following adoption of a 291-cid engine, Daninos launched an improved Vega in 1956. Called FVS (for Facel Vega Sport), it carried an even larger, 330-cid Chrysler hemi with 325 bhp, and was distinguished (if that's the word) by an American-inspired wraparound windshield. Power steering and brakes were offered by 1957, and optional four-wheel disc brakes arrived for 1958, the model's last year, along with a 1.5-inch longer wheelbase and a 225-bhp 354-cid hemi. Alas, these cars suffered poor front-end geometry, which necessitated frequent wheel alignments and suspension overhauls after only 20,000 miles. But performance was terrific: as little as 9.5 seconds 0-60 mph and up to 134 mph all out.

The first-generation Facel Vega was unquestionably in the *grand routier* tradition, spiritual heir to the prewar greatness of Delage and Delahaye. It was also a commendably professional effort for a new manufacturer. In fact, Daninos not only sold all he could build (including 11 special convertibles) but actually made a modest profit, which set the stage for a more ambitious effort, the HK500.

SPECIFICATIONS

Engines: all Chrysler ohv V-8; **1954:** 276 cid/4528 cc, 180 bhp @ 4500 rpm, 255 lbs-ft @ 2000 rpm; **1955-56:** 291 cid/4768 cc, 250 bhp @ 4600 rpm, 255 lbs-ft @ 2000 rpm; **1957:** 330 cid/5407 cc, 255 bhp @ 4400 rpm; **1958:** 354 cid/5801 cc, 325 bhp @ 4600 rpm, 430 lbs-ft @ 2800 rpm

Transmissions:	Pont-à-Mousson 4-speed manual or Chrysler 2-speed PowerFlite (1954-56) or 3-speed TorqueFlite (1957-58) automatic
Suspension, front:	upper and lower A-arms, coil springs, anti-roll bar
Suspension, rear:	live axle on semi-elliptic leaf springs
Brakes:	front/rear drums, front/rear discs (1958)
Wheelbase (in.):	103.5 (1954-57), 105.0 (1958)
Weight (lbs):	3700-4100
Top speed (mph):	110-134
0-60 mph (sec):	9.5-10.5
Production:	**1954-55** 46 **1956-57** 227 **1958** 130

(Note: Some sources list 352 total, including 11 convertibles)

FVS succeeded Facel's original Vega. Styling predicted that of the forthcoming HK500. Swing-out rear quarter windows (**opposite top**) belied hardtop-look roof. Facel interiors (**above**) were typically lush, bright, and woody.

The HK500 continued on the 105-inch wheelbase of the last FVS, so accommodation remained more 2+2 than full four-seater. (One British scribe said it helped if you had *very* small friends for back-seat passengers.) Still, the new envelope was smarter and more contemporary. The FVS had been somewhat rounded, more Forties than Fifties, but the HK500 was crisper and more Detroit-inspired, right down to stacked quad headlamps and a fully wrapped windshield with "dogleg" A-pillars.

The HK500 also continued Facel's fondness for Chrysler V-8 power. Early examples carried the 325-horsepower, 354-cubic-inch hemi engine as in the '58 FVS, but this gave way within a year to the American firm's new 383-cid wedge-head unit, with two four-barrel Carter carburetors and a rated 360 bhp in this application. As the HK500 weighed little more than the FVS, the bigger motor gave truly formidable performance. Top speed was at least 140 mph, and the 0-60 mph sprint consumed less than 8.5 seconds. Fuel economy, though, was more dismal than ever: only about 14 mpg, a big drawback in Europe. Pont-à-Mousson 4-speed manual and Chrysler 3-speed TorqueFlite automatic were available as before. So were the Dunlop all-disc brakes, but Facel sensibly made them standard equipment from 1960 on, along with power steering.

Though faster, more stylish, and more roadworthy than its predecessor, the HK500 was still mainly a grand touring machine a comfortable, lavishly equipped high-speed cruiser of obvious quality. But it was only an interim measure as far as Facel was concerned, because Jean Daninos came up with something even faster and better-looking: the Facel II.

SPECIFICATIONS

Engine: Chrysler ohv V-8, 383 cid/6277 cc, 360 bhp (SAE) @ 5200 rpm, 398 lbs-ft @ 3600 rpm

Transmissions:	Pont-à-Mousson 4-speed manual or Chrysler 3-speed TorqueFlite automatic
Suspension, front:	upper and lower A-arms, coil springs, anti-roll bar
Suspension, rear:	live axle, semi-elliptic leaf springs
Brakes:	front/rear drums; front/rear discs standard from 1960
Wheelbase (in.):	105.0
Weight (lbs):	4035
Top speed (mph):	140
0-60 mph (sec):	8.4

Production: 490 (some sources list 439) incl. 1 special convertible

1959-1963
FACEL VEGA FACELLIA/
FACEL III/FACEL 6

Though Facel Vega was one of history's more successful "hybrid" marques, it went bust after a relatively short 10 years. The main reasons were an over-reliance on high-priced cars, lack of financial depth (which prevented correcting flaws), and stiff competition from thoroughbred marques like Aston, Porsche, and Ferrari. But the deciding factor was the Facellia, a smaller, less expensive car whose poor engine reliability and high resulting warranty claims literally cost Jean Daninos his shirt.

Launched in October 1959, less than a year after the HK500, the Facellia had a distinct Facel look, with the same sort of square central grille, flanking sub-grilles, and vertical head/parklamp clusters. In appearance, it forecast the later Facel II, leading some folks to confuse the two models, though the Facellia was not only smaller and less spacious but a lot slower. A tubular chassis, coil-spring/wishbone front suspension, live rear axle on semi-elliptic leaf springs, cam-and-roller steering, and Dunlop disc brakes were all familiar, though no components were shared with the V-8-powered senior Facels.

That naturally included the body, a new all-steel convertible style that was welded to the chassis on initial assembly. Seating was of the "2+1" variety, and a lift-off hardtop was offered as an optional alternative to the standard folding fabric roof. Dimensionally, the Facellia rode a nine-inch-shorter wheelbase than the HK500 and Facel II, had narrower 51.25-inch front and rear tracks, and weighed almost half as much.

The Facellia engine—and Daninos's ultimate downfall—was a new twincam 1647-cc four, specially designed by Britain's Westlake Engineering and finalized by ex-Talbot engineer Carlo Marchetti. Dual downdraft Solex carburetors were initially fitted, but double twin-choke Webers were also available from mid-1961. Compression ratio was 9.4:1, necessitating high-octane fuel, but the resulting 115 bhp was competitive with the latest Alfa Romeo and MG twincams. Both the engine and 4-speed gearbox (automatic wasn't offered this time) came from Pont-à-Mousson—curious, as the French concern had never built an engine before.

Daninos had conceived the Facellia to rival established small/medium roadsters like the Alfa Giulia, Triumph's TR, and the new MGB, planning to build 5000 a year once production hit full stride. Facel certainly had the facilities to compete in the volume sports-car market, as it had once supplied large numbers of bodies to other automakers. And the car itself was competitive: fast (as one example proved in officially observed speed runs), a decent handler, attractive, and civilized.

But for once, success eluded Daninos. Though the Facellia got an encouraging reception from the press, severe engine problems surfaced almost as soon as deliveries began. The main problem, piston burning, couldn't be traced right away, and it wasn't long before buyer interest evaporated. As with the MGA Twin Cam, which experienced similar traumas, the trouble was eventually diagnosed (poor block cooling), but by then it was too late. American buyers, still Daninos's chief target, didn't expect to have to heave to with wrenches or attend to major engine work every 40,000 miles. Moreover, parts and dealers were both scarce in the U.S., a situation that wreaked havoc with sales.

SPECIFICATIONS

Engines: **1959-62 Facellia:** dohc I-4, 100.5 cid/1647 cc, 115 bhp (SAE) @ 6400 rpm, torque NA; **1963 Facel III:** Volvo ohv I-4, 108 cid/1780 cc, 108 bhp @ 5000 rpm, torque NA; **1964 Facel 6:** BMC ohv I-6, 172 cid/2860 cc, 150 bhp @ 5250 rpm, torque NA

Transmission:	Pont-à-Mousson 4-speed manual
Suspension, front:	double wishbones, coil springs, anti-roll bar
Suspension, rear:	live axle, semi-elliptic leaf springs
Brakes:	front/rear discs
Wheelbase (in.):	96.5
Weight (lbs):	2465-2520
Top speed (mph):	100-120
0-60 mph (sec):	10.5-12.5
Production:	**Facellia** 500 **Facel III** 1500 **Facel 6** 26

As a result, only about 500 Facellias were called for and Facel's fortunes began sinking fast. By 1962, the firm had slipped into receivership.

But the following spring, the receivers attempted a comeback with the Volvo-powered Facel III, basically a Facellia with the Swedish firm's much more reliable 1.8-liter overhead-valve four. Some 1500 were sold, which kept Facel alive through the end of 1963.

Then hope for a rescue appeared as the SFERMA subsidiary of Sud-Aviation agreed to manage Facel for the following 12 months. The new guard briefly considered another derivative powered by an aluminum twincam Facel four with up to 200 bhp, but that only implied more of the problems that had plagued the Facellia. Ultimately, they settled on the BMC 3.0-liter ohv six as used in the Austin-Healey 3000, debored to 2.8 liters and 150 bhp to get under France's 15 *chaveaux* tax limit, for a mildly modified Facellia called Facel 6. But there was still no getting around the Facellia's poor reliability image, and just 26 were built.

By the end of 1964, Facel had negotiated in vain for use of the BMW 2.0-liter sohc six, and SFERMA had refused to continue managing the firm. Facel S.A. was quietly liquidated in early 1965, thus ending Jean Daninos's dream of a new French GT dynasty.

Facel Vega's only convertible was the neat "2 + 1" Facellia and its Facel III and Facel 6 evolutions. A coupe version was also offered. Styling mimicked that of the Facel II but on a smaller scale.

1962-1964
FACEL VEGA FACEL II

While the small Facellia was busy going nowhere, Jean Daninos treated his rugged "senior" chassis to a second restyle. The result, called Facel II, was too costly to generate the kind of sales that might have saved the company, but it was undeniably the best Facel of all.

Styling wasn't the new model's only attraction, just the most noticeable. Glassier and more angular in the contemporary idiom yet unmistakably Facel, it can still turn heads more than a quarter-century later. Compared with the HK500, the Facel II was a tad narrower and lower but rode the same 105-inch wheelbase, so it was just as much a 2+2 rather than a full four-seater.

Nevertheless, it *looked* wider thanks to a lower nose and grille, matched by more neatly integrated Marchal headlamps, still vertically stacked quads. In place of the old wrapped windshield and knee-banging A-posts were simply angled non-dogleg pillars and a taller windshield curved slightly at the top as well as at the sides. The rear window was similarly contoured, both front and rear glass more steeply raked, the roof flatter, C-pillars slimmer. All this gave the Facel II a much airier appearance than the HK500 despite retention of a fairly high beltline. Lower-body contours were squared up, especially at the rear, but deft use of chrome accents kept the car from looking "fat."

Beneath the new exterior was basically the same rolling chassis found on late-

model HK500s. The Chrysler 383 V-8 was now rated at 355 horsepower with optional TorqueFlite automatic transmission or a smashing 390 bhp with the standard Pont-à-Mousson 4-speed manual. Carburetion made the difference: one and two four-barrel Carter instruments, respectively. Standard disc brakes were also retained, as was power steering, still optional with manual transmission and standard on automatic cars.

With its new styling, the Facel II not only looked more aerodynamic than the HK500 but by all accounts *was*. And as curb weight was actually reduced by about 400 pounds, its performance was even more formidable. Curiously, 0-60 mph still took a fraction less than 8.5 seconds, but top speed was up to 150 mph, enough to rival the speediest Italian and British supercars of the day.

Unhappily, the Facel II was as much a victim of the Facellia debacle as Facel Vega itself, and only 184 (some sources quote 182) had been built by the time the firm was forced to close its doors in late 1964. Altogether, Facel completed only some 1270 of its Franco-American GTs in 10 years.

Richard M. Langworth, writing in *Collectible Automobile®* magazine, opined that "it's probably just as well that Facel died when it did. It's difficult to imagine what its cars would have been like in the age of emission controls and 5-mph bumpers. . . . As it stands, the Facel record isn't bad for a firm of its size."

Langworth then went on to quote writer Bernard Cahier, who provided this fitting epitaph: "[The Facel Vega was part of] that elite group of classic, high-powered touring machines which were immortalized in the prewar days by such as Duesenberg, the Talbot, and the Delahaye . . . Daninos created a car of which France could be proud, and much credit must be given to his efforts and persistence in creating such a superb machine."

We can put it more succinctly. A good work is its own reward, and the automotive world is that much better for Jean Daninos and his dream.

SPECIFICATIONS

Engine:	Chrysler ohv V-8, 383 cid/6277 cc, 355/390 bhp @ 4800/5400 rpm (automatic/manual transmission), torque NA
Transmissions:	Pont-à-Mousson 4-speed manual or Chrysler 3-speed TorqueFlite automatic
Suspension, front:	double wishbones, coil springs, anti-roll bar
Suspension, rear:	live axle, semi-elliptic leaf springs
Brakes:	front/rear discs
Wheelbase (in.):	105.0
Weight (lbs):	3640
Top speed (mph):	150
0-60 mph (sec):	8.3
Production:	184 (some sources list 180 and 182)

Arguably the prettiest of the big FVs, the Facel II still looks good today. Aircraft-style instruments and controls were a hallmark of these Franco-American GTs.

1947-1953 FERRARI 166

Enzo Ferrari made his mark in the Twenties as a team driver, then team manager, for Alfa Romeo, and in the Thirties as the driving force behind Scuderia Ferrari, an independent concern that built and raced modified Alfas. After World War II, he began moving toward dual-purpose sports-racing cars of his own design, assisted by the patronage of Enrico Nardi.

Ferrari had set up shop in Maranello, near Modena, but his facilities were small, so his early cars were produced in very limited numbers. In fact, they were virtually handcrafted customs. Just three Ferraris were built in all of 1947, followed by nine in 1948 and 30 in 1949. All were powered by a classic, small-displacement V-12 designed by Gioacchino Colombo in 1946.

The three 1947 cars were 1500-cc road racers designated Tipo (Type) 125. Two then received bored-out 1902-cc engines and were retagged Type 159. Their engines were enlarged again in 1948, to 1995 cc, to create the Type 166, the first of the true roadgoing Ferrari sports cars.

Until recently, Ferrari model numbers always reflected the rounded-off cubic-centimeter displacement of each cylinder (Type 166s had precisely 166.25 cc). Designations also included letters, which meant different things at different times. For example, the first cars carried the suffix "C" for *Corsa* (Italian for "race"), and they were indeed designed more for the track than the street. Later, Ferrari used "C" *(Competizione)* on his single-seat racers and substituted "I," for "Inter," on the sports-racing models. Just to confuse things, there was also a 166 Sport early on, though no more than two were likely built, both compact notchback coupes. The final member of the 166 family was the lovely Spyder Corsa, a cycle-fender two-seat open racer.

Serial numbers initially had three digits, with odd numbers for "street" machines and even ones for competition types. However, the dual-purpose nature of early Ferraris quickly rendered this distinction academic.

Appearing in 1947, the 166 made an auspicious competition debut in April 1948, when an open-body Sport driven by Clemente Biondetti won Sicily's gruelling Targa Florio road race. Biondetti won the Mille Miglia a month later with the same car carrying the Allemano coupe body more familiar today. It was the first of what would be eight outright Ferrari wins in the demanding Mille Miglia, and Enzo

commemorated it by using the "MM" designation on subsequent examples of this chassis.

Now widely termed the "Colombo engine," the 166 V-12 would, with further development, be a Ferrari mainstay until well into the Sixties. A 60-degree design, it employed a single chain-driven overhead camshaft on each cylinder bank to operate two inclined valves per cylinder via rocker arms and finger followers. Each valve was closed by two hairpin-type springs. Carburetion was by a single twin-choke Weber instrument on Inters and Sports, triple twin-choke Webers on MMs. Both fed through siamesed intake ports. Block, heads, and sump were cast of aluminum alloy, with cast-iron cylinder liners. The six-throw crankshaft ran in seven plain bearings, as did the conrods (although one car, the 1949 Le Mans-winning 166 MM, had needle bearings in the rod big-ends). The rods were split at 40 degrees to the centerline, which permitted removing both rod and piston through the top of the engine's small-bore cylinders.

Horsepower of the 166 engine has been variously quoted as between 110 and 150 bhp at 7500 rpm. This is explained not only by the two carburetion setups but different compression ratios, some high enough to permit running on alcohol fuel. Regardless, a single dry-plate clutch and 5-speed non-synchromesh transmission (later 166 MMs had synchronized third and fourth gears) carried power to a live rear axle.

The 166 also set a pattern for roadgoing Ferrari chassis that would persist for many years. Wheelbase varied with each model, but all 166s shared a tubular-steel ladder-type design with oval-section main tubes and round-section cross-tubes. Front suspension was independent via unequal-length A-arms and a transverse leaf spring, while the rear axle was located by a semi-elliptic leaf spring and a pair of parallel trailing arms on each side. Houdaille vane-type lever-action hydraulic shock absorbers were standardized after the first few cars built. Brakes comprised large-diameter aluminum drums with cast-iron liners and hydraulic actuation. Steering was by worm-and-peg. Reflecting Enzo's racing orientation, all 166s had right-hand drive.

Though the Sport was likely Enzo's first attempt at a road car, the 166 Inter was the first Ferrari to see serious production—if 37 units qualifies as "serious." Carrozzeria Touring seems to have supplied most 166 bodies of all types, but virtually every Italian coachbuilder of the day contributed a few. Among them were Allemano, Bertone, Ghia, Ghia-Aigle (a Swiss firm), Pinin Farina, Stabilmenti Farina (founded by Pinin's brother), and Alfredo Vignale.

Of all 166 body styles, the most famous and popular is Touring's Mille Miglia barchetta roadster. The nickname, which did not appear in Ferrari literature, means "little boat," and was prompted perhaps by the full-length bodyside crease suggesting a "waterline." It was this design that would be copied by Tojeiro of Britain for the AC Ace and its Shelby Cobra evolution (see entries).

The first barchetta was also the first Ferrari with a four-digit serial number (0002), again with even numbers for competition cars and odd numbers for road models. The barchetta style also appeared on the later 212 Export and 340 America chassis (see entries). Each was basically stretched from the 166 design, but had the same appealing lines and distinctive Ferrari identity.

SPECIFICATIONS

Engine: sohc V-12, 122 cid/1995 cc, 110-150 bhp @ 7500 rpm (depending on compression and carburetion), torque NA

Transmission:	5-speed non-synchromesh manual
Suspension, front:	unequal-length A-arms, transverse leaf spring
Suspension, rear:	live axle, parallel trailing arms, semi-elliptic leaf springs
Brakes:	front/rear drums
Wheelbase (in.):	86.6 (MM barchetta), 88.6 (MM coupe), 95.3 (Sport), 98.4-103.1 (Inter)
Weight (lbs):	2000 (average)
Top speed (mph):	99-140
0-60 mph (sec):	NA

Production: Inter (1948-53) 37 (some sources list 38) **MM** (1949-53) approx. 32 (incl. 12 closed models) **Sport** (1947-48) 2

*Many different body types graced Ferrari's first roadgoing chassis. Spyder Corsa (**opposite top**) was obviously for competition only. Touring's barchetta roadster (**below**) is the best-known 166 style, but the coachbuilder also produced a trim berlinetta (**opposite bottom**).*

1950-1953
FERRARI 195 AND 212

The pressure of competition both on and off the track had led Ferrari to enlarge his original Colombo V-12 to 1995 cc for the Type 166. The engine was bored out twice more in 1950—from 60 to 65 mm for a total capacity of 2341 cc, and to 68 mm for 2562 cc. Stroke remained at 58.8 mm.

Following Ferrari practice, the cars powered by these enlarged engines were designated Tipo 195 and 212, respectively. Both were offered in several versions, like the 166. The Inter, as before, was the sporty roadgoing model, while the 195 Sport and 212 Export were aimed squarely at competition duty.

Predictably, frame, suspension, steering, and brakes were inherited from the 166, while track dimensions were the same for all 195/212 models (49.8 inches front, 49.2 inches rear). Wheelbases were also in line with the 166. The 195 Sport rode the "short" 86.6-inch span, while the 212 Export's 88.6-inch measure was as for the 166 MM. Inter models in both new series had a still-longer 98.5-inch wheelbase.

Except for their increased bores, the 195 and 212 engines were almost identical with the 166 V-12. Inters had single twin-choke Weber carburetion, while Sport and Export got the triple twin-choke arrangement (reportedly adopted for 1953 212 Inters as well). Also carried over were a 5-speed transmission driving a live rear axle via a single dry-plate clutch. In fact, the 195 and 212 differed so little from the 166 mechanically that most chassis and engine components were apparently interchangeable.

None of this is really surprising. Ferrari was still a small concern whose primary business was competition, so "production" models in these early years were built largely to special order for a discerning, monied clientele.

Thus, Ferrari continued to offer a wide variety of bodies on the new 195 and 212 chassis, with Touring, Ghia, Ghia-Aigle, Pinin Farina, and Alfredo Vignale doing most of the honors. The last two *carrozzeria* had become Ferrari's primary body suppliers by now. Unlike the 166, there was an attempt at "standardizing" 195/212 production around just two body types, coupe (commonly called *berlinetta*, literally "little sedan") and convertible coupe. Even so, there were again many variations in both detail appearance and overall shape. Right-hand steering was used exclusively until 1952, when a left-hand-drive Ghia coupe and Pinin Farina convertible were previewed at the Paris Salon. Later Vignale and Farina styles sported one-piece curved windshields. Touring retained two-piece vee'd windshields, though a curved screen appeared on one of its last berlinettas, whose styling was otherwise dated.

Good though it was, the 195 was overshadowed from the start by the bigger-engine 212 and the even more potent 340 America, which arrived in 1951 (see entry). Buyers opted for the more powerful cars since all three types cost about the same (around $9500). It didn't take Ferrari long to realize he had one too many entries for such a limited market, so the 195 disappeared after just one year and no more than 25 units. A few racing victories might have prevented this early demise, but the 195 had to compete in the same class as the 212, and was thus handily *out*classed.

No such problem for the 212, which enjoyed almost immediate competition success. In Europe alone, Pagnibon and Barraquet drove to victory in the inaugural Tour de France (the car was later sold to American world driving champ Phil Hill), Vittorio Marzotto and Piero Taruffi ran 1-2 in the Tour of Sicily, Luigi Villoresi won the Coppa Inter-Europa and Piero Scotti came home third in the Mille Miglia—all in 1951. That same year, Taruffi paired with Luigi Chinetti and Villoresi with Alberto Ascari to place first and second in the fabled *Carrera Panamericana* (Mexican Road Race).

There's little point in detailed comparisons among the 166, 195, and 212 because they're all so similar aside from bodywork. Moreover, Enzo Ferrari wanted to "win the race" outright, as did his customers, which is why everyone went for the biggest and fastest. In the end, even the 212, which was built through 1953 alongside the 166 MM, was overshadowed by the 340 and the upcoming 250 MM.

Interestingly, most 166, 195, and 212 production seemed to find its way to the United States, where privateers could usually count on winning their class and, quite often, an overall victory too. Though Ferrari would continue with improvements, the 166, 195, and 212 had set a pattern for his touring and sports-racing cars, which would not see fundamental chassis and engine changes until well into the Sixties.

SPECIFICATIONS

Engines: all sohc V-12; **195** (1951): 142.8 cid/2341 cc, 130 bhp @ 6000 rpm (Inter), 160-180 bhp @ 6000 rpm (Sport); **212** (1951-53): 156.3 cid/2562 cc, 130 bhp @ 6000 rpm (Inter), 150-170 bhp @ 6500 rpm (Export); torque figures NA

Transmission:	5-speed manual
Suspension, front:	unequal-length A-arms, transverse leaf spring
Suspension, rear:	live axle, parallel trailing arms, semi-elliptic leaf springs
Brakes:	front/rear drums
Wheelbase (in.):	86.6 (195 Sport), 88.6 (212 Export), 98.5 (Inter)
Weight (lbs):	2100 (approx. average)
Top speed (mph):	110 (195), 120 (212)
0-60 mph (sec):	NA

Production: 195 25 (some sources list 24) **212 Export** 24-26 **212 Inter** approx. 80

Even roadgoing Ferraris had racing-inspired righthand steering through 1952. **Top and opposite:** *This Touring Mille Miglia berlinetta style began with 166 series, continued on the 195 Sport chassis.* **Above:** *Two views of a Vignale-bodied 212 Export. Both were ostensibly competition models, but many were used on the road.*

1950-1955 FERRARI 340/342/375 AMERICA

For most automakers, "racing improves the breed" has usually been more brag than fact. Not at Ferrari. *Auto Avio Costruzioni*, the Ferrari organization's official name in the early Fifties, believed so much in the truth of that old saw that it sold its newest racing cars to private competitors, who not only ran against the factory team but often beat it.

A larger engine was one of the first competition spin-offs to benefit Ferrari road cars. Designed by Aurelio Lampredi, it was conceived around the prevailing Grand Prix formula, which limited displacement to 1500 cc supercharged or 4.5 liters unsupercharged. Enzo had tried the former, but decided that the bigger, normally aspirated engines worked much better.

Lampredi's design followed the earlier Colombo engine in having two banks of six cylinders arrayed in a narrow vee, with a single overhead camshaft per bank and two inclined valves per cylinder with hairpin-type springs. Beyond this, though, the differences were considerable. Bore-center spacing was spread from 90 to 108 mm to allow for greater displacement, roller cam followers were used instead of the Colombo's plain finger-type, intake ports were separate instead of siamesed, and cylinder barrels screwed into the head rather than being pressed into the block. With all this, the Lampredi block ended up 5.1 inches longer than the Colombo's—42.1 inches in all—thus making it the so-called "long-block" Ferrari twelve.

The Lampredi engine first appeared as a 3.3-liter unit in the 1950 Mille Miglia mounts of Luigi Villoresi and Alberto Ascari. The latter's engine was punched out to 4.1 liters by the Swiss Grand Prix in July, and displacement was bumped to the intended 4.5 liters in time for the Italian GP at Monza in September.

Just a month later, a new roadgoing Ferrari called 340 America, powered by the 4.1-liter version, was shown at the Paris Salon. Adorned with open Touring bodywork in the style of the original 166 barchetta, it was described in factory literature as having total displacement of 4101.68 cc from a bore and stroke of 80 × 68 mm. Power was declared as 220 bhp at 6000 rpm with three twin-choke Weber carburetors and 8.0:1 compression. A single-disc clutch transferred power through a 5-speed gearbox, while the rest of the chassis was simply a scaled-up rendition of the now-familiar Ferrari platform. Apropos of its name, several of the barchetta-bodied 340 Americas were sold to Americans: Bill Spear, Jack Kimberly, and Henry Manney (the last subsequently sold his car to John Edgar to be raced by Jack McAfee).

An improved chassis quickly followed, displayed at the Brussels show in January 1951 as the 342 America. Intended strictly for off-track grand touring, it featured a new fully synchronized 4-speed transmission, a much heavier rear-axle center section, and wider tracks. A complete car wasn't seen until the Turin show that spring, but was distinguished by its left-hand drive—an "America" model for America.

The roadgoing 340 was short-lived, as the 342 went into production for model year 1952 to replace it. However, both types were built concurrently for competition, the type of race determining which would be run. Production was extremely limited in either case, and both types gave way to the 375 America in 1953.

The 375 was essentially a big-engine version of the Colombo-powered 110-inch-wheelbase 250 Europa (see entry), identical in all respects save displacement and output. Again Ferrari aimed at Americans, who he believed would want—and could better afford—the big engine's extra performance. The 250 was intended for Europeans, who had to contend with high-priced fuel and high taxes on large-displacement engines. But Europeans who could afford a Ferrari in the first place could also afford these costs, and they wanted the extra power too: 300 bhp at 6300 rpm for the touring cars, 340 bhp at 7000 rpm for the competition models.

There was also a sports-racing derivative on a 102.3-inch wheelbase, the 375 Mille Miglia. Available in roadster and berlinetta styles by Pinin Farina, it was the fastest "roadgoing" Ferrari yet. An even hotter version, a factory-team racing roadster called 375 Plus, arrived in 1954 with 4954.34 cc and 344 bhp at 6500 rpm. It promptly won that year's Le Mans 24 Hours and the *Carrera Panamericana*.

Bodies for all these Lampredi-engine Ferraris came from the usual sources, including Touring, Ghia, and Vignale. (The last was notable for the distinctive long-hood/short-deck berlinetta designed for *Carrera* purposes by Giovanni Michelotti, and thus known as 340 Mexico). But Pinin Farina was increasingly on the scene, and would soon become Ferrari's *carrozzeria* of choice.

SPECIFICATIONS

Engines: all sohc V-12; **340** (1951): 250 cid/4101.6 cc, 280 bhp @ 6600 rpm; **342** (1952-53): 250 cid/4101.6 cc, 200 bhp @ 5000 rpm; **375** (1953-55): 300 bhp @ 6300 rpm; torque figures NA

Transmissions:	5-speed non-synchromesh manual (340), 4-speed all-synchromesh manual (342/375)
Suspension, front:	unequal-length A-arms, transverse leaf spring
Suspension, rear:	live axle, parallel trailing arms, semi-elliptic leaf springs
Brakes:	front/rear drums
Wheelbase (in.):	95.3 (340), 104.3 (342), 110.2 (375)
Weight (lbs):	1980 (340), 2640 (342), 2530 (375)
Top speed (mph):	120-140
0-60 mph (sec):	NA
Production:	**340** 22 **342** 6 **375** 13 (some sources list 12)

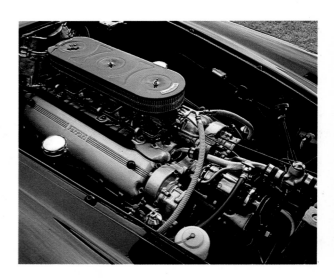

Opposite: Pinin Farina built this one-off convertible on the 375 America chassis (number 0488 AM) for the King of Belgium in late 1954. **Above:** Any Ferrari engine is a feast for the eyes. Here, the so-called long-block Lampredi V-12 of the 375.

1953-1954 FERRARI 250 EUROPA

October 1953 saw the seven-year-old Ferrari organization take a big step. On its stand at that month's Paris Auto Show were two new models: the 250 Europa and 375 America. Built on a 110.2-inch wheelbase, they were not only the largest Ferraris yet but Enzo's most serious attempt at a roadgoing production GT thus far.

As noted (see *340/342/375 America*), the Europa used the 375's chassis but carried a smaller, 2963-cc version of the Lampredi-designed V-12. This and the choice of model names clearly indicated Enzo's desire to satisfy the requirements of two different markets. European car buyers faced stiff purchase taxes based on engine size, plus high-priced fuel, hence the thriftier, small-displacement version. The big-inch model was intended solely for the U.S., where gas was much cheaper and car-purchase taxes nonexistent.

Still, only 17 Europas and 13 Americas were built, starting at around serial number 0295 EU and ending with 0355 AL. As road cars, all had odd serial numbers in keeping with Ferrari practice (even numbers were reserved for competition types). "EU" obviously denoted a Europa, while "AL" stood for America *Lungo* (long wheelbase).

Of the 30, five had Vignale bodies (four coupes, one cabriolet), one was a Ghia coupe, and the rest were dressed by Pinin Farina (22 coupes, one cabrio and one "special"). Two of PF's Europa coupes had right-hand drive, and all of its closed bodies in both the Europa and America series were of 2+2 configuration. Cabriolets and Vignale coupes were strictly two-seaters.

The Farina-bodied Europas are notable as some of the smoothest and least cluttered cars ever seen from this designer, being almost *too* simple in decoration and surface development. Vignale's efforts, on the other hand, seemed to imply a desire to entertain the viewer with every possible form and fillip. They were chiefly the work of Giovanni Michelotti, who would continue to turn out coachwork both beautiful and bizarre.

Because of its precisely "square" cylinder dimensions (bore and stroke: 68 x 68 mm), the Europa V-12 is a rarity among Ferrari engines. Depending on which brochure you read, horsepower was either 200 or 220. Top speed depended more on final-drive ratio; three were available, giving maximum velocities of 115 to 135 mph.

Though it lasted barely a year, the 250 Europa is significant for solidifying Ferrari's reputation as a builder of sophisticated, exotic road cars. As a step beyond the "race-and-ride" concept, it was deliberately larger and lusher than previous models, aimed at more affluent folk who'd always dismissed Ferraris as too high-strung for the road—"racing" machines that were too noisy, uncomfortable, and impractical for everyday use. Unfortunately, the Europa's extra bulk made it almost "American," which wasn't what the typical Ferrari buyer wanted.

Still, some nine Americas and an equal number of Europas survive in the U.S. today and another Europa lives in Canada, so maybe Enzo had the right approach to the North American market. In fact, because of their bulk and rather ponderous handling (for Ferraris), these long-wheelbase models are much more at home in the wide-open spaces Stateside than they'd ever be on the narrow, crowded roads of Europe. And with the high-torque engines and all-synchro transmission, they're fairly easy to drive.

Which is only right. After all, not every Ferrari owner is a Carroll Shelby.

Though not a 250 Europa, this 250 GT Europa displays similar Farina couple styling on that shorter Ferrari chassis. The reduced wheelbase stemmed in part from use of the short-block Colombo V-12 versus the long-block Lampredi engine in earlier 250 Europas.

SPECIFICATIONS

Engine:	sohc V-12, 181 cid/2963 cc, 200 bhp @ 7000 rpm, torque NA
Transmission:	4-speed all-synchromesh manual
Suspension, front:	unequal-length A-arms, transverse leaf spring
Suspension, rear:	live axle, parallel trailing arms, semi-elliptic leaf springs
Brakes:	front/rear drums
Wheelbase (in.):	110.2
Weight (lbs):	2560 (approx. average)
Top speed (mph):	115-130
0-60 mph (sec):	NA
Production:	17 (some sources list 21)

1954-1962 FERRARI 250 GT LONG-WHEELBASE

Early Ferraris were typical of low-volume cars in that there was little apparent consistency among them. In any one year of the early Fifties, Ferrari offerings spanned a variety of wheelbases, engines, and coachbuilt bodies, yet all had a certain commonality in chassis and running gear.

In late 1954, Enzo Ferrari began to bring some order to this model chaos with the 250 GT Europa, generally regarded as his first true production car. Though it retained the familiar ladder-type tubular-steel chassis with leaf-spring rear suspension, it broke new ground with a thoroughly modern independent front suspension, via double A-arms and coil springs. Also new was a 3.0-liter version of the Colombo V-12 (basically, a roadgoing version of the 1953 250 MM competition engine) versus the similarly sized "long-block" Lampredi unit of the previous 250 Europa. (The "GT" suffix was no doubt added to avoid confusion.) At 102.3 inches, the wheelbase was 6.7 inches shorter than the earlier model's. Pinin Farina now moved to the fore, supplying most bodies for the new series, though Vignale contributed some. Virtually all were closed coupes with fastback and semi-fastback rooflines.

Though no one knew it at the time, this new Europa would be the first in a long line of 250 GTs that would stretch into the middle of the next decade. And as Ferrari's newest had been greeted with enthusiasm, spin-offs were not long in coming.

The first was a handsome Farina berlinetta, bowing at the Paris Show in late 1955. An even nicer-looking evolution appeared at Geneva the following March, and joined the line later in '56. Body production was taken over by Scaglietti in Modena the following year.

By that time, the berlinetta had been approved by the FIA—the *Federation Internationale Automobile,* the world motorsports governing body—as a production Grand Touring car. With its lightweight aluminum bodywork, it certainly looked ready to race, and did. Competition versions racked up numerous wins and high finishes in 1956, including a memorable third overall in the Tour de France, and in

'57, when Olivier Gendebien came home third in the Mille Miglia. But it was a string of victories in the French road race that has since earned this model the name "Tour de France."

Meanwhile, a smart PF notchback coupe, another 1956 announcement, had gone into production at Carrozzeria Boano (and is thus known today as the "Boano coupe"). By 1958, founder Mario Boano was working for Fiat and his company was in the hands of Luciano Pollo and Ezio Ellena. But the new owners continued production after raising the roofline and making other modifications. The result was what's now called the "Ellena" or "high-roof" 250 GT coupe.

Geneva 1957 saw a one-off Farina touring cabriolet on the 250 GT chassis. It went into production later that year, thankfully without the show car's notched doors. Partly at the instigation of west coast Ferrari distributor John von Neumann, Farina came up with an even sportier version, an open counterpart to the competition berlinetta. Named Spyder California, it was built by Scaglietti on the same "production line" through early 1960.

Next came a replacement for the Boano/Ellena coupe, shown at the 1958 Paris Salon in October. Another Farina creation and long known as simply "PF coupe," it would continue through 1960. It was a handsome car, though almost plain compared with other Farina designs of the period. Some ruder individuals have even dubbed it the "Italian Thunderbird." Appearing at the same time was a Series II cabriolet with revised coupe-inspired styling. It, too, would be built by Farina, but through 1962.

With the advent of a short-wheelbase series in 1959, these 250 GTs have since come to be called the "long-wheelbase" models, though their 102.3-inch span wasn't the longest in Ferrari history. More significant are the engineering changes that occurred during their production run. Ferrari's first fresh-air heating system arrived in 1959, along with a twin-disc clutch to replace the single dry-plate type. The following year brought tubular telescopic shock absorbers (ousting lever-action hydraulics), disc brakes to replace the 14-inch-diameter drums (which worked pretty well when warm but were usually dodgy when cold), and overdrive for the all-synchro 4-speed gearbox.

No doubt about it: Ferrari had come a long way in a relatively short time. Thanks to its fruitful, well publicized competition efforts and a series of rapidly improving road cars, the marque had, by the dawn of the Sixties, become world famous for exciting, elegant high-performance cars of unsurpassed engineering excellence. Such stature would have seemed almost impossible when the 250 GT first appeared, but Enzo Ferrari was far from ready to rest on his laurels. Even better days were just ahead.

SPECIFICATIONS

Engine: sohc V-12, 180 cid/2953 cc, 220-260 bhp @ 7000 rpm, torque NA

Transmission:	4-speed manual (with overdrive from 1960)
Suspension, front:	upper and lower A-arms, coil springs
Suspension, rear:	live axle, parallel trailing arms, semi-elliptic leaf springs
Brakes:	front/rear drums, front/rear discs from 1959
Wheelbase (in.):	102.3
Weight (lbs):	2100-2815
Top speed (mph):	124-155
0-60 mph (sec):	7.0-8.0

Production: Europa (1954-55) 36 **Berlinetta/Tour de France** (1956-59) 92 (including 7 "interim" 1959 berlinettas) **Boano** (1956-57) 80 **Ellena** (1957-58) 50 **Series I Cabriolet** (1957-59) 40 (including prototypes) **PF Coupe** (1958-60) 350 **Series II Cabriolet** (1959-62) 210 **Spyder California** (1958-62) 47

Pinin Farina crafted this one-off cabriolet on the 250 GT long-wheelbase chassis for Turin 1957. Lines are similar to those of the concurrent Series I cabrio apart from a shapelier snout and door ventwings.

1956-1959 FERRARI 410 SUPERAMERICA

When Enzo Ferrari phased out the 375 America (see entry), he wasn't abandoning the top end of his market. He simply had a better car for it: bigger, beefier, more powerful. Logically, he called it Superamerica—and super it was.

The 410 Superamerica was first shown as a chassis at the Paris Salon in September 1955. Aside from more obvious robustness, its engineering differed little from previous Ferrari practice. Thus, it was a sturdy ladder-type affair comprising oval-section main tubes and round cross-tubes, with the new A-arm/coil-spring front suspension (as seen on the previous year's new 250 GT Europa) and the usual live-axle rear end with trailing arms and leaf springs. As on the 375, wheelbase was 110.2 inches.

Also retained was the Lampredi "long-block" V-12, but the change in type number signified greater displacement. Sure enough, bore was stretched 4 mm, to 86 mm, giving 4962 cc on an unchanged 68-mm stroke. Compression was 8.5:1, one of the lowest yet seen from Ferrari. Nevertheless, factory literature pegged output at a quite healthy 340 horsepower at 6000 rpm. As before, power was taken through a multi-disc clutch and 4-speed gearbox. With a choice of several axle ratios ranging from 3.11 to 3.66:1, claimed top speed ran from 137 to nearly 162 mph.

The first complete Superamerica, clothed in a handsome coupe body by Pinin Farina, starred at the Brussels Salon in January 1956. Though visually much like PF's contemporary Boano/Ellena design on the junior chassis, it offered a little more room and luxury to help justify a considerably higher price. At that year's New York Auto Show, the 250 GT was listed at a lofty $12,800, the Superamerica at an even more stratospheric $16,800. By contrast, Detroit's costliest car that season was the new Continental Mark II, which seemed sufficiently unattainable itself at just under $10,000.

All of which helps explain why only 15 of these Series I SAs were built. Nine were "standard" coupes similar to the Brussels show car. Specials included a finny Ghia-bodied coupe *a la* Chrysler's Virgil Exner, and a coupe and cabriolet with less pretentious Boano coachwork.

An even more spectacular Superamerica appeared at Paris 1956, Farina's new "Superfast" design. A futuristic fastback, it bore a tapered snout, headlamps recessed behind clear plastic covers, and trendy tailfins as wild as any Exner could conceive. Wheelbase was closed up by a full eight inches to 102.3, as on the 250 GT.

The one-off Superfast began a Series II Superamerica. Just eight "standard" Farina-bodied cars were built, all with mild styling updates, plus two specials. Scaglietti did one, a rather tasteless coupe with two-tone paint and too much chrome. The other was a new Farina coupe that he called 4.9 Superfast but is now better known as Superfast II. It was similar to "Superfast I" (the '56 Paris show car) but lacked the fins.

Paris 1958 marked the start of the SA Series III, distinguished by several running-gear changes. Spark plugs moved from inside the engine vee to outboard of the heads (as on the racing 250 Testa Rossa) and compression was raised to 9.0:1, bumping maximum horsepower to 360 at 7000 rpm. The diameter of the all-drum brakes was increased to match those of Ferrari's latest sports-racers, and the gearbox received a normal H-pattern gate, with first at the upper left and fourth at bottom right. (Earlier SAs had a "mirror-image" layout with first at the top right and fourth at the lower left.)

The Series III also looked considerably different, vaguely like Superfast I but more practical. Headlamp covers curved more to match revised front fenderlines, though the last four or five cars were built with exposed lamps. The Series III prototype had an airy, thin-pillar greenhouse with large rear quarter windows, but the latter were exchanged in production (which began in early '59) for louvered metal panels as on Superfast II, so outward vision still left something to be desired.

Not counting specials, it appears that 410 production amounted to 15 Series I cars, eight Series II, and about 15 Series III. Approximately 20 of the total 38 reside in the U.S. at this writing.

SPECIFICATIONS

Engine: sohc V-12, 302.7 cid/4962 cc, 340 bhp @ 6000 rpm (1957), 360 bhp @ 7000 rpm (1958-59); torque NA

Transmission:	4-speed manual
Suspension, front:	unequal-length A-arms, coil springs
Suspension, rear:	live axle, parallel trailing arms, semi-elliptic leaf springs
Brakes:	front/rear drums
Wheelbase (in.):	110.2 (1957), 102.3 (1958-59)
Weight (lbs):	2400-2500
Top speed (mph):	135-155 +
0-60 mph (sec):	NA

Production: Series I (1957) 15 **Series II** (1958) 8 **Series III** (1959) 15

Top and above: Most 1956-57 410 Superamericas wore this Pinin Farina coupe body style with unusual center-mount speedo and tach. Opposite: Appearance evolved into this more rounded form for 1958-59, again by Farina. Nose shaping derived from 410-based '56 Superfast show car.

1959-1964 FERRARI 250 GT SHORT-WHEELBASE

Having reaped great rewards with the roadgoing 250 GT, Ferrari decided to expand on it by contracting it. Thus, the Paris Salon in October 1959 brought a new short-chassis cousin to the so-called "interim" 250 GT berlinetta introduced earlier that year. Designed by Pinin Farina and built by Scaglietti, both were "race-and-ride" two-seaters with the same new rounded contours and tautly drawn body lines. But with 5.7 fewer inches between wheel centers, the shortie looked more integrated and even more aggressive.

Now generally known as the 250 GT SWB (short wheelbase), this tighter, lighter car was even better suited for racing. This explains why even the standard steel bodies employed aluminum for doors, hood, and trunklid. Some all-aluminum bodies were also built for the serious competitor. Still, all SWBs bore odd serial numbers, designating a "touring" Ferrari.

Like LWB 250 GTs, the new SWB used the Colombo-designed V-12, albeit newly modified with spark plugs relocated to the outside of the heads, plus coil instead of hairpin-type valve springs. Though minor, these and other changes added 20 horsepower for a total of 280 bhp at 7000 rpm. Adding to the competitive character of this more compact berlinetta was a choice of six axle ratios: from a relatively long-striding 3.44:1 to the proverbial 4.57:1 stump-puller.

By this time, Ferrari seemed to "own" the Tour de France. It won the gruelling race around the perimeter of France in 1951 and finished runner-up in 1952-53, then swept home 1-2-3 in each year from 1956 to 1960 and took the first *four* places in 1961—an unprecedented showing achieved entirely with both long- and short-wheelbase 250 GT berlinettas.

Perhaps inevitably, the new SWB coupe prompted a companion Spyder California.

It appeared in 1960 to replace the previous long-chassis Spyder, which it closely resembled. (By contrast, the SWB berlinetta bore little resemblance to its long-wheelbase predecessors.) Though production ran from May of that year through February 1963, only 57 were built, again by Scaglietti.

Visual differences between the long- and short-wheelbase Spyders are minimal but worth noting. Front-fender air outlets had three vertical bars on the former, two on the latter, though a few of each model had no outlets at all. SWB Spyders had a horizontal ridge or "shelf" connecting the taillights just below the trunklid; LWBs didn't. Both models sported vertically sited headlamps nestled in scooped-out front fenders, with clear plastic covers conforming to fender shape.

The Spyder California was advertised as a car that could be "driven in normal daily use, or raced." Not surprisingly for Ferraris, a few long- and short-chassis examples enjoyed moderate success on the track. But most Spyders were bought by image-conscious types who liked the aura of a semi-competition machine. For them, racing the car was less important than the fact that they *could* race it if they wanted to.

The final member of the roadgoing 250 GT clan appeared in late 1962, again at the Paris Show, to succeed the SWB berlinetta. Pininfarina (both the man and his company had changed their name to one word the previous year) and Ferrari presented it as the 250 GT/L, but it's now generally known as the Berlinetta Lusso (for "luxury")—and widely regarded as one of the loveliest cars ever created. Its frontal styling recalled that of the SWB, and the smartly chopped Kamm-style tail echoed that of the fabulous 250 GTO competition coupe, but the flowing fastback shape and thin-pillar roofline were new—and timeless. More than 25 years later, the Lusso still draws envious, enthusiastic glances.

Body construction was again entrusted to Scaglietti, virtually a Ferrari subsidiary by now. As with the roadgoing SWB coupe, the Lusso's hood, doors, and trunklid were aluminum, the rest of the structure, steel. Interior design also departed from past Ferrari practice, with a large speedometer and tachometer mounted in the center of the dash and five auxiliary gauges placed directly ahead of the steering wheel.

The Lusso provided a beautiful and memorable conclusion to the 250 GT series, whose total production over 10 years came to some 2500 units, including prototypes and competition models. And that's remarkable, considering that all were high-priced, high-performance thoroughbreds.

They still are, of course, which is why most 250s command six-figure prices. If not always easy to recognize, excellence is invariably coveted and thus never cheap.

SPECIFICATIONS

Engine: sohc V-12, 180 cid/2953 cc, 280 bhp @ 7000 rpm, torque NA

Transmission:	4-speed manual
Suspension, front:	upper and lower A-arms, coil springs
Suspension, rear:	live axle, parallel trailing arms, semi-elliptic leaf springs
Brakes:	front/rear discs
Wheelbase (in.):	94.5
Weight (lbs):	2100-2815
Top speed (mph):	140-150
0-60 mph (sec):	est. 6.5-7.0

Production: Berlinetta 175 Spyder California 57 Berlinetta Lusso 350

Though the dual-purpose 250 GTO has become the most collectible Ferrari, the beautiful Berlinetta Lusso can't be far behind. Farina never really repeated this form and detailing on any other car.

1960-1964 FERRARI 400 SUPERAMERICA

Carmakers do strange things sometimes, even maestros like Enzo Ferrari and Pinin Farina. How else to explain their main attraction at the 1959 Turin show? Apparently the first in a new 400 Superamerica series, it bore a plain, boxy body with a wrapped windshield and an almost square grille flanked by quad headlamps— almost a parody of contemporary American styling. Surely, *this* couldn't be Ferrari's future.

Happily, it wasn't, for the *real* 400 appeared at Brussels in January 1960 as a more conventional, Farina-designed cabriolet. Though mechanically much the same as the superseded 410, it sported a number of interesting changes. It also introduced new nomenclature. Up through the 410 (and continuing with the 250 GTs and the forthcoming 275/330 series), Ferrari model numbers had always represented the cubic-centimeter displacement of each engine cylinder (rounded off, of course). Thus, the 250 GT's total capacity was 3000 cc, that of the 410 engine (which actually had about 413 cc per cylinder) almost 5000 cc. Starting with the 400, the number indicated total displacement in deciliters (in cc's here, 4000).

*The Ferrari 400 Superamerica (**below and right**) superceded the mechanically similar 410, and was fitted with Dunlop four-wheel disc brakes. Body revisions made in 1961-62 resulted in the* Coupe Aerodinamico, *a Pininfarina design that was wind tunnel-inspired and adopted for subsequent 400s.*

More substantive was a new development of the 1947-vintage Colombo V-12, replacing the long-block Lampredi engine that Ferrari now abandoned. As in its other recent applications, spark plugs were mounted outboard of the vee, coil valve springs replaced hairpin-type, and cylinder heads were removable. On 9.8:1 compression, horsepower was an alleged 400 at 6750 rpm, which seems optimistic in view of the fact that the last 410 engine, almost a liter larger, had the same rating. A compression drop to 8.8:1 left later 400s with 340 bhp at 7000 rpm.

Like its contemporary linemates, the 400 received a single dry-plate clutch (replacing the old multi-disc unit) and standard Laycock de Normanville electric overdrive (from Britain) behind a 4-speed all-synchromesh gearbox. Wheelbase shrunk from 102.3 to 95.2 inches (ending up fractionally longer than that of SWB 250 GTs), Koni telescopic shocks replaced lever-action hydraulics, and modern Dunlop disc brakes ousted aluminum drums all-round.

Once again, production of the "senior" Ferrari was extremely limited. Just six 400 SAs were built in 1960, all cabrios with only minor detail differences. An American-style lift-off steel top was offered, and several of these cars were so equipped. There was also one *speciale* on this chassis, a cabriolet with covered headlights as on the Spyder Californias.

But the 400 was far from finished. The next development for this chassis was inspired by a 1960 Turin showpiece called "Superfast II" (not to be confused with the earlier 410 design of the same name). Pininfarina claimed he'd created it with the aid of a wind tunnel, and it showed. The fastback body reminded some observers of an airplane wing: markedly tapered at each end, with retractable headlamps and half-skirted rear wheels. During the winter of 1961-62, a hood scoop was added, the fender skirts removed, and the headlamps exposed behind clear plastic lenses. Called PF *Coupe Aerodinamico* (no translation needed there), this revised body was adopted for all subsequent 400s.

SPECIFICATIONS

Engines: sohc V-12, 242 cid/3967 cc, 400 bhp @ 6750 rpm, later 340 bhp @ 7000 rpm, torque NA

Transmission:	4-speed manual with overdrive
Suspension, front:	unequal-length A-arms, coil springs
Suspension, rear:	live axle, parallel trailing arms, semi-elliptic leaf springs
Brakes:	front/rear discs
Wheelbase (in.):	95.2 (Series I), 102.3 (Series II)
Weight (lbs):	2860
Top speed (mph):	140-160 +
0-60 mph (sec):	NA

Production: cabrio (1960) 6 **"Series I" coupe** (1961-62) 29 **Series II coupe** (1963-64) 19

1964-1967 FERRARI 500 SUPERFAST

Following on the heels of the 1960 Turin show car, the Superfast II (based on the Ferrari 400 Superamerica—see entry), Pininfarina conjured up a *new* Superamerica-based show car, which was seen at the 1962 Geneva Salon in March: the Superfast III. Its main distinctions compared with the "II" were slimmer roof pillars, a new thermostatically controlled radiator cover, and a return to hidden headlamps and partly skirted rear wheels. It was soon followed by Superfast IV, with the same general appearance apart from four exposed headlamps that looked uncomfortable on the ground-sniffing snout. This car, which never appeared at an auto show, was later sold in the United States.

At the end of 1962, the production Superamerica had landed on a long-wheelbase chassis (102.3 inches) and lost its hood scoop for a bulge over the carburetors. This Series II model then stepped aside for the 500 Superfast, which bowed at Geneva in March 1964.

Still a two-seater, it rode an even lengthier chassis (104.3-inch wheelbase) and weighed in about 350 pounds heavier. Though the production Superfast, the final development of the earlier America/Superamerica series, looked much like the last edition of the 400, it sported open headlights and a squared-off tail that gave it a Kamm-style look. As before, the custom-crafted bodywork was executed by Pininfarina.

The Superfast's engine, the largest of Ferrari's then-current single cam V-12s, was unique, with a long block like the Lampredi unit but removable cylinder heads like the Colombo. In fact, the big V-12 was more closely related to the latter than the former. It featured pressed-in cylinder liners. Bore and stroke returned to 410 Superamerica dimensions (88 × 68 mm), so the "500" signified near 5.0 liters displacement (precisely 4961.57 cc). Equipped with three Weber 40 DCZ/6 carburetors and running a compression ratio of 8.8:1, output was rated at a very healthy 400 horsepower at 6500 rpm. The Superfast continued the Dunlop four-wheel disc brakes introduced on the 400, but utilized larger 205-15 tires mounted on Borrani wire wheels. Suspension consisted of unequal-length A-arms and coil springs up front and semi-elliptic leaf springs located by parallel trailing arms at the rear.

Described by some as a "luxury limousine," the 500 would last through two series built over three years. Series I, with a production rate of about one unit per month, retained the 4-speed plus Laycock de Normanville overdrive transmission. It was continued through mid-1966 and about 25 examples were built.

Then the Series II appeared, with a genuine 5-speed gearbox, new engine mounts, and suspended pedals. Externally, the body was the same, but the front-fender panels sported three air outlets per side instead of the 11 small louvers used previously. Only about a dozen were built before the 500 Superfast was phased out in early 1967.

Nonetheless, this Ferrari left its mark, as noted by author Antoine Prunet: "With the 500 Superfast, the refinement, the finish, the comfort, and the immense power which seemed a paradox with such luxury, Ferrari and Pininfarina had, without question, created quite well the Ferrari 'Royale.'"

SPECIFICATIONS

Engine: sohc V-12, 302.7 cid/4962 cc, 400 bhp @ 6500 rpm, torque NA

Transmissions:	4-speed manual with overdrive (Series 1); 5-speed manual (Series II)
Suspension, front:	unequal-length A-arms, coil springs
Suspension, rear:	live axle, parallel trailing arms, semi-elliptic leaf springs
Brakes:	front/rear discs
Wheelbase (in.):	104.3
Weight (lbs):	3200
Top speed (mph):	140-160+
0-60 mph (sec):	NA
Production:	Series I (1964-66) 25 Series II (1966-67) 12

*Aptly named, the Pininfarina-designed and built Ferrari 500 Superfast was not only blindingly fast, but exceptionally luxurious as well. The Series II models (**opposite**) sported three air outlets on the front-fenders as opposed to the 11 small vents on Series I cars.*

1960-1968
FERRARI 250/330 GT 2+2

Carrozzerie Touring, Ghia, and Vignale all built 2+2 Ferrari bodies in the early Fifties, but they were one-off cars with unacceptable rear-seat accommodation for anything longer than a trip around the block. Thus, Maranello fielded nothing but two-seaters until June 1960, when it supplied a 2+2 as the course marshal's car for the Le Mans 24 Hours. It was, in fact, a sneak preview of a new model, which was formally announced at the Paris show in October as the 250 GTE.

Ferrari's first production 2+2 shared its 102.3-inch wheelbase with contemporary long-chassis 250 GTs, but with an engine moved eight inches forward to open up room for a back seat. Other than this and associated modifications, the GTE chassis followed then-current Ferrari specs: double-A-arm front suspension, leaf-sprung live rear axle, all-round telescopic shock absorbers and disc brakes, all-synchro 4-speed gearbox with Laycock de Normanville overdrive.

Also shared with other roadgoing 250s was the 2953-cc V-12 (bore and stroke: 73 x 58.8 mm), with three twin-choke Weber carburetors, 8.8:1 compression, and a rated 240 horsepower at 7000 rpm. Cylinder heads were the now-standard Ferrari design with outboard spark plugs, individual intake ports, and coil valve springs. Body design and construction were by Pininfarina and all-new. Neither changed much through the end of the model run, though 1962 brought minor appearance revisions inside and out, plus a new name: 250 GT 2+2.

Though that model was phased out in late 1963, it was followed by some 50 "interim" examples powered by Ferrari's new Type 209 4.0-liter engine, several inches longer than the familiar 250 unit. The main visual tipoff to this swap was an "America" nameplate at the rear, though not all the cars were so labelled. This and the new engine's individual cylinder displacement account for this model's being known today as the 330 America.

One of Enzo Ferrari's longtime practices was to hold an annual press conference at his Maranello factory to show off his latest cars, showroom and competition models alike. His January 1964 meeting featured a GTE/America replacement, but it met with decidedly mixed reviews. Designated 330 GT 2+2, it combined the 4.0-liter engine with a new body, again designed and built by Pininfarina. Most of the criticism centered on the styling: bulbous and heavy-looking. It even had quad headlights, American-style.

We don't have 1964 sales figures, but it's significant that the 330 2+2 lost two of those headlights for 1965 and beyond. Other than suitably narrowed front fenders with revamped side vents, it would continue in this form through 1968. Total production was about 1000 units over four years.

The 330 GT 2+2 chassis was all-Ferrari in style and substance, though it spanned a longer (104.2-inch) wheelbase than the GTE/America. The drivetrain was strengthened to handle the 4.0-liter engine's extra power, rated at 300 bhp at 6000 rpm. Koni adjustable shock absorbers teamed with concentric coil springs to augment the rear semi-elliptics, and separate front and rear brake systems eliminated the possibility of total braking loss.

Typical of Ferrari, this 330 saw several running changes. Alloy wheels were standardized in 1965, and Borrani wires (both center-lock and knock-off) were offered at extra cost. The following year, a new 5-speed gearbox replaced the old 4-speed-plus-overdrive, in line with other Ferraris.

The 330 2+2s weren't as attractive as the GTE/America, but what they lost visually, they gained mechanically. All-out performance wasn't much better, but the bigger engine's added torque and greater flexibility made driving easier and more enjoyable, while the longer wheelbase and spruced-up interior made the going more comfortable.

In short, this was the "commuter's" Ferrari, a car that could stand the daily stop-and-go grind yet provide a lot of excitement on the right kind of road. No mean feat when you stop to think about it. But then, even "cooking" Ferraris are anything but ordinary.

SPECIFICATIONS

Engines: all sohc V-12; **250 GTE 2+2** (1960-63): 180 cid/2953 cc, 240 bhp @ 7000 rpm; **330 America/330 GT 2+2** (1963-68): 242 cid/3967 cc, 300 bhp @ 6000 rpm; torque figures NA

Transmissions:	4-speed manual with electric overdrive; 5-speed overdrive manual from 1966
Suspension, front:	unequal-length A-arms, coil springs
Suspension, rear:	live axle, parallel trailing arms, semi-elliptic leaf springs
Brakes:	front/rear discs
Wheelbase (in.):	102.3 (330 GT 2+2) 104.2
Weight (lbs):	2820-3040
Top speed (mph):	115-125
0-60 mph (sec):	NA

Production: **250 GTE 2+2** (1960-63) 950 **330 GT America** (1963) 50 **330 GT 2+2** (1964-68) 1000

The 4.0-liter 330 GT 2+2 was much like the original 3.0-liter 250 models, but arrived with a four-lamp front that proved quite controversial. It was used only in 1964. Moving engine forward opened up additional seating space in the 250 LWB chassis.

1964-1965 FERRARI 250/275 LM

Ferrari experimented with mid-engine racing cars as early as 1960, but didn't have one ready until March 1963, when Enzo Ferrari presented the 250P at his annual press conference. Basically, it was an amalgam of the "standard" 3.0-liter dry-sump racing V-12 from the front-engine Testa Rossa (with six DCN Weber carbs) and the chassis from the V-6 and V-8 Dino mid-engine competition cars, albeit with a longer 94.5-inch wheelbase (versus 91.4) to accommodate the longer engine. Soon after its debut, the 250P broke the lap record at Monza in the hands of John Surtees, a recent Team Ferrari recruit.

That November, a closed version called 250 LM (for "Le Mans") was shown at the Paris Salon. Like the 250P, it had all-independent suspension via fabricated tubular A-arms, coil springs, and telescopic shock absorbers, plus four-wheel disc brakes with inboard units at the rear. The engine, again based on the Testa Rossa unit, employed a multi-disc clutch mounted on the flywheel between the engine and transaxle (later versions had the clutch "outboard" behind the transaxle assembly). The non-synchro 5-speed transmission had all-indirect gears, which allowed a low engine position that lowered the center of gravity and reduced frontal area.

Pininfarina supplied shapely berlinetta bodywork whose windshield and side windows would appear on the Series II 250 GTO. In fact, the roof design on both cars was similar, a "flying buttress" style with sloped "sail panels" flanking a vertical

Though designed mainly for competition, the 250 LM was the first mid-engine Ferrari that could be used on the street. This beauty bears the later extended roofline, but most LMs had this basic tunnelback style. One fastback was tested at Le Mans in '64, but never raced.

rear window. Water radiator, an oil cooler, and the reservoir for the dry-sump lubrication system nestled in the nose.

This first 250 LM came to the U.S. in late 1963 (after the fall European show season) and was campaigned by NART (the North American Racing Team of Luigi Chinetti, Ferrari's stateside distributor). After a DNF at Daytona and an undistinguished eighth-place finish at Augusta, Georgia, the car caught fire at Sebring and was totally destroyed.

The LM's next outing was the Le Mans trials in April 1964. By then, the engine had been bored from 73 to 77 mm, which made it a "275," with displacement of 3287.5 cc. On higher, 9.7:1 compression, it packed 330 horsepower at 7700 rpm. Though all subsequent LMs were so equipped, Ferrari didn't change the 250 designation for fear of jeopardizing homologation proceedings. He might just as well have called them 275s, as the FIA took two years to certify the model.

Despite the extra power, the LM's fortunes didn't immediately improve, but the car would acquit itself well over the next two years. In 1964 alone, LMs placed 1-2 at the 12 Hours of Reims, second in the Tourist Trophy, first at Elkhart Lake and Mont Tremblant, 1-2 in the Coppa Inter-Europa and Grand Prix of Angola, and 2-3-6 in the Nassau Trophy. In all, LMs won 10 major events, placed second in six and third in four. Only 10 out of the total 35 entries failed to finish.

Ferrari didn't campaign the 250 LM in 1965 or '66, but privateers continued to race it successfully. In fact, one of its best displays of speed and endurance came at Le Mans 1966, when Jochen Rindt and Masten Gregory finished first in a NART entry, followed by the LM of Pierre Dumay and Gustaf Gosselin. (Willy Mairesse and Jean Beurlys took third overall and first in GT class with their 275 GTB.)

As purpose-designed competition cars, all 250/275 LMs had right-hand drive and a minimal area for a passenger, as regulations specified. Full road equipment—lights, horn, spare wheel and tire, etc.—was also mandatory, thus making the LM seem like a dual-purpose car. But it wasn't. In fact, even the racers ran with only the driver. The earlier 250 GT berlinettas had dominated the Tour de France, Tour of Sicily, and other long-distance events requiring two aboard, but the 250 LM would have been physical disaster for a copilot in one of those week-long contests.

SPECIFICATIONS

Engine: sohc V-12, 200.5 cid/3286 cc, 305 bhp @ 7500 rpm, torque NA

Transmission:	All-indirect non-synchromesh 5-speed manual (in rear transaxle)
Suspension, front:	unequal-length A-arms, coil springs
Suspension, rear:	unequal-length A-arms, coil springs
Brakes:	front/rear discs
Wheelbase (in.):	94.5
Weight (lbs):	1870
Top speed (mph):	160
0-60 mph (sec):	est. 6.5
Production:	35 (some sources list 40)

1964-1967 FERRARI 275 GTB/GTS

A distinctive pair of new Ferraris bowed at the 1964 Paris Salon in October: the 275 GTB, a fastback berlinetta, and GTS spyder. Their shared 94.5-inch-wheelbase chassis was of now-typical Ferrari design with two major exceptions, both firsts for the marque: all-independent suspension, via unequal-length A-arms and coil springs, and a 5-speed gearbox in unit with the differential to form a rear transaxle. Coil springs, tubular shocks, and all-disc brakes continued as before.

Engines were shared, too, being a 3.3-liter V-12 of Colombo origin. But while the spyder unit produced 260 horsepower, the berlinetta's was rated at 280. Reason: the coupe was conceived as a dual-purpose sports-racing machine, the convertible strictly for touring. Accordingly, GTB customers had a choice of either three Weber carburetors (as homologated for the model by the FIA) or six, and steel bodywork (with aluminum hood, doors, and trunklid) or all-aluminum. Campagnolo alloy disc wheels were standard across the board, Borrari wires optional.

Where the 275s differed most was appearance. The spyder body, conceived and executed by Pininfarina, was evolved from that of the 330 GT 2+2, while the berlinetta had a completely new shape. It was, in fact, a replacement for the 250 GT Berlinetta Lusso, and thus softer and more rounded than the spyder. Scaglietti built this body to PF's design.

These cars would be little altered during their three-year production run, with most changes reserved for the GTB. A Series II model appeared at the 1965 Frankfurt show minus chrome headlamp surrounds and driver's door ventwing but with external trunklid hinges (for more luggage space) and a hood bulge over the carburetors. At Paris a month later, Ferrari displayed definitive GTB styling, marked by a lower, longer nose and larger rear window. Marque partisans thus divide the cars into "short-nose" and "long-nose" models. By the Brussels show of January 1966, the open-tube driveshaft had been replaced by a closed torque tube, which eliminated the driveshaft bearing problems that had plagued earlier GTBs and made the car a bit quieter too.

Spring 1966 brought a special competition berlinetta designated 275 GTB/C. Built in more limited numbers, it boasted lightweight aluminum bodywork with Plexiglas windows, dry-sump lubrication system, and special camshafts, valves, pistons, crankshaft, and carburetors.

Even more exciting was a four-cam berlinetta announced at the 1966 Paris show—the first dohc roadgoing Ferrari. Designated 275 GTB/4, it looked much like the twincam coupe but packed 300 bhp at 8000 rpm. The driveline was also revised, with engine, propshaft cover, transmission, and differential all bolted up as one solid unit.

Alas, there was no four-cam spyder, the 275 GTS having given way by now to a larger-displacement 330 evolution. However, Scaglietti built a special berlinetta-based quad-cam cabriolet in 1967 at the behest of Luigi Chinetti, Jr., son of Ferrari's American distributor. Known as the 275 GTS/4 NART Spyder (after the Chinettis' North American Racing Team), it saw only 10 copies, all sold in the U.S.

The 275-series underscored the major change that had taken place in Ferrari's design philosophy over the previous few years. No longer were its road cars thinly disguised racers but comfortable, luxurious GTs. And because of their chassis improvements—mainly the all-independent suspension and the transaxle layout's inherently better weight distribution—the 275s were not only faster but handled better. Though not fast as the later Daytonas, they were more maneuverable and easier to drive, thanks to their smaller size and lower weight.

In fact, superb balance and excellent power make the 275s an absolute delight even among Ferraris, and there isn't much, if anything, on the road that the driver need yield to, especially if he's in a GTB/4. Jean Pierre Beltoise, the noted French GP driver, tested one for l'Auto Journal and reported covering 46 miles in 23 minutes—that's 120 mph—on a Sunday afternoon in spite of "stopping for tollgates." Well, even Ferraris have to slow down sometime.

*Opposite and this page, top: Smooth hood marked the first-year "short-nose" 275 GTB. **This page, center:** Exposed trunklid hinges and larger backlight identify this post-1964 "long-nose" from behind. **Above:** Posh cockpit may seem surprising for an all-out sports car, but then the 275 was conceived to replace the 250 GT Berlinetta Lusso (luxury).*

SPECIFICATIONS

Engines: 1964-66: sohc V-12, 200.5 cid/3286 cc, 260 bhp @ 7000 rpm; **1966-67 GTB/4:** dohc V-12, 200.5 cid/3286 cc, 300 bhp @ 8000 rpm; torque figures NA

Transmission:	5-speed manual (in rear transaxle)
Suspension, front:	unequal-length A-arms, coil springs
Suspension, rear:	unequal-length A-arms, coil springs
Brakes:	front/rear discs
Wheelbase (in.):	94.5
Weight (lbs):	approx. 2500
Top Speed (mph):	148 (GTB), 143 (GTS), 155 (GTB/4)
0-60 (sec):	6.7-7.5

Production: GTB Series I 250 **GTB Series II** 200 **GTS** 200 **GTB/4** 280 **GTB/4 Spyder** 10 (all figures approximate)

1966-1970 FERRARI 330/365 GTC/GTS

As a design principle, "mix-and-match" doesn't produce great cars—except at Ferrari. Introduced at the March 1966 Geneva show, the 330 GTC (for Gran Turismo Coupe) allied the 275 GTB chassis and basic engine of the 330 GT 2+2 with a new Pininfarina body that blended the 275 GTS tail with a front end inspired by that of the 400 Superamerica. Such combinations are often disastrous, but this one worked very well, both visually and mechanically.

Because it inherited the GTB chassis and its rear transaxle, the 330 GT 2+2 engine block had to be redesigned for the GTC to accommodate the different engine and differential mounts. As on late GTBs, the driveshaft passed through a torque tube. Naturally, four-wheel disc brakes and the all-independent double-wishbone/coil-spring suspension were retained, as was the 94.5-inch wheelbase.

Competition and road cars were completely separate by this point in Ferrari history, so the new GTC made no pretense at being anything other than a *grand luxe* touring machine for two. Fast, comfortable, and quiet, it was the sort of car that allowed you to enjoy a good sound system at three-figure speeds. Even air conditioning was an option.

In October '66, a companion convertible bowed at the Paris Salon, designated 330 GTS. About two years later, both GTC and GTS were treated to a larger engine. This

Rear-deck script is about the only external difference between the 330 and 365 GTS cabrios. This example wears an accessory hardtop and Campagnolo alloy wheels.

was created by boring out from 77 to 81 mm (stroke was left at 71 mm) for total capacity of 4390 cc. Designated 365 GTC/GTS, they gained 20 horsepower, up to 320 bhp at 6600 rpm, but nothing in top speed. Still, they were faster off the line and more pleasurable to drive, thanks to the bigger engine's improved torque and low-rpm flexibility.

Regardless of engine, these cars stand as some of the best Ferraris ever built. They make all the right sounds and have all the right moves yet are tastefully conservative in appearance, eye-catching but not extrovert. Naturally, they could be driven at the maximum speed permitted by prevailing conditions and driver skill—and should be— yet provided all the comfort and safety one would expect in a premium GT.

Paul Frère, the noted Belgian racing driver-turned-automotive-journalist, conducted the first test of a 330 GTC, which was duly published in the November 19, 1966 issue of the British magazine *The Motor*. He came away convinced: "The greatest surprise is the silence of the engine . . . In handling, the 330 GTC is exactly like all the Ferraris which I have driven before . . . It is close to being as neutral as one could want . . . But the most impressive feature of the handling of the new vehicle is the solidness with which it changes direction, particularly in S-bends, where it tracks with about the same precision as a modern race car."

Frère made two high-speed runs, lifting his foot only when he encountered traffic. By that point, the speedometer read 146 mph, but "the vehicle was still perceptibly accelerating." He concluded that the car would probably have equalled the factory's claimed 150-mph maximum.

In the standing quarter-mile, Frère measured the 330 GTC at a very lively 14.6 seconds. This dovetails neatly with the 14.9 seconds (at 95 mph) reported by *Road & Track* for its test 330 GTS. That publication listed top speed as 145 mph, exactly matching Frère's result with the coupe.

The 330/365 GTC and GTS aren't the most exciting Ferraris ever built, but their fit and finish, smooth styling, high performance, great comfort, and superb handling make them some of the most sophisticated and elegant cars in the long line of Maranello GTs. And with up to 150 mph on tap, who needs "excitement?"

SPECIFICATIONS

Engines: all sohc V-12; **330 GTC/GTS** (1966-68): 242 cid/3967 cc, 300 bhp @ 7000 rpm; **365 GTC/GTS** (1968-70): 267.8 cid/4390 cc, 320 bhp @ 6600 rpm; torque figures NA

Transmission:	5-speed manual (in rear transaxle)
Suspension, front:	unequal-length A-arms, coil springs
Suspension, rear:	unequal-length A-arms, coil springs
Brakes:	front/rear disc
Wheelbase (in.):	94.5
Weight (lbs):	2650-3200
Top speed (mph):	145-150
0-60 mph (sec):	7.0 (330)

Production: **330 GTC** 600 **330 GTS** 100 **365 GTC** 150-200 **365 GTS** 20

1967-1971
FERRARI 365 GT 2+2

By 1967, Ferrari and Pininfarina had produced over 2000 of the 250 and 330 GT 2+2s, attesting to buyer enthusiasm for a back-seat Ferrari. Not surprisingly, these customers generally cared less about pizzazz and performance than creature comforts and passenger space. Ferrari's next 2+2 would give them more of both.

Premiered at the 1967 Paris Salon in October, it was, in fact, the biggest, plushest Ferrari yet. Wheelbase remained modest at 104.2 inches, but the new Superfast-style fastback body measured 196 inches long overall. This and a curb weight near two tons made the new 365 GT 2+2 about as large—and heavy—as a U.S. intermediate.

Like late 400 SAs and the smaller 330 GTC, styling was clean and conservative, with the same sort of low, rounded nose bearing an elliptical, eggcrate grille. Flanking the latter were slim half-bumpers that undoubtedly looked better than they protected. Headlamps again nestled in nacelles. European models covered these with clear plastic contoured to fender shape, precluded on American models by government regulations. An airy greenhouse with slim roof pillars afforded fine outward vision. Per Ferrari practice, Borrari wire wheels were optional, Cromodora alloys standard. When the high-performance Daytona arrived in 1968 (see entry), its lovely five-spoke rims became standard wear.

Inside, the 365 GT 2+2 was positively sybaritic for a Ferrari. Power brakes and steering, electric window lifts, air conditioning, pleated-leather upholstery, and full carpeting were all standard. So was a full complement of easy-to-read needle gauges directly ahead of the driver. Radio, climate controls, the window switches, ashtray, and lighter were housed in a center console for easy accessibility by driver or front passenger.

There was little new mechanically. The chassis was Ferrari's characteristic steel-tube assembly riding the all-independent double-A-arm/coil-spring suspension as seen on the 275 and 330/365 models. With it came their single-disc dry-plate clutch and 5-speed torque-tube transaxle. The latter helped reduce driveline noise transmission to the cabin. Reflecting the new model's more luxurious character was Ferrari's first rear self-levelling system, developed jointly with Koni. Power was provided by the sohc "365" version of the Colombo V-12, with three downdraft Weber carburetors, 8.8:1 compression, and a rated 320 horsepower at 6600 rpm.

Despite its heft, the new 2+2 could run the standing quarter-mile in 14.7 seconds at 94 mph—"adequate," as Rolls-Royce would say. It reached 149 mph in a European test, about 12 mph faster than its 330 predecessor.

Though purists sneered at its bulk and baubles, the 365 GT 2+2 proved very popular, accounting for more than 50 percent of Ferrari's total production during its three-year life. Ferrari had done its part to make the car state-of-the-art mechanically, and Pininfarina had done its part with the styling, which was not only *au courant* but apparently quite aerodynamic, with details such as flush door handles, modest Kamm-type tail, and that smooth "face." Undoubtedly, this was the best-ever "family" Ferrari—if that's not a contradiction in terms.

Still, neither Ferrari nor PF had achieved their high success by standing still, and the obvious success of the "family" concept guaranteed a new successor model. It arrived in time for the 1971 Geneva show: the 365 GTC/4.

The 365 GT 2+2 was as heavy as it looked, not one of Pininfarina's more memorable Ferraris. Still, this was Il Commendatore's idea of a "family car" in the late Sixties, a role it filled as ably as his earlier 2+2s. Huge air cleaner (above) shrouds durable Colombo V-12.

SPECIFICATIONS

Engine: sohc V-12, 268 cid/4390 cc, 320 bhp @ 6600 rpm, torque NA

Transmission:	5-speed manual (in rear transaxle)
Suspension, front:	unequal-length A-arms, coil springs
Suspension, rear:	unequal-length A-arms, coil springs, hydropneumatic self-levelling
Brakes:	front/rear discs
Wheelbase (in.):	104.2
Weight (lbs):	3500-4000
Top speed (mph):	140-145+
0-60 mph (sec):	7.1
Production:	approx. 800

1967-1969
FERRARI DINO 206 GT

No one knew it at the time, but a car on Pininfarina's stand at the 1965 Paris Salon was a forecast of roadgoing Ferraris to come. Titled "Dino 206 S Speciale," it was a shapely, competition-inspired coupe powered by a twincam, 65-degree Ferrari-designed 2.0-liter V-6 mounted amidships. Unfortunately for would-be buyers, it was a styling exercise, built on a racing chassis (number 0834) with a nonfunctioning engine.

But a *real* mid-engine Ferrari road car was on the way. It first appeared at the 1966 Turin show as a running prototype labelled Dino Berlinetta GT. (As on the earlier V-6-powered sports-racing Ferraris, the Dino name honored Enzo's deceased son.) A year later, again at Turin, Ferrari showed the production version, now simply called Dino 206 GT.

It was a big departure for a Maranello road car: the first with V-6 power and the first to employ the competition-inspired mid-engine configuration, then predicted to be the wave of the future in production sports-car design. It was also *Il Commendatore's* first (and so far only) attempt at a companion marque, the Dino bearing no Ferrari nameplate or prancing-horse badge anywhere.

Like the '66 prototype, the production 206 employed the 2.0-liter V-6 (hence the numerical designation) originally developed for racing, but mounted transversely instead of longitudinally. Though Ferrari engineered it, Fiat mostly built it. The chassis, designed and built by Maranello, had all-independent suspension in the classic mold: upper and lower wishbones and coil springs at each wheel. Scaglietti again supplied bodies to a Pininfarina design, and also assembled the car.

As marque loyalists expected, the new "junior" Ferrari reflected lessons learned from racing, where Maranello now ran nothing but mid-engine cars except for 275 GTBs. Front/rear weight balance was almost ideal, with the heaviest components situated in the middle of the car for a low polar moment of inertia. This made the Dino extremely maneuverable, a car that really shined through tight, twisty stretches thanks to its quick transient response.

But as in other "middies," there were tradeoffs, mainly a *lot* more cockpit noise and marginal luggage space. Dino owners learned to travel light, and it's likely that the cars did most of their miles in the cities and suburbs than on the open road.

Dino styling was equally predictive of future Ferraris, especially the "flying buttress" roofline that would later appear on the flat-12 Berlinetta Boxer and V-8-powered 308. The view to the front and sides was thus good, but terrible astern and over-the-shoulder. Still, owners didn't seem to let such drawbacks overshadow the car's many good points—not the least of which was the fact that this *was* a true Ferrari, even if it didn't have 12 cylinders. It certainly acted and sounded like one.

This first Dino didn't last long, being phased out in late 1969 for the more powerful and refined 246. Most of the 100 or so built were sold in Europe (though a few found their way to other countries), so the 206 isn't as well known in the U.S. as its successor. Indeed, it was conceived mainly for Europe, where smaller engines mean a smaller tax bite on buyers.

Ultimately, though, Ferrari couldn't ignore the U.S., where a larger engine was almost mandatory given the much longer distances between major population centers (in Europe you can drive through several countries in a few hours). It was also a more practical proposition for a land with a seemingly unlimited supply of low-cost fuel.

Then too, Porsche and Lotus both had middies on the market by 1970, and a number of Yankee enthusiasts were drooling at the prospect of a lower-cost mid-engine Ferrari. The Dino 246 GT would answer their prayers—and the competition.

SPECIFICATIONS

Engine: dohc V-6, 121 cid/1986.7 cc, 180 bhp @ 8000 rpm, torque NA

Transmission:	5-speed manual (in rear transaxle)
Suspension, front:	unequal-length A-arms, coil springs, anti-roll bar
Suspension, rear:	unequal-length A-arms, coil springs, anti-roll bar
Brakes:	front/rear discs
Wheelbase (in.):	90.0
Weight (lbs):	1980
Top Speed (mph):	142
0-60 mph (sec):	est. 7.1
Production:	approx. 100 (some sources list 150)

The curvaceous Dino 206 GT set the design pattern for future mid-engine Ferrari road cars. Appearance was virtually the same as that of the later 246, but there was no open version and most 206s had covered headlamps.

1968-1974 FERRARI 365 GTB/4 "DAYTONA" & 365 GTS/4 "DAYTONA SPIDER"

Aside from the 250 GTO, the 365 GTB/4, popularly known as the "Daytona," ranks as perhaps the most coveted Ferrari ever built. It's certainly one of the most remarkable roadgoing Ferraris. First shown at the 1968 Paris Salon, it was not only the costliest such car in Ferrari's 21-year history (just under $20,000) but the fastest. *Road & Track* magazine verified the factory's claimed 174-mph top speed and ran the standing quarter-mile in a blistering 13.8 seconds at 107.5 mph. What Ferrari had here was nothing less than a "muscle car" Italian style.

And what muscle. Replacing the 275 GTB/4, the Daytona rode a similar chassis of identical wheelbase but carried a dohc V-12 bored and stroked to 4.4 liters. With no fewer than six twin-choke Weber carburetors and a fairly high (for the day) 8.8:1 compression ratio, output was 352 thoroughbred horses at 7500 rpm. As on the 275, a single dry-plate clutch sent this power to a 5-speed rear transaxle.

What style, too. Ferrari fans and motoring press alike were initially divided on the Pininfarina design. After almost 20 years, those who merely liked the Daytona now love it, while those who didn't care for it then seem to like it. "Aggressively elegant" describes it; so does "influential." In fact, many Daytona features have since shown up on a number of lesser cars (including a few replicas like the Corvette-based car on TV's "Miami Vice"). One that hasn't is the full-width plastic headlight cover used on early models. U.S. laws prohibited such things, so hidden lamps were substituted for that market and, later, others too.

While Pininfarina designed and built the Paris prototype, Scaglietti again handled production, which began about a year afterwards. Incidentally, the press was responsible for the Daytona name, not the factory, but it stuck anyway, perhaps because it had long been a legend around the world. And really, what better handle for this fastest-ever Ferrari than the name of the Florida beach city that bills itself as "The Birthplace of Speed"?

The Daytona feels heavy behind the wheel—and it is, particularly for a two-seater. Despite aluminum doors, hood, and trunklid, curb weight is near 3600 pounds. But the heft seems to have little effect on handling, which is excellent.

Ferrari made few alterations to the Daytona during its four short years other than the aforementioned headlamp change and the addition of a companion convertible "spider," unveiled at the 1969 Frankfurt show as the 365 GTS/4. It accounted for only 127 of the more than 1300 cars built.

Low production and high appeal explain why Daytona asking prices have soared into the six-figure stratosphere. Convertibles, of course, generally command bigger bucks than coupes—by a factor of 20-100 percent among Ferraris—which explains why several shops now specialize in Daytona spider conversions. While some are done for enthusiasts who simply want an open car and really want it to be a Daytona, we suspect most are motivated by the spider's higher market value and the prospect of further appreciation. If this keeps up, berlinettas could be in shorter supply one day and thus, ironically enough, worth more than spiders, converted *and* original.

A few Daytona berlinettas raced with success, some with all-aluminum bodywork and engines tweaked to 405 bhp. They were formidable track performers, but brakes were a weakness of all Daytonas. Even race-equipped cars tipped the scales near 3600 pounds (bigger wheels and tires and the increased load of larger fuel tanks offset weight savings in bodywork and some mechanical components) and the brakes just weren't up to their 200-mph top speed.

The Daytona's front-engine configuration raised a few eyebrows in the late Sixties, mainly because Lamborghini's V-12 Miura was a mid-engine design, as were Ferrari's own competition cars. But as events soon proved, the Daytona would be the last new two-seat Ferrari in the classic mold.

Which also helps explain today's lofty asking prices—that and a macho character and memorable styling. The Daytona marked the end of an era, and for that reason alone, it will never be forgotten.

SPECIFICATIONS

Engine: dohc V-12, 268 cid/4390 cc, 352 bhp @ 7500 rpm, 365 lbs-ft @ 5500 rpm

Transmission:	5-speed manual (in rear transaxle)
Suspension, front:	unequal-length A-arms, coil springs, anti-roll bar
Suspension, rear:	unequal-length A-arms, coil springs, anti-roll bar
Brakes:	front/rear discs
Wheelbase (in.):	94.5
Weight (lbs):	3600
Top speed (mph):	170 +
0-60 mph (sec):	5.9
Production:	**GTB/4** approx. 1285 **GTS/4** 127

It takes a very pretty penny these days to buy a genuine Daytona Spider. Hidden headlamps were mandated by U.S. law, but replaced the original exposed lights and plastic cover for all markets from 1970. Lush cockpit (above) was especially inviting on a sunny day with the top down.

1969-1973 FERRARI DINO 246 GT/246 GTS

It was only a 206 with a gilded engine, but that hasn't stopped the Dino 246 GT from making its mark. It began doing that, as a prototype, in early 1969, with production commencing at the end of that year.

With two exceptions, the 246 (2.4 liters, six cylinders) was identical with the 206: same basic styling, running gear, and tubular-steel chassis with all-independent wishbone/coil-spring suspension and four-wheel disc brakes. Wheelbase, however, was now 2.1 inches longer for a like gain in cockpit space. As before, Scaglietti supplied the body and Fiat the twincam V-6, still transversely placed twixt cockpit and rear axle. But as the new model number implied, the engine was enlarged (via increased bore and stroke) to 2.4 liters and 175 horsepower (on 9.0:1 compression). Also, it was now made of cast iron instead of Silumin alloy for greater reliability, particularly in the U.S. A single dry-plate clutch continued to take power to a 5-speed transaxle with all-indirect gearing and a 3.62:1 final drive.

The car still bore no Ferrari insignia, the reason for which has never been clear. Some claim the Dino was denied its heritage because of the Fiat-built engine, others because it had only six cylinders instead of 12. The former seems more plausible. After all, Enzo had named his V-6 GP engine Dino, after his late son, a tribute to the young man who'd been working his way up through the Ferrari organization and would likely have taken it over one day. Also, Ferrari had put his name on cars with inline four, straight-six, V-6, and V-8 engines. Why he didn't do it here is known only to *Il Commendatore* himself.

The Dino engine wasn't built entirely by Fiat. Ferrari engineer Franco Rocchi had designed it, and Maranello furnished the lower section containing sump, transaxle,

and halfshafts. The Italian giant manufactured block, heads, manifolds, and accessories.

Fiat used this V-6 in an upmarket sportster of its own, the front-engine Fiat Dino. While the collaboration between automakers of such disparate size might seem strange, Fiat bought a controlling interest in Ferrari in 1969, which would have vast implications for Maranello's future products and production methods.

By mid-1970, the 246's center-lock knock-off Cromodora alloy wheels had been replaced by five-bolt Campagnolo rims. Most U.S. models were so equipped.

Two years later, an open model appeared, the 246 GTS. It wasn't a full convertible, though, being a "targa" design with a lift-off panel above the cockpit. The coupe's rear quarter windows were replaced by metal panels bearing three small louvers, which also contributed to the spider's somewhat different look.

For a "low-line" car, the 246 cockpit was comfortable and relatively plush. The instrument panel, in fact, was almost identical with the Daytona's (albeit suitably scaled down), encompassing eight instruments in an elliptical binnacle set just ahead of the wheel.

Still, not all was bliss. *Road & Track,* in a 1972 coupe test, said that the "Dino's most obvious sacrifice [to practicality] affects the human ear. It is noisy in the extreme. The sounds are exciting to be sure: busy tappets, whining cam chains and transfer drive, a raucous exhaust system. . . . Even on a slow run to the corner drugstore, the Dino seems to be working, snarling, racing. The exhaust note at low speeds gives away its 6-cylinder configuration, but as the engine climbs into its effective rev range (little happens below 3000 rpm) . . . it takes on the characteristic Ferrari sounds despite having only half the number of cylinders."

Of course, with a little less than two-thirds the weight but only half the horsepower, the 246 couldn't match the Daytona in a straight line, but it could outpoint almost any car on a winding road. Even better, it's reasonably reliable, provided the front-cylinder-bank cam chain is regularly checked for proper tension. It's difficult to reach, so some mechanics don't bother, but the wages of neglect are potentially disastrous: a chain that slips a tooth on one of the sprockets can destroy an engine.

You're apt to see some of these Dinos with Ferrari badges now instead of the original emblems. Purists may sneer at such lily-gilding, but it says much about pride of ownership, which the 246 deserves as much as a "real" Ferrari. It did Maranello proud.

SPECIFICATIONS

Engine: dohc V-6, 145 cid/2418 cc, 175 bhp @ 7000 rpm, 160 lbs-ft @ 5500 rpm

Transmission:	5-speed manual (in rear transaxle)
Suspension, front:	unequal-length A-arms, coil springs, anti-roll bar
Suspension, rear:	unequal-length A-arms, coil springs, anti-roll bar
Brakes:	front/rear discs
Wheelbase (in.):	92.1
Weight (lbs):	2800
Top speed (mph):	140
0-60 mph (sec):	8.0
Production:	GT 2800 GTS 1200 (figures approximate)

Though clearly an evolution of the earlier 206 model, the Dino 246 was more aggressive yet practical. The Ferrari tail badge here was not originally fitted.

1972-1988 FERRARI 365 GT4 2+2 /400i/412i

Europeans think of a car like today's "family" Ferrari as a coupe, but some Americans might call it a two-door sedan because of its pillared notchback styling. It certainly looked more like a sedan than the car it replaced, the 365 GTC/4.

Actually though, this model, which bowed at the Paris show in October 1972 as the 365 GT4 2+2, was the lineal successor to the 365 GT 2+2, production of which had ceased a year and half earlier. Such a lag was unusual for Ferrari, which heretofore hadn't discontinued a model without having its replacement ready. In retrospect, then, the GTC/4 was an interim measure. It really wasn't a 2+2, but the GT4 was.

Dimensional comparisons confirm this view. Against the 365 GT 2+2, the GT4 was two inches longer in wheelbase, 7.5 inches shorter overall, fractionally wider, 1.5 inches lower, and up to 300 pounds heavier. The cockpit was 2.5 inches wider in front and over four inches wider in back, while trunk room swelled by a useful 1.2 cubic feet. If all this sounds dull for a Ferrari—and it does—Maranello was only following the contemporary trend among premium GTs: bigger, plusher cars with larger engines and higher prices.

As its model designation suggested, the GT4 carried the quad-cam V-12 as used in the 365 GTC/4, with the same sextet of horizontal carbs and 320 horsepower. Chassis design, suspension, brakes, and steering were also borrowed from the GTC/4, as were the 5-speed manual gearbox and what seemed to be Ferrari's standard road wheel, the lovely five-spoke Cromodora alloys first seen on the Daytona. Power steering and brakes and air conditioning remained standard.

Ferrari fans taken aback by this posh, Yankee-style clipper got an even bigger shock in the updated version announced at the 1976 Paris show. There for all to see was a Ferrari with—could it be?—automatic transmission, the 3-speed Turbo-Hydra-Matic unit from General Motors, recalibrated for the Ferrari V-12. This model was called 400i A, for "Automatic," but the letter could just as easily have meant "American." At least the manual car was still available as the 400i.

Common to both was an engine stroked from 71 to 77 mm, giving total capacity of 4823 cc and an extra 20 horsepower peaking 300 rpm higher with Bosch. Outside were a modest front "lip" spoiler, revamped taillights, and lug nuts instead of knock-off hubs for securing the wheels. Inside, Pininfarina reworked the seats for greater comfort and gave them a slide-forward mechanism to assist rear entry/exit. Ferrari also threw in a four-speaker radio/tape system.

Both 400s continued virtually unchanged until 1985, when they became 412s by dint of a silly millimeter bore increase. The resulting 4942-cc engine also acquired K-Jetronic mechanical fuel injection with Bosch. Marelli Microplex electronic ignition and higher compression (up to 9.6:1 from the previous 8.8:1), but there was no change in rated horsepower except that it peaked at an even lower 6000 rpm. A dual-disc clutch replaced the single-disc unit in manual models, but the most significant change was adoption of Bosch ABS anti-lock electronic control for the all-disc brakes.

"Federalizing" costs soared as much as inflation-fueled car prices in the Seventies, so Ferrari didn't bother certifying any of these models for U.S. sale. Still, a few have been imported privately and through the inevitable "gray market."

Though fast, these are not sports cars but rather the ultimate in a modern grand touring Ferrari—the definitive country-club cruiser, with an unmatched blend of style, comfort, performance, and a panache that is Ferrari's alone. As *Autocar* magazine said in a 1975 group test between the GT4 and a gaggle of British rivals: "Our own cars can compete on one level or another. But none of them can compete with the Ferrari on all levels." So call it a sedan, but just remember it's a Ferrari.

Original 365 GT4 2+2 became the fuel-injected 400i in 1976. Availability of automatic transmission shocked some Ferraristi. The current 412i is basically the same car with a bored-out V-12 and remains the last front-engine Ferrari in the classic mold.

SPECIFICATIONS

Engines: all dohc V-12; **365 GT4 2+2** (1972-75): 267.8 cid/ 4390 cc, 320 bhp @ 6200 rpm, 319 lbs-ft @ 4600 rpm; **400i/400i Automatic** (1976-85): 294.2 cid/4823 cc, 340 bhp @ 6500 rpm, 347 lbs-ft @ 3600 rpm; **412i** (1985-88): 302 cid/4942 cc, 340 bhp @ 6000 rpm, 333 lbs-ft @ 4200 rpm

Transmissions:	5-speed overdrive manual or 3-speed automatic (exc. 365)
Suspension, front:	unequal-length A-arms, coil springs, anti-roll bar
Suspension, rear:	unequal-length A-arms, coil springs, anti-roll bar, hydraulic self-levelling
Brakes:	front/rear discs (with ABS on 412)
Wheelbase (in.):	106.3
Weight (lbs):	4000-4300
Top speed (mph):	145-155
0-60 mph (sec):	7.1

Production: **365 GT4 2+2** 470 **400i/400i A** NA **412i** NA

1973-1979 FERRARI DINO 308 GT4

In 1973, as in so many years past, the Paris Auto Salon witnessed the debut of a new Ferrari. And new it was. A mid-engine design, not only did it have Maranello's first roadgoing V-8—and a twincam at that—but Bertone bodywork, the first production Ferrari in nearly 20 years not designed by Pininfarina.

As a replacement for the 246 GT, the newcomer was called Dino and was equally bereft of Ferrari insignia but looked nothing like its predecessor: more angular in the contemporary idiom, yet still recognizably a Ferrari product. And it was a 2+2—the first mid-engine four-place Ferrari—though the numeral in its 308 GT4 designation represented camshafts, not seats. As in earlier Dinos, the three-digit number signified liters and cylinders, here 3.0 and eight, respectively. Though trim and tidy, the styling didn't win any raves—and still doesn't—but considering the difficulties in shaping a mid-engine 2+2, Bertone handled the assignment well.

This new Dino is also significant for introducing the 90-degree V-8 that would power the 308 and later 328 GTs, the most popular roadgoing Ferraris of all time. As used here, it had four Weber carburetors, 8.8:1 compression, and an advertised 205 horsepower at 6000 rpm. (Another factory folder claimed 240 at 6600; both listed

255 bhp for the European-delivery version.) Unlike the Dino V-6, the V-8 was produced entirely by Ferrari. It also marked the company's first use of a toothed-belt camshaft drive, replacing the traditional chain.

Otherwise, all was as expected from Maranello. Suspension was the traditional all-coil, all-independent double-wishbone system, there were vented disc brakes for all wheels, and a tubular-steel chassis again tied it all together.

The Bertone bodywork continued virtually unchanged during this model's six-year production run, except that the Ferrari prancing horse appeared on the nose, wheel hub centers, and steering wheel in 1976. No explanation was ever given for this sudden and unannounced change, but it likely reflected more astute marketing as much as a change of heart in Maranello.

Though not one of the best-looking Ferraris and short on "+2" space, the first of the 308s was a practical around-town car for four, but more at home with two aboard on the open road. Its performance was certainly nothing to sneeze at. In European tune it needed less than 6.5 seconds in the 0-60 mph dash and could top 150 mph—real thoroughbred stuff. With the rather anonymous styling, this just might be the ultimate "Q-car."

Of passing interest is the 208 GT4, a debored, detrimmed derivative launched in 1975 mainly for the Italian market, where high taxes made cars above 2.0-liters displacement inordinately expensive. With bore and stroke of 66.8 x 71 mm, this car's 1991-cc V-8 was only Ferrari's second undersquare engine. Rated power was 170 bhp, enough for a respectable 137-mph maximum.

Writing in *Road & Track* in 1974, race driver-turned-journalist Paul Frère recalled that "Enzo Ferrari once told me, 'A Ferrari is a 12-cylinder car.' " But the times were a-changin', and if nothing else, the 308 GT4 showed that Ferrari was willing to change with them. *R&T* called it "a worthy addition to the long line of great GT cars from Ferrari," and few, we think, would dispute that.

SPECIFICATIONS

Engine: dohc V-8, 179 cid/2927 cc, 205 bhp @ 6600 rpm, 209 lbs-ft @ 5000 rpm
(Note: A second factory brochure lists 240 bhp @ 6600 rpm; both rate the European model at 255 bhp.)

Transmission:	5-speed manual (in rear transaxle)
Suspension, front:	unequal-length A-arms, coil springs, anti-roll bar
Suspension, rear:	unequal-length A-arms, coil springs, anti-roll bar
Brakes:	front/rear discs
Wheelbase (in.):	100.4
Weight (lbs):	2930
Top speed (mph):	150 +
0-60 mph (sec):	6.4
Production:	NA

Post-1975 308 GT4s like this deviated from previous Dinos in wearing the Ferrari name and prancing-horse badge. U.S. bumpers don't help looks, but aren't bad.

1974-1985
FERRARI 365 GT4 BB &
512 BB/BBi

Ferrari's first horizontally opposed engine was built in 1964, a 12-cylinder, 1.5-liter Formula 1 unit with 11.1 compression, Lucas fuel injection, and 210 horsepower at 11,000 rpm. Flat-opposed engines are often called "boxers" because their pistons move toward and away from each other, like fighters sparring. The term originated in Germany and was first used in reference to early Volkswagen and Porsche engines.

Ferrari built other boxer engines for both GP and sports-racing cars, but didn't get around to a roadgoing model until the 1971 Turin show. That's when a new mid-engine flat-12 prototype appeared, a sort of very grownup Dino GT. It took two years to reach production, in late 1973 as a '74 model to succeed the front-engine Daytona, but it was well worth the wait.

From the start it was labelled 365 GT4 BB: 365 cc per cylinder, grand touring, four-cam berlinetta boxer. As in the Dino, the new 4.4-liter engine sat behind the cockpit and ahead of the rear axle centerline. Of course, the Dino wasn't called a Ferrari, so the BB technically ranks as the first mid-engine production Ferrari.

Like its forebears, the BB's main structure used steel panels and aluminum hood, doors, and "trunklid" (here, an engine access cover). A new wrinkle was fiberglass lower panels, which were always matte black regardless of body color. As on various racing Ferraris and certain production cars like the original Austin-Healey Sprite, the entire front end was hinged to tilt forward as a unit, matched by a similar rear-hinged aft section. Once more, Pininfarina contributed the body design, functional and brutish, with construction by Scaglietti as usual.

Predictably, the BB employed Ferrari's all-independent suspension system, but the chassis broke new ground. It was still a multi-tube affair, but the Turin show car's round- and oval-section members gave way in production to square and rectangular sections that were easier to fabricate. Radiator, spare, and a modicum of luggage space were provided in the nose. Even so, front/rear weight distribution worked out to 43/57 percent. Understeer was designed into the suspension to counteract this, and combined with a low polar moment of inertia (from putting the heaviest components in the middle of the car) to make the Boxer very agile and maneuverable.

Each bank of the Boxer flat-12 employed two overhead camshafts driven by toothed belt, a first for Ferrari. Intake ports were on top, exhaust ports on the lower sides. Two triple-throat Weber carburetors fed each set of intake ports. Connecting rods and valvegear were interchangeable with the 365 GTC/4 V-12. A rated 344 DIN horsepower at 7000 rpm was sent through a single dry-plate clutch to a 5-speed manual transaxle with a choice of 3.90, 3.75, or 3.46:1 final-drive ratios.

Inside was Ferrari's typical slim chrome shifter in a metal gate, which took some practice to work smoothly, what with the long linkage behind. So did the stiff clutch. The unassisted steering was heavy at low speed, though effort lightened up appreciably with speed and was just right for the Boxer's high terminal velocities.

And we mean *high*: 175 mph flat out, according to *Road & Track* magazine's 1975 report, "the fastest road car we've ever tested." Standing-start acceleration was equally vivid: 7.2 seconds 0-60 mph and 15.5 seconds in the quarter-mile at 102.5 mph. Still, *R&T* observed that the "Boxer is surprisingly heavy" (3420 pounds), "1st gear is very tall and the clutch in our test car slipped badly," so these times "aren't as impressive as they should be." By this account, the Boxer was a little faster off the line than the Daytona.

But then, *R&T* described the Boxer as a "dying breed," a semi-prophesy as yet unfulfilled, thank goodness. Indeed, the Boxer quickly went from strength to strength, beginning in late 1976 with the successor 512 BB (Ferrari had again reverted to liters/cylinders numbering). Oddly, it was being built two months before its public debut at the Paris show in October, which we think is another first for Ferrari.

Though the 512 seemed little different from the 365, closer inspection revealed a small chin spoiler in front, NACA ducts on the lower bodysides ahead of the rear wheels, four taillights instead of six, and 1.5 extra inches in tail length. A one millimeter increase in a bore and seven in stroke brought the flat-12 to 4942 cc and horsepower to 360 DIN. Peak revs dropped though, from 7000 to 6200 rpm, making the 512 more tractable.

And faster. In 1978, *Road & Track* recorded 5.5 seconds 0-60 mph, clocked the quarter in 14.2 seconds at 103.5 mph, and estimated top speed at a missile-like 188 mph. Theirs was a privately Federalized example (high certification costs had forced Ferrari to abandon all 12-cylinder cars for U.S. roads) and not as quick as Lamborghini's Countach, "but that was unimportant," said *R&T*. "The Boxer wins a

SPECIFICATIONS

Engines: all dohc flat-12; **365 GT4 BB** (1974-76): 267.8 cid/4390 cc, 344 bhp (DIN) @ 7000 rpm, 302 lbs-ft @ 3900 rpm; **512 BB** (1976-82): 302 cid/4942 cc, 360 bhp (DIN) @ 6200 rpm, 333 lbs-ft @ 4600 rpm; **512 BBi** (1982-85): 302 cid/4942 cc, 340 bhp (DIN) @ 6000 rpm, 333 lbs-ft @ 4200 rpm

Transmission:	5-speed manual (in rear transaxle)
Suspension, front:	unequal-length A-arms, coil springs, anti-roll bar
Suspension, rear:	unequal-length A-arms, twin coil springs, anti-roll bar
Brakes:	front/rear discs
Wheelbase (in.):	98.4
Weight (lbs):	3420-3620
Top speed (mph):	175+
0-60 mph (sec):	5.5-8.7
Production:	365 GT4 BB approx. 400 512 BB/BBi NA

more important award as the best all-round sports and GT car we've tested . . . The Countach is a fascinating design [but] the Boxer has it all: the speed, the handling, the lovely shape, the well done cockpit and, most important of all, a reputation for reliability.'' All it took to own one, then, was a mere $85,000.

The Boxer's last hurrah came in late 1981 with adoption of Bosch K-Jetronic fuel injection for the 512 BBi. Tuning was eased somewhat for new European emissions limits, so DIN horsepower fell to 340. The BB continued in this form for another two years, then moved over for the grandest roadgoing Ferrari yet: the reborn Testarossa.

Ferrari's first-ever flat-12 appeared in the successor to the Daytona, the 365 GT4 BB **(below and opposite)**. *Looks became more aggressive on the even more potent 512 BB* **(this page, bottom)** *and fuel-injected BBi.*

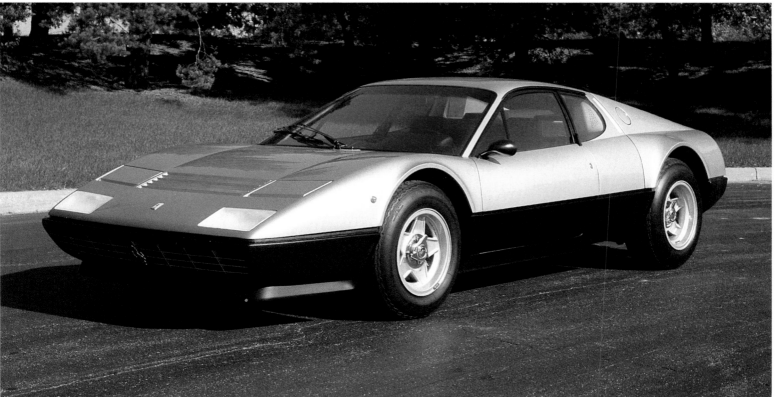

1975-1988
FERRARI 308/308i
GTB/GTS & 328 GTB/GTS

Enzo Ferrari traditionally previewed his new cars at Europe's fall auto shows. Frankfurt always came first (usually held the last two weeks of September, but only in odd-numbered years), followed by Paris (first two weeks of October), London (last half of that month), and Turin (first half of November).

Because of this yearly schedule, most Ferraris were introduced at Paris. In 1975 the firm displayed four cars: 365 GT4 2 + 2, 365 GT4 Berlinetta Boxer, Dino 308 GT4, and a new offering, the 308 GTB, the replacement for the V-6 Dino 246.

As on the 308 GT4, the model number denoted a 3.0-liter eight-cylinder engine— the same four-cam 90-degree V-8, in fact, and also transversely mounted ahead of the rear axle centerline. The four cams were driven by toothed belts. With a quartet of twin-choke Weber carburetors and 8.8:1 compression, rated horsepower was 205 at 6600 rpm. Drive was again taken through a single dry-plate clutch to a 5-speed all-synchromesh rear transaxle, here with a 4.06:1 ratio. Chassis specifications were much like the Dino 246's, right down to the 92.1-inch wheelbase.

Inevitably, bodywork was executed by Scaglietti to a Pininfarina design, but the first few GTB shells were mostly fiberglass, the most extensive use of this material yet seen on a roadgoing Ferrari. (The BB had plastic lower panels, of course, while some single-seat Ferrari racers had all-fiberglass bodies.) But though finish was excellent, conventional steel construction took over very early in production. Ferrari customers just weren't accustomed to "plastic cars."

More appreciated was the 308's styling: taut and muscular yet smooth and sensuous. Highlights included a wide eggcrate grille riding below the bumper, hidden headlamps, "hippy" front and rear fenders set off by aggressively flared wheelarches,

1985-1988 FERRARI TESTAROSSA

There are cars, and then there are *super*cars. The Ferrari Berlinetta Boxer clearly belonged in the latter category, but so did Lamborghini's mid-engine Countach and the more exotic Porsche 911s. In late 1984, and at the Paris show as usual, Ferrari fought back by unveiling a spectacular BB successor that revived the name Testa Rossa ("redhead") of late-Fifties sports-racing fame. It went into production the following year as the first Ferrari specifically conceived with American safety and emissions standards in mind.

Continuing another Ferrari tradition, the Testarossa was designed by Pininfarina, which also built it (Scaglietti had assembled the BB). Unlike most previous roadgoing Ferraris, its body was made of aluminum except for a steel roof and doors. The shape was evolved in the PF wind tunnel with special attention to front and rear aerodynamic downforce, possibly to the detriment of the overall drag coefficient, which wasn't disclosed but worked out to a so-so 0.36 by most estimates.

Perhaps the most striking design feature was a set of long longitudinal ribs or slats on each flank. These were prompted by the use of twin radiators, one per side, aft of the cockpit, with the intakes extending from just ahead of the rear wheels almost to the front door shutlines. Wind-tunnel tests indicated the slats (sometimes called "egg slicers") were needed for more efficient air channeling. They were also needed because some countries require body openings of this size to be covered with some sort of grillework. Placing the radiators aft eliminated a persistent complaint from BB owners about interior heat being generated by radiator-to-engine pipes too near the passenger cell, and also opened up more luggage space in front.

The Testarossa engine was basically an improved version of the BB flat-12, mainly via a new 24-valve head for each cylinder bank (four valves per cylinder), plus a 0.1 point compression drop (to 8.7:1). Bosch K-Jetronic fuel injection and Marelli Multiplex ignition continued from the 512 BBi. All this plus the twin coolers resulted in an extra 40 horsepower, 380 total. As on the 512, it passed through a twin-disc clutch, here enlarged an inch to a 9.5-inch diameter, a necessity with the massive 354 pounds-feet of torque on tap. Suspension, chassis construction, and the longitudinal engine positioning were as for the BB, too.

Dimensionally, though, the Testarossa was larger and a tad lighter (by 44 pounds), though it's hardly svelte at 1.5 tons plus. Wheelbase was two inches longer at 100.4. Tracks were increased, too (to 59.8 inches front, 65.4 rear). In short, it's big for a Ferrari. The 176.6-inch overall length is modest enough, but a 77.8-inch beam makes this one of the widest cars in current production—and results in an overly large (and clumsy) 39.4-foot turning circle.

But low-speed maneuvers are not what this car was designed for, though it *is* relatively docile in traffic. Speed is what the TR is all about, and here it's every bit as spectacular as it looks. How spectacular? Well, one ran the standing quarter-mile in 13.6 seconds at 105 mph in an early road test, while a later report (on a European delivery model) showed maximum velocity of no less than 181 mph. The 0-60 mph time was less thrilling perhaps—"only" 5.3 seconds—but for ground-level flying, the TR was tough to beat. Only the aging Countach had its measure, and the Lambo was far less wieldy and accommodating.

The TR's styling continues to be debated, generally evoking love-it or hate-it responses. But if imitation be the sincerest form of flattery, the design must be considered a success, as its influence has already spread to several high-performance cars of far less stature. We think the TR will go down as one of the more distinctive Ferraris, if not the prettiest.

At over $100,000 at this writing, the Testarossa is not the proverbial "everyman's car," but Ferraris have never been that—and never will be, we reckon. Like its illustrious forebears, it demands respect on the road and a great deal of care off of it. Given these, however, the TR will provide supreme satisfaction to even the most jaded motorists. Breeding shows, you know.

SPECIFICATIONS

Engine: dohc V-12 (4 valves per cylinder), 302 cid/4942 cc, 380 bhp (SAE net) @ 5750 rpm, 354 lbs-ft @ 4500 rpm

Transmission:	5-speed manual (in rear transaxle)
Suspension, front:	unequal-length A-arms, coil springs, anti-roll bar
Suspension, rear:	unequal-length A-arms, twin coil springs, anti-roll bar
Brakes:	front/rear discs
Wheelbase (in.):	100.4
Weight (lbs):	3660
Top speed (mph):	180
0-60 mph (sec):	5.3
Production:	NA (production continues at this writing)

*Though clearly evolved from the Berlinetta Boxer, the brutishly handsome Testarossa has a look all its own. Twin side-mount radiators feed from large "egg slicer" air ducts. Note massive-looking flat 12 (**opposite top**).*

1984-1987 FERRARI GTO

Despite occasional challenges by Jaguar, Porsche, and Aston Martin, Ferrari dominated Grand Touring competition in 1957-61 (with long- and short-wheelbase 250 berlinettas and California Spyders). But Enzo Ferrari was never one to stand still, and in 1962 he introduced a faster, more powerful racer, the fabulous 250 GTO berlinetta.

Those initials, as most everyone knows by now, mean *Gran Turismo Omologato,* literally homologated (approved) for grand-touring-class competition. Ferrari built only enough to satisfy the rulemakers, just 42. Most were fastback coupes with the 3.0-liter "250" V-12—36 in all—but three carried 400 Superamerica engines and the last three built (in early 1964) had the 3.0 engine and notchback styling.

Designed at Maranello and built by Scaglietti, the GTOs remain some of the fastest and most beautiful Ferraris of all. They also marked the ultimate development of the original live-rear-axle Ferrari chassis. Scarcity and well chronicled competition exploits have made them the most sought-after Ferraris among collectors, with prices at this writing running to seven figures.

In 1984, the GTO's originator (you didn't *really* think it was Pontiac) revived the hallowed name for a new sports-racer that was just as handsome and even faster than its forebear but more numerous—if you call a deliberately limited 200-unit production run "numerous." For this reason, the new GTO will probably never command the same high prices, but it's certainly worthy of the name and just as much a track car that's barely usable on the street.

At first glance, the new GTO appears to be a development of the mid-V-8 308/328 berlinetta—which it is, though very little of the production model remains. Immediately noticeable outside are the "flag-style" door mirrors, bulging fenders, large front and rear spoilers, and a pair of driving lamps at the outboard grille ends. Less discernible is the stretched 96.5-inch wheelbase, 4.4 inches longer than the 308's and four inches up on the 328's, necessitated by an engine reoriented from "east-west" to "north-south."

That engine is the familiar quad-cam V-8, enlarged to 2855 cc and fitted with twin IHI turbochargers, each with its own intercooler, for delivering a denser air charge for mixing with fuel supplied by Weber-Marelli port electronic injection. Originally developed for Lancia rally cars (Ferrari and Lancia had long been part of the Fiat empire by this point), the fortified V-8 as installed pumped out a rated 400 horsepower at 7000 rpm and 366 pounds-feet torque peaking at 3800 rpm. Unlike the 308/328, a twin-disc dry-plate clutch was used to transfer power to the 5-speed transaxle. Final drive was surprisingly long-legged at 2.90:1. The result was a claimed 190 mph at maximum revs in fifth gear and, according to *Road & Track,* 0-60 mph in a blistering five seconds flat and a standing-start quarter-mile of 14.1 seconds at 113 mph.

Maranello's primary goal here was a contender for FISA Group B competition, where regulations specified a production minimum of 200 units for a model to qualify. Ferrari built the required number but no more. As a competition car with a high-tune engine, the GTO was never certified for U.S. sale—absolutely no point in that—though a few have inevitably found their way to America via the infamous "gray market." Still, the superficial similarity to the 308/328 boosted the production models' image considerably, one reason their platform was used as a starting point. Cost and time constraints were the main ones.

Per Ferrari tradition, "customer" GTOs were fully equipped for road use. A package option delivered air conditioning, AM/FM/cassette stereo, and electric windows for $1800, which was steep only if you blanched at the $83,400 sticker price. If you have to ask. . . .

It should be noted that this was Ferrari's first race-and-ride sports car since the original GTO was phased out in '64. Though its competition record has yet to be fully written, it would seem a worthy successor to those hallowed cars, judging by specifications and driver reports. In fact, no less an authority than former World Driving Champion Phil Hill, who certainly knows a thing or two about racing and Ferraris, has said just that.

We wouldn't be surprised to see owners of original GTOs looking to add one of the new ones to their stable—and vice-versa. Both are possible. All its takes is a *lot* of money *and* desire—but then, so do most of life's greater rewards.

Mid-Eighties GTO marked the return of the race-and-ride Ferrari epitomized by its like-named early-Sixties forebear. Despite a resemblance to the "everyday" 328, the new GTO differed in many respects. As a homologation special for Group B, only 200 were built, some in road trim.

SPECIFICATIONS

Engine: dohc V-8 (four valves/cylinder), 174 cid/2855 cc, 400 bhp @ 7000 rpm, 366 lbs-ft @ 3800 rpm

Transmission:	5-speed manual (in rear transaxle)
Suspension, front:	unequal-length A-arms, coil springs, anti-roll bar
Suspension, rear:	unequal-length A-arms, coil springs, anti-roll bar
Brakes:	front/rear discs
Wheelbase (in.):	96.5
Weight (lbs):	2555
Top speed (mph):	190 (measured by Ferrari at Italy's Nardo circuit)
0-60 mph (sec):	5.0
Production:	200

1987-1988 FERRARI F40

Enzo Ferrari really knows how to throw a birthday party. With 1988 marking 40 years of cars bearing his name, *Il Commendatore* has given all of us a birthday present in the glorious tradition of the original GTO. Logically and simply, it's called F40.

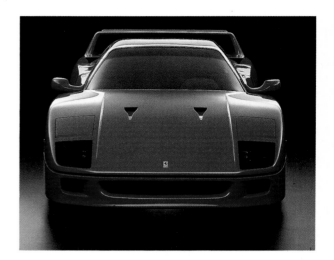

Revealed at Maranello on July 21, 1987, the F40 was born June 6, 1986 when, as Mr. Ferrari told the assembled world press, "I expressed a wish to our executive committee to have a car reminiscent of the original 250 LM [see entry]. Ing. Giovanni Razelli [the firm's managing director] and his collaborators considered my proposal, which had been approved by [Fiat chairman] Mr. Ghidella." The aim, according to Pininfarina general manager Leonardo Fioravanti, was "to recover the spirit of some of the Ferrari cars of the past; that is, to give our customers the possibility of driving objects that are very similar to the racing cars." That they've done. In fact, many old hands at Maranello still shun the prosaic F40 designation, preferring "LM" or "Le Mans" for this latest race-and-ride Ferrari.

And indeed, the F40 is nothing so much as a roadgoing version of the GTO *Evoluzione*, a twin-turbocharged version of the latterday mid-engine GTO (see entry) that would have been Ferrari's Group B contender had the FIA not cancelled the category after two tragedy-plagued seasons (1985-86). The F40 is also nothing so much as a response to Porsche's erstwhile Group B machine, the 959. Italian pride couldn't let Germany lay claim to the world's ultimate roadgoing sports car, hence this new semi-racer, available to only a handful of "qualified"—namely, expert—buyer/drivers.

While it superficially resembles the *Evoluzione*, GTO, and the 308/328 series, the F40 differs in numerous ways. Styling is predictably and obviously PF/Ferrari, but echoes the 959's with wider, more deeply drawn bodywork highlighted by a high-flying rear aerofoil, wheels and tires of near Indy-car proportions, and a profusion of scoops, grids, and louvers. The 0.34 drag coefficient is unexceptional by even road-car standards these days, though PF claims wind-tunnel testing aimed at maximum downforce. Wheelbase is identical with the GTO's, but the F40 is just 2.2 inches shorter than the current Testarossa and an impressive 78 inches wide.

Unlike the lush 959, the F40 has hinged nose and tail sections; its only concession to comfort is a minimal air conditioning system. Carpeting, interior door panels,

sound system, even windup windows have been eliminated (the last replaced by sliding Plexiglas panes) to save weight—and enhance the "race-car" aura. Furthering that impression are form-fitting bucket seats clad in fire-resistant, day-glo-orange Nomex and available in three sizes to suit different physiques. Other competition touches include four-point seat harnesses and a safety fuel bladder (a big sponge encased in rubber holding 31.7 gallons).

The chassis is also racing-inspired, if conventional enough for Ferrari: a steel-tube space-frame carrying classic twin-wishbone all-independent suspension with coil-over-shock units. Remaining basic structure is made of the latest in composite materials reinforced with carbon-fiber and Kevlar; composites are also used for outer body panels. Another high-tech racing touch is three-position ride-height control. At speed the car automatically lowers 20 mm for reduced drag; to clear steep driveways, it can be manually raised 20 mm from "neutral" height.

Again unlike the 959, the F40's steering (rack-and-pinion) and brakes are manual, and there's no anti-lock brake system. But the brakes themselves are Group-C massive: 13-inch-diameter vented, cross-drilled discs with aluminum centers, and cast-iron outers.

Oh, yes: the engine. It's basically a detuned version of the *Evoluzione* V-8, which in turn was a bored, short-stroke derivative of the GTO's twincam *quattrovalvole* unit. Twin air-to-air Behr intercoolers feed dual IHI turbochargers; wastegate control, ignition, and port fuel injection (with two injectors per cylinder) are electronic and combined (via the Weber-Marelli IAW engine-management system). Compression is a modest 7.8:1, but maximum boost is no less than 16 psi—good for a rated 471 horsepower. If that's not enough, Ferrari offers a package with different turbos and cam profiles that adds another *200*.

Power reaches the ground via a GTO 5-speed manual transaxle, albeit with a taller final drive (2.73 versus 2.90:1). To cope with it, the F40 wears Pirelli's latest "P Zero" high-speed tires wrapped around huge, five-spoke Speedline modular wheels and massively sized at 245/40ZR-17 front, 335/35ZR-17 rear—real Formula 1 rolling stock.

Other than a few factory *pilotos*, no one has driven Ferrari's newest at this writing, but the claimed 201-mph top speed and sizzling 12 seconds in the 0-200 km/h (0-124-mph) sprint seem entirely believable. Alas, the price is equally *un*believable—projected around $187,000 at current exchange rates—and with announced production of just 400 or so (beginning in 1988), the F40 will be known first-hand by only a privileged few. The good news is that Ferrari will certify it for U.S. sale.

In all, the F40 is a worthy heir to the Ferrari legend it celebrates; at the very least, it's another instantly collectible Ferrari. Happy 40th, Maranello, and thanks for this very tasty cake.

SPECIFICATIONS

Engine: dohc V-8, twin turbocharged and intercooled, 4 valves/cylinder; 179 cid/2936 cc, 471 bhp (SAE net) @ 7000 rpm (approx. 671 bhp with optional kit), 426 lbs-ft @ 4000 rpm

Transmission:	5-speed all-indirect manual (in rear transaxle)
Suspension, front:	upper and lower unequal-length A-arms, coil springs (concentric with telescopic shocks), anti-roll bar
Suspension, rear:	upper and lower unequal-length A-arms, coil springs (concentric with telescopic shocks), anti-roll bar
Brakes:	front/rear discs
Wheelbase (in.):	94.5
Weight (lbs):	2425
Top speed (mph):	201 (manufacturer's data)
0-60 mph (sec):	est. 3.0
Production:	400 (announced; not begun at this writing)

Purposeful from every angle, the F40 is evolved from the GTO Evoluzione and honors Ferrari's 40th anniversary. More racer than road car, it's fairly stark but blindingly fast, with a claimed 201-mph top speed and acceleration to match.

1959-1966
FIAT 1200/1500/1500S/
1600S

Fiat has been the General Motors of Italy for as long as anyone can remember and, like the American firm, got into the sports-car business relatively late. Fiat's first postwar move in this direction was the 8V of 1952-54, but this was strictly a limited-production indulgence (only 114 built) while the 1100 *Transformabile* of 1955-59 was ugly and unsuccessful. Then, with help from Pinin Farina and OSCA (*Officina Specializzata Costruzione Automobili*), Fiat finally got serious about sports cars in 1959.

One of Fiat's best-sellers at the time was the 1200 sedan, a chunky, uninspired four-door with unit-steel construction, coil-spring independent front suspension, and a live rear axle suspended *and* located by semi-elliptic leaf springs. This hardly seemed the stuff of which sports cars are made, but technical chief Dante Giacosa knew better. Retaining the sedan's powertrain, floorpan and some inner body panels, he called in PF to build him a sports car.

PF (which always insisted it had nothing to do with the *Transformabile*) produced a simple but attractive two-seat convertible complete with wind-down door windows—and consequently landed the contract to build production bodyshells in

*This lightly modified 1600S carries reversed wheels and larger-than-stock tires; it's also missing the central Fiat grille emblem. Tidy Pininfarina styling needed few embellishments anyway, while the civilized cockpit (**below left**) had plenty. Twincam engine (**below**) was a snug fit.*

quantity. Fiat would provide floorpans; PF would build, paint, and trim the bodies before returning them to Fiat's Lingotto factory for final assembly.

Meantime, Fiat had decided to offer a choice of engines: the sedan's plodding 1221-cc ohv four and a newly designed 1.5-liter twincam unit. Fiat had planned to build the latter, but turned instead to OSCA, the Bologna-based engine and race-car specialist then run by the Maserati brothers.

Both new models were revealed in 1959: the 1200 Cabriolet with 58 horsepower and the 80-bhp, OSCA-engine 1500S. As the twincam version wasn't meant to be a volume item, it was left to the pushrod two-seater to establish Fiat's sports-car credentials, which it did in short order. Both were stylish and well equipped little tourers, and the 1500S was as fast as an Alfa 1.3 Giulietta. PF soon produced a removable hardtop as a factory-approved extra. Also with Fiat's blessing, it built and marketed a fixed-roof model that looked rather like PF's later Lancia Flavia coupe design.

The next six years brought numerous improvements to these conventional but sweet-handling open Fiats. The 1500S gained standard front disc brakes at the end of 1960, then became the 1600S via substitution of an enlarged OSCA-built engine boasting 90 bhp. The original 1200 was similarly upgraded in March 1963, being "re-engined" with the latest 1481-cc pushrod four from the new Lampredi-designed sedans to become a 1500 Cabriolet. This brought 72 bhp and more torque, bumping top speed to about 90 mph. At the same time, the 1600S acquired rear disc brakes and a modified four-lamp nose.

The most significant change of all appeared in March 1965: a brand-new 5-speed all-synchro gearbox for both models. It didn't increase their performance, but it did make them easier to drive. It also hinted at Fiat's future, for this same gearbox would return in 1966 for the successor 124 Sport Coupe/Spider and the 124/125 sedans on which they were based—the most successful postwar cars in Fiat history.

SPECIFICATIONS

Engines: **1200** (1959-63): ohv I-4, 74.5 cid/1221 cc, 58 bhp (SAE net) @ 5300 rpm, 61 lbs-ft @ 3000 rpm; **1500S** (1959-63): dohc I-4, 91 cid/1491 cc, 80 bhp (SAE net) @ 6000 rpm, 77 lbs-ft @ 4000 rpm; **1500** (1963-65): ohv I-4, 90.4 cid/1481 cc, 72 bhp (SAE net) @ 5200 rpm, 87 lbs-ft @ 3200 rpm; **1600S** (1962-65): dohc I-4, 95.7 cid/1568 cc, 90 bhp (SAE net) @ 6000 rpm, 98 lbs-ft @ 4000 rpm

Transmissions:	4-speed manual; 5-speed on 1965-66 1600S
Suspension, front:	wishbones, coil springs, anti-roll bar
Suspension, rear:	live axle on semi-elliptic leaf springs, anti-roll bar
Brakes:	front/rear drums, front discs/rear drums (twincams from 1960, ohv models from 1963), front/rear discs (twincams from 1965)
Wheelbase (in.):	92.0
Weight (lbs):	2000-2280
Top speed (mph):	105 (1500)
0-60 mph (sec):	10.6 (1500)
Production:	approx. 43,000

1968-1985 FIAT 124 SPORTS/SPIDER 2000

SPECIFICATIONS

Engines: all dohc I-4; **1968-70:** 88 cid/1438 cc, 96 bhp (SAE gross) @ 6500 rpm, 83 lbs-ft @ 4000 rpm; **1971-72:** 98 cid/1608 cc, 104 bhp (SAE gross) @ 6000 rpm, 94 lbs-ft @ 4200 rpm; **1973:** 97 cid/1592 cc, horsepower and torque NA; **1974-78:** 107 cid/1756 cc, 92 bhp @ 6200 rpm, 92 lbs-ft @ 3000 rpm; **1978-81:** 121.7 cid/1995 cc, 80 bhp @ 5500 rpm, 100 lbs-ft @ 3000 rpm; **1982-85:** 121.7 cid/1995 cc, 102 bhp (SAE net) @ 5500 rpm, 110 lbs-ft @ 3000 rpm; **1982-83:** 121.7 cid/1995 cc turbocharged, 120 bhp (SAE net) @ 6000 rpm, 130 lbs-ft @ 3600 rpm

Transmissions:	5-speed manual, 3-speed automatic
Suspension, front:	unequal-length A-arms, coil springs, anti-roll bar
Suspension, rear:	live axle, trailing arms, Panhard rod, coil springs
Brakes:	front/rear discs
Wheelbase (in.):	89.8 (Spider), 95.3 (Coupe)
Weight (lbs):	2090-2385
Top speed (mph):	95-104
0-60 mph (sec):	9.4-14.5

Production: 1400/1600 Spider 60,233 **1800 Spider** 69,208 **Coupes** 69,208 **2000 Spider/Spider Turbo/Spidereuropa/Spidereuropa Volumex** NA

Sports cars based on workaday sedans are as old as the auto industry itself. And a necessity since World War II, thanks to rising competition and escalating production costs that make wholly separate sports-car designs prohibitively expensive for even the largest volume producers. Postwar history is replete with examples, successful and otherwise: the Austin-Healey, most Mercedes SLs, today's Pontiac Fiero and Toyota MR2, even the original Porsche and Corvette. The most successful such Italian cars were undoubtedly the Fiat 124 Sports Coupe and Spider.

It all started in 1966 with the 124 itself, a boxy little rear-drive sedan and wagon that would rejuvenate Fiat's fortunes in the all-important family-car market. Conventional but modern, they boasted an 1197-cc pushrod four, compact 95.3-inch wheelbase, front-disc/rear-drum brakes, and all-coil suspension with front wishbones and a well located live rear axle. Fiat had done good business in the early Sixties with two-seat cabrios derived from its old 1200 sedan, so a sports-bodied 124 was never in doubt.

It arrived two years behind the sedan and wagon—or rather, they did, for there were two distinct models: an airy Fiat-designed 2+2 coupe on the standard wheelbase, and a shapely two-seat Pininfarina convertible on a 5.5-inch shorter platform. For structural stiffness, the latter had box-section rocker panel reinforcements and rear cross-member, plus strengthened inner wheel housings.

Power was initially supplied by a 1438-cc enlargement of the 124 engine with a new crossflow twincam cylinder head featuring toothed-belt cam drive, a world first. With modified pistons and manifold, special Weber carb, and revised cooling and oiling systems, the Sport Coupe and Spider offered 31 more horsepower than family 124s and a healthy 13 extra pounds-feet torque. The basic 124 chassis was unchanged apart from higher spring rates, wider tracks and wheels, and disc instead of drum rear brakes. The Coupe came with a 4-speed manual gearbox, the Spider a 5-speeder (optional for the Coupe, but standard on U.S. models from 1969).

This formula would be good enough to last over 15 years without fundamental change. Struggling with U.S. emissions requirements more than most, Fiat juggled displacement and engine tuning several times in the Seventies, while tacking on the inevitable "crash bumpers" and other mandated safety equipment with varying degrees of success. The Coupe disappeared after model year 1974 (and a '72 facelift), but the Spider soldiered on, reaching its ultimate form by 1981 as the Spider 2000, with 2.0-liter fuel-injected engine.

That same year, Fiat of North America commissioned a turbocharged Spider from Legend Industries, a conversion sold only in the U.S. It was the fastest Spider yet but no less entertaining. Unfortunately, workmanship still left too much to be desired, as did durability and service backup.

These factors had contributed to a fast fall in Fiat's U.S. sales after 1974. Ten years later, the firm decided to cut its losses and withdraw not only from the U.S. market but from the sports-car business too. As with the X1/9, therefore, Spider production and marketing were turned over to the coachbuilder, and an upgraded edition, the Pininfarina Azzurra (literally, "blue"), was sold in the U.S. by the Malcolm Bricklin group for two years before imports were halted.

For awhile, America's loss was Europe's gain. Fiat hadn't sold the Spider in Europe since the late Sixties, but PF did, starting in 1983 with the Spidereuropa, basically the U.S.-spec 2000 model. There was also a short-lived Volumex version, with Roots-type volumetric supercharger providing power and performance similar to that of the U.S. turbo conversion. Alas, sales were no better there than they'd been here, and PF quietly phased out the winsome convertible after 1985.

Despite their checkered history and Fiat's equally spotty reliability/durability record, the 124-based Coupes and Spiders remain appealing little cars: nice to look at, cheap to buy, thrifty with fuel, fairly easy to work on, and pleasant to drive. They're also roomy and practical for sports cars (the Spider's folding top is still a model of convenience) and most are well equipped. For best performance and driveability, the pre-1973 and post-1977 models are the ones to have.

*Fiat 124 Spider outlived its coupe companion while retaining the same basic appearance and cockpit (**above right**). Spot the differences between this early-Seventies model (**opposite top**) and decade-younger Spider 2000. Once U.S. imports ended, Fiat turned sales over to body supplier Pininfarina, which sold it in Europe as the Spidereuropa.*

1972-1988
FIAT/BERTONE X1/9

Fiat's X1/9 wasn't the first mid-engine production sports car, but it has been one of the most enduring. Announced in 1972, it was elegant, nippy, and full of character, thoughtfully equipped and remarkable value for money. That the X1/9 was "right" from day one is confirmed by the fact that it's still being built 16 years later with few major changes.

It wasn't Fiat's first low-priced sports car, either. The giant Italian automaker had enjoyed good success in the Sixties with coupe and spider versions of its little rear-engine 850 sedan, though these were sporty economy models, not genuine sports cars.

Bertone had supplied bodies for the 850 spider though, and devised the X1/9 (Fiat's internal project code) to replace it. At first the idea was for Bertone to build the new middie on a freelance basis from Fiat-supplied components, but Fiat quickly recognized the design as quite practical for mass production—i.e., "cost effective." The rest, as they say, is history.

The X1/9 followed the Lotus Europa and VW-Porsche 914 in being a "corporate kit car," with two-seat sports bodywork over a rearranged group of components borrowed from a workaday sedan. In this case, the donor was Fiat's front-drive 128, introduced in 1969. It was a simple matter to site its transverse power package midships to drive the rear wheels, thus creating a mini Lamborghini Miura. Steering also came from the 128 shelf, as did brakes, though the X1/9 benefitted from its "kit" composition by getting discs at the rear as well as the front.

Considering its spare 87-inch wheelbase and tidy overall size, the X1/9 was a marvel of space efficiency. Not only was there decent cabin room but two trunks: one fore and one aft (behind the midships powertrain). The fuel tank lived twixt engine bay and cockpit, the spare inside behind the right seat. Bertone's wedgy styling was up to the minute then and still looks good now, while the structure was evidently quite strong.

A good thing, too, because besides having two doors and three access panels (one for each trunk plus engine cover), the X1/9 body had a Targa-style lift-off roof panel above the cockpit that could be stowed in the front trunk. The all-independent suspension was by compact coil-sprung MacPherson/Chapman struts, thus further reducing space intrusion. In all, a clever, well thought-out package.

And a nicely balanced one, thanks to the lower polar moment of inertia and reduced body roll associated with the midships layout. Weight distribution, originally 41/59 percent front/rear, was hardly ideal, but steering and suspension geometry helped compensate, making the X1/9 maneuverable, fun to drive and not at all quirky.

Initially, the X1/9 wasn't as fast as it looked. Its 1.3-liter sohc four, inherited from the 128, may have been okay for Europe but couldn't cut it in the U.S., bogged down by emissions controls and the extra poundage of federally required safety gear (including too-obvious "crash" bumpers). In fact, overall performance wasn't much better than that of the increasingly asthmatic MGB. Fiat partly answered the problem in both markets for 1980 by substituting the 1498-cc engine from its then-new Ritmo/Strada sedan, and junking the original 4-speed transaxle for a longer-striding 5-speed, which also helped economy. The following year, Bosch L-Jetronic fuel injection replaced the previous Weber carburetor for small gains in power and torque.

These and minor yearly cosmetic and equipment revisions are pretty much the extent of changes to date, except that Fiat decided to get out of the sports-car business in the early Eighties and arranged for Bertone to take over complete manufacturing and marketing of the X1/9. This has led to various "special editions" in recent years, though the basic car remains the same.

Meantime, Fiat had decided to bail out of the U.S. market after years of steadily falling sales. Thus, if you want a new X1/9 nowadays, you'll buy it through the Malcolm Bricklin organization and pay upwards of $13,000 for a car with Bertone badges.

A final point. Fiat's Lancia division would use the kit-car approach for the larger (and not very popular) Beta-based Monte Carlo of 1975 (sold briefly in the U.S. as the Scorpion and developed, incidentally, as project X1/20). Today's Toyota MR2 and Pontiac Fiero follow the same pattern. Who's next?

The granddaddy of the Pontiac Fiero and Toyota MR2, the X1/9 has changed remarkably little over the years. **Opposite bottom:** *Fiat's portrait of the 1970 U.S. version.* **Opposite top:** *A British-market 1980 model.* **This page:** *The U.S. Bertone iteration for '84, by which time Fiat had passed production and sales to the coachbuilder. Cockpit is tight but well planned.*

SPECIFICATIONS

Engines: all sohc I-4; **1972-79:** 78.7 cid/1290 cc, 75 bhp (SAE net) @ 6000 rpm, 72 lbs-ft @ 3400 rpm; **1980-81:** 91.4 cid/ 1498 cc, 67 bhp (SAE net) @ 5250 rpm, 76 lbs-ft @ 3000 rpm; **1982-88:** 91.4 cid/1498 cc, 75 bhp (SAE net) @ 5500 rpm, 79 lbs-ft @ 3000 rpm (European version: 85 bhp @ 6000 rpm, 87 lbs-ft @ 3200 rpm)

Transmissions:	4-speed manual (1972-79), 5-speed manual (1980-88); both in rear transaxle
Suspension, front:	MacPherson struts, lower lateral links, compliance struts, coil springs
Suspension, rear:	Chapman struts, lower A-arms, back links, coil springs
Brakes:	front/rear discs
Wheelbase (in.):	86.7
Weight (lbs):	2150-2250
Top speed (mph):	99-105 +
0-60 mph (sec):	11.0-12.5
Production:	NA (production continues at this writing)

211

1955-1957
FORD THUNDERBIRD

Legend says the Thunderbird was born in October 1951, when Ford Division general manager Lewis Crusoe visited the Paris Auto Show with styling consultant George Walker. America had fallen in love with European sports cars in the early postwar years, and both men were taken by the ones they saw there: the curvy Jaguar XK120 and the new Anglo-American Nash-Healey (see entries), GM's experimental two-seat LeSabre. "Why don't we have something like that?" Crusoe asked. Walker replied, "Oh, but we do! "—then hurried to phone Dearborn to get his crew cracking.

Like many apocryphal stories, this one isn't true. Ford stylists had been conjuring two-seaters before this, though there was never a rush to build one because sports-car sales then accounted for a miniscule 0.27 percent of the total U.S. market. But in January 1953, GM threw down a gauntlet Ford couldn't ignore: the Chevrolet Corvette (see entry). Barely a month later, Ford was hard at work on the car that would ultimately be named for the god worshipped by America's Southwest Indians as the bringer of rain and prosperity.

First displayed as a wood mockup at the Detroit show in early 1954, the Thunderbird was a "personal" car, not a pure sports car. It rode the same wheelbase as the first-generation Corvette but was far more luxurious—and practical. In place of creaking fiberglass and clumsy side curtains was a sturdy steel body with convenient roll-up windows. Instead of an ill-fitting soft top there was a snug power top, lift-off hard top, or both. And there was no plodding six-cylinder engine but a burly Mercury V-8.

Bill Burnett supervised the engineering, which relied heavily on standard Ford components. Styling, chiefly the work of young Bill Boyer directed by Walker lieutenant Frank Hershey, couldn't have been better: simple and smooth yet clearly

Ford, with rakish long-hood/short-deck proportions recalling the classic early Forties Lincoln Continental.

With European style and American comfort, convenience, and go, Thunderbird proved well-nigh irresistible. It whipped the rival Chevy in 1955 model-year production by nearly 24 to 1.

You don't mess with such success in Detroit, and Ford didn't with the '56 Thunderbird. Changes were limited to a larger V-8 option, exterior-mount spare (for more trunk space), softer suspension (for a smoother ride), and optional portholes for the hardtop. Production eased but was still five times Corvette's. Trouble was, Ford wanted much higher volume, and had already settled on four-seaters for 1958.

So the '57 was the last two-seat Bird—and arguably the best. A handsome facelift brought a prominent bumper/grille and a longer deck (again enclosing the spare) wearing modest blade-like tailfins. There was more power than ever: up to 285 bhp on the top twin-four-barrel 312 with 10.0:1 compression. Ford even built 208 supercharged "F-Birds" with 300/340 bhp courtesy of Paxton-McCulloch blowers, mainly for racing.

And race the early Birds did, albeit with limited success. A '55 sponsored by *Mechanix Illustrated* magazine's Tom McCahill swept the production sports-car class at that year's Daytona Speed Weeks; Joe Ferguson's two-way average 124.633 mph besting every Austin-Healey, Porsche, and all but one Jaguar XK120. Chuck Daigh did even better in '56 with a Pete DePaolo-prepped car, running 88.779 mph in the standing mile, though Zora Arkus-Duntov's modified Vette was faster (89.735 mph). In '57, Daigh scored 93.312 mph and a privately entered Bird ran the flying mile at 146.282 mph one way, 138.775 mph both ways. Then the Automobile Manufacturers Association issued its infamous racing "ban" and development stopped.

But the Thunderbird had proved its point. If not a true sports car, it could be a high-performance car. That it was also stylish and luxurious made it all the more remarkable—and memorable. An extra-long model year made the '57 the most numerous of the flock, the first American two-seaters to sell in really high numbers.

Which was, of course, the most important point. By proving that two-seaters could be a commercial success, the T-Bird paved the way for the many sports cars that followed it in the U.S., domestic and foreign. For that alone it deserves our respect. For what they were, the early Birds will always have our affection.

SPECIFICATIONS

Engines: all ohv V-8; **292 cid/4785 cc—1955:** 193/198 bhp @ 4400 rpm, 280 lbs-ft @ 2600 rpm; **1956:** 202 bhp @ 4600 rpm, 289 lbs-ft @ 2600 rpm; **1957:** 212 bhp @ 4200 rpm, 297 lbs-ft @ 2700 rpm; **312 cid/5112 cc—1956:** 215 bhp @ 4600 rpm, 317 lbs-ft @ 2600 rpm; 225 bhp @ 4600 rpm, 324 lbs-ft @ 2600 rpm; **1957:** 245 bhp @ 4500 rpm, 332 lbs-ft @ 2300 rpm; 270 bhp @ 4800 rpm, 336 lbs-ft @ 3400 rpm; 285 bhp @ 5200 rpm, 343 lbs-ft @ 3500 rpm; 300 bhp @ 4500 rpm, 340 lbs-ft @ 3200 rpm

Transmissions:	3-speed manual (overdrive optional) or 3-speed automatic
Suspension, front:	upper and lower A-arms, coil springs
Suspension, rear:	live axle, semi-elliptic leaf springs
Brakes:	front/rear drums
Wheelbase (in.):	102.0
Weight (lbs):	2980-3145
Top speed (mph):	105-125
0-60 mph (sec):	7.0-11.5
Production:	**1955** 16,155 **1956** 15,631 **1957** 21,380

Ford's only production two-seater—so far—emerged for 1955 (opposite bottom) to wide acclaim for its styling, luxury, and performance. An outside spare tire marked the '56s (top) while the '57 (below) was heavily facelifted to good effect. It saw the highest production.

1946-1954 HEALEY

Before the Austin-Healey and Nash-Healey there were simply Healeys, sporting cars designed by Donald Healey as an independent manufacturer in the early postwar years. Healey had made his mark in the Twenties as an ace rally driver well known throughout Europe and his native England. In the Thirties he became technical chief for Triumph, and also helped Riley and Invicta win contests like the famed Monte Carlo Rally. By 1946 he was ready to fulfill a long-held ambition of building cars under his own name, and set up a small shop in Warwick, a few miles south of Coventry, then the center of Britain's motor industry.

The Healey was conceived during World War II on the important premise that since the Healey family had virtually no money for tooling, the car would have to be composed almost entirely of components from more established manufacturers. Like many other UK projects of the day, it was specifically designed with an eye to export, particularly the vast and lucrative American market.

Healey ended up buying engines and transmissions but managed his own chassis and suspension. All cars built at Warwick from 1946 to '54 (including the Nash-Healey) rode a sturdy, box-section platform with a 96-inch wheelbase and an odd trailing-arm front suspension inspired by that of Thirties Auto-Union and ERA single-seat racers.

Bodies were farmed out to what few coachbuilders remained in postwar Britain, as Healey had no money or facilities for building his own. The coming years would see four-seat coupes by Elliot, Duncan, and Tickford; convertibles by Westland and Abbott; and a true sports car, the Silverstone, named for Britain's then-new Grand Prix circuit. All could reach at least 100 mph, very creditable for the day.

Most early Healeys carried the 2.5-liter four-cylinder engine and associated gearbox and rear axle from the postwar Riley RM-series sedan, but a few later models employed the more modern 3.0-liter six from the Alvis TA21. An exception, of course, was the Nash-Healey (see entry). The result of a chance meeting aboard the *Queen Elizabeth* between Healey and Nash president George Mason, it used running gear and the 238.4-cubic-inch six from the contemporary Ambassador.

Silverstone apart, most Healey bodies were of "semi-envelope" design, with smooth, flowing lines but distinct fender forms, stylistically closer to prewar than postwar American cars. The Silverstone was a sort of streamlined rendition of the traditional prewar British sports car, a cigar-shaped roadster with cutaway doors, separate "clamshell" fenders, and a smooth nose bearing a "waterfall" vertical-bar grille with two closely set headlights behind (where they interfered somewhat with radiator cooling). Interestingly, it also carried a set of Buick-like portholes.

As a dual-purpose "race-and-ride" sports car, the Silverstone was designed to be as light, simple, and functional as possible. Thus, weather protection was rudimentary, while the spare tire was mounted in the tail and jutted out to do double duty as the back bumper. But the Silverstone weighed 400-500 pounds less than other Healeys, which contributed to its success in competition.

Because they were mostly assembled by hand, these Healeys were quite expensive for their day. Bodies tended to decay rather quickly in hot, damp climates, but chassis and running gear proved strong and durable. In performance they were more than a match for most rivals, especially the Silverstone. Not surprisingly, it's the one with the most appeal today, and is the model described in the specifications panel.

Unlike some other specialty cars of the period, the early Healeys sold in fairly high numbers. A total of 781 were built in less than eight years (plus 506 Nash-Healeys). Only 25 had Alvis engines, but the desirable Silverstone saw 105 copies.

Though little known in America, these cars established Donald Healey's credentials as an engineer and builder, thus setting the stage for his linkup with British Motor Corporation and the first Austin-Healey of 1952 (see entry). That one, of course, would be *very* well known in the "colonies"—and indeed, all over the world.

SPECIFICATIONS

Engine: Riley "RM" ohv I-4, 149 cid/2443 cc, 104 bhp (net) @ 4500 rpm, 132 lbs-ft @ 3000 rpm

Transmission:	4-speed manual
Suspension, front:	trailing arms, coil springs, anti-roll bar
Suspension, rear:	live axle, torque tube, radius arms, coil springs
Brakes:	front/rear drums
Wheelbase (in.):	96.0
Weight (lbs):	2075
Top speed (mph):	approx. 110
0-60 mph (sec):	11.0
Production:	105 (**total all models: 781**)

Distinctive Healey Silverstone roadster mixed prewar-style fenders and windshield with rounded postwar-type main body. Exposed spare tire provided token bump protection. Close-set headlamps behind grille hampered radiator airflow. Note Buick-like fender "ventiports."

215

1965-1974
ISO GRIFO

You may not see a connection between the tiny two-cylinder Isetta "bubblecars" of the Fifties and the mighty Iso Grifo of the Sixties, but it's there. Renzo Rivolta, founder and head of Iso S.p.A. of Bresso, near Milan, was responsible for both.

Iso's business was founded on refrigerators and, later, those strange little 236-cc Isettas. But Rivolta wanted a much more ambitious car, and in 1960 was attracted by the promise of the Chevrolet-powered British Gordon GT prototype. After borrowing it for inspection, he borrowed some of its ideas for a new high-performance 2+2 that would appear in 1962 as the Iso-Rivolta (Renzo was nothing if not immodest about names). Giotto Bizzarrini, the noted freelance Italian engineer who'd been on the staff at Maranello and was largely responsible for developing Ferrari's celebrated 250 GTO, was hired to design a new chassis around Corvette running gear. Bertone was contracted for body styling and production; the youthful Giorgio Giugiaro penned the shape.

The result was a tastefully restrained steel-body notchback coupe with all-independent suspension and a top speed of over 140 mph. Some were fitted with ZF 5-speed gearboxes, others with the Corvette's Borg-Warner T-10 4-speed manual or GM 3-speed automatic. Though sales were as low as production, the Rivolta paved the way for an even more exciting Italo-American hybrid.

A year after the Rivolta debuted, Giugiaro and Bertone produced the stunning Grifo A3L prototype coupe. Though first shown at Turin in early 1963, it wouldn't be production-ready for another two years, by which time several features had been toned down and the car made more civilized. The body was still steel, but this time it was a big, curvy fastback with large engine-cooling grids in the front fenders, gaping twin-mouth grille, a l-o-n-g hood, and a tidy tail chopped Kamm-style. This was welded to a pressed-steel chassis, resulting in a very rigid structure.

Predictably, the Grifo shared running gear and suspension with the Rivolta but was tuned for higher performance. The engine was Chevrolet's 327-cubic-inch small-block V-8 as used in the contemporary Corvette, initially offered with a choice of 300 and 365 horsepower. Front suspension was via conventional wishbones and coil springs, while the rear employed a coil-sprung De Dion live axle located by radius arms and Watt linkage. Brakes were four-wheel discs, of course, steering recirculating-ball.

With a top speed of at least 160 mph in 365-bhp form, the Grifo was as fast as any Italian supercar and as lovely to behold. Yet bluebloods seemed to forget its "native" (Bizzarrini) design, preferring to sniff at the crude, low-cost Yankee mechanicals. A jingoistic attitude, that, for the small-block Chevy proved time and again to be just as powerful as any exotic Latin engine and a lot more durable. As expected of Bizzarrini, the Grifo was solid, handled and stopped well, and generally behaved in a very safe, if extroverted, manner. The main problem was that the Iso marque had nowhere near the prestige and snob-appeal of Ferrari or Maserati (Lamborghini also had the same problem at first), so it wasn't easy to attract orders from the well-heeled types at whom the car was aimed.

The Grifo chassis was also used for a four-door Iso sedan, the Fidia S4 of 1967, and the 2+2 Lele fastback, arriving two years later. But the Grifo was always the fastest, because of its low build (only 47 inches high) and good aerodynamics. By that point, buyers could order the big-block Chevrolet 427 V-8, which brought a central hood section raised not only to clear the engine but provide more effective cooling. So equipped, a Grifo could exceed 170 mph, truly mind-boggling for the time.

With the early Seventies came a facelifted Grifo, marked by a lower nose with semi-hidden headlamps—and a decline in Iso's fortunes. The 1973 Energy Crisis severely hurt sales of all Italian thoroughbreds, but Iso, always a marginal producer at best, suffered more than most. Production duly wound down in 1974 after 412 Grifos had been built, including a few late examples with Ford 351 "Cleveland" engines.

SPECIFICATIONS

Engines: Chevrolet ohv V-8, 327 cid/5359 cc, 300/365 bhp (SAE gross) @ 5000 rpm, 360 lbs-ft @ 4000 rpm (some late examples have Chevrolet 427 and Ford 351 "Cleveland" V-8s)

Transmissions:	4/5-speed manual, 3-speed automatic
Suspension, front:	double wishbones, coil springs
Suspension, rear:	De Dion live axle, Watt linkage, radius arms, coil springs
Brakes:	front/rear discs
Wheelbase (in.):	98.4
Weight (lbs):	2860-3200
Top speed (mph):	150-170
0-60 mph (sec):	6.0-7.5
Production:	412

*Discreet "7-Litre" badge (**opposite right**) and raised hood section identify this as a late-Sixties Grifo with Chevrolet 427 big-block power. Luxurious cockpit (**opposite**) afforded a more comfortable driving posture than in most Italian supercars. Styling, by Giorgio Giugiaro, then of Bertone, managed to be flowing yet muscular, enhanced by a wide, ground-hugging stance and a low 47-inch overall height.*

1948-1954
JAGUAR XK120

It took awhile for William Lyons to go from motorcycle sidecars to cars of his own. Coventry-based Swallow Coachbuilding Company, which he'd founded with William Walmsley in the late Twenties, got into automobiles by turning out special bodies for popular British chassis of the day, notably the cheap Austin Seven. By 1931, this lucrative business had enabled Lyons to turn to complete cars of his own design, built around proprietary components by a renamed company, SS Cars Ltd. The first cars called Jaguar appeared four years later, followed in 1937 by the beautiful SS-100 (later Jaguar 100) roadster.

In 1945, Lyons' company was renamed Jaguar Cars, Ltd. (SS was hardly a sales aid in Hitler's aftermath) and resumed limited production of its prewar models while working on completely new designs conceived during the war by Lyons and his colleagues. Besides an all-Jaguar chassis for a newly styled sedan, plans included a family of twincam four- and six-cylinder engines (previous Lyons cars had engines designed or built by Standard). Called XK-series and engineered by Harry Westlake, it would be the world's first high-volume twincam production engine (though Alfa Romeo soon joined in and the proposed four was abandoned) and would prove remarkably reliable and long-lived.

The new chassis was planned around a 120-inch wheelbase and a new independent front suspension with upper and lower wishbones acting on longitudinal torsion bars (in contrast to the leaf-sprung solid axle of prewar days). Bodies were farmed out to Pressed Steel Ltd.

Delivery delays during 1947-48 left Jaguar with an engine and chassis but nothing to clothe them with. Accordingly, Lyons issued a pushrod-engine Mark V sedan as an interim measure while putting the rush on a short-wheelbase chassis (102 inches) for a new two-seat sports roadster to get the XK some publicity. The result bowed in the fall of 1948 as the XK120.

It was nothing less than a sensation—sleek, beautiful, strikingly modern. Its genesis was the 1938 Jaguar 100 experimental, a streamlined coupe combining a rounded, two-place cabin, sloped tail and fulsome fenders with the SS roadster's long hood and fine-mesh grille. The XK120 retained this basic outline, but substituted a smoother prow with faired-in headlamps flanking a slim, oval vertical-bar grille.

Though the XK120 was intended only as a stopgap, demand was so overwhelming that Lyons quickly put it into production, which didn't begin in earnest until fall 1949. The first 240 cars had aluminum bodies built on a wood skeleton; construction shifted to steel the following spring. Production was earmarked strictly for export in the first few years, with most of it sent to the U.S.

With 160 horsepower in original tune, the XK120 not only looked and sounded magnificent but had performance to match. (The name stemmed from the top speed recorded by prototypes.) And like previous Jaguars, the price seemed too good to be true. The 1951 U.S. figure was around $3500, quite reasonable for a high-performance car with advanced engineering and "tomorrowland" styling.

But though fast for its time, the XK120 was by no means perfect. Cooling capacity was marginal in heavy traffic on hot days, the drum brakes couldn't really cope with the speed, and handling left something to be desired. Still, customers were happy to forgive these and other failings because of all the go and glamour they got for so little money.

Variations on this theme weren't long in coming: a smart if rather claustrophobic, fixed-roof coupe in 1951, a full convertible two years later. Jaguar also offered a "Special Equipment" 180-bhp engine, a 210-bhp alternative called C-Type (after Jaguar's contemporary sports-racer), and a variety of other competition-inspired performance options. Some 120s had steel disc wheels, but many had the extra-cost center-lock wires.

The XK120 wasn't designed for racing, though Jaguar did run off a few specials for that purpose. XK120s also did well in rallies, gymkhanas, and the like, while Coventry set long-distance speed records with them, including a week-long trek at more than 100 mph.

Today, there's still something about the XK120 found in no other contemporary—a combination of style, performance, value, and character. Even its sound set it apart, with a burbling to booming exhaust that was quite unique. Not even other Jaguars could match the XK120's cachet until the sexy E-Type of 1961.

SPECIFICATIONS

Engine: dohc I-6, 210 cid/3442 cc, 160/180 bhp (SAE) @ 5000 rpm, 195/203 lbs-ft @ 2500/4000 rpm

Transmission:	4-speed manual
Suspension, front:	double wishbones, torsion bars, anti-roll bar
Suspension, rear:	live axle on semi-elliptic leaf springs
Brakes:	front/rear drums
Wheelbase (in.):	102.0
Weight (lbs):	2855-3080
Top speed (mph):	120 +
0-60 mph (sec):	10.0

Production: Roadster 7631 **Coupe** 2678 **Convertible** 1769

*A classic today, the Jaguar XK120 seemed ultra-modern in 1948. Many examples wear rear fender skirts as shown here, which enhance the smooth, flowing lines penned by William Lyons. Twincam XK-Series six (**opposite top**) was also quite advanced for its day, and so good that it would continue in production nearly 40 years.*

1954-1957
JAGUAR XK140

The XK120 was so advanced and successful that Jaguar didn't need to replace it for a full six years. This allowed the factory to get heavily involved in motorsports, producing the Le Mans-winning XK120C or C-Type in 1951 and the wind-cheating D-Type three years later.

Predictably, the successor XK140, which also appeared in 1954, was an improved variation on the XK120 theme. It had the same heavy, box-section chassis with wishbone/torsion-bar front suspension, the sterling 3.4-liter XK-series twincam six, and great solidity throughout. Roadster, coupe, and convertible coupe body styles continued too.

Even so, the whole design was thoroughly upgraded, resulting in a more practical, comfortable car all-round. For example, the 140s were about 200 pounds heavier on average, but easier to handle and no less economical than the 120s. Even better, they retained all of the 120's virtues while dispensing with most of its problems.

Though it retained the 120's basic body lines, the 140 was actually modified inside for greater roominess. Changes comprised an engine/gearbox assembly moved three inches forward, a reworked dash and footwells, and higher rooflines. The resulting extra room was great enough to permit a pair of very small "+2" seats in the coupe and convertible. As in so many cars, however, these were really better for carrying

*"Wide-stripe" grille marked Jaguar's XK140, the improved version of the winning XK120. Coupe (**opposite**) and roadster body styles continued along with drophead coupe (convertible). Unlike the 120s, the 140s' top speed didn't match their model number.*

luggage than people, though children could ride without too much trouble, at least for short distances. As before, the roadster came with traditional British side curtains, the coupe and convertible with proper roll-up door glass.

Outside were a new "wide-stripe" grille with fewer vertical bars (for better radiator air flow), a dorsal chrome strip on the hood, and beefier bumpers designed with an eye to U.S. drivers who parked "by ear." Coupe and convertible looked slightly different in profile due to the enlarged cockpits.

Mechanically, the most significant changes were substitution of more precise rack-and-pinion steering for the previous recirculating-ball system and standard horsepower increased by 30 bhp to 190, the same as that of the previous $800 "Special Equipment" package. The 210-bhp engine returned at extra cost. New to the options list were overdrive, which lifted top speed to nearly 130 mph, and Borg-Warner automatic transmission, another concession to the American market, though fitted to fewer than 800 cars.

Incidentally, it's never been explained why the XK140 designation was chosen over the more logical "XK130." By this time, many folks—including, apparently, a few in Coventry—had forgotten that "120" was originally meant to denote maximum speed, for none of the XK140s could approach 140 mph.

Still, if little faster than the 120s and not as "pure" in styling, the 140s proved very popular, especially once word got around that the old overheating and handling problems had been largely eradicated. Prices hadn't gone up much—only by $100 or so in 1955—so high value-for-money was still a big part of the sporting Jaguars' appeal.

Jaguar had become a rapidly expanding company by this time, and changes to both its sedans and sports cars seemed to come thick and fast. Thus, the 140 was dropped after only three years in favor of a third-generation XK, the 150.

SPECIFICATIONS

Engine: dohc I-6, 210 cid/3442 cc, 190/210 bhp (SAE) @ 5500/5750 rpm, 210/213 lbs-ft @ 2500/4000 rpm

Transmission:	4-speed manual
Suspension, front:	double wishbones, torsion bars, anti-roll bar
Suspension, rear:	live axle on semi-elliptic leaf springs
Brakes:	front/rear drums
Wheelbase (in.):	102.0
Weight (lbs):	3135-3245
Top speed (mph):	120 +
0-60 mph (sec):	8.4

Production: Roadster 3347 **Coupe** 2797 **Convertible** 2740

1957-1961
JAGUAR XK150/XK150S

There are those who point to the XK150 as proof that Jaguar's first postwar sports cars hung on too long. But the fact is that the 150 was the most thoroughly developed of the early XKs, if arguably the least sporting.

A changing market hastened the XK140's replacement, which debuted in mid-1957 as the final variation on the original XK120 theme. The 150 was Jaguar's response to recently introduced rivals like the BMW 507 and Mercedes-Benz 300SL, which offered similar performance and roadability while better catering to growing American demands for more comfort and refinement.

The 150 was thus plusher and more civilized than any previous XK. The basic bodyshell was substantially restyled, with higher front fenders, recontoured beltline, wider grille, larger engine-bay aperture, and a curved one-piece windshield (replacing the previous split vee'd type). Critics bemoaned the heavier, more "matronly" appearance, especially since it was matched by higher curb weight. Fortunately, the extra heft didn't spoil overall handling balance.

Aside from a slightly larger (33-foot) turning circle, the familiar XK chassis remained intact for the 150, but Jaguar scored a production first by replacing the old fade-prone drum brakes with servo-assisted Dunlop discs that easily compensated for the extra weight. It was another example of how racing really *can* "improve the breed," as Jaguar had used discs successfully on its D-Type competition cars. Though technically an option, the new brakes were apparently fitted to 100 percent of production.

Initially, the XK150 was offered only as a coupe and convertible, almost as if Jaguar was testing reaction to this obvious fatter cat. However, the roadster was reinstated after nine months, bereft of its cutaway doors but boasting wind-up windows, the only early XK roadster so equipped.

Engine specs were as before, but the 150's extra poundage prompted more buyers to order the 210-horsepower "Special Equipment" option. Overdrive was still popular, while the extra-cost Borg-Warner automatic also garnered more orders, another sign of the changing sports-car market.

Inevitably, the first XK150s were slower than their predecessors, but the deficit was corrected in the spring of 1958 with a 3.4-liter "S" engine featuring straight-port head, three huge SU carburetors, higher (9.0:1) compression, wilder cam timing, and a rated 250 bhp. Then Jaguar bored out to 3781 cc for a more potent pair of powerplants announced in the fall of 1959: a 220-bhp standard (Special Equipment) unit and a new 265-bhp "S." The latter could deliver a top speed in excess of 135 mph and 0-60 mph acceleration of 7.0 seconds or so with two aboard, thus completely restoring whatever verve the 150 had been missing. Fuel economy, all things considered, was excellent: 18-20 mpg on American highways.

In fact, any of the XK litter could return this kind of mileage given a driver skilled with the gearbox. Every XK150S had manual transmission as well as the overdrive; automatic wasn't available. Alas, only 1466 of these cars were built, making them among the rarest of the early XKs and thus among the most coveted today.

If not a volume item, the XK150S helped keep Jaguar's performance image strong pending release of the sensational new E-Type. Of course, that car wouldn't have been possible had the early XKs not succeeded, but succeed they did and beyond all expectations.

Though not the longest-lived, the 150 proved the most popular early XK. Its 40-50-unit weekly production rate was piddling by Detroit standards, but more than sufficient to keep Coventry's cash registers ringing. The roadster accounted for less than a fifth of the total, suggesting William Lyons and friends had correctly read the changing market. With the E-Type, they'd cash in on it big.

The final evolution of Jaguar's original XK sports car was chided in its day for a more "matronly" appearance, which the popular rear-wheel "spats" only seemed to emphasize. Roadster style (opposite top) was initially forgotten, then reinstated with wind-up windows and full-height doors. Cockpits (above) retained central gauges, traditional "fly-off" handbrake. Fixedhead coupe (opposite bottom) shows 150s' larger glass areas, including Detroit-style one-piece curved windshield.

SPECIFICATIONS

Engines: all dohc I-6; **1957-61:** 210 cid/3442 cc, 190/210 bhp @ 5500 rpm, 210/216 lbs-ft @ 2500/3000 rpm; **1958-61 3.4 "S":** 210 cid/3442 cc, 250 bhp @ 5500 rpm, 240 lbs-ft @ 4000 rpm; **1958-61:** 230.7 cid/3781 cc, 220 bhp @ 5000 rpm, 240 lbs-ft @ 4000 rpm; **1958-61 3.8 "S":** 230.7 cid/3442 cc, 265 bhp @ 5500 rpm, 260 lbs-ft @ 4500 rpm

Transmissions:	4-speed manual with optional overdrive, 3-speed automatic
Suspension, front:	double wishbones, torsion bars, anti-roll bar
Suspension, rear:	live axle, semi-elliptic leaf springs
Brakes:	front/rear discs
Wheelbase (in.):	102.0
Weight (lbs):	3220-3520
Top speed (mph):	120-136
0-60 mph (sec):	7.0-8.5

Production: **3.4 Roadster** 1297 **3.4 Coupe** 3445 **3.4 Convertible** 1903 **3.8 Roadster** 42 **3.8 Coupe** 656 **3.8 Convertible** 586 **"S" models** 1466

1961-1971
JAGUAR E-TYPE

Launched in March 1961, the Jaguar E-Type caused as much commotion as the XK120 had in the late Forties. Reason? Enormous sex appeal. Low, curvy and sensual, it shared a good many styling and technical details with the Le Mans-winning mid-Fifties D-Type racer, yet offered great long-distance comfort for two, a docile and tractable engine, all the necessary amenities, even decent luggage space. Per Jaguar tradition, it was readily available and reasonably priced, and there was a choice of roadster or new fast-roof hatchback coupe body styles that looked as good as (some said better than) the D-Type. With all this, the E-Type was the automotive equivalent of dollar caviar.

The E-Type originated in a 1956-57 sports-racing project that was gradually redefined for road use over the succeeding two years. Construction was an improvement on the D-Type's, with a monocoque (unitized) bodyshell bolted up to a multi-tube front structure. As on the racer, sheetmetal ahead of the cowl was made up as a unit and hinged at the front to tilt forward for almost unrestricted engine access. Styling was the work of aerodynamicist Malcolm Sayer, making this the first production Jaguar not shaped by William Lyons (who'd been elevated to the peerage by now). All-independent suspension (via double wishbones with front torsion bars and rear coil springs) and chassis-mounted differential were also new for a production Jaguar.

Mechanically, though, the E-Type was an improved XK150, with an updated 3.8-liter twincam six, all-disc brakes, and front suspension. With 265 horsepower in initial

Later E-Types were more cluttered than early ones thanks to U.S. regulations that dictated exposed headlamps, side markers, larger turn signals, and hammed-up bumpers. Still, this U.S. Series II (early-Seventies) roadster has plenty of sex appeal.

form, plus the much-vaunted "wind-tunnel tested" styling, it could reach 150 mph, which was sensational for the day, let alone a price of some $5500 in the U.S. (where the name was XKE).

Further enhancements began when the E-Type was relaunched as a 4.2-liter model in 1965, with a less undersquare engine whose bigger bore provided better torque but no more horsepower. Together with a new all-synchromesh gearbox, it improved low-speed driving ease. Brakes and electrical components were upgraded too.

The following year brought a 2+2 coupe on a nine-inch longer wheelbase, with the same side-hinged rear hatch but a higher roofline that made appearance more ungainly. An exclusive option for it was Borg-Warner's Model 8 automatic transmission. Greater weight and body drag meant the 2+2 was good for "only" 140 mph, though that was still more than rapid enough for the time.

U.S. E-Types differed little from British-market models through 1967, after which styling suffered due to federal safety standards that resulted in side marker lights, clumsier bumpers, and more upright exposed headlamps (previously mounted behind smoothly faired plastic covers). These Series II cars also received larger (and thus more effective) radiator air intakes and taillamps, Girling (instead of Dunlop) disc brakes, newly optional power steering, and a host of other detail improvements, plus a more steeply raked windshield for 2+2s. Alas, American-market cars began showing the effects of new government emissions limits, and top speed soon fell below 130 mph.

Still, the E-Type managed to retain its sexy character through 10 years and considerably higher production than that of the 1948-61 XK series. And by 1971, Jaguar had an equally exotic answer for the steady decline in its sports cars' performance: a new V-12 engine straight from the competition drawing board.

The Series I and II E-Types would thus be the last "classically" powered sporting Jaguars, an oft-overlooked historical aspect of the cars that marked an important transition in Jaguar engineering history. They remain as exciting and memorable today as they were when new, and always will. Sex appeal, you know, never ages.

SPECIFICATIONS

Engines: all dohc I-6; **1961-65:** 230.7 cid/3781 cc, 265 bhp (SAE gross) @ 5500 rpm, 260 lbs-ft @ 4000 rpm; **1965-71:** 258.4 cid/4235 cc, 265 bhp (SAE gross) @ 5400 rpm, 283 lbs-ft @ 4000 rpm

Transmissions:	4-speed manual with optional overdrive; optional 3-speed automatic on 2+2 only
Suspension, front:	double wishbones, torsion bars, anti-roll bar
Suspension, rear:	lower wishbones, coil springs, anti-roll bar
Brakes:	front/rear discs
Wheelbase (in.):	96.0 (2-seaters), 105.0 (2+2)
Weight (lbs):	2625-3165
Top speed (mph):	125-150+
0-60 mph (sec):	7.2-8.6

Production: 3.8 Roadster 7820 **3.8 Coupe** 7670 **4.2 Roadster** 18,180 **4.2 Coupe** 12,630 **4.2 2+2 Coupe** 10,930

1971-1975 JAGUAR E-TYPE SERIES III V-12

Jaguar began designing a new large sedan in the mid-Sixties while continuing work on a large-capacity V-12 originally intended for racing (tested in a mid-engine 1967 prototype, the then super-secret XJ13). The intent was to launch the new car with the new engine, but the former was ready before the latter, materializing in 1968 as the six-cylinder XK-powered XJ6. Though the twelve would eventually find its way into the four-door, its first home was in a revamped E-Type designated Series III and introduced in 1971.

The sporting Jaguar was due for an update, not only to restore its "novelty value" but performance lost in detuning the venerable six for U.S. emissions rules. The V-12 seemed to answer both needs nicely, especially since the XK six couldn't be easily enlarged anymore (it had, in fact, reached the end of its road in this respect).

Except for Ferrari and Lamborghini, no other automaker offered a production V-12 at the time, and Jaguar soon surpassed the Italians in unit volume with this splendid engine. Massive and complex but beautifully detailed, it featured a 60-degree angle between cylinder blocks, which were made of aluminum, as were the heads and crankcase. Each bank had a single overhead camshaft. Combustion chambers were formed in the top of the pistons rather than in the head casting, which was machined fully flat. Aspiration was via a quartet of constant-vacuum Zenith-Stromberg carburetors. With 272 DIN horsepower in European tune or about 250 SAE net bhp in U.S. trim, this 5.3-liter (326-cubic-inch) marvel was far more powerful than the old six, ensuring respective top speeds of 140 and 135 mph.

To accommodate the bulkier, weightier engine, Jaguar discontinued the two-seat coupe and put the roadster on the same long wheelbase as the 2+2. The central monocoque and tubular front sub-frame were beefed up, wider wheels were specified (slotted steel disc or center-lock wires), the all-disc brakes gained vented (instead of solid) rotors, and power steering (still a rack-and-pinion mechanism) was standardized.

Body modifications comprised a larger hood bulge, re-radiused wheelarches with prominent flares, a somewhat gaudy cross-hatch insert for the "mouth" radiator, the steeper 2+2 windshield for the roadster, dual wipers to clear it and, on U.S. models, big black-rubber bumper guards. A detachable factory hardtop arrived as a new roadster option, while instruments and interior detailing were cleaned up on both models.

The result was an E-Type that not only looked heavier but was: back to XK150 levels, though still sleeker in appearance and much more maneuverable. In fact, the Series III was surprisingly nimble, prompting some to judge it superior to the 3.8-liter original of 1961.

There was no disputing performance: at less than 7.5 seconds in the 0-60 mph test, the Series III offered colossal acceleration of Ferrari/Lamborghini proportions—and for far less money. The U.S. POE price was around $8000 basic in 1972, making this the cheapest 12-cylinder sports car in the world. Moreover, its engine was as smooth and silent as any, if predictably piggish with fuel (14.5 mpg and less in U.S. form).

Still, there was a tendency to view this as new wine in an old bottle, for most of the familiar E-Type problems remained: vulnerable bodywork, tight cockpit, untrustworthy electricals. Indeed, one American magazine summed up the Series III as "a magnificent engine in an outclassed body."

Unique though it was, the Series III was doomed to an early demise by the 1973-74 oil embargo and growing buyer preference for GT-style safety, refinement, and luxury. Jaguar obliged with the four-seat XJS in 1975 after completing the last E-Type roadsters that spring (the 2+2 was discontinued the previous fall). Production stopped at 15,287 units, about a fifth of the E-Type's 14-year grand total.

However clumsy it may have seemed next to earlier E-Types, the Series III was widely mourned, and many enthusiasts still hope for yet another V-12 sports car from Coventry. We're happy to report that, thanks to its Eighties resurgence, Jaguar is working on one for the early Nineties. Let's hope it's at least as good as the underappreciated Series III.

Dark colors help disguise the big, black, American-mandated bumper guards on 1974-75 Series III E-Type V-12s. "Safety" rocker switches and non-glare dash (above) were further concessions. Superb V-12 engine (top) needed no explanations or apologies.

SPECIFICATIONS

Engine: sohc V-12, 326 cid/5343 cc, 272 bhp (DIN) @ 5850 rpm/250 bhp (SAE net) @ 6000 rpm, 304 lbs-ft (DIN) @ 3600 rpm/283 lbs-ft (SAE net) @ 3500 rpm

Transmissions:	4-speed manual or 3-speed automatic
Suspension, front:	double wishbones, torsion bars, anti-roll bar
Suspension, rear:	lower wishbones, trailing arms, fixed-length halfshafts, coil springs, anti-roll bar
Brakes:	front/rear discs
Wheelbase (in.):	104.7
Weight (lbs):	3230-3450
Top speed (mph):	135-142
0-60 mph (sec):	7.0-7.4
Production:	15,287

1975-1988
JAGUAR XJS

The Jaguar XJS appeared in late 1975, less than six months after the last E-Type was built. It's been struggling for acceptance ever since. Marque aficionados were hoping for a direct successor to the fabled sports car. What they got was a plush GT without a soft-top in sight. Disappointed? And how.

But though nearly christened "XKF," the S-Type was never intended to replace the beloved and lovely E-Type. Company founder Sir William Lyons simply wanted to get out of sports cars and into the more profitable GT business. Besides, it seemed that convertibles would soon be outlawed in the vital U.S. market, so who needed a roadster?

Sir William retired in the early Seventies, so the XJS would be the last Jaguar to bear his personal imprint. It was also the last designed by long-time colleague Malcolm Sayer, who died in 1970.

For many, that styling was the other great disappointment. And as Jaguar had recently been folded into the creaky British Leyland conglomerate, there were suspicions that a more beautiful Sayer design had been compromised by committees. Some details were, but not as many as most pundits believed.

Though undeniably awkward from some angles, the XJS was actually developed with the aid of wind-tunnel testing for maximum aerodynamic efficiency. It paid off in a 0.37 drag coefficient, good for the time and a big improvement on the surprisingly mediocre 0.42 of the 2+2 E-Type. Interestingly, one of the car's most criticized elements, its "flying buttress" roof, was lifted largely from a small scale-model coupe that Sayer proposed as one of many ideas for a road car based on the mid-engine XJ13 prototype racer of 1966-67.

That project had spawned the fascinating V-12 that went into Series III E-Types, XJ sedans from 1972, and the new XJC hardtop introduced in late '73. It was naturally specified for the flagship XJS (developed as project XJ27), which arrived with Lucas fuel injection instead of the previous quartet of carburetors to aid emissions cleanup for America. (Jaguar's famous twincam XK six was too tall for the new car.) The all-independent wishbone suspension was basically that of the XJ sedans (praised since their 1968 debut for exceptional ride comfort and uncanny quietness), modified for the more precise handling expected of a GT. The floorpan was borrowed from the original 109-inch-wheelbase sedans, with the rear axle moved forward for a 7.0-inch-shorter wheelbase and cozier 2+2 accommodation.

Nevertheless, the XJS was far roomier than any closed E-Type, partly because it was far wider. Far heavier too, though few seemed to care about the resulting low mileage. Nor was there much grumbling about price, quite a bit higher than the V-12 E-Type's. Per Jaguar tradition, a high center tunnel made things seem rather close behind the wheel, while the low roof and bulky rear pillars limited driver vision.

But all was forgiven once that super-smooth V-12 was into its stride, the XJS wafting you along in leather-lined comfort—a superb highway cruiser. Yet on twisty country lanes it exhibited tenacious grip, plus handling that belied its considerable heft. As for performance, the figures speak for themselves.

The XJS is still with us, as popular as ever (piling up numbers unheard of in E-Type days), and remarkably little changed. Its first major improvement came in 1982 with the high-swirl, high-compression Michael May cylinder head, prompting the H.E. ("High Efficiency") surname. Mileage was somewhat improved, if still not worth writing home about.

But a Targa-roof Cabriolet was, announced the following year along with the new all-aluminum dohc 3.6-liter "AJ6" engine destined for the forthcoming XJ40 sedan. The six-cylinder XJS coupe and Cabriolet haven't come to America—at least not yet—but a V-12 Cabriolet has, along with a full convertible converted by Hess & Eisenhardt of Cincinnati (soon to be replaced by Jaguar's own).

Recent evidence suggests that the XJS has finally received the respect it deserves. And why not? It remains an immensely desirable car, aged but aging gracefully, a lasting tribute to the genius of the late Sir William. There's still nothing else quite like it.

SPECIFICATIONS

Engine: sohc V-12, 326 cid/5343 cc; **1975-81:** 244 bhp @ 5250 rpm, 269 lbs-ft @ 4500 rpm; **1982-88:** 262 bhp @ 5000 rpm, 290 lbs-ft @ 3000 rpm

Transmissions:	4-speed manual (except U.S.) or 3-speed automatic
Suspension, front:	unequal-length A-arms, coil springs, anti-roll bar
Suspension, rear:	halfshafts, lower A-arms, trailing arms, dual coil springs, anti-roll bar
Brakes:	front/rear discs
Wheelbase (in.):	102.0
Weight (lbs):	3850-4050
Top speed (mph):	135+
0-60 mph (sec):	8.5
Production:	29,730 (thru 1/1/85)

*Opposite: Smooth, oval headlamps continue to mark the non-American XJS. Here, the Targa-style Cabriolet, announced in 1983 for Europe and introduced to the U.S. for 1986. **Below:** The familiar XJS coupe has changed little in appearance during its 13 years, but minor front and rear alterations are rumored for '89.*

1972-1976 JENSEN-HEALEY & JENSEN GT

Richard and Alan Jensen had made a good living in the Thirties by turning out custom bodies for various British chassis at their small West Bromwich facilities. After World War II, they began building their own cars: fast if rather odd-looking four-seat GTs with Chrysler V-8 power, sold in very small numbers. Styling improved dramatically in 1966 with a new Interceptor model, designed by Touring of Italy but bodied by Vignale and then Jensen itself, accompanied by the trail-blazing FF version with Ferguson Formula four-wheel drive and Dunlop "Maxaret" anti-skid brakes, both world production firsts.

But these were ambitious cars for a small firm competing against the likes of Ferrari, Porsche, Lamborghini, and Aston Martin. By the Seventies, Jensen was under new ownership—merchant bankers William Brandt, Sons and Co., Ltd.—and in big financial trouble. So when a consortium led by Kjell Qvale, Jensen's San Francisco-based U.S. distributor, came calling with an offer to buy, the Brandt interests were only too happy to sell.

And Qvale had a plan to revitalize Jensen: a new medium-price, medium-size volume sports car, a sort of latterday Austin-Healey. As fate would have it, the chairman of Jensen's new board was none other than Donald Healey himself, a connection made through Qvale, who'd probably sold more A-Hs than any other single U.S. outlet.

Both Qvale and Healey were upset at the 1970 demise of the Austin-Healey marque at the hands of the recently formed British Leyland combine. Both also saw a need for a new "big Healey," again mainly for North America, to fill this gap in the sports-car market. Healey recruited his technical director, Kevin Beattie, to help fill it, and the Jensen-Healey was born.

For both Jensen and Healey, the new J-H was like "coming home." Jensen was certainly no stranger to volume production, having built big-Healey body/chassis structures for the pre-Leyland British Motor Corporation, as well as thousands of complete Volvo P1800s and Sunbeam Tigers.

But the car that went on sale in 1972 wasn't the one envisioned two years before. The original plan called for a relatively inexpensive roadster with Vauxhall (British GM) running gear. But the four-cylinder Vauxhall engine proved unacceptable with the necessary emissions-control gear in place, prompting a frantic search for a replacement. After rejecting both BMW and Ford Europe engines, Beattie settled on a brand-new 16-valve twincam Lotus four derived from the Vauxhall unit. Lotus, then struggling itself, gave it to Jensen before putting it in its own cars, namely the front-engine Elite/Eclat, the later Excel, and the mid-engine Esprit.

Several consultants had a go at styling the all-steel roadster monocoque. The result was as bland as any stew stirred by too many cooks—an uninspired blend of Triumph TR6 tail and MGB front.

Engine apart, the rest of the J-H package was equally unadventuresome. Its all-coil suspension—by twin A-arms in front and a live axle in back—came from Vauxhall's compact Viva GT sedan, as did the rack-and-pinion steering and front disc brakes. A 4-speed gearbox was borrowed from the contemporary Sunbeam Rapier H120, a dumpy little fastback that reached the U.S. in lesser form as the short-lived Sunbeam Alpine.

To no one's great surprise, the Lotus engine developed teething troubles early, and inadequate rust protection soon became depressingly apparent in the unitized structure. At least the J-H handled well, and performance was good—nearly 120 mph even in detoxed, 140-horsepower U.S. form. Alas, cowl shake and a clumsy soft top were throwbacks to the bad old days. All this limited demand, especially in the U.S., and sales never reached expected levels.

After small cosmetic changes in 1973, the Jensen-Healey got a standard 5-speed Getrag gearbox the following year, by which time Donald Healey had disassociated himself with the project. This explains why his name didn't appear on a sportwagon derivative issued in mid-1975 as simply the Jensen GT. Qvale had shifted marketing gears here, offering 2+2 seating and greater utility combined with more lavish trim and equipment. Over the next few months, GT production came to dominate the West Bromwich scene.

But not for long. Thanks to the J-H's high costs and low returns, Jensen was deeply in the red again by 1976, and both the J-H and GT were gone by the end of the year. Ultimately, their failure would spell the end of Jensen itself, though the firm and the big Interceptor have since been revived by yet another new owner.

SPECIFICATIONS

Engine:	Lotus dohc I-4, 120.4 cid/1973 cc, 140 bhp (SAE net) @ 6500 rpm, 130 lbs-ft @ 5000 rpm
Transmission:	4/5-speed manual
Suspension, front:	upper A-arms, lower lateral arms, compliance struts, coil springs
Suspension, rear:	live axle, trailing arms, upper control arms, coil springs
Brakes:	front/rear discs
Wheelbase (in.):	92.0
Weight (lbs):	2155-2400
Top speed (mph):	120-125
0-60 mph (sec):	7.8-9.7

Production: 1972 705 **1973** 3846 **1974** 4550 **1975** 1301 **1976** 51

*California is home to a fair number of Jensen-Healey roadsters (**above and opposite top**) and the sportswagon-style Jensen GTs. Neither car impressed many critics, nor many buyers for that matter, despite involvement by the designer of the beloved Austin-Healey. GT was more civilized but fell victim to Jensen's financial troubles.*

1954 KAISER-DARRIN

By 1952, designer Howard A. "Dutch" Darrin had had it with Kaiser-Frazer. He'd resigned after Willow Run's "orange juicers" meddled with his original 1946 K-F sedan, only to return in 1948 to style the pacesetting '51 Kaiser. But when the firm chose a much dumpier design for its Henry J compact over Darrin's proposal (basically a sectioned, 100-inch-wheelbase '51 Kaiser) Dutch walked again, ostensibly for good.

Still, the great prewar coachbuilder was persistent as well as proud, the Henry J chassis conventional but sound. Dutch realized it "deserved something better than it had received," and decided to make a sports car out of it "without the authorization and knowledge of the Kaiser organization, but spending my own money . . . I built [a] clay model during the first half of 1952 . . . followed by a running prototype."

Typically Darrin, it was a rakish two-seat convertible with several unusual features. Fiberglass body construction was novel enough, let alone a three-position folding top with functional landau irons and—the real conversation piece—sliding doors. The last, which Darrin had patented in 1946, rolled forward into long front fenders, reflecting his dislike for conventional doors. The styling was beautifully proportioned, and handsome except for a small, high shell-shaped grille that "looked like it wanted to give you a kiss," as one wag put it.

Darrin showed his prototype to Henry J. Kaiser himself—and was promptly chewed out. "What's the idea of this?" Kaiser fumed. "We're not in the business of building sports cars." Dutch started to explain when Mrs. Kaiser leaped to his defense (as she had with the '51 Kaiser's "sweetheart" windshield). "Henry," she purred, "This is the most beautiful thing I've ever seen . . . I don't think there'll be many companies after seeing this car that won't go into the sports-car business."

That was all HJK needed, and the Kaiser-Darrin was born. Henry named it, overruling DKF (for "Darrin-Kaiser-Frazer"), his department heads' unanimous

choice. He also ordered up a four-passenger model with backward-sliding rear doors, but it only got as far as a clay model. (Dutch later pitched it to ailing Studebaker-Packard, which was in no better shape to field it either.)

Practical considerations dictated several changes for the production Darrin, but only one aroused Dutch's ire: reworked front fenders to put the headlamps at regulation height. Other alterations comprised separate lids for the trunk and top well (the prototype used a single rear-hinged cover), one-piece (instead of split) windshield *sans* "sweetheart dip," a more professional interior with pleated vinyl upholstery (the prototype's leather trim was made optional) and a revised dash with gauges clustered ahead of the wheel (instead of spread across the panel). Seatbelts appeared for only the second time in U.S. production (Nash had dropped them in '51 after "bad press") and K-F switched to the F-head Willys version of the Henry J six, with single carburetor (instead of three) and 10 more horsepower. Glasspar, pioneer builder of fiberglass boat hulls and kit cars like the Woodill Wildfire, was contracted to supply Darrin bodies.

"The Sports Car The World Has Been Awaiting" bowed in prototype form in late 1952, but the production version (officially DKF-161) didn't reach showrooms until early '54. At a lofty $3668, it cost more than a Cadillac 62 or Lincoln Capri but was at least fully equipped: overdrive 3-speed manual transmission, tachometer, windwings, electric wipers, whitewall tires, and more. Performance wasn't very exciting—less than even Chevy's mild-mannered new Corvette—though a couple of supercharged examples (most production Darrins were "customized" in some way) were among 1954's quickest sports cars.

But the next year, Kaiser-Willys (as the firm had become) bailed out of the U.S. market and the Darrin was finished. Dutch installed 304-bhp Cadillac V-8s in about 100 leftovers and sold them for $4350 apiece. If his cars were going to be changed, *he'd* be the one to change them. These were exciting. A few even won races.

Today they're among more than 300 surviving Darrins, an unusually high percentage of the paltry 435 built. But then, the Darrin itself is unusual—long the most prized of Henry J. Kaiser's automobiles. Dutch was proud of that until the day he died.

SPECIFICATIONS

Engines: Willys ohv I-6, 161 cid/2638 cc, 90 bhp @ 4200 rpm, 135 lbs-ft @ 1600 rpm; Cadillac ohv V-8 (conversion), 331 cid/5424 cc, 304 bhp @ 4400 rpm, 330 lbs-ft @ 2700 rpm

Transmission:	3-speed manual (overdrive optional)
Suspension, front:	upper and lower A-arms, coil springs
Suspension, rear:	live axle, semi-elliptic leaf springs
Brakes:	front/rear drums
Wheelbase (in.):	100.0
Weight (lbs):	2250
Top speed (mph):	98 (I-6), 135 + (V-8)
0-60 mph (sec):	15.0 (I-6), 10.0 (V-8)
Production:	435

Three-way landau top (below) and, of course, novel sliding doors were the Kaiser-Darrin's most unique features. The latter were really too narrow to afford easy access (opposite top). High, shell-shaped grille (opposite bottom) looked to one wag like "it wanted to give you a kiss," and was mimicked in small parking lamps. Curvaceous lines were typical of designer "Dutch" Darrin.

1948-1954 KURTIS

Frank Kurtis was famous for high-performance sports cars long before Colin Chapman or Carroll Shelby appeared on the scene. A chassis designer of enormous skill, he built a series of highly competitive racers beginning in the Twenties, many of them dirt-track midgets powered by that favorite engine of speed merchants everywhere, the flathead Ford V-8. He'd go on to even greater fame in the postwar era with formidable Indianapolis cars that would win the fabled "500" four times between 1950 and 1955. But like Chapman and Shelby, Kurtis couldn't resist applying his competition know-how to a street sports car.

His first attempt was the Kurtis Sport of 1948, a slab-sided two-seat convertible that *Motor Trend* magazine said had "all the features a sports car should have: speed, maneuverability, acceleration, power, and sleek looks." Unusual for the day, its chassis was integral with a body comprising 10 panels, all aluminum except for hood and rear deck, which were fiberglass. Appearance was bulbous but pleasing, aided by a tight 100-inch wheelbase, 169-inch overall length, and 68-inch width. A simple bumper/grille with large guards was mounted on rubber shock absorbers, a forecast of the "safety" bumpers we'd love to hate in the Seventies, and there was a full-perimeter chrome rub rail for bodyside protection. Within the handsomely furnished cockpit was full instrumentation arrayed directly ahead of a big steering wheel on an axially adjustable column, another predictive feature. Side windows were clumsy, clip-in Plexiglas affairs, but a removable rigid top was included besides the expected soft top.

Like interior hardware, the Kurtis Sport's suspension and running gear were mostly proprietary components, though Frank tuned spring and damper rates for optimum handling and roadholding. The powerteam was anything the buyer wanted, though 239-cubic-inch Ford flatheads with Edelbrock manifolds were fitted to most examples. A kit car was also available at prices ranging from $1495 to $3495 depending on completeness.

Light weight gave the Kurtis Sport good go despite the flathead's modest power, and reviewers loved the car's nimbleness and stability. But Kurtis-Kraft was a small outfit, building cars largely—and slowly—by hand, so sales were as sparse as profits. After seeing just 36 Sports out the door through 1950, Frank sold his Glendale, California operation for $200,000 to Los Angeles used-car dealer, radiomaker, and pioneer TV pitchman Earl "Madman" Muntz, who stretched the Sport into a luxury four-seater and sold it with Cadillac or Lincoln power. Called Muntz Jet, it garnered just 349 orders through 1954, forcing Muntz to bail out too.

But Kurtis hadn't given up on a series-production sports car. In 1954, his Kurtis Sports Car Corporation produced 50 chassis based on the tubular 500KK design with which Bill Vukovich had won the 1953 Indy 500. Some 30 of these were sold to individuals who clothed them in various aftermarket bodies, but the remainder got fiberglass roadster coachwork, supplied by McCulloch Motors, and Cadillac running gear (also used in a few Sports).

The result, tagged 500M and priced at $5800, looked something like a scaled-down '54 Buick Skylark but had roughly rectangular bodyside recesses, usually finished in a contrasting color. Wheelbase and track dimensions (56 inches front and rear) were the same as the Sport's, but curb weight was about 200 pounds higher. Still, the 500M was "guaranteed to out-perform any other sports car or stock car on the road." And fast it was: up to 135 mph with the standard GM Hydra-Matic.

Also in 1954, Kurtis fielded the 500S, a stark, Allard-like dual-purpose roadster designed mainly for road courses and dirt-track ovals. It, too, was sold fully built (at around $5000, depending on running gear) or as a kit (in four stages of completeness). The S enjoyed great success in the hands of owner/driver/mechanics like Bill Stroppe, whose flathead-Ford-powered car beat a lot of high-priced foreign machines in 1954 West Coast events.

Vukovich, still in the Kurtis he'd first driven at Indy in 1952, won the 500 again in '54, while seven other of Frank's cars finished in the remaining top nine places. Alas, Kurtis' greatest triumph would be his last, for he soon turned to more mundane endeavors, including the construction of airport service vehicles.

Some of those undoubtedly ended up at Los Angeles International, where Carroll Shelby would set up shop in a few years. But that, as they say, is a whole 'nuther story.

Race-car designer Frank Kurtis' first stab at a production model featured a unit body/chassis skinned with aluminum panels (hood and trunklid were fiberglass). This is one of only 35-36 Kurtis Sports originally built. All had proprietary drivetrains.

SPECIFICATIONS

Engines: Modified Ford L-head V-8, 239.4 cid/3923 cc, 110 bhp @ 3600 rpm, 200 lbs-ft @ 2000 rpm; Cadillac ohv V-8, 331 cid/5424 cc, 160 bhp @ 3800 rpm, 312 lbs-ft @ 1800 rpm

Transmission:	3-speed manual
Suspension, front:	independent, upper and lower A-arms, coil springs
Suspension, rear:	live axle, semi-elliptic leaf springs
Brakes:	front/rear drums
Wheelbase (in.):	100.0
Weight (lbs):	2300
Top speed (mph):	135+
0-60 mph (sec):	8.0-10.0

Production: Sport (1948-49) 35-36 **500M** (1954) 18-20 **500S** (1954) 50 (estimated)

1964-1968 LAMBORGHINI 350 GT/ 400 GT

Heard about the guy so disgruntled with his Ferrari that he decided to build his own? His name was Ferruccio Lamborghini, and in 1962 he was about to start making modern automotive history.

Having owned the best modern Ferraris, Lamborghini decided he could do better than *Il Commendatore*. And having made a considerable fortune in specialized tractors and heating appliances, he certainly had the resources to try.

But Ferruccio didn't intend to dabble. To him, high-performance cars were serious business. Accordingly, he invested in a brand-new factory at Sant'Agata, not far from Bologna—or Modena—in the heart of Italian supercar territory.

Lamborghini knew what he wanted but couldn't design it himself, so he hired Giotto Bizzarrini, the respected freelance engineer who'd already made his mark at Ferrari and was working on new projects for Iso in Milan. Ferruccio's dream was a sleek two-seat coupe with as many unique components as possible. In particular, he was determined to build his own engines, looking down on Iso's use of off-the-shelf Chevrolet power.

Bizzarrini duly ran off a four-cam 60-degree V-12, a design he'd been playing with for some time, and also began laying out a new front-engine chassis with a classic all-independent suspension via double A-arms and coil springs at each corner. Servo-assisted Girling disc brakes would be used all-round. Steering would be ZF worm-and-roller.

In early 1963, Lamborghini hired young Giampaolo Dallara to supervise prototype construction—and to be president of Automobili Ferruccio Lamborghini S.p.A. It was another shrewd choice, for Dallara was not only "ex-Ferrari" but "ex-Maserati," so his supercar credentials—and credibility—were excellent.

The first engine was running by the summer of 1963. It was then mated to a 5-speed ZF gearbox and installed in a prototype called 350 GTV, revealed at the Turin Show that November. Designed by ex-Bertone hand Franco Scaglione and built by Carrozzeria Sargiotto of Turin, it looked rather fussy (despite retractable headlamps), with some apparent inspiration from Aston Martin's DB4GT Zagato and Jaguar's E-Type coupe (see entries).

By the time production began in March 1964, Touring of Milan had rounded off the prototype's angular lower body lines, greatly simplified the tail, and replaced the hidden headlamps and gaping "mouth" intake with exposed, slightly "frogeye" oval lights and a conventional grille. The result premiered at the Geneva show that same month as the 350 GT. Meantime, the V-12 had been given six horizontal Weber carburetors (the GTV had vertical Webers) and finalized at 280 horsepower, and the new factory was ready to produce both engines and the tubular-steel chassis.

Only 13 Lamborghinis were built in '64, but demand grew rapidly as word got around about the 350 GT's splendid engine, excellent handling and roadholding, and very high performance (more than 150 mph flat out). Over the next two years, volume swelled to 120 units, all semi-fastback coupes except for a handful of Touring-built convertibles and one Zagato-styled special.

In 1966, the 350 GT gained a running mate called 400 GT. It carried a 4.0-liter V-12, as the label implied, with 320 bhp, enough to boost top speed to near 160 mph. It also featured the first Dallara-designed Lamborghini gearbox and final drive. Ferruccio was *serious*.

Touring jiggled appearance so that the 400 looked little different from the 350 but shared no common panels. Providing external identification were a quartet of circular headlamps, a scaled-back rear window, and a fractional increase in roof height for a little more interior room. As before, a pair of tiny bucket seats lived in back, and brochures optimistically billed this as the 400 GT 2 + 2. Underneath, a single large fuel tank replaced the 350's pair of smaller ones. Just to confuse matters, there was also an interim 1965/early-'66 350 with the 4.0-liter engine.

In all, these first-generation Lamborghinis represented a very auspicious start for a new marque. As *Road & Track* warned at the time: "Watch out, Ferrari!" The 350 GT remained in production through 1967, but the 400 GT continued into 1968, when it was replaced by a rebodied version called Islero (see entry). Volume was way below Ferrari's, but Ferruccio had fewer models, and his tally wasn't bad.

In fact, Lamborghini had come from nowhere incredibly fast to pose a serious new threat to the performance and prestige of the prancing horse. Worse for Maranello, new models were waiting in the wings that would make the threat even more serious. The rampant bull had arrived.

Opposite: Dual headlamps and high backlight identify the original roadgoing Lamborghini, the 350 GT. Above: Four headlamps, an enlarged V-12 and +2 seating made the successor 400 GT even more attractive. Touring designed and built bodies for both models, but no panels interchange despite similarities in appearance.

SPECIFICATIONS

Engines: all dohc V-12; 211.3 cid/3464 cc, 280 bhp (SAE) @ 6500 rpm, 227 lbs-ft @ 4800 rpm; 239.8 cid/3929 cc, 320 bhp (SAE) @ 6500 rpm, 262 lbs-ft @ 4700 rpm

Transmission:	5-speed manual
Suspension, front:	unequal-length A-arms, coil springs, anti-roll bar
Suspension, rear:	unequal-length A-arms, coil springs, anti-roll bar
Brakes:	front/rear discs
Wheelbase (in.):	100.3
Weight (lbs):	2650-3200
Top speed (mph):	152-156
0-60 mph (sec):	6.8-7.5

Production: **350 GT** 120 **350 GT** "4.0" 23 **400 GT 2+2** 250 (some sources list 247)

1966-1973
LAMBORGHINI MIURA/
MIURA S/MIURA SV

The Lamborghini Miura was one of those rare and wonderful supercars that hardly disappointed anyone. Its exciting mechanical specifications and sensational styling were as effective as they looked. And its performance was incredible, if easy enough to prove. The only problem was that a Miura tended to take off like a jet as it approached maximum speed of—believe it or not—*170-plus* mph.

First shown as a bare chassis at the 1965 Turin show—just two years after Lamborghini's first car, the 350 GTV—the Miura simply astonished the motoring world. A midships V-12 was exotic enough, but its transverse mounting was the real eye-opener. This was a *road* car? No way!

But Lamborghini confounded the critics with the complete car, shown at Geneva 1966. Not only was it a road machine but one straight out of tomorrow, with sexy, aggressively masculine coupe styling by Marcello Gandini of Bertone. The rich and famous quickly lined up to buy, and Enzo Ferrari sent his designers back to their drawing boards.

Bodywork and drivetrain layout aside, the Miura was conventional mid-Sixties Italian supercar. Its chassis, for example, was a fabricated platform affair full of small panels, welded joints, access holes, and other rough-and-ready details, though it was big and brawny but light. The suspension wasn't too special either, being a classic all-independent setup with unequal-length A-arms and coil springs at each wheel. All-disc brakes and rack-and-pinion steering were also as expected for this league.

Nevertheless, the Miura *was* different, a car that looked, handled and ran like a potential Le Mans winner. Even its body panels seemed competition-inspired. The entire front and rear ends were single units hinged to tilt up for chassis/drivetrain access just like on the Ford GT40 endurance racer (which, of course, *was* a Le Mans winner). Yet it was also a practical two-seat tourer with amazing engine flexibility.

The Miura's strengths—pavement-peeling acceleration and towering top speed— were offset by the usual supercar weaknesses and a few that weren't. Most serious

was considerable high-speed lift, a function of the sexy body and suspect aerodynamics. The cabin was tight *and* noisy, ventilation poor, luggage space nil, and vision to any quadrant except dead-ahead limited, if not non-existent. Workmanship also left much to be desired. The car seemed to start crumbling away within months, and a five-year-old example could be a very sorry sight indeed.

Yet the Miura's well-heeled owners didn't seem to mind any of this—maybe because they *were* well-heeled and thus able to take it all in stride. Most were convinced they'd simply bought the world's greatest car, certainly the most charismatic ever seen. *Road & Track* magazine probably summed up their feelings by calling the Miura "one of those beautiful experiences every enthusiast owes himself."

And experience was what the car was all about. You bought a Miura to be noticed, to savor the engine's delicious whoops and wails each time you prodded the accelerator, to thrill at the neck-snapping go and colossal cruising ability whenever conditions and space permitted. No American muscle car ever took on a Miura more than once. Who cared that it cost more than other thoroughbred Italians? This was motoring at its fastest and finest.

But not fine and fast enough for Ferruccio Lamborghini. Thus, the original P400 Miura gave way in 1970 to the tuned P400S with 370 bhp, which quickly stepped aside for the ultimate P400SV of 1971-73, with 385 bhp and a top speed in excess of 175 mph. Not even a Ferrari Daytona could beat that. No wonder Enzo put the rush on a mid-engine reply, the Berlinetta Boxer (see entry).

Though Sant'Agata never got around to an open Miura, a one-off targa-style spider was built for the International Lead-Zinc Research Organization in 1969, predictably with zinc instead of other metals in every possible place. A few closed Miuras were similarly converted by private owners.

Then there was the competition-inspired Jota ("J," for FIA Appendix J rules), a lightweight Miura-based special commissioned by Lamborghini engineer Bob Wallace in 1969 as a "hobby car." With 440 bhp and 770 pounds less weight than standard, it was clocked at an honest 186 mph. The factory later built four Jota replicas to special order, but these were more like the regular article, lacking the Wallace car's dry-sump lubrication, high-tech Avional body construction, flared fenders, superwide wheels and tires, and other features. Predictably perhaps, the Jota touched off a spate of Miura "customizing," some of it of dubious taste.

All of which underscores the Miura's role as the world's first "boutique" car, an ultra-exotic designed for the wealthiest devil-may-care types who tended to treat this machine as a toy and could afford to indulge their whims. But the Miura was nothing compared with what was to follow: the otherworldly Countach.

SPECIFICATIONS

Engines: all dohc V-12, 239.8 cid/3929 cc; **Miura** (1966-70): 350 bhp @ 7000 rpm, 278 lbs-ft @ 5000 rpm; **Miura S** (1970-71): 370 bhp @ 7700 rpm, 286 lbs-ft @ 5750 rpm; **Miura SV** (1971-73): 385 bhp @ 7850 rpm, 294 lbs-ft @ 5750 rpm

Transmission:	5-speed manual (in rear transaxle)
Suspension, front:	upper and lower A-arms, coil springs, anti-roll bar
Suspension, rear:	upper and lower A-arms, coil springs, anti-roll bar
Brakes:	front/rear discs
Wheelbase (in.):	98.4
Weight (lbs):	2850
Top speed (mph):	160-175 +
0-60 mph (sec):	6.3-6.7

Production: **Miura** (P400) 475 **Miura S** (P400S) 140 **Miura SV** (P400SV) 150

Below and opposite bottom: A young Lamborghini company surprised everyone in 1966 with the mid-engine V-12 Miura. Aggressively handsome Bertone styling with predictive rear-window louvers and "reclining" headlamps was noticed as much as the intriguing mechanical layout. Shattering initial performance became even more so with introduction of the fortified Miura S in 1970 (opposite center). The ultimate Miura SV of '71 (opposite top) had even more power. Considerable high-speed lift demanded considerable respect in really fast driving.

1968-1978
LAMBORGHINI ESPADA

Though a mere five years old in 1968, Lamborghini was booming. The Sant'Agata factory was teeming with activity, and Ferruccio Lamborghini was ready to tackle Ferrari on all fronts. His first car had been a front-engine coupe, his second the amazing mid-engine Miura. Now it was time for a full four-seat GT, which arrived that year as the Espada.

The Espada's distinctive styling was inspired by the Bertone-designed Marzal show car of 1966. The one-off's all-glass gullwing doors, honeycomb dash and backlight sunshade motif, and rear (not midships) engine positioning were abandoned, but the basic shape was retained. Like the Miura, the Espada was penned by Marcello Gandini.

Also like Miura, the Espada was engineered largely by Giampaolo Dallara, who stuck to the formula established with the 400 GT 2+2 (see entry): front-mounted quad-cam V-12 bolted up to a 5-speed Lamborghini gearbox directly behind, all-independent wishbone/coil suspension, four-wheel disc brakes. Automatic transmission was conspicuous by its absence in a car of this type, but Sant'Agata belatedly corrected that with optional 3-speed Chrysler TorqueFlite beginning in 1974.

Despite basic similarities with the 400 GT and its Islero successor (see entry), the Espada went its own way in several respects. Its chassis, for example, was a cheap but strong fabricated pressed-steel platform supplied by Marchesi of Modena. Compared with the 400 GT, the Espada engine was tuned for "only" 325 bhp (DIN), and the entire power package rode 7.9 inches further forward. This and an extra 3.8 inches between wheel centers permitted a larger, four-seat cabin despite a half-inch decrease in overall length. The Espada also spanned wider tracks (by 4.2 inches) and, with its many amenities, was inevitably heavier—by no less than 1000 pounds.

Again like the Miura, the Espada was a real head-turner, another feather in Bertone's—not to mention Lamborghini's—cap. A simple nose with circular quad headlamps announced a very wide hood with twin NACA ducts to feed the 4.0-liter V-12's six twin-throat Weber carburetors. Front fenderlines blended seamlessly into the belt, which curved up at the rear to meet an almost horizontal roofline terminating in a chopped tail with a full-width glass panel below the backlight (presumably to give the driver a better view of those trying to keep pace). Once more, hood and upper fenders formed a forward-hinged unit for easier access to a very full engine bay.

Inside were four bucket seats and decent space aft (so long as the front seats weren't pushed all the way back). Initially, the Espada presented its driver with a functionally correct, if aesthetically messy, dash with full instrumentation and a wide, downsloped center console housing shifter, various minor switches, and "eyeball" vents (the last borrowed from Ford of England; the indicator stalk came from the Austin Mini). The original three-spoke steering wheel was rather ugly, but nicer ones appeared later.

Only 37 Espadas were built during 1968, but volume soon rose to a steady, albeit low, level. The Espada made an excellent stablemate for the mid-engine Miura (and, later, the Countach) and its basic chassis would be used for the Jarama (see entry), which replaced the Islero in 1970.

In fact, the Espada was advanced enough to last a full decade with only detail alterations. Series II models arrived in early 1970 with the aforementioned nicer steering wheel, plus a cleaner dash, revised grille, vented brakes, and 25 more horsepower. Two years later, Jarama S-type alloy wheels were specified. The Series III bowed at Turin in late '72 showing another minor grille rework and steering wheel, as well as a redesigned "cockpit" instrument panel with inward-curved center section. Toward the end of the run, Lamborghini claimed 365 bhp.

Though production tailed off rapidly in the aftermath of the first Energy Crisis, the last Espada wasn't built until 1978. Significantly, Lamborghini has yet to field a direct replacement, perhaps because it would be tough to top this exotic Latin flyer. Collectors, take heed.

Evolved from Bertone's Marzal show car, the Espada was long, low, and somewhat "geometric" inside and out. Tiered gauge cluster (above) underwent two revisions before the car's 1978 phaseout. Rear accommodation (top) was quite good for an Italian exotic, though not really suited for long adult trips. Glass panel below backlight helped driver vision astern, has since appeared on the Maserati Khamsin and second-generation Honda Civic CRX.

SPECIFICATIONS

Engines: all dohc V-12, 239.8 cid/3929 cc; **Series I** (1968-70): 325 bhp @ 6500 rpm, 276 lbs-ft @ 6500 rpm; **Series II** (1970-72): 350 bhp @ 7500 rpm, 300 lbs-ft @ 5500 rpm; **Series III** (1972-78): 365 bhp @ 7500 rpm, 300 lbs-ft @ 5500 rpm

Transmissions:	5-speed manual (optional 3-speed Chrysler TorqueFlite automatic from 1974)
Suspension, front:	unequal-length A-arms, coil springs, anti-roll bar
Suspension, rear:	unequal-length A-arms, coil springs, anti-roll bar
Brakes:	front/rear discs
Wheelbase (in.):	104.3
Weight (lbs):	3675-3740
Top speed (mph):	140-160
0-60 mph (sec):	6.5-7.8
Production:	1217

1968-1970 LAMBORGHINI ISLERO

Though Lamborghini's 400 GT 2+2 was still a steady seller in 1967, its Touring body was looking dated and the carrozzeria was falling into grave financial difficulties. The obvious solution was to keep the best and discard the rest, which is what Ferruccio Lamborghini did.

The result was a rebodied 400 called Islero, introduced in 1968 just as the first four-seat Espadas were being built (see entry). Naturally, the original tubular chassis with front-mounted quad-cam V-12 and 100.4-inch wheelbase was retained, but it now wore more contemporary clothes, with hidden headlamps, a glassy notchback greenhouse, and square-cut contours. Ferruccio Lamborghini dictated the general shape, but the styling assignment went to Mario Marazzi, a former Touring employee who'd been associated with Lamborghini for some time and had started his own coachbuilding business in Milan. Though less distinctive than its predecessor, the Islero was at least clean and inoffensive, and its drag coefficient was allegedly quite low despite the blockier lines.

There was progress inside, too, with more rear head- and legroom and standard air conditioning. There was also a new, more restrained instrument panel.

With its rather ordinary looks, the Islero paled next to the sensational Espada and sexy Miura but was as hot-blooded as any Latin supercar. Top speed was in the region of 155 mph, with acceleration to match, and there was still the same superb handling and roadholding that had marked the 350/400 GTs.

Considering how overshadowed it was, the Islero sold well. But it would be a short-timer. After an "S" model took over in 1969, with minor trim changes and 20 more horsepower, the Islero was dropped for yet another iteration of Lambo's small 2+2, the Jarama.

SPECIFICATIONS

Engines: all dohc V-12, 239.8 cid/3929 cc; **Islero** (1969-70): 320 bhp (SAE) @ 6500 rpm, 278 lbs-ft @ 5000 rpm; **Islero S** (1969-70): 340 bhp @ 6500 rpm, 289 lbs-ft @ 5000 rpm

Transmission:	5-speed manual
Suspension, front:	unequal-length A-arms, coil springs, anti-roll bar
Suspension, rear:	unequal-length A-arms, coil springs, anti-roll bar
Brakes:	front/rear discs
Wheelbase (in.):	100.4
Weight (lbs):	2795
Top speed (mph):	156
0-60 mph (sec):	7.5
Production:	**Islero** 125 **Islero S** 100

*Essentially a rebodied 400 GT 2+2, the angular Islero was overshadowed by the Espada and its spectacular styling, but sold well enough despite that. Long-hood/short-deck proportions belie the short 100.4-inch wheelbase. Note impressive Lambo V-12 (**opposite top**).*

1970-1978 LAMBORGHINI JARAMA 400 GT/400 GTS

By 1970, Lamborghini had forged a lineup it hoped would cover the entire supercar market and was ready to proceed with second-generation models. The Jarama, introduced at that year's Geneva show in March, can thus be considered a "Mark II" Islero, though it isn't quite as simple as that.

At the time, Lamborghini's most modern front-engine chassis belonged to the Espada, which dated from 1968, though as with the smaller Islero and mid-engine Miura, its basic suspension and engine engineering went back to 1963. American safety and emissions rules dictated replacing the Islero. As Giampaolo Dallara had left Sant'Agata, the task fell to his former assistant and new chief engineer Paolo Stanzani, who decided that a new body on a shortened Espada chassis would do the trick.

Accordingly, Stanzani removed 10.7 inches from the Espada's wheelbase but left everything else intact, though the steering was geared somewhat lower. Bertone's Marcello Gandini again looked after styling, and body construction was farmed out to Marazzi (who'd both designed and built the Islero's bodywork).

The result was a more distinctive yet still very angular small 2+2, with husky wheelarch flares, Espada-style twin NACA ducts in the hood, and an unusual face with four "eyes" partly concealed by electrically operated "eyelids." Wearing the Espada's wide tracks, the Jarama was broad-shouldered, if a little stubby, on its sectioned chassis. Unfortunately, it was a lot heavier than the Islero, though its claimed 162-mph top speed was the same.

Detail finish on early Jaramas was criticized as poor, but it improved somewhat with time. After three years, the design itself improved, the original 400 GT giving way to the 400 GTS. Changes comprised a modest power increase, a thin but wide hood scoop, air exhaust vents in the upper front-fender sides, and redone wheels. Along the way, the Jarama also picked up some Espada modifications, including availability of optional Chrysler TorqueFlite automatic transmission beginning in 1974.

Nevertheless, this Lamborghini was generally judged a letdown compared to earlier models. Said *Road & Track* in its 1972 test: "Certainly the Jarama is a capable, fast car and an exciting one to look at, but it fails in enough details [ergonomics, noise control, ride, low-speed driveability] that it's only marginally interesting as a total package. The Lamborghini factory has had its problems in the last year or so, with Italian labor unrest and the pains of trying to meet changing American safety and emission rules taking their toll on production, quality and profits . . . The company has changed hands recently, a Swiss firm now holding over 50 percent of capital . . . Let's hope Lamborghini not only continues but gets some of the present problems solved."

Sant'Agata would, but not before things became a lot worse.

SPECIFICATIONS

Engines: all dohc V-12, 239.8 cid/3929 cc; **400 GT** (1970-73): 350 bhp (SAE) @ 7500 rpm, 289 lbs-ft @ 5500 rpm; **400 GTS** (1973-78): 365 bhp @ 7500 rpm, 300 lbs-ft @ 5500 rpm

Transmission:	5-speed manual
Suspension, front:	unequal-length A-arms, coil springs, anti-roll bar
Suspension, rear:	unequal-length A-arms, coil springs, anti-roll bar
Brakes:	front/rear discs
Wheelbase (in.):	93.5
Weight (lbs):	3600
Top speed (mph):	150+
0-60 mph (sec):	6.8-7.2

Production: 400 GT (1970-73) 177 **400 GTS** (1973-78) 150

Essentially a short-wheelbase Espada, the Jarama was squat and angular in the early-Seventies idiom. Espada influence is evident in front, but lidded headlights were unique. A wide hood scoop identified the later, higher-power GTS version (below, both pages).

1970-1979 LAMBORGHINI URRACO P250/P300/P200

When Ferruccio Lamborghini was quizzed about his ambitions in the mid-Sixties, he'd invariably reply: "To build a small car." Not small like a Fiat, you understand, and not cheap. Rather, a compact supercar.

Ferruccio finally realized this dream in 1970 with the mid-engine Urraco, a sort of half-pint Miura that represented a major gamble for his tiny company. Whereas production Lamborghinis had heretofore been powered by 60-degree quad-cam V-12s, the Urraco had a small 90-degree V-8 with only one camshaft per cylinder bank, plus an equally new transaxle and bodywork.

In short, this was Sant'Agata's reply to the Dino 246 GT and Porsche 911. Thanks to Italian pride, however, the Lamborghini would one-up the "budget" Ferrari, with 2+2 instead of two-seat accommodation, a V-8 instead of a V-6, and Bertone rather than Pininfarina styling.

Of course, the German car, produced in much higher volume by a much larger company, could—and did—way outsell the Italians. But the Urraco was further handicapped by a two-year delay in customer deliveries, which reflected—and likely aggravated—Sant'Agata's mounting problems that would come to a head by decade's end.

As "son of Miura," the Urraco used a fabricated pressed-steel chassis with welded-on bodyshell and mounted its engine/transmission package transversely behind the cockpit, ahead of the rear wheels. The usual all-disc brakes and all-independent suspension were on hand, but the latter used MacPherson-strut instead of double-wishbone geometry. Developed under chief engineer Paolo Stanzani, the new single-cam V-8 was less sophisticated than the Lamborghini V-12, though it did have cogged-belt cam drive. The initial 2.5-liter version was the same size as Ferrari's then-current Dino V-6 but delivered 30 more horsepower.

Named for a breed of fighting bull, the Urraco was yet another new Lambo designed by Marcello Gandini. He apparently made little effort to disguise the mid-engine layout, with a short hood and a longish wheelbase on a compact 167.3-inch-long structure. His favored "signature"—a louvered engine bay/rear window area—was in evidence, along with a pointy front bearing hidden headlamps. A steeply raked windshield and a fastback cabin sitting relatively far forward gave the Urraco a definite "mound" profile. The overall effect was low and squat, aggressive, unmistakable.

The Urraco might have given the Dino a good sales fight were it not for several problems. Despite fine performance (up to 143 mph) and real exoticar character, some buyers didn't see it as a "real" Lamborghini. And there were inherent design flaws: poor outward vision, patchwork ergonomics, an odd driving position, mediocre refinement. Worse, a good bit of initial interest undoubtedly evaporated during the long delay in getting cars to customers. Even then, the Urraco didn't seem fully developed somehow. Quality and reliability problems surfaced early, and were publicized as much as the increasing financial and labor problems that prompted rumors of Lamborghini's imminent demise. With all this, a good many buyers likely shied away from the Urraco.

Hoping to recover, Lamborghini brought a pair of improved Urracos to the 1974 Turin show. The big news was the P300, carrying a stroked, 3.0-liter V-8 with new twincam heads designed to counter the power-sapping effects of required U.S. smog gear and establish the Urraco as a genuine Lamborghini. Output rose to 265 bhp (up from a 180-bhp low in U.S. form) and so did performance, though "crash" bumpers and other weight-adding safety equipment cut into both. Even so, driveability remained a problem, and none of the car's other faults were really remedied. The other newcomer was a downmarket 2.0-liter version, the P200, a single-cam "tax break" special for domestic consumption only.

With fewer than 780 examples in six years, the Urraco was not the success it could have been or that Lamborghini needed. When production ended in early 1979, Ferruccio Lamborghini had long since sold out, leaving his company to flounder in a sea of rumors and reorganizations that almost sank it.

But all would not be lost. The Urraco's basic design would survive in the short-lived Silhouette and the more successful Jalpa, both of which would help keep Lamborghini afloat.

SPECIFICATIONS

Engines: **P250** (1970-76): sohc V-8, 150.3 cid/2463 cc, 220 bhp @ 7500 rpm, 166 lbs-ft @ 3500 rpm; **P300** (1974-79): dohc V-8, 182.8 cid/2996 cc, 265 bhp (SAE net) @ 7500 rpm, 202 lbs-ft @ 3500 rpm; **P200** (1974-79): sohc V-8, 121.7 cid/1994 cc, 182 bhp (SAE) @ 7500 rpm, 130 lbs-ft @ 3500 rpm

Transmission:	5-speed manual (in rear transaxle)
Suspension, front:	MacPherson struts, lower A-arms, coil springs, anti-roll bar
Suspension, rear:	Chapman struts, lower A-arms, coil springs, anti-roll bar
Brakes:	front/rear discs
Wheelbase (in.):	96.5
Weight (lbs):	2885-3060
Top speed (mph):	125-155+
0-60 mph (sec):	7.6-10.1

Production: **P250** (1972-76) 520 **P300** (1974-79) 190 **P200** (1974-79) 66

Lamborghini's response to Ferrari's mid-V-6 Dino, the distinctive V-8-powered Urraco looked best in European form. This P300 displays the more coherent dash design (above) used on all Urracos from 1971. Slatted backlight was an obvious visual link with big-brother Miura.

1976-1977 LAMBORGHINI SILHOUETTE

SPECIFICATIONS

Engine: dohc V-8, 182.8 cid/2996 cc, 265 bhp (SAE net) @ 7500 rpm, 202 lbs-ft @ 3500 rpm

Transmission:	5-speed manual (in rear transaxle)
Suspension, front:	MacPherson struts, lower A-arms, coil springs, anti-roll bar
Suspension, rear:	Chapman struts, lower A-arms, coil springs, anti-roll bar
Brakes:	front/rear discs
Wheelbase (in.):	96.5
Weight (lbs):	2750
Top speed (mph):	158
0-60 mph (sec):	7.6
Production:	54 (some sources list 52)

Lamborghini's fortunes were waning in the mid-Seventies. The Urraco had been a costly business, and the firm wasn't doing enough business of any kind to even consider a replacement. But perhaps the Urraco could be redeveloped at low cost into something more saleable. Sant'Agata requested Bertone to do just that, and the result premiered at the 1976 Geneva show as the Silhouette.

Though recognizably Urraco, the Silhouette was obviously different. Most noticeable was the new targa-style configuration, making this Lamborghini's first open production model. A change from 2 + 2 to two-seat accommodation was less apparent. Completing Bertone's restyle were flat-top wheelarches, a squared-off nose, and a deeper front spoiler incorporating an oil-cooler duct and front-brake air scoops, all set off by 15-inch-diameter "five-hole" magnesium wheels (first seen on the 1974 Bravo show car) wearing Pirelli's new state-of-the-art P7 high-performance tires. A roll cage was built into the rear roof "hoop" area for strength, and the roofline recontoured from fastback to "tunnelback." A new, more ergonomic dash was featured inside. The lift-off roof section could be easily stored behind the seats.

Underneath lurked the Urraco's familiar unit body/chassis structure as used in the P300 model, suitably strengthened to go topless. The driveline was the same too, with horsepower from the quad-cam V-8 pegged at 265 in both European and American form.

With all this, the Silhouette was as fast as a 3.0-liter Urraco and had the same excellent road manners. And with the bonus of open-air fun, it should have sold very well indeed.

But it didn't, and the reasons weren't hard to find. First, the Silhouette inherited not only some of the Urraco's design faults but its reputation for indifferent workmanship and suspect reliability. Second, it ran into the same buyer wariness, as Lamborghini's financial and management problems hadn't abated.

A third reason stemmed from the second. Lamborghini in these years was simply in no position to certify cars for the market where they would have sold best: America. In fact, except for gray-market imports, Sant'Agata would be absent from the U.S. scene from 1977 through 1982.

So to no one's great surprise, the Silhouette vanished after just two years and a mere 54 examples. Only a few came Stateside.

But today's defeat often contains the seeds of tomorrow's success, and so it is here. After some very lean years in the economic slowdown of the early Eighties, Lamborghini managed yet another evolution of its small mid-engine V-8 GT, the Jalpa. Together with continuing demand for the low-volume Countach, it kept Sant'Agata solvent until real salvation arrived in 1987 with a complete takeover by the reborn Chrysler Corporation.

A Urraco evolution, the Silhouette was short-lived despite more aggressive looks, new open-air appeal and improved handling and ergonomics (above). The reason was Lamborghini's roller-coaster financial fortunes in the late Seventies and its inability to sell in the U.S.

1974-1988 LAMBORGHINI COUNTACH

As the ultimate supercar of its day, the Lamborghini Miura was going to be tough to top. Sant'Agata knew it. So did many observers. But when a prototype of the Miura's successor was revealed in 1971, there were not only sighs of relief but gasps of astonishment: no one had *ever* seen anything like the Countach.

And it's doubtful we'll soon see another car with the same visual and dynamic impact. More than 10 years later, the Countach still looks like something out of the distant future. And with the possible exception of Porsche's recently arrived 959, there's still no faster car on the planet. Long described as the ultimate automotive fantasy, the Countach remains the sort of thing only a Lamborghini or Ferrari could build. Yet despite its wild styling and exotic mechanicals, Paolo Stanzani's engineers produced, at least by supercar standards, a fairly practical and reliable machine, an "ultracar" that's almost as comfortable in L.A. traffic jams as flat out on the Italian *autostrada*.

Like the Miura, the Countach (pronounced COON-tahsh and roughly equivalent to "Good Lord!") was conceived as a mid-engine two-seater. But except for the famous quad-cam Lambo V-12, it was different in every other respect. Instead of a pressed-steel chassis, it had a complex multi-tubular platform; instead of side-opening doors, articulated doors that swung up as they swung out. Most important, the Countach powerteam was "north-south" rather than "east-west." Better make that "south-north," for the gearbox ran ahead of the engine and into the cockpit between the seats, thus permitting a short, direct linkage for easy, positive cog-swapping.

The sharp-edged, almost pyramidal body design was another effort of Bertone's Marcello Gandini—very modern and geometrical, and enormously popular, of course. General proportions and the semi-gulling doors may have come from Bertone's 1968 Alfa-based Carabo show car, but the Countach was more muscular and menacing, especially in later form with various scoops, scallops and spoilers added. Luggage space? Virtually none, but who cared? Looking at a Countach was almost as good as driving it. This time, Bertone would supply just the body; Sant'Agata itself would handle assembly, paint, and trim.

Although the prototype mounted a 5.0-liter V-12, the initial production Countach, designated LP400, carried the well-known 4.0-liter unit with 375 DIN horsepower.

Sales didn't commence until 1974 (the production version bowed at Geneva the previous year) when only 23 were delivered, but those customers found they had a 175-mph car capable of 0-60 mph in less than seven seconds—and turning *every* head. Handling, braking, and stability were all of race-car caliber, and necessary given the searing performance.

Four years into its career, the Countach received important changes to become the LP400S. Giampaolo Dallara came back from his successful freelancing business to supervise the updates, which included modified suspension geometry, superwide Pirelli P7 tires on broader Bravo-style "five-hole" wheels (as used on the contemporary Urraco-based Silhouette), wheelarch extensions, and a front spoiler. Optional was a huge rear wing, flying on twin struts above the tail, which made the Countach look even more like a racer. It was fitted to most Ss. By 1980, there was a Series 2 S with a tidier, redesigned instrument panel.

With new European emissions standards beginning to take a performance toll almost as high as American ones, Lamborghini upped displacement to 4.75 liters in 1982 for the newly designated LP5000. But horsepower was still 375—and not enough—so in March 1985, Lamborghini unleashed the 5000 Quattrovalvole, which denoted new four-valves-per-cylinder heads for an even larger 5167-cc V-12. With a genuine 455 bhp in European tune, the Countach was again king of the top-speed hill—over 180 mph—though its status as "world's fastest car" was shaky, endlessly debated by the press.

American enthusiasts unwilling to truck with "gray market" importers missed out on the Countach from the mid-Seventies through about 1982, a reflection of Lamborghini's difficulties in those years and its inability to keep pace with changing U.S. rules. But those rules have recently been relaxed, and things are looking up again in Sant'Agata (especially since Chrysler bought the place in 1987) so the Countach is an illegal alien no more. Compared to the 1982 S, the latest U.S. Quattrovalvole packs 420 SAE net horsepower (versus 325), does 0-60 mph in 5.2 seconds (5.7 before) and reaches 173 mph (versus 150). Price has gone up along with performance: from "only" $52,000 in 1976 to near $120,000 now.

And what do you get for it? A rocky ride, tank-like outward vision, engine noise that approaches 747 levels, a driving position only Plastic Man can accommodate, and controls only Arnold Schwarzenegger can manipulate. But oh, that body and, oh, that go!

One American magazine recently called the Countach "bigger than its performance figures, bigger than the sum of its automotive qualities. . . . The Countach's sole reason for existence is that somehow, according to some magic formula, it's bigger than life. The fact that after all these years that is still true, that this car still works the same soul-stopping spell on nearly everyone who sees it, is testament to the success of the Lamborghini concept and the original Bertone design. In fact, if you think it over, it's just a bit miraculous."

Like the car itself.

SPECIFICATIONS

Engines: all dohc V-12; **LP400** (1974-78): 239.8 cid/3929 cc, 375 bhp (DIN) @ 8000 rpm, 268 lbs-ft @ 5000 rpm; **LP400S** (1978-82): 239.8 cid/3929 cc, 375 bhp (DIN) @ 8000 rpm, 268 lbs-ft @ 5000 rpm; **LP5000** (1982-85): 290.3 cid/4754 cc, 375 bhp (DIN) @ 8000 rpm, 302 lbs-ft @ 4500 rpm (U.S. version: 325 bhp [SAE net] @ 7500 rpm, 260 lbs-ft @ 5500 rpm); **LP5000S Quattrovalvole** (1985-88): 315.3 cid/5167 cc, 455 bhp (DIN) @ 7000 rpm, 369 lbs-ft @ 5200 rpm (U.S. version: 420 bhp [SAE net] @ 7000 rpm, 341 lbs-ft @ 5000 rpm); (four valves per cylinder)

Transmission:	5-speed manual (in rear transaxle)
Suspension, front:	unequal-length A-arms, coil springs, anti-roll bar
Suspension, rear:	upper lateral links, lower A-arms, upper and lower trailing arms, dual coil springs, anti-roll bar
Brakes:	front/rear discs
Wheelbase (in.):	98.4
Weight (lbs):	2915-3285
Top speed (mph):	173-192
0-60 mph (sec):	4.9-6.8
Production:	LP400 (1974-78) 150 **Other models** NA

Menacing from any angle, the Countach still looks futuristic more than 15 years after it first appeared. Optional wing spoiler seen on many examples makes it more so, but increases aerodynamic drag.

1974-1975 LANCIA STRATOS

By any standard, the Lancia Stratos was a big success both in and out of competition. Developed as a homologation special for European rallying, it became a cult car after production ceased and is now highly prized as the "modern classic" it is.

The Stratos had no direct ancestors, strictly speaking, though its midships drivetrain was lifted intact from Ferrari's Dino 246 GT (see entry). Here it's important to recall that in 1969, Fiat took over Lancia, then in financial trouble, and also acquired 50 percent of Ferrari.

European rallies had been Lancia's main motorsports venue since the early Sixties, competition that remains much faster, rougher, and tougher than most American-style rallies. The firm's standard-bearer, the front-drive Fulvia coupe, was becoming outclassed by 1970. The Stratos was developed to take over for it and make Lancia the outright world rally champ.

It all began in 1970 when Bertone presented an utterly impractical Fulvia-powered dream car at Turin. Also called Stratos, it prompted Lancia team director Cesar Fiorio to push for a very different purpose-designed rally machine, which the new Fiat managers promptly approved. As ever, there was a minimum production requirement: 500 units, an awkward figure that would necessitate funds for at least semi-permanent tooling as well as design and development. In short, this was a specialized job of the sort long familiar—and thus well suited—to the Italian industry.

Fiorio naturally masterminded the project, which envisioned a short, wide coupe with transverse midships drivetrain. Ing. Tonti lent an assist, as did two consultants: former Lamborghini chief engineer Giampaolo Dallara at first; later, ex-Ferrari engineering chief Mike Parkes. Bertone was immediately contracted to style the beast and build its unit body/chassis structure. Fiorio, having studied every possible powerteam in the Fiat/Lancia group, secured 2.4-liter V-6s and 5-speed transaxles from Ferrari—an ideal choice, as they'd be installed exactly as in the Dino 246. All-independent suspension, rack-and-pinion steering, and four-wheel disc brakes were all specially designed. By November 1971, a prototype was ready for display at Turin.

Bertone's body design was chunky and stubby yet somehow wicked—and predictably minimal, to hold down weight and bulk. Its most distinctive features were semi-concealed A-pillars and a door beltline sharply upswept to the top of the daylight opening. The shape of the resulting unbroken expanse of glass gave the tunnelback roof the appearance of a futuristic crash helmet.

Like the chassis, the main body structure was steel; weight-saving fiberglass was used for tilt-up nose and tail sections. Cargo space was provided by a small box above and behind the powertrain, but the spare wheel precluded any up front. Speaking of helmets, bins were molded into the interior door panels for storing them. Door windows swivelled downwards. Footwells tapered markedly inward.

Stratos prototypes took to the rally circuit in 1972, but didn't score a major victory until the Spanish Rally of April 1973. Another year passed before the roadgoing "production" model appeared. Then, with a rush, Bertone and Lancia built 492 cars before September. Thus homologated (for the Grand Touring class of Group 4), the Stratos went on to win the World Rally Championship three years running—1974-76. Its last major win came in 1979, when a Stratos entered by the Monaco importer won the famed Monte Carlo Rally.

With 190 horsepower in roadgoing trim, the Stratos could exceed 140 mph. With nicely balanced, if slightly nervous, handling, it was as different from, say, a Corvette as a Derby winner is from a plow horse, the kind of car with which you had to become thoroughly familiar before you could really drive flat out. As with the compact mid-engine Ferraris, however, the Stratos was addictive, and most owners fell in love with it.

SPECIFICATIONS

Engine: dohc V-6, 147.6 cid/2418 cc, 190 bhp (SAE net) @ 7000 rpm, 166 lbs-ft @ 4000 rpm

Transmission:	5-speed manual (in rear transaxle)
Suspension, front:	upper and lower A-arms, coil springs, anti-roll bar
Suspension, rear:	upper and lower A-arms, Chapman struts, coil springs, anti-roll bar
Brakes:	front/rear discs
Wheelbase (in.):	85.8
Weight (lbs):	2160
Top speed (mph):	143
0-60 mph (sec):	6.8
Production:	500

Though conceived strictly for rallying, the distinctive Lancia Stratos makes an exciting road car, though it's far from GT standards in luxury and refinement. Cockpit (above) was purposed-designed for fast forest flying. Stratos was world rally champion in 1974-76.

253

1957-1963 LOTUS ELITE

Anthony Colin Bruce Chapman earned fame in his native England with a series of early-Fifties racing "specials," then set up a small company called Lotus to produce small numbers of sports-racing cars to his design. Before long, however, his ambitions turned to road cars, and in 1957 he announced the sleek Elite coupe as his first. Though displayed at that year's London Motor Show, it wasn't fully developed, so customer deliveries didn't begin until 1959.

The Elite was not only the first practical roadgoing Lotus but the world's first production car with unitized fiberglass construction, with no more than a tiny amount of steel stiffening. (This compares with the Chevrolet Corvette, which uses a fiberglass body on a separate steel frame.) Chapman, who liked his cars as light as possible, thought this the ideal way to save weight without compromising structural rigidity. It also seemed the most affordable approach. A separate chassis was old hat, he felt, while a monocoque would have been too costly if built in steel.

Though beautiful and a real image-booster, the Elite was not a corporate success. It was unrefined and unreliable in many ways, which hindered sales, while production costs proved higher than expected, so it never made any money. Worse, the fiberglass monocoque proved such a difficult construction job that Lotus had to switch suppliers in midstream, the later, higher-quality shells coming from a subsidiary of Bristol Aeroplane Company. Nevertheless, this was valuable production experience that would stand Lotus in good stead when it turned to the altogether more practical Elan in the early Sixties.

And despite its problems, the Elite was a technical marvel. The monocoque was extremely light, as was the engine, an all-aluminum overhead-cam four supplied by Coventry-Climax. Chapman had persuaded C-C to productionize its FWA racing engine, which it enlarged into the torquier FWE unit for the Elite (hence the different end initial).

Independent front suspension and all-disc brakes were expected, but ACBC had devised a simple and effective irs that he cheekily called "Chapman strut" suspension. It was simply a modified MacPherson-strut layout transplanted to the rear, but it fit perfectly with the layout and concept of this lean and lovely coupe. Like sports-racing Lotuses, the Elite had soft springs and relatively firm shock absorbers for a comfortable ride with truly excellent grip and handling balance.

The result of all this was a car that weighed half as much as a Jaguar XK140 (see entry) but was almost as fast and far more economical, thus further confirming Chapman's weight-saving design philosophy. Low aerodynamic drag further aided both performance and fuel efficiency, while road manners were responsive—quite feline, in fact.

But refinement—that is, the lack thereof—was the Elite's downfall. With all running gear bolted directly to the main structure, and given the superior noise-transmission properties of fiberglass versus steel, too much mechanical and road ruckus found their way into the cockpit, making the Elite tiring as an everyday car. Also, the barrel-section doors precluded drop-down windows, so occupants either had to swelter in warm weather or remove the windows completely. And with a wheelbase of just 88.2 inches, cockpit room was limited for larger folks, a literal shortcoming that would characterize future Lotuses.

Finally, there was poor workmanship, another failing that would persist far into Lotus's future. The Elite was designed, and largely built, as a kit to take advantage of British tax laws that levied a heavier surcharge on assembled cars. Yet even factory-built Elites were rather fragile, especially in America's more demanding driving conditions. This and the U.S. importer's financial problems and subsequent upheaval did nothing for sales or Lotus's reputation here, especially since the Stateside price was a lofty $4780 POE.

Yet when all was in order, the Elite was a magnificent driving machine: quick, smooth-riding, amazingly obedient. And it became even better. Series II cars, produced beginning in 1960, had revised rear suspension and a ZF gearbox, while a few later examples were built as "Super 95" and "Super 105" models with more powerful C-C engines. Still, the last Elite was essentially the same as the first.

Alas, demand evaporated once the Elan was revealed in 1962, and a tentative proposal to continue the Elite with the new Lotus-Ford twincam engine was abandoned.

But the Elite was certainly an auspicious beginning for a small company entering the production-car lists. More than that, it was a modern milestone that was even recognized as such in its own time. Colin Chapman had done well indeed.

SPECIFICATIONS

Engine: Coventry-Climax sohc I-4, 74.2 cid/1216 cc, 71/83 bhp (DIN) @ 6100/6250 rpm, 77/75 lbs-ft @ 3750/4750 rpm

Transmission:	4-speed manual
Suspension, front:	upper and lower A-arms, coil springs, anti-roll bar
Suspension, rear:	Chapman struts, halfshafts, trailing arms, coil springs
Brakes:	front/rear discs (inboard at rear)
Wheelbase (in.):	88.2
Weight (lbs):	1455
Top speed (mph):	118 (83-bhp engine)
0-60 mph (sec):	11.0-11.8 (83-bhp engine)

Production: 988 (in dispute, as apparently more bodyshells were built than kits or complete cars)

The world's first—and so far only—car with unit fiberglass construction, the Elite proved as delicate as it looked. However, it was a joy to drive when things were working right, though that was seldom. Small cockpit featured no-nonsense dash (top). Light weight enabled small engine (above) to give decent go.

1962-1974
LOTUS ELAN AND
ELAN +2

Though pretty, quick and agile, the Elite wasn't the money-spinner Lotus needed—too complicated and thus too costly to build. In particular, its Coventry-Climax engine had been way too expensive. For the Sixties, therefore, Colin Chapman and company turned to a cheaper, more practical sports car powered by a new Lotus-built engine.

What emerged in October 1962 was what many still regard as the definitive modern British sports car: the two-seat Elan roadster. A fixed-roof coupe was offered beginning in September 1965, followed two years later by a long-wheelbase 2+2 derivative, the Elan +2.

The engine in all Elans combined a four-cylinder British Ford block with a new Lotus-designed twincam head. Also used in the hybrid Lotus Cortina sports sedan, it became increasingly specialized with time and is recognized today as something of a "classic." More than 30,000 would be produced between 1962 and 1975.

There was nothing unusual about the Ford block. A conventional but rugged five-main-bearing cast-iron affair, it was used in various sizes with overhead valves to motivate workaday Anglias, Cortinas, and Corsairs of the period. Lotus's new aluminum head made it something else, however, with twincam valvegear much like that of contemporary Jaguars and Alfa Romeos. Aspiration was initially via twin-choke Weber carburetors; "federal" engines ran twin Zenith-Strombergs beginning in the late Sixties, while European versions were switched to Dell'orto instruments.

Displacement was always 1558 cc in production form, with base output of 105 horsepower. Later "Special Equipment" Elans offered 115 bhp. A so-called "Big Valve" engine with 126 bhp took over in 1971 for the renamed Elan Sprint and +2S 130. In all but the last few cars, the twincam teamed with a 4-speed gearbox based on Ford of Britain's then-current single-rail design, albeit with more closely spaced ratios. A few of the final Big-Valve Sprint two-seaters (likely no more than six) and +2S 130s from late 1972 received the 5-speed unit destined for the new-generation "squareback" Elite of 1974. (So equipped, the 2+2 was badged +2S 130/5.)

Aside from being Chapman's first practical road car, the two-seat Elan is significant for introducing what would become another hallmark of Lotus engineering: the sheet-

SPECIFICATIONS

Engines: all dohc I-4, 95.0 cid/1558 cc; **1962-67:** 105 bhp (net) @ 5500 rpm, 108 lbs-ft @ 4000 rpm; **1967-71:** 115/118 bhp (net) @ 5500 rpm, 108 lbs-ft @ 4000 rpm; **1971-74:** 126 bhp (net) @ 6500 rpm, 113 lbs-ft @ 5500 rpm

Transmission:	4/5-speed manual
Suspension, front:	unequal-length A-arms, coil springs, anti-roll bar
Suspension, rear:	lower A-arms, Chapman struts, coil springs
Brakes:	front/rear discs
Wheelbase (in.):	84.0 (Elan), 96.0 (Elan +2)
Weight (lbs):	1515-1630 (Elan), 2100 (Elan +2)
Top speed (mph):	115-120
0-60 mph (sec):	8.5-9.0
Production:	**Elan** 9659 **Elan +2** 4798

The trim Elan doesn't look that small, but seems to shrink the moment you open the door. Pre-1966 models were completely open; fixed door-window frames were then added to improve weather sealing. Twincam Lotus-Ford four (right) was ultimately tweaked to 126 bhp.

steel backbone chassis. This was split at each end like a tuning fork: at the front to embrace the twincam engine, at the rear to support the Ford-based final drive. The propshaft ran down the backbone, which left a tall center hump but permitted low seating and thus a low center of gravity for minimal body roll in corners.

Each fork also carried components for the all-independent suspension, which comprised classic double A-arms and coil springs fore, coil-sprung Chapman (MacPherson) struts on lower A-arms aft. All-disc brakes and rack-and-pinion steering were also as expected from Lotus. Aside from its longer wheelbase and wider tracks, the +2 chassis was the same as for the two-seaters.

Fiberglass was retained for the simply engineered bodyshells used on all Elans. Two-seaters were neat and rounded in appearance, while the +2 was more overtly styled. Common to all were hidden headlamps, roll-up door glass (with fixed frames on most roadsters), curved windshields (and backlights on coupes), and slender bumpers that were more decorative than protective. As ever, cockpits were tight (even on +2s) and finish patchy, though equipment was gradually upgraded over the years to include niceties like power windows and brakes.

Like the predecessor Elite, the Elans were offered in both factory-built and kit form (the latter still financially advantageous in the UK, where sales tax did not then apply). Also like the Elite, spring rates were relatively soft, shock damping firm, resulting in a surprisingly comfortable ride with race-car-style agility and grip. (What else from a company beginning to dominate Formula and even Indy-car competition?) Low-drag styling combined with Chapman's light-but-strong engineering to give all Elans a good top end and very brisk acceleration, typically 115-120 mph and 8.5-9.0 seconds 0-60 mph.

With updated trim and equipment, the two-seat Elan evolved through Series 2 (1964) and Series 3 (1965-66) iterations before becoming the Series 4 in 1968, by which time Lotus was building "desmogged" cars for U.S. consumption. The Big-Valve Sprint was the final version. The +2 arrived with a 118-bhp "Special Equipment" engine as standard. Capitalizing on the success of its John Player-sponsored Formula racers, Lotus briefly offered a special black-and-gold paint scheme for both two-seaters and the +2 (retagged +2S for the occasion).

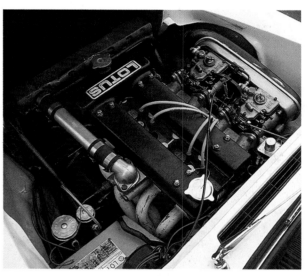

Many were sorry to see the Elans go in 1974, especially the lithe and winsome two-seater (which earned a following on both sides of the Atlantic as Mrs. Peel's car in *The Avengers* TV series). Lately we've seen a UK-built replica, the Evante, while Lotus (now owned by General Motors) continues work on a long-rumored—and eagerly awaited—"new Elan."

Of course, neither is a substitute for the real thing. And fortunately, a good many Elans survive today, thanks to their rotproof bodies, still-ample supplies of most parts, and steady care over the years by loving owners. So there's a good chance you can have one if you want one. The problem will be persuading an owner to part with it. Lotuses inspire that kind of devotion.

1966-1975 LOTUS EUROPA

Lotus's mid-engine racing cars achieved worldwide fame before Colin Chapman got around to a midships road car. Not that he hadn't wanted to offer one, but until the mid-Sixties, he couldn't find a suitable proprietary powertrain available in quantity. Besides, his facilities were already full building Elans. Then Renault introduced its first front-drive car, the 16 sedan, in 1965, and Chapman was intrigued—enough to acquire a more spacious factory at the wartime U.S. Air Force bomber field at Hethel, near Norwich.

Chapman duly arranged to buy modified 16 drivetrains from Renault for a new mid-engine model to be designed and built by Lotus. As part of the deal, sales would be limited to the Continent for the first couple of years, reflecting Chapman's desire to establish a presence in the recently formed European Common Market, another reason for the Renault mechanicals. Chapman diplomatically suggested the name "Europe," which was soon changed to Europa, and the first roadgoing mid-engine Lotus was born.

What Chapman bought was the 16's front-drive transaxle and a tuned, 78-horsepower version of its 1470-cc overhead-valve all-alloy four. Because the powertrain would sit "north-south" behind the cockpit and ahead of the back wheels in the rear-drive Europa, the final drive was modified and the engine turned back-to-front, with the inline gearbox trailing behind. Like other roadgoing Lotuses, a fiberglass body sat atop a steel backbone frame with all-independent coil-spring suspension.

Styling was neat if slightly strange. The low nose with exposed headlamps was no problem (rather like the Elite's, in fact) but the rear quarters were funny, with broad, high sail panels aft of the doors that earned the Europa its "breadvan" nickname. A flat detachable engine cover lived between the sails, just below a slit-like rear window. Bodies and chassis were initially bonded together, which helped structural stiffness but complicated accident repairs.

Retrospectively called "Series 1," the first Europas were delivered in early 1967 after a late-'66 launch, and were sold factory-built or in kit form like other roadgoing Lotuses. Lightweight construction again paid off in surprising performance with great fuel economy, while the midships layout meant little body roll, high grip, and the kind of handling the world had come to expect of Lotus—all this plus the usual fine ride and a very attractive price.

But all was not bliss. Performance disappointed many, as did the cramped interior, fixed door windows, odd styling, and typically patchy Lotus workmanship. The Series 2 Europa, announced in 1968, answered some of these problems. Bodywork was bolted on rather than bonded to ease accident repairs, windows now moved electrically to reduce claustrophobia, the engine cover was newly hinged, and a bit more space was found for luggage (behind the engine) and around the pedals. For the U.S. market, the larger 1565-cc 16TS engine countered power-sapping emissions controls.

British Europa sales commenced in mid-1969, and Chapman hired a new project engineer named Mike Kimberley (Lotus's chief executive at this writing) away from Jaguar. One of his first jobs was to develop an even less quirky, more powerful Europa.

The result appeared in October 1971 as the Series 3 Twin-Cam, with the 105-bhp Lotus-Ford dohc four as used in the front-engine Elan Sprint and Elan +2S 130—and originally ruled out for the Europa! The Renault transaxle was retained. Styling was altered via cut-down rear quarters for improved driver vision, plus new cast-alloy road wheels. In this form, the Europa was good for up to 120 mph flat out (versus the previous 110).

Late 1972 brought the even better Europa Special, with the 126-bhp "Big-Valve" engine and a new 5-speed Renault transaxle, the latter optional at first but made standard in 1974. Top speed improved to 125 mph plus, and there were corresponding gains in standing-start acceleration.

But Lotus was working on a more grown-up middie, the chiseled Giugiaro-designed Esprit, revealed in 1975. Thus, the Europa passed into history much loved, if not overly mourned in light of its stunning successor.

At least U.S. enthusiasts got the best of the breed. Though imports were sporadic through late 1969, the Europa was officially certified for American sale after that, which means most examples on today's market will be the desirable S3 and Special models.

SPECIFICATIONS

Engines: Renault ohv I-4; **1967-71:** 89.7 cid/1470 cc, 78 bhp (net) @ 6000 rpm, 76 lbs-ft @ 4000 rpm; **U.S. 1968-71:** 95.5 cid/1565 cc, 88 bhp (SAE gross) @ 5750 rpm, 87 lbs-ft @ 3500 rpm; Lotus-Ford dohc I-4, 95.0 cid/1558 cc; **1971-72:** 105 bhp @ 5500 rpm, 108 lbs-ft @ 4000 rpm; **1972-75:** 126 bhp (net) @ 6500 rpm, 113 lbs-ft @ 5500 rpm

Transmission:	Renault 4/5-speed manual (in rear transaxle)
Suspension, front:	unequal-length A-arms, coil springs, anti-roll bar
Suspension, rear:	lower A-arms, upper lateral links, upper and lower trailing arms, coil springs, anti-roll bar
Brakes:	front discs/rear drums
Wheelbase (in.):	94.0
Weight (lbs):	1350-1550
Top speed (mph):	109-125
0-60 mph (sec):	7.7-10.7
Production:	9000+

Above: Early Europas had high "breadvan" rear quarters. **Right:** *Cut-down sail panels greatly improved driver vision in later Europas like this Twin-Cam, which belatedly received the capable Lotus-Ford four (this page, top) originally ruled out for the mid-engine Lotus.*

1976-1988 LOTUS ESPRIT & ESPRIT TURBO

Lotus began the complicated and costly job of replacing all its production cars in the early Seventies. New models were definitely needed by then. Not only had the four-cylinder Ford-Lotus engine reached the end of its development road but Colin Chapman had decided to take Lotus into price and performance territory where it had never competed before.

The first of the new breed was a pair of posh front-engine GTs: the square-tailed Elite (named for the first roadgoing Lotus) and a slopeback companion called Eclat (which has since evolved into today's Excel). Once these were locked up, Hethel turned to a new mid-engine coupe. Also envisioned as larger, more powerful and more expensive, it would not directly replace the Europa, though design philosophy and general layout would be much the same, with a fiberglass body and steel "backbone" chassis.

While Lotus would engineer this one too, styling was farmed out to Giorgio Giugiaro and his then-new Ital Design outfit. A prototype on a much-modified Europa platform was ready in time for the November 1972 Turin show, but finalizing chassis and running gear would take much longer. In fact, the production model, which retained Giugiaro's suggested name Esprit, wasn't officially shown until October 1975 and initial deliveries were delayed until mid-1976. In line with Chapman's move upmarket, the Esprit would not be offered as a kit, unlike the Europa.

The Esprit prototype went into production with remarkably few design changes. Typical of then-current Italian trends, it was much more hard-edged than the Europa and quite "wedgy," with a very large, steeply raked windshield; low, slim snout; and a sloped, stubby rump. A lift-up rear hatch incorporated the backlight and covered a small amount of luggage space above the engine cover. A relatively long wheelbase betrayed the mid-engine layout and was five inches up on the Europa's. Tracks were six inches wider.

Like its predecessor, the Esprit had all-independent coil-spring suspension (albeit with more complex geometry) and rack-and-pinion steering, but four-wheel disc

brakes replaced front-disc/rear-drum. High-rate shock absorbers and low-rate springs also continued, so the ride was still soft yet very well controlled.

As expected, Esprit power was provided by the new all-Lotus Type 907 2.0-liter twincam four, first seen in the Jensen-Healey (see entry) and also used in the Elite/Eclat, with all-alloy construction and an easy 160 DIN horsepower in initial form. Positioned fore/aft ahead of the rear-wheel centerline, it was canted 45 degrees to port because it was actually a slant-four, half of a planned V-8 that only existed on paper at that point. Mating with it was a robust 5-speed transaxle, the same one used in the front-drive Citröen SM and Maserati's mid-engine Merak (see entries).

The "Series 1" Esprit was good for 135 mph in European tune. The U.S. version went on sale for 1977 with only 140 bhp (SAE net), so top speed dropped to about 120 mph and the 0-60 mph time, at a tick over 9.0 seconds, was unremarkable.

Alas, running problems again surfaced early in a new Lotus. The most serious were excessive mechanical and road noise transmission through the backbone chassis (it really *did* vibrate like a tuning fork) and marginal engine cooling. Lotus addressed these and other maladies in 1979 with the Series 2, which also sported wider wheels, a front lip spoiler, and revised trim and equipment.

Performance took a great leap forward in 1980 with the new 2.2-liter Turbo Esprit, packing 210 bhp (DIN) along with a more rigid chassis, modified rear suspension, improved brakes, 15-inch wheels, a deep front airdam, and aerodynamic rocker-panel extensions. Top speed jumped to nearly 150 mph, truly incredible for the modest engine size. It was with this car that Lotus would return to the U.S. market in 1983 after being in and out of it since the late Seventies—helped by the Turbo Esprit that starred as the James Bond car in the film *The Spy Who Loved Me*.

The larger engine was also offered in normally aspirated form for an interim 1980-81 Esprit S2.2. In 1983 came the much-changed S3, essentially a re-engineered Esprit with all the Turbo's improvements, plus its wider wheels as an optional extra. The most recent mechanical update was the Turbo's 1986-87 switch from carburetors to Bosch fuel injection.

Lotus remains a tiny company, building small numbers of road and race cars each year. Over the years though, car sales have declined as a share of its total business in favor of consultant contracts with other automakers, mostly in engine design and fiberglass molding techniques. Indeed, Lotus's expertise in these areas was the main reason General Motors bought the company in late 1986. With that, and GM's promise of continued autonomy, Lotus's financial and carmaking future would seem assured.

A restyled Espirit has just arrived at this writing, though there's no all-new model in sight. But it's not really needed. The Esprit still sets design and dynamic standards for the mid-engine brigade, and probably will for some time to come.

SPECIFICATIONS

Engines: all dohc I-4; **1976-80:** 120.4 cid/1973 cc, 160 bhp (DIN) @ 6200 rpm, 140 lbs-ft @ 4900 rpm; **1980-86:** 132.7 cid/2174 cc, 160 bhp (DIN) @ 6500 rpm, 160 lbs-ft @ 5000 rpm; **1987:** 132.7 cid/2174 cc, 160 bhp (DIN) @ 5600 rpm, 160 lbs-ft @ 5000 rpm; **1980-88 Turbo:** 132.7 cid/2174 cc, 210 bhp (DIN) @ 6000 rpm, 200 lbs-ft @ 4000 rpm

Transmission:	5-speed manual (in rear transaxle)
Suspension, front:	upper A-arms, lower lateral links, lower longitudinal links (anti-roll function), coil springs
Suspension, rear:	upper lateral links (halfshafts), lower lateral links and angled trailing arms, coil springs
Brakes:	front/rear discs
Wheelbase (in.):	96.0
Weight (lbs):	2220-2650
Top speed (mph):	120-150
0-60 mph (sec):	6.1-9.2

Production: S1 (1975-79) 1060 **S2** (1979-80) 88 **Other models** NA (S3 and Turbo production continues at this writing)

A more rounded, restyled Esprit, announced as this book went to press, makes this 1987 the last of the original sharp-edged Giugiaro-designed cars. Cockpit has also been freshened and made slightly roomier. Running gear, including fuel-injected 2.2-liter four, is unchanged.

1946-1950 MASERATI A6/1500

Though several coachbuilders' work graced Maserati's first roadgoing chassis, this Pinin Farina coupe was the definitive "production" A6/1500 style, though it didn't appear until the Turin show of 1948. Top speed was only 95 mph, but the chassis was good enough to continue in successor models with more horsepower.

Maserati in Italy built only competition cars in its early years (the Twenties and Thirties), albeit with great success. But there was a change of emphasis soon after the Maserati family sold out to the Orsi group in 1938. After World War II, Maserati began a more serious effort to produce not just race cars but road cars too.

Thus, the first roadgoing Maserati, titled A6/1500, was formally announced in 1947 (after two were built the previous year). Maserati was still a small concern struggling to recover from wartime devastation, so this was a simply engineered machine. As you might guess from the designation, power was supplied by a six-cylinder engine of approximately 1500-cc displacement.

It was, in fact, descended from the supercharged 6CM twincam racing unit of 1936. (Which hadn't been forgotten, just laid aside for still-sportier cars to come.) It was considerably less potent though. With normal aspiration and a single overhead camshaft operating opposed valves through rocker arms, it delivered a mere 65 horsepower compared to its parent's 175 bhp. One reason: tuning for postwar Italy's limited quantities of low-grade fuel. The gearbox was a newly designed 4-speed unit from another of the Orsis' many businesses.

Like other specialist cars of these years, the A6/1500 had a conventional separate chassis, with tubular side-rails and cross-members. Front suspension was independent via coil springs and wishbones; a live axle located by trailing arms rode on coils at the rear.

A6/1500 design work had begun as early as 1943, when Ernesto Maserati laid out the engine, but the war zone crept steadily closer to Modena, so engine bench-testing didn't begin until 1945. The original prototype had a crude, narrow body with separate Allard-like cycle fenders, but was subsequently rebodied by Pinin Farina, whose *carrozzerie* supplied identically styled shells for the entire production run of just 61 units.

Predictably, all these Maseratis were effectively handbuilt cars. After the two 1946 examples, the firm completed three in '47, nine the following year, 25 in 1949, and 22 the year after that. Included in the totals is a handful of Farina spiders and one Zagato-bodied coupe.

As for performance, the A6/1500 was claimed to do 95 mph all out, though it probably couldn't go that fast. But its chassis was a good one, and would serve well with more powerful 2.0-liter and twincam engines to come. The A6 even made one or two competition appearances, though on a private basis.

Humble it may have been, but the A6/1500 was at least a beginning for roadgoing Maseratis. By the Sixties, they'd have engines three times as large producing 500 percent more horsepower—and price tags to match—but from such tiny acorns do mighty oaks grow.

SPECIFICATIONS

Engine: ohc I-6, 90.8 cid/1488 cc, 65 bhp (net) @ 4700 rpm, torque NA

Transmission:	4-speed manual
Suspension, front:	upper and lower wishbones, coil springs
Suspension, rear:	live axle, radius arms, coil springs
Brakes:	front/rear drums
Wheelbase (in.):	102.0
Weight (lbs):	1675
Top speed (mph):	95 (claimed)
0-60 mph (sec):	not quoted
Production:	61

1951-1957 MASERATI A6G & A6G/2000

Although still more interested in and involved with race cars, Maserati was sufficiently encouraged by the success of its first "production" model, the A6/1500, to plan a successor. In retrospect, the new A6G series was a long way from Maserati's first supercar, the 3500, but was definitely a step in the right direction.

Actually, there were two A6G series in 1951-57. Both used an evolution of the A6 chassis, a simple, robust tubular assembly spanning a 102-inch wheelbase. They also had six-cylinder engines. The difference is that the later A6G/2000 had a very different twincam engine.

It was generally agreed, even within the Orsi family, that any A6 replacement would need better handling and more power, if only to keep pace with Ferrari. Accordingly, the A6G received a modified rear suspension with leaf instead of coil springs (it was good enough for Enzo), and a larger 1954-cc engine with 100 horsepower versus the previous 65. The latter retained the previous opposed valves and single overhead camshaft. Body choices were greatly expanded to include cabriolets by Pietro Frua and coupes by Frua, Pinin Farina, Alfredo Vignale, and the occasional Ghia and Bertone one-off.

Despite all this, buyers wanted still more. At a time when twincam Masers were competing successfully against Ferraris on the track, the single-cam A6G had nowhere near the performance of Ferrari's roadgoing V-12s. Thus, after a mere 16 A6Gs, Maserati hustled out the improved A6G54 or A6G/2000.

The "54" in the factory designation stood for introduction year, but the real significance was in the "2000" title, for it signalled that Maserati's first roadgoing twincam engine was ready at last. This wasn't a return to the Thirties 6CM unit or even a twincam conversion of the existing single-cam six. Rather, it was nothing less than a detuned version of Maserati's already famous Formula 2 powerplant. Its bore/stroke dimensions were different from the sohc engine's, giving exact capacity of 1985 cc. At a rated 150 bhp even in "low-output" form, it was a far cry from the 65-bhp engine of just a few years earlier. The basic A6 chassis was retained, and though it had to cope with two-and-half times the power in the 2000, it was well up to the job.

The AG6/2000 bowed at the 1954 Paris Salon, with first deliveries of what was definitely a 120-mph roadgoing Maserati commencing in the spring of 1955. Considering its high price and Maserati's still-primitive manufacturing facilities, the firm did well to sell 61 of these cars in three years.

Here, too, coachwork was farmed out to various *carrozzeria* (again, it was good enough for Enzo). A skim through factory records shows that all 2000s built were two-seat coupes and spiders. Among participating coachbuilders were Frua, Zagato, and Allemano but not Farina, at least on this occasion.

Sad to say, time quickly caught up with the quickest roadgoing Maserati to date. By 1957, the firm's racing program had produced much-modified and much more powerful 3.5-liter twincams, while a new V-12 and V-8 were on the way.

But so was a new grand touring Maserati, one that truly deserved those oft-abused GT initials. With the 3500, Maserati would move to the front ranks of high-performance Italian road cars.

SPECIFICATIONS

Engines:	**A6G** (1951-54): sohc I-6, 119.2 cid/1954 cc, 100 bhp (net) @ 5500 rpm, torque NA; **A6G54/2000** (1954-57): dohc I-6, 121.1 cid/1985 cc, 150 bhp @ 6000 rpm, 123 lbs-ft @ 5000 rpm
Transmission:	4-speed manual
Suspension, front:	upper and lower wishbones, coil springs
Suspension, rear:	live axle, radius arms, leaf springs
Brakes:	front/rear drums
Wheelbase (in.):	102.0
Weight (lbs):	average 1900
Top speed (mph):	100-118
0-60 mph (sec):	10.0-12.5
Production:	**A6G** (1951-54) 16 **A6G/2000** (1954-57) 61

An inside and outside look at an A6G/2000 with spider bodywork by Frua. It's clearly a mid-Fifties design, most evident in the modestly wrapped windshield. A detuned version of Maserati's 2.0-liter Formula 2 twincam six with twin ignition delivered a minimum 150 bhp and brisk performance for the day.

1957-1964
MASERATI 3500GT/GTI

Maserati earned a formidable reputation in the early Fifties with its Formula *monopostos* and two-seat sports-racers, and some of this naturally rubbed off on its road cars. But while Maserati produced a variety of engines to meet all needs, as did Ferrari—inline fours and sixes, V-8s *and* V-12s—its mainstay, especially for road use, was a rugged straight six. Not surprisingly then, this was the engine of choice for the 3500GT, successor to the AG654.

A sturdy, sensibly detailed but very fast grand tourer designed by Maserati chief engineer Giulio Alfieri and his team, the 3500 was previewed at the Geneva Salon in early 1957 and went on sale later that year. It would prove a significant car for Maserati, as its chassis and running gear, with steady development, would remain in production through the end of the Sixties in the Sebring and Mistral (see entries). More important, the 3500 firmly established Maserati as a premier builder of exciting, high-performance cars.

Lovers of advanced engineering need not bother with the chassis specs. Again like Ferrari, Maserati spent most of its effort on running gear in these years. Thus, the 3500's suspension was pretty much like the AG654's, while the chassis was a solid but unadventuresome affair composed mainly of large-diameter steel tubes with various sheet-steel stiffeners. Though British cars like the Triumph TR3A and Jaguar XK150 had already jumped to disc brakes, the 3500 arrived with Maserati's usual massive, four-wheel finned aluminum drums with iron liners. Recirculating-ball steering was another holdover.

Touring-bodied 3500GT gained front vent windows in its doors for '59, tiny triangular panes at the trailing edges for '62. Shown here is the typical production coupe, but Frua, Bertone, and others did various one-offs.

The *pièce de résistance* was the 3485-cc twincam six with twin spark plugs per cylinder, basically a detuned version of the two-seat 350S racing engine but little more civilized. Output was initially rated at 220 horsepower, versus 290 in competition form. In other respects, the 3500 was an "assembled" car in the classic sense. Its 4-speed gearbox came from ZF, its rear axle from Salisbury, its brakes from Girling, and its front suspension from Alford & Adler.

Coachwork still came from the outside too. But with higher volume in mind, Maserati now settled on two "standard" styles: a coupe by Touring of Milan and a convertible by Vignale of Turin, the latter riding a two-inch shorter wheelbase and looking a little like a plumped-up Pinin Farina Alfa spider. Custom bodies from these and other houses could be, and were, supplied.

With a 140-mph maximum and good roadholding (if not sensational handling), the 3500GT readily attracted customers. Even Ferrari's 250 GTs began to feel the pinch. This was obviously a much more serious effort than Maserati's previous production cars, and by 1960 the factory was delivering up to 10 a week.

To keep demand strong, Maserati wasted little time in instituting several important technical changes. First came three new options in 1959: center-lock wire wheels, limited-slip differential, and front disc brakes. The last became standard in 1960, when an extra-cost 5-speed gearbox arrived. The latter was standardized the following year, and the previous trio of Weber carburetors was discarded for Lucas mechanical fuel injection. Signalled by the GTI designation, it added 15 extra horsepower on an unchanged 8.5:1 compression ratio.

But time was running out for the 3500 by then, for 1962 brought a smart new Vignale coupe on the short-wheelbase spider chassis. Called Sebring, it soon elbowed the 3500 into oblivion.

But there was no doubting the 3500's success, for Maserati built 2223 of them in eight years. Even Ferrari would have been proud to do that.

SPECIFICATIONS

Engine: dohc I-6, 212.7 cid/3485 cc, 220/235 bhp (net) @ 5500/5800 rpm, 253/261 lbs-ft @ 3500/4000 rpm (GT/GTI)

Transmissions:	ZF 4-speed manual; 5-speed manual (optional 1960; standard from 1961)
Suspension, front:	upper and lower A-arms, coil springs, anti-roll bar
Suspension, rear:	live axle, radius arms, semi-elliptic leaf springs
Brakes:	front/rear drums (front discs optional 1959, standard from 1960)
Wheelbase (in.):	102.0 (coupe) 100.0 (spider)
Weight (lbs):	average 2800
Top speed (mph):	140
0-60 mph (sec):	8.1
Production:	2223

1962-1966
MASERATI SEBRING

Having earned its stripes in the Fifties as a GT power to be reckoned with, Maserati entered the Sixties intent on expanding this success. With two new models, it would do just that.

First to arrive, and our subject here, was the Sebring, introduced at Geneva in 1962. It combined all the best, newly developed elements of the 3500GTI with more comprehensive equipment and stylish new 2+2 bodywork shaped and supplied by Vignale.

Designer Giovanni Michelotti was still associated with Vignale in those days, so it wasn't surprising that this new notchback coupe looked much like his TR3A-based Triumph Italia being built at the same time. Highlights included quad headlamps, a rectangular mesh grille bearing the famed Maserati trident, a pair of functional air vents behind the front wheelarches just above the rockers, and a straight-through fenderline linking headlamp pods and taillight clusters. B-pillars were raked to match A-pillar angle, glass area was generous, the tail neatly cropped.

Options proliferated, mainly with the American market in mind. Air conditioning and automatic transmission were new—and unheard-of—in a Maserati. Special paint, wire wheels, and radio were also offered.

Beneath this relative luxury was an improved version of the 3500GTI spider chassis with a shorter, 98.4-inch wheelbase. It was more rigid than before, but only an Italian automaker would have bothered with such a labor-intensive design comprising multiple tubes, pressings, stiffeners, and brackets.

A total of 444 Sebrings, all with the same Vignale bodywork, were produced in two series between 1962 and '66. Series I models used the GTI's 235-horsepower twincam six. Most Series II examples, all of which were built in 1965-66, carried a 245-bhp, 3694-cc enlargement, though a few had an even larger 4.0-liter, 255-bhp extension. Both these engines were also used in the contemporary Mistral (see entry).

In its most potent form, the Sebring could touch 150 mph flat out. Alas, that wasn't enough to keep pace with Ferrari's new-generation V-12s and new V-8 models from Maserati itself. But the GTI platform wasn't finished yet: the Mistral had blown in, and it was no ill wind.

*The Sebring in initial Series I form, Series II models wore a lower-profile hood scoop and hooded headlamps. Instrumentation (**opposite top**) was certainly complete. Maser's twincam six (**above**) provided performance aplenty.*

SPECIFICATIONS

Engines: all dohc I-6; **Series I** (1962-65): 212.7 cid/3485 cc, 235 bhp (net) @ 5500 rpm, 232 lbs-ft @ 4000 rpm; **Series II** (1965-66): 225.5 cid/3694 cc, 245 bhp (net) @ 5200 rpm, 253 lbs-ft @ 4000 rpm; 245 cid/4014 cc, 255 bhp (net) @ 5200 rpm, 267 lbs-ft @ 4000 rpm

Transmissions:	5-speed ZF manual or 3-speed automatic
Suspension, front:	upper and lower A-arms, coil springs, anti-roll bar
Suspension, rear:	live axle, radius arms, semi-elliptic leaf springs
Brakes:	front/rear discs
Wheelbase (in.):	98.4
Weight (lbs):	3330
Top speed (mph):	135-150
0-60 mph (sec):	8.4 (3.5-liter)
Production:	**Series I** (1962-65) 346 **Series II** (1965-66) 98

1963-1970
MASERATI MISTRAL

Named for the famous Mediterranean wind, Mistral was the second of Maserati's new six-cylinder Sixties models. Previewed at the '63 Turin show, it aped the Sebring in using an improved version of the 3500GTI chassis but with an even shorter wheelbase. This aided torsional stiffness, as did new folded members along the rocker panels, reinforcements over the rear wheelarches, and more sheetmetal around the tail.

The Mistral was offered in coupe and convertible models, the latter introduced at Geneva in 1964. Both were two-seaters, unlike the 2+2 Sebring. Styling, by Pietro Frua, was different too, more rounded and flowing, with a lower beltline and an airier greenhouse with more markedly curved glass. The coupe featured a large lift-up hatch window somewhat reminiscent of the later Porsche 924/944 treatment. In retrospect, overall appearance forecast the Frua-designed AC 428 of 1968 (even some panels were apparently shared). Doors, hood, and rear deck (hatch on the coupe, trunklid on the convertible) were aluminum; the rest of the shell was steel. Maggiora of Turin supplied both bodies under contract.

While a few early models carried the familiar 3.5-liter Maserati twincam six, most Mistrals had the more potent 3.7- or 4.0-liter versions. Peak power outputs were the same as the Sebring's and allowed Maserati to boast about beating the "1 hp per cu in." figure so magical to Americans in those heady days.

The Mistral proved quite popular. Most of the total 948 units were built in 1964-68 (though the last example, a 4.0-liter spider, wasn't completed until 1970). As ever, coupes way outsold the convertibles, which accounted for just 120 units.

Nevertheless, Maserati was moving on to bigger and better things, so the Mistral would be the last of the traditional front-engine straight-six Masers on which the company had built its great postwar success. Beginning in 1967, the future belonged to the new V-8 Mexico and Ghibli.

Styled by Pietro Frua, the Mistral was the last of the front-engine six-cylinder cars on which Maserati had built its postwar success as a producer of roadgoing GTs. Porsche may have been inspired by the Mistral's lift-up rear window when designing its later 924. Open Spider version was arguably prettier, definitely rarer.

SPECIFICATIONS

Engines: all dohc I-6; 225.5 cid/3694 cc, 255 bhp (net) @ 5500 rpm, 253 lbs-ft @ 4000 rpm; 245 cid/4014 cc, 255 bhp (net) @ 5200 rpm, 267 lbs-ft @ 4000 rpm

Transmissions:	5-speed ZF manual or 3-speed automatic
Suspension, front:	upper and lower A-arms, coil springs, anti-roll bar
Suspension, rear:	live axle, radius arms, semi-elliptic leaf springs
Brakes:	front/rear discs
Wheelbase (in.):	94.5
Weight (lbs):	2800-2860
Top speed (mph):	145-152
0-60 mph (sec):	approx. 8.0-9.0
Production:	**Coupe** 828 **Spider** 120

1965-1973 MASERATI MEXICO

In 1965, Maserati could look back on two decades of steady improvement and steadily increasing success in road cars. While more grand tourer than *pur sang* sports machine, they were still Maseratis, and thus exciting, entertaining, and eminently desirable.

But it was time to move on in '65. Maserati's twincam six had done yeoman service, but was at the end of its development life. Then too, more powerful new V-12 models from Ferrari and upstart Lamborghini represented a competitive challenge that Maserati's pride could not allow to go unanswered.

As with the six, the answer again came from competition. Nine years before, Maserati had fielded a massive and brutishly powerful 90-degree twincam V-8 for the 450S sports-racer, then went on to apply it to the equally famous Type 165 and Type 65 two-seaters of the early Sixties. A detuned version of this 5.0-liter engine had also powered a small run of roadgoing 5000 GTs (31 built) in 1959-64.

Chief engineer Giulio Alfieri set about "productionizing" the V-8 for Maserati's new-generation road cars of the late Sixties and beyond (changing, for example, the cam drive from a train of gears to a simple chain). Its first roadgoing application was Maserati's first sedan, the aptly named Quattroporte (four-door) of 1963.

With a 3.5-inch shorter wheelbase, the QP chassis served as the foundation for a new close-coupled four-seat coupe, unveiled at the 1965 Turin show as the Mexico.

Much more complex than any previous Maserati design, its chassis retained the classic front-engine/rear-drive layout and still took much of its strength from large-diameter tubular members, but was further stiffened with several boxed and fabricated steel sections. In its first two years, the Quattroporte had used a De Dion rear suspension, then reverted to an orthodox live axle on semi-elliptic leaf springs. The latter was retained for the Mexico, along with Maserati's usual coil-and-wishbone front suspension, recirculating-ball power steering, and all-disc brakes.

The V-8 was large and beefy enough to accommodate displacements of 4.2 to 4.9 liters. In initial Mexico guise it was sized at 4.7 liters and delivered 290 horsepower, good for a top speed of over 155 mph. Together with a solid chassis and capable road manners, it made the Mexico one very fast and very desirable GT.

Alas, you wouldn't know it from the Vignale styling, which was obviously Italian but rather bland. Overall, the Mexico resembled a somewhat larger Sebring with most of the character removed.

Which explains why it was overshadowed for sheer beauty and sex appeal by other period supercars, including Maserati's own Ghibli (see entry)—which in turn perhaps explains why it didn't sell as well as Maserati hoped. Historians tell us that most Mexicos went to France and Switzerland. A few landed in Italy, fewer still in the U.S. Certainly none went to Mexico!

In fact, the Mexico virtually disappeared after its erstwhile replacement, the shapely Vignale-designed Indy, came along, but remained in the catalog all the way through 1973, though production was miniscule after 1968. A 4.1-liter option with ''only'' 260 bhp was instituted the following year, mainly to position the car downmarket from the Indy and Ghibli.

As with most ''facts'' concerning Italian specialty marques, it's wise to be cautious about production figures. Several respected sources claim the total was 250 units, while another lists 468. Is the latter more nearly correct?

SPECIFICATIONS

Engines: all dohc V-8; **1965-73:** 287.4 cid/4709 cc, 290 bhp (net) @ 5000 rpm, 290 lbs-ft @ 4000 rpm; **1969-73:** 252.4 cid/4136 cc, 260 bhp (net) @ 5000 rpm, 268 lbs-ft @ 4000 rpm

Transmissions:	5-speed manual or 3-speed automatic
Suspension, front:	upper and lower A-arms, coil springs, anti-roll bar
Suspension, rear:	live axle, radius arms, semi-elliptic leaf springs
Brakes:	front/rear discs
Wheelbase (in.):	103.9
Weight (lbs):	3520-3640
Top speed (mph):	150-158
0-60 mph (sec):	approx. 7.5 (4.7-liter)
Production:	250 (one source lists 468)

Mexico 2 + 2 rode a shortened version of the chassis developed for Maserati's 1963 Quattroporte sedan, was essentially its two-door counterpart. Vignale styling is neat if a tad bland for a Latin exotic.

1966-1973
MASERATI GHIBLI

Has there ever been a car more beautiful than the Maserati Ghibli? Even acknowledging the subjectiveness of the question, few peers come to mind. There's certainly no disputing its tremendous impact. By any standard, the Ghibli was the most memorable Maserati yet. More than two decades after its late-1966 debut, there are those who say it still is.

Like the Mistral and the later Khamsin, the Ghibli was named for a famous European wind (reflecting Maserati's penchant for such names at the time). And indeed, as road tests soon showed, it was a real stormer. But for many, it was enough to simply gaze upon the beast, conceived in 1965-66 by Giorgio Giugiaro, then chief designer at Ghia. No wonder the world motoring press sat up and took real notice of this remarkably gifted young Italian.

Turning to more mundane matters, the Ghibli shared basic chassis and running gear with the Quattroporte sedan and Mexico coupe (see entry), no surprise coming from a small automaker. Wheelbase, however, was reduced 3.5 inches from the Mexico's for this strict two-seater GT. The Ghibli thus had the same tubular chassis stiffened by pressings, foldings, and fabrications, and had to make do with a simple live rear axle on semi-elliptic leaf springs. Like the Mexico, it had disc brakes all-round. If none of this seemed very exciting next to obvious competitors like the Ferrari 275 GTB and Lamborghini 400 GT, nobody seemed to mind, and it didn't hurt performance or roadability one bit.

Fittingly for the prettiest Maserati to date, the Ghibli arrived with the 4.7-liter

version of the firm's excellent twincam V-8 in its most powerful form to date: 330 horsepower. A 5-speed ZF gearbox was standard; Borg-Warner 3-speed automatic became optional in 1969.

The styling, of course, turned every head. Long, low, and wide, the Ghibli crouched on the road like no previous Maserati—which was no illusion. Overall height was only 46 inches, so interior headroom was rather limited, though that didn't dissuade basketball ace Wilt "The Stilt" Chamberlain from Ghibli ownership. At 180 inches long overall, this was also one of the lengthiest European two-seaters ever built, but the long-hood/short-deck proportions were flawless.

The Ghibli's neat, low, hidden-headlamp nose with wide bifurcated grille would show up again on the Giugiaro-designed Bora and Merak mid-engine Maseratis of the Seventies. Some say the Aston Martin DBS of 1967 borrowed some Ghibli details (check the side-window shape and see if you agree), but surely no one except Giugiaro could have produced such an artful yet aggressive car, long on personality if short on practicality.

Some of this applies only to the original fastback coupe, which in 1969 was joined by a spider companion that, if anything, was even lovelier. It was a full convertible, of course, blessedly free of "targa bars" and other excrescences. Its fabric roof stowed completely out of sight beneath a hinged cover behind the cockpit; a detachable hardtop was optionally available for winter driving. At the same time, interiors were spruced up and the dashboard redesigned.

The Ghibli became even more desirable in 1970, when Maserati substituted its ultimate 4.9-liter V-8 with 335 bhp in European trim. This was mainly a concession to emissions controls for the American market, where output was somewhat lower. Spiders so equipped were tagged SS (which must have irked Chevrolet).

Alas, all good things must come to an end. The Ghibli's came in 1973 with the introduction of its direct successor, the Khamsin. Though more technically advanced, it wasn't nearly as inspiring to look at. Which means that the 1274 Ghiblis built still aren't enough to go around.

SPECIFICATIONS

Engines: all dohc V-8; **1966-70:** 287.4 cid/4709 cc, 330 bhp (net) @ 5500 rpm, 290 lbs-ft @ 4000 rpm; **1970-73:** 300.8 cid/ 4930 cc, 335 bhp (net) @ 5500 rpm, 354 lbs-ft @ 4000 rpm

Transmissions:	5-speed manual or 3-speed automatic
Suspension, front:	upper and lower A-arms, coil springs, anti-roll bar
Suspension, rear:	live axle, radius arms, semi-elliptic leaf springs
Brakes:	front/rear discs
Wheelbase (in.):	100.4
Weight (lbs):	3745
Top speed (mph):	154
0-60 mph (sec):	7.5-8.0

Production: **Coupe** 1149 **Spider** 125 (incl. approx. 25 4.9-liter SS)

The Ghiblis were beautiful in any form. Most were fastback coupes **(opposite)** *but a few spiders* **(below)** *were also built (shown with accessory hardtop). Brawny twincam V-8* **(opposite, lower left)** *provided genuine supercar performance despite high curb weight.*

1969-1974 MASERATI INDY

Maserati was positively booming by 1969, and ready to finish overhauling its entire lineup. Straight-six models were being phased out, while their V-8 replacements—the two-seat Ghibli and four-seat Mexico coupe and Quattroporte sedan—were looking after their respective markets. All that remained was a new 2+2. It appeared in '69 as the Indy.

Conceived in 1968, the Indy was first displayed as a Vignale prototype at that year's Turin show, though it was so obviously a production design that no one was surprised when it appeared in Maserati showrooms. It was billed as having unit construction, which meant that the Vignale-built body was now welded to the chassis instead of bolted on.

Carefully sized between the Quattroporte and Ghibli, the Indy rode a 102.4-inch wheelbase but strode wider tracks than either of its stablemates, signalling that Maserati, like most other carmakers, was moving toward wider, roomier bodies. Suspension, steering, and brakes were the usual fare, but the Indy used somewhat simpler chassis construction than other Masers. As announced, it carried the Mexico's smaller 4.1-liter 260-horsepower engine, mating to standard ZF 5-speed gearbox or optional 3-speed Borg-Warner automatic.

Despite a certain visual similarity with the Ghibli, the Indy had nothing in common with it and only a few shared elements, namely hidden headlamps, a high-tailed fastback roofline, and flowing lower-body contours. Aside from standing five inches taller, it differed in having token "+2" seating (assuming small and/or limber back seaters), more prominent B-posts, longer rear quarter windows, and a lift-up rear hatch for cargo-hold access.

It also neither looked as fast nor was as fast as the exceptional Ghibli. But it was a very worthy Maserati. And, of course, a more modern 2+2 than the Sebring and Mexico it effectively replaced.

Changes during the Indy's relatively brief, five-year life consisted mainly of upgraded V-8s that *were* borrowed from the Ghibli: the 290-bhp 4.7, offered beginning in 1970, and the 335-bhp 4.9 from 1973. Some might call this confusing the issue, but Maserati likely viewed it as offering its customers the widest possible choice.

A total of 1136 Indys were produced between 1969 and '74. At one point, the factory was turning out four Ghiblis and five Indys a week. Among the latter was a specially tailored U.S. version, predictably called Indy America.

Alas, time and circumstance precluded a direct Indy successor, at least from Maserati. Alejandro de Tomaso was in control by 1976, and he ushered in a re-engineered version of his Mercedes SL-lookalike Longchamps as Maserati's "new" Kyalami.

SPECIFICATIONS

Engines: all dohc V-8; **1969-70:** 252.4 cid/4136 cc, 260 bhp (net) @ 5500 rpm, 268 lbs-ft @ 4000 rpm; **1970-73:** 287.4 cid/ 4709 cc, 290 bhp (net) @ 5500 rpm, 289 lbs-ft @ 4000 rpm; **1973-74:** 300.8 cid/4930 cc, 335 bhp (net) @ 5500 rpm, 354 lbs-ft @ 4000 rpm

Transmissions:	5-speed manual or 3-speed automatic
Suspension, front:	upper and lower A-arms, coil springs, anti-roll bar
Suspension, rear:	live axle, radius arms, semi-elliptic leaf springs
Brakes:	front/rear discs
Wheelbase (in.):	102.4
Weight (lbs):	3465-3640
Top speed (mph):	136-156
0-60 mph (sec):	7.5
Production:	1136

Clean-lined Indy was Maserati's first V-8-powered 2+2, effectively replaced both the Sebring and Mexico. Its rear hatch was practical but heavy, and thus tended to close by itself rather easily. Vignale styling somewhat disguises the car's true size. Frontal appearance seemed to aim for a family resemblance with the two-seat Ghibli.

1971-1980 MASERATI BORA

Maserati was relatively slow to join the mid-engine brigade. But once the Dino 246, Lamborghini Miura, Lotus Europa, and Porsche 914 had shown that middies could be both practical and saleable, Maserati jumped on the bandwagon, literally with two feet.

As luck would have it, Maserati suddenly had more development money to play with than ever before, thanks to its late-Sixties takeover by Citroën, and a 1968 suggestion by Guy Malleret, the new French administrator, prompted thoughts of two variations on the same new mid-engine theme. The result, appearing at the 1971 Geneva show, was the handsome V-8-powered Bora, followed the next year by a closely related V-6 cousin called Merak (see entry).

Initial design work began in 1968, with Maserati's Giulio Alfieri taking charge of engineering. He not only had the aforementioned cars for inspiration but, soon, a new midships De Tomaso, the Pantera (see entry). The obvious choice for styling was Giorgio Giugiaro, who'd established a phenomenal reputation with Bertone and Ghia and had just set up his own consultancy, Ital Design. In fact, the Bora/Merak project was one of ID's first.

Both mid-engine Masers employed a welded, all-steel unit structure around a longitudinally sited midships drivetrain mounted on a subframe bolted to the hull. Giugiaro's coupe body featured flowing curves, a low snout bearing a stylized Maserati trident, hidden headlamps, and a beltline kicked up sharply at the back of the doors. Both models employed thick B-posts, fastback rear rooflines, and cropped tails, but the deck treatments differed. The Bora had triangular rear quarter windows and a sloping notched fastback roofline. Both models also had spacious cabins divided by a deep "services" tunnel, but the Bora had its own instrument panel and somewhat higher-grade furnishings. There was a small amount of luggage space under the front "hood," more under the rear hatch atop the engine cover.

Matching the Bora's aggressively muscular lines was the famous Maserati twincam V-8 in 4.7-liter form with a rated 310 horsepower. It drove the rear wheels through the 5-speed ZF transaxle as used in Ford's GT40 endurance racers. Suspension was classic coil-and-double-A-arm all-round, steering rack-and-pinion, brakes four-wheel disc. Signalling the new French ownership, the last were actuated by Citroën's unique high-pressure hydraulics, with a conventional brake pedal but the same "no-travel" action as Citroën's floor "button." The system also adjusted all pedals in and out, a real "dream car" feature. A tilt/telescope steering wheel and conventional fore/aft seat adjustment were also provided, so just about any driver short of Bigfoot could get comfortable.

The Bora went on sale almost immediately after its Geneva premiere. Safety and emissions rules excluded it from the U.S. until 1974. The following year, Maserati substituted its 4.9-liter V-8 to compensate for power losses on American models. Rated horsepower was a creditable 280. Beginning in 1976, the larger engine was standardized for Europe too, albeit with more horses.

Like Ferrari's Berlinetta Boxer, its contemporary competitor, the Bora was staggeringly fast but quite practical for an exotic high-performance Latin. Braking and roadholding were impressive, as was top speed: more than 160 mph even in strangled U.S. tune. And though surprisingly comfortable, the Bora felt, sounded, and acted like a thoroughly sorted roadgoing derivative of an all-out racing machine.

And so it was. The only problem was that Maserati ran into a pile of financial problems at mid-decade, when Citroën "divorced" its erstwhile Italian mate. Alejandro de Tomaso soon came to Maserati's rescue and kept the Bora alive too, but no improved versions were ever developed. Then again, the 1973-74 Energy Crisis had decimated the supercar market, making the Bora seem old before its time. The last one was built in 1980, nine years and 571 cars after launch.

Mid-V-8 Bora had performance to match its brutish looks. Unlike its V-6 Merak sister, rear roof was completely enclosed via rear side windows and glassed hatchback. Spare wheel and tire (above) lived in the tail behind the "north-south" engine.

SPECIFICATIONS

Engines: all dohc V-8; **1971-74:** 287.4 cid/4709 cc, 310 bhp (net) @ 6000 rpm, 325 lbs-ft @ 4200 rpm; **1975-80:** 300.8 cid/4930 cc, 320 bhp (net) @ 5500 rpm, 335 lbs-ft @ 4200 rpm (U.S. version: 280 bhp @ 5000 rpm, 275 lbs-ft @ 3500 rpm)

Transmission:	5-speed manual (in rear transaxle)
Suspension, front:	unequal-length A-arms, coil springs, anti-roll bar
Suspension, rear:	unequal-length A-arms, coil springs, anti-roll bar
Brakes:	front/rear discs
Wheelbase (in.):	102.2
Weight (lbs):	3350-3570
Top speed (mph):	160+
0-60 mph (sec):	6.5-7.2
Production:	571

1972-1983
MASERATI MERAK

When Maserati started working on its first mid-engine road car in 1968, it had two versions in mind. One was a V-8 model, which materialized as the Bora (see entry). The other would be a less expensive V-6 car with more components borrowed from new owner Citroën. The result arrived a year behind the big-engine middie as the Merak, which looked back to the great six-cylinder Maseratis of the Fifties and Sixties and ahead to the brave new Seventies world of mid-engine high performance.

The Merak shared the Bora's chassis, suspension, steering, high-pressure hydraulic brakes, basic styling, and forward structure ahead of the B-pillars. The principal differences showed up in and behind the cockpit, and were sufficient to give the Merak its own unique character.

Starting outside, the Bora's heavy rear hatch and triangular side windows were replaced by a flat engine cover flanked by glass-less, unstressed, purely decorative "flying buttresses," thus keeping a fastback profile. Beneath the deck, in longitudinal midships position, was the new 3.0-liter twincam V-6 Maserati had designed for Citroën's front-drive SM sport coupe (see entry), situated to turn the rear wheels through a modified version of the same 5-speed transaxle. The V-6 was shorter than the Bora's V-8, and combined with a fuel tank re-sited to the nose to liberate a little more cockpit space. This was given over to a pair of tiny "+2" seats lacking in the Bora, hard up against the rear bulkhead. They were frankly useless except for carrying luggage, as the cushions were almost on the floor and the backrests bolt-upright.

A more startling difference—and a reminder of the Citroën/Maserati "marriage"—

was the Merak instrument panel, lifted intact from the SM along with its steering wheel. This generated decidedly mixed reactions, and would be abandoned (after Citroën and Maserati "divorced") in favor of a four-spoke wheel and new Italianate dash with proper round (versus oval) instruments.

Unfortunately, sharing so much with the Bora left the Merak barely 150 pounds lighter. And with just 190 horsepower on tap, it was decidedly slower (and disappointing, even, to some critics). On the other hand, it was cheaper by some $5000, still quite a hunk of change in the early Seventies, and its performance wasn't all *that* bad: about 9.5 seconds 0-60 mph and 135 mph flat out.

In fact, many people were happy to settle for a Merak, which looked as good as a Bora, handled and stopped as well, and had the same sort of exoticar prestige. The burly Bora was okay for Europe, but the Merak made more sense and offered better value for speed-limited Americans.

The Merak saw little change through the end of 1975, then gave way to the much-modified Merak SS. This was prompted by the aforementioned "divorce" and Maserati's subsequent takeover by De Tomaso, which quickly set about ridding itself of inherited Citroën engineering influences. Thus, the Bora's ZF transaxle and conventional brakes were substituted along with the new dash, and the body contract shifted from Padane to Osi. Workmanship didn't improve much, but handling did, thanks to wider wheels and tires; a modest chin spoiler was added for better high-speed stability. Performance improved too, in Europe, with a V-6 tuned to 220 bhp. Alas, U.S. models remained at about 180 bhp (SAE net). Shortly afterwards, De Tomaso issued a detrimmed 2.0-liter "tax break" special for Italian buyers only.

Though the Bora disappeared in 1980, the Merak carried on through 1983. Still, it was not a big success volume-wise. Maserati's sporadic presence in the U.S. market after 1975, where the car could have sold much better than it did, hardly helped. The 2.0-liter (dropped in '79) saw only 133 copies, while 3.0-liter production totalled just 1699. Thus ended another one of those good automotive ideas robbed of a fair chance by a combination of unforeseen circumstances and unfortunate timing.

SPECIFICATIONS

Engines: all dohc V-6; **1972-83:** 181 cid/2965 cc, 190/220 bhp (net) @ 6000/6500 rpm, 188/199 lbs-ft @ 4000/4500 rpm; U.S. version: 182/180 bhp (SAE net) @ 6000 rpm, 185 lbs-ft @ 3000 rpm; **1976-79:** 122 cid/1999 cc, 170 bhp @ 7000 rpm, 131 lbs-ft @ 5700 rpm (Italian market only)

Transmission:	5-speed manual (in rear transaxle)
Suspension, front:	unequal-length A-arms, coil springs, anti-roll bar
Suspension, rear:	unequal-length A-arms, coil springs, anti-roll bar
Brakes:	front/rear discs
Wheelbase (in.):	102.2
Weight (lbs):	3200
Top speed (mph):	135 (190 bhp)
0-60 mph (sec):	8.2-9.5
Production:	**3.0-liter** 1699 (incl. SS models) **2.0-liter** 133

Giugiaro-styled V-6 Merak looked much like the V-8 Bora but had a flat deck and "flying buttresses." Between-lamps air intake marks this as a Merak SS.

1974-1982
MASERATI KHAMSIN

Maserati's traditional front-engine GT needed freshening again by the early Seventies. The result was a new model effectively replacing both the Indy and, in fact if not spirit, the Ghibli. Named Khamsin, after the hot violent wind of the Egyptian desert, it bowed at the 1972 Turin show and again at Paris '73, but didn't go on sale until 1974.

The Khamsin was as much a departure for Maserati as the mid-engine Bora and Merak. First, it was a cross between the two-seat Ghibli and 2+2 Indy, a sort of "2+1" if you will. Second, it was the first Maserati shaped by Bertone, with Marcello Gandini of Lamborghini fame doing the honors. Last but not least, it was the first front-engine Maser to bear the unique engineering stamp of Citroën, which then controlled the Italian concern.

Visually, it owed more to Ghibli than Indy, with the same sort of squashed fastback roof and lengthy hood, though the sharply pointed nose and crisp contouring were quite unique. As he had on Lamborghini's Espada, Gandini penciled in a glass panel between the taillamps, and it was just as useful in this low-rider.

Following Indy precedent, the Khamsin employed a unitized steel structure (supplied by Bertone). Some chassis engineering also carried forward, but there were major differences too. Rear suspension was now fully independent (a first for a front-engine Maser), with coil-and-double-wishbone geometry (as on the midships Bora/Merak) matching that at the front. Rack-and-pinion steering was another departure, as was the use of Citroën high-pressure hydraulics to power both steering and the all-disc brakes.

Under the hood and mounted somewhat back in the chassis was the latest version of the familiar twincam V-8. Unlike previous Masers, though, all Khamsins carried the same 4.9-liter unit with a genuine 320 horsepower for Europe, 315 bhp in emissions-legal U.S. trim. Transmission choices still comprised the ubiquitous 5-speed manual (preferred by more sporting buyers) or optional Borg-Warner 3-speed automatic.

The Khamsin was apparently just as slippery as previous Maseratis, for top speed ranged from 140 to 160 mph depending on transmission and engine tune. But less than flat out, it was a curious combination of the traditional and futuristic. The latter was exemplified by the hydraulically powered steering and brakes, both of which took a lot of practice for smooth driving. As on Citroën's SM, the steering would self-center even with the car at rest, was fingertip light, and lightning quick at a mere 2.0 turns lock-to-lock. The brakes were just as touchy, easy to lock up with a shade too much pedal pressure. Handling, by contrast, was easy to get used to, and very balanced thanks to the near even fore/aft weight distribution.

Inside, the driving stance was pure Italian supercar, but ergonomics were far from state-of-the-art and the basic climate system was just that. The ride was harsh, rear-seat accommodations the usual token gesture.

With all this, the Khamsin was not a successful effort even by Maserati standards. Had it not appeared on the eve of the first Energy Crisis, which precipitated Citroën's sudden pullout and several tough years for Maserati, it might have sold better. As it was, only 421 were called for over eight years of production. The peak year was the first, 1974, when a grand 96 were built.

SPECIFICATIONS

Engines: dohc V-8, 300.8 cid/4930 cc, 320 bhp (net) @ 5500 rpm, 354 lbs-ft @ 4000 rpm; U.S. version: 280-315 bhp (SAE net) @ 5000 rpm, 308 lbs-ft @ 3500 rpm

Transmissions:	5-speed manual or 3-speed automatic
Suspension, front:	unequal-length A-arms, coil springs, anti-roll bar
Suspension, rear:	unequal-length A-arms, coil springs, anti-roll bar
Brakes:	front/rear discs
Wheelbase (in.):	100.3
Weight (lbs):	3620-3750
Top speed (mph):	140-160
0-60 mph (sec):	8.1
Production:	421

*The distinctively styled Khamsin was the first Bertone-bodied Maserati. Today it's considered by some as one of the better values among Seventies supercars and a definite "comer" among collectible automobiles. Twincam V-8 **(above)** powered Citroën hydraulic steering and brakes.*

1977-1983
MASERATI KYALAMI

It was the first—and so far only—"badge-engineered" supercar, but the Kyalami had a genuine Maserati heart. To understand why, you have to go back to the early Seventies and the De Tomaso Longchamp.

Alejandro de Tomaso had produced the mid-engine Pantera (see entry) with Ford's help and encouragement. The next of his Dearborn-powered cars appeared at the end of 1970. This was the Deauville, a shapely four-door sedan with front-mounted Ford V-8 and Ghia styling much like that of the Jaguar XJ6, which it also aped in size. The Longchamp arrived two years later on a shortened version of this platform, with trim notchback coupe styling by Frua emulating the lines of Mercedes' SL.

In 1975, De Tomaso took over Maserati after Citroën had decided to solve one of its many financial problems of the time by abandoning its erstwhile Italian partner. In an effort to boost Maserati sales while saving time and money, Alejandro decided to spin off his two "copycat" cars into restyled variants with Maserati power. The respective results were a "new" Quattroporte and the Kyalami, named for South Africa's famous Grand Prix circuit.

Predictably, the Kyalami shared the Longchamp's simple, all-steel unit body/chassis structure and square-rigged Frua styling, but got a reworked front with quad headlamps and a typical Maserati grille, plus minor rear-end changes. The Longchamp's all-independent suspension, which naturally differed from previous Maserati setups, was also retained, but the Italian twincam V-8 was installed instead of the physically similar 351 Ford. De Tomaso was already using the ZF 5-speed gearbox Maserati specified for the Khamsin, so this was retained, but not its optional Borg-Warner automatic, which gave way to Chrysler TorqueFlite (replacing the Longchamp's Ford transmission). The upshot of all this was that De Tomaso had two very similar 2+2s that effectively competed with each other.

In an apparent effort to distance the new hybrid from the 4.9-liter Khamsin, the first 100 Kyalamis carried the 4136-cc V-8, with a rated 255 SAE net horsepower giving a top speed of "only" 147 mph. The big engine became optional in 1978, this time with 280 bhp (SAE net), and both sizes continued for the rest of the car's career.

Despite De Tomaso's intentions, Maserati customers never took to the Kyalami. The thoroughbred Maserati engine was a big plus over the Longchamp's American iron in both performance and prestige, but most buyers understandably viewed the car itself as a half-breed. Production wound down in early 1983 after only 150 units, and the Kyalami quietly faded away in favor of the first "mass-market" Maserati, the very different Biturbo sports sedan.

SPECIFICATIONS

Engines: all dohc V-8; **1977-83:** 252.4 cid/4136 cc, 255 bhp (SAE net) @ 6000 rpm, 289 lbs-ft @ 4000 rpm; **1978-83:** 300.8 cid/4930 cc, 280 bhp (SAE net) @ 5600 rpm, 289 lbs-ft @ 3000 rpm

Transmissions:	ZF 5-speed manual or Chrysler 3-speed TorqueFlite automatic
Suspension, front:	upper and lower A-arms, coil springs, anti-roll bar
Suspension, rear:	half-shafts as upper links, lower lateral links, radius arms, coil springs
Brakes:	front/rear discs
Wheelbase (in.):	104.0
Weight (lbs):	3835
Top speed (mph):	147 (4.1-liter)
0-60 mph (sec):	7.6 (4.1-liter)
Production:	150

Kyalami became the first "badge-engineered" Maserati when Alejandro de Tomaso modified his Mercedes SL-like Longchamps coupe with a trident grille and Maserati twincam V-8. This beauty displays the slightly reworked nose and restyled wheels used on late examples.

1978-1985
MAZDA RX-7

There are three significant things about the original RX-7. First, it almost singlehandedly kept the Wankel rotary engine alive. Second, to the delight of enthusiasts everywhere, it marked the return of the "affordable" sports car for the first time since the late, lamented Datsun 240Z (see entry). Last but not least, it was simply terrific.

Having made the rotary reliable, the main failing of Dr. Felix Wankel and his cohorts at NSU, Mazda nearly went under by selling this efficient, compact engine in otherwise bog-ordinary sedans. Though more powerful than piston engines of the same nominal displacement, the rotary wasn't—and still isn't—as thrifty. But in the panic of the first Energy Crisis, this distinction was lost on consumers, especially in America, who saw the rotary-powered RX-2 and RX-3 as "economy" cars, judged them too fuelish, and quit buying. By 1975, Mazda was on its knees, retreating from rotaries, and relying again on piston-engine cars like the simple little GLC.

But Kenichi Yamamoto, the rotary's patron saint at Mazda (and now company president), kept the faith. If confusing in sedans, why not try the rotary in a sports car? There was even a precedent. Eight years after the Wankel surfaced in Germany, Mazda began building the Cosmo 110S sports coupe (previewed at the '64 Tokyo show), which garnered much press, if not many sales, between 1967 and '72. Market research provided further impetus by showing strong demand, especially in the U.S., for a reasonably priced rotary sports car.

All this came together in Project X605, initiated in 1974 and completed by late '76. The resulting RX-7 went on sale in Japan during 1978 (as the Savanna), but didn't reach U.S. shores until very late in the '78 model year.

Engine apart, it was conventional but thoroughly modern. A small, unitized hatchback coupe, the RX-7 rode an all-coil suspension with front MacPherson struts and a live rear axle located by trailing arms and Watt linkage. Steering was recirculating-ball, brakes front discs and rear drums. Styling was orthodox too, mixing elements of several contemporary cars without looking like any one of them (except maybe around the nose, strongly evocative of Porsche's 924). The 95.3-inch wheelbase limited seating to two Americans, though laughably small "+2" rear seats were offered in Japan and Europe.

Mazda's twin-rotor 12A engine, derived from the earlier RX-3 unit, was small enough to sit behind the front-wheel centerline, making this a "front/mid-engine" car with fine fore/aft weight balance (initially 53/47 percent). As ever, the rotary packed a lot of power for its size: 100 bhp in U.S. form from just 1146-cc nominal displacement.

The RX-7 was, as they say, greeted with enthusiasm. Zesty, nimble, and solidly built, it was long on fun yet quite practical for a sports car and, as events soon proved, boringly reliable—*especially* the engine, thus easing many consumers' fears. And at an initial U.S. POE price of just $6995, it was sensational value.

With all this, one U.S. magazine accurately termed the RX-7 "an enthusiast's dream come true." It wasn't perfect, of course. The ride was a bit stiff, the cabin cramped for larger folks (especially in headroom), and cornering could be a tail-happy exercise on bumpy surfaces or in the wet. But these were hardly major flaws, and the RX-7 sold like the proverbial hotcakes from day one.

As it continued to do for the next six years despite an often difficult market. Most annual changes were of the refinement variety. Transistorized ignition and a larger brake booster improved the '79s, while 1981 brought a revised dash, tidier nose and tail, more efficient emission controls, and larger fuel tank. That same year, the existing S and GS models were joined by a new top-liner, the GSL, with standard rear disc brakes, limited-slip differential, alloy wheels, and power windows. Responding to demands for more power, Mazda brought over its larger 13B engine for a new 1984 entry, the GSL-SE, packing 135 bhp. At the same time, rear control arms were relocated on all RX-7s and the power steering given engine-speed-variable assist.

Unfortunately, American inflation and an appreciating yen had pushed RX-7 prices as high as $15,295 by then. The only consolation was that most rivals cost a lot more.

Meantime, RX-7s went racing around the world in a big way. In America they dominated the GTU class in IMSA endurance events, then started challenging Corvettes and Porsches in GTO. RX-7s also did well in rallying, ran with distinction in SCCA, and even set a few speed records at Bonneville.

But time and changing tastes wait for no car, and the RX-7's huge success inevitably prompted competitors. So although sales remained healthy all along, Mazda knew the RX-7 would have to be changed as early as 1981. It wouldn't be easy, but staying in front never is.

SPECIFICATIONS

Engines: all 2-rotor Wankel; 70 cid/1146 cc, 100 bhp @ 6000 rpm, 105 lbs-ft @ 4000 rpm; **GSL-SE** (1984-85): 80 cid/ 1308 cc, 135 bhp @ 6000 rpm, 133 lbs-ft @ 2750 rpm

Transmissions:	5-speed overdrive manual, 3-speed automatic, 4-speed overdrive automatic
Suspension, front:	MacPherson struts, lower lateral links, compliance struts, coil springs, anti-roll bar
Suspension, rear:	live axle on lower trailing links, upper angled links, Watt linkage, coil springs, anti-roll bar
Brakes:	front discs/rear drums (rear discs on GSL and GSL-SE models)
Wheelbase (in.):	95.3
Weight (lbs):	2440-2640
Top speed (mph):	115-125+
0-60 mph (sec):	8.5-9.7

Production: 1978 72,692 **1979** 71,617 **1980** 56,317 **1981** 59,686 **1982** 59,686 **1983** 57,864 **1984** 63,959 **1985** 63,105

Larger 1.3-liter rotary featured in the RX-7 GSL-SE, introduced to America during 1984. Here, the editors' 1985 test car. New-design alloy wheels carried low-profile Pirelli P6 tires acting on a firmer suspension.

1986-1988
MAZDA RX-7

In greeting the second-generation RX-7, some journalists felt compelled to state that the original would be tough to follow. Unsaid was the equally obvious fact that the '86 couldn't hope to have its predecessor's impact, for the market had changed a lot since 1978—more crowded and competitive than ever. Yet with a little perspective, the second-generation emerges as not only a more mature RX-7 but an eminently desirable one in its own right.

It was born in 1981 as Project P747 (a purely arbitrary number chosen to confuse outsiders). Rotary power, front/mid-engine layout, rear drive, unit construction, and close-coupled hatchback coupe format were never in doubt, but American feedback on the original RX-7, gleaned from several U.S. trips by chief engineer Akio Uchiyama, gave Mazda a whole new perspective on "RX-7ism."

Three possibilities were hatched for P747: a continuation of the existing model, an all-new "high-tech" car with electronic suspension and rear transaxle, and something in between. The last ultimately won out, but the influence of Porsche's 944, which arrived in the program's second year, would be undeniable. Exterior and interior design, features, packaging, and other essentials were determined through a long series of consumer meetings, with counsel from Mazda's California-based U.S. design center.

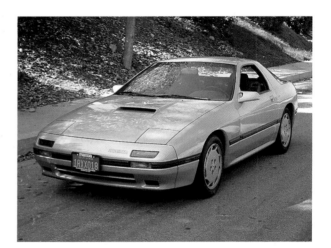

The Porsche's styling had "tested" well, so the new RX-7 looked much like the 944 in front. But the central body bore Porsche 928 overtones, while the compound-curve hatch and bold taillights looked like Chevrolet Camaro copies. A disappointed press termed it all "timid" and "derivative," but at least the new shape was slipperier. The claimed drag coefficient was 0.31, and the optional Sports Package with front air dam, rocker skirts, and loop-type spoiler cut that to a commendable 0.29.

More exciting things hid beneath. Base power was now the six-port 13B rotary with electronic fuel injection, first seen in the U.S. on the '84 GSL-SE but with 11 more horsepower and 6 percent more torque. And there was a production first: an intercooled "Turbo II" version packing an extra 38 horsepower in U.S. trim, a remarkable 182 bhp total. (The blown Wankel was only new to America, however, as Mazda had offered a first-generation "Turbo I" model in Japan.) The extra muscle was welcome. The base '86 weighed about 240 pounds more than the comparable

'85, and the Turbo was some 225 pounds heavier still. Dimensions stayed roughly the same though. The Turbo wasn't available with automatic, but non-turbos were: a new 4-speed overdrive unit, replacing the previous non-OD 3-speeder.

The chassis offered more Good Stuff. Rack-and-pinion steering ousted recirculating ball, and its available power assist was a new electronic system that varied effort with vehicle speed and road surface changes. Front suspension was a simpler MacPherson strut/A-arm setup. Out back, the old live axle was discarded for a new independent Dynamic Tracking Suspension System (DTSS). A rather complex semi-trailing-arm arrangement, it induced a small amount of stabilizing rear-wheel toe-in under high lateral loads and minimized camber changes in cornering, long a problem with this geometry. An intended electronic ride control materialized as Auto Adjusting Suspension (AAS), two-stage manual/automatic shock damping. Finally, all models got low-pressure gas-filled shocks and disc rear brakes instead of drums, vented on the Turbo.

U.S. model choices expanded with the addition of the 2+2 package previously restricted to Europe and Japan. It and the familiar two-seater were offered in normally aspirated base form or as plusher GXLs with standard AAS, power steering, and a host of creature comforts. The Sports Package, which also included power steering and firmer suspension, was limited to the base two-seater, but a Luxury Package with power sunroof and mirrors, premium sound system, and alloy wheels was optional for both it and the 2+2. The Turbo was a two-seater only.

Styling aside, the new RX-7s earned rave reviews. The ride was still a bit firm perhaps and the cockpit too tight for tall types, but the normally aspirated cars were usefully faster and the Turbo was a real flyer, more than a match for the 16-valve 944S in the inevitable comparison tests. One magazine said the new DTSS "occasionally out-tricks itself on the race track," but most critics agreed the new RX-7 was grippier, more nimble, and more forgiving than the old. One said it "raises the standards for sports-car performance."

The second-generation story is far from finished at this writing, and it keeps getting better. The main 1987 development was a new extra-cost anti-lock braking system for the Turbo, GXLs, and Sports Package. Also, a two-seat SE arrived during the year with mid-level trim, extra equipment, and special pricing to combat "sticker shock" caused by worsening yen/dollar exchange rates. The plot thickens for 1988 with the first factory-built RX-7 convertible—and rumors that Mazda may build RX-7s exclusively in the U.S., since that's where most are sold anyway and sports-car demand is now nearly nil in Japan.

Whatever happens, the second-generation story is already a happy one. The original RX-7 may have been tough to follow, but in this case, success has bred success.

SPECIFICATIONS

Engines: all 2-rotor Wankel, 80 cid/1308 cc; 146 bhp @ 6500 rpm, 138 lbs-ft @ 3500 rpm; **Turbo:** 182 bhp @ 6500 rpm, 183 lbs-ft @ 3500 rpm

Transmissions:	5-speed overdrive manual or 4-speed overdrive automatic
Suspension, front:	MacPherson struts, A-arms, coil springs, anti-roll bar
Suspension, rear:	trailing arms with camber-control arms on drop links, semi-trailing links, "Triaxial Floating Hubs," coil springs, anti-roll bar
Brakes:	front/rear discs (rear drums base models)
Wheelbase (in.):	95.7
Weight (lbs):	2625-3030
Top speed (mph):	125-135 +
0-60 mph (sec):	8.5-9.7
Production:	1986 72,760 **1987-88** NA

Opposite top: Turbocharged RX-7s were sold in Japan and elsewhere before 1986, but not in America. Shown is that year's second-generation "Turbo II" coupe. **Below and opposite bottom:** *New-for-'88 convertible is offered in the U.S. only as a 5-speed non-turbo model. It's built on a regular Mazda assembly line.*

1954-1963
MERCEDES-BENZ 190SL

Daimler-Benz was moribund by the time Allied bombers finished with Stuttgart in 1945. Immediate survival hinged on clearing the rubble and rebuilding factories while getting back into production with prewar cars and trucks. There was no time for anything else.

But D-B had bounced back strongly by the mid-Fifties, with new facilities, new postwar products, and a bright future. It had even found the wherewithal to resume racing, in 1952. Two years later, as if to signal the world that all was truly well, D-B announced its first postwar sports cars, the high-performance 300SL (see entry) and a two-seat *boulevardier*, the 190SL. The latter didn't reach production until January 1955.

Like most sports cars of the day, the 190SL was bred from an existing sedan. Here it was the W120-series 180, introduced in 1953 and known as the "Pontoon" (because of the visual and structural character of its steel body/chassis structure). The 190SL, internally coded W121, used an abbreviated version of this platform, to which was welded a neat roadster bodyshell. The 180's all-independent coil-spring suspension was retained, including the infamous high-pivot swing axles that allowed the rear wheels to assume extraordinary camber angles in hard cornering.

Power was supplied by a new 1.9-liter overhead-cam four that was somewhat related to D-B's existing 3.0-liter six. (It would appear in 180 sedans starting in 1957.) In initial form, with twin Solex carburetors and 8.5:1 compression, it produced a creditable 105 DIN horsepower (120 SAE), but a hefty 2500-pound curb weight kept top speed to 105-110 mph. Prototypes were shown with column shift, but production models appropriately carried sportier floor levers.

Like its big brother, the 190SL had rounded overall lines, a low nose, wide "mouth" grille bearing a big Mercedes tristar, and wheelarch "eyebrows" to add interest along the sides. The styling similarity was deliberate, but backfired in unfair performance comparisons with the exotic 300SL. An optional lift-off steel hardtop was added shortly after production began, followed somewhat later by a fixed-top coupe with a similar roofline. Luggage space was unusually generous for a two-seater, with a behind-the-seats hollow in the cockpit supplementing a good-size trunk. The instrument panel also followed 300SL design.

Judged as the sports tourer it was designed to be, rather than an all-out sports machine, the 190SL delivered at least as much as it promised. Had it not looked so much like the big Mercedes sports car, perhaps it wouldn't have been so overshadowed. It was certainly an appealing package: responsive, civilized, adequately fast, well built, and comfortable despite a suspension stiffened considerably to keep those swing axles in line. Then too, it also cost a lot less than a 300SL: $4000-$5000 in 1958 versus nearly $10,000.

The 190SL saw surprisingly few changes in its eight years. The drivetrain was untouched save higher (8.8:1) compression in 1959, while the main visual update was a larger rear window for the coupe and lift-off hardtop, adopted the same year. At 3000-4000 units, annual production was good, all things considered. More important, the 190SL made money, unlike the 300.

By 1963, D-B was ready to change direction with a new two-seater, the "pagoda-roof" W113 SL, which would replace both the 190 and 300. Ironically, it was more like the former than the latter, suggesting that, in commercial terms, the 190 was the better concept.

As indeed it still is. A high proportion of the nearly 26,000 built survive to this day, bringing their owners a lot of practical pleasure—and you can't say that about every sports car.

The four-cylinder 190SL was deliberately styled to resemble the big 300SL, and was thus often unfairly compared with it. But the junior SL succeeded quite well as the sporty tourer Mercedes intended, offering open-air fun, a relatively luxurious cockpit (above) and a decent performance/economy compromise. Longish deck afforded excellent trunk space for a two-seater.

SPECIFICATIONS

Engine: sohc I-4, 115.8 cid/1897 cc, 105 bhp (DIN) @ 5700 rpm, 105 lbs-ft @ 3200 rpm

Transmission:	4-speed manual
Suspension, front:	upper and lower A-arms, coil springs, anti-roll bar
Suspension, rear:	single-joint swing axles as upper lateral arms, radius arms, coil springs
Brakes:	front/rear drums
Wheelbase (in.):	94.5
Weight (lbs):	2550 (roadster), 2600 (coupe)
Top speed (mph):	105 +
0-60 mph (sec):	13.3-14.5
Production:	25,881

1954-1963 MERCEDES-BENZ 300SL

Like the later Jaguar E-Type, the Mercedes-Benz 300SL was conceived as sports-racer, not a road car. Unlike the Jaguar, it proved its mettle on the track before the production model appeared. In subsequent years, 300SLs would also notch up an impressive number of rally successes.

It all began with a small number of racing SL prototypes built in 1952, which won that year's Le Mans 24 Hours and the marathon *Carrera Panamericana*, among other contests. As Stuttgart's first postwar competition cars, they combined suspension and running gear from the then-new 300-series production models with a light, multi-tube space-frame chassis wearing special coupe and spyder bodywork. Full-height side-opening doors would have compromised rigidity in the high-sided chassis, so half-height doors, hinged at the roof center to lift upward, were developed for the coupes, the now-famous "gullwing" design.

American import-car impresario Max Hoffman knew a good thing when he saw it, and suggested that Daimler-Benz offer a roadgoing Gullwing, putting his money where his mouth was by ordering 1000 of them. That was enough for D-B, and the production SL duly debuted at the New York Auto Show in February 1954.

As most enthusiasts know, the Gullwing was replaced in 1957 by the 300SL Roadster, with a modified space-frame permitting conventional doors. Respective production would be 1400 and 1858 units. The peak year was 1955, with 867 units; after 1958, annual volume was only 200-250 units. Of course, demand for costly cars is usually limited, and the SLs cost a bunch: $7300 for the Gullwing in 1956 ($500 more than a Cadillac limo), $11,400 for the 1960 Roadster.

But excellence is never cheap, and the SLs were magnificent: solid, handsome, very fast. In fact, nothing could outpace them except for the occasional Ferrari, which was hardly a "production" car in those days. The SLs' one dynamic problem was Mercedes' favored swing-axle rear suspension. On the Gullwing, this was the original "high-pivot" type that could snap the car into vicious oversteer in hard cornering, especially on wet roads. The Roadster received the new "low-pivot" arrangement designed for the W196 Grand Prix car, with a transverse compensating spring that increased roll stiffness, thereby reducing camber changes so as to keep the rear wheels more firmly planted on the pavement.

Aside from a claustrophobic cockpit, the Gullwing had two other drawbacks, both related to its doors: water-sealing problems and awkward entry/exit. The latter stemmed partly from the high, wide sills and partly from the huge arc the doors scribed, which meant they were impossible to open fully if the car were parked close to, say, a wall. All these factors prompted development of the Roadster, which came with a folding soft top and could be ordered with a lift-off steel top much like that of the 190SL (see entry). Both Gullwing and Roadster bodies used aluminum for doors, hood, and trunklid; the rest was steel. However, all-aluminum competition bodies were available to special order.

The 300SL engine was basically the 3.0-liter 300-series sohc inline six, with dry-sump lubrication and Bosch mechanical fuel injection, the latter a world first for a production car. It was also one of the most potent engines of its day, providing top speeds of 130 to 165 mph (the latter claimed but rarely confirmed) depending on gearing. Transmission, final drive, and suspension were all lifted more or less intact from the 300-series. An interesting Gullwing feature was a steering wheel hinged at the base of its hub to tilt almost upside down, thus easing driver entry/exit.

SL styling hardly needs comment, except to note that it was much lower and sleeker than that of contemporary Mercedes sedans, especially the somewhat baroque 300-series. Distinguishing features such as the big tristar grille emblem, wheelarch "eyebrows," and eggcrate front-fender louvers are well-known. Less obvious, perhaps, is the Roadster's more rounded windshield. Both coupe and convertible were two-seaters, of course, with ample stowage space behind, wind-up windows, and typical no-nonsense Mercedes dashboards dominated by a high-set speedometer and tachometer and plenty of chrome.

In retrospect, the 300SLs were a mixed blessing for Mercedes. On the one hand, they were tremendous symbols of D-B's engineering prowess and terrific image-leaders for the rest of the passenger-car line. On the other hand, they weren't very profitable, and there was the tragedy of Pierre Levegh's 300SLR flying into the grandstand at Le Mans '55, which hastened D-B's retirement from motorsports.

But none of this dims the luster of the 300SLs, long since enshrined in the automotive hall of fame for their performance, heritage, and sheer presence. They will always be counted among the greats.

SPECIFICATIONS

Engines: all sohc I-6, 182.8 cid/2996 cc; **1954-57:** 240 bhp (SAE gross) @ 6100 rpm, 210 lbs-ft @ 5000 rpm; **1957-63:** 250 bhp (SAE gross) @ 6200 rpm, 228 lbs-ft @ 5000 rpm

Transmission:	4-speed manual
Suspension, front:	upper and lower A-arms, coil springs, anti-roll bar
Suspension, rear:	swing axles (high-pivot on Gullwing, low-pivot with camber compensator on Roadster), radius arms, coil springs
Brakes:	front/rear drums
Wheelbase (in.):	94.5
Weight (lbs):	2750 (coupe) 3000 (Roadster)
Top speed (mph):	120-130
0-60 mph (sec):	7.6-8.8

Production: Coupe (1954-57) 1400 **Roadster** (1957-63) 1858

*Top, and opposite top: The original 300SL Gullwing coupe was a racer-turned-road car. Complex high-sided space-frame dictated the high-flying doors, which were less than practical for entry/entry and tight parking places. **Above and opposite bottom:** Conventional doors and open-air appeal made the replacement Roadster somewhat more numerous. Note its slightly more wrapped windshield.*

1963-1971 MERCEDES-BENZ 230SL/ 250SL/280SL

Contrary to oft-repeated statements, the W113 Mercedes-Benz SL, introduced at the Geneva show in March 1963, was not a direct replacement for the 190 or 300SLs (see entries). Instead, it was a ground-up project, an up-to-date sports tourer with 190 size and performance but somewhat more luxury.

Like the 190, this new SL borrowed its chassis and running gear from a volume sedan—here, the finny W111/112 series that began appearing in 1959. Power was supplied by the overhead-cam six of the contemporary 220SE, with a 2-mm bore increase lifting displacement to 2306 cc and new multiport Bosch fuel injection (replacing the previous single-point manifold system) boosting output by no less than 30 DIN horsepower. Retained from the 190 were monocoque body/chassis construction and coil-and-wishbone front suspension; new was a "low pivot" swing-axle rear suspension with transverse camber-compensating spring. Brakes were Girling front discs and Al-Fin rear drums with vacuum assist.

Dimensionally, the 230SL compared almost inch for inch with the 190, with a similar wheelbase and only 1.5 extra inches in overall length. Curb weight was the exception: 2850-3200 pounds depending on equipment (versus 2500-2600 pounds), though the W113 structure would prove to be one of the sturdiest then in production.

Speaking of equipment, it now included the first automatic transmission ever offered on a sporting Mercedes, the new 4-speed Daimler-Benz unit with a simple fluid coupling instead of a torque converter. Fully synchronized 4-speed manual remained standard. Final-drive gearing was initially 3.75:1, but 3.69 and 3.92 gearsets were also offered from September 1965.

The typical 230SL could run the standing quarter-mile in 17-18 seconds and reach 100 mph from rest in 27 seconds—not Corvette-ferocious but more than adequate. As proof, a 230 won the prestigious Spa-Sofia-Liege rally in its introductory year, the first of several rally wins for these SLs. In all, they were rugged cars that could certainly take the rough with the smooth.

Styling was completely fresh—conservative, angular, and obviously related to that of contemporary D-B sedans—though the SL grille and big tristar emblem were carried over from earlier models. An interesting new element was the optional hardtop's "pagoda" roofline, curved upward slightly at the sides to increase rigidity

SPECIFICATIONS

Engines: all sohc I-6; **230SL** (1962-66): 140.8 cid/2308 cc, 170 bhp (SAE gross) @ 5500 rpm, 159 lbs-ft @ 4500 rpm; **250SL** (1966-67): 152.3 cid/2496 cc, 170 bhp (SAE gross) @ 5600 rpm, 174 lbs-ft @ 4500 rpm; **280SL** (1967-71): 169.5 cid/ 2778 cc, 180 bhp (SAE gross) @ 5700 rpm, 193 lbs-ft @ 4250 rpm

Transmissions:	4-speed manual (5-speed from 1969) or optional 4-speed automatic
Suspension, front:	unequal-length A-arms, coil springs, anti-roll bar
Suspension, rear:	single low-pivot swing axles, trailing arms, coil springs
Brakes:	front discs/rear drums (230SL), front/rear discs (250/280SL)
Wheelbase (in.):	94.5
Weight (lbs):	2850-3170
Top speed (mph):	114-120
0-60 mph (sec):	9.9-10.7

Production: 230SL (1963-66) 19,831 **250SL** (1966-67) 5196 **280SL** (1967-71) 23,885

Trunklid badging and minor details are the only visual distinctions among the three variations of the "pagoda-roof" W113-series SL. Like the 190SL, these were sporty tourers rather than out-and-out sports cars, and popular because of it. Note concave windshield header (below).

and glass area. The leather-swathed cockpit offered a pair of large, comfy reclining seats and D-B's then-usual dash motif, with big, round speedometer and tachometer flanking a bank of vertically reading minor gauges. New features included windows-up fresh-air ventilation and one of the industry's first multi-purpose control stalks for lights and wipers. The standard soft top folded away beneath a hinged cover, and the square-cut styling made for considerably more trunk space than on previous SLs.

All this signalled the W113's primary mission as a luxury sports tourer, not all-out sports car. Yet its road manners garnered considerable praise. Bernard Cahier found the 230 "free of handling vices . . . almost neutral with very slight understeer" in sharp corners. Said Hansjorg Bendel: "Body roll is quite pronounced, but the driver never feels it; the steering remains light, accurate and smooth near the limit . . . . This is one of those cars that [impresses as] having [a] center of gravity below road level." Cahier concluded that this SL was "one of D-B's very finest cars."

And so it would remain through a relatively long eight-year production life. There would be only two major changes: a pair of larger engines to counter the extra weight and reduced performance of mandated American safety and emissions equipment.

The first arrived in late 1966 with a revised 250SL. Changes included a 6-mm stroke increase, bringing displacement to 2496 cc, plus a switch from four to seven main bearings and adoption of rear disc brakes, improved seatbelts, and a collapsible steering wheel. Horsepower stayed the same, but torque rose by a useful 15 lbs-ft. Final drive was now 3.69:1 exclusively.

After just 12 months and some 5200 units, the 250 bowed to the 280SL, powered by a new bored-out M130 engine with 2778 cc and 180 bhp (SAE gross) in U.S. trim or 170/180 DIN for Europe. Styling was again basically unchanged. New "federal features" included energy-absorbing steering column, three-point inertia-reel seatbelts, removable top latch handles for the windshield header, and side-marker lights outside. Torque swelled by another 19 lbs-ft, which enhanced low-speed tractability if not mileage, and a new 5-speed ZF manual option helped exploit it. Alas, the 280 had more rubber and thus "slop" in its suspension, and the 5-speed option was pricey ($500), like the car itself. U.S. models came with 4.08:1 final gearing, though the 3.69 and 3.92 ratios were available "upon request."

By 1971, the W113 was old hat, having been denied recent D-B developments like a revised 4-speed automatic, anti-dive front suspension geometry, and new semi-trailing-link rear geometry. All would be rectified with the new R107 generation introduced late that year, a different breed altogether.

In fact, the W113s would be the last two-seat Mercedes true to the original meaning of SL (sehr leicht, very light). They were also far more successful than their Fifties forebears, with annual sales of about 6000 units. So in retrospect, these cars are a bit like the Roman god Janus—looking backward and forward. Today they're valued for precisely that reason: pleasant, well-rounded sporty cars with a certain timeless grace, and an important step in the evolution of Mercedes two-seaters.

1972-1988 MERCEDES-BENZ 350/450/380/500/560SL

Strictly speaking, the R107 Mercedes SL isn't a sports car but a two-seat GT. You may or may not consider that A Good Thing, but it's precisely what Daimler-Benz intended.

D-B began contemplating a successor to the "pagoda-roof" W113 SL in the mid-Sixties. The firm was in an expansionist mood, seeking increased profits (though not necessarily more sales) especially in the lucrative U.S. market. Management realized that bigger, plusher, costlier cars were the way to go. Kicking off another design cycle for the entire Mercedes line, the replacement SL, internally coded R107, was the first model to embody this new philosophy, from which D-B has reaped vast rewards ever since.

Bigger and plusher the R107 certainly was, and very much designed with America in mind. Compared to the 230/250/280SL, it was longer overall (by 3.3 inches) and in wheelbase to provide a little more space behind the cockpit and room ahead for air conditioning, standard for the States. It was also wider to accommodate Washington's required door guard beams as well as bigger tires—almost a necessity, as a switch from aluminum to steel body panels added some 300-400 pounds to curb weight. The extra beef undoubtedly contributed to passive safety, though several other features did more: a fuel tank tucked out of harm's way over the rear axle, safety door handles and steering wheel, new-design seatbelts.

The R107 certainly looked heavier, with none of the previous SL's lithe simplicity. A lift-off pagoda-style hardtop was retained (and even mimicked by a slight trunklid concavity) and there were functional features like ribbed taillamp lenses and A-pillar troughs that shed rain and muck to help the driver see and be seen. Overall, though, the styling was not readily accepted. One U.S. magazine initially described it as "Americanized" and "Anti-agile."

And this weightier SL *was* less agile than its predecessors, though more civilized. Yet its chassis was quite capable, evolved from that of the late-Sixties "New Generation" compact sedans, with D-B's typical rear swing axles (altered to function like semi-trailing arms) and excellent recirculating-ball power steering. To counteract the greater heft and enhance refinement, D-B specified its smooth 3.5-liter V-8 as standard for Europe. American R107s got a 4.5-liter enlargement that emission controls rendered no more powerful. A clumsy four-headlamp treatment, instead of single flush-mount lights, also marred the U.S. version, as did protruding 5-mph "impact" bumpers, federally mandated from 1972-73.

Though far removed from the original "Sports Light" concept, the R107 sold like no previous SL, and has remained popular for a remarkable 16 years without major alteration. Not that Daimler-Benz has ever advocated change for its own sake but, with sales consistently strong, there's been no need to monkey with this assured, polished, and solid sports tourer—timeless in its open-air appeal and always decently quick, sometimes exhilarating.

Which brings us to the changes that *have* been made, mostly in engines. Let's start with Europe, where a 2.8-liter twincam six-cylinder version was added in 1974 as an Energy Crisis special. This ran through 1985, when D-B substituted its new 3.0-liter sohc six (from the W124 sedans) for a new 300SL (though it was nothing like the hallowed Gullwing). A hot 500SL appeared for 1980—just in time for "Energy Crisis II," though inflation had lifted all Mercedes into such rarefied price territory by then that sales were hardly affected by a mere fuel shortage.

Meantime, America got a smaller version of this all-aluminum 5.0-liter V-8 for a 1981-model 380SL, whose tame acceleration led to a "black market" demand for European 500s that frankly embarrassed Mercedes-Benz of North America. This plus an eventual oil glut persuaded D-B to develop a 5.6-liter replacement as a U.S. exclusive for '86. Like the 500, it boasted improved anti-dive/anti-squat control, Bosch anti-lock brakes, and front chin spoiler (but no rear spoiler), plus driver's airbag, limited-slip differential, and upgraded trim and equipment. In Europe, a 420SL replaced the 3.8-liter as the mid-range offering.

Today, the R107 is the senior citizen of the Mercedes line, and engines alone, no matter how good, aren't enough against younger, higher-tech, more aerodynamic competitors. D-B is ready with a new R129SL, for 1989-90, and the R107 will be retired at last.

Many will be sad to see it go, but it will not be forgotten. Good Things never are.

SPECIFICATIONS

Engines: sohc V-8—1970-80: 213.5 cid/3499 cc, 230 bhp @ 5800 rpm, 231.5 lbs-ft @ 4200 rpm; **1972-81:** 276 cid/4520 cc, 190 bhp @ 4750 rpm, 240 lbs-ft @ 3000 rpm; **1980-85:** 234 cid/3839 cc, 155 bhp @ 4750 rpm, 196 lbs-ft @ 2750 rpm; **1980-88:** 303.5 cid/4973 cc, 231-240 bhp @ 4750-5000 rpm, 297 lbs-ft @ 3200 rpm (DIN); **1985-88:** 256 cid/4196 cc, 218 bhp @ 5200 rpm, 242 lbs-ft @ 3750 rpm (DIN); **1986-88:** 339 cid/5547 cc, 227 bhp @ 4750 rpm, 279 lbs-ft @ 3250 rpm; **dohc I-6—1974-85:** 168 cid/2746 cc, 177-185 bhp @ 5800-6000 rpm, 176 lbs-ft @ 4500 rpm (DIN); **sohc I-6—1985-88:** 181 cid/2962 cc, 188 bhp @ 5700 rpm, 192 lbs-ft @ 4400 rpm

Transmission:	3/4-speed automatic
Suspension, front:	unequal-length A-arms, coil springs, anti-roll bar
Suspension, rear:	semi-trailing arms, coil springs, anti-roll bar, "torque compensating axle" (560SL)
Brakes:	front/rear discs
Wheelbase (in.):	96.7
Weight (lbs):	3550-3880
Top speed (mph):	110-130
0-60 mph (sec):	7.5-11.0

Production: 350SL (1970-80) 15,304; **450SL** (1971-80) 66,298; **280SL** (1974-85) 22,598; **380SL** (1980-85) 45,056 (through 1984); **500SL** (1980-87): 1299 (through 1981); **300SL** (1985-87) NA; **420SL** (1985-87) NA; **560SL** (1986-87) 12,565 (1986 U.S. sales)

The current R107-series SL has seen several engines over the years but little external change. **Opposite bottom:** *The editors' test 1984-model 380SL.* **Opposite top:** *New flat-face wheels arrived with 1985's engine revisions. The editors drove this 1986-model 560SL.*

1945-1949
MG TC

Britain's beloved T-Series MG was born in 1936, a year after Lord Nuffield (the former William Morris) turned over Morris Garages (which he personally owned) to the Nuffield Organisation (which had grown out of his original Morris Motors). The move closed MG's design office, so the T-Series was developed by Morris at Cowley.

The first of the breed, logically called TA, used an old long-stroke four. Then came the TB of 1939, the same car with a new overhead-valve "short-stroke" engine (but still markedly undersquare) designated XPAG. Immediately after World War II, as MG reorganized for peacetime production, the TB was lightly modified to become the TC, introduced in late 1945.

As the first MG exported to the U.S. in significant numbers, the TC has long been credited with sparking the sports-car love affair that would sweep America beginning in the early Fifties. This is hard to understand in a way, for the TC was a slow, hard-riding, crude little traditional British roadster, and never sold with left-hand drive. But America took to it because, like the TA and TB, it had oodles of character and looked *right:* classically pure and very different from anything Detroit had to offer.

Character, of course, doesn't result from conscious, logical design but breeding, over many years and by managers who have a sixth sense about what customers want. Now in truth, the TC had none of the things most Americans wanted in the late Forties. It wasn't big, powerful, flashy, or even particularly comfortable. But a relatively small yet vocal group of buyers—people who enjoyed driving, as opposed to just getting someplace—found it well-nigh perfect: compact, responsive, and "urgent" somehow despite its leisurely acceleration. The TC also offered good fuel economy plus cheap and easy maintenance—a good thing, the latter, as it was needed often. Like the Tin Lizzie of earlier times, you either put up with the TC's idiosyncrasies or you didn't. It was the sort of car that demanded involvement. And isn't that the way love affairs begin?

· Except for being foreign, the TC offered nothing exotic for Americans. Like the TA/TB, it rode a simple, rather "whippy" ladder-type chassis with channel-section side members. Suspension was equally old-fashioned: just a rigid axle on short, hard semi-elliptic leaf springs front and rear, allied to hydraulic lever-arm shock absorbers.

The charming two-seat roadster body was merely an update of the original mid-Thirties design, with rear-hinged cutaway doors, sweeping separate fenders, a traditional radiator and freestanding headlamps, even running boards (which Detroit had abandoned years before). Steel panels fastened to a wood skeleton, real Twenties-style construction. Weather protection, such as it was, comprised a shallow windshield that could be folded down for *real* wind-in-the-hair (or bugs-in-the-teeth) motoring, plus snap-in side curtains and a soft top stretched over a complicated metal framework. TC owners typically proved their hardiness by driving almost always with top and curtains removed—and their enthusiasm by waving frantically at passing fellow MG'ers.

Beneath the TC's rakishly long hood sat the 1250-cc XPAG engine, virtually unchanged since 1939, hooked to a 4-speed floorshift gearbox with no synchromesh on first—all very modest. Yet though its natural cruising gait was a mere 60-65 mph, the TC looked, sounded, and acted like a more "important" car. It seemed tiny to Americans, of course. Wheelbase was just 94 inches, curb weight less than 1750 pounds. But that only made it very agile, ideally suited for those funny European contests called rallies and gymkhanas, and a revelation next to the dull, bulky Detroiters of the day.

Racing a TC was usually frustrating because of its poor aerodynamics, though the very "tuneable" engine made up for a lot of that. On the road, the TC was all bouncy and busy, for wheel travel was limited and springing hard. Even mild bumps could be real kidney-jolters, while cornering on less than perfectly smooth surfaces could send it skittering sideways, though the steering was so direct that a skilled driver could counteract the tendency.

It all added up to enjoyable, unforgettable motoring, completely foreign to most Yanks at the time and utterly infectious because of it. Today, there are almost as many TCs around as there were 40 years ago, making memories for a new generation of enthusiasts while teaching them what *real* sports cars are all about.

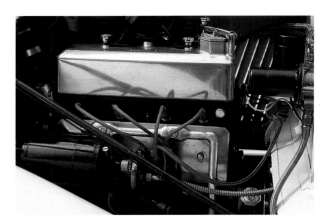

The TC was the last classically styled MG sports car in the Thirties mold and, as the firm would say later, "the sports car America loved first." Though merely an update of the prewar TB, it was a revelation to Yankee driving enthusiasts. Small XPAG four (top) was no powerhouse, but rakish looks and "trad" cockpit (above) compensated a lot for many.

SPECIFICATIONS

Engine: ohv I-4, 76.3 cid/1250 cc, 54 bhp (net) @ 5200 rpm, 64 lbs-ft @ 2600 rpm

Transmission:	4-speed manual
Suspension, front:	rigid axle, semi-elliptic leaf springs
Suspension, rear:	live axle, semi-elliptic leaf springs
Brakes:	front/rear drums
Wheelbase (in.):	94.0
Weight (lbs):	1735
Top speed (mph):	75
0-60 mph (sec):	22.7
Production:	10,000

1949-1953
MG TD

Replacing the TC would have been easy enough, but the Nuffield Organisation insisted that MG develop a successor as quickly, simply, and cheaply as possible. "Traditional" looks were also decreed, as this seemed an MG selling point (especially in the States), yet there was an equal demand for independent front suspension.

Inspiration for the last came from MG's contemporary Y-Series, a sedan which had been conceived in 1938 (and looked it) but which had a fairly modern ifs via coil springs and wishbones. MG engineers duly rushed out a new version of the Y-Series box-section platform in 1949, retaining the TC wheelbase and adopting hypoid-bevel final drive. They also provided a frame kickup over the rear axle for increased wheel travel, so that softer springs could be used to match the more supple new front end. A cost-cutting oddity that attracted much criticism was the use of 15-inch steel disc wheels in place of the previous 19-inch-diameter wires. And the traditional wires wouldn't even be available at extra cost.

The result, called the TD, retained the TC drivetrain with only minor modifications. Road tests recorded a slightly higher top speed but less rapid acceleration, mainly due to significantly more weight. Body construction and general appearance stayed the same too, but the TD was wider and sat much lower than the TC, and every body panel was different. In all, the TD was obviously new yet very much a traditional MG.

For U.S. buyers though, the TD's main improvement was its availability with left-hand drive, which made navigating a lot easier on increasingly crowded American roads. The softer suspension and fatter tires also made driving this MG less taxing than the TC. Still, the TD remained rather crude, with the same primitive top and clumsy side curtains, plus limited cockpit space.

In mid-1951, the TD became the TD II, with a larger clutch and (eventually) oil pan, plus other updates. This should not be confused with the TD Mark II, a much rarer and more specialized version intended for racing. This used a more powerful XPAG engine with 60 instead of 54 horsepower, and was occasionally seen with modified suspension components and other items from MG's competition catalog. MG also marketed engine-tuning kits (called Stage II, Stage III, etc.) for all TDs to match specific customer needs.

The TD proved even more successful than the popular TC, especially in the U.S. The TC's best production year had been 1948 and 3085 units; the TD handily beat it, the Abingdon factory building 10,838 in 1952 alone. Nearly 30,000 would be built in all, with a remarkable 23,488 of them sold in the U.S.

By 1953, however, the TD was in trouble, mainly due to strong new competition from Triumph's faster, more civilized TR2. MG's response was to update the classic T-Series formula once more. The result appeared late that year as the new, and somewhat controversial, TF.

SPECIFICATIONS

Engine: ohv I-4, 76.3 cid/1250 cc, 54 bhp (net) @ 5200 rpm, 64 lbs-ft @ 2600 rpm

Transmission:	4-speed manual
Suspension, front:	double wishbones, coil springs
Suspension, rear:	live axle, semi-elliptic leaf springs
Brakes:	front/rear drums
Wheelbase (in.):	94.0
Weight (lbs):	1930
Top speed (mph):	80
0-60 mph (sec):	23.5
Production:	29,664

TD looked somewhat more modern than the TC due to a lower stance (via a 4-inch reduction in wheel diameter) and a less angular front end. Unlike the TC, lefthand drive was available; it helped the TD become the most popular T-Series MG, mainly due to strong U.S. demand.

1953-1955
MG TF & TF 1500

MG had already devised a replacement for the TD when the model reached peak sales in 1952, but company bosses wouldn't approve it for production. The TD definitely need replacing, however, so there was nothing to do but give it a facelift and a new name.

What emerged after a great deal of hurrying in 1953 was little more than a TD with revised styling at each end and slightly more power. It was designated TF, not TE, which sounded too much like the slightly ribald "tee hee" to British ears. Though roundly criticized in its day as too little, too late, the TF has since become regarded as the most graceful and desirable T-Series of all.

The nose-and-tail job was exactly that, for the TD's central structure—wood skeleton, steel panels and all—was left intact. Ahead, the hood sloped more sharply to a smaller, newly raked radiator flanked by reprofiled fenders with faired-in

Simple but effective nose and tail restyling turned the TD into the more streamlined TF, which was originally chided for being almost too modern but has since come to be regarded by many as the best-looking T-Series MG. Here, a lovely example of the end-of-the-line TF 1500, whose larger, somewhat more powerful engine was prompted by price/performance competition from Triumph's new TR2.

headlamps. Out back, the familiar fuel tank and exposed spare were angled more rakishly. Completing the visual package was a new instrument panel with gauges shaped in MG's trademark octagon instead of the usual circles. Purists applauded the return of center-lock wire wheels as a regular (and eventually popular) option.

All was as before underneath, except for minor engine adjustments that added 3 horsepower to the total. The TF thus went, sounded, and handled just like any TC or TD. Unfortunately for MG, it ran smack into Triumph's TR2, priced exactly the same but offering 90 bhp and a 105-mph top speed. Though sleeker, the 57-bhp MG was still hampered by barn-door aerodynamics and couldn't exceed 80 mph. No wonder the press gave it a hard time—or that MG was reluctant to lend TFs to enthusiast magazines.

To help remedy the situation, MG rushed through a revised block casting that allowed the 1250-cc XPAG engine to be enlarged into the 1466-cc XPEG. The result was 17 percent more torque but only a 10-percent gain in peak power, to 63 bhp. So equipped, the revised TF, which became known and was often badged as the TF 1500, was 5 mph faster all out and quicker off the line but still not competitive with the TR2 in either performance or sales, especially in America.

Thus, after just two years of TFs, MG finally laid the classic T-Series to rest and returned to the more modern sports car it wanted to build back in '52. And a good one it would be. With the MGA, Abingdon would make up for a lot of lost time.

SPECIFICATIONS

Engines: all ohv I-4; **TF** (1953-54): 76.3 cid/1250 cc, 57 bhp (net) @ 5500 rpm, 65 lbs-ft @ 3000 rpm; **TF1500** (1954-55): 89.5 cid/1466 cc, 63 bhp @ 5000 rpm, 76 lbs-ft @ 3000 rpm

Transmission:	4-speed manual
Suspension, front:	double wishbones, coil springs
Suspension, rear:	live axle, semi-elliptic leaf springs
Brakes:	front/rear drums
Wheelbase (in.):	94.0
Weight (lbs):	1930
Top speed (mph):	80-85
0-60 mph (sec):	16.3-18.9
Production:	**TF** (1953-54) 6200 **TF 1500** (1954-55) 3400

1955-1962
MGA AND MGA DeLUXE

The T-Series never sold better than in 1952, but MG was already thinking about a replacement. A prototype was completed that year, only to be mothballed by managers refusing to allocate production funds. In a couple of years, though, the T-Series had reached the end of the sales road, so its erstwhile successor was hauled out of mothballs. The result was the very different MGA of 1955.

It was virtually all-new, starting with the chassis: a modern, massively strong affair with the basic TD/TF independent front suspension and all-drum brakes. Wheelbase was unchanged, but more space-efficient chassis packaging and a smooth new envelope body provided more cockpit and luggage room than any T-Series ever knew.

While the 1952 prototype carried TD running gear, MG had become part of British Motor Corporation by the time the project was revived in 1954, so the MGA was reconfigured around newly developed "corporate" hardware as fitted to MG's latest ZA Magnette sports sedan. It thus became the first MG sports car to employ the BMC "B-Series" four-cylinder engine, its associated 4-speed gearbox, and a new type of hypoid-bevel rear axle. The powerplant initially chosen was the 1489-cc version with a rated 72 horsepower, just enough for a top speed around the magic "ton" (100 mph).

In appearance and body construction there was no comparison with the old T-Series. The MGA's fully welded all-steel body had the same long-hood/short-deck proportions, but was lower and wider and looked at *least* 20 years newer. Instruments reverted from octagonal to circular, while the dash provided for fresh-air ventilation and radio installation. Separately adjustable seats returned to MG for the first time in years, and turn indicators were standard. Body styles were initially confined to the traditional roadster, but a fixed-roof "bubbletop" coupe arrived within a year, boasting roll-up door glass and exterior door handles (both lacking on the roadster) plus a curvier windshield.

Fast, safe, and well balanced, the MGA was such an advance on even the TF1500 that it could have come from another make. Though not quite as fast as the rival Triumph TR3 (see entry), it was prettier to most eyes and sold far better than any T-Series. In fact, just over 100,000 MGAs of all types would be built through 1962.

Along the way, the MGA was treated to gradual but perceptible improvements in displacement, power, and equipment. The introductory model (retrospectively known as 1500) was replaced in 1959 by the MGA 1600, with 1588 cc, 80 bhp, and standard front disc brakes. Mid-1961 brought the 1600 Mark II, with 1622 cc and 86 bhp, plus a revised grille that made the car look as if it had been "kicked in the teeth." The hot Twin Cam variant had come and gone by then (see entry), but its suspension, all-disc brakes, and center-lock wire wheels were fitted to pushrod-engine 1600s and Mk IIs to create new DeLuxe variants beginning in late 1960. Except for superior braking power, they performed exactly as "non-DeLuxe" models. Most were loaded with extras rarely ordered on MGAs, and were pretty rare themselves.

Because weight seemed to rise in step with horsepower, late MGAs weren't much faster than early ones (Twin Cam apart, that is) but all these cars were well loved by their owners—and still are, come to that. The production figures tell the story; sales were truly excellent by European standards.

But it was time to move on again by 1962, the year that brought a new MG sports car destined to be even more popular and long-lived. Sadly, it would also be the last.

SPECIFICATIONS

Engines: all ohv I-4: **1500** (1955-59): 91 cid/1489 cc, 72 bhp (net) @ 5500 rpm, 77 lbs-ft @ 3500 rpm; **1600 "Mark I" and DeLuxe** (1959-61): 97 cid/1588 cc, 80 bhp (net) @ 5500 rpm, 87 lbs-ft @ 3800 rpm; **1600 Mark II and DeLuxe** (1961-62): 99 cid/1622 cc, 86 bhp (net) @ 5500 rpm, 97 lbs-ft @ 4000 rpm

Transmission:	4-speed manual
Suspension, front:	upper and lower A-arms, coil springs
Suspension, rear:	live axle, semi-elliptic leaf springs
Brakes:	front/rear drums (1955-59); front discs/rear drums (1959-62), front/rear discs (1960-62 DeLuxe)
Wheelbase (in.):	94.0
Weight (lbs):	1988-2105
Top speed (mph):	98-101
0-60 mph (sec):	13.7-15.6

Production: **1500** (1955-59) 58,750 **1600 "Mark I"** (1959-61) 31,501 **1600 Mark II** (1961-62) 8719 **1600 "Mark I" DeLuxe** (1960-61) 82 **1600 Mark II DeLuxe** (1961-62) 313

*A complete departure from the T-Series, the MGA maintained a clean basic appearance throughout its life as a roadster (**opposite top**) and fixed-roof coupe (**bottom**). Only the latter carried external door handles, but both styles were far more civilized than any previous sporting MG. Initial 1.5-liter engine gave way to a 1.6 in '59; it continued in Mark II models, which gained more upright grille bars for i.d.*

1958-1960
MGA TWIN CAM

Even before the MGA appeared, plans were laid to offer it with a more powerful twincam engine at extra cost. Two four-cylinder units were built and tested, and one was chosen to power a pair of prototypes in the September 1955 British Tourist Trophy race. Ultimately, though, it was decided to offer the other one in a production model, which arrived less than three years later as the MGA Twin Cam.

Though more potent, the new dohc engine was a lot costlier and more complicated than the overhead-valve B-Series four in "cooking" MGAs, so Abingdon decided to make the car around it a more upmarket product. There was no money for even minimal styling changes, but wheels, brakes, and steering could be and were upgraded.

While the twincam engine originated as a simple B-Series conversion, it became increasingly specialized as development progressed, and little of the original engineering was left by 1958. (However, its cylinder dimensions would eventually be shared with the pushrod 1588-cc unit of the MGA 1600s.) The head, made of alloy, was laid out in classic Jaguar XK fashion, with valves opposed at 80 degrees from vertical and operated via inverted bucket tappets enclosing coil springs around the valves themselves. Combustion chambers were hemispherical. Initial compression ratio was very high for the day at 9.9:1. With all this, horsepower was a rated 108 at 6700 rpm, versus 80 bhp at 5600 rpm for the ohv 1600.

To match this bulkier, beefier engine, MG altered the steering (mainly for clearance), specified Dunlop disc brakes all-round, and fitted special Dunlop center-lock disc wheels of the type made famous a few years earlier by Jaguar's D-Type sports-racers. The result was a good-handling car made even more stable and agile, so MG's hopes were high when the Twin Cam went on sale in the summer of 1958 in the same roadster and coupe styles as other MGAs.

Unhappily, numerous quality and reliability problems plagued early Twin Cams, and it didn't take long for the word to be heard through the enthusiast grapevine. In particular, the engines were often serious oil-burners and needed very-high-octane fuel to give of their best—not to mention avoiding harmful detonation. Many of these early engines suffered damage when either problem got out of hand.

A pity, because the Twin Cam was fast for a 1600, fearsomely competitive when running right. But because it was so specialized, it was merely a side show for most MG dealers, and owners found it hard to find one able to keep their cars in proper shape. Not that there were that many owners to begin with, because the Twin Cam arrived with a 27-percent price premium over a comparably equipped ohv model.

No wonder, then, that production was very slow at first—about 100 units a month. It peaked at only 313 units monthly in February 1959, before word of engine troubles got out and sales fell away. Production dropped to a trickle by fall, and only 90 were completed during the Twin Cam's last nine months.

By that time, MG had cured the oil-burning and "fixed" detonation bothers (by lowering compression), but the Twin Cam had been branded a dog and that was that. Production ended in the spring of 1960, and the balance of Twin Cam frames, wheels, and brakes were used for a small number of pushrod-engine MGA DeLuxe models (see entry).

Not surprisingly, the low-volume high-performance Twin Cam is now regarded as the most desirable MGA bar none. Many have survived and been rebuilt. Ironically, they're now running better than they ever did when new.

SPECIFICATIONS

Engine: dohc I-4, 97 cid/1588 cc, 108 bhp (net) @ 6700 rpm (low compression: 100 bhp), 104 lbs-ft @ 4500 rpm

Transmission:	4-speed manual
Suspension, front:	upper and lower A-arms, coil springs
Suspension, rear:	live axle, semi-elliptic leaf springs
Brakes:	front/rear discs
Wheelbase (in.):	94.0
Weight (lbs):	2185-2245
Top speed (mph):	113
0-60 mph (sec):	9.1
Production:	2111

*Center-lock disc wheels were one way to distinguish the hot Twin Cam from other MGAs—that and its faster getaway. Hemi-head twincam four (**opposite top**) was potent for a late-Fifties 1.6-liter four, but high compression dictated premium fuel and the engine soon became known as a serious oil-burner. The latter was eventually cured, but contributed to the model's early demise.*

1961-1979
MG MIDGET

MG's first Midget was the 1928 M-Type. The name disappeared after the last K3 model of 1934, but the T-Series were Midgets in spirit.

By 1958, MG was under the British Motor Corporation roof with Austin-Healey and producing the original A-H Sprite at its Abingdon factory. The "bugeye" proved so successful, especially in the U.S., that BMC decided to restyle it for 1961 and sell it in a second version as a new Midget.

Through 1971, the Sprite and Midget were built side-by-side as fraternal twins differing only in badges, grilles, and minor trim and equipment. The Midget then carried on alone through 1979. Basic design stayed the same throughout these 19 years, though there were running changes to engines, transmissions, brakes, suspension, top mechanisms, trim, and equipment. Of course, what applies to the Midgets also goes for the Sprites (badged simply as Austin Sprite in 1971 *only*).

Visually, the rebodied '61 Sprite/Midget was boxier and more conventional than the "bugeye," its lift-up nose section replaced by fixed front fenders with integral headlamps, plus a rear-hinged hood. The tail was also squared up and given a conventional trunklid. Sliding side curtains for the doors and British-traditional build-it-yourself soft top were retained, as were the central body section, diminutive 80-inch wheelbase, the willing little 948-cc four-cylinder engine, rack-and-pinion steering, coil-spring independent front suspension, and a live rear axle on cantilevered leaf springs, located by radius arms.

With all this, the new-design Sprite/Midget was much like its predecessor: a cheeky, high-revving little roadster that handled like a go-kart, wasn't very fast, and had *just* enough room for two adults. Nevertheless, sales picked up in a big way, reaching 15,000-20,000 a year. This rate would be maintained (with many ups and downs) through 1979, with the U.S. taking the bulk of production as usual.

Model changes began with the '63s, which received the larger 1098-cc version of the BMC A-Series four and 56 horsepower. A Mark III Sprite and Mark II Midget arrived in the spring of '64 with 59 bhp, taller windshield, wind-up door windows, and conventional semi-elliptic rear leaf springs. Fall 1966 brought the Sprite Mk IV and Midget Mk III with a more rugged, 65-bhp 1275-cc A-Series, followed in 1969 by minor styling changes arranged to eliminate virtually all remaining differences between the two versions.

With the Sprite retired after 1971, the Midget progressed to Mark IV form in 1974, identified by fully radiused rear wheelarches, plus a larger fuel tank and collapsible steering column, the latter prompted by U.S. regulations. Smog standards had stolen a lot of American engine power, so the Midget became a 1500 for 1975 via a drivetrain donation from the latest Triumph Spitfire. Flat-top rear wheelarches returned along with a jacked-up suspension to get the headlights up to U.S. regulation height, and a protruding black bumper/grille to satisfy new American impact standards. The latter two followed MGB changes and reflected the apparent unwillingness—or inability—of troubled British Leyland to do more than meet the letter of U.S. law in the cheapest, most expedient ways possible. Thus, the Midget acquired a third wiper beginning with the '76 models to comply with another new visibility standard.

As the production figures show, these dreary changes plus steadily falling horsepower took a sales toll after 1974, though the Midget remained quite popular right to the end—and likely profitable, what with tooling costs written off by the mid-Sixties. But BL was in desperate straits by 1979 and willing to do anything to increase its survival chances, even abandon sports cars. Thus, the last Midgets came off the line that autumn. A year later, MG's historic Abingdon works would close forever.

MG revived the prewar Midget name when BMC decided to market a second version of the rebodied 1961 Austin-Healey Sprite. Both shared new squared-up looks and conventional front end, but the Midget stood apart by dint of its vertical-bar MG-style grille, retained as shown here through 1969. Cockpit (above) remained spartan but serviceable, A-series four (top) rugged but none too powerful in initial 948- and 1088-cc sizes.

SPECIFICATIONS

Engines: all ohv I-4; **1961-62:** 57.9 cid/948 cc, 43 bhp (net) @ 5200 rpm, 52 lbs-ft @ 3300 rpm; **1962-66:** 67 cid/1098 cc, 56/59 bhp @ 5750 rpm, 65 lbs-ft @ 3500 rpm; **1966-74:** 77.8 cid/1275 cc, 65 bhp (net) @ 5000 rpm, 72 lbs-ft @ 3000 rpm (U.S. version: 55-62 bhp); **1974-79:** 91.1 cid/1493 cc, 65 bhp (net) @ 5500 rpm, 77 lbs-ft @ 3000 rpm (U.S. version: 50-55 bhp)

Transmission:	4-speed manual (non-synchro first gear through 1974, then all-synchromesh)
Suspension, front:	upper and lower A-arms, coil springs, anti-roll bar
Suspension, rear:	live axle, cantilever leaf springs (1961-64), semi-elliptic leaf springs (1964-79)
Brakes:	front discs/rear drums
Wheelbase (in.):	80.0
Weight (lbs):	1575-1700
Top speed (mph):	85-101
0-60 mph (sec):	14.7-18.3

Production: Mark I (1961-62) 16,080 **Mark II** (1962-66) 36,202 **Mark III** (1966-74) 99,896 **Mark IV/1500** (1974-79) 72,185 [**A-H Sprite** (1961-71): 80,360]

1962-1980
MGB AND MGB GT

Abingdon did such good business with the MGA that it waited seven years before fielding a replacement, though it was working on one by the end of the Fifties. Announced in the fall of '62, the new MGB would go on to set the marque's all-time production record: 18 years and over half a million units. Sadly, the last Bs built would also be the last MG sports cars—at least so far.

If the MGA had been a technical leap forward, the B was a smaller one. Its main innovation—for MG anyway—was modern monocoque construction, replacing the A's separate body and sturdy chassis, still a two-seat roadster but far more rigid. BMC's B-Series four-cylinder engine was retained with capacity stretched to 1798 cc, and the 4-speed gearbox could be supplemented with optional Laycock de Normanville electric overdrive for the first time. Like the A, the 95-horsepower B could just beat 100 mph, but was faster off the mark. In some respects, though, it was still quite dated. Suspension and brakes were as for the A, which meant that the independent front-end geometry harked back a decade to the TD.

At least the B was better packaged than the A, with more cockpit and luggage room despite a 3-inch-shorter wheelbase. Styling was smooth, if boxier than on the curvaceous A, slightly Italianate but conceived in Abingdon without outside help. Highlights included a wide, shallow rendition of the traditional MG grille, fender headlamp nacelles, slab sides, and neat, vertical taillamp clusters. The B's other big "technical" innovation showed up inside: wind-up door windows. Marque partisans were stunned—and quite divided on this break with roadster tradition.

Still, the B was stylish and quick—enough to keep pace with Triumph's latest (the TR4, launched in '61)—and blessed with idiotproof handling plus a supple ride. The price was right too: around $2500 at introduction. Altogether, it was a winning combination. U.S. sales, which began at the end of '62, were strong. More than 23,000 Bs were built in calendar 1963, a new yearly record that MG promptly shattered with 26,542 units in '64.

For some years, the MGB could do no wrong, and numerous running changes kept it competitive against other sports cars in its size and price bracket. The engine, for example, was switched from a three- to five-main-bearing crankshaft at the end of '64, followed in the autumn of '65 by a pretty hatchback coupe derivative called MGB GT, which *had* been designed with a Latin assist—from Pininfarina. Elegant yet practical, the GT could double as daily transportation for a small family. Two years later, a B "Mark II" appeared with a new all-synchromesh gearbox and stronger rear axle, plus MG's first-ever automatic transmission option. The last wasn't popular though, and quietly disappeared in 1973 after only about 5000 installations.

Alas, this would be the high point of MGB development. By 1968, MG had been stirred into the British Leyland stew, where Triumph was favored for future sports cars. The B was thus allowed to limp through the Seventies with only minor annual refinements and, for the U.S., steadily decreasing horsepower and cheap, cheerless solutions to safety and emissions standards. The nadir was the '75 model, with a suspension cranked up 1.5 inches to meet regulation U.S. headlight height and marred by big, black energy-absorbing bumpers, including a front "bra." U.S. engines were down to an asthmatic 62 horsepower, and the BGT had been withdrawn.

With all this, late-model U.S. Bs couldn't top 90 mph, even though overdrive was standardized in 1975. Meantime, Americans missed out on the desirable BGT V-8. Introduced for the British market in 1974, it packed the 3.5-liter aluminum engine that General Motors had devised for its 1961 B-O-P compacts, later sold to Rover and hence BL. No heavier than a standard BGT, the V-8 could hit 60 mph from rest in 7.7 seconds, versus 18.3 for the four-cylinder U.S. car. Still, only 2591 were built.

Age, familiarity, and worsening pound/dollar exchange finally caught up with the B in 1980. The last one was built in October that year, after which the historic Abingdon factory was closed in another of BL's many attempts to cut costs and stay afloat. It's likely that at least half of all four-cylinder Bs came to the U.S., perhaps more. Among the various limited-edition cosmetic specials offered over the years were 1000 farewell 1980 models for the home market only: 420 bronze roadsters and 580 pewter GTs.

Enthusiasts everywhere mourned the B's demise, but we may yet see a new MG sports car, perhaps a production version of the stunning 1986 EX-E experimental. Let's hope the state-owned Rover Group (as BL has since become) can get its act together and build it. A sporting MG for the Nineties might help the firm out of its 20-year doldrums.

SPECIFICATIONS

Engine: ohv I-4, 109.7 cid/1798 cc, 62-95 bhp (SAE) @ 5400 rpm, 87-110 lbs-ft (SAE) @ 3000 rpm

Transmissions:	4-speed manual with optional overdrive (standard U.S. from 1975), 3-speed automatic (1967-73)
Suspension, front:	upper and lower A-arms, coil springs, anti-roll bar
Suspension, rear:	live axle, semi-elliptic leaf springs
Brakes:	front discs/rear drums
Wheelbase (in.):	91.0
Weight (lbs):	2030-2600 (Roadster) 2190-2260 (GT)
Top speed (mph):	90-103
0-60 mph (sec):	12.2-18.3
Production:	**Roadster** 387,675 **GT** 125,597

Opposite top: Early Bs, like this circa-1968 roadster, were the cleanest-looking and best-performing of the four-cylinder breed. Above: By 1975 they stood higher, were slower and wore a controversial protruding snout, all to satisfy U.S. regulations. Opposite bottom: Rapid Rover-engine BGT V-8 evolution, shown here in 1974 form, never made it to America. Fewer than 2600 were built.

1967-1969
MGC AND MGC GT

By the mid-Sixties, British Motor Corporation had too many sports models for the number it was selling, and set about reorganizing the ranks. The Austin-Healey Sprite had been cloned into an MG Midget twin at the start of the decade. Before long, the A-H 3000 was looking the odd man out at the Abingdon sports-car factory. This prompted a new project coded ADO51/ADO52 (ADO for Austin Drawing Office).

Its object was a successor for the "Big Healey," which did not share body or chassis with any other BMC car. The plan was a six-cylinder derivative of the successful MGB to be sold in A-H (ADO51) and MG (ADO52) versions. But Donald Healey refused to have his name on a car he hadn't had a hand in, so only the MG appeared.

Tagged MGC, it was cleverly designed to use as many components from the BMC bins as possible. Starting with the MGB monocoque, engineers installed a new front suspension with longitudinal torsion bars to accommodate a 2912-cc straight six. Though similar in size and output to the 3.0-liter Healey engine, this ohv unit was completely different: shorter, a little lighter, and allegedly more efficient. BMC, then reorganizing its passenger cars as well, had devised it for transverse installation in the new front-drive Austin 3-Litre sedan, revealed along with the MGC, which used a tuned version. Still, this was a fairly long power unit and thus a tight fit in the B's engine bay, and it made the C quite nose-heavy. Predictably, the C got the new all-synchromesh gearbox, heavy-duty Salisbury rear axle, and new automatic transmission option developed for the Mark II MGB, also released at this time.

Outside, there was little to distinguish the C from the then five-year-old B. Even their badges looked alike. The newcomer's most obvious differences were 15-inch wheels (versus 14s) and hood bulges to clear the bulkier six-cylinder engine. Like the B, the C was offered as a roadster and GT hatchback coupe.

The MGC got off to a bad start with the British press, which judged its handling inferior to the big Healey's, its steering too heavy, and its general feel sluggish. It had, wrote one, lost "the Abingdon touch." Sales were also sluggish as BMC merged with Leyland Motors to form British Leyland, then picked up to about the same rate as that of the last Healeys. But the MGC never quite recovered from the press drubbing and disappeared after just two years.

Initially, final-drive gearing was perhaps too tall and the gearbox ratios on non-overdrive models weren't as sporting as they might have been. But BMC changed this on the '69s, which felt livelier but weren't actually faster. (One problem: a conspicuous lack of torque.) At the same time, reclining seats were standardized and pretty "Rostyle" wheels became an option to plain disc rims.

But the public never seemed to accept the C after its 1968 "character assassination." The last one was completed in September 1969, just 26 months after quantity production had begun. Of the 8999 built, about half (4256) were sold in the U.S.

SPECIFICATIONS

Engine: ohv I-6, 177.7 cid/2912 cc, 145 bhp (net) @ 5250 rpm, 170 lbs-ft @ 3400 rpm

Transmissions:	4-speed manual (overdrive optional) or 3-speed automatic
Suspension, front:	upper and lower A-arms, longitudinal torsion bars, anti-roll bar
Suspension, rear:	live axle, semi-elliptic leaf springs
Brakes:	front discs/rear drums
Wheelbase (in.):	91.0
Weight (lbs):	2460 (Roadster), 2610 (GT)
Top speed (mph):	120
0-60 mph (sec):	10.0
Production:	**Roadster** 4550 **GT** 4449

*The MGC, shown here in fastback GT form, was outwardly little different from the four-cylinder B except for badges, inch-larger wheels, and a rather ungainly hood bulge. U.S. versions (**opposite**) wore side marker lights and other required equipment fitted to contemporary Bs.*

1967-1977 MONTEVERDI 375-SERIES

Although Switzerland stands proudly independent amidst Italy, France, and Germany, it has never developed a strong native motor industry. Observers were thus quite surprised in 1967 when Binningen-based businessman Peter Monteverdi announced that he would not only build a car in Switzerland but that it would take on the world's premier high-performance makes.

Monteverdi was a successful, well-established motor trader, having been the Swiss BMW importer and manufacturer of the MBM single-seat racers. Predictably, he took the simplest and most practical route to his new GTs, designing the chassis himself but looking to the Italians for styling help and to Detroit for drivetrains.

The first Monteverdi was a two-seat semi-fastback coupe dubbed 375S, built on a separate tubular-steel chassis with coil-spring front suspension and De Dion rear. The latter, of course, isn't the best solution for fast-car handling, as it's halfway between a live rear axle and a fully independent setup. But Monteverdi, with neither time nor money for his own irs, decided that what was good for Aston Martin was good enough for him.

Monteverdi also had his own ideas about styling, but wisely enlisted Pietro Frua to refine them. The result looked like a slightly sleeker rendition of two Frua-designed contemporaries, the AC 428 and Maserati's Mistral (see entries). Bodyshells were supplied by Fissore in Italy.

The Ferrari-esque model designation referred to the SAE gross horsepower of the standard 440-cubic-inch Chrysler V-8 (re-rated by the mid-Seventies to 305 bhp SAE

net). For a not-so-few dollars more, you could order a "High Speed" model powered by the famed 426-cid hemi with 450 bhp (SAE gross). Either could be teamed with Chrysler 4-speed manual or 3-speed TorqueFlite automatic transmission. The latter would end up being fitted to most of the relatively few 375s built during the series' 10-year lifespan.

Soon after announcement, the 375S was joined by a companion 2+2 called 375L, followed in 1969 by a two-place cabriolet, logically designated 375C. All rode a 105.5-inch wheelbase. The chassis was stretched to no less than 125 inches between wheel centers for a large, heavy four/five-seat sedan, the 375 Limousine. Then in the spring of '75, the Cabriolet was put on a 98-inch wheelbase and given a restyled front to become the Palm Beach Spider. Chassis and mechanical specifications were otherwise the same for all models, and largely unchanged during the entire production run. Styling was typical late-Sixties Italian supercar: rather angular contours, glassy greenhouse with slim pillars, shapely tails, and broad eggcrate grilles with quad headlamps.

As the Chrysler engines were designed to motivate heavyweight New Yorkers and Imperials, they returned somewhat better performance in the lighter Monteverdis. The 440 could see all but the Limousine to over 150 mph, competitive with most Maseratis if not the magnificent Ferrari Daytona. The hemi-engine cars were faster still, as quick as most any Ferrari or Lamborghini save the mid-engine Berlinetta Boxer and Miura.

Though reliable figures are hard to come by, it's doubtful Monteverdi production exceeded 50 cars in any one year, and was probably much lower in most. Sales were confined mainly to Europe, as there was no U.S. marketing effort, and prices were towering for these largely handbuilt machines. In retrospect, the lack of U.S. sales seems odd, as the use of Chrysler drivetrains would have made meeting federal emissions regulations a lot easier for Monteverdi than most other exoticar builders. Perhaps the whole thing was nothing more than a hobby for Mr. Monteverdi.

Regardless, by 1977, perhaps a little earlier, the 375-Series was gone and Peter Monteverdi had turned to selling plushed-up, slightly restyled Dodge Aspen sedans, called Sierra, through his handful of European dealers. He later applied a similar "boutique" treatment to the four-wheel-drive Range Rover.

SPECIFICATIONS

Engines: all Chrysler ohv V-8; 440 cid/7210 cc, 375 bhp (SAE gross) @ 4600 rpm, 480 lbs-ft @ 3200 rpm; 426 cid/6974 cc, 450 bhp (SAE gross) @ 5000 rpm, 489 lbs-ft @ 4000 rpm

Transmissions:	Chrysler 4-speed manual or 3-speed TorqueFlite automatic
Suspension, front:	upper and lower A-arms, coil springs, anti-roll bar
Suspension, rear:	De Dion live axle, Watt linkage, radius arms, coil springs
Brakes:	front/rear discs
Wheelbase (in.):	105.5, 98.0 (Palm Beach)
Weight (lbs):	3345-3630
Top speed (mph):	152 (440 cid)
0-60 mph (sec):	6.3 (440 cid)
Production:	NA

*The two-seat 375S was the first effort of Swiss motor magnate Peter Monteverdi. Styling, by Frua of Italy and executed by Fissore, differed from that of later models in having only twin headlamps and low-profile grille. Back seat (**opposite center**) was strictly for show, as evidenced by the long-wheelbase 375L 2+2 in 1968.*

1950-1968 MORGAN PLUS 4

Although Morgan began building three-wheelers in 1910, it didn't get into four-wheelers until a quarter-century later with the 4/4 model. It was typical of mid-Thirties British sports cars in appearance and body construction, but Morgan and its customers found this very satisfactory—so much so that today's Morgans aren't all that different. Panels, dimensions, drivetrains, and details *have* changed, but not the basic look, engineering, or appeal. In every way, Morgans have become their own replicars.

Morgan stuck with the original 1935 design through 1950, then introduced a 4/4 replacement called Plus 4 on a four-inch longer wheelbase and with a different, more powerful engine. Like its predecessor, the Plus 4 had a separate steel chassis topped by a choice of traditional-looking roadster bodies erected from steel panels over a wood frame. Morgan built and trimmed its own bodies but bought nearly everything else: chassis, running gear, steering, and brakes.

The chassis was a simple ladder type with what became known as "Z-section" side members (not channel-section and nowhere near box-section) and underslung rear axle. Independent front suspension was via coil springs and sliding pillars, an arrangement said to have been copied from Lancia and one that's figured on every Morgan ever built. Springs and shock absorbers were *very* hard on all Morgans (some say frame flex was the actual "suspension"), so the cars leaped from bump to bump and had a bone-shattering ride. But the stiff chassis meant next to no body roll and wheels that always stayed vertical, so roadholding on smooth surfaces was excellent.

Plus 4 power was initially supplied by a wet-liner four-cylinder engine from the postwar Standard Vanguard sedan, mated to a separately mounted Moss gearbox of the type used on Jaguar's then-new XK120 (see entry). With 68 horsepower and the sub-one-ton curb weight, top speed was 86 mph.

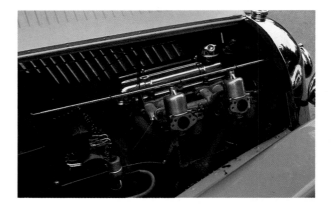

Styling, as ever, was strictly Thirties, with flowing separate fenders, vestigial running boards, a two-piece hood hinged "butterfly" style, and freestanding headlamps. The fuel tank was concealed, but the spare tire (two at first) was exposed in the time-honored way. Body styles initially comprised two- and four-seat roadsters and a two-seat convertible coupe, all on the same 96-inch wheelbase. The four-seater was like a 2+2, with rear riders sitting atop the back axle where the going was very lively indeed.

The basic Plus 4 design would continue for 19 years with occasional updates but, of course, no radical change. The Vanguard engine was replaced by the more powerful Triumph TR2 unit from 1954, and every time Triumph improved it, Morgan picked up the changes. Displacement thus eventually rose from 1991 to 2138 cc and horsepower from 90 to 100. The little Worchester-based firm even managed a pepped-up (by Lawrencetune) 115-bhp version. Disc front brakes were adopted in 1959, when center-lock wire wheels became an optional alternative to the standard steel disc rims.

Fifties styling changes saw the old flat-face radiator replaced by a raked grille (after 1950), a smoother tail, just one spare, and semi-faired headlamps. A four-seat convertible was briefly offered, there was a short run of fiberglass-bodied Plus 4 Plus coupes (see entry), and aluminum bodywork was available to special order.

Yet for all these apparent improvements, the mid-Sixties Plus 4 looked and acted just like the mid-Fifties model, which explains why demand steadily drained away. Also, the Triumph four had reached the end of its development road. This prompted a V-8 replacement, the Plus 8 (see entry), at the end of 1968, just as vintage in most ways but a lot more exciting.

Flat-face radiators were a Morgan hallmark through 1950, after which a cowled "fencer's mask" style took over. Thus, the only Plus 4 to have the traditional style was the first-year 1950 model (top). Cockpit (above center) was stark but functional, another marque tradition. Standard-Triumph four (above) powered all Plus 4s through '68, resided under Thirties-era butterfly-hinged hood. Twin spare tires (opposite) continued through the mid-Fifties, as on this rare two-seat convertible coupe, which could be used semi-open as shown.

SPECIFICATIONS

Engines: all Standard-Triumph ohv I-4; **1950-54:** 127.4 cid/ 2088 cc, 68 bhp (net) @ 4800 rpm, 108 lbs-ft @ 2000 rpm; **1954-62:** 121.5 cid/1991cc, 90 bhp (net) @ 4800 rpm, 117 lbs-ft @ 3000 rpm; **1962-68:** 130.5 cid/2138 cc, 100/115 bhp (net) @ 5000 rpm, 117 lbs-ft @ 3000 rpm

Transmission:	Moss 4-speed manual
Suspension, front:	sliding pillars, coil springs
Suspension, rear:	live axle, semi-elliptic leaf springs
Brakes:	front/rear drums (front discs from 1960)
Wheelbase (in.):	96.0
Weight (lbs):	1950-2100
Top speed (mph):	86-96
0-60 mph (sec):	13.3-17.9
Production:	**1950-54** 245 **1954-68** 3390 **115-bhp** 102

1955-1988 MORGAN 4/4

With its 1950 Plus 4, Morgan moved upmarket in size, weight, power, and price. The little British concern realized it might lose some potential customers, but was happy to live with the situation for awhile. By mid-decade, though, the Plus 4 had become more potent, and Morgan felt it should again field a lower-power car. This explains the revival of the 4/4 model, though it was completely from the car that carried that title in 1935-50.

In fact, the new 4/4 was closely related to the Plus 4. The main difference was engines, purchased from Ford Britain instead of Triumph. Gearboxes were now in unit with the engine, not separated as on the Plus 4, but the rock-hard ride, crude weather protection (including removable side curtains), vintage styling, and ultra-low driving position were all there.

The reborn 4/4 has been around for more than 30 years now and shows no signs of dying away. Like other Morgans, it's always had the same antique chassis design, body construction, and styling—a kind of technological time-warp that customers keep coming back for nevertheless. Engines have changed several times over the years, and the model has picked up most of the improvements made to the Plus 4 and Plus 8.

The original Series II 4/4 of 1955 arrived with the cowled radiator, semi-faired headlamps and sloped tail of the then-new Plus 4, none of which have changed since.

Morgan styling hasn't changed much since World War II, but modern instruments and steering wheel (above) mark this 4/4 as a post-Sixties model. Note traditional passenger tonneau (opposite), hood tie-down (below).

But unlike bigger-engine Moggies, body styles were limited to just a two-seat roadster at first. Thus, three decades of 4/4 evolution have centered almost entirely on engines and transmissions, ranging from a 36-horsepower/3-speed drivetrain to a 98-bhp/5-speed team, though standard front disc brakes were a notable Sixties "innovation."

Let's chart the changes. First up was the old 1172-cc Ford UK side-valve four. In 1959 came the new oversquare overhead-valve 997-cc "Kent" unit and 4-speed gearbox from the 105E Anglia. Ford spun off larger and powerful versions of this in the next few years, and Morgan always hurried to fit the best available. Capacity rose to 1340 cc in '62, to 1498 cc from 1963, and finally to 1599 cc and 88 bhp in 1968. (The last, incidentally, would be familiar to Americans in Ford's imported Cortinas and Capris of 1968-72 and early Pintos, not to mention Formula Ford racing.) By that time, the Plus 8 (see entry) had replaced the Plus 4, so the 4/4 was also offered as a four-seater.

The name changed too, to 4/4 1600, and specifications were frozen for the Seventies, when production averaged 6-8 a week. (The big automakers may have had problems, but "cottage industry" Morgan somehow muddled through that turbulent decade.) Top speed was up to 100 mph despite awful aerodynamics, and acceleration was brisk if hardly breathtaking.

The next turning point didn't occur until 1982, when Morgan actually offered a *choice* of engines, both 1.6-liter fours: the sohc Ford "CVH" four, European cousin to the American Escort unit, and the twincam Fiat unit familiar from the 124 sports cars, each mated to a 5-speed gearbox. Three years later, Morgan substituted a 2.0-liter derivative of the Fiat unit for a revived Plus 4, thus coming full circle.

Production continues, and seems likely to for some time to come. The total recently passed 6500 units, paltry by Detroit standards, let alone for 30-plus years. But then, Morgan builds old-fashioned cars the old-fashioned way, and things like that just won't be hurried.

SPECIFICATIONS

Engines: **1955-59:** British Ford L-4, 71.5 cid/1172 cc, 36-39 bhp (net) @ 4400 rpm, 52 lbs-ft @ 2500 rpm; **1959-61:** British Ford ohv I-4, 60.8 cid/997 cc, 54 bhp (net); **1962-63:** 81.8 cid/1340 cc, 60 bhp (net); **1963-68:** 91.4 cid/1498 cc, 78 bhp (net); **1968-82:** 97.6 cid/1599 cc, 88 bhp (net) @ 5400 rpm, 96 lbs-ft @ 3600 rpm; **1982-87:** British Ford ohc I-4, 97.4 cid/1596 cc, 96 bhp (DIN) @ 6000 rpm, 98 lbs-ft @ 4000 rpm; **1982-88:** Fiat dohc I-4, 96.7 cid/1585 cc, 98 bhp (DIN) @ 6000 rpm, 94 lbs-ft @ 4000 rpm

Transmissions:	3-speed manual to 1960, 4-speed manual to 1982, 5-speed manual since 1982
Suspension, front:	sliding pillars, coil springs
Suspension, rear:	live axle, semi-elliptic leaf springs
Brakes:	front discs/rear drums (front drums through 1959)
Wheelbase (in.):	96.0
Weight (lbs):	1570-1700
Top speed (mph):	92 (1.3-liter) to 102 (1.6 ohv)
0-60 mph (sec):	9.8 (1.6 ohv) 10.5 (1.3-liter)
Production:	6500 + (production continues at this writing)

1963-1966
MORGAN PLUS 4 PLUS

As Morgan carried on with its Thirties-style cars through the Forties and Fifties, customers kept buying and the press started complaining. The Morgan family—particularly Peter Morgan, who'd become managing director at the end of the Fifties—listened politely but resisted change—until 1963, when they suddenly unveiled a very different car, the Plus 4 Plus.

This was Malvern Link's first (and so far only) attempt at anything like modern styling, with a smooth "bubbletop" coupe body on an unaltered Plus 4 chassis. Its other novelty was that the body was made of fiberglass by an outside supplier instead of by Morgan using its traditional steel-over-wood construction.

Announcing the Plus 4 Plus was a laid-back grille of familiar Morgan design above a normal Plus 4 bumper. The windshield was curved and the roof fixed, both firsts for Morgan, as were glass door windows, which slid up and down via contact with the leading edge of the door frame. Seating remained strictly for two, but with a large cargo hold behind and a separate trunk with lid, two other Malvern Link "breakthroughs." The roof was almost bell-shaped and the lower body square-cut, with slab sides, large wheel cutouts, straight-through fenderlines, and a simple tail.

Triumph's 2.1-liter TR4 engine had recently been adopted for the Plus 4 roadsters, so the coupe had it too, along with front disc brakes and, on most examples, center-lock wire wheels. Modern it may have looked, but the Plus 4 Plus had the same very hard ride, limited suspension travel, and jackhammer back axle as other Morgans. So primitive is this chassis, in fact, that experienced Morgan owners are said to be able to run over a coin on the road and tell whether it's up heads or tails.

Though smart-looking if no head-turner, the Plus 4 Plus was too radical for marque loyalists and too crude for non-Morgan owners. Malvern intended to build 50, but completed just 26 before abandoning this experiment in modernity after only three years.

SPECIFICATIONS

Engine: Triumph ohv I-4, 130.5 cid/2138 cc, 100 bhp (net) @ 4600 rpm, 128 lbs-ft @ 3350 rpm

Transmission:	4-speed manual
Suspension, front:	sliding pillars, coil springs
Suspension, rear:	live axle, semi-elliptic leaf springs
Brakes:	front discs/rear drums
Wheelbase (in.):	96.0
Weight (lbs):	1820
Top speed (mph):	approx. 110
0-60 mph (sec):	approx. 12.5
Production:	26

Awkwardly named Plus 4 Plus saw Morgan flirt briefly with modern styling, coupe coachwork, and fiberglass construction. Lower-body lines were conventional enough, but bell-like roofline wasn't. Spare was enclosed by a trunk with external lid, three more items new to Morgan.

1968-1988 MORGAN PLUS 8

When Triumph's four-cylinder TR4/4A engine ran out of development potential, Morgan began seeking substitute power for its Plus 4 roadster, a change that took on greater urgency when the TR4A was dropped in favor of the six-cylinder TR5PI/TR250 in 1967. But as one door closed, another opened. Rover was just putting its new ohv V-8 into production, and speedily offered it to the Worcestershire company. The result was the Plus 8, the first high-performance Morgan, introduced in early 1968. It's still in production more than 20 years later and as popular as ever.

The Plus 8's 3.5-liter Rover engine was a license-built version of the all-aluminum General Motors unit developed for the Buick Special, Oldsmobile F-85, and Pontiac Tempest compacts of 1961, abandoned for cast-iron V-8s three years later and subsequently sold to Rover. Except for slightly different production methods and the use of British SU instead of American Rochester carburetors, it was nearly identical with the GM original. Although bulkier than the Triumph four, it was no heavier, so it worked performance wonders for both Rover and Morgan. In the Plus 8, it initially teamed with the separately mounted Moss gearbox from the Plus 4.

Engine transplant aside, the Plus 8 was basically a Plus 4 with numerous detail changes. Wheelbase was stretched two inches for a little extra underhood space to accommodate the V-8. For the same reason, chassis side-members were set further apart, bringing a slight increase in track to the benefit of handling, and cast-alloy road wheels replaced the Plus 4's less rigid center-lock wires. Most everything else was left alone: front disc brakes, live rear axle with very limited travel, the sliding-pillar ifs, rock-hard ride.

Styling changed little too. Fenders were widened to cover broader wheels and tires, but that was about it. Only a single two-seat roadster style was offered, with the usual wood-framed, steel-panelled bodywork, though some aluminum-panelled cars have also been produced. The cockpit bore signs of safety design, with non-protruding rocker switches instead of the traditional toggles and matte-black instrument bezels, replacing chrome.

With little extra weight and nearly 50 percent more horsepower, the Plus 8, not surprisingly, was much faster than four-cylinder Moggies—provided the hard-sprung, lightly loaded back end could get a grip. Assuming you avoided unwanted wheelspin, the Plus 8 could outdrag an E-Type Jaguar, though only up to about 90 mph. Awful aerodynamics worked against it at higher speeds, so maximum velocity was only about 125 mph.

What made this car so appealing, of course, was its unique combination of Morgan traditionalism and near supercar performance. "Traditionalism" here means vices often seen as virtues: rudimentary weather protection, jolting ride, minimal people and package space. So while the Plus 8 was as much a masochists' car as any Morgan, the newfound performance gave it even more of the "character" for which Britons—and Morgan fanciers—are willing to put up with shortcomings, that would cause ulcers in Tokyo or Detroit.

The Plus 8 has evolved but slowly since introduction. Track and fenders have been widened a couple of times, several wheel designs have been tried, and there have been four fairly significant running-gear changes. The first came in May 1972, when the old Moss gearbox was finally junked in favor of an all-synchro Rover 4-speed (from the SD1 fastback sedan, sold briefly in the U.S. as the 1980-model 3500) in unit with a slightly uprated engine. Early '77 brought yet another revised V-8 plus standard 5-speed gearbox, followed in the mid-Eighties by adoption of the new fuel-injected Rover Vitesse engine with 190 horsepower. Rack-and-pinion steering arrived at the same time.

Plus 8 production has always been low even for Morgan, with a good year seeing just 150-180 units (3-4 cars per week). This means that volume wouldn't exceed 2500 until the mid-Eighties. Only 484 examples were built with the old Moss gearbox. A few Plus 8s have come to the U.S., beginning in the late Seventies as propane conversions, more recently with the normal gasoline unit now that the Range Rover (which has the same basic engine) has been made emissions-legal.

How long will this rare, modern anachronism go on? Your guess is as good as ours, but let's hope it's a long, long time. The motoring world would be a lot duller without cars like this, and individualism deserves a place in these conformist times.

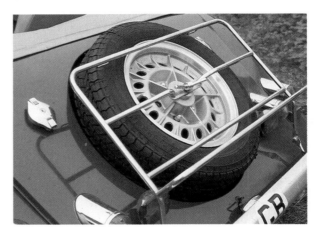

Cast-alloy wheels and a more ground-hugging stance enhanced by wider fenders and track dimensions are telltale hallmarks of the high-performance Plus 8, as on this circa-1982 example. "Safety" version of traditional Morgan dash (top) was used from the first.

SPECIFICATIONS

Engines: all Rover ohv V-8, 215 cid/3528 cc; **1967-72:** 143 bhp (DIN) @ 5000 rpm, 202 lbs-ft @ 2700 rpm; **1972-77:** 151 bhp (DIN) @ 5000 rpm, 210 lbs-ft @ 2700 rpm; **1977-85:** 155 bhp @ 5200 rpm, 198 lbs-ft @ 2500 rpm; **1985-88:** 190 bhp (DIN) @ 5200 rpm, 220 lbs-ft @ 4000 rpm

Transmissions:	4-speed manual through 1977, then 5-speed manual
Suspension, front:	sliding pillars, coil springs
Suspension, rear:	live axle, semi-elliptic leaf springs
Brakes:	front discs/rear drums
Wheelbase (in.):	98.0
Weight (lbs):	approx. 1900
Top speed (mph):	125
0-60 mph (sec):	5.6-6.5
Production:	2500+ (production continues at this writing)

1951-1954 NASH-HEALEY

Almost anything can happen on an ocean liner. Take the Nash-Healey. In late 1949, Nash-Kelvinator president George Mason was returning from Europe aboard the *Queen Elizabeth* when he bumped into famed British sports-car builder Donald Healey. Mason was looking to boost Nash's stolid image; Healey was seeking a supply of Cadillac V-8s for a new project. By the time they docked, the two had hatched a plan for an Anglo-American sports car built around Nash mechanicals.

The result appeared in prototype form barely nine months later at the 1950 London and Paris auto shows: a smooth two-seat roadster called Nash-Healey, with aluminum bodywork (supplied by Panelcraft) on Healey's usual chassis with its unusual trailing-link front suspension. Nash's conventional torque-tube drive took power from a modified Ambassador six with twin SU carburetors, hotter cam, and aluminum cylinder head with sealed-in intake manifold and higher (8.0:1) compression. Grille, headlamps, and other body hardware also came from the contemporary Ambassador Airflyte.

Production began at Healey's small Warwickshire works (newly expanded for the N-H) before the end of 1950, initially for Canada, Great Britain, and Europe as well as the U.S., though sales were soon restricted to America alone. The N-H made its home debut at the 1951 Chicago show in February priced at $4063, a third again as much as an Ambassador. It was well equipped though, with leather upholstery, adjustable steering wheel, whitewall tires, and 3-speed manual transmission with overdrive.

The N-H had already made an impressive competition debut. The very first one built, a special *monoposto*, finished 9th in the 1950 Mille Miglia, then 4th at the Le Mans 24 Hours in France (among 29 survivors from 66 starters). At Le Mans '51, the same car, rebodied as a coupe, finished 3rd in its class and 6th overall, ahead of two Ferraris.

But such doings didn't count for much in the States, and press reaction to the new transatlantic hybrid was guarded enthusiasm. Still, veteran tester Tom McCahill said he'd "never driven a sports car that handled better or gave the driver so much control," while *Motor Trend* reported that "the Nash-Healey rides far better than the average sports car without any apparent ill effect upon handling qualities."

Mason hadn't cared for the original slab-sided styling, but as he'd contracted Batista "Pinin" Farina to design the senior '52 Nashes, he asked the Italian master to freshen up the N-H too. What emerged was more visually pleasing, with a lower, one-piece windshield, pronounced rear fender bulges, and a plain oval grille encircling the headlamps. Steel bodywork replaced aluminum, yet careful engineering actually reduced curb weight. A larger Nash six with Carter carbs and 10 more bhp arrived during the year, and would continue through the end of production.

Alas, the 1952 price was hiked to $5858—over $1500 above Cadillac's Sixty Special—reflecting the huge shipping costs involved in N-H production. Nash first sent drivetrains and other components to Healey, which completed rolling chassis that then went to Italy, where Farina mounted the bodies and completed final assembly before shipment back to the States. Few automobiles have been so well travelled.

The N-H continued to impress at Le Mans in 1952. An open car based on the '51 coupe placed 3rd overall and 2nd in the Index of Performance. (An N-H also finished 4th in its class and 7th overall in that year's Mille Miglia.) Honoring the feat, a pretty new LeMans coupe on a six-inch longer wheelbase joined the open N-H for '53. The latter, now called a convertible, was up to $5908, while the coupe cost a towering $6399.

Only the LeMans returned for '54, little changed except for a three-piece wraparound rear window and a lower price ($5128). But Nash was in trouble by now, no longer able to afford the Healey's meager 100-unit annual volume. Accordingly, N-H production was halted in August. Exactly 506 were built, some say because Donald Healey had ordered only this many sets of front trailing links and had simply run out.

A Nash dealership was the last place enthusiasts expected to find a sports car, and this plus high price and Nash's fast-faltering fortunes ultimately did in the N-H. But not before a final triumph at Le Mans, where a '53 convertible managed 11th overall in the 24 Hours at a higher average speed than the 3rd-place '52 car. Not until the Sixties would an American-powered sports car do as well at the legendary French circuit.

*A pair of 1953 Nash-Healey convertibles (**opposite**) show off the Pinin Farina styling applied for '52. Le Mans coupe (**below**), also new for '53, honored N-H doings in the famed 24-hour race. Tuned Ambassador six (**bottom**) was named "Le Mans Dual Jetfire" in this application.*

SPECIFICATIONS

Engines: all ohv I-6; **1951:** 234.8 cid/3848 cc, 125 bhp @ 4000 rpm, 215 lbs-ft @ 2500 rpm; **1952-54:** 253 cid/4140 cc, 135 bhp @ 4000 rpm, 230 lbs-ft @ 2000 rpm

Transmission:	3-speed manual with overdrive
Suspension, front:	trailing lower links, coil springs
Suspension, rear:	live axle, coil springs
Brakes:	front/rear drums
Wheelbase (in.):	102.0
Weight (lbs):	2690 (1951)
Top speed (mph):	102-104
0-60 mph (sec):	11.5-12.0
Production:	**1951** 104 **1952** 150 **1953** 162 **1954** 90

1984-1988
NISSAN 300ZX

History probably won't be kind to the 300ZX. Though barely five years old at this writing, it's aged with surprising speed. That's understandable when you consider that though all-new, it was conceived as little more than a cautious update of the lumpy but loveable 280ZX—so conservative, in fact, that many motor-noters wondered aloud whether Nissan hadn't lost its way—or at the very least its nerve.

A Nissan executive has since confirmed such speculation, blaming former company chairman Takashi Ishihara for being interested only in "building 'nice' cars...in making money and fighting Toyota." As Nissan has discovered, playing it safe doesn't necessarily improve sales. It certainly doesn't produce innovative or even memorable cars like the original Datsun 240Z.

The name was Nissan on this third-generation Z-car, but journalists could hardly disguise their disappointment in the new model's evolutionary nature. "The same— only more so," said one buff magazine. "It all seems to add up to a change for the difference," said another. In dimensions, chassis specifications, even styling, the 300ZX was amazingly similar to the 280ZX.

Not that there weren't differences. One of the most important was what one writer termed the 300ZX's "heart of a gold": a new single-overhead-cam 3.0-liter V-6 (hence the model designation)—smoother, quieter, and significantly more powerful than the 280ZX's inline six. Styling was leaner and cleaner, with small gains in aerodynamic efficiency. Detail improvements included wider wheels and tires giving fractionally wider tracks, a new 4-speed automatic transmission option with electronic control and three shift modes (replacing the previous 3-speeder), a slightly roomier cockpit, marginally better outward vision, and even more creature comforts than the lush 280ZX possessed.

The 300 continued with the same three models as the last of the 280s: normally

aspirated two-seat and 2 + 2 coupes and turbocharged two-seater. The last came with a new suspension gimmick: electronically adjustable shock-absorber valving via a cockpit switch marked Soft, Normal, and Firm. As with Goldilocks though, only the middle setting was just right. Soft produced too much porpoising and cornering roll, Firm excessive ride jitters. The optional electronic instrumentation/leather-upholstery package returned with a new gimmick too: an instrument measuring g-force in acceleration and braking. It wasn't as silly as it sounds, for squat and dive were notably reduced from 280ZX levels, and Turbo acceleration was vivid, even if it didn't feel so.

In fact, refinement is one of the 300ZX's great strengths. We still fondly remember a short California blast in an '85 T-top Turbo from a mountain photography site to Newport Beach. The car really came into its own on empty two-lanes, powering through high-speed sweepers with great ease yet never pummeling itself—or us—with a rocky ride or excessive engine noise. Turbo lag was a nuisance at times but, overall, the V-6 felt and sounded as though it came from BMW, high praise indeed.

Fortunately, this basic mechanical goodness hasn't been compromised since, nor has the 300 changed all that much. The '85s were the first with a standard T-top, and Nissan wisely separated the flashdance instruments and hide upholstery options. Solid-roof non-turbo models with lower prices reappeared for 1986, along with fender flares, rocker skirts, body-color bumpers, new sports seats, and minor interior revisions for all models, plus 16-inch wheels for Turbos. Styling was slicked up for '87 with a smoother nose, new wheels, and full-width taillamps, while rear brakes were newly vented, the power steering pump recalibrated for better response, and the Turbo given a low-friction blower (though rated power was unchanged).

For all the fiddling, though, the 300ZX has been on steady sales slide since introduction, paralleling that of Nissan itself. The good news is that Nissan shows signs of returning to the kind of thinking that produced the original 240, which bodes well for the next-generation Z.

For 1988, a new "high-flow" blower and tighter compression (8.3:1 versus 7.8) added five horses to the Turbo, which also got a limited-slip differential as standard. Induction changes also upped the non-turbo unit by five bhp, and trim was shuffled for all models.

SPECIFICATIONS

Engines: all sohc V-6, 181 cid/2960 cc; **1984-87:** 160 bhp @ 5200 rpm, 174 lbs-ft @ 4000 rpm; **1984-87 Turbo:** 200 bhp @ 5200 rpm, 227 lbs-ft @ 3600 rpm; **1988:** 165 bhp (SAE net) @ 5200 rpm, 173 lbs-ft @ 4000 rpm; **1988 Turbo:** 205 bhp (SAE net) @ 5200 rpm, 227 lbs-ft @ 3600 rpm

Transmissions:	5-speed overdrive manual or 4-speed overdrive automatic
Suspension, front:	MacPherson struts, lower lateral arms, compliance struts, coil springs, anti-roll bar
Suspension, rear:	semi-trailing arms, coil springs, anti-roll bar
Brakes:	front/rear discs
Wheelbase (in.):	91.3 (2-seater), 99.2 (2 + 2)
Weight (lbs):	3050-3150
Top speed (mph):	125-130
0-60 mph (sec):	7.2-9.1
Production:	NA (production continues at this writing)

The name was Nissan, not Datsun, on the third-generation Z-car, represented here by the editors' test 1985 Turbo two-seater. Cabin (opposite top) was more luxurious and begadgeted than ever, but also roomy and versatile. Lift-off twin T-tops were standard equipment that year.

1968-1973
OPEL GT

Germany's Adam Opel AG in Russelsheim built sewing machines and bicycles before turning to cars. Like General Motors, which acquired Opel in the late Twenties, its stock-in-trade was practical, reliable family transportation at a fair price, and it maintained an enviable reputation for same right into the Sixties.

It was in that expansive decade that Opel, like most everyone else, responded to the growing demand for sportier, more youthful cars. One of its earliest and most visible moves in this direction appeared at the 1965 Frankfurt show, a slick one-off two-seat fastback coupe simply called Opel GT. At the time, Opel said it had no intention of selling copies, but the show car generated intense public interest that couldn't be ignored, and a production version appeared just three years later with the same name.

The Opel GT was styled chiefly by GM's Clare MacKichan, who'd played a big part in designing the 1955 Chevrolet before his tour of duty in the Russelsheim studios. This may explain the up-front similarity between the GT and the newly styled '68 Corvette, with the same low, sharply profiled nose, blade-type bumper, and hidden headlamps. The latter operated manually on the Opel, revolving up out of their recesses to give the car something of a frogeye look. Another difference was the pair of cooling slots between the Opel's lamps. From the cowl back, the production GT was broadly the same as the show car, with an abbreviated tail bearing four round lights (again echoing Corvette), plus shapely flanks and doors predictively cut up into the roof (with hidden drip rails). Somehow, though, the production styling wasn't as graceful, though you wouldn't know that if you hadn't seen the show car.

Beneath this sporty exterior were the chassis and running gear of Opel's humble

little Kadett in its beefier GT form. That meant transverse-leaf front suspension, front-disc/rear-drum brakes, ordinary worm-and-roller steering, and a coil-sprung live rear axle located by radius arms and Panhard rod. There were two engine choices, both ohv fours: 60-horsepower 1.1-liter and the new 1.9-liter cam-in-head unit developed for the mid-range Ascona sedan (which served as the basis for the 1969 Manta coupe series styled by Chuck Jordan, now GM Vice-President of Design but then an Opel colleague of MacKichan's). Only the 1.9 came to America and was favored in Europe, as the smaller engine had too little power. A telling comment on Opel's vision of GT buyers is that the 1.9 was offered with automatic transmission as an optional alternative to the standard 4-speed manual. No self-respecting enthusiast would have a "slushbox" in Sixties Europe—or in America, come to that.

Despite its fairly pedestrian mechanicals, the Opel GT was a winsome little car: stylish, obedient, practical, refined, and quick enough with the 1.9-liter engine and manual gearbox. It could even boast "custom" coachwork, as the independent French body builder Brissoneau & Lotz fashioned its unit body/chassis structure from Opel-supplied Kadett floorpans. The cockpit was unusually roomy and functional, with full instrumentation set in an impressive-looking dashboard. Like Corvettes since '63, the GT lacked an external trunklid, so luggage had to be loaded from inside, behind the seats, where it was concealed by a little curtain. Why a German car had to inherit this American inconvenience remains a mystery.

There's no mystery about GT popularity, which was high for a European sports coupe of the day. It has yet to develop much of a collector following, probably because it's an Opel, a make still not closely tied to high performance in most minds. But at least the GT got people to notice that Opels could be something other than dull people-movers.

The Kadett's 1972 redesign on the then-new T-car platform (later borrowed for the American Chevrolet Chevette) effectively ended GT production, and there was no direct replacement. Despite early rust problems, GTs are still running around in the care of loving owners with a taste for the unusual. A mini-Corvette was no bad thing to be 20 years ago, and it wouldn't be a bad idea now. How about it, GM?

SPECIFICATIONS

Engines: all ohv I-4; 65.8 cid/1078 cc, 60 bhp (DIN) @ 5200 rpm, 61 lbs-ft @ 3800 rpm; 115.8 cid/1897 cc, 90 bhp (DIN) @ 5100 rpm, 108 lbs-ft @ 2500 rpm

Transmissions:	4-speed manual or (1.9 only) 3-speed automatic
Suspension, front:	upper and lower A-arms, transverse leaf spring
Suspension, rear:	live axle, Panhard rod, radius arms, coil springs
Brakes:	front/rear discs
Wheelbase (in.):	95.7
Weight (lbs):	1865-2110
Top speed (mph):	115 (1.9-liter)
0-60 mph (sec):	12.0
Production:	1.1-liter NA 1.9-liter 103,373

*Pretty four-spoke steel wheels for 1973 was the Opel GT's only major styling change. Front was very Corvette-like, which was deliberate, but the rest of the car, including its roomy cockpit (**opposite top**), was quite individual.*

1984-1988
PONTIAC FIERO S/E & GT

Fiero means "very proud" in Italian, and that's how Pontiac feels about its car of that name. Why? Because Fiero is not just Detroit's first mid-engine production effort but only its second volume two-seater since the mid-Fifties Ford Thunderbird.

Yet within Pontiac itself, the Fiero had more significance as a moral victory: the sports car for which the division had fought for the better part of 20 years, an alternative to the Corvette from rival Chevrolet. Not that it started out as such. Rather, it was broached in 1978 as a "commuter car," a high-mileage mini to help General Motors meet the government's new corporate average fuel economy (CAFE) standards that took effect that year.

But the urge toward a full-fledged sports car was irresistible, especially since even the "commuter" concept envisioned a mid-engine/rear-drive layout with a transplanted power package from the forthcoming X-body front-drive compacts. In October 1978, GM president Elliott M. "Pete" Estes okayed the idea—perhaps for sentimental reasons: He himself had pleaded for a two-seat Pontiac as division chief back in the Sixties.

Unusually for a GM project, Fiero engineering development was assigned to an outside firm, Entech of Detroit, with Hulki Aldikacti as overall director. Basic styling evolved under Ron Hill in Advanced Design III, then finalized from April 1980 in Pontiac Exterior Studio II under John Schinella, who also came up with the Fiero name. Corporate cash-flow problems almost killed the project several times in 1980-82, but Aldikacti ultimately convinced management that the Fiero not only made financial sense for GM but was vital for injecting new life into a Pontiac image that had become confused and stale.

The result was a "corporate kit car," with a 2.5-liter four-cylinder engine mounted transversely behind the cockpit on an X-car engine cradle. The compacts also donated their 4-speed manual and optional 3-speed automatic transaxles, plus front suspension and brakes, used aft, of course. Up front were Chevy Chevette steering, suspension, and brakes. A major innovation was the fully driveable space-frame chassis structure to which various Enduraflex plastic (not fiberglass) body panels attached, construction that would make style changes easy, cheap, and fast. Only four color choices would be offered at any one time in the interest of quality control, which was claimed to represent a new Pontiac peak.

Arriving in base and spiffier S/E trim, Fiero received wide and mostly favorable press coverage. "Buff books" applauded the handsome styling, practical packaging, and overall roadability, but longed for a quieter, lighter car with more oomph, a 5-speed gearbox, smoother ride, and less twitchy cornering.

Pontiac responded. Fiero was named Pace Car for the 1984 Indy 500, which spawned replicas with a snarky new ground-hugging nose. This returned for 1985 on a new GT model powered by Chevy's fine port-injected V-6 (also from the X-cars) with 52-percent more power than the base four. Standard rear spoiler, "ground effects" body addenda, uprated Y99 suspension, and a mellow exhaust system enhanced the newcomer's mini-muscle-car aura.

Sans V-6, this package became the 1986 S/E model, followed at mid-season by a new GT with revised rear flanks and "flying buttress" fastback roofline. The promised 5-speed, a Getrag design built by GM under license, didn't arrive until June. Changes for 1987 were limited to a larger fuel tank (12 versus 10.2 gallons, answering a persistent complaint) and additional minor trim and equipment revisions.

The sporty twosome became even more so for 1988 as Fiero finally got its own suspension. Though geometry stayed broadly the same, the new components made handling tighter, cornering more predictable and fun. A new Formula package option with GT-style appearance and chassis specs arrived to spice up the S/E notchback, and an improved linkage made 5-speed shifting a genuine pleasure in V-6 models. Alas, steering remained manual—and heavy at low speeds—though Pontiac hinted that power assist was in the offing.

The Fiero will no doubt continue to mature. It's already evolved into base-model "commuters" as originally envisioned, but the S/E and GT are the ones to have: genuine sports machines that are downright exciting with the right options. They're cars to do any enthusiast proud.

SPECIFICATIONS

Engines: all ohv V-6, 173 cid/2837 cc; **1984-86:** 140 bhp @ 5200 rpm, 170 lbs-ft @ 3600 rpm; **1987-88:** 135 bhp @ 4400 rpm, 165 lbs-ft @ 3600 rpm

Transmissions:	4/5-speed manual or 3-speed automatic (in rear transaxle)
Suspension, front:	upper and lower A-arms, coil springs, anti-roll bar
Suspension, rear:	Chapman struts, lower A-arms, tie rods, coil springs
Brakes:	front/rear discs
Wheelbase (in.):	93.4
Weight (lbs):	2750-2860
Top speed (mph):	105-120
0-60 mph (sec):	7.7-8.5

Production: **1984 SE** 67,671 (incl. 6000 Pace Car replicas); **1985 SE** 24,734 **1985 GT** 22,534 **1986 SE** 22,231 **1986 GT** 12,786 **1987 SE** 3629 **GT** 15,967

*This page, above: A 1987 S/E shows the Fiero's original notchback styling. **Opposite top:** New-for-'88 Formula bears rear wing, plus the smoother nose applied to all Fieros. **Opposite bottom:** Tunnel-fastback GT debuted at mid-'86. Here, the 1988 version. **This page, top:** Driver sits low, center tunnel rides high in wide Fiero cockpit.*

1950-1955
PORSCHE 356

Ferdinand Porsche, like Henry Ford, was around at the automobile's birth and dreamed of cars for the common man. As an engineer at Austro-Daimler, Daimler-Benz, NSU, and Auto Union, he won renown for inventiveness—not to mention all-conquering competition cars—then went on to design what everyone thought impossible and Adolph Hitler demanded: a cheap "people's car."

After an unwarranted two-year imprisonment in France, Porsche returned to Gmünd in his native Austria. There, with son Ferry, this artistic genius would create his last and greatest work: the first of the great sports cars to bear his name.

Designated Type 356, the first Porsche was based on the prewar Type 114 F-Wagen, conceived as a sporting evolution of the bug-shaped *Volkswagen*. The original prototype, a spartan mid-engine roadster, was built in 1947, then reconfigured as a cabriolet with VW-style rear engine (sited behind the rear-wheel centerline); a beetle-backed coupe companion was also developed. Production was underway in Gmünd by 1948, when Porsche Konstruktionen GmbH completed just four of these 356/2 cars, followed by 25 in '49 and 18 in 1950. All were handbuilt. Though painfully halting, it was the start of a modern dynasty that Ferdinand Porsche barely lived to see. Following a stroke in November 1950, just two months after his 75th birthday, he died in January 1951.

In 1949, Porsche had begun moving operations to Zuffenhausen, a suburb of Stuttgart in the newly created nation of West Germany, and it was here that serious production began. The first German-built cars were delivered in April 1950, by which time the company name had changed to Dr. -Ing. h.c. F. Porsche KG, indicating Porsche's honorary engineering doctorate (h.c. for the Latin *honorus causa*) and that the firm was incorporated (KG denoting limited partnership). Production briefly overlapped between Gmünd and Stuttgart during 1950.

Early 356s made heavy use of modified Volkswagen components: engine, transmission, suspension, brakes, wheels, and steering. This was a deliberate decision, and sensible. Dr. Porsche had designed the VW, and using proprietary parts would hold down costs.

As on the "Type 1" VW, the 356 employed unit construction, with the floorpan welded to a boxed, pressed-steel chassis. Suspension was fully independent via parallel trailing arms on each side in front and rear swing axles with single, flexible trailing arms for longitudinal location. Springing was by transverse torsion bars. Shock absorbers were hydraulic, tubular fore, lever-action aft. Gmünd cars had cable-operated mechanical brakes, but VW's new 1950 hydraulic brakes were fitted to Stuttgart cars.

Power was provided by a Porsche-modified Volkswagen air-cooled flat four with special heads and 1131-cc displacement, though some Gmünd cars had only 1086 cc to qualify for 1100-cc-class racing. In both, drive went through a single dry-plate clutch and VW non-synchromesh 4-speed transaxle.

With the move to Stuttgart, the 356/2 became the 356 and received cleaner styling by Erwin Komenda. The windshield was larger but still two-piece, flat to within four inches of the outboard ends, then curved to meet the A-posts. Wing vents were removed, the beltline raised, an oil temperature gauge added, and the clock moved from over the glovebox to beside the speedometer. There was still no gas gauge, Porsche relying on VW's reserve-tank arrangement and a wooden measuring stick. The engine gained different Solex carbs.

By 1951, the VW brakes had been ousted for twin-leading-shoe Lockheed-type drums from Ate, and tube shocks took over for the outmoded lever-action rear dampers. Appearing at the same time was a bored-out 1286-cc engine option, with aluminum cylinder liners (replacing cast iron) and a rousing four extra horsepower.

At the Frankfurt show in October 1951, Porsche announced a new 1488-cc engine with roller-bearing rod journals. A one-piece windshield with two flat sections and vertical center crease was adopted, brakes were increased from 230- to 280-mm diameter and from 30 to 40 mm in width, and a new transmission arrived with the famous Porsche-patented split-ring synchromesh on all gears.

The following year, Porsche built some 20 "America" roadsters, lightweight 1500-cc specials intended mainly for racing. This was at the behest of U.S. import-car baron Max Hoffman, who sold most of them. Also in 1952, the now-familiar Porsche emblem was created. It bore the Stuttgart coat of arms with a rampant black horse on a yellow shield, representing an old part of the city where a stud farm had once been (*Stuotgarten*); surrounding this were the colors and six staghorns from the crest of the state of Baden-Württemberg.

After a quiet '53, Porsche had a busy 1954. Engine choices during the year

SPECIFICATIONS

Engines: all ohv flat four; **1100** (1950-54): 66.7 cid/1086 cc, 40 bhp (DIN) @ 4200 rpm (46 bhp SAE), 50 lbs-ft @ 2800 rpm; **1300** (1951-54): 78.7 cid/1286 cc, 44 bhp (DIN) @ 4200 rpm (50 bhp SAE), 58 lbs-ft @ 2500 rpm; **1500** (1951-52): 90.6 cid/1488 cc, 60 bhp (DIN) @ 5000 rpm (70 bhp SAE), 73 lbs-ft @ 2800 rpm; **1500** (1952-55): 90.6 cid/1488 cc, 55 bhp (DIN) @ 4400 rpm (64 bhp SAE), 76 lbs-ft @ 2800 rpm; **1500 Super** (1952-55): 90.6 cid/1488 cc, 70 bhp (DIN) @ 5000 rpm (82 bhp SAE), 77 lbs-ft @ 3600 rpm; **1300 Super** (1953-55): 78.7 cid/1286 cc, 60 bhp (DIN) @ 5500 rpm (70 bhp SAE), 63 lbs-ft @ 3600 rpm

Transmissions:	4-speed manual; VW non-synchromesh (1950-52), Porsche all-synchromesh (1952-55) (all in rear transaxle)
Suspension, front:	twin parallel trailing arms, transverse laminated torsion bars, anti-roll bar (1954-55)
Suspension, rear:	swing axles, transverse torsion bars
Brakes:	front/rear drum
Wheelbase (in.):	82.7
Weight (lbs):	1675-1830
Top speed (mph):	95-111
0-60 mph (sec):	10.3-15.4

Production: 1950 coupe 410 **1951 coupe** 170 **cabrio** 999 **1952 coupe** 1057 **cabrio** 240 **1953 coupe** 1547 **cabrio** 394 **1954 coupe** 1363 **cabrio** 328 **Speedster** 200 **1955 coupe** 1992 cabrio 278 **Speedster** 1700 (all calendar year production; 1955 includes 356A)

numbered six—1100, 1300, 1300S (Super), 1300A, 1500 and 1500S. Only the last two were sold in America. The 5000th Porsche was completed on March 15.

September 1954 saw introduction of another Max Hoffman idea, the sporty, loveable Speedster, a detrimmed cabriolet with cut-down one-piece windshield, priced at $2995 (1500) or $3495 (1500S). Sales were initially restricted to the States. Like other early 356s, it rolled on 16-inch wheels.

Changes for '55 were mainly mechanical. A three-piece 4.5-liter aluminum crankcase replaced a two-piece, 3.5-liter magnesium one. Most internal engine dimensions stayed the same, but there were fewer interchangeable parts as Porsche moved further from dependency on VW components. U.S. models were called Continental this year—and this year only, because Lincoln "owned" the name and was bringing out its new Continental Mark II.

Reutter supplied most early 356 bodies, though Heuer built some cabriolets and Gläser did the 1952 America models. Naturally, Porsche production increased as body supplies improved, eventually reaching 12 cars a day and 2952 units for the 1955 model run.

The bargain-priced 356 Speedster bowed in late 1954 at the behest of U.S. distributor Max Hoffman. It featured a cut-down windshield (below) and spartan interior (opposite).

1955-1959 PORSCHE 356A

It would become traditional for Porsche to introduce its really new models at the Frankfurt show in September (held only in odd-numbered years). The 1955 exhibition brought the first variation on the 356 theme. Logically designated 356A, it went into production a few weeks later for model year 1956.

As in '55 there were coupe, cabriolet, and Speedster, with bodies supplied exclusively by Reutter in Stuttgart. Styling was subtly altered. Most obvious were a one-piece curved windshield and rocker rub rails on coupes and cabrios, but all 356As hunkered closer to the road on 15 × 4.5-inch wheels, replacing 16 × 3.25-inch rims.

European buyers now had five engine choices: 1300, 1300 Super, 1600, 1600S, and 1500GS. Only the last three went to America. All were still air-cooled flat fours, and all but the 1500GS retained overhead valves actuated by pushrods and rocker arms. The new 1.6-liter had been created simply by fitting larger cylinder barrels to the previous 1500, thus enlarging bore. All body styles were available with all engines except that there was no 1300 Speedster.

The 1500GS unit was a detuned version of the twincam 550 Spyder engine introduced in Porsche's 1954 sports-racing cars. It was dubbed "Carrera" in honor of the famed Mexican Road Race (*Carrera Panamericana*) where Porsche had competed with distinction in 1953-54. Featured were a Hirth built-up crankshaft with one-piece connecting rods, roller bearings for both mains and rods, 8.7:1 compression, and dry-sump lubrication. Output was an impressive 100 DIN horsepower (115 SAE gross).

Other changes, major and minor, marked the 356A. Suspension was softened a bit by removing leaves from the laminated torsion bars in front and at the rear by lengthening the bars (from 21.8 to 24.7 inches) and reducing their diameter (by 1 mm, to 24). This together with the lower-profile wheels helped to improve roadholding. Inside was a new flat-face dash with padded top, ousting the previous center-bulge all-metal panel, with a large tachometer flanked by speedometer (on the left) and a combined fuel level/oil temperature gauge. A floor lowered 1.5 inches afforded better legroom and easier entry/exit, the ignition switch gained a starter detent, and more sound insulation material was applied at strategic points.

The '57 models were initially unchanged but received some detail refinements in the spring of that year. The speedometer exchanged places with the combination gauge, horizontal teardrop taillights substituted for the previous four round units, and the license-plate/backup-lamp bar moved from above to below the plate.

Evolutionary changes were again seen in '58. Vent wings appeared in cabriolet doors, and coupes sprouted windwings on the outside of their window frames. Exhaust tips on all but Carrera models now poked through the lower part of the vertical bumper guards, and a double-bow front bumper overrider replaced the former single-bow item. Speedster and cabriolet tops got larger rear windows, and the Speedster was offered with a lift-off fiberglass top as a factory option (made by Brendel in Germany for Europe, Glasspar in California for America).

On the mechanical front, the 1300 engines were dropped, the 1600 N and S engines reverted to plain bearings, and cast-iron cylinders returned on the 1600 Normal to reduce both cost and noise for what was basically a touring Porsche. The Carrera unit grew to 1588 cc and also got plain bearings. (Some 1500 Carreras were still being built too, some with plain bearings and some with the rollers.) Carburetors were now Zenith NDIX instruments, a Hausserman diaphragm clutch replaced the coil-spring Fitchel & Sachs unit, and the old worm-and-peg VW steering gave way to a Ross-type mechanism by ZF.

In August 1958, Porsche got a head start on model year '59 by introducing the Speedster D to replace the original Speedster. This had a taller, chrome-framed windshield and a top somewhere between the original low, simple design and the cabrio's deluxe padded top. The Speedster's bodyside chrome strip was retained, giving the D some of its visual character, but the higher top was far more practical. Bodies were supplied by Drauz, hence the "D," though the car was renamed Convertible D before its public introduction. Reutter supplied coupe and cabriolet bodies as before.

These are only the highlights of the 356A's evolution. Porsche continuously improved the car through roughly four years of production, not always waiting for the next model year to do so. With each improvement, Porsche handling and driveability gained new respect in the eyes of owners and the automotive press.

SPECIFICATIONS

Engines: ohv flat four—**1300** (1955-57): 78.7 cid/1290 cc, 44 bhp (DIN) @ 4200 rpm (50 bhp SAE); **1300 Super:** 60 bhp (DIN) @ 5500 rpm (71 bhp SAE); **1600** (1955-59): 96.5 cid/1582 cc, 60 bhp (DIN) @ 4500 rpm (70 bhp SAE); **1600 Super:** 75 bhp (DIN) @ 5000 rpm (88 bhp SAE); dohc flat four—**1500GS/GT Carrera** (1955-57): 90.6 cid/1498 cc, 100/110 bhp (DIN) @ 6200 rpm, 85/88 lbs-ft @ 5200 rpm; **1600GS/GT Carrera** (1958-59): 96.9 cid/1588 cc, 105/110 bhp (DIN) @ 6500 rpm, 86 lbs-ft @ 5000 rpm

Transmission:	4-speed manual (in rear transaxle)
Suspension, front:	twin parallel trailing arms, transverse laminated torsion bars, anti-roll bar
Suspension, rear:	swing axles, transverse torsion bars
Brakes:	front/rear drum
Wheelbase (in.):	82.7
Weight (lbs):	1800-2000
Top speed (mph):	98-125
0-60 mph (sec):	10.5-14.4

Production: **1955 coupe** 390 **cabrio** 69 **Speedster** 100 **1956 coupe** 2921 **cabrio** 430 **Speedster** 850 **1957 coupe** 3283 **cabrio** 542 **Speedster** 1416 **1958 coupe** 3670 **cabrio** 1382 **Speedster** 556 **Convertible D** 386 **1959 coupe** 2743 **cabrio** 944 **Convertible D** 944

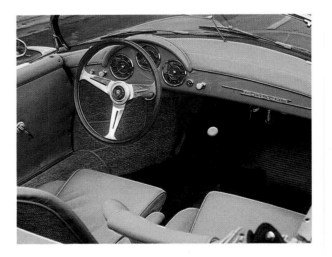

Above and opposite top: Sporty Speedster continued in the 356A series, still cheaper than other Porsches and with its own appearance and dash design. Opposite bottom: A 1958 European 356A coupe sans U.S. bumper overriders.

1960-1965
PORSCHE 356B/356C

Visitors to the 1959 Frankfurt show saw the best-looking Porsche yet: the new 1960-model 356B. Higher bumpers (raised 3.75 inches front, 4.1 inches rear) with large vertical guards appeared, primarily to improve protection of the relatively delicate body, but they also improved looks. Headlights were raised, too, so that fenderlines ran almost straight back from the tops of the chrome rims. Parking lamps were set below, outboard of small grilles covering the horns. Air intakes, for front-brake cooling, were cut in below the bumper. The Convertible D was renamed Roadster.

Inside the 356Bs, rear seats were lowered to increase headroom, and the folding seatback, a feature since the early 356 days, was split so that three persons and some luggage could be carried inside. All models acquired door vent windows, and defroster vents were added below the rear window.

Underneath, brake drums with circumferential fins were replaced by new cast-aluminum drums with 72 radial fins, plus cast-iron liners held in by the Alfin process. Engines were almost unchanged, but the new 1600 Super 90 unit (named for its rated DIN horsepower) announced at Frankfurt didn't appear in production until March 1960.

For 1961, Koni shock absorbers were installed as standard equipment on 1600S and Super 90 models, and rear roll stiffness was reduced by the use of 1-mm-smaller torsion bars (now 23 mm in diameter). A transverse leaf spring, called a "camber compensator," was standard for S-90s, optional elsewhere.

Models and coachbuilders began proliferating. Bodies for the Drauz-built Roadster, which was built into the early part of model year '62, were now also supplied by D'Ieteren Frères, and Karmann in Osnabrück began production of a new fixed-roof notchback coupe looking much like the cabriolet with optional lift-off top in place.

Reutter, meantime, supplied lightweight GT coupes with Carrera-tune engines for 1960-61. These were the first Porsches with 12-volt electrical systems.

The 356Bs entered model year '62 with subtle body changes: a flatter front "trunklid," twin air-intake grilles in the rear engine lid, an external gas filler (hidden under a flap in the right front fender), and larger rear windows for coupes. Spring brought the last and fastest of the 356 Carreras: the new 2.0-liter Carrera 2. Appropriate for the hottest roadgoing Porsche ever, it had all-disc brakes of the same Porsche design as used on the firm's single-seat Formula 1 and Formula 2 racers.

With little change, the 356B continued to July 1963, when its successor appeared. Visually, the 356C was a twin to the B save for flat-face hubcaps covering standard disc brakes all-round. Porsche had been experimenting with two disc systems since 1958: its own (as on the Carrera 2) and a Dunlop design made by Ate (the Alfred Teves company). The choice came down to economics and logic. Using its own system would make Porsche unique among the world's automakers; the Dunlop system meant reduced cost and increased parts availability, so it was the one selected.

Engines were down to three: Carrera 2, 1600C, and 1600SC, the last two respectively derived from the 1600S and Super 90, with positive crankcase ventilation for the U.S. market. All were available in both coupe and cabriolet, the only body styles remaining. A corporate move with lasting implications for Porsche design and construction occurred in 1963, when Porsche absorbed Reutter and spun off a seatmaking division that has since become the world-famous Recaro company (from *Reutter Carozzerie*).

After more than 15 years and 76,303 units, the 356-Series was honorably retired in September 1965. Porsche had come a long way with this basic car since the struggling days in Gmünd, now internationally respected as a builder of fast, durable, superbly engineered performance machines at home, on road, and track alike. Prosperity and rapid corporate growth naturally accompanied this growing renown. Porsche had needed four years to build its first 5000 cars (April 1950 to March 1954). With the 356B, it exceeded that figure in each calendar year.

But, of course, there were even better days ahead. With the new six-cylinder 911, Porsche would succeed in ways its founding father could never have imagined.

Opposite: This 356B cabriolet displays the raised headlamps, modified sheetmetal, and higher, sturdier front bumper that set the 1960 models apart from earlier Porches. This page: Flat-face hubcaps and larger coupe windows were in place for the 356C.

SPECIFICATIONS

Engines: ohv flat four, 96.5 cid/1582 cc—**1600** (1960-63): 60 bhp (DIN) @ 4500 rpm (70 bhp SAE), 78 lbs-ft @ 2800 rpm; **1600 Super:** 75 bhp (DIN) @ 5000 rpm (88 bhp SAE), 83 lbs-ft @ 3700 rpm; **1600 Super 90:** 90 bhp (DIN) @ 5500 rpm (102 bhp SAE), 86 lbs-ft @ 4300 rpm; **1600** (1963-65): 75 bhp (DIN) @ 5200 rpm (88 bhp SAE), 88 lbs-ft @ 3600 rpm; **1600 Super:** 95 bhp (DIN) @ 5800 rpm (105 bhp SAE), 88 lbs-ft @ 4200 rpm; **Carrera 2** (1961-64): dohc flat four, 120 cid/1966 cc, 130 bhp (DIN) @ 6200 rpm, 116 lbs-ft @ 4600 rpm

Transmission:	4-speed manual (in rear transaxle)
Suspension, front:	twin parallel trailing arms, transverse laminated torsion bars, anti-roll bar
Suspension, rear:	swing axles, transverse torsion bars
Brakes:	front/rear drums (356B), front/rear discs (356C, Carrera 2)
Wheelbase (in.):	82.7
Weight (lbs):	1940-2250
Top speed (mph):	110-130
0-60 mph (sec):	9.2-14.5

Production: 356B—**1959 coupe** 1320 **cabrio** 468 **Roadster** 561 **1960 coupe** 4413 **cabrio** 1617 **Roadster** 1529 **1961 coupe** 4176 **cabrio** 3257 **Roadster** 563 **1962 coupe** 4092 **cabrio** 1667 **hardtop** 2171 **1963 coupe** 2197 **cabrio** 932 **hardtop** 2229 **356C**—**1963 coupe** 2104 **cabrio** 832 **hardtop** 1738 **1964 coupe** 3823 **cabrio** 1745 **hardtop** 4744 **1965 coupe** 3 **cabrio** 588 **hardtop** 1097 (figures incl. **Carrera 2**—**356B** 1810 **356C** 2134)

1963-1964
PORSCHE 904 GTS

After two years of somewhat less-than-spectacular results in GT racing, Porsche fielded a new contender. Called 904 GTS, it was a surprise in many ways.

For example, it retained the 2.0-liter quadcam Carrera four even though the roadgoing 901 (later, 911) had just been introduced with a new air-cooled flat six, though it did use the new 901 5-speed transaxle. Moreover, the 904 body was fiberglass, not metal, bonded to a sturdy boxed-rail chassis and built by Heinkel, a firm better known for aircraft. All-coil suspension was another departure, borrowed from Porsche's eight-cylinder Formula 1 car, with wishbones in front and reversed wishbones and parallel trailing arms at the rear. Finally, the 904 was a true mid-engine car, its power pack sited behind the cockpit, ahead of the rear-wheel centerline.

Work on the 904 began in 1962, when a wood body buck was built to a design by Ferdinand "Butzi" Porsche, grandson of the company founder (he also designed the 901/911). This was sent to Heinkel in February 1963, which returned the first finished body the following November. For a purpose-built machine, Butzi's styling was quite pretty: smooth, shapely, and distinctive.

To speed pit stops, bodywork behind the doors was a one-piece assembly that lifted up on rear hinges, and the engine could be easily removed for more serious servicing. This convenience didn't extend to body repairs, however, as Porsche found it extremely difficult to fix broken panels quickly.

FIA rules at the time required 100 units to qualify a car for GT-class racing, and Porsche completed the requisite number of 904s by April 1964. The first six were retained as factory team cars and were eventually seen with four-, six-, and eight-cylinder engines. The first dozen or so customer cars went to the U.S., where the racing season started earlier than Europe's. Unfortunately, only these 100 would be built. All were quickly snapped up, but a number of buyers were left wanting, as orders far exceeded cars.

The 904 emerged heavier and slightly less aerodynamic than expected, but when factory pilot Herbert Linge drove an early one around the Nürburgring in 9 minutes, 30 seconds, it looked like a sure winner. And though the weight reduced the 904's effectiveness in short-distance "sprint" contests, it proved no great handicap in longer races on less-than-perfect surfaces. A 904 might not outrun competitors, but it could almost certainly outlast them.

A bit pudgy it may have been, but the GTS was the first Carrera with a sub-10 pounds/bhp power-to-weight ratio, about 8 lbs/bhp. It could thus do 0-60 mph in less than six seconds yet would run at 160 mph in fifth gear—all day long if necessary. At $7500, it was a real racing bargain. The quadcam Carrera four was 10 years old by now but at its development peak, while the mid-engine layout made for superb handling. All-disc brakes rounded out a *very* competitive track performer.

Racing success, both factory and private, came quickly for the 904, with longer events the predictable forté of this almost too-sturdy machine. Clutch problems prevented a finish at Sebring 1964, the car's debut outing, but things went better a month later when 904s ran 1st and 3rd in the Targa Florio, followed by a 3rd overall in the Nürburgring 1000 Kilometers. Five cars were entered for that year's Le Mans enduro, and all finished in the top 12, the highest placing 7th overall. In the Tour de France, 904s ran 3rd through 6th (behind a brace of Ferrari GTOs) and were 1st and 2nd on handicap. For the 1965 Monte Carlo Rally, Porsche acquired the services of ace Mercedes driver Eugen Bohringer, who drove his 904 to 2nd overall in one of the snowiest Montes ever, one of 22 to finish out of 237 starters.

Porsche planned a roadgoing 904, and a few were built with slightly milder engine tuning. Even so, the Carrera four didn't like stop-and-go traffic, and the car as a whole wasn't as successful for touring as it was in racing. Most of those now used on the road have been retrofitted with 911 engines, but that does nothing for non-existent sound insulation nor a cockpit that was never designed for relaxed highway cruising.

Nevertheless, the 904 remains one of the most desirable Porsches ever built. Besides excellent performance, pretty styling, and a great competition record, it has historic significance as the Porsche that closed the book on the four-cylinder/quadcam decade.

SPECIFICATIONS

Engine: dohc flat four, 119.9 cid/1966 cc, 155/180 bhp (DIN) @ 6900/7800 rpm (road/race tune), 133/144 lbs-ft @ 4800/5000 rpm

Transmission:	5-speed manual (in rear transaxle)
Suspension, front:	unequal-length A-arms, coil springs, anti-roll bar
Suspension, rear:	four links with radius arms, coil springs, anti-roll bar
Brakes:	front/rear discs
Wheelbase (in.):	90.6
Weight (lbs):	1430
Top speed (mph):	150-160
0-60 mph (sec):	5.3-6.4
Production:	100

The mid-engine Type 904 Carrera GTS was pretty for a competition car and hasn't dated much in 25 years. Young "Butzi" Porsche, who styled the 911 prototype, designed the body, which was executed in fiberglass.

1965-1969/1976
PORSCHE 912/912E

The 911 ushered in a new era of Porsche luxury, high performance and, inevitably, higher prices. The cheapest 911 cost some $5500 in West Germany, about $1500 more than a comparable 356SC—quite a difference. Zuffenhausen managers were convinced they'd sell all the 911s they could build, but feared losing 356 customers for whom a 911 was simply out of reach. Their answer to the problem was quick, direct, and logical: install the old pushrod four in the new platform to produce a less costly model. The result, called 912, became available for Europe in April 1965 but didn't reach America until September, when 356 production stopped.

Lifting a 912's engine lid revealed the familiar 1582-cc flat four, taken almost directly from the 356SC. It was slightly detuned, from 95 to 90 horsepower, but provided a bit better performance thanks to the 911's superior aerodynamics—specifically, a top speed of 115 mph and 0-60 mph acceleration of just over 11.5 seconds. Like its big-engine brother, 912 employed 12-volt electrics and offered a choice of 4- and 5-speed transmissions, the latter with the racing-style gear pattern that put first on the dogleg to the lower left.

Inside, the 912 was more 356C than 911, so whether it qualified as "spartan" depended on your frame of reference. The 911's teakwood dash appliqué was deleted, and instead of five instrument dials there were three: centrally placed tachometer and flanking speedometer and fuel/oil gauge, again lifted from the 356C. Safety and some convenience features were shared with the 911 though, including three-speed wipers, windshield washers, rear-window defroster, backup light, and reclining seats. As on the 911, a Webasto auxiliary gasoline heater was offered during 1965 and, in September that year, the Targa body style.

The 912 may have had less oomph than the 911 (which had 40 horsepower more) but its smaller, lighter engine meant more even weight distribution (44/56 percent

At a glance, it was tough to tell a four-cylinder 912 from the costlier, more potent six-cylinder 911—which, of course, was the whole point. Five-dial 911 gauge set (above) and lack of side-marker lights identifies this U.S. version as a '67 model.

front rear versus 41/59). Of course, much lower price was its main attraction. Interestingly, *Car and Driver* magazine listed the 5-speed model at $4696 in its October 1965 issue, while *The Autocar* showed about $6500 (at then-current exchange rates), this at a time when the U.S. 911 was selling for about $6300. As usual, American buyers fared better than British ones.

Improvements came steadily, in typical Porsche fashion, as the 912 picked up most running changes made to each year's 911s, a production economy that also benefitted buyers. Thus, the 912 gained the 911's new-for-'67 safety door locks and also acquired its five-dial instrumentation. For 1969, both 911 and 912 shared a 2.25-inch longer wheelbase (achieved by lengthening the rear semi-trailing arms) and mildly modified rear flanks. By 1969, the 912's base price had swelled to more than $5000, though that was still reasonable and only topped $6000 with all the extras. At year's end, the junior Porsche was phased out in favor of the new mid-engine "people's Porsche," the VW-powered 914 (see entry), which was cheaper still.

But the 914 provided a sales disappointment, and by late 1975, Porsche was regrouping around the new front-engine 924, due for '77. To fill the gap, the 912 was revived for a year as the 912E (for *Einspritzung*, fuel injection). It still looked a lot like the 911, sharing the smooth integrated bumpers adopted there for '74. This time, though, its flat-four engine wasn't a Porsche but a VW unit, the same 1971-cc pushrod affair from the last 914s (originally inherited from VW's abortive 411 sedan). Horsepower remained at 90 but, somehow, the car had gained an extra 400 pounds since '69. Nevertheless, the VW engine's superior torque and a standard 5-speed combined for small gains in acceleration and top speed.

As for price, the 912E sold for nearly $11,000 in U.S. trim, a considerable jump over the 914. But that was still much less than a 911, which had also been climbing the ladder, and the 912E had the same lovely Butzi Porsche body, fine handling, great comfort, and superb workmanship, including 1976's new fully galvanized structure.

Despite the fuel injection's tendency to misbehave in extreme cold, the 912E sold relatively well during its one-year encore. Today it's regarded by Porsche enthusiasts as one of the more desirable four-cylinder models.

SPECIFICATIONS

Engines: all ohv flat four; **1965-69:** 96.5 cid/1582 cc, 90 bhp (DIN) @ 5800 rpm (102 bhp SAE), 87 lbs-ft @ 3500 rpm; **1976:** 120.2 cid/1971 cc, 90 bhp (DIN) @ 4900 rpm (86 bhp SAE net), 98 lbs-ft @ 4000 rpm

Transmissions:	4-speed manual, 5-speed manual (1966-69, 1976) (in rear transaxle)
Suspension, front:	MacPherson struts, lower A-arms, longitudinal torsion bars, anti-roll bar
Suspension, rear:	semi-trailing arms, transverse torsion bars
Brakes:	front/rear discs
Wheelbase (in.):	87.1 (1965-68), 89.3 (1969), 89.4 (1976)
Weight (lbs):	2140-2560
Top speed (mph):	115-119
0-60 mph (sec):	11.3-11.6

Production: **1965** 6440 **1966** 8700 **1967** 3239 **1968** 11,921 (incl. 1969 models) **1976** 2099

1969-1973 PORSCHE 911

Porsche's 911 had gotten off to a fine start in its original A-Series form. The new B-Series introduced for 1969 was even better, differing in subtle but significant ways.

They started with a wheelbase stretched 57 mm (2.24 inches), to 2268 mm, via lengthened rear semi-trailing arms, though the engine and transaxle stayed in their original position. The old Nadella halfshafts were replaced by Löbro shafts with Rzeppa constant-velocity joints, with the shafts canted rearward from the inner to outer joints. All this improved fore/aft weight distribution from 41.5/58.5 percent to 43/57, and ride benefitted too.

Models were much as before: base 911T, 911E (replacing the L), and 911S. The last returned to the U.S. market after a one-year hiatus, while the T was a new Stateside entry. E and S gained thicker, vented disc brakes that widened track about 0.4-inch, which necessitated flared wheel openings, carried by all versions. The S rolled on six-inch-wide wheels, the E was equipped with Boge self-levelling hydropneumatic front struts instead of the usual MacPherson struts and torsion bars, and the Targa rear window was changed to fixed wraparound glass, replacing the zip-out plastic section that had proven both leaky and noisy.

Significant engine changes also occurred. While the T had two Weber 40IDT carburetors, the E and S employed Bosch high-pressure mechanical fuel injection, with a Bosch fuel pump driven by toothed belt from the left camshaft. With 9:1 compression, the E delivered 140 DIN horsepower, while the S was up to 170 on a 9.8:1 squeeze. E and T transmission choices comprised standard 4-speed or optional 5-speed manuals and the extra-cost Sportomatic, while the S came with only the 5-speed.

The 1970 C-series 911s bowed at the September 1969 Frankfurt show with a 2195-cc engine (via a 4-mm bore increase) and substantially more horsepower. The T, now with twin Zenith 40 TIN carbs, went from 110 to 125 bhp DIN, the E to 155 bhp, and the S to 180. Front suspension attachment points were moved ahead 14 mm (0.55-inch), which reduced steering effort and kickback, and limited-slip differential was added to the options list. The E's self-levelling Boge struts were phased out during the year as unpopular in that model, and as options in the S and T.

After a little-changed 1971 D-series, the E-series 1972 models received another displacement boost (this time via a longer stroke). Engine-lid badges read "2.4," but actual capacity was 2341 cc. T,E, and S engines continued as before, all with slightly increased horsepower despite lower compression ratios. Detroit says "there's no substitute for cubic inches," but Zuffenhausen's aim was not higher performance but more low-end torque for greater flexibility in low- to medium-speed driving with U.S. emission controls. The T picked up the Bosch fuel injection, and all American 911s now ran on regular-grade fuel. Transmissions were unchanged, but the optional 5-speed was strengthened, made easier to shift, and given a more logical gate, with fifth on a dogleg to the right and first in the upper left of the normal H.

There were two small appearance changes, both functional. The oil tank for the dry-sump lubrication system was resited from the right rear wheelarch to a position between it and the right door, hidden beneath a flap like the one for the gas filler on the *left* front fender. This was abandoned after '72 because service station attendants tended to put fuel into the oil tank by mistake—with unfortunate results. As an aid to high-speed stability, the S got a small under-bumper lip spoiler in front. The result of aerodynamic work by Porsche engineers, it reduced lift from 183 to 104 pounds at 140 mph, which was purely academic in America. The spoiler was optional for the T and E, but became so popular that it was made standard 911 wear for '74.

The '72s and the F-series '73s were mechanically little changed from the 1969-71 models, but wheelbase again lengthened, this time by a mere 3 mm (0.12-inch), to 2271 mm. No explanation has ever been offered for this. It's not easily noticed—or even measurable without an accurate steel tape.

In 1972, Porsche had revived the Carrera name (last seen on the mid-engine Type 906 Carrera 6 Makes Championship racer of 1967) for a special 911-based racer with a 2687-cc engine. Officially tagged 911RS, it was lightened in every way possible: thin-shell front seats, thinner sheetmetal and windshield glass, fiberglass engine lid, and no sound insulation, rear seats, or non-essential road equipment. There was no detox gear, of course, so the RS couldn't be sold in the U.S. as a road car. But it became available here for track use during 1973. Approximately 1600 were built that year, of which 600 were trimmed to 911S specs for European road use.

With all this and more, these were eventful years for the 911—and there was more to come. If anyone had doubts about the durability of the basic 911 design—or Porsche's ability to keep it in step with ever-shifting regulations and a changing market—the '74s would erase them pronto.

*Porsche offered three 911 models for 1969-73 in coupe (**opposite bottom**) and Targa (**above, opposite top**) styles. S and mid-range E wore five-spoke Fuchs alloy wheels.*

SPECIFICATIONS

Engines: all sohc flat six; **2.0** (1969)—121.5 cid/1991 cc; **911/ 911T:** 110 bhp (DIN) @ 5800 rpm (125 bhp SAE), 112 lbs-ft @ 4200 rpm; **911E:** 140 bhp (DIN) @ 6500 rpm, 125 lbs-ft @ 4500 rpm; **911S:** 170 bhp (DIN) @ 6800 rpm,130 lbs-ft @ 5500 rpm; **2.2** (1970-71)—133.8 cid/2195 cc; **911T:** 125 bhp (DIN) @ 5800 rpm, 126 lbs-ft @ 4200 rpm; **911E:** 155 bhp @ 6200 rpm, 137 lbs-ft @ 4500 rpm; **911S:** 180 bhp (DIN) @ 6500 rpm, 142 lbs-ft @ 5200 rpm; **2.4** (1972-73)—142.9 cid/2341 cc; **911T:** 130 bhp (DIN) @ 5600 rpm, 140 lbs-ft @ 4000 rpm; **911E:** 165 bhp (DIN) @ 6200 rpm, 147 lbs-ft @ 4500 rpm; **911S:** 190 bhp (DIN) @ 6500 rpm, 154 lbs-ft @ 5200 rpm

Transmissions:	4- and 5-speed manual, optional 4-speed semi-automatic (all in rear transaxle)
Suspension, front:	MacPherson struts, lower A-arms, longitudinal torsion bars, anti-roll bar except 911T
Suspension, rear:	semi-trailing arms, transverse torsion bars, anti-roll bar on S
Brakes:	front/rear drums
Wheelbase (in.):	89.3 (1969-71) 89.4 (1972-73)
Weight (lbs):	2250-2600
Top speed (mph):	110-140
0-60 mph (sec):	6.6-9.1

Production: **1969** 14,446 **1970** 10,234 **1971** 12,422 **1972-73** 15,061 (all calendar year)

1970-1976
PORSCHE 914 & 914/6

Porsche's mid-engine racing cars have most always been successful, starting with the prewar V-12 and V-16 Auto Unions and continuing into the Fifties and Sixties with the 550 Spyder, 550A/1500RS, RSK, 904 GTS, 906, and 908. By the mid-Sixties, Porsche engineers, like their colleagues at some other auto companies, saw the mid-engine layout as the wave of the future for production sports cars, and they wanted to build one. Thanks to Volkswagen, they got their chance.

At the time, VW president Heinz Nordhoff wanted a new sports model to get away from the make's utilitarian image. The squarish Type 3 Karmann-Ghia hadn't done that, and it wasn't selling well anyway. Porsche, meantime, was eyeing a less expensive car to replace the 912. Given the historic links between the two firms, this coincidence suggested that perhaps one car could serve both needs.

That's apparently what Nordhoff and Ferry Porsche thought, for they agreed to what we'd now call a "joint venture" car, one that would also give the Wilhelm Karmann works something to build once VW gave up on the Ghia. The plan called for Karmann to supply finished cars to Volkswagen and bodies of the same design to Porsche. But when Nordhoff died in April 1968, his successor, Kurt Lotz, reneged on some terms of his original verbal agreement with Ferry.

Porsche and VW thus entered into a joint sales venture with the new sports car as its cornerstone. A new company called VG (for *Vertriebsgesellschaft*, literally "Motors Inc.") was created, each partner owning 50 percent, to handle Porsche, Volkswagen, and Audi (the last now part of VW) in Europe. Porsche could still buy bodies for the new sports car from Karmann, though the unit price ended up much higher than Zuffenhausen expected.

What emerged from all this was a mid-engine two-seat targa-roof coupe designed by Porsche around VW power and built by Karmann on a "turnkey" basis. Designated 914, it bowed at the 1969 Frankfurt show with a new "VW-Porsche" badge and reached German showrooms the following February. U.S. cars arrived in March bearing Porsche badges only.

The 914 was essentially a "cocktail." Front suspension was lifted almost intact from the 911, as was the rear suspension, albeit with new links and coil springs. Anti-roll bars were omitted as unnecessary. Boge shock absorbers were standard and gas-

pressurized Bilsteins optional. Non-vented disc brakes appeared all-round. Power was supplied by an air-cooled flat four in the best VW/Porsche tradition, the 1.7-liter unit from VW's new "big" car, the dumpy 411. Standard electronic fuel injection, devised by Bosch under Bendix patents, allowed the 914 to clear U.S. emissions limits without an air pump. All this plus a 5-speed 911 transaxle mounted in an all-steel monocoque structure with rather square styling that was a bit odd in front.

Despite a well-planned cockpit, surprising luggage space, open-air appeal and mid-engine mystique, the 914 was pretty tame stuff. Horsepower was only 80, there were too many VW bits inside, and trim was functional, bordering on spartan. The price was right—initially $3495 in the U.S.—but critics sneered at the VW engine and Porsche partisans refused to accept the 914 as a "real" Porsche.

Zuffenhausen was uncomfortable with it too, and decided to *make* it a real Porsche by slotting in the 110-bhp 911T engine, with capacitive-discharge ignition and two triple-choke Weber carbs. To handle the extra performance, Porsche specified wider, light-alloy wheels, fatter tires, and slightly larger brakes (vented in front), along with deluxe trim and 911-style full instrumentation. The result, called 914/6, was built entirely by Porsche and badged as such. Introduced in late 1970, it cost quite a bit more than the four-cylinder job: $5595 in the U.S.

Alas, the 914/6 proved even harder to sell, and was quietly canned after model year '72. The four-cylinder version, by then known as 914/4, soldiered on into early '76 with only two important changes. One was a bored-out 2.0-liter option for 1973 and beyond. The other was adoption of a slightly larger and torquier standard unit, also by VW, beginning with the '74 models.

The "people's Porsche" was a good idea that was ultimately defeated by a half-breed image and VW's marketing policies. As Karl Ludvigsen wrote: "The new...VW-Porsche [marque] had neither image nor tradition. At the same time it was both VW and Porsche and neither VW *nor* Porsche."

Had things worked out differently, we might have seen a 916. A swoopy evolution to challenge Ferrari's Dino 246 (see entry), it would have had fixed-roof 914 bodywork with bulging wheelarches, five-spoke 911 wheels, color-keyed bumpers and deep front airdam, plus leather interior, beefed-up suspension, and 2.4-liter, 190-bhp 911 six. Price was pegged at $14,000-$15,000, 0-60 mph at under seven seconds, but the 916 was cancelled as unprofitable after 20 prototypes had been built.

Happily, the 914s have since come to be appreciated. If not the handsomest or most collectible of Porsches, they're reasonably practical sports cars and fun to drive, with great road manners and adequate-to-brisk performance. They've also proved to be great competitors, particularly in weekend club racing. A pity they didn't sell better, but they set the stage for another "people's Porsche": the front-engine 924.

SPECIFICATIONS

Engines: **914**—VW ohv flat four; **1970-73:** 102.3 cid/1679 cc, 80 bhp (DIN) @ 4900 rpm (76 bhp SAE), 95 lbs-ft @ 2700 rpm; **1974-76:** 109.5 cid/1795 cc, 85 bhp (DIN) @ 5000 rpm (72/76 bhp SAE net), 97 lbs-ft @ 3400 rpm; **1973-76:** 120.3 cid/1971 cc, 95/100 bhp (DIN) @ 4900 rpm (91 bhp SAE net), 112 lbs-ft @ 3500 rpm; **914/6**—Porsche sohc flat six; 121.5 cid/1991 cc, 110 bhp (DIN) @ 5800 rpm (105 bhp SAE net), 112 lbs-ft @ 4200 rpm

Transmission:	5-speed manual (in rear transaxle)
Suspension, front:	MacPherson struts, lower A-arms, longitudinal torsion bars
Suspension, rear:	semi-trailing arms, coil springs
Brakes:	front/rear discs (vented front on 914/6)
Wheelbase (in.):	96.4
Weight (lbs):	2085-2195
Top speed (mph):	109-123
0-60 mph (sec):	8.7-13.9

Production: **914 1969** 13,312 **1970** 16,231 **1971** 21,440 **1972** 27,660 **1973-74** NA **914/6 1969** 2668 **1970** 443 **1971** 240 (all calendar year)
(Note: One source lists total 914/4 production as 78,643)

Opposite: Most 914s had four-cylinder power. Early ones carried logo-less VW hubcaps. Vinyl on roof "basket handle" was part of a U.S. Appearance Group option. *Below:* Porsche flat six and 911S-type alloy wheels featured on the 914/6.

1974-1977 PORSCHE 911

Still seeking more horsepower and better flexibility, Porsche upped displacement of the production 911 engine a third time, for model year 1974. The T and E were dropped, leaving base and 911S to bow at the Frankfurt show in September '73.

More evident were beautifully integrated new body-color bumpers, in line with that year's U.S. 5-mph impact standards front *and* rear. Porsche met them by simply pulling the bumpers out from the body and putting them on aluminum-alloy tubes that collapsed when struck at 5 mph or above. This meant replacing the tubes after a crunch, but better body protection. The bumpers themselves were aluminum, again to save weight. Hydraulic shock-absorber attachments that didn't need replacing post-impact were standard on UK cars and optional in other markets. Accordion-pleat rubber boots filled the gaps twixt body and bumpers.

It was a typically thorough Porsche solution to a problem no one could foresee when the 911 was designed, and it made most other "crash" bumpers seem clumsy. Not that Zuffenhausen didn't have an incentive to do it right, because the U.S. was now taking more than 50 percent of production. By contrast, U.S. sales for BMW and Mercedes were still well under 20 percent of total volume.

As on 1973's semi-competition Carrera model, displacement stood at 2687 cc, achieved via a 6-mm bore increase. Bosch K-Jetronic fuel injection, sometimes called CIS (Continuous Injection System) and introduced on the 1973 T model, replaced the previous mechanical system across the board, thus further rationalizing the 911 series and contributing to useful gains in both power and torque.

Better yet, there was now a road-legal U.S. Carrera. Relegating the 911S to mid-line status, it used the same 167-horsepower (SAE net) engine, but stood apart with bigger wheels and tires that were wider aft (7 inches) than fore (6 inches). It also had bold i.d. lettering on the lower bodysides, and a racing-style "ducktail" engine-lid spoiler (rimmed in rubber to protect pedestrians per *German* government regulations).

This Carrera was essentially a U.S. version of the European Carrera RS, minus its extra performance. Of course, Porsche hadn't been idle on the race-and-ride front. This year's 911-based "customer" racer was the RSR, with an even larger bore, 2993 cc, aluminum (instead of magnesium) crankcase, and 315 DIN horsepower, upped during production to 330 (320 SAE). Planned production was 100 units to satisfy homologation requirements, but the FIA still classified this as a road car, not a racer. Accordingly, only 49 of the 109 RSRs eventually built were stripped for the track. The others were used on public roads, but only in Europe. Needless to say, it was one of the hottest cars on *any* road.

Back in the showroom, all '74 911s boasted a front spoiler, redesigned steering wheels, new high-back front seats with winged backrests and integral headrests, new dash vents, and a larger fuel tank (21.1 gallons, up from 16.4). High-pressure headlight washers were a new feature for European models, mounted on the front bumper just ahead of each lamp. They'd arrived on U.S. models for '75.

The 911 took a breather that year. U.S. offerings were pared to S and Carrera, both with 157 bhp (SAE net). The latter sprouted a deeper front spoiler and the now-famous "whale tail" rear spoiler, while both models benefitted from extended service intervals (now 15,000 miles).

America's bicentennial year brought new 911 excitement in the rapid Turbo Carrera (see separate entry), plus thoughtful S. improvements. Among them were cruise control, mainly for the American market and new to Porsche, a second round of heating system revisions including optional automatic temperature control, and a double-sided zinc coating for all body/chassis metal that allowed Porsche to introduce a pioneering six-year anti-rust warranty.

The 1976 S had most equipment seen on the '74 Carrera and was now quite lush compared to earlier 911s. Tinted glass, two-speed-plus-intermittent wipers, two-stage rear-window defroster, anti-roll bars at each end, and 5-speed transaxle were all standard—which was only right, as base price had risen to over $14,000, versus $9950 just two years earlier. (The U.S. and UK importers specified the 5-speed as standard; the 4-speed was standard elsewhere.) Options ran to Koni adjustable or Bilstein gas/oil shocks, external oil cooler (in the right front fender), forged alloy wheels, sport seats, electric sunroof for the coupe, and air conditioning.

After minor refinements for '77, including revised dash vents and antitheft flush door locks, the 911 was ready for its next major change. Against all odds, this aging design was not only surviving but thriving—fully up to date yet a classic in its own time. An elegant example of Porsche engineering excellence, wouldn't you say?

The 911's first major facelift occurred for 1974; this basic look has changed little since. Engine-lid "whale-tail" was developed for the forthcoming 911 Turbo (Type 930).

SPECIFICATIONS

Engines: all sohc flat six, 164 cid/2687 cc; **911** (1974): 150 bhp (DIN) @ 5700 rpm (143 bhp SAE net), 168 lbs-ft @ 3800 rpm; **911S/Carrera** (1974): 175 bhp (DIN) @ 5800 rpm (167 bhp SAE net), 168 lbs-ft @ 4000 rpm; **1975-77:** 165 bhp (DIN) @ 5800 rpm (157 bhp SAE net), 161/168 lbs-ft @ 4000 rpm

Transmissions:	4/5-speed manual (in rear transaxle)
Suspension, front:	MacPherson struts, lower A-arms, longitudinal torsion bars, anti-roll bar
Suspension, rear:	semi-trailing arms, transverse torsion bars, anti-roll bar
Brakes:	front/rear drums
Wheelbase (in.):	89.4
Weight (lbs):	2370-2460
Top speed (mph):	130-145
0-60 mph (sec):	7.5-8.5

Production: **1974 911** 7124 **911S** 2257 **Carrera** 2243 **1975 911** 2236 **911S U.S.** 3827 **911S** 651 **Carrera** 715 **Carrera U.S.** 395 **1976 911** 3444 **911S U.S.** 4254 **Misc** 283 **1977 911** 4173 **911S U.S.** 6135 (all calendar year figures)

1975-1988 PORSCHE 924/924 TURBO/924S

It was the first front-engine water-cooled Porsche to reach production, but the 924 actually followed a pattern set with the 356. The very first Porsche used Volkswagen suspension, brakes, steering, and a modified version of VW's air-cooled flat four, mounted at the rear. Those same components in the 924 were also from a contemporary VW. Aside from engine position and cooling medium, the big difference was that the 356 had been designed *as* a Porsche, while the 924 was designed *by* Porsche to be a Volkswagen and ended up as a Porsche.

Because it was conceived as a sporty upscale VW (project EA425), the 924 employed as many production parts as Porsche engineers could lift from VW shelves. The selected engine, for example, was a 2.0-liter inline four designed by VW but built by its Audi division. Features included a single overhead cam (driven by toothed belt), cast-iron block, slightly oversquare cylinder dimensions, and Heron-type combustion chambers with dished pistons and flat-face head.

This powerplant was also used in carbureted form on VW's European Type LT van (not sold in the U.S.) and, briefly, American Motors' Gremlin. For the 924 (and Audi 100 sedan) it received Bosch K-Jetronic fuel injection and, in U.S. trim, lower compression (8:1 versus 9.3:1). DIN horsepower was 125 for British and European models, 95-100 for emissions-regulated Canadian, U.S., and Japanese cars. On the last three, compression was raised half a point with the optional fully automatic transmission—a first for a Porsche, incidentally—boosting DIN output to 115.

The 924 hewed with Porsche tradition in another way: a rear transaxle. With the engine up front, this meant a long driveshaft, a tiny 20-mm-diameter affair, straight and without U-joints, encased in a tube and running in four strategically placed bearings. The engine and gearbox were each supported on two rubber mounts. The clutch bolted up directly behind the engine. A rear "clutch housing" was provided for the automatic's torque converter.

Though some 10 inches longer between wheel centers than the 911, the 924 also emerged as a 2+2. Styling broke new ground for Porsche: rounded (though different than the 911) and sleek, dominated by a large compound-curve rear window that doubled as a luggage hatch. Rear suspension was 911-like (though not interchangeable) while the front employed conventional MacPherson struts, lower A-arms, and coil springs. Rear brakes were drums instead of Porsche's usual discs, but then, this was the "budget" model.

Like its engine, the 924 was built by Audi, at the one-time NSU factory in Neckarsulm, West Germany. The first cars rolled off the line in November 1975 as '76 models for Europe. U.S. versions arrived in April 1976 as early '77s. At first, 4-speed manual was the only transmission available, but Audi's new 3-speed automatic became optional for Europe in late 1976, for America from March '77. A new 5-speed Getrag manual became an option with the '78 models (revealed at Frankfurt '77).

High-volume engineering and all the borrowed parts made for bargain prices. The 1976 tags read $8900 in West Germany and $9395 in America. Besides automatic, options included air conditioning ($548), tilt/take-out sunroof ($330), alloy wheels and larger tires ($295), metallic paint ($295), front and rear anti-roll bars ($105 the pair), and antenna and three radio speakers ($240 the lot).

As the effective replacement for the 914, the 924 got somewhat better treatment from the press. Performance was judged good if not great, road manners excellent (thanks to near-equal weight distribution with the rear transaxle), ergonomics and general practicality much improved. But critics carped about the rough, noisy engine, and purists moaned that this and being assembled by Audi left the 924 hardly more a "real" Porsche than the 914.

Again, Porsche hustled to make an erstwhile VW its own. The 5-speed became standard for '79, but the big news that year was the 924 Turbo, identified by four nasal air slots, functional NACA hood air duct, unique alloy wheels, and front and rear spoilers.

This time, Porsche built both car and engine. The latter employed the standard block (shipped from Neckarsulm) topped by a new Porsche-designed head with modified hemispherical combustion chambers and suitably lower compression (7.5:1). Plugs moved from the exhaust to intake side, and the water seal between head and block was by copper gasket and silicone rings. CIS fuel injection was retained, but with two pumps to assure full fuel pressure. Fitting the turbocharger, a German KKK

(Kuhnle, Kopp & Kausch), on the engine's right (exhaust) side necessitated moving the starter to the left.

With 33 more horsepower in U.S. form, plus a beefier chassis for all versions, the Turbo was a more serious 924—"another *real* Porsche," said Britain's *Autocar*. Some problems remained, however—mainly a still-buzzy engine and an even lumpier ride—so the critics weren't completely silenced.

For 1980, the base 924 got a new standard 5-speed, the previous 4-speed with an extra gear. The Turbo retained its Getrag 5-speed. The 1981s received standard halogen headlamps, rear seatbelts and, belatedly, rear disc brakes (standard on previous Euro-Turbos).

Porsche, meantime, had been working on a thorough overall of the 924, and it arrived for 1982 as the 944 (see entry). With that, both 924s were withdrawn from the U.S., but continued in production for Europe and the UK.

Four years later, the 924 was upgraded for all markets to become the 924S. This latest "entry-level" Porsche was essentially the original 924 with 944 chassis hardware and running gear, plus a good many standard extras (including air, tinted glass, heated power-remote door mirrors, and power steering, windows, and antenna). With the 944's smoother, more potent all-Porsche engine in the lighter 924 shell, the normally aspirated S was faster flat out than even the Turbo, and nearly matched its acceleration. And by late Eighties standards, this 924 was still a bargain.

That brings the story up to date. And if you missed its moral, it is that, if you're Porsche, you *can* teach an old dog new tricks.

Below and opposite bottom: The 924 left the U.S. after 1981 but continued in Europe, then returned to America for '87 as the 924S. The latter was visually distinguished by 928-type "telephone-dial" wheels. Opposite top: The editors' test 1981-model 924 Turbo.

SPECIFICATIONS

Engines: **924** (1975-86): Audi sohc I-4, 121.1 cid/1985 cc, 125 bhp (DIN) @ 5800 rpm, 118 lbs-ft @ 3500 rpm (U.S. version: 95 bhp SAE net 1976-77, 110 bhp @ 5750 rpm 1977-81); **Turbo** (1979-82): 125 bhp (DIN) @ 5500 rpm, 181 lbs-ft @ 3500 rpm (U.S. version: 143 bhp SAE net, 147 lbs-ft @ 3000 rpm) **924S:** Porsche ohc I-4, 151 cid/2479 cc; **1986-87:** 147 bhp (SAE net) @ 5800 rpm, 144 lbs-ft @ 3000 rpm; **1988:** 158 bhp @ 5900 rpm, 155 lbs-ft @ 4500 rpm

Transmissions:	4/5-speed manual (see text), 3-speed automatic (all in rear transaxle)
Suspension, front:	MacPherson struts, lower A-arms, coil springs
Suspension, rear:	semi-trailing arms, transverse torsion bars
Brakes:	front discs/rear drums; front/rear discs European Turbo and 1981 U.S. models
Wheelbase (in.):	94.5
Weight (lbs):	2380-2735
Top speed (mph):	110-134
0-60 mph (sec):	7.5-12.5
Production:	NA (production continues at this writing)

1975-1988 PORSCHE TURBO CARRERA & 930

Porsche began experimenting with turbochargers in the late Sixties, testing its technology with the mighty 917 flat-12s in GT and Can-Am competition, plus a variety of 911-based production-class racers. By 1975, Porsche was ready with a roadgoing model, the 911 Turbo. Available only for Europe that year (as the Carrera 3.0), it was so heavily re-engineered from standard that it received its own type number: 930.

Despite the recent Energy Crisis, the new SuperPorsche was federalized for model year 1976, when it bowed in the States as the Turbo Carrera. Road tests promptly confirmed it as the fastest roadgoing Porsche ever sold in the U.S. Some said it was America's fastest production car, period.

At its heart was the latest 3.0-liter version of the amazingly adaptable 911 flat six, the larger displacement chosen for better off-boost performance with the lower compression (7:1) then necessitated by turbocharging. The blower itself was placed on a cast-aluminum manifold studded to the heads, with Ultramid plastic tubes for the Bosch K-Jetronic fuel injection placed between manifold and intake ports. Boost pressure was set at 11.5 pounds per square inch.

In U.S. tune, the blown 911 belted out 234 emissions-legal SAE net horsepower. Torque was equally prodigious—so much so that Porsche decided a wide-ratio 4-speed transaxle was a better match than the normal 911's close-ratio 5-speed. Predictably, performance was awesome, as they used to say. One magazine reported a 0-60 mph time of just 4.9 seconds, the standing quarter-mile in 13.5 seconds, and a top speed of 156 mph. Yet the Turbo was quite civilized: tractable in city traffic and a bit quieter than the non-turbo car.

Outside, the Turbo Carrera wore the now-familiar "whale tail" plus new massively flared wheelarches shrouding ultrabroad high-performance tires on handsome cast-aluminum wheels, with the rears notably wider than the fronts. A suitably beefier chassis included the Bilstein gas/oil shocks optional on the standard 911. An oil cooler was standard too.

Inside was most every comfort and convenience feature Porsche could pack in: air conditioning, power windows, AM/FM stereo, leather upholstery, and more. Options

were confined to electric sliding sunroof, limited-slip differential, heavy-duty starter, and "Turbo" bodyside graphics. Targa bodywork and Sportomatic weren't available.

After being virtually unchanged for '77, this remarkable missile was bumped to 3.3 liters and 253 bhp (SAE) for 1978 and renamed Porsche Turbo. Adding to its extra muscle was an air-to-air intercooler, shoehorned into the engine compartment to push the A/C condenser to the right side of the spoiler's air intake.

Performance didn't change much, as the larger engine was adopted mainly to keep pace with U.S. emissions limits and new European standards then creeping in. For the record, *Motor* magazine in England ran 0-60 mph in 5.3 seconds and 0-100 in 12.3—still phenomenal going by any standard. To cope, the Turbo now received the ventilated cross-drilled disc brakes with four-piston calipers from the fabled 917. *Motor* reported they'd stopped the car from 70 mph in an excellent 174 feet, and didn't fade at all in 20 successive stops from 100 mph (made at 45-second intervals).

The 930 would continue in this basic form through 1986, but was temporarily withdrawn from the U.S. market after 1979, a public-relations nod to a second energy crunch. Of course, there are always those with extra will, and the notorious "gray market" provided the way for a handful of European 930s to reach determined (and wealthy) U.S. buyers.

By 1986, Zuffenhausen had taken direct control of its U.S. distribution (from VW of America). It was also moving toward common specifications—and performance—for all its models regardless of where they were sold, to simplify production and eliminate the bothersome gray-market traffic in its cars, particularly in the U.S.

One result of this is that the 930 was recertified and reintroduced to America for 1986. This time, the U.S. version was all but identical with the European. Performance was little changed despite an increase in rated power, but interim chassis refinements made the beast more predictable and safe in really fast work. Though specifications changed little for '87, the Turbo could be ordered as a Targa for the first time—and with the full 911 cabriolet body introduced for 1983.

By that point, the "Turbo look" had been widely copied in aftermarket body-restyling kits for ordinary 911s, as well as the hidden-headlamp "slant nose" first seen on certain late-Seventies 935 racers. Porsche decided to end *those* ripoffs too, first with a 1984 "Turbo Look" package for the normally aspirated 911 Carrera (the option also included the Turbo's uprated chassis) and a 1987 "Turbo slant-nose modification option" for the 930, stupefyingly priced at near $24,000—*not* counting the car! The latter becomes a separate model for 1988, called 930S. It's all part of the factory's new "Porsche Exclusive" customizing service, which will happily help you run a Turbo's tab to over $106,000.

That's a breathtaking sum, but then the Turbo has always been a breathtaking car. But just how long can it go on? Like the 911 itself, seemingly forever—defying the rules, the odds, and the naysayers. Anachronistic? Maybe. A high-performance classic? Definitely.

Below and opposite bottom: "Whale tail" and massively flared rear wheelarches are evident on this 1979 U.S.-market 930 Turbo. Opposite top: New-for-'88 930S has a "slant nose" and other body addenda similar to these.

SPECIFICATIONS

Engines: all sohc flat six turbocharged; **1976-77:** 182.6 cid/2993 cc, 234 bhp (SAE net) @ 5500 rpm, 246 lbs-ft @ 4500 rpm; **1978-85:** 201 cid/3299 cc, 253 bhp (SAE net) @ 5500 rpm, 282 lbs-ft @ 4000 rpm; **1986-88:** 201 cid/3299 cc, 282 bhp (SAE net) @ 5500 rpm, 288 lbs-ft @ 4000 rpm

Transmission:	4-speed manual (in rear transaxle)
Suspension, front:	MacPherson struts, lower A-arms, longitudinal torsion bars, anti-roll bar
Suspension, rear:	semi-trailing arms, transverse torsion bars, anti-roll bar
Brakes:	front/rear discs
Wheelbase (in.):	89.4
Weight (lbs):	2960-3112
Top speed (mph):	150-156
0-60 mph (sec):	4.9-5.3

Production: NA (production continues at this writing; est. 6000 through 1987)

1978-1988 PORSCHE 911

When Porsche unveiled its '78s at the September 1977 Frankfurt show, there were only two 911s: 3.3-liter Turbo (see entry) and the new normally aspirated 3.0-liter 911SC. The latter, for all practical purposes, was the old Carrera without the name, with the same mechanical specifications, styling, and general features.

Though horsepower was down from the Carrera's 200 (DIN) to 180, a flatter, fuller torque curve made the SC more enjoyable and somewhat easier to drive. Mechanical improvements included a new, stronger crankshaft with larger bearings, and the return of an aluminum crankcase (used on 1964-67 models, after which a pressure-cast magnesium piece took over).

In line with Porsche's new policy of a "world" specification and performance level, breakerless CD distributor and U.S.-style air pump were adopted for all 911s regardless of market. American models still differed in one respect, however, as the more efficient catalytic converter replaced thermal reactors as the main emissions-control device, thus improving driveability.

Servo-assisted brakes became standard for '79, and a new clutch-disc hub for the 5-speed transaxle eliminated gear chatter at low speeds. The latter necessitated moving the engine back 30 mm (about 1.2 inches), but no handling difference was noticeable in any but race-track conditions. Porsche engineers also decreed that rear tire pressure be elevated from 34 to 43 psi, and offered American models with extra-cost 16-inch wheels and tires. Finally, the never-popular Sportomatic transmission option was dropped.

Except for Porsche's typical on-going improvements and one major development that we'll get to shortly, the 911SC would continue in this form with little change through 1983. U.S. models became somewhat plusher in these years. Air conditioning, power windows, center console, and matte-black exterior trim were no-cost extras for 1980, along with a three-way catalytic converter that allowed slightly higher compression for even better driveability and fuel economy. Halogen headlamps and rear seatbelts were added for '81, when Porsche extended its rust warranty from six to seven years. The 1982s received standard headlight washers, leather front seats, and upgraded audio system.

But 1982's happiest happening came at the Geneva show in March: the long-rumored 911SC cabriolet, the first true factory-built Porsche convertible since the last

356 model of 1965. (Because of its fixed rollbar, the versatile Targa was never considered a true convertible.) As with its fondly remembered predecessor, the new ragtop's body was built by Porsche's Reutter division.

For 1984, the SC became the 911 Carrera, again reviving the famous model name used on and off since 1953. Reflecting both the times and Porsche philosophy, the long-running flat six was enlarged to 3.2 liters, the fifth such increase since 1964, achieved by combining the Turbo engine's 74.4-mm stroke with the SC's 95-mm bore. That brought total capacity to more than 50 percent above the original 2.0 liters, eloquent testimony to this engine's design durability. Fuel injection was changed from Bosch K-Jetronic to the same firm's new Digital Motor Electronics (DME) or "Motronic" system with integrated electronic ignition. All this brought SAE net horsepower to 200, yet gas mileage was better than ever.

Other 1984 changes included brakes with thicker rotors (by 3.5 mm), larger ventilation passages, and 928 proportioning control. Foglights now nestled in the front spoiler, and a new "Turbo Look" package option gave you the looks and chassis prowess of the mighty 930.

Apart from an electrically adjustable driver's seat, the main 1985 news was a much-expanded warranty: two years/unlimited miles on the car itself (formerly one year/unlimited miles), 10 years on rust perforation (up from seven), and five-year/50,000-mile powertrain coverage. The '86s arrived with lowered front seats, short-travel gearshift, revised climate system, and a second, heavy-duty windshield washer. Horsepower rose by 14 for 1987, which also brought a new hydraulically actuated clutch, smoother-shifting transaxle, and a thermostatic electric fan for the oil cooler. New colors arrived, and options expanded to include full power seats and separate electric lumbar-support adjustment. Top speed was up to 149 mph and 0-60 mph acceleration down to 6.1 seconds.

The 911 rolls on into 1988—its 24th year—with three-point rear seatbelts (replacing simple lap belts), electronic cruise control (previously pneumatic), and a new Club Sport option for the coupe. In the grand Porsche tradition, the last is for weekend racing, deleting such things as air conditioning and sound insulation in exchange for fortified shock absorbers, sports seats, and a higher rpm limit.

And so it goes. An "all-new" 911 is rumored for 1989 or '90, with the same beloved looks but many new features, some inspired by Zuffenhausen's latest technical marvel, the 200-mph four-wheel-drive 959. Sadly, prices seem destined to keep climbing. By May 1987, the Carrera coupe was up to over $40,000, the cabriolet a whopping $46,725.

Of course, the 911 is a lot better equipped than it once was, and there's U.S. and West German inflation plus shifting dollar/D-mark rates to contend with. So in today's money, the 911 is as good a value as it ever was—better, really—and even more rewarding to drive and own. How nice to be able to count on more of the same for a good many more years.

SPECIFICATIONS

Engines: all sohc flat six; **1978-83:** 182.6 cid/2993 cc, 172 bhp (SAE net) @ 5500 rpm, 189 lbs-ft @ 4200 rpm; **1984-88:** 193 cid/3164 cc, 200/214 bhp (SAE net) @ 5900 rpm, 185/195 lbs-ft @ 4900 rpm

Transmission:	5-speed manual (in rear transaxle)
Suspension, front:	MacPherson struts, lower A-arms, longitudinal torsion bars, anti-roll bar
Suspension, rear:	semi-trailing arms, transverse torsion bars, anti-roll bar
Brakes:	front/rear discs
Wheelbase (in.):	89.4
Weight (lbs):	2740-2750
Top speed (mph):	126-149
0-60 mph (sec):	6.1-6.7
Production:	NA (production continues at this writing)

Opposite: Classic 911 coupe, here in non-turbo 1986 Carrera trim, has hardly aged in 25 years. Neither has its flat-six. **Below:** *Full convertible returned in 1982.*

353

1978-1988 PORSCHE 928/928S/ 928S 4

No car lasts forever, but the 911 may be an exception. It's certainly surprised the powers in Zuffenhausen by hanging on long after so many predicted its demise—including Porsche itself, which first contemplated a replacement way back in the early Seventies. Today we know it as the 928.

Development of this erstwhile 911 successor was headed by Dr. (later Professor) Ernst Fuhrmann, president of Porsche from 1972 to '82. Foremost among project goals were that the new car "have all the quality and performance of previous Porsches" and "be capable of meeting any and all government regulations that might be conceived in the foreseeable future." The latter applied to Europe as well as export markets. Yet in view of the fact that the U.S. absorbed about 50 percent of Porsche's total production, any new model would have to be designed primarily with that market in mind.

Taking all this into account, the technical brief called for a water-cooled engine in front, rear transaxle, all-independent suspension, and all-disc brakes. The result was the first Porsche designed with a clean sheet of paper to be all-Porsche. In retrospect, the decision to proceed with this bigger, plusher car seems courageous, as it was taken just as the first Energy Crisis hit in late 1973.

Porsche traditionally premiered new models at Frankfurt, its biennial "home" show, but chose Geneva for introducing the 928, in March 1977. It seemed a fitting choice, as the original 356 had had its public debut there back in 1950.

What showgoers saw was a sleek and futuristic, if bulbous and somewhat heavy-looking, hatchback 2+2 designed by American-born chief stylist Anatole "Tony" Lapine. Highlights included a long nose with exposed headlamps that laid back in recesses when switched off, parallelogram-shaped door windows, body-color bumpers, smooth flanks, and a shapely fanny. Unit-steel construction was per production Porsche practice, with aluminum hood, doors, and hatchlid to save weight.

Inside was the most sumptuous cockpit ever seen from Zuffenhausen, with all the usual features and a few that weren't. Among the latter: a combined height-adjustable steering wheel/ instrument cluster, rear-seat sunvisors, and air conditioning ducts for the glovebox.

While the 924 (see entry) had established rear transaxles and water-cooled front engines at Zuffenhausen, the 928 broke new ground for a production Porsche with its 90-degree 4.5-liter V-8. Both block and heads were cast of Reynolds 390 aluminum alloy (which required no cylinder liners), a Gilmer-type toothed belt drove a single overhead camshaft per bank, and fuel was delivered via Bosch K-Jetronic injection. Drive went through a 200-mm-diameter Fitchel & Sachs twin-disc clutch and torque-tube-contained solid driveshaft to 5-speed manual or 3-speed automatic transaxles, the latter supplied by Daimler-Benz.

Like the drivetrain, the all-coil suspension was new, though based on Porsche racing experience. The front end was conventional enough, but rear geometry was by something called a "Weissach axle." Named for the Porsche research center where it was created, it comprised an upper lateral arm and lower semi-trailing arm per side. The four disc brakes were ventilated, and there were dual diagonal circuits.

With all this, nobody was indifferent to the 928. Porsche purists scratched their heads, while status seekers seeking high-performance luxury promptly queued up to buy. Not that many did, for it landed on U.S. shores for 1978 at a hefty $26,000. One magazine beamed that the 928's "combination of comfort, sportiness, and civility...rank it with the world's great GTs," then cautioned that, as with the 911, "if you want one, you pay the price or do without."

More than enough folks have been wanting and willing, and subsequent changes have only made the 928 even more desirable. For 1980, a 2-mm bore increase brought displacement to near 4.7 liters on the new European 928S, and higher compression (10.5:1, up from 8.5) boosted horsepower. America got a lookalike S without the more potent powerplant through 1982. Then a real S arrived with a new 4-speed automatic (as before, Daimler-Benz gubbins within a Porsche-designed case) as standard (the manual 5-speed became a no-cost option). With a top speed of 146 mph, Porsche claimed it as the fastest street-legal car on the U.S. market.

It became even faster in 1985 thanks to a new 5.0-liter engine (achieved via a 3-mm bore stretch) with Bosch LH-Jetronic injection and—the big event—freer-breathing twincam heads with four valves per cylinder. The result in U.S. tune was 288 horsepower, versus the original 219 and the interim S's 234. Unusually, this development was a U.S. exclusive at first, though Europe eventually got it too. To

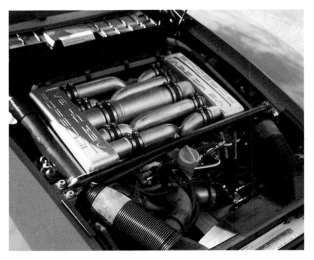

Opposite top: Smoother tail, "detached" rear spoiler identify the latest 928S 4. Other photos: The 1985-model 928S introduced an enlarged 5.0-liter V-8 with 32 valves.

SPECIFICATIONS

Engines: (U.S. versions; SAE net figures) **sohc V-8—1978-82:** 273 cid/4474 cc, 219 bhp @ 5250 rpm, 254 lbs-ft @ 3600 rpm; **1983-84:** 283 cid/4644 cc, 234 bhp @ 5500 rpm, 263 lbs-ft @ 4000 rpm; **dohc V-8—1985-86:** 302 cid/4957 cc, 288 bhp @ 5750 rpm, 302 lbs-ft @ 2700 rpm; **1987-88:** 302 cid/4957 cc, 316 bhp @ 6000 rpm, 317 lbs-ft @ 3000 rpm

Transmissions:	5-speed overdrive manual, 3-speed automatic, 4-speed overdrive automatic (all in rear transaxle)
Suspension, front:	upper A-arms, lower trailing arms, coil springs, anti-roll bar
Suspension, rear:	upper transverse links, lower semi-trailing arms, coil springs, anti-roll bar
Brakes:	front/rear discs
Wheelbase (in.):	98.3
Weight (lbs):	3410-3505
Top speed (mph):	138-165
0-60 mph (sec):	6.3-7.0
Production:	NA (production continues at this writing)

match the extra go-power, '86s received standard anti-lock brakes, plus an automatic shift quadrant in the tachometer face, newly optional heated front seats and, as with other Porsches, extended warranties.

Model year 1987 brought the 928S 4 (the "4" denoting "fourth series"). Larger ports, recessed combustion chambers, and tuned intake manifold added another 28 bhp. To handle it, a large-diameter single-disc clutch replaced the small twin-disc unit. Outside was a reshaped nose with a deep front airdam incorporating fog and driving lights, plus ducts for engine and brake cooling. Wraparound flush taillamps and a larger "detached" rear spoiler (replacing the previous lip type at the rear window base) were also applied. All this got the claimed drag coefficient down to 0.34 (from the original 0.41) and, with the added power, got top speed up to 165 mph with manual.

Despite still-controversial looks, the 928 has been an unqualified success, on roads and sales charts alike. Of course, it's still a fairly young design, barely 10 years old at this writing, one reason Porsche says it will carry on into the 21st century. What can we expect to see between now and then? The mind boggles, but you can bet it'll be spectacular. After all, this *is* a Porsche.

1982-1988 PORSCHE 944/944 TURBO/944S

In September 1981, like so many times before, the biennial Frankfurt Auto Show witnessed the public unveiling of a new Porsche: the 1982-model 944. Basically, it was the familiar 924 (see entry) with different nose and tail styling, plus "blistered" fenders to accommodate wider wheels and tires. But the real news was under the hood, for here was the first junior Porsche with a real Porsche engine.

As on the 924, it was a single-overhead-cam inline four—water-cooled, of course—but looked very much like half of the current 928 V-8. It was. They even shared the same stroke (78.9 mm), but wider bore (100 versus 95 mm) put displacement at over half the V-8's: 2479 versus 4474 cc. Block and head were cast of Reynolds 390 aluminum-silicon alloy, also like the V-8. For all the similarities, though, there were no interchangeable parts.

Four-cylinder engines of more than 2.0 liters are usually rough runners, so Porsche looked to an idea developed way back in 1911 by Frederick W. Lanchester and more recently resurrected—and patented—by Mitsubishi of Japan. This involved the use of twin counterweighted balance shafts, mounted in the block, turning at twice crankshaft speed and in the opposite direction to dampen the vibrations (technically termed "coupling forces") inherent in big fours. A Gilmer-type cogged belt drove the single overhead camshaft; a second belt, with teeth on each side, drove the balance shafts.

On 9.5:1 compression, U.S. 944s offered 147 SAE net horsepower, while the Euro version had 153 (160 DIN) thanks to a tighter 10.6:1 squeeze. The former would run 0-60 mph in a brisk 8.3 seconds, slightly slower than its transatlantic cousin. Still, the 944 was superior to the 924 Turbo in acceleration (8.3 and 9.1 seconds European/American models) and nearly as good in top speed (130 versus 134 mph)—all without the blower's complexity. Strict weight control helped. The 944 engine weighed just 340 pounds dry, while curb weight was initially 2778 pounds, making the 944 slightly heavier than a 924 Turbo. The latter's vented disc brakes were used all-round.

Needless to say, the engine swap made all the difference, and the 944 was immediately hailed as a true Porsche—and thus eminently desirable—by enthusiasts, motor-noters, and buyers. The new engine was not just smooth but very torquey, strong and quiet—just what the 924 had needed. Strong sales confirmed the appeal

*"Aero" nose and tail revisions marked the 944 Turbo **(below and opposite bottom)** on its 1986 U.S. debut. 16-valve 944S **(above)** premiered that same year.*

of this winning package. Porsche had only to attend to refinements and a couple of significant evolutions.

The first occurred for 1984, when the original Bosch LE-Jetronic fuel injection gave way to the same company's more advanced DME (Digital Motor Electronics) setup that used one computer to control both injection and ignition. At the same time, the welded front-suspension A-arms were replaced by alloy castings. A reworked interior arrived at mid-1985, with a new instrument panel (replacing the 924 dash on early models) and more readable instruments, plus a smaller, round steering wheel for better under-rim thigh clearance, long a problem with the previous oval wheel.

As if to answer speculation about the return of a blown junior model, Porsche released the 944 Turbo for 1986. Aside from the turbo and correspondingly lower compression (8.0:1), its engine was basically stock but delivered a healthy helping of extra power and torque. Comparing the normally aspirated and turbocharged '44s, one U.S. magazine recorded respective quarter-mile times of 16.6 and 16.4 seconds and terminal speeds of 85 and 97.5 mph. Of course, the Turbo was also faster off the line—6.1 seconds to 60 mph—but its real advantage was in the upper range. This may have been rather academic in speed-limited America, but it certainly enhanced prestige.

Enhancing Turbo appearance were a revised nose with wide cooling slots and combination bumper/spoiler, a rear underbody pan (to smooth airflow leaving from beneath the car, again for better high-speed stability), and a more prominent rear spoiler at the base of the big hatch window. Wider wheels and tires were naturally included, the wheels being the five-hole 928 design.

The newest member of the 944 family arrived at mid-model year '86: the 944S. Here, Porsche took an intermediate road to performance via a new twincam head with four valves per cylinder for better breathing. It's similar to the head on the latest 928S 4 but, again, no parts interchange. Valvegear is unusual. A single toothed belt drove the exhaust cam, which in turn drove the intake shaft via a chain between cylinders two and three. Other changes include larger ports and beautifully cast manifold runners for both intake and exhaust. The result of all this was not only more power and a fatter torque curve compared with the 2-valve 944 but smoother power delivery than the Turbo and almost as much go.

For 1987, four-channel anti-lock brakes arrived as 944S and Turbo options, and airbags for both driver and passenger were newly standard for the Turbo and optional for other models. The 944 thus became the first car to offer a passenger airbag at any price—which sounds anti-performance but only reflects Porsche's longstanding concern for safety.

Progress has its price, of course. Though initially spotted at just under $20,000, the 944's sticker read $25,500 by the start of the '87 season, while the Turbo stood at a lofty $33,250. Porsche isn't entirely to blame, as worldwide inflation and, lately, a falling dollar have taken their toll. And let's not forget the old law of supply and demand, the principal factor that props up Porsche prices and resale values year after year. Obviously, popularity has a price too.

SPECIFICATIONS

Engine: (U.S. versions; SAE net figures) all sohc I-4, 151 cid/2479 cc; **944—1982-87:** 147 bhp @ 5800 rpm, 140 lbs-ft @ 3000 rpm; **1988:** 158 bhp @ 5900 rpm, 155 lbs-ft @ 4500 rpm; **944S** (1986-88): 188 bhp @ 6000 rpm, 170 lbs-ft @ 4300 rpm; **Turbo** (1986-88): 217 bhp @ 5800 rpm, 243 lbs-ft @ 3500 rpm

Transmissions:	5-speed manual (in rear transaxle; 3-speed automatic optional 944 only)
Suspension, front:	MacPherson struts, lower A-arms, coil springs
Suspension, rear:	semi-trailing arms, transverse torsion bars
Brakes:	front/rear discs
Wheelbase (in.):	94.5
Weight (lbs):	2900-3060
Top speed (mph):	123-153
0-60 mph (sec):	6.1-9.0
Production:	NA (production continues at this writing)

1987-1988 PORSCHE 959

Enthusiasts have long dreamed of the "everything" car—the one that can do it all. The Porsche 959 is that dream come true. Just two small problems: only 200 or so will be built, and they're all spoken for—at upwards of $180,000 apiece!

Created in 1983 for the now-abandoned Group B racing series, the 959 is based on the current 911 Carrera, with a similar steel center section and the same wheelbase. The cockpit is also familiar fare. Otherwise, most everything else is different.

Start with a lower body reshaped for good surface aerodynamics, and with a profusion of ducts and vents for controlled airflow *through* it. The results: a 0.31 drag coefficient and—the real achievement—*zero* lift. To save weight, doors and front lid are made of aluminum, the nose cap of polyurethane, the remainder of fiberglass-reinforced Kevlar.

Rolling stock comprises 17-inch alloy wheels wearing ultra-wide super-performance Bridgestone RE71 tires (235/45VR-17 fore, 255/40VR-17 aft). Hollow wheel spokes (first used on Porsche's 1980 Le Mans racers) provide more air for the tires and a smoother ride than would otherwise be possible. There's no spare; the tires can run flat for at least 50 miles after a blowout. Electronic sensors within the wheels warn of any pressure loss.

Power is provided by an exotic short-stroke version of the famous 911 flat six, with twin overhead cams per bank, four valves per cylinder, water-cooled heads, titanium con rods, and twin KKK turbochargers. Crossover pipes and bypass valves provide "staged" turbo operation. Only the port blower is used below about 4000 rpm; the starboard unit is phased in as revs approach that. Despite 8.3:1 compression, DIN horsepower is a heady 450.

Putting it to the ground are a unique full-time four-wheel-drive system and *six*-speed gearbox, basically the five-speed Carrera unit with an extra-low first gear added, ostensibly for off-road use. Power is taken aft in the usual way, forward via a tube-encased driveshaft running from the gearbox to a front differential with an integrated multi-plate clutch in an oil-filled chamber. Varying clutch oil pressure determines front torque delivery, so there's no center differential. A locking rear differential is provided.

Torque apportioning is manual or via one of four computer programs. "Traction" locks the front clutch and rear diff for maximum pulling power in mud and snow. "Ice" splits torque 50/50. "Wet" divides it 40/60, increasing rear-wheel power with acceleration. "Dry" also offers a 40/60 split, but can provide up to 20/80 in all-out acceleration. It's all done via the wheel-mounted speed sensors of the anti-lock braking system, which is essentially 911 Turbo with larger front discs.

The suspension employs classic double-wishbone geometry plus twin shock absorbers and concentric coil springs at each wheel. The shocks in each pair have separate damping functions, again computer-controlled; one set stiffens as speed rises, the other lowers the car slightly from 95 mph to improve aerodynamics. A manual override is also provided.

One of the few ever likely to drive a 959 is British journalist Mel Nichols, whose report appeared in the November 1987 *Automobile.* His was a "sport" model, lacking the rear seats, air conditioning, and additional sound insulation of the so-called "comfort" version but weighing 110 pounds less. That made for just 6.1 lbs/bhp (versus 7.1) and, as the data table shows, truly phenomenal performance. Even more impressive, the 959 was as docile in town as any 911, much quieter, and so stable on the highway that 100 mph felt more like 60, even in driving rain. In corners, it was simply a revelation: "At different times, I lifted off when near maximum power, and all the car did was tighten its line neatly at the front. There was no way that tail—so deadly in these circumstances in a 911—was going to come around. So here was the 959's supreme message...supreme safety. What I liked was the clarity and accessibility of the handling that went with it.

"No car has ever affected me as deeply as this one," Nichols concluded. "Its performance alone makes it more thrilling than any other car I have driven, but I love it most because it gave so much and asked for so little . . . . That is Porsche's achievement. It has built a racing car for road drivers . . . As magnificent as that achievement is, the good news is that it is the tip of an iceberg: Other Porsches will gain the 959's technology and degrees of its prowess. And other manufacturers have been shown the challenge and given the notion of what is possible"—good news indeed for dreamers everywhere.

Though obviously 911-based, Porsche's wild 959 was created under the direction of Dr. Helmut Bott specifically for the short-lived Group B racing series and differs greatly from the production 911. All 200 or so examples are already sold.

SPECIFICATIONS

Engine: dohc flat six, 174 cid/2849 cc, 4 valves/cylinder, dual turbochargers; 450 bhp (DIN) @ 6500 rpm, 369 lbs-ft @ 5500 rpm

Transmission:	full-time 4-wheel drive via 6-speed manual transmission to front differential and rear transaxle
Suspension, front:	unequal-length upper and lower A-arms, coil springs, anti-roll bar (dual shock absorbers)
Suspension, rear:	unequal-length upper and lower A-arms, coil springs, anti-roll bar (dual shock absorbers)
Brakes:	front/rear discs
Wheelbase (in.):	89.4
Weight (lbs):	2977/3088 (Sport/Comfort models)
Top speed (mph):	190 + *
0-60 mph (sec):	3.7*

Production: 200 (built 1987-88; at this writing, Porsche indicates a few additional units may be built)
* manufacturer's data

1966-1970
SAAB SONETT II

The name SAAB stands for *Svenska Aeroplan AB*, which, as you might guess, was founded to build aircraft for the Swedish air force. That was in 1937. When military orders dried up in the wake of World War II, the firm decided to bolster its business with a very different product: automobiles.

What emerged was a streamlined but dumpy-looking little fastback sedan with front-wheel drive (a postwar pioneer in this respect) and a German DKW-inspired two-stroke twin for power. It went on sale in 1949 as the Saab 92. (Like Porsche's, Saab projects have numbers, be they cars or airplanes.) Later models had three-cylinder two-strokes, but remained two-door sedans or three-door station wagons.

Humble they may have been, but these early Saabs proved quite worthy: solid, reliable, and able to cope easily with the harsh Swedish winters for which they were designed. Not surprisingly, they began to do well in European rallying, so the idea of a sporting model wasn't as far-fetched as it might have seemed.

Saab's first move in this direction was the Sonett I of 1956-57, a fiberglass-bodied two-seat roadster based on standard production components. Only a handful were built though, all essentially prototypes, and the company wouldn't try again until 10 years later.

This second effort was somewhat more successful. Internally designated Saab 97 and sold as the Sonett II, it employed rather modest coupe bodywork, again of fiberglass, over the floorpan and running gear of the latest Saab 96 Monte Carlo sedan. That meant a 60-horsepower 841-cc two-stroke three, front drive, front disc brakes, and a 4-speed manual transaxle with Saab's usual column-shift control. Styling was smooth if a bit odd, with a long, pointy front, prominent hood bulge, fixed compound-curve backlight, and abbreviated tail. The design came from Malmo Aircraft Industry (MFI), while bodies were initially built by the Swedish Railway Works (ASJ) in Arlov, many miles from any other Saab production facility. As on the Austin-Healey Sprite and Jaguar E-Type (see entries), hood and front fenders were a single-hinged unit.

Like other Saabs, the Sonett II didn't have much performance at first. The two-stroke three had reached the end of its development by the time sales began in 1966, and was hard pressed to cope with a 1565-pound curb weight. So although handling and durability were of a high order, only 60 Sonnetts were built that first year, followed by 455 in 1967.

That was no way to make money, so the 1968 model received the same engine transplant applied to other Saabs that season: the narrow-angle 1.5-liter V-4 from the German Ford Taunus. Horsepower rose by only five (though the rating was likely conservative), but superior torque greatly improved low-speed tractability. Even better, the V-4 acted and sounded like a "real" engine, a welcome change from the quirky, poppity two-stroke.

Known as the Sonett V-4, Saab's revised sportster was sold in the U.S., though on a very limited basis. One reason is that many showroom browsers found it difficult to take the car seriously. Saab advertising didn't help, defining "Sonett" as "Swedish for 'expensive toy.' You can find it in the toy department."

Nevertheless, this was a very nimble, fun-to-drive little car, with decent luggage space (but no external access) and passenger room, plus the practicality of front-wheel drive and that rustproof body. Though not as well balanced as the two-stroker, the V-4 was far more "sloggable," and its 100-mph performance made it far better for a wider range of driving conditions.

Saab would have loved to have sold more Sonett IIs in the U.S., but dumpy looks and competition from established sports cars like MG and Triumph continued to limit demand. Production ended in 1970, but only because Saab had something better: the new Sonett III.

Though sportier, Sonett II maintained Saab's reputation for distinctive styling (opposite). Two-stroke inline three (above) sat well forward under the hood, which acquired a very prominent bulge when the German Ford V-4 took over for '68. Instrumentation (top) was complete, businesslike.

SPECIFICATIONS

Engines: **1966-67:** two-stroke I-3, 51.3 cid/841 cc, 60 bhp (SAE net) @ 5200 rpm, 69 lbs-ft @ 4000 rpm; **1968-70:** German Ford ohv V-4, 91.4 cid/1498 cc, 65 bhp (net) @ 4700 rpm, 85 lbs-ft @ 2500 rpm

Transmission:	4-speed manual (in front transaxle)
Suspension, front:	upper and lower A-arms, coil springs
Suspension, rear:	beam axle, central locating bracket, radius arms, coil springs
Brakes:	front discs/rear drums
Wheelbase (in.):	85.0
Weight (lbs):	1565-1700
Top speed (mph):	100 (V-4)
0-60 mph (sec):	12.0 (V-4)
Production:	1868

1970-1974
SAAB SONETT III

By most accounts, the report card on the Sonett II and V-4 was, "Tries hard, but could do better." With the Sonett III, aimed directly at the U.S. market, that's precisely what Saab did.

Because this remained a specialty model with limited sales potential, and because of Saab's small size, there was no way to justify the cost of a completely new design. It might have made good *technical* sense to switch the sports car to the chassis of the then-new 99 sedan, but this wasn't seriously considered.

Accordingly, the Sonett III, which bowed publicly at the 1970 New York Auto Show, was simply a restyled version of the previous 96-based Sonett II. Most of the design work was done by Italian freelancer Sergio Coggiola (also well known to Swedish rival Volvo), with Saab's own studio applying final touches.

Retaining the Sonett II's central body, Coggiola lengthened the tail, discarded the ungainly wrapped backlight, and substituted a proper fastback roof with convenient hatch window. Up front was a longer, smoother nose with conventional hood, pop-up headlamps, and a wide, shallow grille with driving lamps behind its thin horizontal bars. Other changes included rear quarter windows, more aggressively flared

wheelarches, a stylish new dashboard, and a choice of two models: standard and luxury. As before, the body was fiberglass, and ASJ in Arlov handled both body production and final assembly.

Also retained were the underframe and front-drive running gear from Saab's V-4 96 sedan/95 wagon, but a more powerful, 1.7-liter version of the German Ford engine was adopted in deference to tightening American safety and emissions standards. Alas, its 10 more horsepower and nine extra pounds-feet of torque were offset by a considerable gain in curb weight, so the III was no faster than the II all out and actually a bit slower off the line. Sales weren't any better either: just 940 units for the entire calendar year.

Changes were simple and few in subsequent years. The '71s wore redesigned wheels, and the alloy rims previously offered on the luxury model were eliminated. Saab's new "corporate" grille motif marked the '72s, which were also reruns otherwise. The following year brought U.S.-inspired front and rear "impact" bumpers much like those applied to the previous season's 99 sedans. Of the last, Saab's own historians said: "No one in the world could say that they did much for the car's design."

Unfortunately for Saab, sales were still a long way from viable, and this plus the 96's planned North American phaseout meant that the Sonett would also vanish after 1974. A successor was considered but would never reach production.

Saab has yet to try another sports car, and may never. It has since found sports sedans—especially the turbocharged variety—to be much more profitable. Today, the closest thing to a Saab sports car (which still sounds like a contradiction in terms) is the 900 Turbo convertible—very able but, as they say, a horse of a different color.

SPECIFICATIONS

Engine: German Ford ohv V-4, 103.7 cid/1699 cc, 75 bhp (DIN) @ 5000 rpm, 94 lbs-ft @ 2500 rpm

Transmission:	4-speed manual (in front transaxle)
Suspension, front:	upper and lower A-arms, coil springs
Suspension, rear:	beam axle, central locating bracket, radius arms, coil springs
Brakes:	front discs/rear drums
Wheelbase (in.):	85.0
Weight (lbs):	1785
Top speed (mph):	100
0-60 mph (sec):	14.4
Production:	8351

Italian designer Sergio Coggiola turned Sonett II into the more handsome Sonett III. Dash was more "grownup."

1965-1966 SHELBY GT-350

Ford hit the jackpot with the Mustang, the first of the sporty compacts later termed "ponycars" in its honor. Nearly 691,000 were delivered for debut 1965, another 608,000 for '66. But marketer Bob Johnson discovered that even the most potent factory Mustang didn't have enough beef for hard-core enthusiasts, many of whom bought Corvettes instead. That didn't please Ford division chief and Mustang "father" Lee Iacocca, who knew that racing not only improves the breed but profits.

So Mustang would join Ford's other "Total Performance" cars on the track. But who could make it a winner? Iacocca knew: Carroll Shelby, the ex-Ferrari team driver and sometime chicken rancher who'd stuffed a Ford 289 V-8 into the light British AC Ace roadster to create the beautiful, brutal Cobra (see entry).

Shelby went to work at his small Venice, California shop, aided by race driver Ken Miles, who'd helped develop the Cobra, and engineer Chuck Cantwell. Because product recognition was vital to give showroom Mustangs a "race-proved" image, their efforts focused on B-Production, one of the stock classes in Sports Car Club of America competition. By the fall of '64 they'd built two prototypes based on the recently introduced Mustang fastback. A dozen handbuilt cars were ready by Christmas and 88 assembly line examples by New Year's, thus satisfying the SCCA's 100-unit homologation minimum. The car was announced January 27, 1965 at Riverside Raceway as the Mustang GT-350, a strictly arbitrary designation; most everyone soon started calling it Shelby-Mustang or Shelby GT-350.

Two versions were planned from the start: a street car, called "S", and a full-bore R-model racer. Both began as white fastbacks produced at Ford's San Jose, California plant *sans* hood, exhaust system, and rear seat but with the "Hi-Performance" 289, Borg-Warner T-10 4-speed gearbox, front disc brakes, and Galaxie rear axle and drum brakes (the last replacing the stock Mustang's lighter Falcon components). Once moved to larger quarters in a hangar at Los Angeles International Airport, Shelby-American set up a small assembly line where it installed rear trailing radius rods, Detroit No-Spin "locker" differential, bigger-than-stock front anti-roll bar, Koni adjustable shocks, quick-ratio steering box, hefty 15-×6-inch wheels mounting Goodyear Blue Dot high-speed tires, and a fiberglass hood with functional scoop. Aluminum high-rise manifold and a larger carb added 35 horsepower, and blue racing stripes were applied to rocker panels and atop the car nose-to-tail.

R-models got a blueprinted Cobra racing engine with oil cooler, an even bigger carb, still-hotter cam, enlarged and polished ports, and other tweaks. Insulation, carpeting, door panels, and window-winders were omitted, the front bumper was replaced by a fiberglass apron with brake and oil-cooler air ducts, and Plexiglas was used for all windows save windshield. A long-range 34-gallon fuel tank and five-spoke 7×15 magnesium wheels completed the package.

Bargain-priced at $4547, the GT-350S garnered rave reviews while the $5950 R-model cleaned up in B-Production, winning the 1965 national championship and four out of five regional championships. The same cars won again in '66, when Walt Hane took the trophy, and in '67, with Fred Van Buren the national champ.

Those '65s kept running because the '66s weren't quite the all-out racers they were. Though there's no clear distinction, the first 250 or so '66s were actually leftover '65s fitted with Plexiglas rear quarter windows instead of the stock air vents, plus a Revised grille and working rear-fender air scoops. But the "real" '66s came in more colors; had the stock back seat, underhood battery, and 14- instead of 15-inch wheels; and offered the "locker" diff as an option—along with automatic transmission. Ford just couldn't resist broadening the car's market appeal. Shelby even built a limited run of cushy gold-on-black GT-350H models for Hertz, which lost a bundle on weekend rentals. The one bright spot was the arrival of a Paxton supercharger as a $670 option (also sold as a $430 kit). It allegedly boosted horsepower beyond 400 and cut the claimed 0-60 mph time to a mere 5.0 seconds, but very few cars were so equipped.

From here on, the Shelby GT would never be the same. A Mustang gave Ford the manufacturer's trophy in the 1966 inaugural of the SCCA's Trans-American road-racing series for ponycars and compact sedans, but it was a Shelby-prepped notchback, not a GT-350.

An interesting postscript: At the end of '66, Shelby had six prototype GT-350 convertibles built as gifts. Exactly 15 years later and with his blessing, another 12 were converted from restored '66 Mustang convertibles, essentially brand-new cars identical with the originals. All sold quickly despite costing around $40,000 apiece.

All 1966 GT-350s had rear quarter windows and side scoops **(opposite)**. *Cockpit* **(above)** *was mostly stock Mustang. Shelby-Tuned 289 V-8* **(top)** *was a powerhouse.*

SPECIFICATIONS

Engine: ohv V-8, 289 cid/4736 cc, 306 bhp @ 6000 rpm, 329 lbs-ft @ 4200 rpm (R model: 324-328 bhp @ 6500 rpm)

Transmissions:	4-speed manual; 3-speed automatic (optional 1966)
Suspension, front:	independent, upper A-arms, lower control arms, coil springs, anti-roll bar
Suspension, rear:	live axle, semi-elliptic leaf springs, torque control arms
Brakes:	front discs/rear drums
Wheelbase (in.):	108.0
Weight (lbs):	2800
Top speed (mph):	120+
0-60 mph (sec):	6.8

Production: 1965 562 (incl. 12 R-model) **1966** 2378 (incl. 936 GT-350H, 3 R-model, and 6 prototype convertibles)

1967-1969 SHELBY GT-350/GT-500/ GT-500KR

Mustang put on pounds and inches for '67, so the Shelby GT-350 did too. But that wasn't the half of it. Ford now offered its big-block 390 V-8 as the top Mustang performance option. Typical of the man, Carroll specified the physically identical 428 engine for a second Shelby called GT-500. It was a popular move, the newcomer outselling its smaller-capacity stablemate two-to-one.

Still, performance began taking a back seat to styling and luxury with the '67s, because that's where the money was spent. Ford was still spending it, of course, but was now more intimately involved with the Shelbys—and more determined that they turn a profit.

Because Mustang was heavier for '67, and with customers wanting a more manageable Shelby, power steering and brakes became mandatory Shelby options. Mustang's newly reworked '67 interior was little altered for the Shelbys, though they continued with several unique touches: distinctive racing steering wheel, additional gauges, and a genuine roll-over bar with built-in inertia-reel shoulder harnesses. Comfort and convenience options proliferated: air conditioning, tinted glass, tilt steering wheel, and more.

Outside, Ford's Chuck McHose and Shelby-American's Pete Brock styled a new fiberglass nose to match Mustang's longer '67 hood, with a "big-mouth" grille bearing twin center-mount high-beam driving lamps (since moved outboard on some cars to comply with headlight-spacing regulations). Scoops were everywhere—hood, lower bodysides, sail panels—all functional and, of course, larger. Out back, a special trunklid with integral spoiler appeared above wide taillamp clusters purloined from the new Mercury Cougar.

All these touches plus Mustang's new full-fastback styling made the '67 Shelbys handsome, fast-looking cars. Alas, GT-350 performance sagged under the weight of

all the new fluff. Its horsepower was ostensibly the same as before but surely less in actuality, as the steel-tube exhaust headers had disappeared.

The new GT-500 *was* quick, but curiously disappointing. Carmakers began using more conservative horsepower ratings for '67 as a sop to insurance companies. The Shelby's 428 had an advertised 335, though again it was probably more. *Car and Driver,* whose test car took 6.5 seconds 0-60 mph, said that while the 428 "isn't the Le Mans winner," the GT-500 "does with ease what the old [GT-350] took brute force to accomplish." But *Road & Track,* which recorded 7.2 seconds for the same sprint, said the GT-500 "simply doesn't have anything sensational to offer . . . . A [standard] Mustang with the 390 cu. in. engine option does as well." As ever, Shelby had an answer: an optional 427—which *was* the Le Mans engine—rated at 390 bhp. Still, not many were ordered.

Dearborn's control over the Shelby-Mustangs became total for '68. Production was moved from Los Angeles to Michigan, where stock Mustangs (from Ford's Metuchen, New Jersey plant) were converted into Shelbys by the A.O. Smith Company under contract. The fastbacks gained convertible companions with built-in roll-over hoop, and all four models sported a full-width hood scoop, new hood louvers, a larger grille with square running lamps (not driving lights), sequential rear turn signals, and minor trim changes.

With federal emissions limits in force, the GT-350 was switched to Ford's newly enlarged 302-cid small-block—and lost a lot of power. However, the Paxton supercharger option returned from '66 to add about 100 horses, though it, too, found few takers. The GT-500 initially retained its 428, now at 360 bhp. A few, however, got ordinary 390 V-8s. This probably stemmed from a shortage of 428s due to an engine-plant strike, but buyers weren't told about the substitution, which was nearly impossible to spot.

Mid-year brought some redress, however, in the GT-500KR (for "King of the Road"). This had the new Cobra Jet engine, basically the existing 428 with big-port 427 heads, larger intake manifold and exhaust system, and an estimated 40 extra horses. Ford also tossed in wider rear brakes.

Shelby production rose for the fourth straight year in 1968, but would go no higher. The press mostly yawned at the plusher '68s, and Ford made no effort to race either the '67 or '68 Shelbys. Not that they'd have been competitive. They'd grown too big, too soft, too heavy—not at all the race-bred stormers their predecessors had been. And Ford only managed to dilute their appeal further with Shelbyesque showroom Mustangs like the '68 GT/CS ("California Special") notchback. With all this, the Shelby-Mustang wasn't dead by the end of '68, but it didn't have long to live.

Shelby's busier, bulkier '67 styling was mildly warmed over for '68. Here, the GT-500KR ("King of the Road"), a mid-year substitution for the GT-500, powered by the then-new Cobra Jet version of Ford's big-block 428 V-8.

SPECIFICATIONS

Engines: all ohv V-8; **GT-350** (1967): 289 cid/4736 cc, 306 bhp @ 6000 rpm, 329 lbs-ft @ 4200 rpm; **GT-350** (1968): 302 cid/4949 cc, 250 bhp @ 4800 rpm, 310 lbs-ft @ 2800 rpm or 315 bhp @ 5000 rpm, 333 lbs-ft @ 3800 rpm; **GT-500/500KR** (1967-68): 428 cid/7014 cc, 355-360/400 bhp @ 5400 rpm, 420 lbs-ft @ 3200 rpm; **GT-500 "Special"** (1967): 427 cid/6998 cc, 390 bhp @ 5400 rpm, 465 lbs-ft @ 3200 rpm

Transmissions:	4-speed manual or 3-speed automatic
Suspension, front:	independent, unequal-length A-arms, coil springs, anti-roll bar
Suspension, rear:	live axle, semi-elliptic leaf springs, torque control arms
Brakes:	front discs/rear drums
Wheelbase (in.):	108.0
Weight (lbs):	2920-3300
Top speed (mph):	125 +
0-60 mph (sec):	6.5-8.0
Production:	**1967** 3225 **1968** 4450

1969-1970
SHELBY GT-350/GT-500

There's little to say about the 1969-70 Shelby GTs, other than that they were even more like production Mustangs than the 1967-68 editions and thus further removed from Carroll Shelby's original concept. Of course, they'll always be treasured as the last of a special breed, but that'll likely be the only reason.

Not that these cars weren't, er, interesting. Mustang got a much swoopier new bodyshell for '69, so the Shelbys did too. Both fastback and convertible returned in GT-350 and 500 form, differentiated from the weightier, lengthier, much busier production cars by a three-inch longer hood, reshaped front fenders, and a new nose with a big loop-style bumper/grille (all made of fiberglass to hold down weight), plus a clipped tail still bearing a lip spoiler and Cougar sequential turn signals. Scoops were everywhere—five NACA ducts on the hood alone—and wide reflective tape stripes ran midway along the flanks. Said *Car and Driver* magazine's Brock Yates: "I personally can't think of an automobile that makes a statement about performance...any better than [this Shelby]."

But brag is one thing, fact another. And the fact was that stiffening emission controls and the new Mustang's greater weight made the '69 Shelbys somewhat tamer. The GT-500 was no longer labelled "King of the Road" but retained that '68 model's 428 Cobra Jet engine, still at a nominal 355 horsepower, though actual output was down 25 horses by most estimates. The GT-350 was promoted to Ford's new 351-cubic-inch "Windsor" small-block, with hydraulic-lifter cam, big four-barrel carb, aluminum high-rise manifold, and low-restriction exhaust system. Advertised horsepower was unchanged from that of the previous 302—but then, this engine was standard in the new Mach 1 fastback, which cost much less than the Shelby.

Yates derisively described the '69 GT-350 as "a garter snake in Cobra skin." But if the magic was gone—and it was—part of the problem was that Ol' Shel had long ceased to be involved with his cars. In fact, the '69s were built at Ford's Southfield, Michigan plant right alongside box-stock Mustangs.

The other part of the problem was new competition from the Mustang line itself. The Mach 1 was interference enough, but mid-year brought the hot Boss 302, a thinly disguised Trans-Am racer for the street, and the incredible Boss 429, a thinly disguised drag racer stuffed full of Ford's potent "semi-hemi" big-block. Of course, the Bosses were no cheaper or more readily available than the Shelbys, but they were "a curious duplication of effort," as Yates put it, that only dimmed what luster the Shelbys still had. "The heritage of the GT-350 is performance," he mused, "and it is difficult to understand why the Ford marketing experts failed to exploit its reputation."

Perhaps they'd learned Ol' Shel was tiring of the car business. Ever the individualist, he'd begun by building machines he himself wanted to drive, then watched his Cobras and the original GT-350 dominate SCCA competition. His efforts with Ford's assault on the World Manufacturer's Championship had helped the mid-engine Ford GT racers win Le Mans two years in a row (1966-67) and vanquish Ferraris and Porsches all over the world. But racing was becoming ever-more competitive and costly, and rapidly advancing technology was making it hard for all but a few specialists to apply new engineering principles successfully. By 1970, Shelby had decided that racing wasn't fun anymore; it was business.

So was building his own cars once Ford muscled in and started calling the shots. And Shelby hated design by committees, where accountants and lawyers often overruled engineers and test drivers. The Bosses and Mach 1 were only last straws.

In a way, time had caught up with both Shelby and his cars. Carroll knew it, and urged Lee Iacocca to end the Shelby-Mustang program after 1970. Iacocca agreed. These final cars were merely leftover '69s with Boss 302 front spoilers, black hoods, and new serial numbers. At Riverside in October 1969, Shelby announced his retirement as a race-car developer and team manager.

But the last Shelby-Mustangs would not be the last Shelbys. Being who he is, Carroll couldn't stay away from the car business forever. Today, thanks to his friend Iacocca, he's working the same kind of magic at Chrysler that he did for Ford, and we enthusiasts are all the better for it.

*The final Shelby-Mustangs were arguably the raciest-looking of the breed, but they were also most like the hotter stock Mustangs under the hood (**above**) and inside (**top**). As before, front and tail styling was unique. Note standard twist-type locks on hood.*

SPECIFICATIONS

Engines: all ohv V-8; **GT-350:** 351 cid/5752 cc, 300 bhp @ 5400 rpm, 380 lbs-ft @ 3400 rpm; **GT-500:** 428 cid/7014 cc, 355 bhp @ 5200 rpm, 440 lbs-ft @ 3400 rpm

Transmissions:	4-speed manual or 3-speed automatic
Suspension, front:	upper and lower A-arms, trailing links, coil springs, anti-roll bar
Suspension, rear:	live axle, semi-elliptic leaf springs
Brakes:	front discs/rear drums
Wheelbase (in.):	108.0
Weight (lbs):	3000-3200
Top speed (mph):	120+
0-60 mph (sec):	7.5
Production:	**1969** 3150 **1970** 601

1959-1968
SUNBEAM ALPINE &
HARRINGTON Le MANS

When Rootes discontinued the original Sunbeam Alpine in 1955 (see entry), it didn't even attempt a replacement, mainly because it was going to start overhauling its entire passenger-car fleet that year. But the task was completed by 1958, and Rootes could again take up a sports car. The result appeared the following year as a new, very different Alpine.

Like its predecessor, this Alpine borrowed liberally from Rootes' ordinary family sedans. But instead of a middle-class medium-size platform, its basis was the smaller and cheaper unit-steel structure that mostly made up the new corporate line. Variations comprised of a basic four-door sedan, the Hillman Minx; an upmarket version, the Singer Gazelle; and a derivative hardtop coupe, the Sunbeam Rapier. Convertible and station wagon were also offered, along with a two-door short-chassis wagon/panel van, the Hillman Husky. (All these were seen in the U.S., some more often than others.) So though it had the same name, the new Alpine had no technical or styling links with the earlier one.

In an interesting joint venture, Alpine engineering and initial assembly was handed to Armstrong-Siddeley of Coventry in exchange for a new six to power Rootes' next generation of big Humber cars. Styling was an in-house job, still an open two-seater but much more contemporary, right down to a curved, but not wrapped, windshield and trendy tailfins. "Modern" features abounded, including roll-up door windows, an easily erected soft top, proper heater, and fully outfitted dash. Options ran to a detachable steel hardtop and electric overdrive. With all this, plus Americanized styling, the Alpine was widely regarded as more sports tourer than traditional sports car.

About the same size as an MGA or Triumph TR3 (see entries), the Alpine used the short-wheelbase Husky underframe combined with slightly improved Rapier running gear. Power initially came from the 1.5-liter version of the corporate overhead-valve four, rated at 78 horsepower and good for nearly 100 mph in magazine road tests (of cars that were probably tweaked a bit). Needless to say, the new Alpine

was lighter and more nimble than the original, and thus keen competition for the MG and TR. It was slightly heavier and less powerful than they were, but offered superior structural stiffness.

Not that Rootes, its dealers or customers complained, especially as the Alpine was progressively improved. Like America's Corvette, in fact, it seemed to get worthwhile changes almost every year, thus gaining a distinct sales advantage over most rivals.

The progression was simple and fairly rapid. Autumn 1960 brought a Series II model with an 80-bhp 1.6-liter engine. The Series III followed at the beginning of 1963 with a second model called GT. This featured a slightly detuned engine, walnut-covered dash and the removable hardtop but, curiously, no folding top. The fins were cut back for the Series IV, which bowed in early '64 with a new extra-cost automatic transmission. An all-synchromesh manual arrived later that year. Last came the late-1965 Series V, *sans* automatic option but boasting 1725 cc and 92 bhp. It was predictably the fastest accelerating Alpine, but maximum speed was somehow stuck at 98-100 mph. Even so, this winsome little car carried on successfully into early 1968, by which time Chrysler Corporation had taken over Rootes and was directing new products, some good, some dreadful.

The rarest of these Alpines was the 1962-63 Le Mans, a unique fastback coupe conversion by the Harrington coachworks. It began with a Series II roadster shorn of fins and fitted with a smooth fiberglass roof terminating in a reverse "ducktail." Discreet coachlines (pinstripes) hid the seams where plastic met metal toward the rear, making the finished product look almost as if it had been the original design. Seats were trimmed in leather or vinyl (it varied from car to car), the dash in traditional walnut. The 1.6-liter engine was tuned to "Stage 2" specs, as on the factory fastbacks that had won the Index of Thermal Efficiency at the 1961 Le Mans 24 Hours. This improved acceleration but didn't much affect top speed. Even hotter "Stage 3" tuning couldn't lift the maximum beyond 110 mph.

As custom-built jobs, the "Harringtons" (Rootes didn't use this name in the U.S.) weren't cheap. The Le Mans cost $3995, which was close to Corvette territory, versus $2800 or less for a contemporary Alpine. Harrington did other Alpine conversions, including a lower-powered GT fastback, but the Le Mans was the best-selling one, though it only saw 250 copies.

There would be one more Alpine, a product of the Chrysler regime and not to be confused with these two-seaters. This was little more than a pillarless fastback version of the mundane late-Sixties Hillman Hunter sedan (Sunbeam Arrow in the U.S.) and just as dull, barring a hot Holbay-tuned British-market model called H120 (for its alleged 120-mph maximum). Chrysler made a half-hearted U.S. sales effort in 1969-70, then cast its captive-import lot with Mitsubishi of Japan—which is a story for another book.

SPECIFICATIONS

Engines: all ohv I-4; **1959-60:** 91.2 cid/1464 cc, 78 bhp (net) @ 5300 rpm, 89 lbs-ft @ 3400 rpm; **1960-65:** 97.2 cid/1592 cc, 80 bhp (net) @ 5000 rpm, 94 lbs-ft @ 3800 rpm; **1965-68:** 105.3 cid/1725 cc, 92 bhp (net) @ 5500 rpm, 103 lbs-ft @ 6200 rpm (Respective horsepower with available Harrington tuning kits: 88 bhp @ 5500 rpm, 93 bhp @ 5700 rpm, 100 bhp @ 6200 rpm)

Transmissions:	4-speed manual with optional Laycock de Normanville overdrive or (1964-65) 3-speed automatic
Suspension, front:	upper and lower wishbones, coil springs, anti-roll bar
Suspension, rear:	live axle, semi-elliptic leaf springs
Brakes:	front discs/rear drums
Wheelbase (in.):	86.0
Weight (lbs):	2135-2240
Top speed (mph):	92-100 (Harrington: 99-109)
0-60 mph (sec):	13.6-18.8 (Harrington: 10.6-13.1)

Production: **Series I** (1959-60) 11,904 **Series II** (1960-63) 19,956 **Series III** (1963-64) 5863 **Series IV** (1964-65) 12,406 **Series V** (1965-68) 19,122 **Harrington Le Mans** (1962-63) 250

Opposite: Alpine was a Fifties design, so its curved windshield and trendy tailfins were no surprise. The latter were shaved off for '64. *Below:* Harrington Le Mans fastback conversion featured high-tune engine.

1964-1967 SUNBEAM TIGER

SPECIFICATIONS

Engines: all Ford ohv V-8; **1964-66:** 260 cid/4261 cc, 164 bhp (SAE gross) @ 4400 rpm, 258 lbs-ft @ 2200 rpm; **1967:** 289 cid/ 4737 cc, 200 bhp (SAE gross) @ 4400 rpm, 282 lbs-ft @ 2400 rpm

Transmission:	4-speed manual
Suspension, front:	upper and lower wishbones, coil springs, anti-roll bar
Suspension, rear:	live axle, Panhard rod, semi-elliptic leaf springs
Brakes:	front discs/rear drums
Wheelbase (in.):	86.0
Weight (lbs):	2560
Top speed (mph):	117-122
0-60 mph (sec):	7.5-9.5
Production:	**Tiger** (1964-66) 6495 **Tiger II** (1967) 571

Carroll Shelby had stuffed a lithe British sports car full of American V-8 without much regard for cost. Rootes Group did the same thing, but its car was a lot more affordable yet just as exciting. Carroll's invention, of course, was the A.C. Shelby-Cobra (see entry). The Rootes hybrid was named Sunbeam Tiger and bore strong Shelby influence, for the prototype was built by his company around the same basic Ford V-8.

The four-cylinder Sunbeam Alpine (see entry) had earned a fine reputation by the mid-Sixties, especially in the U.S., but everyone agreed it deserved a more potent engine. Trouble was, Rootes didn't have one. It was thus left to Ian Garrad, an American-based Rootes executive, to "invent" the idea of an Alpine with Ford small-block power, and to get Shelby to work out the details.

The result debuted at the New York Auto Show in April 1964 (the same month as Ford's trend-setting Mustang), with deliveries commencing that summer. Because the Rootes plants in Coventry were taken up with the Alpine and family car production, Tiger assembly was farmed out to Jensen of West Bromwich (logical, as that firm had supplied Austin-Healey 3000 tubs to BMC and had recently completed the first of Volvo's P1800s).

Visually, the Tiger was much like the Alpine Series IV except for the requisite badges, different wheel covers, and discreet full-length bodyside chrome strips. This similarity partly explains limited Tiger sales, as American buyers presumably wanted their neighbors to *know* they had something special. It also seemed a problem in the UK, where sales began during 1965.

Like the first Shelby-Cobra, the Tiger arrived with the 260-cubic-inch version of Ford's sterling new-for-'62 "thinwall" V-8, albeit in a much milder state of tune. Then again, even its 164 horsepower was more than twice what the Alpine had, and thus sufficient to say the least. The live rear axle and 4-speed gearbox with central floorshift also came from Ford. There was no overdrive option, but none was really needed.

The chassis was the Alpine's conventional affair, but Shelby took the opportunity to change from recirculating-ball steering to rack-and-pinion, specified considerably stiffer springs and shocks, and added a Panhard rod to help keep the back end from doing the watusi in hard takeoffs. Brakes remained front discs and rear drums.

Motor-noters raved about the two-seat Sunbeam's new-found go. The Tiger cut the Alpine's 0-60 mph time almost in half, and its top speed was some 18 mph higher. Handling, roadholding, and ride comfort all earned high marks, though the combination of skinny tires (5.90-13s) and that torquey engine meant startling axle hop and poor off-the-line traction. But this was easy to forgive in light of the spirited performance and a practical basic package inherited from the Alpine. The Tiger may have been a lot slower than a Cobra, but was far more civilized, better equipped, and much cheaper. In fact, at $3499, it was almost a steal.

The problem for Rootes wasn't selling the car but a change in corporate politics, for Chrysler bought into the firm just as the Tiger was being launched. With Lord Rootes' death, Chrysler was calling the shots in Coventry within two years despite lacking a majority interest. As the Tiger put Chrysler in the embarrassing position of having to guarantee a Ford engine, Rootes scrambled to fit a politically correct substitute, but even the smallest Chrysler V-8 was just too big.

An improved Tiger II was already in the pipeline, and it duly went on sale in 1967. The main change was adoption of the 289 Ford small-block with a rated 200 bhp, plus a restrained eggcrate grille insert, not-so-restrained twin rocker-panel stripes, and revised badges reading "Sunbeam V-8" instead of "Powered by Ford 260." By one U.S. account, the extra power did nothing for 0-60 mph acceleration (though Britain's *Autocar* magazine reported a two-second improvement, to 7.5 seconds), but top speed rose by 5 mph despite no gearing or tire alterations. Regardless of such discrepancies, the Tiger II was the equal of Jaguar's E-Type in traffic-light *grands prix* and significantly quicker than the last of the big Healeys or the first of Triumph's six-cylinder TRs.

But it didn't matter. Chrysler's corporate pride couldn't countenance a Ford-powered car for long, and the Tiger II was unceremoniously dumped during 1967. Some folks still haven't forgiven Chrysler for that.

The rapid Sunbeam Tiger was a sort of "budget" Cobra built to much the same formula. Series I models like this bore a single grille bar with large medallion.

1965-1970
TOYOTA 2000GT

It would have been credible enough for an established sports-car builder. But coming from a Japanese automaker with no sporting tradition, the Toyota 2000GT was simply astonishing—and all the more welcome for it.

Toyota had been building cars for some 30 years before the 2000GT, but they'd been uniformly mundane: solid, stolid people-movers of high reliability but no technical interest or sophistication. By the late Sixties, the archetypical Toyota was a Corolla or Corona, built by the tens of thousands like so many refrigerators and possessing about as much soul.

The car that would change that image came about through a quirky turn of events. It started with Count Albrecht Goertz, the industrial designer who'd shaped the mid-Fifties BMW 503 and 507 (see entry). Goertz went to Japan as a freelancer in the early Sixties and did a two-seat coupe for Nissan. Yamaha, the pianos-to-motorbikes firm, built a running prototype that Nissan eventually turned down, though some of its styling themes were further developed for the Datsun 240Z (see entry).

But Yamaha also had ties with Toyota and pitched the prototype its way. Toyota liked it and modified it a little. *Voila!* The 2000GT was born. Chassis work began in May 1964, the production prototype was unveiled at the Tokyo Motor Show in October 1965, and sales began in May 1967.

Toyota's lack of high-performance engineering experience at the time suggests that the 2000GT was merely a means of obtaining same and that it was never envisioned as even a limited-production item. It was "series built" to be sure, but in such low numbers as to preclude volume sale at a reasonable price.

This also explains the heavy technical borrowing from contemporary European GTs. The chassis, for example, was a box-section steel backbone affair clearly inspired by that of the Lotus Elan, as was the classic all-independent wishbone suspension. Rack-and-pinion steering, Dunlop four-wheel disc brakes, and magnesium-alloy road wheels were also *de rigueur* in Europe but unheard-of for an Oriental. Power was supplied by a Yamaha-developed 2.0-liter twincam conversion of the 2.3-liter *single-cam* straight six from Toyota's big Crown sedan, linked to a 5-speed overdrive manual gearbox. With 150 horsepower and slippery coupe bodywork of lightweight aluminum, the 2000GT was claimed to do 135 mph flat out.

In appearance, the 2000GT was predictive of the 240Z that followed it, though rounder and a touch more "Oriental." Some were reminded of the Jaguar E-Type, though detailing was completely different. The front was both advanced and traditional. The main headlights were hidden, flipping up from the nose when switched on, but were supplemented by a pair of large glass-covered driving lamps within a rather geometric grille. Again foreshadowing Nissan's Z-car, "production" 2000GTs were all two-seat fastback hatch coupes, though a couple of special convertibles were run off for a starring role in the James Bond film *You Only Live Twice*.

As Toyota's first venture into high-performance territory, the 2000GT was an indulgence for both company and consumer. The 1967 Japanese price was 2.4 million yen, while *Road & Track* magazine estimated the U.S. POE charge at $6800, well above the E-Type or Porsche's 911. Equipment, however, was downright luxurious for a sports car: self-seeking AM radio, "rally" clock/stopwatch, telescopic steering wheel, full instrumentation, a modern heating/ventilating system, and a comprehensive tool kit.

But Toyota was just testing the waters. As proof, the 2000GT was built only with righthand drive, which made it less-than-practical in the U.S. and most of the rest of the world, while the cockpit was decidedly tight for other than Oriental physiques.

Such problems would doubtless have been ironed out in a more serious production effort. But publicity, not profits, was the mission, and the 2000GT accomplished it admirably. Prototypes performed well in Japanese sports-car races (3rd overall in the '66 Japanese GP and 1st at that year's Suzuka 1000 Kilometers), and set records by running at 128 mph for up to 72 hours and 10,000 miles.

In retrospect, the 2000GT was merely a warm up for Toyota's high-volume mini-Mustang, the 1970 Celica. That car was a long way from the GT in both presence and performance, but it began a whole new breed that's with us yet. In fact, there's a little 2000GT in today's twincam Supra, and we can all be grateful for that.

SPECIFICATIONS

Engine: dohc I-6, 121.4 cid/1998 cc, 150 bhp (net) @ 6600 rpm, 130 lbs-ft @ 5000 rpm

Transmission:	5-speed manual
Suspension, front:	unequal-length A-arms, coil springs, anti-roll bar
Suspension, rear:	unequal-length A-arms, coil springs, anti-roll bar
Brakes:	front/rear discs
Wheelbase (in.):	91.7
Weight (lbs)	2480
Top speed (mph):	128-137
0-60 mph (sec):	8.4-10.0
Production:	337

Smooth-lined Toyota 2000GT was styled by Albrecht Goertz and somewhat predictive of his Datsun 240Z design, yet also had strong Jaguar E-Type flavor. Large driving lights behind clear covers flanked the grille. The normal headlamps swivelled up from above.

1985-1988
TOYOTA MR2

Japan's first mid-engine production car has been greeted as one of the best sports cars around regardless of price—which it is. That the MR2 comes from a firm not long known for sporting machinery only makes it all the more significant.

Like its contemporary American rival, the Pontiac Fiero, MR2 (which means something like "Mid/Rear-engine 2-seater") is what might be described as a corporate kit car: an amalgam of existing components arranged in a new way. It's an idea as old as the first hot rod or, more recently, the Lotus Europa, Porsche 914, and Fiat X1/9. If the MR2 has any distinction here, it may be the superior components Toyota was able to pull off its shelves.

The MR2 was born in the late Seventies when a project team led by Akio Yoshida began looking at sports-car possibilities using components from the first front-drive Toyota, the small Tercel economy model. Later, Toyota re-engineered its popular Corolla sedans for front drive, and their components became the building blocks. A prototype dubbed "SV-3" was shown about a year ahead of the production MR2, which went on sale in Japan in June 1984 and arrived in the U.S. the following February.

There's nothing mysterious about "Mister Two's" mechanical makeup. A transverse four-cylinder engine and transaxle are lifted from the front-drive Corolla and put behind a two-seat cockpit in a unitized coupe hull; the same car's front MacPherson-strut suspension and disc brakes are used at both ends. While an ordinary 1.5-liter engine powers the base Japanese model, uplevel versions and all U.S.-market MR2s have the twincam 16-valve unit first seen in the rear-drive 1984 Corolla Sport coupes. Steering is the expected rack-and-pinion *sans* power assist, though none is really needed with the lightly loaded nose (front/rear weight distribution is 44/56 percent).

Critics have almost all been disappointed with MR2 styling—conservative, angular, and not that pretty. But beauty is only skin deep, and the MR2 has many inner charms.

One of them is the snug but surprisingly airy cockpit, a modern yet practical design with a more normal, upright driving position than Fiero's (a lower center tunnel helps immeasurably), ideally located pedals and shifter, fine ergonomics, and body-hugging

Below and opposite: "Mister Two" appearance has seen little change so far. An optional "aero" body kit with rocker skirts and decklid spoiler was added for 1986. *Above:* New-for-'88 MR2 Supercharged comes only with the T-roof option in the U.S. Note its deeper front airdam.

sports seats with more adjustments than an income-tax form. Amenities are equally charming: tilt steering wheel, AM/FM stereo radio, and electric remote-adjustable door mirrors are all standard, and there are optional goodies like leather upholstery, alarm system, tilt/takeout glass sunroof, air conditioning, and power windows and door locks. Factor in reasonable base prices of $11,000-$14,000, and it's easy to understand the MR2's instant sales success.

Comparisons between MR2 and the more comely Fiero were inevitable given their similarities in concept, packaging, and marketing. Perhaps the best way to contrast them is to say that the Toyota does more with less. Being much lighter than the Pontiac (generally judged needlessly heavy for its size), the Toyota is easier to drive, its low-effort primary controls (steering, shifter, and clutch) making stop-and-go traffic a breeze. Both cars are set up for mild initial understeer in hard corners and exhibit lift-throttle oversteer in fast ones, but the MR2 lacks the unnerving, pendulous tail wag that afflicts early Fieros. Neither car is really quiet, a traditional mid-engine drawback, though both make nice noises.

But it's the twincam engine that gives the MR2 so much of its charm and is, perhaps, its biggest advantage over the Fiero. Quite simply, this four-valver loves to rev—as indeed it must for best performance—but it's so smooth and willing and the shifter so quick and precise that you'll soon think you're ready for Formula 1. Few cars make their drivers look so good or smile so much.

Fortunately, the MR2 has been little changed, its high fun quotient undiminished. The '86 models offered several new options, including 4-speed automatic transmission, T-bar roof, and add-on aerodynamic body kit, while the '87s received minor cosmetic changes inside and out, larger rear brakes, and a transverse brace for the front strut towers.

Now we have a more grownup MR2, the new supercharged model with a Roots-type blower that operates only on demand to minimize fuel-wasting drag. Engagement is computer controlled via an air bypass valve and electromagnetic clutch. Also featured are an air-to-air intercooler; stronger, heat-resisting forged-aluminum pistons; wire-reinforced head gasket; lower compression (8.0:1 versus 9.4:1); high-speed anti-knock system; revised manifold, camshaft, and valve timing; and new two-aperture fuel injectors. The result is 30 percent more horsepower and 45 percent more torque: 145 bhp at 6400 rpm and 140 lbs-ft at 4000 rpm. Matching the increased power are a larger clutch and wide-ratio gears for the 5-speed, and strengthened internals for the automatic.

It's still not perfect, but the MR2, especially the new blown version, remains "a whole bunch of fun to drive," as *Consumer Guide®* magazine put it, "the kind of car that begs to be pushed hard." And isn't that what sports cars are all about?

SPECIFICATIONS

Engines: all dohc I-4, 97 cid/1587 cc; **1985-87:** 112 bhp (SAE net) @ 6600 rpm, 97 lbs-ft @ 4800 rpm; **1988:** 115 bhp (SAE net) @ 6600 rpm, 100 lbs-ft @ 4800 rpm; **1988 Supercharged:** 145 bhp (SAE net) @ 6400 rpm, 140 lbs-ft @ 4000 rpm

Transmissions:	5-speed overdrive manual or 4-speed overdrive automatic (in rear transaxle)
Suspension, front:	MacPherson struts, lateral links, compliance struts, coil springs, anti-roll bar
Suspension, rear:	Chapman struts, lateral links, trailing arms, toe links, coil springs
Brakes:	front/rear discs
Wheelbase (in.):	91.3
Weight (lbs):	2290
Top speed (mph):	115-120
0-60 mph (sec):	8.5-9.0
Production:	NA (production continues at this writing)

1946-1949 TRIUMPH 1800/2000 ROADSTER

Triumph of Coventry began with pedal cars and progressed to motorcycles before building its first proper cars in 1923. After severe financial problems during the Depression, it went into liquidation, was briefly taken over by a Sheffield concern, then sold in 1944 to Standard Motor Company, Ltd. under Sir John Black. Though Triumph would live on for another three decades, its postwar models had no links at all with prewar products (some of which were quite splendid sporting cars).

Predictably, the first postwar Triumphs were based on existing Standard components, including suspension, running gear, and a new chassis. Spring 1946 brought two very different models: a four-door sedan with Rolls-like razor-edge styling, and a fulsome roadster that Sir John hoped would outgun Coventry rival Jaguar (though he didn't know about the forthcoming XK120). Both used the same overhead-valve Standard four of 1776 cc and were thus logically designated "1800."

As in America, getting back to production was Standard's top postwar priority, so both models were simply engineered to avoid costly, complex tooling. This meant a straightforward ladder-type tubular chassis, to which was grafted the transverse-leaf independent front suspension of the Thirties-era Standard Flying Fourteen sedan. The Standard-built engine, also used by Jaguar for its late-Forties 1½-Litre sedans, teamed with a 4-speed column-shift gearbox.

In concept and appearance, the Roadster was a throwback to the mid-Thirties. The styling, which could be termed "Early Streamlined," was actually the work of two Standard draftsmen: Frank Callaby, who did the front, and Arthur Ballard, who labored aft of the cowl. "Modern" touches like roll-up windows were balanced by the world's last production rumble seat, easily the car's most striking feature and one Sir John had insisted upon. It even had a flip-up secondary windshield. Access was a matter of clambering over the rear quarters and bumper, not the most dignified arrangement for milady. In the best British tradition, the body comprised a light-alloy "skin" over an ash frame, the panels being produced on wartime rubber "stretcher" tooling used for military aircraft parts.

The 1800 Roadster neither looked nor acted like a sports car. With just 65 horses to pull some 2500 pounds, it was hard pressed to beat 70 mph, and its gearchange was ponderous and none too precise. But a war-weary, car-starved public would buy almost anything in those days, so the sporty tourer sold reasonably well (though the stablemate Town & Country sedan did better).

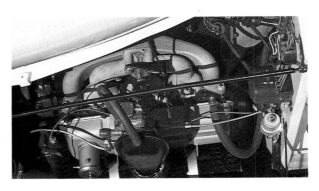

Standard's postwar design policy was evident by 1948, when old models like the Flying Fourteen were swept away in favor of a new "world car," the Standard Vanguard. This provided a new set of running gear for the Roadster (and the sedan a bit later), which became a 2000 via substitution of the Vanguard's 2088-cc four and 3-speed gearbox. The latter retained the vague steering-column control but was now fully synchronized. Equally welcome were the Vanguard's more modern coil-and-wishbone front suspension and new rear axle.

Despite a mere 5 extra horsepower, the 2000 Roadster was up to 7 mph faster than the 1800. It still wasn't a true sports car, but it now had plenty of competitors that were, including Jaguar's sensational new XK120 and MG's updated TC. Sales languished, and the model was discarded after a single year.

Standard considered a Roadster replacement, the futuristic TRX, but decided not to proceed. A good thing too, because it hastened the development of a real Triumph sports car. The first of the memorable TRs was at hand.

*This handsome example of the one-year-only Triumph 2000 Roadster (**opposite**) shows few external changes from the earlier 1800 model. However, it was somewhat quicker, if still no sports car, thanks to a torquier 2.0-liter engine (**above**). Auxiliary windscreen swung up for passengers in the rumble seat (**top**), a feature dictated by Standard-Triumph chief Sir John Black. The 1800/2000 Roadster was the last series-production car to have one.*

SPECIFICATIONS

Engines: all Standard ohv I-4; **1946-48:** 107 cid/1776 cc, 65 bhp (SAE) @ 4500 rpm, 92 lbs-ft @ 2000 rpm; **1949:** 128 cid/2088 cc, 68 bhp (SAE) @ 4200 rpm, 108 lbs-ft @ 2000 rpm

Transmissions:	4-speed manual (1946-48); 3-speed manual (1949)
Suspension, front:	rigid axle, transverse leaf springs (1800), upper and lower wishbones, coil springs, anti-roll bar (2000)
Suspension, rear:	live axle, semi-elliptic leaf springs
Brakes:	front/rear drums
Wheelbase (in.):	108.0
Weight (lbs):	2460-2540
Top speed (mph):	70-77
0-60 mph (sec):	27.9-34.4
Production:	**1800** (1946-48) 2501 **2000** (1949) 2000

1953-1955
TRIUMPH TR2

The TR2 was a major turning point for Triumph. Since the war, the marque had adorned rather dowdy, upmarket versions of the Standard automobile. But with the TR2, Triumph earned worldwide renown as a maker of rugged, high-value sports cars while establishing a line that would run nearly 30 years.

The TR2 was really conceived "on the rebound." Jealous of MG's export success, Standard chief Sir John Black had tried to buy up Morgan but was rebuffed, so he ordered his engineers to design a new sports car. The result was unveiled at the London Motor Show in October 1952 as the 20TS or "TR1."

Because Standard-Triumph had no sports-car tradition, the 20TS had several big flaws. Its chassis (basically that of the Thirties-era Standard Flying Nine with front suspension from the little postwar Triumph Mayflower sedan) was too flexible, so handling was mediocre, while its overhead-valve 2.0-liter four (borrowed from the new Standard Vanguard sedan) had too little power. Appearance was flawed too: neat and distinctive ahead of the cowl but stubby and awkward at the rear, especially the exposed spare tire. Cost considerations dictated simple engineering and construction, so a steel body was mounted atop the uninspired box-section chassis.

Still, the 20TS looked promising, and a complete redesign during the winter of 1952-53 only made it more so. Masterminded by Harry Webster with an assist from development engineer Ken Richardson, it involved a sturdy new frame, modified tail styling, and a more thoroughly developed "wet liner" engine with 90 horsepower.

The revised car, tagged TR2, looked a lot more saleable. Like the 20TS, it was a two-seat roadster with a distinctive recessed radiator opening, cutaway doors, and flowing fenders integral with the body, all fashioned by Triumph's Walter Belgrove. The new rear-end restyle finished it off beautifully and brought the added bonus of a trunk that was relatively roomy for a sports car.

Even better was the price: just under $2500. This would have been good for any early Fifties sports car, let alone one capable of just over the magic "ton" (100 mph). Yet the TR2 could be quite frugal: up to 26 mpg (U.S.) in some British tests, equally remarkable for the day.

It wasn't perfect, of course. The ride was hard and handling somewhat mulish, mostly due to restricted rear suspension travel that also meant a degree of bump-steer through rough corners. The drum brakes weren't fully developed, and there were oddities like full-depth doors that couldn't be opened near some curbs without scraping.

But it was another promising start and, after a mere 250 units in all of 1953, demand and production picked up smartly. Of no little value were the TR2's well-publicized 120-mph speed run on Belgium's Jabaekke Highway, outright victory in the British RAC (Royal Automobile Club) rally of March 1954, and a steady, if not sensational, showing by a private entry at Le Mans '54.

Though its lifespan was a short two years, the TR2 was steadily improved. Center-lock wire wheels, electric overdrive, radial tires, and lift-off hardtop became available at extra cost, while brakes were beefed up and the doors shortened. But none of this disturbed the little car's charm or rugged reliability, and the TR2 was soon seen as much better value than MG's antiquated TF and a cheaper, if less elegant, alternative to the Austin-Healey 100 (see entries). A legend had been born, and enthusiasts everywhere rejoiced.

SPECIFICATIONS

Engine: ohv I-4, 121.5 cid/1991 cc, 90 bhp (SAE) @ 4800 rpm, 117 lbs-ft @ 3000 rpm

Transmission:	4-speed manual (overdrive optional)
Suspension, front:	upper and lower A-arms, coil springs
Suspension, rear:	live axle, semi-elliptic leaf springs
Brakes:	front/rear drums
Wheelbase (in.):	88.0
Weight (lbs):	1850
Top speed (mph):	103
0-60 mph (sec):	11.9
Production:	8628

*Considerably modified and more practical than the "TR1" prototype, the TR2 established the now-familiar basic shape (**opposite**) of the successor TR3 and 3A models. Lift-off hardtop (**above**) is rare now, 2.0-liter four (**below**) rugged and reliable, dash (**below left**) nicely laid out.*

1955-1957
TRIUMPH TR3

The well-received TR2 suffered a sales slowdown in 1954 as production ran ahead of demand and inventory piled up. Nevertheless, Standard-Triumph was sufficiently confident about its sports car's future to proceed with an updated successor. Predictably called TR3, it bowed in the fall of 1955 just in time to do battle at home and overseas with the smart new MGA 1500 (see entry).

Changes abounded. Outside, an eggcrate grille filled the 2's open "mouth" with recessed mesh, badges bore the new model number, and you could now order an "occasional"—i.e., token—rear seat. Under the hood, larger-choke SU carburetors and modified ports upped output of the 2.0-liter four by five horsepower. Even so, performance suffered due to a slight increase in weight, and some road testers pointed out that fuel economy suffered too. Whereas the TR2 could return 26 miles to a U.S. gallon, the TR3 was good for only about 22 mpg. But no one complained since gas was still dirt-cheap, and reliability was as good as ever.

Cylinder heads changed twice in the TR3's first year, though it's hard to tell from chassis numbers when these occurred. Regardless, the introductory "Le Mans" casting gave way after about 3300 engines to a new "high-port" design that added another five horses, again to the detriment of fuel efficiency.

A more noteworthy running change occurred in the autumn of 1956, when the TR3 became the first series-built British car with standard front disc brakes. Supplied by Girling, they were accompanied by modified rear drums attached to a new and more robust axle. The car was already selling well, but it did even better once stopping power was equal to go-power. As proof, calendar 1956 export sales totalled 4726 units, but the '57 tally was 10,151. The figure would go even higher in 1958, and again in '60.

The TR3 also introduced an interesting new factory option, the so-called "GT Kit," inspired by Triumph's designs on two different rally classes: "Sports" and "GT." The kit simply comprised the optional lift-off hardtop and a set of exterior door handles, but satisfied class requirements.

Like its predecessor, the TR3 would last only two years. Triumph was now moving full steam toward all-out success among production sports cars. Next stop: the TR3A.

SPECIFICATIONS

Engine: ohv I-4, 121.5 cid/1991 cc, 95/100 bhp (SAE) @ 4800/5000 rpm, 117 lbs-ft @ 3000 rpm

Transmission:	4-speed manual (overdrive optional)
Suspension, front:	upper and lower A-arms, coil springs
Suspension, rear:	live axle, semi-elliptic leaf springs
Brakes:	front/rear drums; front discs/ rear drums from late 1955
Wheelbase (in.):	88.0
Weight (lbs):	1990
Top speed (mph):	102
0-60 mph (sec):	12.5
Production:	13,378

*Forward-mount eggcrate grille distinguished the TR3 from the TR2 **(opposite top)**. Cockpit **(below)** was much the same save availability of "occasional" rear seat. Engine **(below left)** gained 5-10 horses, negated by a slight weight gain.*

1958-1962
TRIUMPH TR3A &
TR3B

Had things worked out differently, we might never have had a TR3A. By the time it appeared, Triumph had already done a great deal of work toward a rebodied sports car. But none of it was deemed satisfactory, so another TR2 update was decreed for the interim. The result, as the production figures show, was one of the most successful "interim" cars ever built.

Launched in early 1958, this revised TR3 never had a suffix letter in factory literature or on its badges, but was obviously different. In fact, initial changes were confined solely to appearance. The most noticeable was a full-width grille that earned the nickname "wide mouth" (as opposed to the "small-mouth" 1955-57 models). Exterior door handles (from the previous GT Kit) and a locking trunklid handle appeared, headlights were slightly recessed (instead of protruding), and there were new, trendier paint colors. Options were as plentiful as ever. Indeed, it was rare to find a "basic" 3A with steel wheels and no overdrive.

There was also a new mechanical option beginning in 1959: a 2138-cc enlargement of the regular 2.0-liter four, though installations were apparently few. A bit later, the brakes were again completely revised, though the basic front-disc/rear-drum Girling system was retained.

But the TR was growing old and sales were withering. By the end of 1960, Standard-Triumph found itself in financial trouble due to overproduction during the previous two years as much as falling demand. Fortunately, the replacement TR4 would be ready for a fall 1961 debut, but the classic TR wasn't quite finished. Having seen the new model, Triumph's U.S. importer decided to hedge its sales bets and asked that the 3A be continued at least another year. With leftovers piling up, Triumph was only too happy to oblige.

The result was the TR3B, not an official factory model but a converted 3A built only for the U.S. at a satellite factory in Birmingham (Triumph's Coventry plant had already changed over to TR4 production by 1961). Appearance was unchanged, but almost all these cars got the TR4's new all-synchromesh gearbox, and all but the first 500 carried its 2138-cc engine. Later models also had vinyl in the center dash area.

The upshot was that Americans immediately took to the TR4 in a big way, which convinced Triumph that it was finally time to retire its original sports-car design. Thus, the last of the classic TRs rolled out the door in October 1962. Nowadays, the (unofficially named) 3B is the most collectible early TR.

SPECIFICATIONS

Engines: all ohv I-4; **1958-62:** 121.5 cid/1991 cc, 100 bhp (SAE) @ 5000 rpm, 117 lbs-ft @ 3000 rpm; **1962:** 130.4 cid/ 2138 cc, 100 bhp (net) @ 4600 rpm, 127 lbs-ft @ 3350 rpm

Transmission:	4-speed manual (overdrive optional)
Suspension, front:	upper and lower A-arms, coil springs
Suspension, rear:	live axle, semi-elliptic leaf springs
Brakes:	front/rear drums
Wheelbase (in.):	88.0
Weight (lbs):	2050
Top speed (mph):	102
0-60 mph (sec):	12.5
Production:	TR3A (1958-62) 58,236 **TR3B** (1962) 3331

*"Wide-mouth" grille **(opposite top)** set the TR3A/B apart from the TR3. Late examples like this one had vinyl on dash **(opposite, lower left)**. Original 2.0-liter four **(opposite, lower right)** made its last appearance on the TR3A. U.S.-only B used the enlarged 2.2-liter TR4 engine.*

1961-1967
TRIUMPH TR4/TR4A

Triumph found it very difficult to replace the much-admired TR3A. To change a car without changing its basic character, to modernize it without spending a fortune for tooling, to make it more civilized without losing sportiness...it wasn't an easy job.

Coventry's own designers had made repeated attempts at a new sports car before Triumph hired Italian stylist Giovanni Michelotti as a consultant. His first job had been shaping the small Herald family car; the next TR was soon on his "to do" list.

Numerous concepts were floated in 1957-60, at least four of which progressed to the prototype stage: a way-out "dream" design; the Italia, built in small numbers by Vignale; a short, narrow coupe; and a wider, smoother long-wheelbase coupe. The last was cloned for Le Mans racing with special overhead-cam engines. The definitive design emerged in 1960, code-named "Zest" but soon to be TR4. Production commenced in the fall of '61.

Despite its "all-new" aura, the TR4 was essentially just a rebodied TR3A. Michelotti's styling was much squarer than that of any previous TR and thus more contemporary, helped by a new wide-track stance and straight-through fenderlines. The grille was also wider and more assertive, headlamps nestled under "eyelids" formed by humps in the hood, and the windshield was both larger and slightly curved. Wind-up door windows, a first for a TR, literally enhanced the modern air, as did a new face-level ventilation system (a first for a British car). The optional accessory hardtop returned with a novel new feature: a center section that could be lifted out and replaced with canvas to form a "surrey" top. In all, the TR4 was undeniably Michelotti and quite distinct from any other sports car.

Beneath the new clothes were some significant running-gear changes to the basic 3A chassis. Tracks, as mentioned, were widened (by three inches at each end) and steering was now the preferred rack-and-pinion type. Power was supplied by the 2138-cc engine fitted to a few 3As (the previous 1991-cc unit was optionally available to qualify for 2.0-liter-class racing) and the gearbox was reworked with synchromesh on all forward gears.

As you might expect, the TR4 was comparable to the 3A in performance, though it could rarely better 20 mpg (U.S.) in everyday driving. Despite the new looks and plusher cockpit, the ride remained rock-hard and "vintage," and bump-steer was still a problem. But the TR4 was only a first step, because Triumph (now owned by Leyland) was readying a better version.

It arrived in 1965 as the TR4A, little different outside but very different underneath. The 2.0-liter option was gone, while the standard engine was slightly tweaked, boosting top speed to nearly 110 mph.

But the big change was a new and stiffer chassis with coil-spring/semi-trailing-link independent rear suspension. However, Triumph's U.S. distributor again had reservations, so American buyers could have the new chassis with the old live axle for a time. It wouldn't last: irs was overwhelmingly preferred. No wonder. It gave a more supple ride while banishing bump-steer.

Unhappily, the TR was being outclassed for performance and refinement (rival twincam Italian sportsters didn't cost that much more) yet the ancient wet-liner four offered no hope for improvement. More cylinders was the obvious solution, and Triumph would apply it to the next evolution of its classic sports-car formula.

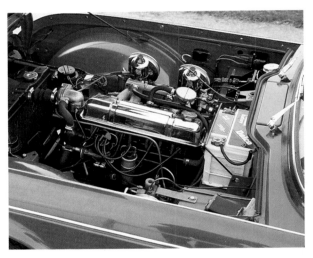

A handsome example of an early British-market TR4A displays the chrome side trim and front-fender "repeater" lamps not found on TR4s. Big four (above) was slightly tweaked, but fully independent rear suspension was the main attraction. Cockpit (top) was spruced up some.

SPECIFICATIONS

Engines: ohv I-4, 130.4 cid/2138 cc, 100/104 bhp (net) @ 4600/4700 rpm, 127/132 lbs-ft @ 3350/3000 rpm

Transmission:	4-speed manual (electric overdrive optional)
Suspension, front:	upper and lower A-arms, coil springs
Suspension, rear:	live axle, semi-elliptic leaf springs (TR4); semi-trailing arms, coil springs (TR4A)
Brakes:	front/rear drums
Wheelbase (in.):	88.0
Weight (lbs):	2130/2240 (TR4/4A)
Top speed (mph):	102-109
0-60 mph (sec):	10.9-11.4
Production:	**TR4** (1961-64) 40,253 **TR4A** (1964-68) 28,465

1962-1967
TRIUMPH SPITFIRE
MARK 1 & 2

Sports-car fans were delighted when British Motor Corporation brought forth the cheap, cheerful Austin-Healey Sprite (see entry), and they were quite spoiled when Triumph followed suit with the Spitfire. Both catered to the growing demand for smaller, lower-priced sports cars by enthusiasts who couldn't afford—or didn't want—"big guns" like the Healey 3000 or Triumph's own TR4.

It's no secret that the Spitfire was derived from Triumph's family-toting Herald, a car that got off to a very troubled start. But the Spitfire was successful right out of the box and would continue for 18 years, during which it would consistently outsell the rival Sprite and MG Midget *combined.*

To back up a bit, the Herald replaced Standard's unitized 8/10/Pennant sedans of the Fifties and employed body-on-frame construction. There were two reasons for this: it would facilitate overseas assembly, as the frame could double as a jig; also, Standard-Triumph wasn't able at the time to find a contractor who could supply suitable unit structures. Even so, Herald assembly quality was initially poor, though it improved after S-T was taken over by the Leyland combine.

Though Leyland put it into production, Triumph's new small sportster was conceived in the pre-Leyland days of 1960. Styling was entrusted to Italian consultant Giovanni Michelotti, while the name came from the World War II fighter plane that played a key role in the Battle of Britain. Sales began in the autumn of 1962.

The Spitfire was built on a new backbone-style chassis with a shorter wheelbase than the Herald's, but carried the family car's all-independent suspension and a

modified version of its 1147-cc overhead-valve four with 63 instead of 51 horsepower. A 4-speed gearbox was on hand as expected, and the Herald-based steering provided a tight 24-foot turning circle that enabled the "Spit" to outmaneuver a London taxi. The body was a welded steel monocoque (the Herald's was simply bolted together).

With its graceful styling and somewhat larger package size, the Spitfire was more elegant and "grownup" than the Sprite/Midget, with a roomier cockpit, better equipment, and nicer trim. Trunk space was a little better too, and front disc brakes were standard. As on the Herald and the "bugeye" Sprite, the hood and front fenders were a unit that tilted up and forward for superb service access.

The Spitfire was nippy and reasonably quick for its price class, but the Herald's swing-axle rear suspension made it quite skittish in hard cornering, prone to sudden, alarming oversteer caused by large camber changes that let the outside rear wheel tuck under, thus upsetting stability. But this didn't deter buyers, especially in the U.S., who just loved the pert styling and carefree character. In 1963, the Spitfire's first full year, 6224 were sold in America; the total was 9097 two years later, when production was racing along at over 20,000 units a year.

Several popular options arrived in 1963: overdrive (effective on both 3rd and 4th gears), center-lock wire wheels, and a pretty, detachable steel hardtop. In December 1964, Triumph switched to a Mark 2 model with an extra four horsepower, more luxuriously trimmed seats, vinyl-covered dash (replacing painted metal) and floor carpeting instead of rubber mats. Pricing was as attractive as ever. The 1965 U.S. POE figure was a low $2199; the hardtop added $100.

As you might expect, the Spitfire quickly became popular among weekend racers, and Triumph urged them on beginning in 1964 with a trio of tuning kits: Interim, Stage I, and Stage II. The first was the most common, comprising revised manifolds and a downdraft Solex carb to produce 70 bhp. The Stage II gave you twin DCOE Weber carbs, higher-lift cam and an exhaust header, but was extremely rare and is all but impossible to find today.

In retrospect, the Mk 1 and Mk 2 Spitfires marked Triumph's return to the original TR concept: a versatile, high-value basic sports car of enormous charm. Alas, some of that charm would be lost in subsequent editions, as we relate a little further on.

SPECIFICATIONS

Engines: all ohv I-4, 70 cid/1147 cc; **1962-64:** 63 bhp (net) at 5750 rpm, 67 lbs-ft @ 3500 rpm; **1964-67:** 67 bhp (net) @ 6000 rpm, 67 lbs-ft @ 3750 rpm

Transmission:	4-speed manual; overdrive optional from 1963
Suspension, front:	upper and lower wishbones, coil springs, anti-roll bar
Suspension, rear:	swing axles, radius arms, transverse leaf spring
Brakes:	front discs/rear drums
Wheelbase (in.):	83.0
Weight (lbs):	1570
Top speed (mph):	92
0-60 mph (sec):	15.5-16.5

Production: Mark 1 (1962-64) 45,573 **Mark 2** (1964-67) 37,409

A more grownup basic sports car than its Sprite/Midget rivals, the Spitfire was a solid sales success. Early models like this UK-registered car wore small hubcaps.

1966-1968 TRIUMPH GT6

It was almost inevitable that Triumph's four-cylinder Spitfire would get a six-cylinder running mate. After all, it had evolved from the Herald sedan that was offered in a six-cylinder version called Vitesse (sold briefly in the U.S. as the Sport Six). Such conversions were easier to talk about than realize, but sports-car enthusiasts thought that if Triumph could engineer one miracle, the Spitfire, it could conjure up another.

At first, Triumph had no thoughts of a small six-cylinder sports car, though it did build a batch of Spitfire-based racing prototypes in 1963-64 with four-cylinder power and fixed fastback roofs. These Spitfire GTs ran with determination, if not stunning success, at Sebring and Le Mans, but Triumph realized that the stock-tune Spitfire engine wouldn't provide decent performance in a roadgoing version. Triumph thus decided to "do a Vitesse" on the GT, and it arrived in the fall of 1966 as the GT6.

Predictably, the GT6 chassis was virtually identical with that of the then-current Mark 2 Spitfire. Its engine was closely related too, being machined on the same transfer-line tooling as the Spitfire four. This was the same basic 2.0-liter six that powered the Vitesse and Triumph's larger 2000 sedan. (Its next tour of duty would come a year later in the TR5/TR250.) Because of its extra length and the fact that the gearbox couldn't be moved rearward, the GT6 carried a lot more of its total weight on the front wheels than the much better-balanced Spitfire, and was thus less rewarding in corners.

But it came into its own on straightaways. The six was not only smoother but packed 28 more horsepower than the Spitfire four, so the GT6 could top 100 mph

SPECIFICATIONS

Engine: ohv I-6, 121.9 cid/1998 cc, 95 bhp (net) @ 5000 rpm, 117 lbs-ft @ 3000 rpm

Transmission:	4-speed manual; overdrive optional from 1963
Suspension, front:	upper and lower wishbones, coil springs, anti-roll bar
Suspension, rear:	swing axles, radius arms, transverse leaf spring
Brakes:	front discs/rear drums
Wheelbase (in.):	83.0
Weight (lbs):	1905
Top speed (mph):	106
0-60 mph (sec):	12.0-12.3
Production:	15,818

and offered effortless performance at other times. As on the roadster, its standard and only gearbox was a 4-speed manual, albeit a new, all-synchromesh unit, and overdrive was optional. Spring and damper rates were recalibrated for the altered front/rear weight distribution, as was the steering, which was geared slightly lower than the Spit's for easier parking. All this made the GT6 more refined than its open cousin, and more than one observer described it as a mini-XKE.

The styling furthered that impression; the steel fastback roof with top-hinged hatch looking quite good on the unchanged Spitfire lower body. With roll-up windows (inherited from the roadster), well-stocked dash and cushy seats, the GT6 seemed for all the world like a shrunken E-Type coupe, which was hardly bad. It even sounded a little like the six-cylinder Jaguar, with the same sort of exhaust.

Alas, it neither performed nor handled like an E-Type. The GT6 wasn't as light as it looked, and the front-end weight bias combined with the quirky swing-axle rear suspension to make it even more wayward in hard cornering than the Spitfire. Then too, its cabin was cramped even for a two-seater, and provision for windows-up ventilation was conspicuous by its absence.

But the GT6 was much faster than its obvious rival, the MGB GT (see entry) and almost matched its U.S. sales. Some 2000 reached American buyers in the first year, double that in the second.

Still, it wasn't fully developed, and critical comments about handling and general equipment prompted second thoughts. The result appeared just two years after the original in a much-improved GT6 Mark 2, which we cover elsewhere.

Install a hatchback top and stuff a small two-liter six into a Mark II Spitfire roadster and—voila!—enter the Triumph GT6. More powerful and refined than the Spitfire, it cast the aura of a mini Jaguar XK-E coupe. Alas, it was let down by tricky handling, caused by the front-end weight bias and the quirky swing-axle rear suspension.

1967-1968
TRIUMPH TR5 PI/TR250

Triumph's rugged, easily tuned wet-liner four had done yeoman sports-car service since 1953 but was literally out of breath by the mid-Sixties, when it became clear that the larger new TR4/4A (see entry) would need more power to stay competitive. More cylinders seemed the answer, and Triumph had them.

Back in the Fifties, Standard had introduced a small inline four that was later developed for Triumph's compact Herald sedan and the "junior TR," the Spitfire (see entry). There was also a derivative six, first seen in Standard's four-door Vanguard Six and later used in the Triumph 2000 sedan. With modifications, this 2.5-liter engine was duly installed in the TR4 to create a more potent successor.

Despite its greater displacement, the six was no heavier than the old four, though it was significantly longer. Luck was on Triumph's side, though, as the six just fit the TR4 engine bay and proved relatively easy to clean up for the new U.S. emissions standards that were being enacted during its development.

Nevertheless, Triumph ended up producing two versions of its latest TR. America got the TR250 with a detoxed 104-horsepower six fed by twin Zenith-Stromberg carburetors. Europe and the rest the world enjoyed the 150-bhp TR5 PI, the suffix

denoting petrol (fuel) injection by Lucas, the same basic system used by Maserati on its contemporary 3500GTI and Sebring (see entries). Needless to say, the performance of these cars was utterly different.

Visually, they differed little from the TR4A, with changes confined to the grille (now minus its vertical support bar), nameplates, and minor trim. The TR5 even retained the original hood bulge needed for carburetor clearance on the TR4. Both rolled on standard steel wheels, adorned (if that's the word) with "mag-look" covers, but many examples were treated to the traditional center-lock wires. TR250s wore rather silly transverse racing stripes on their noses, and their soft tops had reflective tape above the doors and rear window for nighttime safety.

Chassis specs remained much as before, but radial tires were standard and the rigid rear axle option for American models was scratched. Final-drive ratios were numerically lowered to suit the torquier six.

Returning to performance, the TR250 was no faster than the TR4A from standstill or flat out—no surprise, since it had no more horsepower. But, of course, the six was a lot smoother than the old four, and its extra torque greatly improved driveability at low speeds in the intermediate gears. By contrast, the TR5 would wind to an easy 6000 rpm and near 120 mph, while cutting no less than 20 seconds from the 4A's 0-100 mph time. Unfortunately, it idled like a race car and used a lot more gas than the 250 (perhaps as much as 16 mpg U.S.), and the fuel injection proved far more finicky than the 250's good old-fashioned carburetors.

Despite their six-cylinder smoothness and greater flexibility, the TR5 and TR250 were seen by many as new wine in old bottles. What was needed, some said, was fresh styling to match the new engine and its more "manly" character. Triumph, in fact, was already working on it, which explains why TR5/250 production lasted just a year and a half. The TR6 was on the way.

SPECIFICATIONS

Engines: all ohv I-6, 152.4 cid/2498 cc; **TR5 PI:** 150 bhp (net) @ 5500 rpm, 164 lbs-ft @ 3500 rpm; **TR250:** 104 bhp (net) @ 4500 rpm, 143 lbs-ft @ 3000 rpm (111 bhp, 152 lbs-ft SAE gross)

Transmission:	4-speed manual (electric overdrive optional)
Suspension, front:	upper and lower A-arms, coil springs
Suspension, rear:	semi-trailing arms, coil springs
Brakes:	front/rear drums
Wheelbase (in.):	88.0
Weight (lbs):	2270
Top speed (mph):	107-120
0-60 mph (sec):	8.8-10.6
Production:	TR5 2947 TR250 8484

Fuel-injected TR5 PI departed from TR4A appearance mainly in badges and standard mag-look wheel covers.

1967-1970 TRIUMPH SPITFIRE MARK 3

Like the rival Sprite/Midget, the Triumph Spitfire took a few years to mature. Its basic concept was always right, and everyone loved the Marks 1 and 2, but a fully developed, better balanced car took time. The Mark 3, introduced in early 1967, was just such a Spitfire: faster than the earlier models, a little more stylish and better equipped.

Triumph had neither the money nor desire for many changes in its small sports car, but the few it did make were definitely for the better. The main one was substituting the larger, 1296-cc SC ("Small Car") four from the front-drive 1300 sedan of 1965 (soon to be used in the Herald too). With a proper eight-port cylinder head (the previous engine had siamesed intake ports) and 75 horsepower, it made the Mk 3 a near-100-mph car and, as events would prove, the fastest Spitfire of all. A more substantial clutch was specified to cope with the extra power.

The front disc brakes were more substantial too. Otherwise, the chassis was left alone, which meant that with the bigger engine's extra torque, snap oversteer was even easier to provoke. In general, though, the Spitfire remained an eager, very responsive little car — and safe when you respected its limits.

Imminent U.S. regulations prompted the major appearance alteration: a raised front bumper suggesting a dog with a bone in its teeth. Some thought it cute, others ghastly. For Triumph, it was merely an easy answer to an irksome Yankee requirement. Revised parking/turn-signal lights sat below, while the rear quarter-bumpers were reshaped (and still quite dainty). The top now had a proper folding mechanism and was permanently attached, making it much easier to operate than the previous do-it-yourself affair of slot-in sticks with canvas cover, though it took up more space when lowered. The cockpit itself was again spruced up, this time with handsome walnut veneer on the dash.

The Mk 3 would continue in production through December 1970 with few interim changes, none mechanical. A rearranged dashboard appeared on 1969 U.S. models only, with instruments grouped directly ahead of the wheel instead of in the center (universally adopted with the Mark IV). All the 1970s were treated to wider wheels (4.5 versus 3.5 inches) and gained sportier steering wheels, improved cockpit padding, and other cosmetic touch-ups.

By this point, complaints about the ill-handling swing-axle rear suspension were louder and more frequent than ever, but Triumph finally had an answer here too. No quick fix, it would help make the next Spitfire even more mature.

SPECIFICATIONS

Engine: ohv I-4, 79.1 cid/1296 cc, 75 bhp (net) @ 6000 rpm, 75 lbs-ft @ 4000 rpm

Transmission:	4-speed manual; overdrive optional
Suspension, front:	upper and lower wishbones, coil springs, anti-roll bar
Suspension, rear:	swing axles, radius arms, transverse leaf spring
Brakes:	front discs/rear drums
Wheelbase (in.):	83.0
Weight (lbs):	1570
Top speed (mph):	95
0-60 mph (sec):	14.0
Production:	65,320

*Mark 3 bore "interim" Spitfire styling with a higher, more protective front bumper on an otherwise unaltered body. Cockpit (**opposite, lower left**) was again spruced up. Access to new 1300-cc four (**lower right**) remained superb.*

1969-1976 TRIUMPH TR6

Triumph was working on a restyled six-cylinder sports car even before the TR5/TR250 appeared. The result was the TR6, introduced at the start of 1969.

Basically, it was the existing TR with a simple but adroit facelift at each end of the original Michelotti-designed bodyshell. Michelotti himself was now Triumph's "resident" design consultant and fully occupied with family models, so the sports-car makeover was assigned to Karmann of West Germany (and of VW Karmann-Ghia fame), partly because it could produce the necessary tooling in double-quick time.

Retaining the center body and general proportions, Karmann tacked on a little more front overhang, flattened the hood, moved the headlamps down and fully outboard, added a wider grille, reshaped the stern with a fashionable Kamm chop (a "signature" of the early-Seventies Stag and Spitfire Mark IV), and applied new bumpers and taillamps. The accessory hardtop was also revamped, becoming more angular and of one-piece construction (to replace the two-piece "surrey" top).

Technical changes were few: a front anti-roll bar and half-inch wider wheels. There were still two versions, fuel-injected European and carbureted American, but no more name distinction, though some insisted on calling the former "PI," the latter "Carb."

*Below: An early U.S. TR6 with an accessory roll bar of the type favored by weekend racers. **Opposite:** A late British-market example with accessory hardtop.*

U.S. models initially had the same 104 net horsepower as the superseded TR250, and Triumph held the line despite progressively tighter emissions standards; it even managed two additional horses later on. Still, the "Carb" remained at TR250 performance levels throughout its life.

The injected European engine returned with the 150 bhp it had in the TR5, and continued to be criticized for its lumpy idle and inflexible habits. Triumph responded in early 1973 with a more moderate camshaft profile that increased smoothness and tractability in exchange for a slight drop in power and top-end performance.

The TR6 would soldier on for some seven years with few interim changes. Internal transmission ratios were altered beginning in mid-1971, mainly to standardize gearboxes with the then-new V-8 Stag four-seater (performance was unchanged), and a different, more modern Laycock overdrive became available (still at extra cost) from early 1973. A modest front "lip" spoiler and restyled gauges also arrived that year, while 1974 brought large black bumper guards at each end to meet America's new 5-mph impact-protection standards.

This lack of change seems sad, but this was an aging design. And despite organizational chaos and deteriorating finances, British Leyland had plans for a very different Triumph sports car. Though it bowed in spring 1975, TR6 production continued through July '76, albeit at a slower pace.

Thus ended 23 years of the traditional "hairy-chested" TRs loved all over the world. The successor TR7 would generate nowhere near as much affection.

SPECIFICATIONS

Engines: ohv I-6, 152.4 cid/2498 cc, 150 bhp (net) @ 5500 rpm, 164 lbs-ft @ 3500 rpm (**U.S. version:** 104/106 bhp SAE gross @ 4900 rpm, 142 lbs-ft @ 3000 rpm)

Transmission:	4-speed manual (electric overdrive optional)
Suspension, front:	upper and lower A-arms, coil springs, anti-roll bar
Suspension, rear:	semi-trailing arms, coil springs
Brakes:	front/rear drums
Wheelbase (in.):	88.0
Weight (lbs):	2475
Top speed (mph):	119 (European model), 109 (U.S. version)
0-60 mph (sec):	8.2 (European model), 10.7 (U.S. version)
Production:	94,619

1968-1973 TRIUMPH GT6 MARK 2/GT6+ & GT6 MARK 3

Triumph's GT6 became a Mark 2 in the autumn of 1968, and a much better car. In less than two years, engineers and sales staff had not only weighed press and public reactions to the "Mk 1" but had devised improvements, tested them, and got them into volume production. The result was nothing less than a transformation, with a completely new rear suspension, a more potent and efficient engine, and better equipment, all within the original envelope.

By far the most significant change was the new rear suspension, where the Mk 1's crude and quirky swing axles were ditched in favor of what was effectively a double-wishbone system. Cleverly, the original transverse leaf spring now doubled as the "top wishbones," working in concert with double-jointed halfshafts, new lower A-arms, and re-sited radius arms and shock absorbers. The resulting geometry minimized camber changes in hard cornering, thus providing the balance and predictability that had always been so sorely needed. At last, GT6 handling was all most anyone could desire.

In fact, the revised chassis could handle more power, which was provided via a reprofiled camshaft, a new cylinder head, and freer-breathing manifolds. Emissions controls kept 1969-70 U.S. models— called "GT6+"—at their previous 95 horsepower, but the figure for other markets was now 104 bhp.

Cosmetics and convenience came in for attention too. Among new features common to all these cars were standard mag-style wheel covers, a raised front bumper *a la* Spitfire 3 (see entry), revamped dash and interior trim, and air exhaust grilles aft of the rear side windows for flow-through interior ventilation.

Yet for all this, sales stayed virtually the same. U.S. deliveries numbered 4254 in 1969 and 4066 the following season, while total calendar-year production continued at the 1967-68 pace of 6000-6500 units.

By 1971, it was time for another change. Because the GT6 and Spitfire shared so many components, they evolved more or less in parallel. Thus, when the roadster was restyled at the end of 1970 to become the Spitfire Mk IV, the GT6 was too.

Called Mark 3 in all markets, the revised fastback Triumph received the Spitfire IV's smoother bumpers, modest wheelarch flares, and crisp new tail styling, plus a few touches all its own: recessed exterior door handles, extra air extraction vents, and rear quarter windows that swept back a little more. Inside was a modified dash, a new steering wheel and, when equipped, an overdrive control switch sensibly relocated from the dash to the shift knob.

Alas, U.S. models had to be detuned each year to meet progressively tighter emissions limits. Thus, while UK-spec cars remained at 104 bhp, the '71 federal Mk 3 had only 90 bhp, then slumped to a miserable 79 bhp. Of course, the GT6 wasn't alone in this, but fading performance put a big dent in the U.S. demand on which Triumph relied so heavily; 1972 American sales amounted to just 2753 units. The first Energy Crisis provided a logical reason for euthanasia, and the GT6 was quietly killed after 1973.

Opposite: A British-registered GT6 Mark 2 circa 1970. U.S. version was called GT6+. Both shared "bone in the teeth" front end with contemporary Spitfire. This page: Restyled rear a la Spitfire Mark IV distinguished the final Mark 3 GT6. Here, another home-market example, a very late '73.

SPECIFICATIONS

Engines: all ohv I-6, 121.9 cid/1998 cc; 104 bhp @ 5300 rpm, 117 lbs-ft @ 3000 rpm; **U.S. version 1969-70:** 95 bhp (SAE) @ 4700 rpm, 117 lbs-ft @ 3400 rpm; **1971:** 90 bhp @ 4700 rpm, 116 lbs-ft @ 3400 rpm; **1972-73:** 79 bhp @ 4900 rpm, 97 lbs-ft @ 2900 rpm

Transmission:	4-speed manual with optional overdrive
Suspension, front:	upper and lower wishbones, coil springs, anti-roll bar
Suspension, rear:	double-jointed half-shafts, lower A-arms, radius arms, transverse leaf spring
Brakes:	front discs/rear drums
Wheelbase (in.):	83.0
Weight (lbs):	1905-2030
Top speed (mph):	95-112
0-60 mph (sec):	10.1-12.0
Production:	Mark 2/GT6+ 12,066 Mark 3 13,042

1970-1980 TRIUMPH SPITFIRE MARK IV & 1500

After eight successful years, the jaunty little Triumph Spitfire was restyled and thoroughly overhauled for its next 10. Although this Mark IV (*not* the expected "Mark 4") was similar in many ways to the Marks 1 through 3, it had much better handling, more modern fixtures and fittings and, eventually, different running gear. Above all, it remained an honest little sports car in the hallowed British tradition, and would swell Spitfire production to a grand 18-year total of 314,342 units.

The Mark IV originated in the late Sixties, when Triumph requested design consultant Giovanni Michelotti to produce a completely reskinned Spitfire on the existing backbone chassis, retaining the same proportions and as many body panels as possible. As with the TR6 (see entry), the result was more a major facelift than a completely new design.

Michelotti had proposed flip-up headlamps, but the Mark IV front was like the Mark 3's aside from a larger grille opening and a recontoured bumper (still the bone in the dog's teeth) with black guards below it instead of overriders on it. Two-piece fenders were discarded for single units at the front but retained for the rear, which was nicely reshaped along TR6 lines, as was the accessory hardtop. Other recognition points included GT6-style recessed door handles, reshuffled trim and, on U.S. models, distinct side marker lights as required by law. Inside was the more logically ordered instrument panel first seen on the American-market 1969-70 Mk 3.

But the most important change was down under, where the deadly old high-roll-center swing-axle rear suspension was junked in favor of a new "swing-spring" layout. This referred to a transverse leaf spring that was now free to pivot atop the differential, thus greatly reducing rear roll stiffness. The new arrangement looked

virtually the same as the old but virtually eliminated rear-wheel tuckunder at high cornering loads for altogether safer and more predictable handling. Up front, the Mk 3's 1296-cc engine was retained in slightly detuned form, and now mated with the new all-synchromesh 4-speed gearbox from the GT6.

U.S. Mark IVs followed the GT6 in another way, with performance that declined each year as emissions standards tightened. The '71 models had only a single carburetor and 58 horsepower—even less than on the original '62 model. Output faded to a pitiful 48 bhp on the '72s, which could only reach about 80 mph, yet no fewer than 9687 were delivered that year.

There's no substitute for cubic inches—er, centimeters—even where the goal is cleaner air, not higher performance. Accordingly, 1973-74 U.S. Spitfires received the stroked, 1493-cc engine (still with single carb) that would go into the MG Midget beginning in late '74 (see entry), a move that would simplify emissions certification for British Leyland, which was home to both these cars by now. Available horsepower rose to 57—better, if not quite adequate. At the same time, a two-inch-wider rear track, cleaned-up instrument panel, fire-retardant trim materials, and standard reclining seats were adopted.

The name was Spitfire 1500 on the '74 U.S. models, which gained a protruding lower "jaw" spoiler and big fat bumper guards (a hasty solution for that year's new 5-mph impact-protection standards). Another sign of the times: the optional wire wheels were no longer available. Non-American Spitfires received most of these changes— including the new name—for 1975, only their 1500 engine packed 71 DIN horsepower, making these the lustiest Spitfires of all. Top speed, for example, was back to around 100 mph.

Sadly, the Spitfire was an orphan by then. The parent body-on-frame Herald/Vitesse sedans had been dropped in 1971, and the last GT6 had been built in late '73. Production economics and BL's red-washed balance sheet meant the Spitfire would have to go soon. Somehow, though, sales remained strong enough (and even went up for a time) to keep it alive through August 1980. Then BL gave up on sports cars altogether in another of its many gropes toward profitability.

But the Spitfire had served long and well, and many were sad to see it go. The good news is that many of these cars are still around, and dirt cheap. It may never be a collector's item, but the Spitfire will always be hard to beat for low-cost sports-car fun.

SPECIFICATIONS

Engines: all ohv I-4; **1970-74:** 79 cid/1296 cc, 63 bhp (net) @ 6000 rpm, 69 lbs-ft @ 3500 rpm; **1971-72 U.S. version:** 58/48 bhp (SAE net) @ 5200/5500 rpm, 72/61 lbs-ft @ 3000/2900 rpm; **1974-80:** 91.1 cid/1493 cc, 71 bhp (DIN) @ 5500 rpm, 82 lbs-ft @ 3000 rpm; **U.S. version:** 57 bhp (SAE net) @ 5000 rpm, 74 lbs-ft @ 3000 rpm

Transmission:	4-speed manual; overdrive optional
Suspension, front:	upper and lower wishbones, coil springs, anti-roll bar
Suspension, rear:	swing axles, radius arms, pivoting transverse leaf spring
Brakes:	front discs/rear drums
Wheelbase (in.):	83.0
Weight (lbs):	1720-1750
Top speed (mph):	80-100
0-60 mph (sec):	13.2-15.9

Production: Mark IV (1970-74) 70,021 **1500** (1974-80) 95,829

*More prominent bumpers for the U.S. and a recontoured rear identified the Spitfire Mark IV. Even bigger bumper guards appeared on the last 1500-cc models (**below and opposite bottom**). British cars (**opposite top**) weren't so afflicted.*

401

1975-1981
TRIUMPH TR7

The Leyland company gradually became Britain's native motor industry during the Sixties, successively absorbing Standard-Triumph, AEC, Rover/Alvis and, in 1968, British Motor Holdings (BMC with Jaguar). Thus it was that two old foes, MG and Triumph, found themselves under the vast new roof of British Leyland.

BL management was initially top-heavy with former Triumph executives, so Triumph was given design responsibility for the new firm's future sports cars, which would wear the Triumph badge, leaving MG out in the cold. An early result of this decision was a new program initiated in 1970-71 to create a single replacement for BL's two aging "big" sports cars, the MGB and Triumph TR6—a modern design with worldwide buyer appeal and engineered for high-volume production. It emerged some four years later as the Triumph TR7.

Though it carried the famous TR initials, this new Triumph was completely different from the TR6 it would eventually oust from the lineup. Instead of a six-cylinder roadster with Italian styling, all-independent suspension, and body-on-frame construction, it was a British-designed unitized coupe with a four-cylinder engine and beam rear axle.

As originally envisioned, the basic TR7 platform would have spawned a whole sports-car family with engines ranging from a 2.0-liter four through a 16-valve version and on up to a 3.5-liter V-8, the light-alloy GM unit recently acquired by Rover. All would have fixed-roof coupe bodywork and were planned to be on the market within three years of the introductory four-cylinder model.

TR7 styling originated at BL in Longbridge, not at Triumph itself, with an off-hand sketch by designer Harris Mann—"off-hand" in that it wasn't a serious proposal. But his "bubbletop wedge" shape appealed to management, and they stuck with it all the way through to production despite, some say, sage counsel to the contrary. What emerged was by no means as graceful as Giugiaro's Lotus Esprit or any of the Italian supercars it tried to emulate, being stubby and wide, almost as cartoonish as Mann's original drawing. The interior was nicely done but rather cramped, thanks to a very bulky dashboard, and though the trunk was useful enough, there was little in-cabin stowage space.

Production economics and corporate politics dictated chassis components and driveline be taken from the BL bins. The engine, for example, was an enlarged version of the Triumph-designed 1.7-liter sohc four supplied to Saab for its period 99 sedans

(since re-engineered by the Swedes, who still build it for their current 900 and 9000 models). It also showed up in Triumph's small Dolomite sedan, a rear-drive derivative of the earlier front-drive 1300/1500, for which a twincam 16-valve version was developed (but would never appear in a TR7 as planned). The standard gearbox was a 4-speed manual, but there were two options: an overdrive 5-speed (borrowed from Rover's big SD1 hatchback-sedan series) and British-built Borg-Warner 3-speed automatic.

Chassis specs were conventional. The all-coil suspension employed front MacPherson struts and a live rear axle located by radius arms. Steering was the expected rack-and-pinion, brakes servo-assisted front discs and rear drums.

Still struggling to come to terms with more automated manufacturing, BL set up TR7 production at its brand-new Speke plant near Liverpool. It was a big mistake. The workforce not only had no experience building sports cars but, egged on by ever-stubborn union leaders, tended go on strike even more often than other British factory workers. Not surprisingly, workmanship was highly variable and production erratic, neither of which did anything for sales.

Properly put together, though, the 7 was a much sweeter-handling TR than the 6, about as fast, and more practical if less romantic. But the oddball styling, indifferent quality control, and the tarnished reputation of British cars in general took a big sales toll, especially in the U.S., where demand would never meet expectations.

After yet another management shuffle, BL closed Speke in 1978 and shifted TR7 tooling to Triumph's Canley plant near Coventry, a process that left a six-month gap in production. Things were uprooted again just two years later, when the TR7 was sent to Rover's Solihull facility in the face of BL's large, continuing cash shortfalls and its ever-more desperate need to economize.

Hoping to turn the TR7 around, BL issued a smart new convertible version in 1979. Bereft of the coupe's foreshortened roof and dippy side window line, it looked miles better, and BL attended to details inside and out. But none of this did anything for sales. Neither did the planned V-8 derivative, which arrived the following year as the TR8 (see entry).

Because by then, it was all over. With BL's waning American sales, continuing huge losses, and soaring development costs for new mass-market family models like the Metro and Maestro, Whitehall stepped in and nationalized the firm, which remains on the dole at this writing. This brought another new management team and yet another recovery plan that included doing away with sports cars. The TR7 thus went to its grave in October 1981, shortly after the MGB and Triumph Spitfire had been killed off; the TR8 went with it, of course.

It was a sad end for the once-great TR, and Triumph itself was gone by the mid-Eighties. Alas, neither is likely to make a comeback. Still fighting to stay alive, today's Rover Group, the last remnant of the ill-fated BL empire, bravely talks about a new sports car for the Nineties, but if it appears at all, it'll be an MG, not a Triumph. In view of what happened with the 7, TR fans might be grateful for that.

Except for details, the rather odd "flying doorstop" shape of the TR7 coupe was unchanged through the model's troubled production run. Here, a 1981 British example with aftermarket sunroof.

SPECIFICATIONS

Engines: sohc I-4, 121.9 cid/1998 cc, 105 bhp (DIN) @ 5500 rpm, 119 lbs-ft @ 3500 rpm; **U.S. version:** 86-90 bhp (SAE net) @ 5000-5500 rpm, 102-106 lbs-ft @ 3000-3250 rpm

Transmissions:	4/5-speed manual, 3-speed automatic
Suspension, front:	MacPherson struts, coil springs, anti-roll bar
Suspension, rear:	live axle, radius arms, coil springs, anti-roll bar
Brakes:	front discs/rear drums
Wheelbase (in.):	85.0
Weight (lbs):	2205-2470
Top speed (mph):	105-110
0-60 mph (sec):	9.1-11.5
Production:	112,368

1980-1981 TRIUMPH TR8

Triumph's fastest sports car was also its last, which should make the TR8 something of a milestone. Alas, it's more like an epitaph for the sad TR7 that sired it.

The TR7 is covered elsewhere, so we need only observe that it was poorly built and unreliable like too many British cars and styled like nothing else ever seen. As basically a V-8-powered TR7, the TR8 inherited these traits, but its smooth, all-aluminum small-block engine gave it some big advantages over the four-cylinder version.

Designer Harris Mann, whose impromptu sketch led to the TR7's unfortunate "flying doorstop" shape, had anticipated a V-8 installation, so both TR7 and TR8 evolved more or less in parallel and with the American market very much in mind. The TR8 engine was, of course, a mildly modified version of the one developed for the 1961-63 Buick Special/Olds F-85 compacts. General Motors had abandoned it when those cars grew to intermediate size for '64, but sold the tooling to Rover shortly before Rover and Triumph became relatives in the unwieldy British Leyland family.

Powerplant apart, the differences twixt TR7 and TR8 were relatively few. The TR8's hood was bulged to clear the taller engine, which reached U.S. shores with twin Stromberg carbs except for California, where stricter emissions standards dictated Bosch L-Jetronic fuel injection (used on all '81 models). The TR7 offered 5-speed manual or 3-speed automatic transmission (the latter a first for a TR), so the 8 did too, though the V-8's greater torque allowed a longer-striding final drive (3.08:1 versus 3.90:1) for maximum mileage. Springs and shocks got the obligatory stiffening, larger pads helped the front disc brakes cope with the V-8's greater performance, and the TR7's rack-and-pinion steering gained standard power assist and faster gearing. Finally, the battery was moved to the TR8 trunk in the interest of better fore/aft weight balance, and the 7's optional cast-alloy wheels were made standard along with wider, 185-section tires (versus 175s). Tinted glass, AM/FM stereo, and metallic paint were included. Air conditioning was the sole factory option.

With the chaos that reigned supreme at British Leyland throughout the Seventies, the TR8 didn't make its official U.S. debut until model year 1980. Coupe and convertible body styles were offered as per TR7, but prices ran some $2000 higher. Interestingly, 202 American-spec TR8 coupes, most with automatic transmission, were sent over for preliminary evaluation in 1978-79, then privately sold by importer Jaguar-Rover-Triumph.

The open TR8 garnered the most press attention (the TR7 convertible had appeared only a year before) and accounted for most TR8 sales. And why not? It was much prettier than the coupe, and the V-8 made both TR8s a lot quieter than the 7s. And a lot faster: about 8.5 seconds 0-60 mph, enough to unnerve a Corvette.

Even better, this new-found power didn't harm handling much. Still, axle tramp was a problem in bumpy corners and hard acceleration, power oversteer was easy to provoke, and some testers judged the power steering twitchy because of excess assist and a curious over-center action. Naturally, the 8 inherited the TR7's roomy, well-planned cockpit, with body-hugging bucket seats, full instrumentation, and generally good ergonomics.

Unfortunately, it also inherited the same sloppy workmanship and that classic bane of British roadsters: cowl shake. Indeed, *Consumer Guide®* magazine's test TR8 roadster had so much body flex that parking on even shallow inclines was enough to keep the doors from opening or closing.

We also remember that car for a temperature gauge that kept crowding its red zone. On checking with a dealer about possible overheating, we were told that you had to keep a screwdriver handy for tightening hose clamps during the first 1000 miles!

And that in a nutshell is why British cars have all but disappeared from the U.S. and why Triumph itself is no more. Still, low production, high performance, and end-of-the-line status mark the TR8—especially the convertible—as a future collector's item to rival the Sunbeam Tiger, a more pleasing epitaph for Triumph's sports-car farewell.

SPECIFICATIONS

Engine:	Rover ohv V-8, 215 cid/3528 cc, 133 (carburetor) or 137 (fuel injection) bhp @ 5000 rpm, 165 lbs-ft @ 3200 rpm
Transmissions:	5-speed manual or 3-speed automatic
Suspension, front:	MacPherson struts, lower lateral arms, coil springs
Suspension, rear:	live axle, lower trailing arms, upper angled arms, coil springs
Brakes:	front discs/rear drums
Wheelbase (in.):	85.0
Weight (lbs):	2655
Top speed (mph):	135
0-60 mph (sec):	8.5
Production:	2497 (incl. 2308 U.S. models)

This 1981 American-market TR8 convertible is similar to the one that underwhelmed these editors. Rover-built ex-GM small-block V-8 (above) gave terrific performance, but workmanship left much to be desired.

1963-1965
TVR GRIFFITH

TVR is one of those tiny, peculiarly British "cottage industry" automakers that's managed to survive its own checkered history. Founded in 1954 by Trevor (TreVoR) Wilkinson, it began with kit cars designed around British and West German components. Every TVR ever since has been assembled in Blackpool, a seaside resort in the northwest of England.

In 1956, Wilkinson joined forces with Bernard Williams, owner of nearby Grantura Plastics, and together they set up a small assembly line. Two years later, they began building an oddly styled fiberglass-bodied coupe called Grantura, sold as a kit and fully assembled, with a tubular backbone chassis designed to accept a variety of proprietary engines and suspension components. But TVR's fortunes were decidedly mixed in these years. By the early Sixties, it had been reorganized and refinanced no fewer than three times.

Three MGA-powered Granturas ran at Sebring in 1962. As it happened, two of the team drivers had their personal cars maintained at the New York workshops of Jack Griffith. One of these was an early Shelby-Cobra (see entry), the other a '62-model Grantura. As the story goes, Griffith's mechanics decided one day to see whether the Cobra's Ford V-8 would fit the TVR. Amazingly, it did.

Griffith saw the potential, had the conversion more professionally engineered, and took the idea to Blackpool, asking TVR to build him some Granturas that would take the Cobra drivetrain, which he would install Stateside. Ever desperate for cash, TVR said yes, and a new model, the TVR Griffith, duly went on sale in 1963. It was built strictly for export only through early '65, when British sales began on a limited basis.

Drivetrain apart, the Griffith was basically the latest Grantura Mark 3, which meant a multi-tube chassis with an 85.5-inch wheelbase (previous TVRs had an 84-inch span) and most of its strength in the central backbone. Independent double-wishbone suspension was used at each end, and stronger wire wheels with wider rims were specified.

Power was supplied by the new 289-cubic-inch version of Ford's lightweight small-block V-8, available in two states of tune: stock 195 horsepower or 271-bhp "high performance." A Ford-built 4-speed gearbox mated with it, sending drive to the rear wheels and a BMC-type differential.

Like other early TVRs, the Griffith had a cramped cockpit and as little luggage space (with no exterior access), plus a very hard ride and the patchy workmanship typical of "cottage cars." Except for a pronounced hood bulge (to clear the V-8) it looked almost exactly like the MGB-powered Grantura Mk 3.

The original Griffith, later known as the 200, was far from fully developed, suffering various quality problems as well as a serious tendency to overheat. The Griffith 400, which arrived in spring 1964, was better-engineered if not better-looking. This was the first TVR with the sharply truncated tail and enlarged rear window that would persist at Blackpool through the end of the Seventies. Bringing up the rear were large "pie-plate" taillamps, borrowed from the British Ford Cortina sedan. Kenlowe thermostatically controlled cooling fans and a larger radiator addressed the overheating problem, but didn't entirely cure it.

Introduced at the April 1964 New York Auto Show, the 400 was well received, and TVR was soon sending Griffith five engineless cars a week. With so many horses pulling less than a ton of curb weight, performance was shattering (road testers mentioned 155 mph all out), and the stiff suspension and tidy dimensions added up to nimble handling and tenacious roadholding.

But the Griffith wouldn't last long, done in by its own quality problems and, more seriously, a prolonged U.S. dockworkers strike. Griffith soon gave up, thus shattering TVR's fragile finances and forcing the Blackpool concern into liquidation. Of course, there were more TVRs to come, but they'd be nowhere near this hairy for a long time.

SPECIFICATIONS

Engine: Ford U.S. ohv V-8, 289 cid/4727 cc, 195/271 bhp @ 4400/6500 rpm, 282/314 lbs-ft @ 2400/3400 rpm

Transmission:	Ford 4-speed manual
Suspension, front:	upper and lower wishbones, coil springs, anti-roll bar
Suspension, rear:	upper and lower wishbones, coil springs
Brakes:	front discs/rear drums
Wheelbase (in.):	85.5
Weight (lbs):	1905
Top speed (mph):	150 +
0-60 mph (sec):	5.7
Production:	300

Anglo-American Griffith combined TVR's Grantura Mark 3 body with small-block Ford V-8. Truncated tail set the later 400 model (shown) apart from the initial 200 version. A few Griffiths, like this one, were sold in England.

1967-1971
TVR TUSCAN

As a result of its 1965 liquidation, TVR was acquired by Martin Lilley and his father Arthur, who reconstituted the firm as TVR Engineering, Ltd., and set it on a path to prosperity. Among the assets they inherited was a sound basic chassis that could accept MG four-cylinder and Ford V-8 engines. Martin decided to develop this further, and over the next four years created several variations on the original model theme.

For a time, Blackpool concentrated solely on the MGB-powered Grantura 1800S, for which demand remained steady in Britain. Compared with cars built under the previous, rather discredited regime, it had distinctly higher-quality fittings, especially the "Mark IV" model that took over in the autumn of '66.

The following year, Lilley revived the Griffith 400 in spirit, if not name, with the Mark IV as a starting point. Called Tuscan V-8, it was newly distributed in the U.S. by Gerry Sagerman but couldn't escape the Griffith's poor reputation. Only 28 were built, some with the 195-horsepower Ford 289, some with the "hi-po" 271-bhp engine. All but four were sold in America.

Tuscan V-6 was the most successful of TVR's late-Sixties vee-engine models, though only 101 were built. A few came to America.

Lilley's next salvage effort was a stretched, 90-inch-wheelbase Tuscan, achieved by lengthening the floorpan to make all the extra space available inside. Identified by different taillamps (from the British Ford Cortina Mk II) and a revised hood, this Tuscan V-8 SE was built in 1967-68 and fared even worse than its predecessor: just 24 built, half of which went to the States.

Undaunted, Lilley announced yet another Tuscan at the 1968 New York Auto Show. This time, however, the familiar chassis was covered with a longer, wider, and much smoother body, a step toward the definitive M-Series design of 1972. Alas, it sold no better than previous Tuscans: a mere 21 were built between April 1968 and August 1970 (two had right hand drive). At this point, TVR belatedly gave up on a Ford V-8 model.

Somewhat more successful was an "in-between" TVR that neatly bridged the price-and-performance gap between the V-8s and the Cortina-powered Vixen. Introduced in October 1969 as the Tuscan V-6, it was basically a Vixen with Ford Britain's fine 60-degree 3.0-liter "Essex" V-6 and 4-speed gearbox (a drivetrain already seen in such diverse places as the British Ford Capri "ponycar" and Zephyr/Zodiac sedans, the Reliant Scimitar GTE sportswagon, and the odd-looking Marcos GT). The V-6 delivered 136 bhp (versus the Vixen's 88) and had a very lusty torque curve.

Still, there must have been something about these vee-engine TVRs that turned off potential buyers, for the V-6 didn't sell as well as it deserved. Yet magazine road tests showed a top speed of near 125 mph, brisk acceleration, and surprising fuel economy (about 28 mpg U.S.). Nevertheless, production stopped in early 1971 at just 101 units, most of which remained in Britain.

SPECIFICATIONS

Engines: Tuscan V-8 and V-8 SE (1967-70): Ford U.S. ohv V-8, 289 cid/4727 cc, 195/271 bhp (SAE gross) @ 4400/6500 rpm, 282/314 lbs-ft @ 2400/3400 rpm; **Tuscan V-6** (1969-71): Ford Britain ohv V-6, 182.7 cid/2994 cc, 136 bhp (net) @ 4750 rpm, 173 lbs-ft @ 3000 rpm

Transmission:	4-speed manual; overdrive optional
Suspension, front:	upper and lower wishbones, coil springs, anti-roll bar
Suspension, rear:	upper and lower wishbones, coil springs
Brakes:	front discs/rear drums
Wheelbase (in.):	85.5 (V-8, V-6), 90.0 (V-8 SE)
Weight (lbs):	1905-2240
Top speed (mph):	125-155
0-60 mph (sec):	5.7-8.3

Production: V-8 (1967-68) 24 **V-8 SE** (1968-70) 21 **V-6** (1969-71) 101

1972-1979 TVR 2500/3000M & TAIMAR

Six years after the Lilleys rescued it, TVR introduced a completely new chassis, its first basic design change since 1962 and only the third distinct platform in TVR history. With it came a new generation that would continue all the way to 1980.

As with past TVR chassis, this new one was designed to accept a variety of proprietary engines to suit the legislative requirements and price classes of various markets. However, it would be the first to carry more than one body style, as a convertible and hatchback coupe would eventually complement the familiar TVR fastback, though this wasn't planned when the chassis was designed.

It was superficially like the old Tuscan SE chassis in that both were 90-inch-wheelbase affairs made of small-diameter tubes, with a strong central backbone, coil-spring all-independent suspension, front-disc/rear-drum brakes, and rack-and-pinion steering. The difference is that the new one was a "space frame" rather than a simple platform design, strode wider tracks (53.75 inches front and rear), and employed a mixture of square and circular tubing.

Called M-Series, the new TVR was visually similar to the short-lived "wide-body" Tuscan V-8 SE, with a longer nose and tail than on the old Vixen/Griffith models but the same characteristic TVR look. Seating remained strictly for two, and there was still no external trunk access. As in the V-8 Tuscans, engines mounted behind the front-wheel centerline in "front mid-engine" position, which left sufficient room for stowing the spare ahead, just above the radiator.

This chassis would carry the following engines during its eight-year life, all with overhead valves: 1.3-liter Triumph Spitfire four, Ford Britain's crossflow 1.6-liter "Kent" four-cylinder, the 2.5-liter Triumph straight six from the TR6, and Ford's 3.0-liter "Essex" V-6 as used in the British Capri and TVR's own Tuscan. The last was also turbocharged but rarely seen here.

The best-sellers in the new range were the 1.6-liter 1600M, 2.5-liter 2500M, and 3.0-liter 3000M. The last was treated to a simple hatchback conversion in late 1976 and renamed Taimar. A companion ragtop, prosaically called Convertible, was issued two years later and—lo and behold—it had a proper trunk with lid.

There was also a "pre-M" 1971 model simply called 2500. Devised especially for the U.S., it was basically the old V-6 Tuscan fitted with the American-spec TR6 engine. Exactly 289 were built in less than a year, along with 96 examples of another "cocktail" model, this one with the old-style bodywork atop the M-Series chassis.

But the definitive TR6-powered model was the 2500M, almost all of which were sold in the U.S. Production ended in 1977 because British Leyland had cancelled the TR6 the previous year and engine supplies soon dried up. As it weighed about the same as the Triumph, the 2500M naturally had similar performance, with a top speed of about 110 mph.

The 3000M, always available in Britain, then took over for the U.S. 2500M, with sales continuing through 1979. It was basically the same car, of course, except for its British Ford V-6, which had been improved since Tuscan days (and should not be confused with Ford's 2.8-liter German-designed V-6 of this period). In U.S. trim, the 3000M could reach close to 115 mph. The Taimar and Convertible were a tad slower owing to the higher weight of their extra equipment.

The 3.0-liter Turbo was a rare but rapid bird. Top speed was 140 mph and 0-60 mph acceleration took just 5.8 seconds. Just 63 were built, though that encompassed all three body styles.

SPECIFICATIONS

Engines: **1972-77 2500M:** Triumph ohv I-6, 152.4 cid/2498 cc, 106 bhp (net) @ 4900 rpm, 133 lbs-ft @ 3000 rpm; **1972-79 3000M/Taimar/Convertible:** Ford Britain ohv V-6, 182.7 cid/2994 cc, 138 bhp (DIN) @ 5000 rpm, 174 lbs-ft @ 3000 rpm; **U.S. version:** 142 bhp (SAE net), 172 lbs-ft: **Turbo:** 230 bhp (DIN) @ 5500 rpm, 273 lbs-ft @ 3500 rpm

Transmission:	4-speed manual; overdrive optional
Suspension, front:	upper and lower wishbones, coil springs, anti-roll bar
Suspension, rear:	upper and lower wishbones, coil springs
Brakes:	front discs/rear drums
Wheelbase (in.):	90.0
Weight (lbs):	2240-2335
Top speed (mph):	109-139
0-60 mph (sec):	5.8-9.3

Production: 2500M (1972-77) 947 **3000M** (1972-76) 654 **Taimar** (1976-79) 395 **Convertible** (1978-79) 258

*Opposite page: TVR's M-Series began with a choice of several engines in what was largely the "long-wheelbase" Tuscan V-8 body. **This page:** Later 3.0-liter V-6 models were turbocharged by both private tuners and TVR itself. M-Series dash remained typical TVR, but was updated for safety.*

1980-1988
TVR TASMIN FAMILY

Tiny TVR entered the Eighties with a new and very dramatic-looking replacement for the M-Series/Taimar. In the eight years since, its chassis has carried Rover and Ford Europe engines, manual and automatic transmissions, and convertible, coupe, and 2+2 body styles. Add in interim facelifts and model-name changes and you have a complex story. U.S. models are much easier to track; so far, all have had a German Ford 2.8-liter V-6, and most have been ragtops.

Despite the different variations and their differences from previous models, all these TVRs share two traits. First, they're hairy-chested sports cars in the great British tradition. Second, they're the most thoroughly sorted and best-built TVRs ever.

The first of the breed appeared in January 1980: a wedgy two-seat hatchback coupe called Tasmin. The derivative 2+2 and convertible appeared within a year on the same 94-inch wheelbase.

Though its engineering was new, the Tasmin hewed to TVR's usual design philosophy and layout. Despite the longer wheelbase, its chassis was basically the same "space frame" used on the M-Series/Taimar, made up of small-diameter tubes, some round in section, some square. All-independent coil-spring suspension and rack-and-pinion steering were also inherited, but disc brakes were now used at the rear as well as at the front. As before, bodies were built up from fiberglass moldings, and major components like engines, transmissions, and differentials were purchased from volume automakers.

Styling was where the Tasmin most obviously broke rank. Here was the first TVR that could honestly be called pretty instead of just "distinctive" (often the motoring journalist's synonym for ugly). Contours were of the "folded paper" school popularized by Giugiaro, perhaps a little dated for the "aero-look" Eighties but a vast improvement on previous TVRs.

In front three-quarter view the Tasmin was quite reminiscent of the Lotus Excel, but an unusually long hood (necessary for the favored "front mid-engine" positioning) gave it an entirely unique profile. The "anteater" nose, sloped down ahead of the hood and from a breakline above the front wheelarches, looked a bit odd, as did the quite lengthy front overhang and abbreviated rear overhang. Aside from fattish B-pillars, coupe roofs seemed almost delicate.

The coupes were difficult to distinguish at a glance, but their proportions differed in detail. Since the 2+2 shared the two-seater's wheelbase, its back seats were a tight fit and thus a token gesture for all but the smallest living beings. Happily, the convertible pretended to be nothing but a two-seater, and its fold-away Targa-style hoop was a novel idea welcomed by fresh-air fiends.

The principal engine during the Tasmin's first four years was the fuel-injected version of Ford Cologne's 2.8-liter ohv V-6, familiar on both sides of the Atlantic from the early Seventies through its 1987 phaseout (in favor of a reengineered 2.9-liter evolution). It had already been desmogged, which allowed TVR to resume U.S. sales in 1983 after an absence of several years. With about 145 SAE net horsepower, the federal Tasmin could see 125 mph all out.

Though ride was still quite hard by most any standard, the Tasmin was far more modern and integrated than any previous TVR, with eager handling and thoroughbred road manners, plus those striking looks. Unfortunately, it also cost a lot more to build. TVR tried to recoup with a detrimmed price-leader powered by Ford Britain's 2.0-liter "Pinto" four, but sold only 61 in three years.

Meantime, TVR changed hands again, with Peter Wheeler taking over from Martin Lilley in 1981-82. Wheeler wanted more performance and, like TVR's previous owners, began dabbling with engine swaps. After trying a turbo V-6 (two prototypes were built) he settled on Rover's all-aluminum 3.5-liter V-8, basically the early-Sixties Buick unit that had since gone into the Triumph TR8 and Morgan Plus 8 (see entries) and still powers the luxury Range Rover four-wheel-drive wagon. In its latest fuel-injected form it delivered 190 bhp.

By 1984, the V-6 Tasmin had been renamed 280i and the new V-8, called 350i, was on the road. The latter was rumbly and muscular, a true supercar, with top speeds in the 135-140 mph range and acceleration to match.

But it was only a first step. Late '84 brought the 390SE, a bored-out 3.9-liter limited edition that could "outdrag a Porsche Turbo," according to one British magazine. Styling was smoothed out a little for 1986, when the even hotter 420SEAC arrived, boasting no less than 300 bhp from a newly enlarged 4.2-liter V-8, plus swoopy rocker-panel skirts and full color-matched exterior. With a top speed in excess of 150 mph and a British-market price of around $45,000, it's a long way from early TVRs, and a welcome addition to the growing ranks of high-performance cars that will take us into the Nineties.

SPECIFICATIONS

Engines: Tasmin/280i (1980-87): Ford Germany ohv V-6, 170 cid/2792 cc, 160 bhp (DIN) @ 5700 rpm, 162 lbs-ft @ 4300 rpm; **U.S. version:** 145 bhp/150 lbs-ft (SAE net); **350i/390SE/ 420SEAC** (1984-88): Rover ohv V-8; 215.2 cid/3528 cc, 190 bhp (DIN) @ 5300 rpm, 220 lbs-ft @ 4000 rpm; 238.3 cid/3905 cc, 275 bhp (DIN) @ 5500 rpm, 270 lbs-ft @ 3500 rpm; 258 cid/ 4228 cc, 300 bhp (DIN) @ 5500 rpm, 290 lbs-ft @ 4500 rpm

Transmissions:	4/5-speed manual, 3-speed automatic
Suspension, front:	upper and lower wishbones, coil springs, anti-roll bar
Suspension, rear:	upper and lower wishbones, coil springs, anti-roll bar
Brakes:	front discs/rear drums
Wheelbase (in.):	94.0
Weight (lbs):	2365-2535
Top speed (mph):	108-150+
0-60 mph (sec):	5.6-11.8
Production:	NA (production continues at this writing)

*Opposite: Tasmin convertible was announced in October 1980, 10 months behind the initial coupe. Styling has stayed basically the same for both models. **This page:** Coupe is also offered with several engine choices.*

1961-1971 VOLVO P1800/1800S/ 1800E

Some car companies seem so sober that it's difficult to imagine them producing a sports car, or even a sporty coupe. Volvo, which began building cars in 1927, was just such a company, so sensibly Swedish that its P1800 was a complete surprise.

Volvo had built a handful of fiberglass-bodied sporty convertibles in the Fifties, though this wasn't a serious production effort. But the P1800 was. In fact, Volvo spent a lot of time on the new coupe before putting it on the market. One reason: there was no room for another model on assembly lines that were already overflowing. For this reason, tooling for the P1800's unit body/chassis structure was contracted to Pressed Steel in the UK, which also built the shells initially and sent them on to Jensen in West Bromwich for final assembly.

There was nothing startling about the P1800 apart from its looks, which were only startling for a Volvo. Running gear was borrowed from the firm's existing 120-Series "Amazon" sedans, which meant a sturdy but orthodox 1.8-liter overhead-valve four (initially rated at 100 horsepower) and a 4-speed all-synchromesh gearbox with overdrive turning rear wheels attached to a coil-sprung rigid axle with Panhard-rod location. Front suspension was equally ordinary: independent with unequal-length A-arms and coil springs.

Styling, curiously enough, was a mixture of Frua and Ghia ideas, and rather dated by the car's late-1961 debut. The lines were curvy, the nose jutted out to an eggcrate grille, and there were modest tailfins above bullet-shaped pod taillights. The roof was quite low, but so was the seating, which gave a real "bathtub" feel. Though mainly marketed as a two-seater, the P1800 did have a small back seat that was more like a shelf—good for parcels, bad for people.

It all added up to a more stylish Volvo with a sporty air but no sports-car credentials. Ride and road manners were able enough, but performance was pedestrian. Still, the P1800 had much to offer: comfortable seats, an effective heating/ventilation system, an orderly dash with full instrumentation, rugged construction, even a useful trunk. In short, it was an honest car that was still dashing enough for the country club—exactly what Volvo wanted. Helping its image in the UK and, to a lesser extent, the U.S. was *The Saint* TV series, where Simon Templar (a.k.a. Roger Moore) drove a P1800 in almost every episode.

With annual volume of only about 5000 units, the P1800 wasn't going to make Volvo rich, but it proved a steady seller while benefitting from a number of changes. In late 1964, after the first 6000 or so had been built, production was transferred from England to Sweden and the name changed to 1800S. There were also some minor cosmetic alterations, mainly a less gaudy grille insert and bodyside chrome repositioned to de-emphasize the curious upswept character line in the doors.

Displacement went to 2.0 liters for 1968, in line with other Volvos, though the model designation stayed the same. The following year brought Bosch fuel injection for what was now called 1800E (the letter denoting *Einspritzung,* German for fuel injection). Also on hand were a black grille, rearranged dash, a new steering wheel, flow-through ventilation system (identified by small exhaust grids on the rear flanks), the beefed-up gearbox from Volvo's six-cylinder 164 sedan, four-wheel disc brakes, and new five-spoke cast-alloy wheels (which looked like wheel covers).

By this time, top speed was up from 109 to 115 mph, the 0-60 sprint down to 10 seconds or so from the original 14. Still, the 1800 mainly appealed as a snug, fairly agile little "sedan" able to cruise all day at a comfortable 90 mph—the sort of solid, sturdy, reliable, and functional car for which Volvo had become famous.

If the original 1800 had seemed dated in 1961, it *really* looked old-hat 10 years later. But Volvo still had one more trick up its sleeve that would keep the 1800 going a few more years. To find out what it was, just read on.

SPECIFICATIONS

Engines: all ohv I-4; **1961-67:** 108.5 cid/1778 cc, 100/108/115 bhp @ 5800 rpm, 108/110/112 lbs-ft @ 4000 rpm; **1968:** 121.2 cid/1986 cc, 118 bhp @ 6000 rpm, 123 lbs-ft @ 3500 rpm; **1969-71:** 121.2 cid/1986 cc, 130 bhp @ 6000 rpm, 130 lbs-ft @ 3500 rpm

Transmissions:	4-speed manual with overdrive (3-speed automatic on a few late-production examples)
Suspension, front:	unequal-length A-arms, coil springs, anti-roll bar
Suspension, rear:	live axle, Panhard rod, coil springs
Brakes:	front discs/rear drums (1961-68), front/rear discs (1969-72)
Wheelbase (in.):	96.5
Weight (lbs):	2400-2535
Top speed (mph):	107-115
0-60 mph (sec):	10.1-13.9

Production: **P1800** (1961-64) 6000 **1800S** (1964-68) 23,993 **1800E** (1969-71) 9414

Small C-pillar script distinguishes the P1800 from its evolutionary 1800S successor. Driving position (opposite top) is low, underhood installation (center) crowded.

415

1971-1973
VOLVO 1800ES

The Volvo 1800 was safe, solid, and sporty, but also overweight, rather cramped, visually dated, and not all that fast. Of course, it was never intended as an all-out sports car, but it *was* the Swedish automaker's image-leader and, as such, quite in need of updating by 1970.

Volvo toyed repeatedly with plans for restyling the 1800 during the Sixties, but could never justify a completely new body. Finally, in 1967, it came up with a clever solution that would not only give the car a new lease on life but answer complaints about lack of people and package space: a restyled roof that would turn the coupe into a sporty station wagon.

Called 1800ES, this new version didn't appear for another four years, leading some to speculate that Volvo merely copied the 1968 Reliant Scimitar GTE, an identical wagon-out-of-coupe conversion. However, there's no way Volvo could have known in advance about that British car. Put it down as just another of those "simultaneous creations" that occasionally pop up in automotive history as the result of coincidental timing. Then again, perhaps both had been inspired by Chevrolet's mid-Fifties Nomad, a sporty wagon if ever there was one.

Still, a good idea most always remains a good idea, and it worked just as well for Volvo as it did for Reliant and Chevrolet. The transformation was certainly easy enough. Starting with the existing fuel-injected 2.0-liter 1800E, Volvo simply lopped off the coupe roof and substituted a "squareback" style with long rear quarter

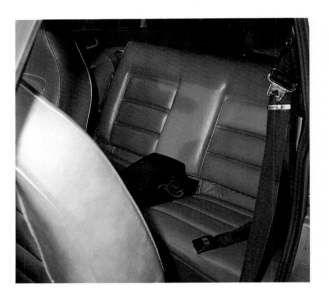

windows, rakishly slanted C-pillars, and a frameless, liftup glass hatch. Lower-body sheetmetal aft of the doors was ostensibly unchanged, but differed slightly in detail.

Aside from improving looks, the new roofline brought welcome gains in rear headroom and cargo space. The back seat was still no fit place for adults and the load deck stood rather high off the ground, but the rear backrest could be flopped down to extend the flat-floor bay to a full five feet in length, and children at least could now ride in back without feeling tortured. As a stylish smaller hauler for the buyer who'd outgrown sports cars, the 1800ES was hard to beat. A 200-pound gain in curb weight was an acceptable tradeoff for the greater utility, even if it did negate the long roof's superior aerodynamics.

The rest of the package was mostly left alone, though Volvo widened wheels and tires to cope with the ES's expected heavier cargo loads, and Borg-Warner automatic transmission was a new option (actually introduced toward the end of coupe production). European models naturally remained at 1800E power levels, but tightening emissions standards strangled the American ES, which suffered a 1.8-point compression drop (to 8.7:1) to accommodate low-lead fuel. So saddled, the ES took a bit more than a second longer to reach 60 mph from rest compared to the previous U.S.-spec coupe, though reported top speed was still in excess of 115 mph.

A practical sporty car may seem a contradiction in terms, but buyers still liked the sportwagon idea and the ES actually sold at a faster pace than previous 1800s. Still, time waits for no car, this one's basic design was ancient, and Volvo would have had to spend lots of money to bring it in line with even tougher American rules for 1974 and beyond (especially that year's 5-mph bumper standard). That made no economic sense, so the 1800 series was put to rest in June 1973.

But the 1800ES made a lot of friends for Volvo, and the company wouldn't forget it. The Dutch-built 420ES, introduced in 1986, is very much the same sort of car, as many observers have been quick to note. As we said, a good idea most always remains a good idea.

SPECIFICATIONS

Engines: ohv I-4, 121.2 cid/1986 cc, 120 bhp (DIN) @ 6000 rpm, 124 lbs-ft @ 3500 rpm; **U.S. version:** 112 bhp (SAE net), 115 lbs-ft

Transmissions:	4-speed manual with overdrive; optional 3-speed automatic
Suspension, front:	unequal-length A-arms, coil springs, anti-roll bar
Suspension, rear:	live axle, Panhard rod, coil springs
Brakes:	front/rear discs
Wheelbase (in.):	96.5
Weight (lbs):	2490-2570
Top speed (mph):	110-115+
0-60 mph (sec):	9.7-11.3
Production:	8078

*The Volvo 1800 coupe worked remarkably well as a sporty wagon. Rear seat (**opposite top**) remained mainly for show, but luggage space was much more suitable for long jaunts.*